THE HANDBOOK OF THE CRIMINAL JUSTICE PROCESS

EDITED BY

MIKE McCONVILLE

AND

GEOFFREY WILSON

OXFORD
UNIVERSITY PRESS

OXFORD

UNIVERSITY PRESS

Great Clarendon Street, Oxford OX2 6DP

Oxford University Press is a department of the University of Oxford.
It furthers the University's objective of excellence in research, scholarship,
and education by publishing worldwide in

Oxford New York

Auckland Bangkok Buenos Aires Cape Town Chennai
Dar es Salaam Delhi Hong Kong Istanbul Karachi Kolkata
Kuala Lumpur Madrid Melbourne Mexico City Mumbai Nairobi
São Paulo Shanghai Singapore Taipei Tokyo Toronto

with an associated company in Berlin

Oxford is a registered trade mark of Oxford University Press
in the UK and in certain other countries

Published in the United States
by Oxford University Press Inc., New York

© Mike McConville and Geoffrey Wilson, 2002

The moral rights of the authors have been asserted
Database right Oxford University Press (maker)

First published 2002

British Library Cataloguing in Publication Data
Data available

Library of Congress Cataloging in Publication Data
Data available
ISBN 0–19–925395–1 (pbk.)
ISBN 0–19–925460–5 (hbk.)

Typeset by RefineCatch Limited, Bungay, Suffolk
Printed in Great Britain by
T.J. International Ltd.,
Padstow, Cornwall

THE HANDBOOK OF THE CRIMINAL JUSTICE PROCESS

ENTERPRISE LTD.

PREFACE

We have been impressed over the last few years by the interest shown in the working of the English legal system in the People's Republic of China, as evidenced by the number of delegations we have hosted at the Law School of the University of Warwick during their tours of the United Kingdom, as well as the requests for seminars and lectures and information and advice which we have received together and individually. On his many visits to China, Mike McConville has seen at first hand how interest in the English legal system and the methods of the common law has spread throughout China's legal system as well as to the students who will run the system in the future.

In early discussions with Dr David Li Kwok-po, who amongst many other things is a member of the Legislative Council of Hong Kong and chairman of the Bank of East Asia there, our first thoughts were that we might help to satisfy this interest by organizing a conference on the English criminal process to which we could invite a selection of Chinese lawyers, judges, administrators, and scholars and at which their United Kingdom equivalents could provide an overview of the English scene, highlighting the main features of the process and the problems it faced and the ways in which it was trying to tackle them. This, we thought, would be a far more economical and efficient way of spreading information and understanding than by drip-feeding delegations as they passed through. We soon came to the conclusion, however, that it would still be only a limited number of participants who could benefit directly from such a conference and that a wider audience would be reached only if and when the papers given at it were published. We decided therefore to go straight for the papers and ask a number of experts to contribute to a collection of papers—we have hovered between calling it a Handbook, and Encyclopædia or simply Essays—it is not as practical as a Handbook, nor as encyclopædic as an Encyclopædia, but is more than just a collection of *Essays*—on various aspects of the English criminal process which would be published in both mainland China and Hong Kong and in both Chinese and English. David Li agreed to sponsor the project through the Geoffrey Wilson–Dr David Li Kwok-po Innovation Fund whose terms of reference, 'to promote the understanding and improvement of the world's legal systems', seemed to be exactly in keeping with the spirit of the enterprise.

We have used the words criminal process to emphasize that we meant something much more than the bare legal bones of criminal procedure, though we recognize that even to draw a line between process and the substantive law is somewhat arbitrary if one is trying to understand the ways in which the process is intended to work and works in practice. Many of the matters discussed, for example, assume a wider context in which criminal offences are limited in their scope and clearly defined, and in which there is sufficient respect for the law and the notion of due process to make any limitations on the exercise of powers and guarantees of a fair process effective.

In our note of guidance to the contributors we made it clear that the English criminal process was not being presented as a model to be followed, but as an *example* of the ways in which one legal system was trying to cope with the problems it had identified as being central to its criminal process. And the essays were to be something more than a simple description, and in particular something more than a simple description of the relevant legal rules. They were to include wherever possible an explanation of how the present positions had been reached and the choices involved in reaching them. And they were to include critical comments where contributors thought these to be appropriate. The essays also illustrate the characteristically English and common law pragmatic way in which the system has responded to changes in circumstances, views, and values.

Our overall view was that whatever differences there may be between the contexts, traditions, and cultures, both legal and beyond, of different countries, there was still something to be learned from looking at the English experience, including even the way in which those engaged closely with it responded to a request to describe it.

We wish to thank Dr David Li for his personal support and encouragement at every stage of the project. We wish to thank Aileen Stockham at Warwick and Sandy Li at City University for their patience in preparing the scripts for publication and of course the contributors, all of whom have taken time out from their busy schedules to assist in a project which they thought worthwhile.

MIKE McCONVILLE AND GEOFFREY WILSON

OUTLINE CONTENTS

CONTENTS

CONTRIBUTORS

ROB ALLEN joined the Esmee Fairbairn Foundation in January 2001, directing 'Rethinking Crime and Punishment', a three-year project about public attitudes to imprisonment and other forms of punishment. Rob was previously director of Research and Development at NACRO, where he was responsible for the organization's work on crime reduction, youth justice, and mental health, as well as its fundraising department. In the early 1990s, he was seconded for three years to the criminal policy directorate in the Home Office. In 1997 Rob was awarded a Winston Churchill Travelling Fellowship to study youth crime prevention programmes in the USA, and he has undertaken consultancy work in a number of countries. Rob is a member of the Youth Justice Board for England and Wales.

PROFESSOR KEITH BOTTOMLEY is Professor of Criminology and Director of the Centre for Criminology and Criminal Justice at the University of Hull. He is the author of numerous books in the fields of criminology and criminal justice, including *Decisions in the Penal Process* (1973), *Criminology in Focus* (1979), *Understanding Crime Rates* (1981), *Crime and Punishment: Interpreting the Data* (1986), and *Privatizing Prisons* (1997). He is a member of the Editorial Boards of the *Howard Journal of Criminal Justice, and Punishment and Society: the International Journal of Penology*, and served on the Experts' Group for the Home Office Review of Crime Statistics (2000–2001). He is currently President of the British Society of Criminology (1999–2002).

PROFESSOR LEE BRIDGES, BA (Dartmouth) is Head of Department of the School of Law, University of Warwick. He has written widely on criminal justice, legal aid, and race. Among his publications are: *Legal Services in Birmingham* (1975); *The Duty Solicitor's Handbook* (1988); *Advice and Assistance at the Police Station and the 24 hour Duty Solicitors Scheme* (1989); and *Standing Accused: The Organisational Practices of Criminal Defence Lawyers in Britain* (1994). He has worked as a consultant to the Law Society and the Legal Aid Board.

PROFESSOR ED CAPE, B.Tech., LL.M., Solicitor, is Professor of Criminal Law and Practice at the University of the West of England, Bristol. A former partner and solicitor in private practice, he has a special interest in both criminal defence practice and quality. His publications include *Defending Suspects at Police Stations* (3rd edition, 1999), and joint authorship of *Evaluation of the One Stop Shop and Victim Statement Pilot Projects* (1998) and *Quality in Criminal Defence Services* (2000). He has recently acted as consultant to the Law Society developing a duty solicitor accreditation scheme, and is currently part of a team evaluating the pilot public defender service.

DR SATNAM CHOONGH graduated from Warwick University in 1990, was awarded his D.Phil. by Trinity College, Oxford, in 1994, and was called to the Bar that same year. Dr Choongh has published extensively in the field of criminal justice. His publications include 'Understanding the Long-term Relationship between Police and Policed', in M. McConville and L. Bridges, *Criminal Justice In Crisis* (1994); *Policing as Social Discipline* (1997); *Review of Delay in the Criminal Justice System* (1997); *Improving Custodial Legal*

Advice: The Impact of the Accreditation Scheme for Police Station Advisers (co-authored with Lee Bridges) (1998); *Ethnic Minority Defendants and the Right to Elect Jury Trial* (2000).

DR PENNY DARBYSHIRE, Ph.D., MA is a senior lecturer in law at Kingston University. She has written widely on criminal justice issues, especially relating to justice in the lower courts (magistrates' courts), an area that too often gets overlooked by researchers. She has just completed a lengthy review of jury research throughout the world for the *Criminal Courts Review* 2001.

PROFESSOR SEAN DORAN teaches at Queen's University Belfast. He is also a practising member of the Bar of Northern Ireland and a member of the Council of Legal Education for Northern Ireland. His main research interests are in evidence and criminal procedure. He is co-author with Professor John Jackson of *Judge Without Jury: Diplock Trials in the Adversary System* (1995) and co-editor with Professor Jackson of *The Judicial Role in Criminal Proceedings* (2000). He is a member of the editorial board of the *International Journal of Evidence and Proof* and co-editor of the electronic journal, *International Commentary on Evidence (ICE)*.

DR CAROLYN HOYLE is Lecturer in Criminology based in the Centre for Criminological Research and Fellow of Green College, University of Oxford. She has a BA from the University of Kent and an MSc. and a D.Phil. from the University of Oxford. She is the author of *Negotiating Domestic Violence* (1997) and various articles on restorative justice, victims, and domestic violence. She is co-editor (with Richard Young) of *New Visions of Crime Victims* (forthcoming). She is currently engaged in directing three different studies of restorative justice (in police cautioning, in Youth Offender Teams, and in the police complaints process).

DR ANTHEA HUCKLESBY is Lecturer in Criminology at the University of Hull. She was formerly Lecturer in Criminal Justice at the University of Leicester. She has a BA in Social Science (1987, CNAA), an MA in Criminology (1989, Hull), and was awarded her doctorate in 1994 (Glamorgan). She has published extensively in the area of bail. Recent relevant publications include: 'Police Bail and the Use of Conditions', *Criminal Justice* (2001); 'Tackling Offending on Bail' with E. Marshall, *Howard Journal* (2000); 'Court Culture: An Explanation of Variations in the Use of Bail in Magistrates' Courts', *Howard Journal* (1997); 'Remand Decision Makers' [1997] *Criminal Law Review*.

PROFESSOR JOHN JACKSON, BA, LL.M, Barrister at Law, is Professor of Public Law at Queen's University and is currently Director of the Institute of Criminology and Criminal Justice at Queen's Law School. His interests lie in the areas of evidence, criminal justice, and human rights. He is the author of several major articles in the fields of evidence and criminal procedure and has conducted a number of empirical studies on criminal justice in Northern Ireland. He is co-author (with Sean Doran) of *Judge without Jury: Diplock Trials in the Adversary System* (1995) and of *The Judicial Role in Criminal Proceedings* (2000).

ROGER LENG is a Reader in Law at the University of Warwick and is currently editor of *The International Journal of Evidence and Proof*. His research includes a study of the processes of investigation and prosecution (with Mike McConville and Andrew Sanders) published as *The Case for the Prosecution* (1991) and a study of *The Right to Silence in*

Police Interrogation, conducted for the Royal Commission on Criminal Justice in 1993. More recently he has been involved in interpreting and commenting on new criminal justice legislation. Recent books in this area include: *Guide to the Criminal Procedure and Investigations Act 1996* (with Richard Taylor), *Guide to the Crime and Disorder Act 1998* (with Richard Taylor and Martin Wasik), and *Guide to the Youth Justice and Criminal Evidence Act 1991* (with Di Birch).

PROFESSOR MICHAEL LEVI, MA (Oxon), Dip. Crim. (Cantab), Ph.D. (Southampton) is a graduate of Oxford, Cambridge, and Southampton Universities, and has been a full Professor of Criminology at Cardiff University since 1991. His major research contributions have been in the fields of white-collar crime and corruption, organized crime, money-laundering, and violent crime. His books include *The Phantom Capitalists*; *Regulating Fraud: White-Collar Crime and the Criminal Process*; *The Investigation, Prosecution, and Trial of Serious Fraud*; *Money Laundering in the UK: An Appraisal of Suspicion-Based Reporting*; and *Financial Havens, Banking Secrecy and Money-Laundering* (1998). His most recent book (with Andy Pithouse), *White-Collar Crime and its Victims*, will be published in 2002.

PROFESSOR RONNIE MACKAY, Barrister-at-law, is Professor of Criminal Policy and Mental Health at De Montfort University Law School. He researches and teaches in Criminal Law and Medical Law. In particular, he has a longstanding research interest in Mental Health Law and has conducted a number of empirical research studies dealing with mentally abnormal offenders. He is author of *Mental Condition Defences in the Criminal Law*, and has written numerous articles for scholarly journals including the *Criminal Law Review* and the *British Journal of Criminology*. He was a member of the Parole Board of England and Wales from 1996–2001.

PROFESSOR MIKE MAGUIRE is Professor of Criminology and Criminal Justice at Cardiff University. He has conducted research and written extensively on many aspects of policing and the criminal justice system, including the regulation of police investigations and the operation of the Police and Criminal Evidence Act 1984. With Clive Norris, he conducted research for the Royal Commission on Criminal Justice, and more recently has been examining the effectiveness and the regulation of new forms of 'intelligence led' policing. He is also a co-editor of a major textbook, the *Oxford Handbook of Criminology* (1994, 3rd edition, 2002).

PROFESSOR MIKE McCONVILLE is Dean, City University School of Law and Professor, University of Warwick. He has written widely in the general area of policing, prosecutions, plea bargaining, jury trial, defence practices, and legal history. His writings include: *Negotiated Justice* (1977); *Jury Trials* (1979); *Courts Prosecution and Conviction* (1981); *The Case for the Prosecution* (1991); *Watching Police Watching Communities* (1992); and *Standing Accused* (1994).

PROFESSOR JENNY McEWAN has published widely in the fields of criminal law and criminal evidence. She has taken particular interest in the effect of the adversarial trial upon the content of the law of evidence, and its effect on vulnerable witnesses. She has participated in television programmes highlighting these problems. She is the author of *Evidence and the Adversarial Process: The Modern Law* (1998). She has participated in judicial training courses and training for the Crown Prosecution Service. Since 1999 she has been Professor of Criminal Law at Exeter University.

SIR PHILIP OTTON was a Lord Justice of Appeal from 1995–2001. He was concerned with both criminal and civil appeals. He was a High Court Judge from 1983 until his appointment to the Court of Appeal. He previously practised as a Barrister. In 1998 he accompanied Prime Minister Tony Blair to Beijing when he was the leader of the delegation of 140 lawyers for British Law Week. In 1999 he took a delegation to Beijing, Chong Ching, and Shanghai. In 2001 he returned to Beijing with another delegation and presided over a televised mock trial and chaired the ensuing in-depth discussions with Chinese judges, lawyers, and academics on issues of criminal justice common to both countries.

NICOLA PADFIELD, BA (Oxon), Dip. Crim. (Cantab), DES (Aix-Marseille) is a Lecturer at the University of Cambridge Institute of Criminology and a Fellow of Fitzwilliam College, Cambridge. A qualified barrister, she has written widely on criminal law and criminal justice, including sentencing. She is the editor of *Archbold News*, the *Commonwealth Judicial Journal*, and *Butterworths Core Law Series* of student textbooks, to which she has contributed the book on criminal law. She is currently writing a book on the release of life-sentence prisoners.

PROFESSOR ROSEMARY PATTENDEN, B.Comm. (NSW), LL.B (NSW), D.Phil. (Oxon) has been examining aspects of criminal evidence and procedure since 1976. She is currently a professor of law at the University of East Anglia, Norwich. Her published work includes *Judicial Discretion and Criminal Litigation* (1990), *English Criminal Appeals 1844–1994* (1996) and many articles on the law of evidence. Her books and articles have been cited in the judgments of superior courts including the High Court of Australia, the Supreme Court of Canada, the South African Constitutional Law and the English Court of Appeal.

PROFESSOR ROBERT REINER is Professor of Criminology in the Law Department, London School of Economics. He was formerly Reader in Criminology at the University of Bristol, and at Brunel University. He has a BA in Economics from Cambridge University (1967), an MSc in Sociology (with Distinction) from the London School of Economics (1968), a PhD in Sociology from Bristol University (1976), and a Postgraduate Diploma in Law (with Distinction) from City University, London (1985). He is author of *The Blue-Coated Worker* (1978), *The Politics of the Police* (1985; 2nd edition 1992; 3rd edition 2000), *Chief Constables* (1991), and editor (with M. Cross) of *Beyond Law and Order* (1991), (with S. Spencer) of *Accountable Policing* (1993), of *Policing* (1996), and (with M. Maguire and R. Morgan) of *The Oxford Handbook of Criminology* (1994; 3rd edition, 2002). He has published over 100 papers on policing and criminal justice topics. He was editor (with Rod Morgan) of *Policing and Society: An International Journal of Research and Policy from 1989–98*, and review editor of *The British Journal of Criminology* from 1986–88.

PAUL ROBERTS, BCL MA (Oxon) M.Phil. (Cantab) is Reader in Criminal Justice in the University of Nottingham School of Law, where his teaching and research focus on the philosophical, comparative, and international dimensions of Criminal Justice and the Law of Evidence. His publications on expert and scientific evidence include (with C. Willmore) *The Role of Forensic Science Evidence in Criminal Proceedings* (1993). He is also Reviews Editor of *Evidence and Proof*, and an editorial board member of *Law, Probability and Risk* and the on-line *International Commentary on Evidence (ICE)*.

PROFESSOR ANDREW SANDERS is Professor of Criminal Law and Criminology at the University of Manchester. He is author of *Community Justice* (2001), is co-author (with Richard Young) of *Criminal Justice* (2nd edition, 2000) and co-author (with Mike McConville and Roger Leng) of *The Case for the Prosecution* (1991). His recent empirical research includes several projects on victims funded by the Home Office, including the negotiation of the criminal justice system by victims with learning disabilities and two evaluations of aspects of the Victims' Charter. He is currently evaluating (with Roger Evans) provisions for vulnerable and intimidated witnesses arising from *Speaking up for Justice*. He was a member of the Parole Board for England and Wales from 1995–2001, was appointed to the Attorney-General's Advisory Board for HM CPS Inspectorate in January 2001, and was made a Transitional Life Sentence Commissioner for Northern Ireland in October 2001.

SYBIL SHARPE, LL.M, Barrister, has lectured and researched in the field of criminal evidence for many years. Her books include *Judicial Discretion and Criminal Investigation* (1998) and *Search and Surveillance: The Movement from Evidence to Information* (2000). She has also contributed articles in journals such as the *Criminal Law Review, Anglo-American Law Review*, and the *International Journal of Evidence and Proof* and a published conference paper delivered to the Second World Congress on Evidence and Proof held in Amsterdam in 1999.

PROFESSOR SIR JOHN SMITH, BA 1949, LL.B 1950, LL.D 1975 (Cambridge). Hon. LL.D, Sheffield 1984, Nottingham 1989, Villanova 1993, De Montfort 1995. FBA 1973. Barrister, 1951, QC 1979. CBE 1983, knighted 1993. Professor of Law, University of Nottingham, 1958–87. Professor Smith is a world-renowned expert in criminal law and evidence. His publications include: (with Brian Hogan) *Criminal Law* (1965, 9th edition, 1999) and *Criminal Law, Cases and Materials* (1975, 7th edition, 1999), *Law of Theft* (1968, 8th edition, 1997); *Codification of the Criminal Law* (with I. H. Dennis and E. J. Griew, 1985); *Justification and Excuse in the Criminal Law* (1989); *Criminal Evidence* (1995). He has written monthly commentaries on criminal cases in the *Criminal Law Review* between 1956 and 2001.

STEPHEN SOLLEY QC is Head of Chambers of Charter Chambers, 2 Dr Johnson's Buildings, Temple, London EC4Y 7AY. He was called to the Bar in 1969, became a Crown Court Recorder in 1988, and a Queen's Counsel in 1989. Since 1999 he has been Chair of the Human Rights Committee of the Bar of England and Wales. His practice encompasses criminal commercial fraud and grave crime, with an emphasis on human rights.

JOHN SPRACK, BA, LL.B is a barrister and Chairman of Employment Tribunals. He was formerly Reader at the Inns of Court School of Law. He is editor of the Procedure section of *Blackstone's Criminal Practice*, author of *Emmins on Criminal Procedure*, joint author of *Criminal Evidence and Procedure: The Essential Framework*, and a contributor to the electronic service *Crime Online* on developments in criminal procedure.

D. A. THOMAS was until recently Reader in Criminal Justice at Cambridge University. He is a fellow of Trinity Hall, one of the colleges of the University. His main writing has been on the subject of sentencing; *Principles of Sentencing* (1970 and 1979), and *Current Sentencing Practice* (first published 1982, updated continuously). He is a regular contributor to the *Criminal Law Review* and the editor of the *Criminal Appeal Reports (Sentencing)*.

He was appointed Queen's Counsel (honoris causa) in 1996 and is a barrister in practice at 2 Bedford Row, London.

PROFESSOR CLIVE WALKER is Professor of Criminal Justice Studies and Head of the Department of Law at the University of Leeds. His books have focused upon terrorism, including (with G. Hogan) *Political Violence and the Law in Ireland* (1989) and *The Prevention of Terrorism in British Law* (2nd edition, 1992), and upon miscarriages of justice, including (with K. Starmer), *Miscarriages of Justice* (1999). He has also considered the impact of the Internet on criminal justice in (with Y. Akdeniz and D. Wall) *The Internet, Law and Society* (2000).

PROFESSOR GEOFFREY WILSON is Emeritus Professor of Law at the University of Warwick. Having been a fellow of Queens' College, Cambridge he became the Founding Professor of the Law School at Warwick in 1967. He has published books and articles on the English legal system, the British constitution, and comparative law. He was made Doctor of Law Honoris Causa of the University of Giessen in 1999. His publications include: *Cases and Materials on Constitutional and Administrative Law* (1966), *Cases and Materials on the English Legal System* (1973), and, as editor, *Frontiers of Legal Scholarship* (1995).

PROFESSOR ROBIN C. A. WHITE is Dean of Law at the University of Leicester. He holds degrees from the University of Oxford and the University of Virginia. He is a Solicitor of the Supreme Court, and sits as a Deputy Social Security Commissioner for England and Wales. He is the author of *The English Legal System in Action: The Administration of Justice* (3rd edition, 1999).

DR RICHARD YOUNG, LL.B, Ph.D., is Assistant Director of the Centre for Criminological Research, University of Oxford. He has written widely on criminal justice and restorative justice, and conducted a number of empirical studies in these areas. His main publications include *Criminal Justice* (2nd edition, 2000) co-authored with Andrew Sanders, and 'Just Cops Doing "Shameful" Business: Police-led Restorative Justice and the Lessons of Research', in A. Morris and G. Maxwell (eds.), *Restorative Justice for Juveniles* (2001). He is currently co-directing a project examining the use of restorative justice within the police complaints system.

INTRODUCTION
Mike McConville

The ambition of the project that gave rise to this book was to explain what it means to try to understand a criminal justice process and what needs to be thought about in setting out to establish or reform an existing system. The idea led naturally away from a mechanical account of criminal procedure law, and instead sought to identify the values and principles that underlie any mature criminal justice process, the choices that have to be made, and the attendant costs and benefits.

In setting out on this task, we had in mind separate audiences. On the one hand, we wanted to address the concerns of policy-makers throughout the world as they struggle to reform systems that are thought to be outdated, inefficient, or unfair. In our discussions in many countries, it became clear that those charged with changing their own systems wanted to see and would benefit from seeing a description of a more fully worked out system so that a rounded view of legal change could be taken.

For policy-makers in countries in social transition, the criminal justice process in England and Wales is often viewed as a model. After all, the common law is often celebrated by its leading practitioners as a system in apogee, fit to be emulated as 'the best in the world'. Indeed, it is a remarkable fact of modern times that the adversarial system of the common law is so manifestly in the ascendant and the inquisitorial system so clearly in retreat.[1]

Despite these international trends, we do not present the criminal justice process in England and Wales as a *model*, either in the sense that it has reached a state of perfection or in the sense that it is fit to be directly copied by transitional societies. Rather, for policy-makers everywhere, we have used England and Wales as an *example* of how one system has confronted in more or less successful ways the problems that beset any system. As will become clear from the detailed accounts in the chapters in this volume, the criminal justice process in England and Wales is marked by failures as well as successes, and, indeed, there are significant disagreements about whether particular features count as successes or as failures. It will be equally apparent that the whole process is, in significant ways, always under discussion and scrutiny, and in a real sense is in a state of almost continuous change.

At the same time, it became clear that students would also benefit from an

---

[1] The early examples of Spain (1882), Norway (1887), and Denmark (1916) have been followed more recently by countries such as Argentina, China, Colombia, Estonia, the Czech Republic, Guatemala, Italy, Japan, Portugal, and Sweden, all of which have adopted versions of the adversarial system in criminal cases.

approach that went beyond description and consciously sought to engage with the underlying values and principles. It is these underlying values and principles that represent the glue that holds the system together. And an important part of this inquiry is to understand how those values and principles come into existence and are themselves contestable and contested domains.

When looked at from this vantage point, it becomes clearer that the criminal procedure of any country is simply today's account of a process in continuous evolution that is best understood by looking at its animating principles and values, rather than as, on the one hand, a system that has arrived at its destination or, on the other, a system in permanent crisis.

Our starting point was a set of problems that almost all systems of criminal justice have to confront at some point in their history and that most systems have to confront on a regular basis. In looking at legal systems as they are today, it is all too easy to fall into the trap of seeing them in some sense as natural or inevitable or as having a clear and compelling rationale, even if this is not readily ascertainable. Our intention here, by contrast, is to stimulate the reader to ask some basic questions that should always be put when reform of any legal system is on the agenda.

For example, what sort of powers should a police force have over those suspected of involvement in criminal activity? When and under what conditions should a police officer be permitted to deprive citizens of their freedom to go about their business and take them into custody for questioning? What rights should citizens have when held in police custody, and what powers and responsibilities should officers have in relation to those held in their custody? What considerations should be given to dealing with individuals who have broken the law outside the formal criminal justice process by using alternative systems of social control? Should a person under arrest be allowed access to a lawyer, and, if so, under what conditions, and should provision be made by the State if the individual is unable to afford a lawyer? What principles should govern the distribution of functions between police officers and those individuals responsible for conducting prosecutions in court? How should defence lawyers be organized and funded? What rules should govern the acquisition, disclosure, and admissibility of evidence in a criminal case? Should there be special rules and procedures for particular categories of case, such as economic crime, or people, such as juveniles? What are the functions and responsibilities of the legal profession towards clients and towards the court? What is the responsibility of the judge for the conduct of a criminal case? What are the objectives in bringing a criminal prosecution and could these be better secured by other means?

These are just some of the questions that consideration of any criminal justice process raises. They are also the sorts of questions that the authors of the various chapters were asked to bear in mind when looking at particular aspects of the criminal justice process, so that the choices confronting law-makers at any time are more transparent and the difficulties inherent in system-building more apparent. The various contributions illustrate not only how difficult these policy choices are, but also how decisions about one part of the process have an impact upon other parts that may seem at first sight disconnected and remote. They also show how the answers to these questions shift over time as the social environment in which they are located alters.

One of the advantages of using the English and Welsh system as an example is its essentially pragmatic character. Unlike codified systems that aspire to provide in advance for all eventualities, the English criminal justice process assumes the impossibility of pre-determined answers to future questions whose contours cannot even be predicted. Whilst a code seeks to put up one umbrella to provide shelter against all storms, the English system proceeds on the principle that continual adjustments will need to be made depending upon the direction and force of the weather. It is the job of the judges to reflect upon the law and to respond intelligently to the challenges that advocates pose. And both lawyers and judges need to keep an eye on the wider society to see whether changes there should be reflected in any way by changes to the law. It is in this process of adjustment and refinement that the values and principles become clearer, are contested, and may change.

The English and Welsh system also has the advantage that the architecture of the process is always regarded as provisional and subject to challenge. This occurs on a case-by-case basis in which the overall quality of the process is very much interrelated to the quality of the lawyers—judges, barristers and solicitors—who run the system on a working basis. There is no point in having a framework that encourages scrutiny and inquiry if the courtroom actors lack training or competence.

The choice of England and Wales also offers an example of an alternative way of thinking about law reform because the approach used by the judges is also used outside the judge-made law. Piecemeal reform rather than seismic change has been the English tradition. As can be seen in many of the contributions to this volume, law reform in England and Wales is never off the agenda: often tardy and faltering, rarely sudden and decisive, changes are gradual and attended by a process of refinement so that the process is more or less continuous.

Increasingly in modern times, this process of reform and the questioning of existing arrangements have given space and importance to research. Indeed, until recently it was difficult to imagine how any major reform process, as, for example, consideration of an area of law by a Royal Commission, could be undertaken without the assistance of an accompanying body of commissioned research.[2]

As socio-legal research has matured, so research has come to act as an independent check upon the working system and to help prevent practitioners from falling into the trap of assuming that what they happen to do or experience necessarily represents general or best practice. And research too can feed directly into the process if it is used by advocates or judges to ground discussions about the direction of the law with an empirical dimension. What emerges then is a system under continual interrogation rather than a system that is either permanently fixed or subject to periodic convulsion.

Seen in this way, there emerge several values that underpin the criminal justice process and should figure more prominently in law reform discussions but that are

---

[2] The review of the criminal justice system undertaken by Auld LJ (2001: **www.criminal-courts-review.org.uk**) did not, however, commission its own research, although it did pay attention to much of the considerable body of research that was already in the public domain in both England and Wales and elsewhere. Even so, the Auld Report goes against the principle that a process of reform should be underpinned by empirical research.

under-recognized in traditional accounts and policy debates. One of these is the need for mature systems to be self-aware. In addition to correcting an over-emphasis on the procedural law by looking at the whole process and those engaged in it, what is stated as the law in the books has to be matched by an evaluation of the way the process works in practice. Observers need to know if the process is effective in fulfilling the aspirations set out in its law. This is one of the functions of research.

Equally, in the English and Welsh system, it is no longer possible or plausible to imagine that law reform is the privilege of a few 'experts' working in private. Whether the criminal justice process is working well or is misfiring has become a concern for a wide range of groups in society, all of which are now seen to have a legitimate voice in any reform discussion.[3] The introduction into the law reform process of a democratic element, more or less successfully achieved, is perhaps another feature of the English and Welsh criminal justice process that deserves study and even emulation.

Whilst this volume has sought to provide a broad coverage of one criminal justice process, the task of creating a complete account proved beyond us. We could neither give the depth of treatment we wished to the topics dealt with nor find space for other areas that deserve discussion and the inclusion of which would make our effort more comprehensive. In particular, we felt unable to address some of the real problems confronting those who have to administer the process on a daily basis, such as managing case load and controlling budgets, even though the way these issues are responded to has an important influence upon the make-up and character of the whole process.

Nor could we find space to include specific discussion of the increasing influence that international standards are having upon the criminal justice processes of national systems. Whilst the extent of that influence is still to be worked out, it is now difficult to imagine how any country can engage in a process of law reform without paying close attention to the norms and standards that are increasingly shared by the broader international community and against which more and more systems are beginning to be judged. The criminal justice process of England and Wales, for so long largely self-contained, is no longer, as the various contributors indicate, immune from this wider dimension, and this external element will increasingly be a part of criminal justice processes everywhere.

---

[3] The Auld Report *ibid.*, will provide a good example of this process in one jurisdiction. Auld LJ was asked by the Lord Chancellor in 1999 to conduct a review into 'the practices and procedures of, and rules of evidence applied by, the criminal courts at every level, with a view to ensuring that they deliver justice fairly, by streamlining all their processes, increasing their efficiency and strengthening the effectiveness of their relationships with others across the whole of the criminal justice system, and having regard to the interests of all parties including victims and witnesses, and thereby promoting public confidence in the rule of law'. The report is wide-ranging and includes recommendations to replace the existing courts with a unified Criminal Court consisting of three Divisions one of which (the District Division) would be wholly new and would handle many cases currently dealt with by juries; to give trial judges the power in serious and complex fraud cases to direct trial by a judge and two lay members; to codify and simplify the rules of evidence; and, if race is an important issue in the case, to ensure that three members of the jury are from ethnic minorities. The recommendations have already sparked considerable public debate and the Government has acknowledged that it can see difficulties in proceeding with some of the proposals, as for example those that undercut the principle of random selection of jurors.

1

THE STRUCTURE AND ORGANIZATION OF CRIMINAL JUSTICE IN ENGLAND AND WALES

An overview

Robin C. A. White

INTRODUCTORY THOUGHTS

The structure and organization of criminal justice in England and Wales are charac-terized by fragmentation, differences in roles and aims among institutions forming parts of the system, the absence of a single Government department responsible for criminal justice policy and implementation,[1] and a continuing concern that crime is a growing social evil which must be brought under control without the miscarriages of justice which so frequently hit the headlines.

The complexity of what passes for a criminal justice system is such that some might challenge whether it is a system at all. But in any modern society, criminal justice is certain to be complex. Once that complexity is recognized, then the nature and operation of the system can be discerned more readily. There is a multiplicity of actors in a multiplicity of processes, but the overarching objectives of the system are to regulate 'potential, alleged and actual criminal activity within procedural limits supposed to protect the citizen from wrongful treatment and wrongful conviction'.[2] One constant theme in the process in England is that the system remains adversarial, in that perpetrators of crime are not normally required to co-operate in the building up of the case against them. That is a matter for the investigating and prosecuting authorities who may ultimately be called upon to prove in accordance with well-established rules of evidence before a court all the required ingredients of a particular offence. So the presumption of innocence and

---

[1] The Home Office, the Lord Chancellor's Department, and the Attorney-General's Office are the three main government departments with responsibility for criminal justice.

[2] A. Sanders and R. Young, *Criminal Justice* (2nd edn., London: Butterworth, 2000).

the requirement that proof be beyond reasonable doubt remain two key aspects of its criminal process.

In England and Wales there have been two major Royal Commissions on the criminal process in recent decades. The Royal Commission on Criminal Procedure[3] (Philips Commission) of 1981 was noteworthy for the volume of original research which it commissioned in order to provide a sound empirical basis on which its recommendations could be based. That Commission had as its philosophical base the concept of a fundamental balance between the interests of the community in bringing offenders to justice and the liberties of persons suspected of crime. The recommendations of the Royal Commission resulted in a complete re-writing of the system for the investigation and prosecution of offenders, which can now be found in the Police and Criminal Evidence Act 1984 (PACE) and the Prosecution of Offenders Act 1975.

The Philips Commission had addressed the investigation of offences and the decision to prosecute, but a number of high-profile miscarriages of justice called into question the ability of the institutions of the criminal justice system to catch the right offender in the first place and, in particular, of the courts to rectify mistakes. Hence the establishment of the Royal Commission on Criminal Justice (Runciman Commission).[4] The political climate in which the Runciman Commission deliberated included not only concern over an appalling series of miscarriages of justice, but also a feeling that it was sometimes too easy to avoid conviction. The Commission reported in 1993 and made 352 recommendations. Notably, the systems of criminal appeals and of pre-trial disclosure of information were adjusted, and a new institution, the Criminal Cases Review Commission, designed to be more robust in investigating potential miscarriages of justice, was established.

Recent years have also seen a debate about the ability of the various institutions forming the criminal justice system to work together more as a system, and the demands of a value-for-money culture in government which has also affected criminal justice.

What follows will examine the key roles of seven institutions in the criminal process:

- The police
- The Crown Prosecution Service
- The Criminal Defence Service
- The Courts
- The Probation Service
- The Prison Service
- The Criminal Cases Review Commission
- The Criminal Injuries Compensation Authority

---

[3] Royal Commission on Criminal Procedure, Report, Cmnd 8092 (1981).
[4] Royal Commission on Criminal Justice, Cm 2263 (1993).

The Government has set aims and objectives for the criminal justice system which indicate the current policy agenda underlying the programme for the modernization of the criminal justice system which the Home Secretary presented to Parliament in February 2001.[5] The first aim is 'to reduce crime and the fear of crime and their social and economic costs', with the following objectives attached to it:

- to reduce the level of actual crime and disorder;
- to reduce the adverse impact of crime and disorder on people's lives;
- to reduce the economic costs of crime.

The second aim is 'to dispense justice fairly and efficiently and to promote confidence in the rule of law', with the following associated objectives attached to it:

- to ensure just processes and just and effective outcomes;
- to deal with cases throughout the criminal justice process with appropriate speed;
- to meet the needs of victims, witnesses, and jurors within the system;
- to respect the rights of defendants and to treat them fairly;
- to promote confidence in the Criminal Justice System.

Operating an effective criminal justice system is not cheap. In 2000–01 some £13 billion was spent on the criminal justice system in England and Wales. Of that, 59 per cent was spent on the police, 2.5 per cent on the work of the Crown Prosecution Service and the Serious Fraud Office,[6] 7.5 per cent on legal aid, 4.5 per cent on the Probation Service, and 16 per cent on the Prison Service.

Though respect for defendants' rights has always been a feature of the criminal justice system, the recent incorporation of the European Convention on Human Rights into English law by the Human Rights Act 1998 has given a new impetus to the consideration of human rights questions in the criminal process. It has already called into question some recent policies contained in legislation.[7]

THE POLICE

England and Wales have a decentralized police force. There are forty-three local police forces.[8] Each of the police forces is maintained by a police authority composed of local government councillors, magistrates, and independent members, which is

---

[5] *Criminal Justice: The Way Ahead*, Cm 5074 (Feb. 2001).

[6] The Serious Fraud Office investigates and prosecutes cases of serious or complex fraud.

[7] E.g., the circumstances in which a judge will be able to invite a jury to draw adverse inferences from a defendant's election not to respond to certain questions either during the investigation of the offence or in court, and the requirement that certain repeat offenders are to be given extended mandatory prison sentences.

[8] There are some differences in relation to the City of London Police and the Metropolitan Police Service.

funded by a combination of local and central government money. The police authority appoints the Chief Constable of the local police force, subject to the approval
of the Home Secretary who is the Minister responsible for policing in the central
government. Chief Constables are responsible for publishing annual policing plans
and annual reports, and for setting local objectives. The Home Secretary retains a role
in relation to those matters which require national regulation, such as matters of
police rank and disciplinary rules. All police forces are subject to inspection by Her
Majesty's Inspectors of Constabulary, who act on behalf of central government.

It is a peculiar feature of the English system that each police officer is a constable,
and as such an office-holder in his own right rather than an employee subject to
directions by line managers. Constables, as independent office-holders, enjoy a degree
of independence in the exercise of the powers given by legislation to the constable.
However, that independence is affected by the culture in which the police work, and
constables are subject to organizational and occupational rules and norms just like
any employee in a large organization. The police are the gatekeepers of the criminal
justice system who exercise considerable discretion over whether a person enters the
criminal justice system or stays outside it. So police officers on the street will exercise
discretion over whether to stop and question an individual, whether to stop and
search an individual, or whether to arrest a person and take him to the police station
for further processing. Police officers in the police station will exercise discretion
about the level of police resources to be devoted to a particular reported crime, while
senior officers will exercise discretion in the allocation of the overall resources of
the force.

Discretion both by the police and by other criminal justice agencies is increasingly
being managed by the expectation that it will be exercised in accordance with a
published code. In the case, for example, of the exercise of powers of stop and search,
PACE Code A has been approved by Parliament and carries the full authority of
Parliament in the values it embodies. In this way discretion is subject to some form
of accountability, particularly when, as with stop and search, it is coupled with
a recording, reporting, and monitoring system with the person searched being
entitled to a copy of the national search record. Clearly balancing discretion and
accountability are key themes in policing.

There is no doubt that the adversarial nature of the criminal process has an impact
upon pre-trial procedures. The essence of the adversarial trial is that the trial takes the
form of a contest between prosecution and defence which is governed by strict rules
of evidence and which alone determines whether the accused committed the crime
charged. The pre-trial stages merely represent the collection of evidence and preparation of cases by prosecution and defence. Disclosure rules take on a particular significance in an adversarial system. The key point is that in such a system convictions
are secured in one of two ways. First, the prosecution may succeed in adducing
admissible evidence which persuades the finder of fact beyond all reasonable doubt
that the accused committed the act constituting the offence with the requisite intent.
Alternatively, the accused may plead guilty, bypassing completely the necessity for
proof of commission of the offence. It is accordingly unsurprising that the police will
go to considerable lengths to secure a criminal trial which involves a guilty plea rather

than a not guilty plea. There is no uncertainty about the outcome, and the result will be seen by the police to accord with what they know rather than what they can prove in court. The evidential burdens of the adversarial system invariably mean that the police will 'know' more than they can prove. The adversarial system also leaves the pre-trial stages of the process in the hands of the police, largely uncontrolled by outside interference until the point at which the police decide to put a case forward for consideration by the criminal courts.

In an inquisitorial system there is much earlier judicial involvement in the criminal process. Typically an investigating judge will supervise the investigation and be much more involved in the preparation of evidence by the police and in how the various parties will present their cases in court. So the judge will question witnesses, with prosecutor and defence able to ask supplementary questions. There is much less of a contest between the parties, and more of an inquiry to determine the truth. The Royal Commission on Criminal Justice of 1993 considered but did not recommend any change to the adversarial system and concluded that it was fundamental to the system that the prosecution should be obliged 'to establish the defendant's guilt on the basis of evidence which the defence is entitled to contest'. Though there are certain fundamental differences of approach in the two systems, ultimately there are as many similarities as there are differences. For example, the European Convention on Human Rights is able to lay down requirements for a fair criminal trial which apply equally to countries with adversarial and inquisitorial systems.

THE CROWN PROSECUTION SERVICE

The Crown Prosecution Service (CPS) is a national agency, created in 1985 and operational from October 1986, which provides the bridge between the police investigation of cases and the determination of guilt or otherwise by the criminal courts. Once the police have decided to bring a charge against a suspect, the file in that case is passed to the CPS which reviews the file and determines whether there is sufficient evidence to offer a realistic chance of securing a conviction of the accused. The decision is made by applying the Code for Crown Prosecutors, a set of official guidelines on the factors to be taken into account in deciding whether to proceed with the prosecution or to discontinue it. The CPS is also responsible for the presentation of all cases in the criminal courts. The CPS is available to advise the police at any time if they seek it.

The underlying reasons for the establishment of a separate CPS to review police files and to present cases in court were a belief that having the police bear sole responsibility for the decision to prosecute was inconsistent with their duty to investigate. The police were considered to lack the necessary objectivity to throw out weak cases in which they had invested much time and energy in investigating. It was argued that this led to weak cases remaining in the system longer than necessary and increased the risk of miscarriages of justice.

The CPS has had something of a mixed history, culminating in a very critical government report in 1998.[9] The Glidewell Report led to the reorganization of the CPS into forty-two areas largely coinciding with the forty-two police areas (counting the Metropolitan and City Police areas as one). Each area has a Chief Crown Prosecutor who manages a team of lawyers and case workers. Like the police, the CPS is subject to inspection by a central CPS Inspectorate. This reflects a current view that criminal justice agencies will become more efficient if they are run with a greater application of business principles. The inspectorate offers the opportunity for institutional appraisal against stated aims and objectives, as well as checking that the statutory responsibilities of the agency are fulfilled and that inter-agency co-operation is working.

Prosecutions will be undertaken by lawyers working for the CPS, including some prosecutions tried in the Crown Court;[10] for other Crown Court work, the CPS lawyer will instruct a barrister to appear on behalf of the prosecution in that court.

THE CRIMINAL DEFENCE SERVICE

Article 6(3) of the European Convention on Human Rights[11] guarantees certain minimum rights to defendants. The criminal justice system seeks to secure legal representation for those accused of crime by giving them a statutory right to consult a lawyer in private at any time while in a police station for questioning.[12] This statutory right is converted into reality through a system of publicly funded duty solicitors on call to attend at police stations where persons are detained who need their assistance. There is also a duty solicitor scheme operating in the lower criminal courts,[13] though it does not extend to representation for a contested trial.

The old legal aid system which provided representation in court, as well as some office-based advice, has recently been taken over by a new Criminal Defence Service

---

[9] *Review of the Crown Prosecution Service (Glidewell Report)*, Cm 3960 (1998).

[10] See below. Only Crown Prosecutors trained as higher court advocates can appear in the Crown Court.

[11] Everyone charged with a criminal offence has the following minimum rights:

  (a) to be informed promptly, in a language which he understands and in detail, of the nature and cause of the accusation against him;

  (b) to have adequate time and facilities for the preparation of his defence;

  (c) to defend himself in person or through legal assistance of his own choosing or, if he has not sufficient means to pay for legal assistance, to be given it free when the interests of justice so require;

  (d) to examine or have examined witnesses against him and to obtain the attendance and examination of witnesses on his behalf under the same conditions as witnesses against him;

  (e) to have the free assistance of an interpreter if he cannot understand or speak the language used in court.

[12] Police and Criminal Evidence Act 1984 s. 58.

[13] The magistrates' courts: see below.

(CDS) operated by the Government's Legal Services Commission. The function of the CDS is to ensure that people suspected or accused of a crime have access to advice, assistance, and representation where the interests of justice so require. Contracting with lawyers for block services rather than case-by-case services is a feature of the CDS in a measure intended to control the costs of legal defence work. In addition the Legal Services Commission is piloting its own defender service in a four-year project. Six public defender offices will be established using lawyers directly employed by the Commission.

The use of state power in prosecuting criminal offences requires that there is an effective, and sometimes fearless, criminal defence service. Unfortunately, there is some evidence to suggest that defence lawyers too often tend to assume their client's guilt, and through inexperience or inadequate training contribute to the reinforcement of the case constructed against them by the police and the CPS.[14]

COURTS

TWO DIFFERENT SYSTEMS

An appreciation of the distinction between the two types of criminal court in England and Wales is fundamental to an understanding of the criminal justice system. In essence, the distinction is simple: magistrates' courts deal in bulk with less serious or routine crime, while the Crown Court deals with a comparatively small number of more serious criminal offences. Magistrates' courts dispose of the overwhelming majority of criminal business; figures commonly cited show that they dispose of around 95 to 97 per cent of total criminal business. The Crown Court is responsible for no more than 3 to 5 per cent of total criminal business.

But beneath this simple distinction is a far more complex difference: the process by which each court fulfils its functions is dramatically different. It would be quite misleading to think of the process in magistrates' courts as simply a quicker and less formal process than that in the Crown Court.

The use of lay decision-makers is common to both forms of trial. Magistrates' courts are most often composed of three lay magistrates who determine the defendant's guilt or innocence. They are advised on the law by a lawyer clerk. In a contested trial in the Crown Court, a jury of twelve ordinary men and women is the tribunal of fact, determining guilt or innocence after hearing the case for the prosecution and for the defence and the judge's summing up of the case before them. The lay element in the criminal trial is perceived as a great strength of the English criminal justice system, and many argue that it contributes to public support for the system. It is certainly true that attempts by government to change the law, sometimes successful and sometimes not, so as to transfer the trial of particular offences from jury trial to trial before

---

[14] See generally M. McConville *et al.*, *Standing Accused: The Organisation and Practices of Criminal Defence Lawyers in Britain* (Oxford: Clarendon Press, 1994).

the magistrates are inevitably controversial matters accompanied by many public statements on the fundamental nature of the right to be tried before a jury.

Lay decision-makers act as a counter to excessive legal technicality, but there is the risk that complex cases may be beyond lay decision-makers. Some concerns have been expressed that juries composed of ordinary men and women may not be able to cope with the complexity of modern fraud trials, but so far proposals for special juries or specially composed courts to deal with such cases have not been implemented.

MAGISTRATES' COURTS

There are two types of magistrates: lay magistrates, known as justices of the peace (JPs), and stipendiary magistrates, now renamed District Judges. The history of lay magistrates goes back at least to the twelfth century. Today there are 328 independent magistrates' courts, known as Petty Sessional Areas, operating in around 430 courthouses; they are administered locally by Magistrates' Courts Committees.[15] Stipendiary magistrates have a much shorter history than lay magistrates. They first came to be appointed in the eighteenth century as an alternative to corrupt lay magistrates in some urban areas; stipendiaries survive in many of those areas, but District Judges are now commonly used wherever the volume of business is such that lay magistrates cannot cope with all the business. There are sometimes suggestions that District Judges[16] work much faster than lay magistrates because such a system is inherently more efficient than a system of deliberation by magistrates advised by a lawyer clerk.

Magistrates and District Judges exercise a wide variety of powers. They try less serious criminal cases, but they also have important powers in relation to accused persons prior to their trial. Among the most important are bail or jail decisions, since detention in custody by the police is permitted only for a short period of time following a charge, after which the accused person must be brought before a magistrates' court. It is then for the magistrates' court to determine whether the accused person is to be kept in custody pending trial or released into the community on either unconditional or conditional bail. In exercising this function, they are guardians of the liberty of accused persons.

THE CROWN COURT

The Crown Court is formally a single court, part of the Supreme Court, with power to sit anywhere in England or Wales. There are seventy-eight main Crown Court centres divided into six regions, known as Circuits. The administration of the Crown Court is the responsibility of the Court Service, an executive agency of the Lord Chancellor's Department. It deals, for example, with the appointments of both judges and of magistrates.

---

[15] There are around 31,000 serving lay magistrates.

[16] There are 106 full-time and 169 part-time District Judges working in this capacity; the title is also used for certain judges undertaking civil work.

The Crown Court consists of a full-time or part-time judge empowered to sit in the Crown Court who sits with a jury in contested trials. The Crown Court deals with the most serious criminal offences, together with those cases where the magistrates' courts have committed a defendant for trial in the Crown Court, either because some factor in their view justifies trial in the higher court, or because the defendant has refused to consent to be tried in the lower court where he or she has the choice of being tried[17] in the higher court. The Crown Court also deals with those defendants convicted in the magistrates' courts where, on conviction of an offence which can be tried either in the magistrates' court or the Crown Court (either-way offences), the magistrates' court concludes that its limited sentencing powers are inadequate to deal with the defendant, who is committed to the Crown Court for the sentencing decision to be made in the higher court.

Trial in the Crown Court is the epitome of the ordinary citizen's popular view of the criminal process. A robed judge presides over a court in which silken-voiced advocates employ formidable forensic skills in examining and cross-examining witnesses in order to persuade the jury of the guilt or innocence of the accused. The pace is measured and the details frequently gripping even in a routine case.

Though the process of jury trial appears to be a model of fairness, it is wrong to isolate it from the processes which have gone before. There is evidence to suggest that the outcome of cases in the Crown Court is as much dependent on what happens to accused persons in the police station and in the magistrates' courts[18] as upon the process of jury trial.

However, the full panoply of a contested trial occurs only in three in ten cases tried before the Crown Court. As elsewhere in the criminal justice system, the guilty plea dominates and is by far the most common method by which a criminal trial comes to its conclusion.

Because the outcome of trial in the Crown Court (whether contested or on a guilty plea) is inevitably serious for the defendant, representation by a lawyer is common. Representation is mainly the province of barristers, though Crown Prosecutors qualified as higher court advocates and solicitors with corresponding qualifications are entitled to appear in the Crown Court.

THE RELATIONSHIP BETWEEN THE TWO MODES OF TRIAL

It will be clear that it is, broadly, the seriousness of the offence which determines the distribution of business between the magistrates' courts and the Crown Court. All offences are classified as either triable only on indictment, that is, in the Crown Court, triable only summarily, that is, in the magistrates' courts, or triable either way. Offences classified as triable either way may be tried either in the magistrates' courts or in the Crown Court. Where an accused person is charged with an either-way offence, the magistrates' court must decide which court is more suitable for the trial of the particular defendant. The nature and seriousness of the offence are the most significant factors taken into account. Both prosecution and defence can make

---

[17] See below.　　[18] E.g., whether bail was granted or refused.

representations to the court about this. If the magistrates' court decides that trial before the magistrates is more appropriate, it offers the defendant trial in the magistrates' court. Defendants can, at this point, consent to trial in the magistrates' court or refuse their consent. If they refuse consent, they must be committed to the Crown Court for trial even if the circumstances of the offence seem trivial to the magistrates' court. If, on the other hand, the magistrates' court considers that trial in the Crown Court is more appropriate, the defendant has no choice in the matter.

There are national guidelines designed to ensure some consistency in decision-making on the determination of the mode of trial of either-way offences by the hundreds of courts making such decisions each day.[19]

APPEAL COURTS

Because there are two separate systems of criminal trial, there are also two separate systems of appeal. Appeal following trial in the magistrates' courts is far more generous than the system of appeal following trial in the Crown Court. This reflects a deep-rooted respect for decision-making by juries. Indeed, it was not until 1907 that there was anything resembling a proper system of appeal following trial by jury, and it was not until 1966 that this appeal became part of the mainstream system of appeal courts in England and Wales.

Perhaps surprisingly, the appeal system is not designed primarily to ensure that a correct decision has been reached, though that is, of course, one of its underlying purposes. Apart from an appeal from the magistrates' courts to the Crown Court against conviction, there is never a re-run of the trial before the appeal court.[20] There are said to be three main purposes of a system of criminal appeals. The first is to ensure that the defendant's trial was fair and that there was no material irregularity in the proceedings. The second is to allow for the development of rules of criminal procedure and of the substantive criminal law. The third is to ensure some degree of consistency in the administration of criminal justice and in the sentencing of convicted offenders.

There are, however, procedures by which a defendant can seek to undo a miscarriage of justice, but the time limit for appealing[21] often militates against this. The adversarial nature of the trial, which permits both prosecution and defence to select the case they will put before the magistrates' court or the jury in the Crown Court, also means that appeal courts are reluctant to offer opportunities for a fresh trial which can be run in a different way. For many, the hope of overturning their conviction will turn on some new evidence coming to light, and this is likely to occur outside the normal time limits for appealing.

None of this is to undermine the importance of a properly functioning system of criminal appeal, which is a vital ingredient in any criminal justice system.

---

[19] Practice Note: Mode of Trial Guidelines [1990] 3 All ER 979, as amended in 1995.
[20] Though the Court of Appeal has the power to order a re-trial on the quashing of a conviction.
[21] Usually 28 days from the date of the decision of the trial court.

THE PROBATION SERVICE

Probation officers are successors to the church workers who, in the nineteenth century, agreed to be responsible for juvenile offenders in order to keep them out of prison. The Probation of Offenders Act 1907 established probation officers on a statutory rather than charitable footing to advise, assist, and befriend offenders. The Probation Service has grown into an important agency in the criminal justice system with responsibility for advising the courts in pre-sentence reports about the options available for dealing with convicted offenders, and for supervising offenders in the community under a variety of non-custodial sentences. Probation officers also work with officers of the Prison Service in assessing prisoners' suitability for early release from a prison sentence. They also work in prisons to assist offenders to address their offending so that they can be rehabilitated.

The Probation Service has recently become a single national service operating under a National Director, who is accountable to the Home Secretary. The Service is organized into forty-two areas corresponding to police force and CPS areas. Like other criminal justice agencies, it is subject to inspection, in this case by Her Majesty's Inspectorate of Probation. There have been suggestions from a minority of courts that probation officers can become too 'offender-biased' and make unrealistic recommendations to courts on the treatment of offenders.[22]

THE PRISON SERVICE

Views of punishment for crime have changed dramatically over time. Punishments that were once commonplace are now regarded as barbaric. Execution, flogging, and transportation were once common penalties. Considerable public support remains for the re-introduction of the death penalty, but this form of punishment has been abolished in England and Wales, and its abolition is encouraged for all members of the Council of Europe.[23]

There are currently 137 Prison Service establishments in England and Wales, of which seven are privately managed under a contracted-out arrangement permitted by the Criminal Justice Act 1991. There are different categorisations of men and women prisoners. All adult male prisoners are allocated to one of four categories:

Category A: those whose escape would be highly dangerous to the public
Category B: those whose escape would pose a risk but who do not require the highest levels of security

---

[22] Home Office, *Magistrates' Views of the Probation Service* (London: Home Office, 1997).
[23] See Protocol No. 6 to the European Convention on Human Rights.

Category C: those with neither the will nor the resources to make a determined escape

Category D: those who pose no risk and are unlikely to attempt an escape.

Prisons holding categories A to C prisoners are known as 'closed' prisons, while prisons holding category D prisoners are 'open' prisons with little external security. Women and young prisoners of either sex may be placed in Category A accommodation, but are not otherwise categorized.

Arrangements for the detention of juveniles are currently being reorganized, because of their vulnerability and the inappropriateness of their being housed with adult offenders. The Prison Service's statement of purpose retains some of the language of an earlier age:

Her Majesty's Prison Service serves the public by keeping in custody those committed by the courts. Our duty is to look after them with humanity and help them lead law-abiding and useful lives in custody and after release.

Prisons (whether managed by the Prison Service or a private prison) are subject to inspection by the Prisons Inspectorate.

Custody has become a more common form of punishment in recent years, and sentences have lengthened. In 1993 the prison population was 45,000, of whom 11,000 were on remand (i.e. detained) awaiting trial. Five years later the prison population was 65,000, of whom 13,000 were on remand awaiting trial. The average length of prison sentences for males aged 21 or over and sentenced in the Crown Court rose in this period from 21.8 months to 23.6 months. England and Wales imprison people at a somewhat higher rate than most of our European neighbours, but at a significantly lower rate than the United States.

THE CRIMINAL CASES REVIEW COMMISSION

Those for whom the time limits for appeal had long passed, but who believed there were grounds for questioning the correctness of their conviction could formerly write to the Home Secretary putting their case. The Home Secretary could cause inquiries to be made, and in some cases would refer the case back to the Court of Appeal for further consideration. The system was haphazard and felt not to be a proper response to the problems of miscarriages of justice. Following recommendations made by the Royal Commission on Criminal Justice, the Criminal Cases Review Commission (CCRC) was established by Part II of the Criminal Appeal Act 1995. The Commission started work in April 1997 and has been a considerable success.

The CCRC is an independent body with fourteen members supported by case workers and support staff. It has responsibility for reviewing convictions and sentences both in the magistrates' courts and in the Crown Court. Reviews of convictions are conducted to identify whether the conviction may have been unsafe, while reviews of sentences seek to identify whether a point of law was not raised in the court proceedings or new information is now available which has a bearing on sentence. In both cases the CCRC has to decide whether there is a real possibility of success. Where there is, the CCRC will refer the case back to the appropriate appeal court. The Commission has no power of its own to overturn a conviction or alter a sentence. In addition to its functions of reviewing cases, the CCRC can be asked by the Court of Appeal to investigate matters for it which will assist it to resolve a case before it. The CCRC has no investigative staff of its own, but can appoint a police officer to conduct inquiries on its behalf.

CRIMINAL INJURIES COMPENSATION AUTHORITY

A noticeable and noteworthy feature of the criminal justice system in recent years has been its increasing concern with the victims of crime. Their interests have come to be seen as an important aspect of the system. A sentencing policy based on restorative justice pays much greater regard to the views of victims; there is also more use made of victims in persuading offenders to understand the trauma their offences cause, whether offences against the person or against property.

The criminal justice system has long recognized the need to offer compensation to those who suffer personal injury as the result of criminal acts and who cannot recover compensation from the perpetrator of the criminal act, either because he cannot be found or because he is impecunious. The Criminal Injuries Compensation Authority, as successor to the Criminal Injuries Compensation Board, adjudicates on claims by victims of crime and seeks to offer the same levels of compensation to these victims that the civil law of obligations would provide. Many claimants are police officers who have been injured in the line of duty, though it would probably be better if there was a separate system to provide compensation in such cases.

MODERNIZING THE SYSTEM

Despite an intense period of reform of the criminal justice system over the past three decades, there is still seen to be a need to modernize the criminal justice system.[24] The historical division between magistrates' courts and the Crown Court is being questioned. A number of submissions to the Auld Review have argued for the creation of a single criminal court supported by a unified and nationally funded administration, but which would retain some form of local accountability.[25] This would mirror

[24] Evidenced by the Criminal Courts Review under the chairmanship of Auld LJ ('the Auld Review') which is due to report later this year, and the Government's Command Paper, n. 5 above.

[25] See now *Report on the Review of the Criminal Courts of England and Wales (Auld Review) October 2001* (London: Stationery Office, 2001), which recommends the creation of a unified Criminal Court with 3 levels of jurisdiction: the existing magistrates' courts, the existing Crown Court, and a new District Division to exercise jurisdiction over a range of middle-ranking cases.

developments in the civil justice system, where the historic division of jurisdictions between locally based county courts and a nationally based High Court has been replaced by a system which retains the local and national institutions but super-imposes upon them a single national system for the allocation of civil litigation.

Another theme which is emerging is the effectiveness of managing the criminal justice system through three government departments. Recent co-operative mechanisms have sought to ensure that there is a common approach to strategy and planning. This is achieved through a Ministerial Steering Group, chaired by the Home Secretary but including the Lord Chancellor and the Attorney-General. This is supported by a Strategic Planning Group consisting of senior officials in the relevant departments. Two interdepartmental units also seek to co-ordinate activity. The Criminal Justice Joint Planning Unit consists of staff from the Home Office, the Lord Chancellor's Department, the Crown Prosecution Service, and the Treasury. The Integrating Business and Information Systems Unit (IBIS) is a joint initiative to ensure better integration of information systems. Beneath these lead bodies is a whole host of units and organizations providing inputs into policy and strategy for the criminal justice system. Information technology is seen as a vital tool in improving case management.

There has been recognition that the system moves too slowly at times. This is seen to have a number of adverse impacts. Petty criminals can delay the moment of their conviction, while the delays inherent in trial in the Crown Court can result in lengthy periods of remand in prison for those awaiting trial. Initiatives have already been set in place to address some of these problems, and changes made to the substantive law, but there remains some concern that tinkering with the system may not be enough to achieve lasting and permanent acceleration of the processes while retaining due process. This has allowed more radical solutions to be considered, and is reviving interest in the codification of the substantive criminal law coupled with a simpler single code of criminal procedure.

A key challenge in modernizing the system is to ensure that speedy justice remains fair. In a seminal work,[26] Herbert Packer, an American scholar, argued that systems of criminal justice could usefully be examined to see to what extent they corresponded to two theoretical models: the due-process model and the crime-control model.

The due-process model corresponds to the rhetoric of the English criminal justice system. The hallmarks of this model are the presumption of innocence and the requirement of proof of guilt beyond all reasonable doubt. At all stages of the process suspects and defendants enjoy safeguards against self-incrimination. There are obstacles in the face of the police and prosecutors which operate as a form of quality control, ensuring that the criminal process constantly weeds out all those who appear to be innocent. At the centre of the due-process model is the trial stage, which is again marked by restrictions on the introduction of prejudicial material not directly relevant to the offence or of doubtful probative value. Ultimately the due-process model accepts that the price paid for the certainty that no innocent person is convicted will be the occasional acquittal of the guilty.

The contrasting crime-control model replaces the judicial procedures with

---

[26] H. Packer, *The Limits of the Criminal Sanction* (Stanford, Cal.: Stanford University Press, 1968).

administrative procedures and formal processes with informal processes. Great trust is placed on informal fact-finding, that is, what the police know rather than what is admissible in a process of formal adjudication. The conclusions of the police as fact-finders are the principal determinants of guilt. Repression of criminal conduct is seen as the most important function of the criminal process. Criminal procedure becomes geared to the speedy processing of suspects and defendants. The obstacles of the due-process model disappear to be replaced by low visibility administrative processing. Packer comments that:

If there is confidence in the reliability of informal fact-finding activities that take place in the early stages of the criminal process, the remaining stages can be relatively perfunctory.[27]

The presumption of innocence in the due-process model is replaced by an implicit presumption of guilt, so that the police are relied upon by courts to weed out the innocent at the investigation stage.

The crime-control model is usually rejected as inapplicable to the English criminal justice system. But the rejection seems premature if there is routine violation of the rules governing the police powers of arrest, search and seizure, and interrogation, and if one adds to this evidence showing how rarely suspects relied on the right to silence and the overwhelming number of guilty pleas, where no proof of guilt is required, where there is currently no independent assessment of the evidence, and where there are no adversarial procedures, and the crime-control model begins to look remarkably apposite. Much writing on the criminal justice system in England and Wales has shown that there is a gap between the rhetoric of the system and its delivery in practice.

An important contribution to the debate on underlying values was made in 1994, and this has taken on added significance in the light of the Government's decision to incorporate the European Convention on Human Rights into United Kingdom law by the Human Rights Act 1998. Ashworth,[28] discussing the pre-trial stages of the criminal process, argues for a rights-based approach based on the values implicit in the protec-tions to be found in the European Convention. He regards the search for a balance between the community interest in securing the conviction of offenders and the protection of the civil liberties of the citizen as misplaced, and as giving no clue to which objectives are to be accorded priority when conflicts arise. He advocates a more principled approach which would identify key values and require any derogation from them to meet tests of necessity and proportionality.

CONCLUSION

There can be few institutions more central to modern society than a criminal justice system, and there can be few greater challenges than the continuing delivery of an effective criminal justice system.

---

[27] *Ibid.*, 160–1.
[28] A. Ashworth, *The Criminal Process. An Evaluative Study* (Oxford: Clarendon Press, 1994: see now 2nd edn., (1998)).

In introducing the Government's current thinking on the modernization of the criminal justice system in England and Wales, the Home Secretary commented:

An effective criminal justice system is a vital part of a fair, just and tolerant society. We need to make sure that law enforcement agencies have the right tools, that prosecutors and courts are operating with fair and simple rules of evidence and that prisons and probation deliver punishment that works to protect the public and prevent reoffending.

That is an enormous challenge laid out in a simple way. But it disguises the essential debate on values, principles, and structures that will deliver the promise. Despite centuries of tradition in the development of a legal system, the criminal justice system of England and Wales cannot yet claim to have got it right. But it continues to try to do so.

Further Reading

ASHWORTH, A., *The Criminal Process: An Evaluative Study* (2nd edn., Oxford: Oxford University Press, 1998).

McCONVILLE, M., and BALDWIN, J., *Courts, Prosecution and Conviction* (Oxford: Oxford University Press, 1981).

—— SANDERS, A., and LENG, R., *The Case for the Prosecution* (London: Routledge, 1991).

—— HODGSON, J., BRIDGES, L., and PAVLOVIC, A., *Standing Accused. The Organisation and Practices of Criminal Defence Lawyers in Britain* (Oxford: Clarendon Press, 1994).

SANDERS, A., and YOUNG, R., *Criminal Justice* (2nd edn., London: Butterworths, 2000).

WHITE, R. C. A., *The English Legal System in Action. The Administration of Justice* (3rd edn., (Oxford: Oxford University Press, 1999).

Further information can be obtained from the following websites:

The Court Service	www.courtservice.gov.uk
Criminal Cases Review Commission	www.ccrc.gov.uk
Criminal Courts Review (Auld Review)	www.criminal-courts-review.gov.uk
Criminal Injuries Compensation Authority	www.cica.gov.uk
Criminal Justice System	www.criminal-justice-system.gov.uk
Crown Prosecution Service	www.cps.gov.uk
HM Inspector of Constabulary	www.homeoffice.gov.uk/hmic/hmic.htm
HM Inspector of Prisons	www.homeoffice.gov.uk/hmipris/hmipris.htm
HM Inspector of Probation	www.homeoffice.gov.uk/hmiprob/hmiprob.htm
HM Magistrates' Courts Inspectorate	www.open.gov.uk/mcsi
Home Office	www.homeoffice.gov.uk
Just Ask	www.justask.org.uk
Legal Services	www.legalservices.gov.uk
Lord Chancellor's Department	www.open.gov.uk/lcd
Magistrates Association	www.magistrates-association.org.uk
Magistrates' Courts Service	www.open.gov.uk/lcd/magist/magistfr.htm
Police Services in the United Kingdom	www.police.uk
Prison Service	www.hmprisonservice.gov.uk
Probation Service	www.homeoffice.gov.uk/new_indexs/index_probation.htm
United Kingdom Parliament	www.parliament.uk
Victim Support	www.victimsupport.com

2

THE ORGANIZATION
AND ACCOUNTABILITY
OF THE POLICE

Robert Reiner

INTRODUCTION: THE CONCEPTS OF
POLICE AND POLICING

The very idea of policing is in many ways fundamentally problematic for democracy and the rule of law. Controlling the police has always been seen as one of the most difficult aspects of statecraft, as the Roman writer Juvenal's famous question '*quis custodiet ipsos custodes?*'—'who guards the guards?' indicated two millenia ago. The problems are apparent as soon as we consider what policing is.

Policing refers to the set of activities directed at preserving the security of a particular social order, through the creation of systems of surveillance coupled with the threat of sanctions for discovered deviance. Policing may be carried out by a variety of people and techniques. It may be done by professionals employed by the State in an organization with an omnibus policing mandate—the archetypal modern idea of *the* police. It may also be carried out by state agencies with other primary purposes (such as the military), private security companies, citizen volunteers, or as a by-product of other activities (such as care-taking or bus-driving).[1] Policing may be carried out by technology, like CCTV cameras or listening devices. Policing may even be designed into the architecture and furniture of streets and buildings. All these policing strategies are proliferating in Britain today.

Until modern times policing functions were primarily carried out as a by-product of other social relationships. Specialized policing institutions appear only in relatively complex societies. Police forces developed hand-in-hand with the development of social inequality and hierarchy. They are the product of the emergence and protection of more centralized and dominant state systems.[2] The complex and contradictory function of contemporary police, as simultaneously embodying the quest for general

---

[1] L. Johnson, *Policing Britain: Risk, Security and Governance* (London: Longman, 2000).

[2] C. Robinson and R. Scaglion, 'The Origins and Evolution of the Police Function in Society' (1987) 21 *Law and Society Review* 109.

and stratified order—'parking tickets' as well as 'class repression'[3]—is thus inscribed in their birth process.

British police ideology has always rested upon the myth of a fundamental distinction between its model of community-based policing and an alien, 'Continental', state-controlled system. Conventional histories of the British police attempt to trace a direct lineage between ancient tribal forms of collective self-policing and the contemporary 'bobby'. Many European systems of police did develop more overtly as instruments of state control,[4] but British police development is equally intertwined with the shifting structures of class and politics. The supposedly benign 'British' police model was in any case for home consumption only. A more militaristic and coercive style was from the outset exported to colonial situations, including Ireland.[5]

It is problematic to define contemporary police mainly in terms of their supposed crime functions. The police are called upon routinely to deal with a bewildering miscellany of problems, from traffic control to terrorism. The common feature of the tasks that have come to be seen as police work is that they all involve 'something that ought not to be happening and about which someone had better do something NOW!'.[6] In other words, policing tasks arise in emergency situations, usually with an element of at least potential social conflict. This does not imply that all policing is about the use of force. On the contrary, 'good' policing is the craft of handling trouble without resort to coercion, usually by skilful verbal tactics.[7]

The governance of the police as a specialist body with the power to exercise legitimate force is a particular problem for democracies. The very existence of a specific police institution implies at least potential social conflict and the absence of complete consensus. Policing is always at least partly an exercise of power *against* someone. Who decides when force is needed, how much force is justified, and how it should be exercised are vexed issues for any democracy purporting to be based on the rule of law.

Although they are the institution charged with the ultimate power of legitimate force, the police have not been mere tools of the State faithfully carrying out tasks determined from above. Whether this is regarded as legitimate or not, all police forces have been characterized by the discretion exercised by the lowest ranks in the organization. This discretion is facilitated above all by the low visibility of police work, which consists mainly of dispersed patrol, surveillance, and investigation. The reality of much operational street-level policing is thus hidden from managerial and legal scrutiny and accountability. The definition of police work in practice is

[3] O. Marenin, 'Parking Tickets and Class Repression: The Concept of Policing in Critical Theories of Criminal Justice' (1983) 6 *Contemporary Crises* 241.

[4] R. Mawby, *Comparative Policing Issues* (London: Unwin, 1991); J.-P. Brodeur (ed.), *Comparisons in Policing* (Aldershot: Avebury, 1995).

[5] M. Brogden, 'The Emergence of the Police: The Colonial Dimension' (1987) 27 *British Journal of Criminology* 4.

[6] E. Bittner, 'Florence Nightingale in Pursuit of Willie Sutton: A Theory of the Police' in H. Jacob (ed.), *The Potential For Reform of Criminal Justice* (Beverly Hills, Cal.: Sage, 1974) 30.

[7] R. Reiner, 'Process or Product? Problems of Assessing Individual Police Performance' in J.-P. Brodeur (ed.), *How to Recognise Good Policing* (Thousand Oaks, Cal.: Sage, 1998) 55.

achieved by the interplay of a variety of processes and pressures, amongst which formal law and policies determined at the top have been of relatively little significance.[8]

This chapter will review the development and current organization of policing in Britain. Its particular focus will be on how the British police have struggled with the problem discussed above: how to render an institution for regulating conflict, by force if necessary, acceptable and accountable to the public.

THE BRITISH POLICE TRADITION AND POLICING BY CONSENT

It is a central part of British police mythology that policing in this country rests on a particular style, often referred to as 'policing by consent'. An official report summed this up by describing the British police officer as a 'citizen in uniform', armed not with special legal powers but with public support.[9] The construction of this traditional image was a long, complex, and conflict-ridden process.

The modern British police were established during the first half of the nineteenth century in the face of massive opposition from a wide range of political interests and philosophies.[10] While middle- and upper-class suspicions were rapidly allayed, working-class resentment lived on, expressed in sporadic physical violence. Yet by the mid-twentieth century the police had become not merely accepted but a symbol of national pride.

The 1950s were the zenith of police acceptance by the public. This was shown most clearly by a national opinion survey conducted for the Royal Commission on the Police in 1959, which found 'an overwhelming vote of confidence in the police', in all social classes.[11] Police *power*, i.e. the capacity to inflict legal sanctions including force, seems to have been transmuted into *authority*, power that is accepted as at least minimally legitimate.

The achievement of consensus policing in Britain was partly the product of specific aspects of police organizational policy. However, an essential precondition was the process whereby the working class, the main source of initial hostility to the new police, came to be incorporated into the political and economic institutions of British society. Police acceptance was mutually interdependent with a wider process of the pacification of social relations.

The architects of the benign and dignified English police image were Home Secretary Robert Peel and the two Commissioners of the Metropolitan Police he appointed in 1829 when the Metropolitan police force was created, Colonel Charles Rowan and Sir Richard Mayne. They adopted a set of policies aimed at securing

---

[8] R. Reiner, *The Politics of the Police* (3rd edn., Oxford: Oxford University Press, 2000) chaps. 3 and 6.

[9] Royal Commission on the Police, *Final Report*, Cmnd 1728 (1962) 11.

[10] See Reiner, n. 8 above, chaps. 1 and 2.

[11] B. Weinberger, *The Best Police in the World* (London: Scolar Press, 1995) 1–2.

public acceptance in the face of strong opposition to the very existence of the police, by encouraging a low-profile, legalistic policing style. The following policies were crucial for the creation of consent.

BUREAUCRATIC ORGANIZATION

The basis of the 'new' police idea was the establishment of a full–time force of professional police officers, organized into a bureaucratic hierarchy. This contrasted with the previous reliance on part-timers and amateur volunteers. Entry and promotion were meritocratic, not partisan or nepotistic.

A chain of command was constructed on quasi-military lines, and at first the policy was to appoint former non-commissioned military officers to the higher ranks, because of their experience as disciplinarians. This later changed in favour of internal promotion from the ranks. By the 1870s the notion of policing as a career offering status and security began to emerge, and a sense of professional identification and commitment developed.

THE RULE OF LAW

The way in which the police maintained order and enforced the law was itself supposed to be governed by legalistic procedures and constraints. The Commissioners were well aware of the importance of the police maintaining an image of subjection to the rule of law as a way of alleviating opposition. They laid down strict regulations and sanctions governing the use of the wide discretionary powers conferred on constables by statutes such as the Vagrancy Act 1824. While the Commissioners believed such powers were needed by constables, they imposed strict disciplinary sanctions in cases of abuse, and encouraged 'all respectable persons' to bring complaints to them.[12]

THE STRATEGY OF MINIMAL FORCE

All police forces would claim to use as little force as necessary. The British tradition stands out, however, for its avoidance of arms. With characteristic forthrightness, Sir Robert Mark once articulated the crowd-control strategy of the Metropolitan Police thus: '[t]he real art of policing a free society or a democracy is to win by appearing to lose'. Their secret weapon was not water cannon, tear gas, or plastic bullets, but public sympathy.

Constables' weapons were limited to the truncheon, carried concealed until 1863, and intended as a last resort. On specific dangerous assignments or beats, specially selected officers might carry a pistol or a cutlass, but each occasion when such a weapon was used was closely scrutinized.

The army was available as the ultimate back-up for dealing with civil disorder, and it was used on many occasions in the latter part of the nineteenth and early twentieth

---

[12] W. Miller, *Cops and Bobbies* (2nd edn., Columbus, Ohio: Ohio State University Press, 1999) 4–12, 56–66.

centuries. But gradually the non-lethally-armed civilian police force became the sole means of riot control in mainland Britain.

Although they have certainly never acted with kid gloves, there is no doubt that the British police developed a tradition of containing industrial disputes and political demonstrations with minimum force when contrasted with the experience of many other countries. Nonetheless anxiety and controversy about political and industrial conflict have recurred many times, with complaints of police brutality and right-wing bias.

NON-PARTISANSHIP

Peel, Rowan, and Mayne recognized that public acceptance depended upon the police not being seen as political. They insisted on strict exclusion of patronage in appointments and promotions at a time when this was normal civil service practice. Police officers were also denied the vote until 1887. The insistence on suppressing indications of overt political control or partisanship softened the initial conception of the police as a tool of government oppression.

ACCOUNTABILITY

The police were portrayed as accountable in two ways. First, the legality of police action was reviewable by the courts. Secondly, they were portrayed as accountable through an almost mystical process of *identification* with the British people, not the State. Although lacking any tangible control by elected institutions, they were supposed to be in tune with the popular will because of their social representativeness. The recruitment policies of the police reflected this principle, drawing upon recruits from manual working-class backgrounds representative of the mass of the people. Since the Second World War this principle has even governed the selection of chief officers in all forces: Chief Constables work their way up through the ranks and share working-class origins.

THE SERVICE ROLE

The nineteenth-century police reformers quite deliberately cultivated a service role for the police in order to secure legitimacy for more coercive policing functions. These were often regarded by the police themselves as unwelcome 'extraneous' duties. Many of the service tasks benefited the middle class at the expense of the working class, such as the enforcement of nuisance laws. But others did benefit the working class too. Arguably the criminal prosecution role of the police was a more valued and useful service to the mass of the population than the 'friendly' non-coercive 'services' to which the term is usually confined. But the 'service' role played a part in securing police legitimation.

PREVENTIVE POLICING

The primacy of prevention over detection was emphasized in the famous opening lines of Peel's celebrated instructions to the Metropolitan Police's first batch of recruits (which are still used today). The practical implementation of this principle meant the concentration of the force's manpower on regular 'beats' by uniformed police. This was motivated not only by a belief in the efficacy of the constable's 'scarecrow function'. It was also a response to widespread fear of undercover police spies.

Hostility to the idea of plain-clothes police delayed the formation of detective branches for many years. A separate Criminal Investigation Department was established only in 1877. By the 1880s the police had gained sufficient public confidence for the formation of a specifically political unit, the Special Irish Branch, initially to deal with terrorism. It subsequently acquired a wider remit and became the Special Branch. But during the nineteenth century the emphasis on crime prevention by uniformed patrols was a factor in the achievement of police legitimation, quelling early fears about undercover spies.

POLICE EFFECTIVENESS

The final aspect of police policy contributing to their legitimation was the appearance of effectiveness in the core mandate of crime control. How effective the police actually were in reducing crime remains debatable, but certainly the image of success was cultivated.

THE SOCIAL CONTEXT OF POLICE LEGITIMATION

Gradually even most of the working class became reconciled to the criminal justice system and used its services when they were the victims of theft or assault. Slowly the new police inserted themselves into working-class life, not only as an intrusive controlling apparatus but also as a potential source of security, although this was at times threatened by heavy-handed control of industrial or political conflict.

The all-important background precondition for police legitimation was not any aspect of police policy, but the changing social, economic, and political context. The working class, the main original opposition to the police, gradually, unevenly, and incompletely came to be incorporated as citizens into the political institutions of British society. This process had very clear limits. It enabled the bulk of the working class to share in the growth of the economy, but class inequality remained largely unaltered, and has widened substantially since the return of free market economics in the late 1970s.[13]

---

[13] I. Taylor, *Crime in Context: A Critical Criminology of Market Societies* (Cambridge: Polity Press, 1999).

Nonetheless, the wide gulf between 'two nations', which was sharply manifest in the mid-nineteenth century as the new police came into being, had become blurred by the 1950s, the high point of police legitimation. From a widely hated and feared institution, the police came to be regarded as the embodiment of impersonal, rule-bound authority, enforcing democratically enacted legislation on behalf of the broad mass of society rather than any partisan interest, and constrained by tight legal requirements of due process.

POLICING BY CONSENT: RECENT CHALLENGES

Since 1959 British policing has been beset by controversy and competing proposals for reform, and the policing by consent tradition has been threatened. Survey evidence in the 1970s and 1980s suggested a hæmorrhage of public confidence in the police. This decline slowed down a little in the late 1990s, and more than three-quarters of the public still say their local police do a very or fairly good job.[14] Nonetheless, during the last quarter of the twentieth century, all the factors that had produced the earlier 'policing by consent' tradition came under pressure.

RECRUITMENT, TRAINING, AND DISCIPLINE

The image of the police as a disciplined bureaucracy was gradually eroded. Partly this was a question of standards of entry and training that had not kept up with general improvements in education. In the 1960s various schemes were introduced to attract university graduates to the service, and encourage higher education for serving police officers. However, significant results were achieved only during the 1980s, when as a result of the 1978 Edmund-Davies pay award (and unemployment outside the service) the intake of graduates accelerated sharply to about 12 per cent of recruits *per annum*. Significant changes have occurred in recruit training too, largely following from the 1982 Scarman Report. Despite these developments, however, they have not prevented the erosion of public confidence in police professional standards.

Perhaps the single worst blow to the image of the British police as a disciplined, impersonal bureaucracy was the series of corruption scandals that began in 1969. Since then the police have experienced a repeated cycle of scandal and reform. The standard methods of criminal investigation, especially the cultivation of close relations with criminals as informants, operate perennially on the borderline of legality. There was extensive corruption behind the façade of legitimacy even in the 'Golden Age' of high public confidence in the police. The explosion of corruption scandals in the 1970s was the product of the dangers inherent in traditional detective methods, coupled with new pressures. These included the rise of large-scale organized crime, and growing toleration of some still illegal activities (like drug-taking or pornography)

---

[14] L. Sims and A. Myhill, *Policing and the Public: Findings From the 2000 British Crime Survey* (London: Home Office Research and Statistics Directorate, 2001).

which increased their profitability. Declining public deference also made it much more likely that police wrongdoing would come to light and that allegations against officers would be believed.

THE RULE OF LAW

The issue of police violations of legal procedures in the course of dealing with offences became acutely politicized in the 1970s. On the one hand groups like the National Council for Civil Liberties publicized evidence of widespread police malpractice, while on the other the police began to lobby for greater powers to aid the 'war against crime'. This conflict resulted in the establishment in 1979 of the Royal Commission on Criminal Procedure (RCCP), which reported in 1981. After much argument and modification, the RCCP Report eventually resulted in the Police and Criminal Evidence Act 1984 (PACE). This purported to provide a balanced codification of police powers and safeguards over their exercise, synthesizing the concerns of the 'law and order' and the civil liberties lobbies, although there has been extensive debate about whether it has succeeded.[15]

What is certain is that controversy about police abuse of powers increased rather than abated. Between 1989 and 1991 public confidence in the police was further shaken by a series of scandals revealing serious malpractice. In October 1989 the Court of Appeal released the 'Guildford Four', three men and a woman sentenced to life imprisonment in 1974 for the bombing of public houses in Guildford and Woolwich. A further blow to confidence in the police was the release in March 1991 of the 'Birmingham Six', who had been convicted in 1975 of the bombing of a Birmingham pub. Several other *causes célèbres* were considered by the Court of Appeal in the early 1990s, revealing yet more miscarriages of justice.[16] The anxiety produced by these revelations of abuse was enough to make the Home Secretary announce in 1991 the establishment of a Royal Commission on Criminal Justice, the first Royal Commission in twelve years of Conservative government.

THE STRATEGY OF MINIMAL FORCE

In the last thirty years a clear trend of harder-line policing of political and industrial conflict has also threatened the traditional British police strategy of 'winning by appearing to lose'. The capacity of the police to cope with public order problems expanded during the 1970s. Militarization of policing proceeded apace in the 1980s in the wake of yet more serious conflicts, notably the 1981 and 1985 urban riots, and the 1984–5 miners' strike.[17] Several Public Order Acts (notably in 1986 and 1994) enhanced police powers.[18]

[15] M. McConville, A. Sanders, and R. Leng, *The Case for the Prosecution* (London: Routledge, 1991); Reiner, n. 8 above.

[16] M. McConville and L. Bridges (eds.), *Criminal Justice in Crisis* (Aldershot: Edward Elgar, 1994).

[17] C. Critcher and D. Waddington (eds.), *Policing Public Order* (Aldershot: Avebury, 1996).

[18] P. A. J. Waddington, *Liberty and Order* (London: UCL Press, 1994).

Without much public debate *de facto* specialist 'third forces' developed, specifically trained and readily mobilizable to cope with riots. All police forces now have such units (under various names), specially trained in riot control, use of firearms, plastic bullets, and CS gas. Since 1974 all forces have also formed Police Support Units to help in controlling crowds, strikes, and demonstrations. These are specially trained for public-order duties, including the use of shields, though they are normally engaged in ordinary policing at local level. However they are readily mobilizable to deal with problems arising outside their own force under mutual aid arrangements. During the 1984 miners' strike a massive, centrally co-ordinated police operation was directed by the National Reporting Centre, with much criticism of 'police-state' tactics. During the trial of miners on riot charges, it was revealed that in the early 1980s the Association of Chief Police Officers (ACPO) had produced a secret document, the *Tactical Options Manual*. This set out the blueprint for a finely graded response to public disorder, culminating in the militaristic tactics used during the strike.

In the mid-1990s there arose a variety of new forms of political protest. On the one hand there was a spread of protest against specific issues, such as live animal exports and the building of new roads in rural areas. These brought together groups with long experience of the hard end of public-order policing with middle-aged, middle-class people, including many women, who would traditionally have been stalwart police supporters. This combination created especially acute policing problems. In the late 1990s there has also been a resurgence of left-wing protest about financial globalization and its consequences of deepening inequality, including major clashes in the City of London in 1999 and 2000 (with counterparts in the USA in Seattle and Washington). Although the British police response to riots has remained lower in profile than that of most foreign forces, there has undoubtedly been a tougher strategy, and more resort to technology, equipment, and weaponry.

Apart from the growing use of riot-control hardware, there has been a rapid proliferation of firearms use by the police in Britain.[19] Although still unarmed (apart from the traditional truncheon) on routine patrol, the number of occasions on which firearms are issued to the police has escalated inexorably. Many forces now deploy cars carrying guns in their lockers, which can be used on orders from headquarters. The number of times guns are used by the police remains small, and the rules are tight. Most police officers are adamant in wishing to remain unarmed for routine work, but there is a growth of support for being armed. Whatever the justifications in terms of the growing violence faced by police, the traditional unarmed image of the British bobby has been undermined. Debate has raged about whether this has aggravated the violence that it is supposed to deal with.

ACCOUNTABILITY

Until relatively recently the independence of the British police force from control by any elected governmental institutions was portrayed as a virtue, although there has

---

[19] P. Squires, *Gun Culture or Gun Control?* (London: Routledge, 2000); I. McKenzie, 'Policing Force' in F. Leishman, B. Loveday, and S. Savage (eds.), *Core Issues in Policing* (2nd edn., London: Longman, 2000) 176.

also been a long-standing radical critique arguing that it was anomalous in a democracy. As policing became more controversial the perception of accountability changed. Police identification with the public came under strain as the police came to be seen as unrepresentative in terms of race, gender, and culture, and alienated from the groups they typically dealt with as offenders and victims.

Throughout the 1980s radical critics pinpointed the police as being out of control by any outside bodies, the dark side of their vaunted independence, and hence unresponsive to the popular will. They sought to reform the structure of police governance so as to make police policy-making fully accountable to the electoral process.

All governments have wanted to maintain the constitutional *status quo*. They have, however, become increasingly concerned to render the police more accountable for their use of powers, and, even more crucially, the effective use of resources, as will be discussed below in the section on police governance. The widely perceived lack of adequate accountability has been a major factor undermining police legitimacy in recent years.

NON-PARTISANSHIP

During the 1970s the police at all levels from the Police Federation (the rank-and-file quasi-trade union) to chief officers began to campaign increasingly about criminal justice issues and broader social and political matters, marking a fundamental departure from the tradition of non-partisanship. At times they seemed to set the terms of debate on law and order and social policy. During the 1979 General Election campaign (which brought Margaret Thatcher to power) a stream of strikingly similar and much-publicized pronouncements appeared from the police and Tory (Conservative) politicians. In the early 1980s there was a particularly close relationship between the new Conservative government and the police. The police were pivotal in controlling the disorder resulting from neo-liberal economic policies in the urban riots and industrial disputes, and in turn received 'special case' treatment largely exempting them from public expenditure cuts.

The love affair between the Conservatives and the police cooled in the early 1990s as public expenditure cuts began to bite on the police, and they feared a hidden agenda of incipient privatization. The Labour Party tried hard and ultimately successfully to repair broken bridges with the police. There has emerged a new kind of consensus, largely because the Labour government has accepted most of the policy changes of the Thatcher years. Its electorally successful soundbite 'tough on crime, tough on the causes of crime' has increasingly emphasized the former. Political party conflict on law and order has become confined to a contest about who supports the police more effectively. Nonetheless, the years of partisanship had tarnished, possibly irretrievably, the sacred aura hitherto enjoyed by the British police of being outside party politics.

THE SERVICE ROLE

The service role continues to be emphasized rhetorically by Chief Constables. Indeed, an influential current of police thinking stresses the fact that most uniformed police work (measured by time or number of incidents dealt with) consists of service calls for help. The 'community policing' philosophy has become an influential movement amongst progressive police chiefs around the world.[20]

The very energy put into this campaign is an index of the degree to which the service aspects of policing have been devalued and downgraded by the operative force status system. There is copious evidence that most rank-and-file policemen believe the service aspects of the work should have low or no priority.

The response of many Chief Constables was to set up specialist community relations units to provide an artificial surrogate for what tradition had held to be part of basic constabulary duty. Such specialist liaison units began to proliferate in the late 1960s as forces grew larger, more distant from their communities, and as specialization of all kinds multiplied.

The decline in public support in the late 1980s led to a redoubling of the effort to define policing in service terms, culminating in the Metropolitan Police '*Plus*' *Programme* and the 1990 Association of Chief Police Officers' (ACPO) *Statement of Common Purpose and Values*.[21] However, these efforts were largely overturned by the Conservative government's reform package, launched in 1993, which explicitly sought to make 'catching criminals' the primary, if not sole, job of policing. New Labour's Crime Reduction Programme, launched in 1998, continues this emphasis in a somewhat moderated form.

PREVENTIVE POLICING

The meaning of police crime prevention has shifted in recent years.[22] Originally it referred to the 'scarecrow' function of regular uniform patrols, augmented by the deterrent value of detection after the event. But the development of 'intelligence-led', risk-oriented, inter-agency, and 'partnership' policing methods has accentuated the breadth and depth of pre-emptive surveillance and analysis in all police forces.[23]

There has been an expansion of specialist crime-prevention departments in police forces, providing advice to citizens on methods of minimizing the risk of becoming the victims of crime, and alerting them to the dangers of some kinds of offences. The impact of such vaunted crime-prevention efforts as Neighbourhood Watch is mixed however.[24]

In the view of some critics the community policing philosophy, emphasizing

[20] J. Skolnick and D. Bayley, *Community Policing* (Washington, DC: National Institute of Justice, 1988); J.-P. Brodeur (ed.), *How to Recognise Good Policing* (Thousand Oaks, Cal.: Sage, 1998).

[21] I. Waters, 'Quality and Performance Monitoring' in Leishman, Loveday, and Savage, n. 19 above.

[22] G. Hughes, *Understanding Crime Prevention* (Buckingham: Open University Press, 1998).

[23] M. Maguire, 'Policing By Risks and Targets: Some Dimensions and Implications of Intelligence-Led Social Control' (2000) 9 *Policing and Society* 315.

[24] M. McConville and D. Shepherd, *Watching Police, Watching Communities* (London: Routledge, 1992).

both service and crime-prevention work, is itself only a more covert (and therefore insidious) means of penetrating communities to acquire information. Its equally proactive cousin 'Problem-Oriented Policing'[25] has been subject to the same accusation, although it purports to have a more finely targeted scope, aimed at specific problems. What seems clear is that the pursuit of greater crime-prevention effectiveness has meant a proliferation of proactive tactics, and specialist and plain-clothes units, reversing the original strategy of Peel, Rowan, and Mayne. These policies are themselves a response to the apparent decline of police effectiveness in crime control.

POLICE EFFECTIVENESS

Police effectiveness is a notoriously slippery concept to define or measure. But the official statistics routinely produced by police forces and published by the Home Office seem to record an inexorable rise in serious offences and decline in the clear-up rate since the mid-1950s. Fewer than half a million indictable offences *per annum* were recorded by the police fifty years ago, but the annual figure is now over five million. Before the Second World War the percentage of crimes recorded as cleared-up was always over 50 per cent: it is now well under 40 per cent.

The inadequacy of all these figures is well known.[26] Many crimes are not reported to the police, so increases in the rate may mean a greater propensity to report rather than rising victimization. The clear-up rate is affected by many other determinants apart from detective effectiveness, including faking the figures. Nonetheless it is hard to argue that the recent recorded trends (in particular the spectacular rise since the 1950s) do not reflect basic changes.[27] They are certainly associated with a growing public fear of crime and a popular sense that police effectiveness is declining.

In the 1980s the Home Office Research Unit produced a growing volume of evidence (paralleling earlier American findings) indicating that current methods of patrol and detection were of dubious effectiveness.[28] During the 1990s, however, there has been a rebirth of police and political belief in the possibilities of crime control by the police, with support from some criminological researchers.[29] Others maintain that policing alone can have only a relatively marginal impact on crime.[30] Whatever the outcome of these debates is, there can be no doubt that public concerns about apparently declining police effectiveness have been a major factor in reducing public confidence since the 1970s.

---

[25] M. Maguire, 'POP, ILP and Partnership' (1998) 32 *Criminal Justice Matters* 21.

[26] M. Maguire, 'Crime Statistics, Patterns and Trends' in M. Maguire, R. Morgan, and R. Reiner (eds.), *The Oxford Handbook of Criminology* (2nd edn., Oxford: Oxford University Press, 1997).

[27] R. Reiner, 'Crime and Control in Britain' (2000) 34 *Sociology* 71.

[28] R. Clarke and M. Hough, *Crime and Police Effectiveness* (London: Home Office, 1984).

[29] P. Jordan, 'Effective Policing Strategies for Reducing Crime' in C. Nuttall, P. Goldblatt, and C. Lewis (eds.), *Reducing Offending* (London: Home Office, 1998).

[30] R. Morgan and T. Newburn, *The Future of Policing* (Oxford: Oxford University Press, 1997).

THE SOCIAL CONTEXT OF DECLINING
POLICE LEGITIMACY

Police activity has always borne most heavily on the economically and socially marginal elements in society. Such groups have aptly been named 'police property'—they are excluded from full 'citizenship' and bear the brunt of policing.[31] Whereas the incorporation of the working class modified its systematic resentment at policing, police conflict with those at the base of the social hierarchy remained. Drawn mostly from the respectable working class, the police are responsive to their moral values and adopt a disdainful scorn for groups whose life-styles deviate from them. The decline of policing by consent in the 1960s and 1970s was partly because social changes increased the size of the 'police property' groups, as long-term unemployment and poverty returned, and industrial and political conflict became more militant.

A crucial change has been the catastrophic deterioration of relations with the black community. There is a long history of police prejudice against ethnic minorities and complaints of racial harassment. By the mid-1970s clear evidence mounted of blacks (especially black youths) being disproportionately involved in arrests for certain offences, partly (though not only) because of police discrimination. The consequential disastrous ebbing away of black confidence in the police has been crystallized in recent years by the Stephen Lawrence case, in which the police over many years have failed to bring to justice the murderers of a black teenage boy. This dramatically illustrated the inadequacy of police protection of black people, who are disproportionately the victims of crime.[32]

Research on police–public relations suggests clearly that while these remain harmonious with the majority of the population (including most of the working class) they are tense and conflict-ridden with the young, the unemployed, and black people.[33] Since the 1970s the size of these critical groups has grown, primarily because of the increasing social exclusion that results from free-market policies, and a heightening of their self-consciousness as targets of policing.

However, the key to how this is translated into political debate is a long-term cultural change amongst the articulate opinion-forming middle class. A crucial development was the growth of middle-class political protest since the early 1960s, and the politicization of forms of marginal deviance that involve some middle-class people, notably drug-taking and homosexuality. These trends gave groups that hitherto were bastions of support for the police a taste of being at the receiving end of police powers. In addition, as high-volume crime rates grew, more privileged social groups that had hitherto been relatively shielded from crime experienced it, and lost confidence in police effectiveness. The gradual disenchantment of the middle class with the police has been of enormous significance in converting policing into an overt political issue.

[31] P. A. J. Waddington, *Policing Citizens* (London: UCL Press, 1999).

[32] B. Bowling, *Violent Racism* (Oxford: Oxford University Press, 1999).

[33] C. Mirrlees-Black, *Confidence in the Criminal Justice System: Findings From the 2000 British Crime Survey* (London: Home Office Research and Statistics Directorate, 2001).

CONTROLLING THE CONTROLLERS:
DEVELOPMENTS IN POLICE ACCOUNTABILITY

British police rhetoric tends to celebrate their unique accountability to the law.[34] There are four main ways in which the law can regulate police conduct:

(i) Police officers may be prosecuted for crimes, for example arising out of serious complaints;

(ii) Civil actions may be brought against police officers for damages;

(iii) Judges have discretion to exclude evidence obtained in violation of their powers, as defined primarily by the Police and Criminal Evidence Act 1984;

(iv) Judicial review of police policy decisions may be sought if they are claimed to be *ultra vires*.

In practice none of these has operated effectively. This may change after 2000, when the Human Rights Act 1998, which incorporated the European Convention on Human Rights into domestic UK law, has become operational.[35]

Police officers are rarely prosecuted for crimes arising out of wrongful performance of their duties. The Director of Public Prosecutions (DPP) and the Crown Prosecution Service (CPS) have demanded stricter standards of evidence before recommending the prosecution of police officers than other suspects, because of the difficulty of persuading juries not to give special credence to police testimony. During the 1990s there has been an increase in the number of officers convicted of criminal offences (other than traffic offences) from thirty-five in 1992 to sixty-five in 1998. However the number remains small when compared with the approximately 35,000 complaints against the police recorded *per annum*, or the 1,367 people awarded damages for police wrongdoing after a civil action was settled or won.[36] The burden of proof in civil actions is the lesser standard of 'balance of probabilities' but the problems of cost, time, and access to lawyers mean that such actions are rarely resorted to (and are rarely successful), even though they have significantly increased in recent years.

THE COMPLAINTS SYSTEM AND CIVIL ACTIONS

The Police Act 1964 laid down the basic pattern for the current system for making complaints against the police. From the start it was subject to severe criticism because complaints were investigated and adjudicated by the police. After many years of

---

[34] D. Dixon, *Law in Policing* (Oxford: Oxford University Press, 1997).

[35] F. Klug, *Values for a Godless Age: The Story of the United Kingdom's New Bill of Rights* (London: Penguin, 2000), 40–9.

[36] B. Dixon and G. Smith, 'Laying Down the Law: The Police, the Courts and Legal Accountability' (1998) 26 *International Journal of the Sociology of Law* 419.

pressure to introduce an independent element into the assessment of complaints against the police, resisted by most police opinion, the Police Act 1976 established the Police Complaints Board. The Board received a copy of the investigating officer's report, and could recommend that disciplinary charges be brought.

In 1984 PACE replaced the Complaints Board with the Police Complaints Authority (PCA), which was required to supervise the investigation of complaints alleging death or serious injury. The Act also established procedures for resolving minor complaints informally, if complainants agree to this.

During the late 1990s pressure for fundamental reform of the system mounted. In 1998 the Parliamentary Home Affairs Committee (HAC) published a Report, *Police Disciplinary and Complaints Procedures*, that recommended radical changes. It supported the principle of independent investigation, and recommended that the Home Office mount a feasibility study of how to implement this. It also concluded that the terms on which officers were investigated was as important as who did the investigating. Consequently, it recommended the removal of the 'right to silence' from police disciplinary proceedings, and held that the civil balance of probabilities, standard of proof, should apply, not the criminal one of beyond reasonable doubt. It also recommended enhancing the PCA role in the investigation and adjudication of complaints, and that the PCA itself should be able to receive complaints directly. The Report concluded that the complaints process should be more open and transparent, with disclosure of the reports of investigations, and public disciplinary hearings. It also suggested the establishment of a fast-track disciplinary procedure with a higher standard of proof than balance of probabilities, where this would not be prejudicial to subsequent criminal proceedings. The HAC Report supported the earlier agreement between the Home Office and the police staff associations for a procedure to handle unsatisfactory performance by police officers. It expressed concern about CPS decisions about the prosecution of police officers, urging the DPP to give written reasons when prosecution was not recommended.

The Home Secretary's response was largely favourable. A feasibility study of an independent system for investigating complaints against the police was conducted. Finally, in December 2000 the Home Office published a consultation document proposing an independent system for investigation of complaints against the police,[37] along the lines of the HAC Report.

In the light of the poor prospects of the substantiation of complaints against the police (currently about 2 per cent), it is hardly surprising that civil actions have become a major growth industry as an alternative means of redress. The 1964 Police Act section 48 made police forces liable for wrongs committed by officers, making it financially worthwhile to sue officers for torts they may have committed. The means for suing frequently came from legal aid. The lower burden of proof in civil actions compared to the criminal standard required for complaints also made the prospects of success much greater. In London (the Metropolitan Police or Met) in particular, settlements and damages for civil actions rose from £471,000 to 127 claimants in 1991 to £2,309,000 to 295 claimants in 1998–9. As a result police policy appears to have

---

[37] *Complaints Against the Police: Framework for a New System* (London: Home Office, 2000).

changed in the mid-1990s from settling to contesting actions wherever possible. In 1997 the Met was successful in getting the Court of Appeal to suggest more restrictive guidelines for damages. On the other hand the grounds for civil actions were extended in 1996 in *Swinney* v. *Chief Constable of Northumbria*, when the Court of Appeal held the police liable for negligence.[38] Reform of the complaints system may limit the growth of civil actions in the future. At present, however, they appear to many as a preferable means of redress for police wrongdoing.

POLICE GOVERNANCE

The Police Act 1964 consolidated the governance structure that had developed in the previous century. For provincial forces (of which there are at present forty-one in England and Wales) the 1964 Act continued the 'tripartite' system, whereby police governance was divided between the Chief Constable, the local police authority, and the Home Secretary. The majority of police authority members (two-thirds) were elected councillors, and the other third were Justices of the Peace. The Act defined the police authority's responsibility as 'to secure the maintenance of an adequate and efficient police force for the area' (section 4(l)).

The precise relationship between police authority, Chief Constable, and Home Office has been a complex and much debated matter.[39] Although the 1964 Act purported to clarify and rationalize the situation, it failed to do so. Its statements were self-contradictory or vague at crucial points. The police authority was explicitly empowered to appoint the Chief Constable, to secure her retirement (subject to the Home Secretary's agreement) 'in the interests of efficiency', and to receive an annual report from her. It could also ask her to submit further reports on 'matters connected with the policing of the area' (section 12(2)). However, the Chief Constable could refuse to give such a report if she deemed it inappropriate, and the dispute was then to be referred to the Home Secretary as arbiter. The 1964 Act was not clear either about the possibility of the police authority being able to instruct the Chief Constable on general policy concerning law enforcement in the area (as distinct from the immediate, day-to-day direction and control of the force which is clearly precluded). Again, in cases of conflict it was for the Home Secretary to arbitrate.

Altogether the Act strengthened the power of the Chief Constable and the Home Office at the expense of the local police authority. The police authorities shared policing costs with central government but had no independent power. They determined the force's establishment and rank structure, and appointed the Chief Constable, but only subject to Home Office approval. The Chief Constable had sole responsibility for deployment of the force, as well as for appointments, promotion,

---

[38] Dixon and Smith, n. 36 above, at 424–6.

[39] L. Lustgarten, *The Governance of the Police* (London: Sweet and Maxwell, 1986); N. Walker, *Policing in a Changing Constitutional Order* (London: Sweet and Maxwell, 2000).

and discipline. The authority could dismiss the Chief Constable for good cause, but, again, only subject to a Home Office veto. In practice most police authorities did not even use the limited powers envisaged by the Act.

Until 1999 the Metropolitan Police, the largest in the country, had elected the police authority. The Home Secretary acted as its police authority, so that Londoners lacked even the limited form of financial accountability available in the provinces. In 1999 the Greater London Authority Act finally ended the anomalous lack of a local police authority in London, with the establishment of the Metropolitan Police Authority (MPA).

The Court of Appeal judgment in R. v. *Secretary of State for the Home Department, ex parte Northumbria Police Authority*,[40] confirmed the powerlessness of local police authorities. The Northumbria Police Authority sought a judicial review of a Home Office Circular that authorized Chief Constables to obtain plastic bullets from central supplies if their local police authorities objected to their purchase. It argued this was outside the Home Secretary's powers under the 1964 Police Act, which placed primary responsibility for 'maintaining an adequate and efficient' police force on the authority (section 41). The Court of Appeal rejected this argument. It held that the Home Secretary had power under the Royal Prerogative to do what he felt necessary for preserving the Queen's Peace, irrespective of the Act. It also interpreted the Home Secretary's statutory powers under the Police Act (as in sections 28 and 41), as enabling him to override the police authority's views on necessary expenditure and equipment. This seemed to underline the impotence of local police authorities *vis-à-vis* the other two legs of the tripartite system of police governance, making them only a token of local influence in a highly centralized structure.

In the early 1990s a number of other developments continued this centralizing trend.[41] Talk of a 'hidden agenda' of regionalization or even a national force was common amongst the police elite. Central government increasingly achieved effective control of policing, but without the overt creation of a national force. Its instruments for this were Her Majesty's Inspectorate of Constabulary, the Association of Chief Police Officers (ACPO), the Met, and the creation of specialist national policing units.

The cutting edge of the thrust to greater centralization has been the government's tightening control of the police purse-strings. Concern about 'value for money' from policing, as from all public services, was a major theme of the Thatcher Government throughout the 1980s. Home Office Circular 114 of 1983 signalled the Government's intention to make additional police resources conditional on evidence that existing resources were being used as efficiently, effectively, and economically as possible, and this was confirmed by the tougher Circular 106 of 1988.

The new financial regime was not only tighter but more centralized. The Audit Commission, the independent body established by the government to monitor local authority spending, became a key player, with a series of hard-hitting reports

---

[40] [1988] 2 WLR 590.
[41] B. Loveday, 'New Directions in Accountability' in Leishman, Loveday, and Savage, n. 19 above.

aimed at enhancing value for money. In addition the role of HM Inspectorate of
Constabulary was considerably enhanced after the mid-1980s, as the linchpin of
a more centralized co-ordination of standards and procedures.[42] In 1987 the HM
Inspectorate launched a complex computer-based management information
system, the Matrix of Police Indicators, as the basis for its annual inspections. Since
1990 inspection reports on individual forces have been published. Inspections now
involve the collation of considerable data on a standardized basis, shaping police
activity into centrally determined channels. The change in the role of the
Inspectorate has been accompanied by a change in the character of appointments to it. Inspectors are now chosen mainly from relatively young Chief Constables,
in the prime of their careers, and with the prospect of advancement in terms
of operational command still ahead of them. There are also specialist civilian
HMIs.

The Home Office has also encouraged the Association of Chief Police Officers
(ACPO) to develop a much higher profile and expand its role, as a means of
enhancing the standardization and centralization of policing. Successive Home Secretaries have encouraged ACPO to become the pivotal body for harmonizing policies
between forces. The Home Office increased funding to professionalize the ACPO
secretariat. In 1989 ACPO appointed a civilian, Marcia Barton, to the new post of
general secretary, at a salary comparable with that of serving chief officers, and with
responsibility for a policy analysis unit. ACPO is now the linchpin of what has become
a centralized 'policing policy network'[43] which includes the Home Secretary and
Home Office civil servants, Her Majesty's Inspectorate of Constabularies, the Audit
Commission, together with some input from the staff associations representing lower
ranks (the Police Federation and Superintendents' Association), individual chief
officers, and police authorities.

In addition to the growth in importance in recent years of the HM Inspectorate and
ACPO as co-ordinating bodies, there has been a proliferation of specialist national
policing units. The most significant have been the National Criminal Intelligence
Service (NCIS) and National Crime Squad (NCS), established by Parts I and II of the
Police Act 1997, growing out of a variety of specialist national and regional organizations that had proliferated in the previous decade. They are the core agencies in the
development of intelligence-led and proactive policing throughout the country, and
with strong links with international policing bodies.

Concern about the quality of police leadership has been a major source of the
impetus towards centralization in recent years. A Parliamentary Home Affairs Committee (HAC) Report in 1989 attributed most of the shortcomings of police leadership to lack of adequate central control, leading to a deficient career structure and
unco-ordinated training. It recommended a number of measures to enhance the
extent of rational central control over the careers and training of senior officers,
such as making successful completion of the Senior Command Course at Bramshill a

---

[42] M. Weatheritt, 'Measuring Police Performance: Accounting or Accountability?' in R. Reiner and
S. Spencer (eds.), *Accountable Policing* (London: Institute for Public Policy Research, 1993).

[43] S. Savage, S. Charman, and S. Cope, *Policing and the Power of Persuasion* (London: Blackstone, 2000).

condition of promotion above Assistant Chief Constable rank. This was a formal ratification of the *status quo*, in which the Home Office already exercised a considerable measure of control over who becomes a Chief Constable.[44]

The centralizing trend became more apparent still as a result of the profound restructuring of police governance in the 1990s. Originally announced by Home Secretary Kenneth Clarke in March 1993, and published by his successor, Michael Howard, in the June 1993 White Paper *Police Reform*, the reforms culminated in the Police and Magistrates' Courts Act 1994. The Police Act 1996 consolidated the Police Act 1964, the Police and Criminal Evidence Act 1984 Part IX, and the Police and Magistrates' Courts Act 1994 into the currently definitive statutory statement of the structure of police governance.

The most controversial changes were to the structure of police authorities. Section 4 of the 1996 Act now limits the normal size of police authorities to seventeen (although the Home Secretary has discretion to increase this under section 2). This uniform size, regardless of the area or population covered, itself signified a departure from the conception of police authorities as primarily *representative* local bodies. The specific functions of police authorities have also been altered from the 1964 Act section 4 formulation, which was the 'maintenance of an adequate and efficient' force. Section 6 of the 1996 Act changed to a force that is 'efficient and effective'. The precise scope of this responsibility remains as ambiguous as in the 1964 version, but the symbolism is obvious. The prime motif of the new police authorities is that they are to be 'businesslike' bodies—the local watchdogs of the managerialist ethos underpinning the whole reform package.

The democratically elected councillor component of police authorities was reduced from two-thirds to just over a half (nine out of the normal total of seventeen members) (Police Act 1996, Schedule 2, section, 1(1)(a)). Three members are magistrates (i.e. just under one-sixth instead of one-third: section 1(1)(b)). The remaining five members are appointed under an astonishingly complex and arcane procedure detailed in Schedule 3 to the 1996 Act. The rationale running through the fourteen sections and numerous subsections of the complex selection process seems to be to allow the Home Secretary as much influence as possible, without simply letting him or her choose the members directly. The original version of the Bill did indeed do precisely this, but so overtly centralizing a measure drew the wrath of a number of former Conservative Home Secretaries in the House of Lords, who staged a revolt against this aspect of the legislation. Under the process embodied in the Act, the Home Secretary appoints one of the three members of the selection panel, the police authority itself appoints another, and the two members thus selected appoint the third. They then nominate four times as many people as the number of vacancies on the authority to the Home Secretary, applying criteria specified by the Home Secretary. The Home Secretary shortlists half of these nominees. If the selection panel nominates fewer people than twice the number of vacancies to be filled, the Home Secretary makes up the shortfall. This brief summary of the arrangements cannot do

[44] R. Reiner, *Chief Constables* (Oxford: Oxford University Press, 1991); D. Wall, *The Chief Constables of England and Wales* (Aldershot: Avebury, 1998).

justice to their complexity, but it does show how the Home Secretary remains the pivot of the process.

The Chair of the police authority is chosen by the members themselves. This was another concession resulting from the House of Lords revolt against the clear centralizing thrust of the original Bill. It was originally intended that the Home Secretary would appoint the Chair directly. Overall the final version of the Act leaves police authorities with a slight preponderance of elected members, but this barely disguises the centralization that was nakedly apparent in the Bill as originally presented to Parliament.

The police authorities have more explicit functions and powers than their 1964 Police Act predecessors. They have new duties to issue an annual policing plan for their area (Police Act 1996 section 8) and local policing objectives (section 7). The Chief Constable has the same general function of 'direction and control' of the force as in the 1964 Act, but this must now be exercised with regard to the local policing plan and objectives that the authority draws up in liaison with her (section 10). This is an empowerment of the police authority compared to the 1964 Act, but it has to act as a conduit for the Home Secretary's priorities. The Home Secretary decides the codes of practice for police authorities (section 39), sets national objectives and performance targets which local plans must incorporate (sections 37, 38), determines the central government grant to police forces (section 46), and can direct police authorities about the minimum amount of their budgetary contribution (section 41) and any other matters (section 40).

Overall it seems clear that the Police and Magistrates' Courts Act substantially shifts the balance of power to central government. Nonetheless it was officially represented by the Conservative Government as doing precisely the opposite. This claim was based on the relaxation of the detailed controls that used to exist on precisely how chief officers spent their budgets. Chief Constables are now free to allocate their budgets in whatever way they feel is best suited to carry out the policing plan. Chief Constables' new budgetary independence may prove somewhat illusory in the context of the other elements of the government's police reform package. The Sheehy Inquiry into Police Responsibilities and Rewards, which reported in the same week of June 1993 as the *Police Reform* White Paper, recommended that all police officers should be appointed on short-term contracts and subject to performance-related pay (PRP). The criteria for successful performance, and the assessment of whether these have been satisfied, would be governed by the Home Secretary via the new police authorities.

This constituted a formidably centralized system of control over policing. Without abandoning the constabulary independence doctrine in any formal way, the Home Secretary can influence the use of discretion by constables by setting and assessing the criteria for performance that determine pay and job security. The police are no longer accountable in the gentlemanly 'explanatory and co-operative' style that characterized the 1964 Police Act.[45] Nor are they subject to the 'subordinate and obedient' style of accountability to democratically elected local authorities which was demanded by the

---

[45] G. Marshall, 'Police Accountability Revisited' in D. Butler and A. H. Halsey (eds.), *Policy and Politics* (London: Macmillan, 1978).

Act's radical critics. Instead they have become subject to a new market-style discipline which can be called 'calculative and contractual'.[46]

A 1998 House of Lords judgment underlined the significance of the Home Secretary's national policing plan and objectives in setting the framework for operational policing throughout the country (*R. v. Chief Constable of Sussex, ex parte International Trader's Ferry Limited*, available on the House of Lords website). This upheld the legality of a Chief Constable's decision which restricted the level of police protection for live animal exporters against protestors. The decision was based in part on the Chief Constable's statutory obligation to pursue the objectives set by government. 'The chief constable has operational command of the force. . . . But he is now also required to have regard to the objectives and targets set out in an annual plan issued by the police authority pursuant to section 8 [of the 1996 Police Act]. . . . In preparing the plan, the authority will have regard to what it perceives to be the policing priorities of its area and also to any national objectives and performance targets set by the Home Secretary under sections 37 and 38' (*per* Lord Hoffmann).

The traditional common law doctrine of constabulary independence was given lip-service in the House of Lords judgment, and indeed in this case it was supporting the Chief Constable's decisions. However, there was also recognition of the way that the Police and Magistrates' Courts Act 1994 and subsequent legislation obliges the Chief Constable to pursue objectives specified by central government. This leaves the doctrine of police operational independence an empty shell. Whatever the eventual impact of the reforms in practice, there has certainly been a profound transformation in the formal organization of police governance since 1994.

Greater centralization is not a new development but the accentuation of a process that goes back to the initial creation of policing on a uniform basis throughout the country in the nineteenth century. Every major piece of legislation concerning the police has imposed greater uniformity. Arguably, attempts to re-localize control now are like pushing a stream uphill. As 'law and order' has become increasingly politicized it becomes more unlikely that any government would wish to relinquish control over it. The myth of a 'tripartite' structure of governance for essentially local policing, with constabulary independence for operational decisions, has become useful for legitimating a system of *de facto* national control.

Nonetheless, concern to give local communities effective control over policing remains a live issue in England and Wales as well as elsewhere. It has been argued, most authoritatively by the Patten Independent Commission on Policing for Northern Ireland, that instead of talking about accountability for *police* we should talk of *policing*, hence its recommendations for a Policing Board regulating the whole complex of policing processes.[47] The proliferation of policing institutions and processes beyond the conventional Home Office police discussed earlier clearly poses even more acute accountability problems than before. Given how chimerical the pursuit of adequate police accountability has been in the past, however, it is hard to be optimistic about the implications of current developments.

---

[46] Reiner and Spencer, n. 42 above.

[47] C. Patten, *A New Beginning: Policing Northern Ireland* (Norwich: HMSO, 1999) chap. 6.

Further Reading

There are several recent books that offer general surveys of policing in Britain:

JOHNSTON, L., *Policing Britain: Risk, Security and Governance* (London: Longman, 2000).

LEISHMAN, F., LOVEDAY, B., and SAVAGE, S. (eds.), *Core Issues in Policing* (2nd edn., London: Longman, 2000).

MORGAN, R., and NEWBURN, T., *The Future of Policing* (Oxford: Oxford University Press, 1997).

REINER, R., *The Politics of the Police* (3rd edn., Oxford: Oxford University Press, 2000).

WADDINGTON, P. A. J., *Policing Citizens* (London: UCL Press, 1999).

Two recent texts on police accountability are:

DIXON, D., *Law in Policing* (Oxford: Oxford University Press, 1997).

WALKER, N., *Policing in a Changing Constitutional Order* (London: Sweet and Maxwell, 2000).

Much information about recent trends, policies, and statistics are available on the internet, especially at:

www.homeoffice.gov.uk/rds/index.htm
www.homeoffice.gov.uk/hmic/hmic.htm
www.homeoffice.gov.uk/pcrg/policec.htm

3

POLICE INVESTIGATIVE POWERS

Satnam Choongh

INTRODUCTION

A police force equipped with an array of powers to detect crime, apprehend offenders, and gather the evidence necessary to secure their conviction is a central element of the modern criminal justice system of England and Wales. Such is the significance and presence of the police force within the criminal process that it is now difficult to imagine a system of law enforcement without a police force. However, a look at the history of English criminal justice reveals that the police are a relatively recent innovation. The fact is that until the last quarter of the nineteenth century this country enforced its quite extensive criminal law without the assistance of an institutional police force with special investigative powers. The story of how and why the English system moved from that position to its current position provides a means through which to explore wider political issues about policing which are likely to be common to all forms of government.

The theme that runs through the development of police powers in England and Wales is the tension between the ideals of liberal legalism, with their emphasis on protecting the citizen from the coercive potential of the State, and the need to have a police force with sufficient powers to enforce the law effectively and efficiently. The powers currently enjoyed by the police were not bestowed without controversy and debate. Present police investigative powers are the product of choices made by courts, Royal Commissions, and successive governments between the competing value systems prayed in aid by the protagonists in what was at times a heated debate. This chapter provides a brief review of that debate, explains what compromises the English system of policing has struck, and describes the structure of the legal regime governing police powers and suspects' rights.

THE ADVERSARIAL SYSTEM

One of the main causes of the confusion and controversy surrounding the development of police powers in this country is the fact that these powers developed in the context of an *adversarial* system of justice.

Although it is difficult to be precise about the origins of the adversarial system, its growth probably stemmed from the time of the Glorious Revolution in 1688. This signalled the beginning of the gradual process by which the 'subject' (an individual who enjoyed rights and liberties merely on licence from the monarch) was converted into the 'citizen'. Fundamental to the idea of the State/citizen relationship is the view that the State is to be looked upon with suspicion. The development of liberal constitutionalism during the eighteenth century called for political structures and legal rules designed to minimize the ability of the State to intervene in the lives of its citizens. Under this new theory of governance, officials were viewed as servants of the law rather than of the State, and when they acted officially they had to do so within the rule of law.[1]

The nineteenth century witnessed the consolidation of individualism, marked in part by the creation of a canopy of rights and safeguards to protect individuals from the possibility of the State abusing its powers. Nowhere was this more apparent than in the form of trial adopted to try those accused of criminal conduct, perhaps because at no point of interaction between State and citizen does the State reveal its coercive potential more explicitly. The rules governing the criminal trial were based on the firm belief that 'Government in its various aspects . . . is now immeasurably stronger than it ever was before', and as such society is 'capable of inflicting so very much more harm on the individual than the individual as a rule can inflict upon society'.[2]

The system of trial by jury was deeply influenced by this underlying suspicion of State power and the desire to restrict the ability of the State to order the lives of its citizens. In this system the judge was marginalized. He had no right to determine the evidence to be called, or how the prosecution and defence should present their respective cases. His role was limited to ensuring that the proceedings were conducted according to the law, and to pronouncing sentence in the event of a conviction. As a State appointee, it was considered dangerous for the judge to decide on the merits or otherwise of a case brought by the State. The issue of guilt or innocence was the preserve of the jury, and its right to find the accused guilty was dependent on it being satisfied of his guilt 'beyond reasonable doubt'. Perhaps most importantly, the rules made it clear that suspicion alone was insufficient to empower the State to intervene in the life of the citizen beyond the bare right to put him on trial. State officials were barred from torturing the accused, and he was given the right to remain silent should such officials seek to interrogate him.[3] The central tenet around which this entire set

---

[1] E. P. Thompson, *Whigs and Hunters: The Origins of the Black Act* (London: Alan Lane, 1975) 263–6.

[2] J. Stephen, *History of the Criminal Law of England* (London: Macmillan, 1883) i, 354 and 356.

[3] *Felton's case* [1628] 3 How St. Tr. 371.

of rules operated was that the accused, until proven guilty by due process of law, was to be treated as though he were innocent.

POLICE INVESTIGATIVE STRATEGIES IN AN ADVERSARIAL SYSTEM

A police force is of course the most readily identifiable representation of the coercive power of the State. Given the triumph of constitutionalism with its emphasis on restricting State power, it was no surprise that plans put forward in the early decades of the nineteenth century for the establishment of a modern police faced massive opposition.[4] Law enforcement had prior to this been a local affair, organized on semi-private lines. The prosecution of offenders was a matter left almost entirely to the discretion of victims themselves. The entire idea of a professional police force was viewed as un-British, and fears were voiced that it would be used as a tool of government oppression. The story of how that opposition was appeased is told elsewhere,[5] but suffice it to say that the police were sold to the public on assurances that there would be strict limits on the extent of their powers, that they would operate within the confines of the rule of law, that they would not act as state prosecutors, and, in short, would have no powers over and above the power of all citizens to apprehend offenders.

Following the acceptance of Home Secretary Peel's Bill for the establishment of a police force for the Metropolis in 1829, there was by 1856 a legal obligation on all counties to maintain efficient police forces. Having gained a foothold, the new police were reluctant to accept the role of mere foot-soldiers who patrolled the streets in a mainly preventive capacity, being called upon now and again to apprehend suspected offenders. The police force wanted a more proactive role for itself, and this desire manifested itself in individual constables acting as prosecutors, collating evidence and conducting prosecutions in court. Within a decade of their establishment, the Metropolitan Police were conducting a significant proportion of the prosecutions in the capital's criminal courts, and by 1854 the evidence throughout the country was that the 'vast majority' of prosecutions were being conducted by the police.[6]

It can be seen, therefore, that the police acquired the very important power of prosecution despite a prevailing ideology which opposed trusting officials of the State with this power. A similar process was to take place in respect of what are today considered central police investigative powers. The power of arrest provides one example. As explained above, in the theory of the adversarial system the citizen is innocent until proven guilty. It is a corollary of this that at every stage prior to conviction his freedom is not to be unnecessarily restricted. This was reflected in the

---

[4] L. Radzinowicz, *The History of English Criminal Law* (London: Stevens, 1968) 158.

[5] R. Reiner, *The Politics of the Police* (Brighton: Wheatsheaf, 1985).

[6] D. Hay and F. Snyder, *Policing and Prosecution in Britain 1750–1850* (Oxford: Clarendon, 1989) 44.

original rules governing arrest powers. The only common law power of arrest without a warrant was for breach of the peace. In all other cases, there was prior judicial scrutiny of arrest, in that a person could be arrested only if a magistrate issued a warrant for his arrest. Over the course of the nineteenth century the legislature created a number of offences for which an arrest could be made on the basis of 'reasonable suspicion' and without the need for a warrant. However, these statutes made no distinction between police officers and the ordinary citizen. The Royal Commission on Police Powers and Procedure of 1929 argued that as far as the law was concerned there was no distinction between the powers of the police and those of the ordinary citizen, stating that 'the principle remains that a policeman, in the view of the common law, is only "a person paid to perform, as a matter of duty, acts which if he were so minded he might have done voluntarily"'.[7]

Despite the increasing number of offences for which persons could be arrested without warrant, the purpose of arrest at common law remained that of ensuring the suspect attended court for trial. If there was no danger of the suspect absconding, there could be no justification for pre-trial detention and the police were obliged to proceed by way of a summons (a written notice). Even if the initial circumstances warranted an arrest (for example to stop a crime taking place or continuing), the law required a suspect to be released on bail with a direction to attend court unless there was a risk that he would abscond. In the latter type of case, the law sought both to restrict the period of his detention and to make public the fact of his detention as soon as possible. It did this by a requirement that the suspect had to be presented before a court as soon as practicable, which was interpreted to mean within twenty-four hours. The extent to which the common law resented detention without trial was perhaps underlined by the rule that if the suspect could not be brought before a court within twenty-four hours, the authorities were obliged to release him.[8]

From a police viewpoint this interpretation of the purpose of arrest is unduly restrictive. Arrest provides a mechanism not merely to deliver a suspect to the court-room but to enhance crime detection and investigation. The arrested person can be searched, and his premises raided whilst he is out of the way. This may lead to the discovery of incriminating evidence, in respect either of the crime for which the person is initially arrested or other crimes about which the police would otherwise remain ignorant. Those suspected of criminal activity can be put out of operation, albeit temporarily, without the need for trial. This provides an opportunity, through interrogation, to sift through what may be a trawl of the 'usual suspects'. The pressures induced by interrogating suspects in isolation can produce intelligence about the criminal fraternity and the unearthing of crimes which would otherwise go undetected.

It is perhaps unsurprising that by the early twentieth century the police were astute enough to see that they could discharge their function far better by more aggressive use of their powers of arrest, coupled with detention and interrogation. In 1929 the Royal Commission on Police Powers and Procedure reported that the police were well

---

[7] Quoted in Royal Commission on Criminal Procedure, Cmnd 8092–1 (1981) 2.
[8] *Ibid.*, at para. 64.

aware that, in the absence of a magistrate's warrant, they had no power to search an arrested individual's premises, and that any such unauthorized search constituted trespass. However, the information generated by the Commission showed that the police routinely raided the premises of arrested persons. Furthermore, the Commission found that police forces across the country used arrest as a mechanism for detaining suspects at the police station, where they could be questioned and held whilst their answers were investigated, and that such detention could run into days. Finally, it was clear to the Commissioners that for the police 'reasonable suspicion' did not always mean particular and specific grounds for suspecting that the individual to be arrested was guilty of the offence being investigated. The police were quite prepared to gather up a whole group of individuals in the wake of a serious crime on the basis that they constituted the 'usual suspects'.[9]

Interrogation during detention was also to become the norm. Indeed, the 1929 Commission discovered that the police arrested individuals for minor offences (for which they could show reasonable suspicion) in order to interrogate them about more serious offences (for which there was no reasonable suspicion). Although the common law had long since developed a rule that confessions induced by threats or promises of favour, or by oppressive behaviour, would not be admitted in evidence, the Commissioners found that the police deployed a variety of ploys to pressurize suspects into confessing. Indeed, there was a widespread suspicion by this time that confessions were often the product of unacceptable pressures being applied, or were entirely fabricated.

THE LEGAL RESPONSE TO POLICE INVESTIGATIVE TACTICS

The political and legal response to the reality of police practices was to prove a template for how the politico-legal system was to grapple with the contradictions between, on the one hand, an overarching philosophy committed to restricting the powers of state officials, and, on the other hand, increasing acceptance of the idea that in a modern society the police provided the most efficient agency for enforcement of the law and that they should not be unduly hampered in their attempts to enforce it.

It was the role of police as prosecutors that attracted particular attention. Neither Parliament nor the common law had sanctioned such a role for the police, and the idea that prosecution was not the monopoly of any state agency but a right of all citizens was one of the cornerstones of the liberal conception of the State/citizen relationship. Lawyers and politicians alike called for a strict demarcation between the roles of policing and prosecuting, and it was argued that if there was a need for a more co-ordinated response to prosecutions these should be conducted by a public

---

[9] Report of the Royal Commission on Police Powers and Procedure, Cmd 3927 (1929), paras. 32, 33, 153–159, 268.

prosecutor who could be subjected to proper control and scrutiny. Much of this criticism was grounded in a distrust of the police. It was believed that the power to instigate a prosecution was too important to be placed in the hands of policemen, 'a class over whom the most incessant vigilance [is] requisite to prevent flagrant and cruel abuses of their authority'. The Attorney-General branded their presence in court as prosecutors a 'great scandal', arguing that it made them 'over-zealous' in search of convictions because their chances of promotion hinged on success in court.[10]

This concern led to a number of parliamentary reports and inquiries to consider the possibility of setting up a public prosecutor system. Matters even went so far as the introduction of a Public Prosecutors Bill in Parliament. However, nothing came of these concerns and initiatives. In the course of thirty years or so, the police succeeded in persuading the magistracy, judiciary, and politicians that they were indispensable as a prosecution agency. Those officials involved in and responsible for the efficiency of the criminal justice system realized that in practical terms the introduction of public prosecutors would introduce an unnecessary layer of bureaucracy, for the prosecutors would be dependent upon the police for the information and evidence necessary actually to mount prosecutions. The net result was that prosecution in the lower courts became a virtual police monopoly, and was to remain so until the establishment of the Crown Prosecution Service in 1985.

This *de facto* acquisition by the police of the power to prosecute, followed by legal and political acceptance and endorsement of such behaviour, was to be repeated in respect of the investigative powers which the police had seized. The only difference was to be that the tension between police demands for greater powers and the hitherto accepted orthodoxies of the adversarial system was to prove more difficult to resolve in respect of powers of arrest, detention, and interrogation than it had in respect of the power to prosecute. It was left to the courts to confront issues about the role of the police and the rights of the citizen in the adversarial system in the course of making decisions about the admissibility of evidence. The courts had to face the key question of whether evidence tainted by false arrest, wrongful detention, and illegitimate questioning should be put before the jury.

When evidence of police questioning initially came before the courts in the last quarter of the nineteenth century, the judiciary was united in condemning it as unconstitutional and illegal. Judges took the view that 'a constable has no more right to question than a judge has to cross-examine',[11] and it was made clear that once a policeman had:

taken anyone into custody, and also before doing so when he has already decided to make the charge, he ought not to question the prisoner. A magistrate or judge cannot do it, and a police officer certainly has no more right to do so.[12]

---

[10] See Select Committee on the Public Prosecutors Bill (Parl. Papers) 1854 (vol. 12) and 1856 (vol. 7); The Fifth Report of the Judicature Commission (Parl. Papers) (1874); Parl. Debates (HC) 3rd Series, 17 May 1855 and 20 Feb. 1855.

[11] *R. v. Gavin* (1885) 15 Cox C C 656.

[12] *Knight and Thayre* (1905) 20 Cox C C 711.

Police interrogation was considered to be not only unconstitutional, but also dangerous in that it produced inherently unreliable evidence. In 1893 Cave J declared that:

it would be monstrous if the law permitted a police officer to go, without anyone being present to see how the matter was conducted, and put a prisoner through an examination, and then produce the effects of that examination against him.[13]

Later that year, the same judge made his concerns yet more explicit: 'I always suspect these confessions, which are supposed to be the offspring of penitence and remorse and which nonetheless are repudiated by the prisoner at trial.'[14]

Despite agreement that police interrogation was unconstitutional, the judges were split on whether a confession made in response to such questioning ought to be admitted as evidence. Some judges wanted such confessions automatically excluded, but the majority were of the view that sufficient protection against wrongful conviction was provided by the old common law rule that a confession would be ruled inadmissible unless made freely and voluntarily. Different decisions by different judges were sending confusing messages to police forces throughout the country. By the first decade of the twentieth century a consensus emerged in favour of the rule that the courts should concern themselves primarily with whether a confession was voluntary, but that in applying this rule judges ought to take into account the manner and duration of questioning and whether the suspect had been cautioned (told that he was under no obligation to answer questions).[15] This important shift from *prohibition* to *regulation* was formalized through what became known as the Judges' Rules. First issued in 1912, expanded in 1918 and in 1930, and re-drawn in 1964, the Rules (and accompanying Administrative Directions) forbade the use of threats and inducements, and stipulated that persons under arrest should not be questioned without first being cautioned, ought to be allowed to make a voluntary statement without being cross-examined by police officers, and ought to be informed of their right to consult privately with a solicitor at any time.

The Rules were inspired by the idea of striking some sort of balance between police powers and the rights of the suspect, but over the course of the twentieth century concern grew that a proper balance had not been struck. Through their spokesmen, the police argued that laws regulating arrest, search, seizure, detention, and interrogation were unduly restrictive, and hampered the fight against crime, especially serious, organized crime. The police stated it was unfair that they should be forced to ignore these restrictions in practice, thereby placing themselves at risk of legal challenge and punishment, simply in order to bring offenders to justice. The Commissioner of the Metropolitan Police questioned the rationale of a system which gave 'every advantage to the defence', and argued that these rules from a previous age were 'not suited to the trial of an experienced criminal, using skilled legal assistance, in the late twentieth century'.[16] The provision in the Judges' Rules guaranteeing access to legal advice was attacked on the basis that it allowed lawyers to concoct defences for their clients, and

---

[13] *R. v. Male* (1893) 17 Cox C C 689.   [14] *R. v. Thompson* [1893] 2 QB 12.
[15] *Best* [1909] 1 KB 692.
[16] R. Mark, *Minority Verdict* (London: BBC Publications, 1973) 63–4.

the right not to answer questions (popularly known as the right to silence) was said to be illogical, in that it provided a means by which the guilty could conceal their guilt with impunity.[17]

In the period from the first introduction of the Judges' Rules in 1912 to their replacement by the Police and Criminal Evidence Act in 1984, the courts showed themselves extremely reluctant to exclude evidence, despite breaches of the Rules and despite the fact that the police had engaged in activities not sanctioned by the law, and they refused to discipline the police by excluding the evidence obtained in an improper way unless it was in the form of an illegally obtained confession. Worse still, they were willing to admit evidence obtained as a result of the confession. Judges attached little importance to the fact that suspects were frequently not cautioned before being questioned, that they were regularly denied access to legal advice, and that they were held in detention for longer than the twenty-four hours permitted by the common law. The sentiments expressed by trial judges and the Court of Appeal showed that the judiciary had a great deal of sympathy with the view that the law in these respects was outdated and inimical to public policy.

In one case the Court of Appeal justified the admission of a confession despite the absence of a caution on the basis that 'the police must investigate matters of this kind or there will be no protection for anybody'.[18] Judges regularly argued for the abolition of the right to silence,[19] and the Court of Appeal restricted the right in a decision in which it ruled that trial judges could inform juries that, although the accused did not have to answer police questions, 'there are . . . those who think that the law should be altered in that it operates to protect the guilty'.[20] Trial judges interpreted in as restrictive a manner as possible the provision in the Judges' Rules which guaranteed access to legal advice,[21] and in doing so were probably influenced by the announcements of senior judges that the presence of lawyers hampered interrogation.[22] In another case, the Court of Appeal refused to rule inadmissible a confession made by a suspect who had been unlawfully arrested, detained for five days without access to legal advice, and questioned without caution. The court's position in respect of these rules was that they 'hinder[ed] the police in bringing criminals to justice'.[23] Police powers of search and seizure were greatly expanded by the courts in this period, with judges making it clear that 'in these present times . . . honest citizens must help the police and not hinder them in their efforts to track down criminals'.[24] Finally, the High Court redefined the purpose of arrest by ruling that it was both lawful and reasonable for the police to arrest rather than proceed by summons if a person was more likely to confess if subjected to 'the greater stress and pressure involved in arrest and deprivation of liberty'.[25]

Underpinning these sentiments was a change in the way in which the police were perceived by judges, politicians, and the vast majority of the public. From being

---

[17] R. Mark, *Minority Verdict* (London: BBC Publications, 1973) at 65; (1975) 128 *New Law Journal* 769–70.

[18] *Wattam* (1952) 36 Cr. App. R 1972.   [19] See *The Times*, 8 Apr. 1971.

[20] *R.* v. *Gilbert* (1977) 66 Cr. App. R 237.   [21] *Stephen King* [1978] *Crim. LR* 632.

[22] See *The Times*, 17 July 1971.   [23] *Houghton and Franciosy* (1979) 68 Cr. App. R 197.

[24] *Chic Fashions* v. *Jones* [1968] 2 QB 299.   [25] *Holgate-Mohammed* v. *Duke* [1983] 3 WLR 598.

distrusted and seen as corrupt and overbearing, they came during the course of the twentieth century to be seen as 'the embodiment of impersonal, rule bound authority, enforcing democratically enacted legislation on behalf of the broad mass of society . . . constrained by tight legal requirements of due process'.[26]

This change in perception directly affected judicial attitudes towards police powers, with the courts willing to expand those powers in the hope that this would assist the fight against crime. The dangers of expanding police powers in this way were no longer felt to be as great as they once had been—as one Court of Appeal judge expressed it, the restrictions on police powers were the product 'of earlier times when the police were not to be trusted, as they are now to be trusted in almost every single case, to behave with complete fairness towards those who come into their hands'.[27]

POLICE POWERS AND SUSPECTS' RIGHTS

The current legal regime governing police powers and rights of those suspected of crime is contained in the Police and Criminal Evidence Act 1984. The provisions of the Act are based upon the recommendations contained in the Report of the Royal Commission on Criminal Procedure, which was established in 1977 and reported in 1981. As will be readily apparent from the above brief history of police powers, the law in this field had developed in an *ad hoc* fashion against a backdrop of confusion and conflicting public-policy arguments. The purpose of the Commission was not only to clarify and rationalize the existing law but to see if some consensus could be reached on what powers the police ought to have and how suspects ought to be protected from undue and unnecessary coercion.

The Commission stated in its final report that the fundamental philosophy underlying its recommendations was the need to strike an 'appropriate balance between the individual's rights and the community's interest'. In determining what powers the police ought to have, the Commission sought to give effect to the view that 'coercive powers cannot and should not be exercised against a person, his property or his liberty unless he himself is known to have committed or is suspected on reasonable grounds to have committed a specific crime'. Accordingly, the scheme of the Act is to confer powers on the police, but then to seek to protect suspects from the abuse of such powers by granting to suspects certain rights and protections. The Act sets out in an extremely detailed manner the circumstances in which the police can exercise their powers, and is supplemented by five codes of practice containing yet further detailed guidance on powers of stop and search, search of premises and seizure of property, the detention, treatment, and questioning of suspects, identification of suspects, and the tape-recording of interrogations.

It is not the intention here to set out the whole array of powers the police now possess, but merely to provide an overview of some of the key provisions of the

---

[26] Reiner, n. 5 above, 61.   [27] Winn LJ in *R. v. Northam* (1968) 52 Cr. App. R 97 at 102.

relevant legislation to show how the English system has sought to balance the needs of law enforcement with the need to protect civil liberties.

STOP AND SEARCH

The police have several statutory powers to stop, detain, and search persons and vehicles. Many of these powers are limited and arise only where the police have suspicion in respect of particular specified crimes, and these powers pre-date PACE. Concerns were expressed to the Commission that existing stop and search powers were used disproportionately against certain ethnic minorities, and that they did not contribute much to the fight against crime, because for the most part they proved unsuccessful in uncovering wrongdoing. Nonetheless, the Commission recommended and PACE introduced a general power for the police to stop and search persons and vehicles, because it was felt that 'people in the street who have committed property offences or have in their possession articles which it is a criminal offence to possess should not be entirely protected from the possibility of being searched. The availability of powers to search is of use in the detection of crime and the arrest of offenders'.[28]

PACE confers powers to stop and search for stolen goods, prohibited articles, articles intended to be used in connection with offences of dishonesty, and offensive weapons. Offensive weapons are defined to mean not only articles offensive *per se*, but any article which the police believe the suspect has in his possession with the intention of using for an offensive purpose. However, in line with the Commission's view that 'the exercise of the powers must be subject to strict safeguards', the Act does provide protections for the suspect.

First, the power of stop and search can be exercised only if the constable has reasonable grounds for suspecting that stolen or prohibited articles will be found. There must be something which gives rise to the suspicion. This may relate to the article itself being visible, the time and place, information received, or to the behaviour of the suspect. The code makes it clear that a person's age, colour, style of dress or hairstyle, or previous conviction is an insufficient factor to amount to reasonable suspicion. Secondly, the suspect can be detained for only such time as is reasonably required to carry out the search. Thirdly, suspects cannot be directed to remove in public anything other than an outer coat, jacket, or gloves. If a more detailed search is required the suspect must be removed to a nearby place where members of the public are not present. Finally, a search cannot be carried out without the suspect first being told of the constable's name and police station, the object of the proposed search, the grounds for the proposed search, and told that a copy of a written record of the search will be made available if requested.

---

[28] N. 7 above, at para. 3.17.

ARREST

The Royal Commission recommended that arrest, as a coercive power, should not be resorted to as a matter of course, and that greater reliance should be placed on the summons procedure. In theory, therefore, the use of arrest powers is regulated by the criterion of necessity. The Commission stated that arrest could only be justified if one of the following applied:

(a) the refusal by a suspect to reveal his identity so that a summons could be served;

(b) the need to prevent continued repetition of the offence;

(c) the need to protect the arrested person or property;

(d) the need to secure or preserve evidence;

(e) the likelihood that the suspect would fail to appear at court to answer the summons.

Despite this, the police have wide-ranging powers of arrest under PACE. The Act sets out a long list of what are known as 'arrestable offences', and the term is defined to include all offences punishable by imprisonment for five years or more. The Act provides that a constable with reasonable grounds for suspecting that an arrestable offence has been committed may arrest without a warrant (prior authority of a magistrate) anyone whom that constable has reasonable grounds for suspecting to be guilty of the offence. The police can arrest for such offences even when it would be practicable to proceed by way of summons.

In addition, the police have a general power to arrest for all other offences if any of the 'general arrest conditions' set out in the Act is satisfied. This provision of the Act operates to provide the police with a wide and general power of arrest for all offences, no matter how minor or petty, because the conditions to be satisfied confer a great deal of discretion on the arresting officer. He or she can arrest if there are reasonable grounds for doubting that the name or address given by the suspect is correct, or if the officer believes that arrest is necessary to protect a child 'or other vulnerable person' from the person to be arrested, or to prevent the suspect causing harm to him/herself or others.

Despite the assumption built into these rules that the normal process should be by way of summons rather than arrest, the evidence suggests that since the introduction of PACE the police proceed by way of arrest as opposed to summons even more than they did in the pre-PACE era. Research carried out in the late 1980s showed that the summons procedure is used in a mere 2 per cent of all cases.[29]

---

[29] See M. McConville, *et al.*, *The Case for the Prosecution* (London: Routledge, 1991) 39.

DETENTION AND INTERROGATION

The Act balances these extended powers of detention for the police with greater safeguards and protections for suspects First, key decisions are taken away from the arresting and investigating officers and given to the 'custody officer'. Secondly, the Act states that a suspect has the right to have a friend or relative or other person informed of his or her arrest and whereabouts at public expense. Thirdly, and perhaps most importantly, the Act grants the suspect the right to free legal advice whilst in custody. Finally, the Act regulates quite closely the recording of interrogations with the aim of ensuring that the court is provided with an accurate record of what was said by both the police and suspect during interrogation.

Under the Act those arrested have to be presented before a custody officer, and it is the duty of the custody officer to determine whether grounds exist to justify detention. The custody officer is permitted to authorize detention where he believes that it is necessary in order to 'secure or preserve evidence of or relating to [the] offence or to obtain such evidence from the suspect by questioning him'. The Act therefore gave statutory recognition to the practice of detaining suspects for the sole purpose of questioning, following the Commission's acceptance of the argument that there was 'no substitute for police questioning in the investigation and, ultimately, in the prosecution of crime'.

With regard to the duration of questioning, the Commission argued that, whilst due regard had to be paid to the rights of suspects, the time limits must 'enable the police to do their job properly'. It rejected the idea of 'short and absolute time limits', stating that these were 'not possible' given the demands on police time and the varying nature of investigations. To meet these concerns, the Act allows the police to detain a suspect for up to thirty-six hours without charge and, if further time is required, the police can make an application to a magistrate to extend the period of detention for up to ninety-six hours.

Many of the concerns which the judiciary had in the early part of the twentieth century were about the reliability of evidence produced through police questioning behind the closed doors of the police station. The current legal regime in England and Wales seeks to remove these concerns by providing the suspect with a set of protections so that the courts can safely rely upon evidence emerging from the police interrogation. As the Commission itself stated, its aim was to ensure 'that the maximum possible reliance for evidential purposes can be placed upon the suspect's statements in all cases where they are made'. The shift from denying the police investigative powers to granting such powers but making them subject to rights and protections, however, has not eliminated entirely the thorny question of when the courts ought to exclude evidence in order to protect the suspect.

EXCLUSIONARY RULES

Although PACE regulates police interrogation indirectly by laying down rules about refreshments and rest breaks for the suspect, it does not lay down detailed guidance about the content of police interrogation itself. Instead, it seeks to exclude unreliable confessions by adopting the old common law rule that a confession can be admitted in evidence only if the prosecution proves that it was not obtained by oppression, or as a result of anything said or done which was likely in the circumstances to make it unreliable. It also preserves the common law rule that even if a confession is excluded on this basis, any other evidence obtained as a result of the tainted confession remains admissible.

This latter rule provides one example of the general rule which the common law has always operated, namely that evidence is not to be excluded merely because it has been obtained in an unlawful or improper way.[30] This perhaps explains why the courts in the early part of the twentieth century were reluctant to exclude confessions secured through police interrogation solely on the basis that the police had in law no power to question suspects. The judiciary preferred to operate a rule of exclusion which stressed the need for reliability rather than legal or constitutional propriety. As explained above, although the courts initially said that breaches of the Judges' Rules would be taken into account when deciding whether a confession would be admitted in evidence, it soon became clear that unless the breach could be said to render the confession involuntary the courts would in all likelihood admit it in evidence.

The Act marks to some extent a departure from this approach, in that it confers on the court a broad discretion to exclude evidence obtained 'unfairly'. Under this provision, the courts can exclude any category of evidence, not simply confession evidence. The courts have refused to lay down general guidelines on how this discretion ought to be exercised, stating that circumstances vary infinitely and decisions have to be taken on a case-by-case basis. However, the rule which appears to have emerged is that evidence will be excluded if there are significant and substantial breaches of the codes of practice. The courts have been particularly ready to exclude evidence in cases where there is a suspicion that the police have deliberately sought to evade the recording provisions of PACE, denied or delayed access to a solicitor, or have deceived suspects into making confessions.[31]

CONCLUSION

The legal regime in England and Wales governing police powers is organized and structured so as to permit almost limitless flexibility. That this should be so is particularly ironic when one considers that the starting point for the development of such

---

[30] *Sang* [1980] AC 402.
[31] See H. Levenson, F. Fairweather, and E. Cape, *Police Powers* (London: Legal Action Group, 1996) 288–300.

powers was almost complete prohibition, justified by reference to a fairly well-defined and overarching philosophy of governance. Over the course of the twentieth century, an almost universal consensus has emerged that effective crime control requires that the police be equipped with extensive powers of control and surveillance over citizens. From prohibiting interference by the police in the affairs of the citizen, the law has moved to regulating what is accepted as unavoidable interference. Ideals and philosophy have given way to a pragmatic approach, in which the law can respond quickly to new public concerns and changing legal challenges by expanding or restricting police powers without any seismic effect on the underlying rationale of a regulatory system built around compromise and balance.

Examples of the system's ability to change, even in respect of fundamental issues, without major organizational difficulties are numerous. For instance, although the Royal Commission in 1981 argued that the police should have the power to interrogate, it continued to be influenced by traditional adversarial thinking because it rejected the idea that the suspect should have an obligation to answer. It noted that the right to silence must be retained because abolition would 'amount to requiring a person during investigations to answer questions based on possibly unsubstantiated and unspecific allegations or suspicion, even though he is not required to do that at trial'. Accordingly, many of the provisions of PACE and the codes of practice were written to accommodate this enunciation of principle. However, the government became increasingly convinced that the right to silence was hindering the fight against crime. Therefore, in 1994, the law was amended to require suspects to put forward their defence when questioned by the police or risk the court drawing adverse inferences from their failure to do so. PACE and the codes of practice were amended to change the wording of the caution, and now if the police want to rely on this provision they must warn the suspect during interrogation of the risk he runs by remaining silent.

Another example is provided in respect of police powers of stop and search. Despite the entire scheme of PACE being built around the notion of reasonable suspicion (the concept which justifies official intrusion into the citizen's right to go about his business), when the public were believed to demand extra protection from terrorism the government responded by granting to the police in some instances the power to stop and search for 'articles of a kind which could be used for a purpose connected with the commission, preparation or instigation' of acts of terrorism 'whether or not [the police officer] has any grounds for suspecting the presence of articles of that kind'.

The system has proved sufficiently flexible to respond to concerns that some of the protections provided by PACE to suspects were inadequate. For example, following research findings that the police were using a range of strategies to dissuade suspects from requesting legal advice, changes were made to the codes to strengthen this right. These included, for example, the provision that the police had to record on the custody record the reasons given by the suspect for declining the offer of free legal assistance. Indeed, PACE and the codes are structured in such a way that there would be no fundamental difficulty in introducing new conditions which would need to be met before a suspect could be stop and searched, arrested, detained, or made to provide bodily samples, were it to be felt that new protections were needed for suspects. Although the incorporation of the European Convention on Human Rights into English domestic law can be expected to provide challenges to the system of police powers and their regulation, the English law is well positioned to deflect such challenges given the flexibility of such provisions as section 78 of PACE, which allows the court to exclude evidence where it would be 'unfair' to admit it.

Further Reading

ASHWORTH, A., *The Criminal Process* (Oxford: Oxford University Press, 1998).

BROGDEN, M. *et al.*, *Introducing Police Work* (London: Unwin, 1988).

CHOONGH, S., *Policing as Social Discipline* (Oxford: Clarendon, 1997).

JEFFERSON, T., and GRIMSHAW, R., *Controlling the Constable* (London: Muller, 1984).

McCONVILLE, M. *et al.*, *The Case for the Prosecution* (London: Routledge, 1991).

NEWBURN, T., *Crime and Criminal Justice Policy* (London: Longman, 1995).

REINER, R., *The Politics of the Police* (Oxford: Oxford University Press, 2000).

4

COVERT SURVEILLANCE
AND THE USE
OF INFORMANTS

Sybil Sharpe

In England and Wales, traditional forms of police investigation (for instance, the obtaining of confessions from suspects and physical searches of persons and premises) have been regulated, since 1985, by the Police and Criminal Evidence Act 1984 (hereinafter PACE). The purpose of this regulation is to ensure that certain procedures are adhered to in respect of these investigative techniques and that proper records (electronic recordings in the case of confessions) are kept by the police of actions taken in respect of suspects. Whilst PACE imposes procedures on the police which involve not only recording action taken, but also notification to suspects of the basis upon which actions are being taken, PACE also assists law enforcers because it confers statutory powers upon them. The Act states the criteria for arrest, and for the search for and seizure of evidence. It gives statutory authority to the police to detain suspects for questioning. Within these statutory criteria, there is an element of discretion enabling the police to act on belief based on reasonable grounds. Investigation under PACE is therefore overt and the procedures or criteria adopted in any particular case may be challenged in a court of law.

The use of covert investigation in relation to criminal suspects allows law enforcers to obtain evidence not only without the co-operation of a suspect, but also without the awareness of a suspect. In traditional forms of policing, even those techniques, such as physical search, which do not necessarily require co-operation for their efficacy if authorized by statute or by warrant, take place with the awareness of the target of the search. The target is also made aware, through notification, of a package of due-process protections in respect of any search of his person or premises and, if arrested, of the grant of certain rights whilst detained in custody.[1] These protections and rights are necessary to protect the vulnerable and also to maintain basic standards of ethical behaviour by the police. For the police and other law enforcers the disadvantage of overt investigation is that some offenders may utilise due-process protections

---

[1] See Codes of Practice A and B on the conduct of searches. Custodial protections include notification of the right to free and private legal advice and the right to be cautioned on arrest and prior to questioning; see PACE, s. 58 and Code C of the Codes of Practice.

to defeat the search for incriminating evidence. It is not surprising, therefore, that there has been an increasing tendency on the part of law enforcers to rely on practices that are not regulated by PACE.[2]

In practice, covert investigation is not confined to the most serious offences that threaten the fabric of society, but has become sufficiently commonplace and sophisticated for it to be a common practice amongst law enforcers. It is important, therefore, to ensure that similar due-process rights are applied to protect all suspects who are subjected to surveillance or to covert 'interviewing' as are available in relation to overt investigations. If such rights do not exist, the police have no incentive to act ethically, the human right to privacy and autonomy of person will be substantially weakened, and ultimately society may lose respect for the law itself.

Statutory control does now exist in relation to many forms of covert investigation. However, these controls have evolved in a pragmatic way in respect of different kinds of activity. There has been a recent attempt in the Regulation of Investigatory Powers Act 2000 (hereinafter RIPA) to legislate for various forms of surveillance within a single statute. However, the Act largely consolidates existing practices and the substance of previous statutes. It does not provide a new Code based upon a fundamental reassessment of the use by police and other law enforcers of new methodologies. Further, some forms of covert investigation still fall outside the regulation of this Act.

One method of surreptitious investigation is the use of wired civilian informants or of undercover officers to obtain incriminating evidence or admissions. A secretly recorded statement made by a target that incriminates him in past or planned criminal activity may be used in evidence and may do away with the need for a confession to be obtained in a formal interrogation. The suspect often believes that he is having a conversation with a friend or criminal collaborator, and has no awareness that his words will be used against him in criminal proceedings. At the stage of the secretly recorded conversation the police may not have sufficient grounds to arrest and interrogate the suspect; they may simply suspect that he is planning some sort of future criminal activity. Frequently this method of investigation is used to infiltrate conspiracies involving crimes such as the importation of drugs. Customs and Excise officials, rather than the police, may therefore be the investigating and prosecuting officers in the case. There has never been any statutory regulation of secretly recorded conversations where these take place face to face between the parties. RIPA section 26 states that the use of an individual to establish a personal relationship in order to gain information is a form of covert policing, but section 48 of the same Act excludes 'information disclosed in the presence of the source'.

The electronic bugging of premises is another form of covert investigation. Bugging may preclude the need for any interrogation or any physical search. There is, of course, the possibility of law enforcers carrying out covert visual surveillance without the help of electronic devices. However, such surveillance (the taking of photographic evidence apart) does not provide an incontrovertible record of what occurred. It does

---

[2] Audit Commission Report, *Helping With Enquiries: Tackling Crime Effectively* Police Papers, n. 12, and HMIC *Policing With Intelligence: HMIC Thematic Inspection Report On Good Practice* (1997).

not allow a criminal court to hear the verbatim words spoken by an individual or to see the actions of an accused caught on a hidden video camera.

As with the wiring of individuals, the use of such techniques allows the police to target potential offenders rather than past offences. It allows for a proactive role to be taken in gathering information about future crime. A proactive approach is particularly effective when used in respect of victimless crimes, such as the importation and supply of narcotics, or in respect of serious international crimes, such as terrorism or large financial frauds. Premises may be bugged by means of attaching a device to the wall of the premises or by hiding an electronic recording device inside the property. There may also be a hidden video tape or digital recorder so that actions as well as words may be recorded. If the device is placed without the consent of the occupier, there is an interference with his civil rights (known as a trespass), which gives in theory a claim to compensation though it is not in itself a criminal offence. The police are authorized to commit such an interference by the Police Act 1997 section 93 provided that it is likely to be of substantial value in the prevention or detection of serious crime. Increasingly, advanced technology will allow the police to eavesdrop into premises without the need physically to locate a recording device in them. Such remote surveillance was not previously subject to statutory control, and it is still not covered by the Police Act 1997, but it now falls under RIPA. RIPA makes a distinction between remote surveillance of residential premises and surveillance of other premises, regarding only the former as 'intrusive'. Strangely, the Act also treats surveillance of an individual in a private vehicle as more intrusive than that carried out in respect of individuals whilst they are on business premises. Of course, not all remote surveillance involves surveillance of individuals as such. Vehicles may have tracking devices placed on them, and these will do no more than locate the route travelled by the vehicle. In common law jurisdictions such devices are considered not to violate the privacy of any individual since they reveal no human communication and their use is not regulated by statute.

A third form of surveillance is the interception of telephone communications and electronic mail. These communications may be intercepted and recorded with the consent of one party to the conversation or may be effected, by warrant, without the knowledge of either conversant. Inevitably, when a telephone line is being intercepted, people other than the targets may find that their conversations are being listened in to. RIPA controls this form of surveillance, substantially re-enacting an earlier statute that dealt with the interception of public telephone systems only. RIPA regulates the interception of public telephone systems, private telephone systems (so long as they are ultimately attached to a public system), and stored electronic mail.

As with vehicular tracking devices, there is no statutory protection for traffic data (known as a pen register in the United States), i.e. data simply identifying that calls were made to a specific telephone number and which do not reveal the content of those calls. Traffic data may be useful in their own right. For instance, the fact that a large number of calls is made to a particular number, the subscriber to which is thought to be a drug dealer, may justify the police in applying for a warrant to intercept the calls or may form the basis of a decision to watch the premises.

THE COMPETING INTERESTS OF CRIMINAL INVESTIGATION AND INDIVIDUAL AUTONOMY

What has been said so far is subject to the impact on English law of the European Convention on Human Rights and its enactment into English law by the Human Rights Act 1998.

As has already been mentioned, the covert monitoring of a suspect may not involve a physical search for tangible evidence, nor any trespass onto property. However, it has been recognized in many jurisdictions that there is a right to privacy which applies to persons rather than to places, and to freedom from eavesdropping as well as to physical intrusion. This recognition was expressed nearly thirty years ago in the United States of America in the seminal case of *Katz* v. *US*,[3] where the interception of a telephone conversation originating from a public call box was said to be in breach of the Fourth Amendment to the United States Constitution. The human right to be free from unreasonable searches is thus applied to surveillance and to undercover operations. In this way, the fundamental protection of privacy is preserved in the face of modern technological developments. The right to be free from state intrusion, whether that intrusion is intercepting written communications and telephone calls or eavesdropping on conversations, is maintained in various other human rights documents, some national and some international. The wording in all of these is, in substance, remarkably similar. There is no absolute right to privacy. There is a right to be free from 'arbitrary' or 'unreasonable' interference with personal privacy, home, or correspondence.[4] It is the concept of reasonableness that is crucial here. In all the jurisdictions where such a right is recognized, it is accepted that those reasonably suspected of crime have forfeited their right to the extent that an investigation will tend to prove or disprove their involvement in an offence.

In the United States and Canada, there is a body of case law that considers those factual situations that constitute a search (and thus require reasonable grounds) and those that do not. Such case law provides useful guidance for those countries such as England and Wales, where the legality of electronic surveillance by law enforcers is only now being tested for compliance with the Human Rights Act 1998. The following general propositions can be extracted from the case law. First, in the United States and in England, a target, who in 'mistaken confidence' chooses to confide in an undercover agent, cannot object when his words are secretly recorded and used in court against him, even though there may have been deception about the role of the undercover confidant.[5] Secondly, certain covert investigations will not be 'searches' because

---

[3] (1967) 389 US 374.

[4] The Universal Declaration of Human Rights 1948 uses the word 'arbitrary', as does the International Covenant on Civil and Political Rights 1966. However, the Fourth Amendment to the United States Constitution speaks of 'unreasonable searches', as does s. 8 of the Canadian Charter of Rights and Freedoms 1982. The European Convention on Human Rights 1950 uses the drafting device of a presumptive absolute right that can then be abrogated by a public authority 'in accordance with the law' to the extent 'necessary' to prevent crime.

[5] See *US* v. *White* (1971) 401 US 745; *Christou* v. *Wright* [1992] QB 979 and compare the different position in Canada as stated in *Duarte* v. *The Queen* (1990) 65 DLR (4th) 240.

of the fact that there is no 'reasonable expectation of privacy' in the information thereby obtained. Thus records of numbers dialled from a particular telephone or the records of an electricity company in respect of the supply of electricity to particular premises can be obtained without objective grounds for suspicion and without formal authorization.[6] Thirdly, the place where the surveillance takes place may be crucial to whether or not a target has an expectation of privacy. In the United States there is no expectation at all in respect of open land (even if the land is privately owned and the proprietor has fenced that land to avoid observation). The position is less clear in Canada where, in the absence of compelling and urgent circumstances, a visual search of private open land without reasonable grounds to suspect the target may be a violation of privacy.[7] On the other hand, there is no requirement that, for a right to privacy to exist, the building targeted has to be a private residence. A hotel room is protected by this right. This has been held to be the case even when the room was not used as a bedroom but for gambling activities that were advertised to the public at large.[8]

Where reasonable grounds have to be established before surveillance is authorized by law, there is no rigid requirement on how these grounds have to be established. A classic statement of this principle comes from the case of *Illinois* v. *Gates*.[9] In that case the point was made that probable cause, too, is a fluid concept and turns on the assessment of probabilities in particular factual contexts. It is not readily, or even usefully, reduced to a neat set of legal rules. Relying on information from informants may or may not provide probable cause, since informant tips come in many shapes and sizes from many different persons.

Whilst there is no rule that the investigative information that forms the reasonable grounds (or probable cause, since the two terms are interchangeable) must take any particular form, an official authorizing the surveillance will be expected to take account of certain factors. One is the source of the information. Others are the amount of detail provided and whether an informant has a past record of providing reliable information. Even an anonymous source may be relied upon, so long as law enforcers confirm this anonymous information with their own investigations.[10] One difficulty with this flexible approach is that the previous bad character of the target may be used to support information provided to the police. Such a practice may lead to an individual being 'set up' for reasons of personal gain to the informant. The ethical dilemmas and risks of injustice posed by reliance on informers are discussed in more detail below.

---

[6] See *Smith* v. *Maryland* (1979) 442 US 735 and *R.* v. *Plant* (1993) 84 CCC (3d) 203.

[7] *California* v. *Ciarolo* (1986) 476 US 207 and compare *R.* v. *Grant* (1993) 84 CCC (3d) 173 and *R.* v. *Plant*, n. 6 above.

[8] Compare the Police Act 1997 s. 97; *Lustig* v. *US* (1949) 338 US 74 and *R.* v. *Wong* [1990] 3 SC 36. Note that the RIPA (discussed below) states that 'intrusive surveillance' affects 'residential premises'. This term is further defined in the Codes as meaning premises used for residential purposes or living accommodation, albeit on a temporary basis.

[9] (1983) 496 US 213.

[10] See *R.* v. *Garofoli* (1990) 60 CCC (3d) 161 and *R.* v. *Plant*, n. 6 above.

FORMS OF COVERT INVESTIGATION AND
THEIR REGULATION

As stated earlier, there are various ways in which surveillance may be effected and electronically recorded. Historically, the oldest method is to provide an informant or an undercover officer with a hidden recorder. The conversation takes place face to face between the target and the individual, who poses as a trusted friend or as a fellow conspirator. The conversation may be contemporaneously transmitted to law enforcers or may simply be recorded by the wearer of the wire. In either case, the fact that the evidence is incontrovertible means that it is a very effective investigative tool. There has been a refusal to accept that this form of monitoring involves an infringement of privacy, since the target is aware that he is confiding information (albeit under a false sense of trust). Equally, the argument that such a practice leads to a breach of the right against self-incrimination has been rejected in many common law jurisdictions on the basis that there is usually no active pressure by the informant to compel the target to make admissions.[11] Despite being the earliest form of electronic surveillance, the wiring of persons is the least regulated form of covert evidence gathering. In England and Wales, under voluntary codes adopted by the police prior to RIPA 2000, there was a belated acknowledgement that such activity should be authorized only where the information could not 'reasonably' be achieved by other means and that confidential information (such as medical records and communications between lawyer and client) should be acquired only if 'serious crime' was being investigated. Reasonableness, as defined in the voluntary codes, did not mean that the police had to show that evidence could *only* be obtained in this way and that the use of overt interrogation would, in all likelihood, be ineffective. Rather it was a practical question. The question was whether it was possible to achieve the objective sought in a reasonable time and to a reasonable standard other than by such measures.[12] This approach probably remains under the RIPA. RIPA section 26 has given statutory recognition to the fact that a 'covert human intelligence source' is a tool in the surveillance activities of the police because the police set up a relationship or use one that exists for a covert purpose. However, the Act does not cover communications made in the *presence* of an informant or undercover operative (RIPA section 48). There is, therefore, no statutory control over those conversations where, arguably, admissions are obtained through deceptive conduct that induces a false sense of confidence. And even where the use of a covert human intelligence source does fall within the regulating statute, the grounds upon which authorization may be given are very wide and include not simply the prevention or detection of crime or disorder, but also the interests of national security, the protection of public health, the interests of public safety, and the assessment of taxes and other duties. The generality of the justifications for the use of this type of surveillance activity, incidentally, also

---

[11] S. Sharpe, *Search and Surveillance: The Movement From Evidence to Information* (Aldershot: Ashgate, 2000) at 162–6.

[12] National Criminal Intelligence Service Voluntary Codes and see Sharpe, n. 11 above, at 113–4.

demonstrates the linkage between governmental control and crime control. The bases for authorization, which are repeated in respect of certain targeted electronic surveillance and, in part, in respect of telephone interceptions,[13] show that covert surveillance may be used as much to prevent civil disorder and disobedience, or to effect public compliance in respect of the payment of government taxes and duties, as to deal with criminal conduct. Such multifarious usage has attracted criticism on the ground that the functions of the security services and of the civilian police are not clearly differentiated.[14] The new legislation now governing England and Wales does not adequately address this criticism.

The use of persons as 'electronic eavesdroppers' is, of course, based upon the co-operation and participation of an undercover operative. Such co-operation may exist, but is not essential, for other forms of surveillance activity, and these other forms of covert investigation are therefore potentially more useful to the police. In the United States and Canada, the bugging of premises and the interception of telephone conversations are treated as different methods of achieving the same goal, that is to say, effecting electronic search.[15] The requirement of a judicial warrant applies to all such searches and their validity requires probable cause.

In England and Wales, because the statutory regulation of electronic eavesdropping has been a piecemeal development, the absence of a unified perspective has led to an *ad hoc* approach to control. The Interception of Communications Act 1985 was the first statute passed. It governed only telephone tapping and was a direct response to an adverse decision of the European Court of Human Rights in *Malone* v. *United Kingdom*,[16] which held that the existing use of purely administrative guidelines for the use of telephone tapping were insufficient to ensure that interceptions were 'in accordance with law' as required by Article 8 of the European Convention on Human Rights, which guarantees a right to privacy. The 1985 Act did little more than put the existing guidelines into statutory form and did not provide for any form of judicial supervision. What was required was a warrant approved by the Home Secretary, a minister of the central government, whenever the purpose of the interception was the detection of serious crime.[17] It was a minimalist response to the *Malone* decision. The Act has now been repealed, but the current provisions of RIPA are substantially based upon it. Again, out of concern that the English courts might face criticism from the Human Rights' Court in Europe and following judicial criticism in the House of Lords, sitting as the highest appeal court in the country,[18] the Police Act was passed in 1997. It was introduced to the legislature with the declared intention that it would

---

[13] See RIPA ss. 5, 26, and 28, discussed below.

[14] See I. Cameron, 'Telephone Tapping and the Interception of Communications Act 1985' [1986] *Northern Ireland Law Quarterly* 126 at 136.

[15] In the USA, the Electronic Communications Privacy Act 1986 and Title 18 USC and, in Canada, the Criminal Code RSC 1985 regulate the issuance of warrants.

[16] (1985) 7 EHRR 14.

[17] Retrospective annual judicial review was provided by a Commissioner (a high-ranking judicial officer). However, this review tended to be based on a sample of cases extracted from the list of all warrants issued during the review period and was uncritical, despite some errors found in the issuance of warrants. See, for instance, the Annual Report on IOCA, Cm 4364 (1999) HMSO.

[18] *R. v. Khan (Sultan)* [1996] 3 All ER 289.

control the use by the police of bugging equipment generally. In fact, the Act controls only those actions that involve entry onto property without the owner's consent or an interference with property. The Act remains in force, but is now supplemented by RIPA in respect of the use of remote surveillance and the installation of bugging equipment that involves no trespass (for instance where one occupier gives consent). The major criticism of both statutes is that the power to authorize bugging is vested in the police themselves and not in any independent judicial body. The Police Act, section 93, contains a detailed list of senior officers, such as Chief Constables, Police Commissioners, and the Director of the National Criminal Intelligence Service, who may give authorization. RIPA, in sections 30 and 32, again gives power to senior officers or, in cases of urgency, to their deputies. Thus, the North American model has been rejected in favour of internal control. This issue is further discussed below.

The position is further complicated by the fact that, in England and Wales, surveillance activity is divided into categories depending on the level of intrusiveness into personal privacy resulting from the surveillance or whether trespass is involved. There are different justifications and different authorizations needed for each category. When the bugging of premises takes place, intrusiveness is measured in terms of whether actions in a residence or a private vehicle are being monitored. It is not measured in terms of the confidentiality of the information obtained from the monitoring exercise. The statutory justifications allowing the surveillance of business premises without physical intrusion or by consent are as wide as those permitting the use of a covert human intelligence source, even though the information obtained may relate to the target's private or family life. This could occur where the premises are the offices of a doctor, lawyer, or counsellor. The grounds permitting surveillance of a private home or car are much narrower and are confined to the protection of national security, the national economy, and to the prevention or detection of serious crime. The law therefore focuses on property rights rather than on privacy. English legislation has not yet fully accepted that privacy applies to persons and not to places. The only concession that is made to the acquisition of confidential material is that, under the Codes that govern best practice under RIPA, a higher-ranking officer must authorize the acquisition of such material. English law does not completely follow the wider North American model of a reasonable expectation of privacy that developed from the case of *Katz* v. *US*.[19] This obsession with interference in property rights is further demonstrated by the fact that, when the placing of a surveillance device involves entering a property without consent or a physical interference with the property of the target under the Police Act 1997, there is only one basis for the authorization, that it is believed that the action specified is 'likely to be of substantial value in the prevention or detection of serious crime'.[20]

In respect of telephone interception there has been a recognition that technology has outpaced legislation. The Interception of Communications Act in 1985 regulated

---

[19] N. 3 above. Mr Katz was making a call from a public telephone booth. He was not in a private residence.

[20] Police Act 1997 s. 93. Serious crime, as defined in the Police Act and in RIPA, could include a vast amount of middle-range criminality such as public disorder, minor assaults, or a first offence of dishonesty where a large sum of money was involved.

only the public telephone system and did not extend to private telephone systems. Further, mobile phones and pagers were not within that Act. In 2000, RIPA extended the need for authorization to the interception of these methods of communication as well as stored electronic mail. However, the revised legislation does not restrict the grounds for authorization of interception. Indeed, it gives ministers of the central government wider powers than previously existed to sanction interception as part of a mutual assistance agreement with another jurisdiction. National security, the prevention and detection of serious crime, and the national economic well-being are retained from the earlier legislation as further bases upon which a minister may issue a warrant. The permission of a government minister is still required unless one of the parties to the conversation consents, in which case a law enforcement agency may legitimate the interception. There has been no move towards independent judicial authorization despite the fact that on mainland Europe this is a normative requirement.

The lack of any requirement of prior judicial approval in any of the surveillance activities outlined above differs from the legal position in North America, Australia, and many countries in Europe. However under the Police Act 1997 and RIPA, where surveillance activities involve monitoring activities in residential premises, the prior approval of a Commissioner (who is a judge) is required.[21] Yet even this requirement can be avoided in circumstances of urgency. In all other circumstances, in England and Wales, a Commissioner has power only to review covert policing retrospectively and to quash any improper authorizations after they have taken effect. There is an even greater potential problem with the self-regulating nature of the English system. This is that the statutes and codes governing surveillance and interception expressly incorporate safeguards that claim to make investigative practices compliant with human rights law. These safeguards are known as the proportionality principle and the necessity principle, both concepts which also appear in the United States and in Canada.

The first principle (proportionality) requires that the action is no more intrusive than is necessary to carry out the investigation and demands that particular attention be given to those innocent parties whose privacy may be invaded as a consequence. It also limits the duration of the surveillance. The second (necessity) requires that the action is necessary in order that an investigation may proceed without undue delay or obstruction; in other words, that it is a reasonable course of action.

These principles are of paramount importance, but they cannot be effectively enforced when the individuals sanctioning the activities of law enforcers are part of the organization involved. A police officer, even though he may be of senior rank, should not be considering issues of necessity and proportionality in the applications made by more junior officers within the force. This is because he is not a detached and neutral arbiter. English practice on covert investigations generally offends against the principle adopted in relation to the physical searches of premises that a warrant must be issued by an independent judge who has no interest in the outcome of the investigation.[22]

---

[21] RIPA s. 36 and the Police Act 1997 s. 97.

[22] In the USA, ostensible bias will invalidate the issue of *any* search warrant. See *Coolidge* v. *New Hampshire* (1971) 403 US 443; *Connally* v. *Georgia* (1977) 429 US 245; *Commonwealth* v. *Davis* (1973) 310 A 2d 334.

A further difficulty arises in connection with the use of material obtained through surveillance. Telephone conversations that have been intercepted by a government warrant may not be used directly in evidence in criminal proceedings (though they may lead to evidence found as a consequence of the interception which can be used). However, telephone interceptions made with consent of one party may be used as evidence in a criminal trial. This inconsistency is significant because RIPA provides that there can be no questioning in any trial that may tend to suggest that an interception has occurred illegally. Thus an accused who argues that the taped telephone conversation used in evidence against him was intercepted without the consent of one party or without proper police authorization is not allowed to challenge this at trial. The European Court of Human Rights has, perhaps surprisingly, stated that this situation does not violate the right to a fair trial.[23] The English House of Lords had disagreed and held that no intercepted telephone conversations should be put before the court however they were obtained.[24] But the statute law followed the European Court's decision and is an example of the view, discussed in the next section, that if evidence is inherently reliable, it does not matter whether it was illegally obtained.

ETHICAL PROBLEMS INHERENT IN THE USE OF COVERT SURVEILLANCE AND INFORMANTS

Once the prosecution seeks to use evidence that has been obtained by the use of covert investigation in a criminal trial, it is not only the fundamental right to human privacy that may be infringed. There is also the basic right to a fair trial. This second right consists of various due-process protections including the right to legal representation, the right to know the allegations that form the prosecution case, the right to test the prosecution case through examination and cross-examination of witnesses, and the right to be presumed innocent until proven guilty. The right of a suspect not to be compelled to incriminate himself forms part of the right to a fair trial even though the incrimination may have occurred at an investigation prior to the trial itself. These protections are contained in the European Convention on Human Rights as well as in the Canadian Charter of Rights and the Constitution of the United States. In countries that have a common law tradition there is a further protection granted to accused persons. This protection consists of exclusionary rules excluding particular kinds of evidence. These rules will be discussed in more detail in a later chapter. In essence, a trial judge has a discretion and, sometimes, an obligation, to refuse to permit the prosecution to put evidence that has been improperly obtained before the court. There is, however, considerable uncertainty about how judges will exercise their powers in relation to exclusion and the issues, so far as they relate to covertly obtained evidence, will be outlined below.

There is also a more drastic power vested in judges to stop a criminal trial

---

[23] *Choudhary* v. *United Kingdom*, App. No. 40084/98.   [24] *Morgans* v. *DPP*, 17 Feb. 2000 (HL).

altogether for an 'abuse of process'. This abuse of process could in principle include morally flagrant and, possibly, illegal behaviour on the part of criminal investigators. It has been said that the power to stop the proceedings exists in order to give the accused a fair trial, or because it offends the court's sense of justice and propriety to be asked to try the accused in the particular circumstances of the case.[25] There are therefore two separate rationales for stopping a criminal trial. The first is a determination that an accused would lose his right to a fair trial if the case were to proceed. The second is that, irrespective of whether the fairness of the trial process itself has been affected by misconduct on the part of law enforcers, the behaviour of those investigators is so outrageous that a court of law cannot be seen to condone it by continuing to try the case. In England and Wales, the power to stop proceedings for impropriety during the course of an investigation is used extremely sparingly. In two relatively recent cases, proceedings were stopped because of abuses of the extradition procedure in returning offenders to the United Kingdom.[26] These were situations involving physical coercion or breach of international law but, up till now, the use of entrapment and even the incidental commission of crime on the part of investigators have been insufficient to give rise to a finding that the public conscience would be shocked that a criminal trial is based on such conduct.

There is frequently a fine dividing line between covert policing and entrapment. A covert human intelligence source can easily cross the line between purely passive observation and incitement to offend. Although the RIPA Code states that a human source of information has no licence to commit a crime, it is conceded that, in the context of an authorized operation, the source 'may infiltrate a criminal conspiracy or be a party to the commission of criminal offences'. Entrapment is no defence in English law, but a judge has the power to include evidence obtained as a result under PACE section 78 which gives a judge statutory discretion to exclude potential prosecution evidence should he or she consider that its admission would have an adverse effect on the fairness of the proceedings. The factors that may incline a judge to exclude entrapment evidence have been stated in the seminal English case of R. v. Smurthwaite.[27] They include the degree of incitement offered to the target and the nature of the entrapment, the degree of activity or passivity of the undercover operative, and whether there is an incontrovertible record of what occurred. These factors bear some similarity to the application of the entrapment defence in the United States, in that where an otherwise innocent target (one with no previously known inclination toward crime) is actively encouraged and pressured to offend, it is more likely that the evidence will be excluded than in the case of a target who has a previous criminal

---

[25] R. v. Horseferry Road Magistrates' Court, ex parte Bennett [1994] 1 AC 42. See also judicial dicta in R. v. Latif, R. v. Shazad [1996] 1 All ER 353, although the proceedings were not in fact stayed in Latif and Shazad. Echoing this approach, it has been stated by the Canadian Supreme Court in Collins v. The Queen (1987) 38 DLR (4th) 508 that the two separate reasons to exclude evidence are first, to permit a fair trial and, secondly, to prevent the administration of justice coming into further disrepute. Proceedings will be stayed in Canada on the same principles as apply to the exclusion of evidence.

[26] R. v. Horseferry Road Magistrates' Court, ex parte Bennett, n. 25 above, and R. v. Mullen [1999] 2 Cr. App. R 143.

[27] [1994] 1 All ER 898, and see Latif and Shazad, n. 25 above.

disposition. However, a proper exercise of the discretion under PACE should take account of matters other than the predisposition of the suspect. One matter that seems to have become crucial to any decision-making is the reliability of the evidence obtained by the undercover agent. If the actions and/or words of the suspect have been electronically recorded, then the fact that the actions took place or the words were said is beyond challenge. The background leading up to the recorded evidence may be contested, but that has not weighed heavily with the courts. This emphasis in English legal practice on reliability as the ultimate criterion of admissibility has had serious implications beyond the challenge to alleged entrapment evidence.

The use of new technology in the covert investigation of suspects has created a new form of 'incontrovertible' evidence. The approach of the judiciary to the admission of such evidence is that where investigators have used deception, or even illegal practices, the courts will condone their actions in order to allow evidence of guilt to be put before the court. It is still rare for evidence obtained through the use of informants and undercover agents to be excluded.[28] The English courts have effectively retreated to a position that was frequently adopted prior to the passing of PACE when illegally acquired evidence was admitted. A problem with this approach is that it does nothing to encourage or exhort police officers to uphold the law and to conduct ethical investigations. Indeed, in the leading case of *Chalkley* v. *Jeffries*,[29] the Court of Appeal stated that exclusionary powers could not be utilized simply to mark disapproval of the way in which evidence had been obtained by law enforcers if that conduct was the only basis of a claim of 'unfairness' by a defendant. It has also been reaffirmed recently that 'fairness' must include a consideration of the interests of the victim and of the public as well as those of the defendant.[30] It may well be considered unfair to both the victim and the public to exclude evidence the content of which is indisputable because it has been acquired through electronic recording.

Of course, if the police do not need specific higher authorization to conduct an investigation, no formal rules are broken and the possibility that the evidence will be excluded is even more remote. One method by which the police may circumvent the need for such authorization is to seek the agreement, or at least the compliance, of someone known to a target. In this way, provided that one party consents, intrusive surveillance inside private premises may be conducted without governmental authorization or the prior approval of a Commissioner. The ethics utilized by police officers in persuading a person to co-operate in this way may be as tainted as those that sometimes occur in the use of informants. Deals may be agreed to the effect that there is to be immunity from prosecution for the enterprise under investigation, or that unrelated criminal conduct of the participant is to be condoned. Indeed an informant is likely to fulfil both the role of undercover agent and also of an instrument of surveillance by wearing a recording device whilst entering a target's home, or by

---

[28] Two cases reported in 2000 (*R.* v. *Shannon* [2000] *Crim. LR* 1001 and *R.* v. *Bow Street Magistrates' Court and others, ex parte Proulx* [2000] *Crim. LR* 997) both raised entrapment as a basis for the exclusion of evidence without success.

[29] [1998] 2 All ER 155.

[30] See the House of Lords in *Attorney-General's Reference No. 3 of 1999*, 14 Dec. 2000.

consenting to the tapping of his telephone and then instigating an incriminating conversation with the target. It is never possible to challenge the reality of any bargaining that may have taken place between the participant and the police because the principle of public-interest immunity (which allows public bodies to refuse to disclose information where this would be contrary to the public interest) prevents such information being made available. In some ways, therefore, the potential for unethical practice is even greater because, on the face of the investigation, no illegality has taken place.

SURVEILLANCE AND INTERNATIONAL DATABASES

Increasingly, covert surveillance is used not to obtain specific evidence against a target who is suspected of having committed or is in the course of committing a crime, but to gather information that may, at some later date, prove useful to law enforcers. Such information is held on databases of increasing size and scope of application. In England and Wales, there are several databases created for the use of criminal investigation and the maintenance of public order. Not all of these contain covertly obtained data. The DNA database, for example, holds DNA details relating to convicted persons for the purpose of cross-matching samples taken at a later date from crime scenes or the victims of crime. This information is obtained with the full knowledge, though without the need for the consent, of a suspect.[31] Other databases contain information that has been acquired without either the consent or the knowledge of the subject. The National Criminal Intelligence Service holds and analyses data in order to discharge its statutory function of providing criminal intelligence to police forces and other law enforcement agencies throughout the United Kingdom. The use of sophisticated surveillance equipment is recognized as a means for acquiring this intelligence.[32] Thus bugging activities under the Police Act 1997, telephone interceptions under RIPA, and the use of human intelligence sources under the same statute may all be used to provide data which are then available to NCIS. Material may be retained on the basis of possible relevance in any future investigation and its use is not, therefore, confined to the investigation in which it was obtained. If the subject of the information is unaware that the information is being compiled against him, he cannot seek to challenge its reliability. In any event, the Data Protection Act 1998, in sections 28 and 29, precludes access by a subject of recorded data in respect of data processed for the purpose of safeguarding national security, or for the prevention or detection of crime, where this would be likely to prejudice police operations. It is extremely unlikely, therefore, that a target will be aware that personal information is being held in respect of him and, even if he is, he will rarely succeed in establishing the nature of this information and, therefore, whether it is correct.

---

[31] See PACE ss. 62–65.
[32] HMIC, *Policing With Intelligence HMIC Thematic Inspection Report On Good Practice* (1997).

National databases pose a significant threat to personal privacy, but, increasingly, in our global society data may also be transferred to the law enforcers of another jurisdiction or be held on an international database. An obvious example of this is the exchange of intelligence that occurs between members of the European Union. The establishment of a formal mechanism for the cross-border exchange of information concerning the maintenance of public order and crime control is often included as part of a wider political agreement between Member States. Thus the Schengen Agreement,[33] originally signed in 1985, led to a Convention giving powers to foreign police officers to carry out surveillance in the territory of another 'Contracting Party' with the authorization of that other country. Perhaps more importantly, the Convention also provides that the Contracting Parties are to set up and maintain the Schengen Information System. This system is used to exchange data on asylum seekers, undesirable aliens, persons expelled or extradited, and persons wanted for criminal prosecution. Where a person is suspected of intending to commit 'extremely serious' offences,[34] information will be stored as a result of surveillance, including the identities of those accompanying the target and of other occupants of any vehicle being observed. Whilst the holding of this information may be a matter of concern, there are certain safeguards. The data must be used for the specified purposes only and there are restraints on those having access to the data. These safeguards, however, do not attach to a second network of police and security operations, SIRENE, which exists, virtually unregulated and confidential, under the Schengen Agreement.[35]

The Europol Convention[36] is another example of a co-operative information exchange system that is part of a wider political comity between European Union Member States. It does not provide for an integrated police unit along the lines of the American Federal Bureau of Investigation, but it does provide for the sharing of criminal information and technical support. A computerized system for the collection of information has been established. The range of offences to which the Convention applies is to be incrementally increased to include not just drug trafficking and serious international crime, but also crimes such as offences against the person and fraud. Data stored may also be held in a temporary 'work file' for the purposes of analysis. This file may include details of persons who are not suspected of criminal activity such as victims, witnesses, and associates of the target. Information on the database may be communicated to third (non-member) States and may be obtained under other Conventions. Thus the acquisition and disclosure of information is not limited to the European Union.

---

[33] The objective of the Agreement was the abolition of internal border controls and greater co-operation between States endorsing the Agreement. The Implementation Convention was signed in 1990. The Agreement is incorporated into European Union law through the Amsterdam Treaty.

[34] Art. 99 of Schengen.

[35] SIRENE is a network for police and security co-operation between Schengen countries. National SIRENE offices handle non-standardized information (including written text, photographs, and telephonic exchanges between officers). Such information will not be regulated by the Schengen Convention. Any public knowledge of the workings of the SIRENE network has been acquired through unauthorized leakage of information since the operating manual is not available for public scrutiny.

[36] The Europol Convention came into force in the UK in 1998 and has been operational since 1999.

Theoretically the safeguard for a citizen against wrongful inclusion on these criminal databases or against the storage of erroneous information is that the information is to be disclosed only to authorized individuals for authorized purposes.[37] However, the major limitation on this safeguard is that a target of criminal surveillance has virtually no right of access to it. This means that he or she is not allowed to discover whether the database does contain material relating to him or her, let alone whether this material is correct or is the result of malicious misinformation by others, or even the result of a genuine mistake. As stated above, the Data Protection Act 1998 contains certain exceptions to the presumptive right of a subject to be told in 'intelligible form' of any personal data held upon him by another person (the data controller). The exception relating to criminal investigation, which exempts information concerning the prevention and detection of crime and the apprehension or prosecution of offenders from disclosure, applies equally to international databases. Even if the information were to be forthcoming because, as is unlikely, the police considered that it would not prejudice police operations, there are further constraints on disclosure once the data reach European systems such as Europol or Schengen, when the interests and objectives of all Member States will be considered paramount.[38]

It is evident that, whilst surveillance and the storage of information may be necessary tools in the fight against sophisticated, serious, and international crime, there are serious concerns about the privacy and security of individuals who may wrongly be caught up in a surveillance operation. These individuals have no right to discover the existence of or to challenge the reliability of the information obtained by a covert investigation, nor to control the dissemination of information obtained as a result of that investigation. In this respect, covert policing is arguably more oppressive than the physical search of individuals or their property and even more oppressive than regulated custodial interrogation.

Further Reading

ASHWORTH, A., 'Should The Police Be Allowed To Use Deceptive Practices?' (1998) 114 *Law Quarterly Review* 108.

Justice Report, *Under Surveillance* (London: Justice, 1998).

MATHIESON, T., *On Globalisation Of Control: Towards an Integrated Surveillance System in Europe* (London: Statewatch, 1999).

POWER, R., 'Technology and the Fourth Amendment: A Proposed Formulation For Visual Searches' (1989) 80 *The Journal of Criminal Law and Criminology* 1.

SHARPE, S., 'Covert Policing: A Comparative View' (1996) 25 *Anglo-American Law Review* 163.

---

[37] Europol Arts. 10 and 18 and Schengen Arts. 101 and 102.

[38] Europol Art. 19 and Schengen Art. 109.

5

REGULATING THE POLICE STATION

The case of the Police and Criminal Evidence Act 1984

Mike Maguire[*]

INTRODUCTION

The principle famously articulated by Winston Churchill, that a country's level of civilization can be judged from the state of its prisons, could plausibly be extended to include those areas of police stations where arrested people are detained and questioned. Like prisons, these areas—variously referred to as 'charge rooms', 'the cells', or (in the current euphemistic language of UK criminal justice) 'custody suites'—are places hidden from public view, where people are held against their will by representatives of the State who possess potentially far-reaching powers over their physical welfare. The reality of detainees' experience around the world ranges from beatings and torture at one extreme to something approaching respect and fair treatment at the other, but even in countries which are serious about human rights, allegations of oppressive behaviour are common and deaths in custody are anything but rare events (Harding 1995; Evans and Morgan 1998; Morgan and Evans 1999). Equally important, of course, evidence from questioning in pre-trial custody often determines the outcome of court proceedings, and hence the manner in which interrogations are conducted and recorded can have huge consequences for the suspect's future, including his or her liberty, reputation, employment prospects, and, in countries with the death penalty, even life itself. There are many notorious examples, from Britain and elsewhere, of miscarriages of justice caused by unreliable interview evidence or false confessions. For these reasons, the regulation of regimes of detention and questioning is an issue of central importance to the quality, integrity, and legitimacy of any country's system of criminal justice.

---

[*] Full citations for all books and articles cited in this chapter are to be found in the Bibliography and Further Reading section.

The ubiquity of cases of mistreatment of suspects and unreliable confessions is not convincingly explained as the result of some kind of free-floating tendency towards brutality or dishonesty by police officers around the world.[1] It is better understood through an examination of some fundamental pressures, problems, and dilemmas which are common to all criminal justice systems. Equally, regulatory regimes governing detention and questioning—an important example of which was created in England and Wales by the Police and Criminal Evidence Act 1984, the main focus of this chapter—can be regarded as the results of different countries' attempts to resolve some of these key contradictions.

'CRIME CONTROL' AND 'DUE PROCESS'

At the heart of the matter is the problem of reconciling two aims which are frequently in conflict: obtaining enough evidence to convict offenders in court, while at the same time protecting the rights of all suspects and preventing wrongful conviction of the innocent. McConville *et al.* (1991), reinterpreting a distinction originally made by Herbert Packer (1969), contrasted two 'ideal types' of criminal justice process: the 'crime control' model (in which the end—convicting the guilty—is held to justify the means) and the 'due process' model (whereby procedural propriety is considered more important than obtaining convictions). Describing the situation in England and Wales in the late 1980s, they argued that, while the legal processes and rhetoric surrounding detention and questioning reflected at least some commitment to the ideal of due process,[2] the beliefs and behaviour of the police continued to exhibit almost total adherence to a crime control approach. While some aspects of this account attracted significant criticism from other academics (see, for example, Morgan 1995; Dixon 1992, 1995), it provides a useful broad framework for discussing the key issues.

In more concrete terms, the designers of any regulatory system for pre-trial processes have to confront some basic problems regarding the production of evidence. Clearly, statements by a suspected offender are potentially a fertile source of evidence and, from a 'crime control' perspective, formal questioning of suspects is an important weapon in the investigator's armoury. In the ideal scenario, their answers assist a rigorous 'search for the truth' about a particular offence, increasing the chances of convicting the guilty and—equally important—offering the 'truly' innocent a chance to demonstrate that the suspicions are unfounded. However, this assumes that (a) it is already clear what offences have been committed, (b) there is other good evidence available, (c) the police will approach the interview with an open mind, and (d) the

---

[1] It is recognized that in many inquisitorial (as opposed to adversarial) systems of criminal justice, pre-trial questioning is sometimes carried out by an examining magistrate or judge, rather than a police officer (e.g., in France, by a *procureur* or *juge d'instruction*). However, this often applies only to a minority of cases, and anyway does not preclude the possibility of mistreatment in detention before or after the formal interview.

[2] They are, however, critical of claims (such as those by McBarnet 1981) that legal forms and rhetoric in this area are *primarily* driven by due process ideals. They argue that legislation is strongly influenced by police lobbying for greater powers and that, far from inhibiting police officers from abusing the rights of individuals, the law often facilitates such abuses.

suspect is willing to answer questions. In reality, many interviews take place without some or all of these conditions being present, making the encounter between investigator and suspect (or, in symbolic terms, the interface between state and citizen) a much more problematic event.

First of all, in a primarily adversarial (as opposed to inquisitorial) system of justice such as that in England and Wales, where the onus is upon the prosecution to prove guilt 'beyond reasonable doubt', it is often in a suspect's interest to decline to answer any questions. Although seriously undermined in recent years,[3] the 'right to silence' is a traditional element of such a system, justified by the aim of achieving 'equality of arms' between prosecution and defence. This raises serious questions about the use of detention without charge to assist investigations and, in particular, to persuade suspects to answer questions (which may harm their own defence).

An extreme version of the 'due process' position would be that it is wrong in all circumstances for a non-judicial body like the police to deprive people forcibly of their liberty when it has insufficient evidence to bring criminal charges against them. Indeed, in nineteenth-century Britain, this was a highly sensitive issue, and the fiction of asking people 'voluntarily' to accompany an officer to a police station in order to 'assist the police with their inquiries' was created partly in order to avoid the problem and stave off challenges (Sanders 1997). However, the general trend in the twentieth century, in Britain and elsewhere, was towards acceptance of the practice of routinely detaining suspects for questioning, and there are now few, if any, jurisdictions in the world which do not permit this in some form. This is partly a result of a pragmatic shift towards 'crime control' approaches to criminal justice in the face of growing concern about crime, but it can also be argued that in certain circumstances—and given adequate safeguards—it is quite justifiable in principle to detain suspects against their will for a short period, even though there is as yet insufficient evidence to bring charges. For example, a person's observed behaviour, or presence at the scene of a crime, may create enough suspicion to warrant asking him or her in a formal setting to provide an explanation. Detention may also be justified as a means of preventing suspects from destroying evidence or warning associates, once they learn that an investigation is in progress. However, as any form of detention constitutes a major intrusion on liberty, it is essential for advocates of this view to establish where the line is to be drawn in terms of the seriousness of the offences under investigation and the strength of the grounds for suspicion: without this, there is a risk of people being 'pulled in' on any minor pretext in the hope that they will admit to an offence (such practices are sometimes referred to as 'fishing expeditions'). Equally close attention has to be paid to the 'robustness' with which questions can be put, and the length of time for which people can be held. Moreover—especially if one accepts the view of police as driven by a 'crime control' model of criminal justice—it is necessary to ask who has effective control of decision-making 'on the ground', as there will inevitably

---

[3] The Criminal Justice and Public Order Act 1994 allowed courts, under certain circumstances, to 'draw such inferences as appear proper' from a person's silence under questioning. Most importantly, this applies when a defendant uses a defence in court which s/he failed to mention earlier when questioned or charged by the police (s. 34). For a broad discussion of issues surrounding the right of silence see Morgan and Stephenson (1994).

be wide scope for individual judgement in virtually any set of rules that are devised.

Furthermore, it is clear that interview evidence is not simply the 'icing on the cake', but is of central importance to the prosecution process. Only a small minority of all interviewed suspects remain silent or refuse to answer questions, and in well over half of all court cases the evidence includes a 'confession'—many of these cases, of course, involving a guilty plea (Zander and Henderson 1993; Morgan and Stephenson 1994). There is little doubt that, without this highly convenient combination of confession and guilty plea (in other words, in the extreme case, if every suspect both refused to answer police questions and pleaded not guilty), the criminal justice system would fall into serious crisis. Although some corroborating evidence is usually produced to support confessions (McConville 1993), such evidence would often be insufficient without the confession, and a great deal more investigative effort would be needed to maintain anything like current conviction rates; obviously, too, the need to more than double the number of contested trials would produce enormous strains on time and resources.

It is important to note that interviews can be used, in a sense, to 'create' crime. Investigative work often does not conform to the ideal model of systematic collection of evidence in relation to specific reported offences: rather, it tends to be driven by hearsay and suspicions about the activities of offenders already 'known to the police' (for classic studies demonstrating this see Skolnick 1966; Ericson 1981). In these circumstances, police interviews can become a vehicle for what McConville *et al.* (1991) call 'case construction'—a process whereby experienced detectives use their knowledge of the law to manœuvre suspects into making a series of self-incriminating statements that can be woven together into an apparently coherent 'story' of a sequence of criminal actions, and used to produce charges for a variety of offences beyond those originally under investigation. In short, the importance of interviewing for the production of charges and convictions creates a strong temptation for investi-gators (who tend to be motivated above all by a desire to 'convict the guilty') to ignore principles of due process and to treat interviewing as nothing more than a convenient tool for 'obtaining a confession'. This situation contains a built-in probability that some will employ improper or oppressive interrogation techniques to achieve their aims, and that a number of unsafe convictions will result.

Finally, it is important to add that interviews can be experienced by suspects as oppressive without any conscious attempt on the part of the police to 'bully' them. Detention is *inherently* coercive, and detained persons often experience it as a fright-ening and psychologically disorienting situation—one in which the police are, to use a sporting analogy, 'playing at home' and the suspect, already suffering the shock of being arrested, is on unfamiliar and apparently hostile territory. In such circum-stances, people may unfairly be persuaded to make self-incriminating statements, especially in response to hints that 'co-operation' will bring quicker release or more lenient treatment. Some, too, may be vulnerable to suggestion and even find them-selves making false confessions to crimes mentioned by interviewers (Irving and Hilgendorf 1980; Gudjonsson *et al.* 1992).

REGULATORY SYSTEMS

Every criminal justice system has to deal in some way with fundamental issues of the above kinds. Although most legislators and policy-makers are keen not to hinder the gathering of evidence necessary to convict guilty people, they are also aware of the dangers of allowing *carte blanche* to investigators. Over the years, each country has therefore developed its own rules and traditions for controlling, to a greater or lesser extent, the grounds on which people may be detained, the length of time they can be held without charge, the ways in which they can be questioned, the extent to which legal advice and independent scrutiny are allowed, how what is said is recorded, and so on. These range from highly formalized codes of procedure to informal practices that have evolved under legal frameworks which allow wide discretion to police or prosecutors. However, it is important to emphasize that, even among jurisdictions with tightly specified regulations, there are significant variations in the extent to which these are actually observed. At one extreme are criminal justice systems in which rules are blatantly flouted and physical mistreatment (even torture) is known to be a routine element of police questioning; at the other extreme are those in which, although individual deviance may occur, the normal expectation is that suspects' rights will be respected. Such differences, it should be noted, may be easiest to observe at the 'ground level' of culture and practice among low-ranking officers, but explanations may be best sought by looking at attitudes and behaviour 'higher up the chain'. Where abuses are rife, it is partly because their perpetrators run little risk of disciplinary interventions by senior officers and/or the exclusion of evidence by judges (see, for example, Maguire and Norris 1991, 1994; McConville *et al.* 1991; Maguire 1994).

This chapter focuses on one prominent example of a systematic attempt to regulate the process of detention and questioning. This is the comprehensive set of rules governing police procedures in England and Wales, which were introduced under the Police and Criminal Evidence Act 1984 (commonly known as 'PACE'). It provides an important and instructive case study of a new system which emerged out of a high-level review of fundamental principles (the 1981 Royal Commission on Criminal Procedure) and one in which conscious attempts were made to create a 'balance' between what could be broadly described as 'crime control' and 'due process' concerns. It is also interesting, in that the legislation represented a sudden and radical change from traditional approaches in England and Wales, which had relied mainly on trust in the police to treat suspects in accordance with vague principles articulated over the years through case law. As will be described in more detail below, the system is highly codified, with detailed rules covering each stage of the process and an obligation on the police to keep contemporaneous written records of everything of significance that happens.

The main aim of the discussion will be to assess broadly the impact that PACE has had over the last fifteen years upon the capacity of the police to bring good evidence before the courts, upon their willingness to observe the letter and the spirit of the regulations, and, most importantly, upon the risks of mistreatment of suspects, false confessions, and miscarriages of justice—concern about which was the initial driving force behind the new legislation. In contrast to the situation in many other countries, several British researchers have been granted open access to police stations to study the operation of PACE, so this task is greatly assisted by the availability of strong empirical evidence.

The chapter begins with a brief account of the background to PACE and the broad nature of the regulatory mechanisms it introduced. This is followed by a more detailed discussion of rules relating to the authorization of detention, the physical welfare of suspects, access to legal advice, and the conduct and recording of interviews. Research evidence is then used to assess how effective these mechanisms have been in practice. Finally, it is asked what general lessons may be learned from the British experience.

THE 'PACE' REGULATIONS

BACKGROUND AND RATIONALE

The Police and Criminal Evidence Act 1984 ('PACE') was the outcome of a lengthy, and often heated, political and legal debate. The single event which did most to set this in motion was the Maxwell Confait case, in which three mentally impaired teenagers were wrongly convicted of murder on the basis of 'confessions' made under oppressive police questioning and in the absence of any legal advice or other support. When it emerged that they were innocent, a major inquiry (Fisher 1977) was instigated, and its critical comments contributed in turn to the decision to set up a full-scale Royal Commission to undertake a fundamental examination of criminal procedure in England and Wales. The Royal Commission on Criminal Procedure (1981), under the chairmanship of Sir Cyril Phillips, produced recommendations for radical change in a number of key areas, including the regulation of detention and questioning in police stations. Many of these recommendations were eventually turned into legislation in 1984, albeit in an altered form after lengthy political debate which took account of strong lobbying from the police and other interested groups (Zander 1985).

The central rationale behind the system of regulation that PACE introduced—at least, as this was expressed by both the Royal Commission and the architects of the Act—was the notion of achieving a 'balance' between competing rights and interests. The Royal Commission's remit required it to 'have regard both to the interests of the community in bringing offenders to justice and to the rights and liberties of persons suspected or accused of crime' (RCCP 1981: iv). This idea was translated into legislation by efforts to balance limitations on the powers of the police in some areas with increases in their powers in others: for example, while detained persons gained the rights to notify friends or relatives of their arrest and to receive legal advice, the police gained greater powers to enter and search their homes.

The Commission's report identified three criteria by which any system of crime investigation and criminal procedure should be judged: 'fairness', 'openness', and 'workability'. It was seen as particularly important that rules are applied consistently and equitably; that suspects are clearly informed of what is happening and why; and that actions and the reasons for them can be properly reviewed by others after the event. At the same time, it was emphasized, regulatory procedures should not be so complex and time-consuming that they paralyse the work of investigators.

The mechanism eventually designed to put these principles into practice was a set of detailed Codes of Practice issued by the Home Secretary under the provisions of PACE (first implemented in 1985, the Codes were revised in 1991 and 1995). These place clear duties and responsibilities upon police officers to ensure that stipulated procedures are followed during their dealings with suspects. The Codes do not have the full force of law and breaching them is not a criminal offence; however, it is punishable under police disciplinary procedures and hence potentially damaging to an officer's career.

The Codes of Practice set out rules covering many aspects of investigative procedure, both inside and outside police stations. In accordance with the principles of 'fairness' and 'openness', these place strong emphasis on ensuring that suspects are made aware of their rights—for example, by stipulating that they must sign a declaration of whether they want legal advice. More generally, the Codes attempt to maximize the accountability of police officers, and the visibility and reviewability of their actions, through requirements that they make and retain *systematic written records of key decisions, actions, and events.* The architects of the Act placed considerable faith in the notion that police behaviour could be largely controlled by these 'paper' procedures: indeed, it can be argued that the effectiveness of the whole regulatory system depends critically on whether they were right. Important examples include the stopping and searching of people in the street, which should be recorded on a form stating the reasons for the search, a copy being given on request to the person stopped; and the entry and search of arrested people's homes, which should be authorized by an inspector and a full record kept of what occurred. As will presently be discussed, however, the most substantial (and arguably the most important) record-keeping requirements concern detention and questioning in the police station.

Finally, the Royal Commission's other defining criterion of an effective regulatory system—that it should be 'workable'—is reflected in the common use, throughout the PACE Codes of Practice, of the phrase 'where practicable'. This indicates that there are many situations in which the police may temporarily bypass the required procedures if insufficient resources are currently available. For example, if a particular action should be authorized by an inspector but all the inspectors are dealing with other urgent matters, a sergeant may perform the task and it may be authorized retrospectively by an inspector. As will be discussed presently, such 'let out clauses' may be sensible in principle, but contain an inherent risk of abuse.

KEY ELEMENTS OF THE SYSTEM

Having outlined the broad background to PACE and some of the main principles and assumptions on which it was based, it is time to look in more detail at the resulting framework of regulatory mechanisms, as set out both in the Act and in the Codes of Practice. As noted above, PACE brought about significant changes in several other areas of investigative practice, but the focus here will be solely upon the detention, questioning, and treatment of suspects, which are covered in Parts IV and V of the Act.

The regulatory framework can be summarized most simply as a combination of (a) the formal appointment of selected police officers as 'custody officers', independent of the investigation and with specified duties in relation to the welfare and rights of detained persons; (b) strict limits on the length of time for which suspects can be deprived of their liberty; (c) a set of specific rights for suspects, including the rights to be offered free legal advice and to have someone informed of their detention; (d) stipulated levels of authority for decision-making and the use of discretion; (e) rules against oppressive styles of interviewing; and (f) record-keeping requirements. The formal requirements in each of these respects will be outlined briefly in turn, followed by a discussion of some of their limitations and of research evidence about how they have worked in practice.

The custody officer

The role of the 'custody officer' is central to the system set up by PACE. He or she acts in theory as an independent gatekeeper to detention, guardian of the rights of those detained, and overseer of their treatment and welfare. Section 36 of the Act states that the custody officer shall be of at least the rank of sergeant, and must not be involved in the investigation of offences for which people in custody have been arrested. Sections 37 to 39 in Part IV set out the custody officers' main 'gatekeeping' and welfare duties in relation to arrested persons. In summary, these are:

- To determine whether there is sufficient evidence to charge the person with the offence for which s/he was arrested (if so, s/he must be charged; if not s/he must be released without delay);

- To decide whether there are 'reasonable grounds for believing that his detention without charge is necessary to secure or preserve evidence relating to an offence for which he is under arrest or to obtain such evidence by questioning him' (in which case, the custody officer may authorize detention for up to six hours);

- If authorizing detention, to make a written record, in the presence of the arrested person, of the grounds for the decision;

- If the arrested person is a juvenile, to identify a person responsible for the latter's welfare and to inform that person of the arrest and detention. Equally, if the custody officer suspects that the detainee may be 'mentally disordered or mentally handicapped', s/he must ensure the attendance at the police station, and the presence at interviews, of an 'appropriate adult' (see below);

- After a charge has been made, to decide whether there are 'reasonable grounds for believing' that it is necessary to keep the person in police detention until he or she appears in court (for the suspect's own protection, the protection of other people or property, or the prevention of interference with the process of justice; other acceptable reasons are doubts about a suspect's identity and a belief that s/

he will fail to appear in court). Again, the grounds for this decision should be recorded in writing in the presence of the charged person;

- A general duty to ensure that all persons in police detention are treated in accordance with the Act and the Codes of Practice, and that proper records are made of the times at which they are given food, transferred to investigating officers for interviewing, and so on.

The Codes of Practice on 'Detention, Treatment and Questioning' (Home Office 1985, 1991, 1995) spell out most of the above duties in more detail, and add specific rules and notes of guidance—stipulating, for example, that the custody officer must summon immediate medical assistance if a detained person appears to be ill or 'fails to respond normally to questions'. In addition, the custody officer is responsible for several of the actions which must be carried out under Part V of the Act, including searching arrested persons and recording a list of their possessions; informing a friend or relative of the suspect that s/he is in detention; and informing suspects of their right to legal advice (and arranging this where necessary).

It should be noted that custody officers' decisions on matters for which they are responsible cannot be arbitrarily overruled by an investigating officer, whatever the latter's rank. In cases where an investigator wishes to dispute a decision—for example, that there is sufficient evidence to charge without further questioning, or that there are insufficient grounds for detention—the matter must be resolved by referral to a superintendent or other senior officer in charge of the police station.

Limits on detention

As described above, the initial decision to detain an arrested person—for up to six hours—is made by the custody officer, who should be of the rank of sergeant, and who should have 'reasonable grounds for believing' that detention without charge is necessary to secure or preserve evidence or to obtain evidence through questioning. Sections 41 and 42 of PACE allow further detention after reviews of the case by more senior officers, but stipulate that nobody can be detained without charge for longer than twenty-four hours, unless they are being held in relation to a 'serious arrestable offence' (the definition of which will be discussed presently). Moreover, the absolute limit of police powers to detain is thirty-six hours (the last twelve hours of which have to be authorized at superintendent level—see below). Beyond this, a 'warrant of further detention' must be obtained from a magistrate, who can authorize up to sixty more hours, giving a maximum detention period of ninety-six hours in all but terrorist cases (the latter are covered under separate legislation, which allows detention without charge—again, authorized by a court—for up to seven days).

Suspects' rights to advice and communication

Sections 58 and 59 of PACE give to any detained person the right of access to legal advice. Moreover, unless the suspect wishes to pay for the services of a solicitor of his or her own choice, legal advice has to be provided under a rota system at the expense of the State. Detained persons are also given a right (section 56) to 'intimation'—in other words, to have someone known to them informed that they have been arrested, and told where they are being held. Suspects must be formally told that they have these rights, and sign a record that they have been so informed.

However, the police retain the right to delay both intimation and access to legal advice in cases where a serious arrestable offence is under investigation, and there are 'reasonable grounds for believing' that telling the named person of the arrest will lead to 'interference with or harm to evidence connected with a serious arrestable offence' or 'the alerting of other persons suspected of having committed such an offence but not yet arrested for it', or will 'hinder the recovery of any property obtained as a result of such an offence'. Such decisions have to be authorized by a senior officer (see next section).

Levels of authority

PACE introduced an elaborate system of authorization whereby, in broad terms, the greater the impact of a decision on a person's rights or liberty, the higher the rank of officer by whom it should be made. For example, as already stated, a sergeant can authorize an initial period of detention up to six hours. This can be extended by eighteen hours (i.e. to a total of twenty-four hours) on the authority of an inspector, who must review the case at the six-hour and fifteen-hour points. Any detention beyond twenty-four hours has to be authorized by a superintendent.

Other major intrusions on liberties, including the conduct of intimate searches (i.e. of bodily orifices), the taking of samples from the person's body, and delays in informing relatives of the arrest or in granting access to a lawyer, can likewise be authorized only by a superintendent or above. In each case, the senior officer must have 'reasonable grounds for believing' that this is necessary in order to achieve specific aims referred to in the Act (e.g. the safety of officers or the suspect, or the acquisition of evidence that will tend to prove or disprove the suspect's involvement in the offence).

Interviewing conditions and style

The Code of Practice (though not the Act itself) lays down a number of restrictions on the conditions and manner in which suspects can be questioned. The police have a general responsibility to provide interview rooms which are 'adequately heated, lit and ventilated'. All interviews must be recorded. Everyone present during an interview must be identified on tape. Suspects cannot be required to stand during the interview, and they must be given breaks for meals 'at recognized meal times' and short breaks for refreshments at intervals of approximately two hours. Moreover, in any period of twenty-four hours, they must be allowed a continuous period of at least eight hours for rest, free from questioning or travel. However, as with many other PACE rules, exceptions are allowed (see below).

The suspect is allowed the presence of a solicitor throughout the interview, provided that the latter does not 'obstruct' the interview (interviewers may remove a solicitor who persistently obstructs questioning).[4] Where both juvenile and

---

[4] The following are not, however, sufficient basis for removal of a legal adviser from the interview: advising the suspect not to answer particular questions; challenging improper questions; requesting a break to give the client further advice (Code C, 6D).

'mentally disordered' or 'mentally handicapped' suspects are concerned, an 'appropriate adult' must be present during any interview—although, as usual, this can be waived in 'exceptional circumstances' (Code 11.16). The appropriate adult is usually a parent, guardian, social worker, or trained volunteer; his or her role is principally to advise the detained person and to observe the interview to ensure that it is conducted fairly.

In relation to the process of questioning itself, neither PACE nor the Codes of Practice are very clear about what kinds of styles or 'tactics' are acceptable. Section 76 of PACE allows the courts to exclude evidence on the ground that it has been obtained by 'oppressive' questioning or that police actions have rendered a confession 'unreliable'. However, there is no clear definition of oppressive behaviour, nor any guidance to the police on what particular tactics may be used. Generally speaking, it has been left to the police to develop their own guidelines and training for interviewers. Further comment on this issue—which is central to concerns about false confessions—will be made below.

Record-keeping

Finally, two of the most important of all the changes introduced under PACE concerned record-keeping. The first was an obligation upon the custody officer to maintain a comprehensive 'custody record' on each detained person. This is a standard form on which should be recorded ('as soon as practicable') all significant aspects of his or her progress through the various stages of detention, each entry being signed, timed, and dated. The custody officer is responsible for the record's accuracy and completeness, as well as for ensuring that it accompanies the person if they are transferred to another police station (where it must be continued). Detained persons are also entitled to copies of their custody record after they have left police detention, if they make a formal request to that effect.

The Codes of Practice specify a large number of matters which must be recorded (for a full list, see Zander 1990: 388–415). These include:

- the grounds for detention;
- the suspect's signature that s/he has been informed of the rights to consult a solicitor, have someone informed of the arrest, and read the Codes of Practice (or a note by the custody officer that the suspect has refused to sign);
- any waiver by the suspect of his or her right to legal advice;
- details of any intimate search, the reasons for it, and its result;
- requests to inform a friend or relative of the arrest and actions taken in response;
- grounds for delaying intimation or access to legal advice;
- details of meals served to the suspect;
- details of any complaints by suspects about their treatment;
- details of any medical treatment;
- times at which suspects are handed over to, and back from, other officers for interview;

- grounds for any decision to start interviewing a suspect before a requested solicitor (or, in the case of a juvenile, an 'appropriate adult') has arrived;
- details of reviews of detention and the grounds for any delay to a review;
- the time at which a suspect is cautioned when charged, and details of any reply.

The second important change in the area of record-keeping was a new requirement on the police to make what is usually referred to as a 'contemporaneous' record of any interview with a suspect. In other words (although exceptions are allowed—see below), the record must be made *during the course of the interview*. Moreover, the initial Code of Practice emphasized the need for accuracy in such records, stating that they 'must constitute either a verbatim record of what has been said or, failing this, an account of the interview which accurately and adequately summarizes it' (Home Office 1985: para. 11.3). The main reason for this reform was widespread concern in the pre-PACE period about 'verballing'—the practice of police officers getting together after interviews in order to write up notes of what the suspect had said, in some cases embellishing his or her statements to sound as though clear admissions had been made.

When first introduced, these requirements had to be met mainly by police officers writing down in longhand what was said during interviews—a process which was widely found to be unwieldy, time-consuming, and disruptive to the 'natural flow' of interviews. However, within a few years—a process accelerated by the dissatisfaction with contemporaneous note-taking—all police stations designated for the detention and questioning of suspects[5] had been fitted with facilities for the tape-recording of interviews, and this quickly became standard practice.

DISCRETION, EXCEPTIONS, AND THE 'SPIRIT OF THE LAW'

As already noted, many of the PACE rules contain phrases which allow them to be circumvented—albeit in some cases only temporarily—if conformity would cause practical difficulties for the police. Several are also worded in such a way that the police are granted a considerable amount of discretion in defining the particular people or situations to which the rule applies.

Many exceptions to rules are allowed, under the banner of 'practicability', on the grounds of temporary unavailability of resources. For example, officers below the rank of a sergeant may perform the duties of custody officer 'if a custody sergeant is not available to perform them' (section 36) and reviews of detention may be postponed 'if at that time no review officer is available' (section 40). These kinds of exception are relatively unimportant, so long as the police do not exploit the flexibility of the rules on a frequent basis. However, in some cases the concept of 'practicability' has been extended to include situations in which the normal safeguards to suspects can be sidestepped in order to assist the investigators in much more significant ways.

---

[5] PACE stipulated that the detention and questioning of suspects should normally take place only in police stations officially 'designated' for this purpose, where minimum conditions for the welfare of suspects are met and custody officers are officially appointed.

For example, in the initial Code of Practice, it was stated that records of interviews had to be made during the course of the interviews 'unless in the investigating officer's view this would not be practicable or would interfere with the conduct of the interview' (paragraph 11.3). While this has been superseded by the advent of universal tape-recording, it clearly gave interviewers an opportunity to avoid recording parts of interviews which they might find it inconvenient to put in writing. Another example—still in force—is the power of the interviewing officer to delay breaks for meals or refreshments, or to delay or interrupt the stipulated eight-hour period for rest, if s/he has 'reasonable grounds for believing' that a break at that time would 'prejudice the outcome of the investigation'.

There is also a certain amount of discretion in the categorization of offences as 'serious' or not, which has consequences for the powers available to the police in particular cases. For example, if a person is deemed to have been detained on suspicion of having committed a 'serious arrestable' offence (as opposed to simply an 'arrestable' offence), he or she may be detained, on the authorization of a superintendent, for an extra twelve hours. However, the definition of such an offence includes any criminal offence that is considered by the police to have led, or to be likely to lead, to any of a list of serious consequences (for example, serious harm to public order, death or serious injury, or serious financial loss)—a formulation that allows the senior officer considerable scope for interpretation (Zander 1985: 152).

What these examples illustrate (and there are many more that could be cited) is that, although the Codes of Practice look rigorous at first reading, on closer inspection there are so many potential 'escape clauses' that the effectiveness of the PACE regulations in protecting suspects is dependent in large degree on the willingness of the police to obey the rules not just in 'letter' but in 'spirit'. In other words, it is vital to the well-being and fair treatment of suspects that all the key police officers involved— the custody sergeant, the interviewer, the more senior officers reviewing cases— approach cases with an acceptance of the basic philosophy behind PACE and a willingness in the final analysis to recognize that suspects' rights must be respected, even at the cost of 'losing' some cases in which they are sure that the detained person is guilty. Consequently, any overall assessment of PACE has to take account of the findings of empirical research examining actual practice in police stations. These are discussed in the next section.

PACE IN PRACTICE: EMPIRICAL RESEARCH FINDINGS

There have been several major empirical studies of the operation of PACE within police stations, although most of these were conducted in the first few years after its introduction and recent information is more scarce. Most of these studies have focused on the extent to which police officers have complied with particular requirements of the Codes of Practice, the extent to which suspects have exercised their right to legal advice, and any measurable outcomes in terms of numbers of arrests, lengths of detention, confessions, convictions, and so on. Some researchers have also interviewed police officers and suspects to obtain their views of the system. In interpreting the results, there have been some major disagreements between those who conclude that PACE has brought about some significant changes in the behaviour (and to some extent attitudes) of the police *vis-à-vis* detained persons, and those who argue that the police have merely 'adapted' their activities to the existence of PACE, complying with the rules at a superficial level, but circumventing them and exploiting them in subtle ways so that there has been little meaningful change in reality (see, for example, Dixon 1992, 1995; Morgan 1995; Sanders 1997).

The main findings will be presented under three headings: (a) numbers of arrests and lengths of detention; (b) level of independence of custody officers; and (c) interviewing practice.

Numbers of arrests and lengths of detention

Much of the early research on PACE paid particular attention to its impact on the overall level of pre-charge detention. This was important, as one of the main conclusions of the Royal Commission on Criminal Procedure (1981) had been that that there was too much use of police detention for the purpose of questioning: it had become too common for police officers simply to 'round up the usual suspects' and, under the fiction of 'voluntary' attendance at police stations, to conduct what often amounted to 'fishing expeditions' through unregulated interrogation. For this reason, PACE strongly encouraged the replacement of 'voluntary' attendance with a system whereby people would be arrested and detained only if there were concrete reasons for suspecting them of a particular offence and the detention was necessary to the quest for further evidence. Moreover, in less serious cases, it encouraged greater use of summons rather than arrest.

The broad consensus from research in the 1980s was that, overall, PACE did not bring about a great deal of change in either the numbers of arrests made, or the lengths of time for which suspects were held. Maguire (1988) noted a significant dip in arrests in the forces he studied during the first few months of implementation, probably due to caution on the part of officers unfamiliar with the new rules, but within a short time the figures appeared to be returning to previous levels. Irving and McKenzie (1989), Bottomley *et al.* (1991), and Brown (1991) all expressed caution about the interpretation of arrest figures, which are lacking in detail, but none noted any clear evidence of changes in the use of arrest. The only researchers to do so were McConville *et al.* (1991), who concluded that, based on a sample of 1,000 arrests and summonses in three forces, far from reducing the use of arrest, PACE had led to major *increases* in its use: police officers, they argued, took the option of an arrest at almost every opportunity, primarily because it offered them the chance of questioning suspects. The evidential basis for this conclusion has been questioned (Brown 1997), but it certainly remains a possibility. Be that as it may, it seems fair at least to conclude that PACE has not achieved the original goal of significantly reducing the overall use of arrest and detention.

This does not necessarily mean that it has not led to any improved practice in the area of decisions to arrest. In fact, there is some evidence to suggest that officers may be *delaying* arrests more often than in the past, in order to ensure they have a sufficient amount of evidence to justify questioning. For example, Irving and McKenzie (1989) concluded that the strength of initial evidence was 'good' in around half of all arrests in their sample in 1986–7, compared with under one-third of arrests in a pre-PACE sample (see also Bottomley *et al.* 1991; Brown 1991, 1997). In other words, there may not be fewer arrests, but there may be fewer unjustified arrests.

Finally, PACE does not appear to have had a major impact on the lengths of time for which suspects are held. The majority of studies conclude that the average length of detention has either remained virtually unchanged or has fallen slightly. Some researchers have noted a tendency for detention lengths to increase at the 'lower end'—i.e. in straightforward cases involving minor offences—owing to a rise in the proportion of cases in which solicitors attend (necessitating waiting time) and to a tendency for the police sometimes to hold people until the six-hour review point is approaching. However, increases in detention in these kinds of cases appear to have been offset or outweighed by earlier releases or charges in other kinds of cases (see, for example, Maguire 1988; Irving and McKenzie 1991; Morgan *et al.* 1991; Bottomley *et al.* 1991; Brown 1991, 1997).

Level of independence of custody officers

The main issue addressed in research on custody officers has been the extent to which they display independence in their work. One of the areas in which their independence has been most strongly questioned is that of the 'gatekeeper' role they are supposed to perform when arrested people are brought to the police station. It has been found consistently that custody officers very rarely refuse to authorize detention in this situation. For example, Morgan *et al.* (1991) found only one case of refusal among a large sample of arrests, concluding that the authorization procedure was a 'presentational fig-leaf'. Bottomley *et al.* (1991) and McConville *et al.* (1991) came up with similar findings and conclusions, while Irving and McKenzie (1989) found that custody officers often failed to ask for any details of the evidence on which the decision to arrest had been based.

The inference generally drawn from these findings—even by writers such as Brown (1997) who conclude that PACE has been for the most part effective—is that this is an important area in which neither the letter nor the spirit of the Act has been followed by the police. Major critics of the legislation, such as McConville *et al.* (1991) and Sanders and Young (1995), see this as a prime example of the failure of PACE to change police practice: in essence, they argue, police officers remain free to arrest people for questioning on flimsy grounds without any serious concern that the custody officer might not endorse their decision. The possibility remains, of course, that the low 'refusal rate' for detention is a result of a major change in the practice of operational officers, whereby they are now less likely to arrest people without some evidence and hence there are relatively few cases which custody officers *should* refuse. Certainly, the delaying of arrest until more solid evidence has been gathered is a recommended feature of 'intelligence-led' policing, which is currently practised in many forces (Maguire and John 1995). However, many arrests—particularly for the less serious offences—are still unplanned, immediate responses to events 'on the street', and it is improbable that virtually all of these are justified under the PACE guidelines. Overall, it has to be concluded that custody officers do not display much independence from the wishes or demands of operational police officers in this 'gate-keeping' aspect of their role.

A second area of concern regarding the independence of custody officers has surrounded their duty to inform suspects of their rights to legal advice. Several of the major PACE research studies found that, although custody officers are obliged to inform suspects of the possibility of receiving free legal advice (and must obtain their signature that they have been so informed), in reality this task was often performed in such a way that it appeared to the suspect as an unattractive option. McConville *et al.* (1991)—whose basic argument was that most custody officers display little independence from the police 'culture', continuing to think and act as police officers and giving greater priority to 'crime control' than to 'due process'—identified a number of 'ploys' that were used to dissuade detainees from taking up the offer of legal advice, including reading them their rights in a perfunctory or inaudible manner and telling them that waiting for a solicitor was likely to delay their release for several hours. Other researchers, while not always imputing base motives to custody officers, also found many cases of poor communication of rights to suspects (see, for example, Morgan *et al.* 1991).

The lack of clear information and the negative tone in which it tended to be delivered were thought by many observers to be partly responsible for what remained a surprisingly low take-up rate for a free service: although many more people were requesting legal advice after PACE than before it, the proportion doing so was still only about one in four in the late 1980s. It was as a result of such concerns that revisions were made to the Code of Practice, whereby it is now explicitly forbidden for a custody officer to attempt to dissuade a suspect from requesting advice, and suspects must be clearly informed that the provision of legal advice is without cost and that the adviser is independent of the police. In a 'before and after' study of the impact of these revisions, Brown (1992) found that the majority of custody officers were giving fuller information to suspects, and that there was an increase in the proportion of suspects requesting legal advice (from 24 per cent to 32 per cent). Even so, he found that a significant minority of custody officers were not following the new guidelines.

Other evidence of a lack of independence in the attitude or behaviour of custody officers includes Bottomley *et al.*'s (1991) observation of access being given to investigating officers to talk to prisoners informally in their cells—euphemistically recorded in custody records as 'welfare visits', but sometimes in reality for 'off the record' bargaining. It is not known how widespread such practices are, but they are clearly against the intentions of PACE that all interviews should be recorded.

On the other hand, the evidence regarding the performance of custody officers in ensuring the physical and mental welfare of suspects is generally more positive. For example, they have been found to call doctors to suspects who are ill or intoxicated much more readily than in the past (Brown 1989), and to be stricter in ensuring that mentally handicapped people are not interviewed without an appropriate adult present (Irving and McKenzie 1989)—although there remain concerns in the latter area due to doubts about their ability to recognize mental problems. These improvements may be due more to fear of disciplinary consequences than to concern about the welfare of suspects (Dixon 1992), but they do provide evidence of some beneficial changes in police practice 'on the ground' as a result of the establishment of the role of custody officer.

Interviewing practice

Potentially the most important outcome of the regulations established under PACE is the prevention of unfair or oppressive interviewing—which, in turn, may help to reduce the number of miscarriages of justice due to 'false confessions' or other unreliable interview evidence. It is clear from a number of well publicized post-PACE cases that it is still possible for people to be convicted on the basis of clearly oppressive interviews which the system has failed to control and which have not been effectively challenged either in the police station or in court (Rozenberg 1992). One of the most notorious is the case of the 'Cardiff Three', in which three defendants were convicted of murder mainly on the strength of a series of lengthy and oppressive interviews with a mentally impaired suspect, at which a solicitor was present but failed to intervene. Empirical research has also revealed the continuing use of improper tactics in a significant proportion of cases. For example, Moston *et al.* (1990), Baldwin (1992), and McConville and Hodgson (1993), all of whom analysed samples of taped or videoed interviews, found between them numerous examples of coercive, repetitive, or unfair questioning, as well as a number of inducements to confess. Nevertheless, there is evidence that the extent of such practices has decreased markedly as a result of the tape-recording of interviews. In particular, Irving and McKenzie (1989) reported from a replication of an earlier study that the use of 'tactics' in interviews had roughly halved between 1979 and 1987.

It may be asked why such tactics persist at all in a situation where interviews are taped. One reason seems to be that although the tapes are available, they are rarely played in court. Instead, police officers make transcripts in which they summarize much of the material, recording verbatim only those parts of the interview which they consider directly relevant as evidence (Baldwin and Bedward 1991). Consequently, if the defence lawyer is not vigilant or strongly committed to the case, it can easily fail to emerge that a confession was obtained by improper tactics. Importantly, too, although PACE proscribes the use of 'oppressive' tactics and the offering of 'inducements', and allows the courts to exclude evidence that would have an adverse effect on the fairness of proceedings (section 78), there are no clear definitions of any of these terms. Generally speaking, their interpretation has been left, on the one hand, to police trainers and, on the other, to judges and magistrates. The courts have excluded interview evidence only on rare occasions and have provided little clear guidance to interviewers on what is permissible, and the running has been made mainly by the police themselves. In particular, efforts have been made to develop training in 'investigative' or 'ethical' interviewing styles, in which two of the main messages are that the aim of the interview should be to 'search for the truth' rather than 'extract a confession', and that questioning should be open-ended and non-aggressive (see, for example, McGurk *et al.* 1993; Stockdale 1993; Williamson 1996). However, changing what is still a strongly ingrained element of police culture—the view that the overriding aim of an interview is to obtain a confession—is an ambitious task, and there is little doubt that poor interviewing practices still persist to a considerable extent.

Finally, it is interesting to note that, despite the PACE rules on oppressive questioning on the one hand, and the removal of the unconditional 'right to silence' on the other (see note 3, above), there appears to have been little change over the last twenty years in the proportions of interviews which result in a 'confession'. Measurement in this area is difficult, but it is generally agreed from research that the figure has remained around 60 per cent over many years. This suggests that, at ground level, both police practice and the behaviour of suspects may have been affected less by the changes in formal rules than the designers of such rules expected.

CONCLUSIONS

The implementation of those sections of PACE (and its associated Codes of Practice) which govern the detention and questioning of suspects in police stations, provides an unusual and instructive national case study of a carefully designed, comprehensive, and well-resourced attempt to regulate this complex and relatively hidden area of police activity, which is of such huge importance for the integrity of criminal process. The particular means chosen to achieve this in England and Wales is essentially one of self-regulation by the police, guided by a complex set of guidelines and open to a degree of external scrutiny after the event. The *post hoc* scrutiny is made possible by the obligation on the police to create detailed records of everything significant that occurs while the suspect is in custody, as well as to record reasons for key decisions such as those to authorize or continue detention, or to charge, bail, or release. There are also potential sanctions for breaches of the regulations, including disciplinary actions against individual police officers, as well as the possible exclusion by judges of evidence which is found to have been obtained by unfair means.

Academics have been seriously divided over the impact of the legislation. What is agreed, however, is that it brought much-needed clarity to an area in which there had previously been no clear rules. Prior to 1984, there had been no formal regulation of detention and questioning in England and Wales: many people were held in police stations on flimsy grounds, ostensibly agreeing 'voluntarily' to be questioned, but in practice not free to leave; even after arrest, there were no official time limits on detention, and no rights to obtain legal advice or to contact relatives; and there were no formal controls over the length or style of questioning. The only protection against abuses of police powers lay in the so-called 'Judges' Rules', a set of somewhat vague precepts developed by the courts over the years to define the limits of fairness in the production of evidence. However, as it was very difficult for a defendant to prove that these limits had been overstepped, the fairness of the system relied almost entirely on the integrity of the police in following the spirit of these 'rules'.

By establishing a clear statutory framework for detention and questioning, with defined time limits, rights to advice, duties of care, individual police accountability for decisions, and strict record-keeping requirements, PACE has undoubtedly brought about a huge improvement in structural terms. In theory, both police officers and suspects now 'know exactly where they stand' once a person has been arrested. What is at question, however, is the extent to which the theory is translated into practice, and how far it remains possible for the police—either 'routinely' or by deliberate deviance in individual cases—to circumvent the rules and frustrate the aims of the Act, hence increasing the risk of miscarriages of justice.

The main critics of the Act have argued that, in reality, many aspects of the legislation have made little or no difference to police behaviour: rather, the police have become adept at satisfying the letter (but not the spirit) of the law through the payment of lip service to the rules and the skilful manipulation of written records—sometimes referred to ironically as 'account-ability'. One of the main focuses of attention has been upon the work of custody officers, who, it is pointed out, often alternate their performance of this role with that of an operational police officer. Many, it is claimed, fail to 'internalize' the philosophy behind the PACE regulations: in other words, they are unable to detach themselves from the prevailing 'crime-control' thinking of the police and to see the world, if only temporarily, from an independent, 'due-process' perspective. Thus, for example, it has been shown that custody officers almost never refuse to authorize the detention of people brought to the police station—indeed, they often do not ask any questions about the evidence on which an arrest has been made. Instead, they learn a number of standard phrases with which to fill in the appropriate part of the custody record, which can cover almost any situation and which are difficult to challenge later. Equally, they learn ways of informing suspects of their right to legal advice which meet the requirements of the Act, but are understood by many suspects to mean that it will not be in their interests to request the presence of a lawyer (concern on this matter led to revisions to the Code of Practice in order to prevent such 'ploys', but even this met with limited success—Brown 1992, 1997). While by no means every custody officer behaves in these ways on a regular basis, it is clear from research that a significant number do, that it is easy to do so, and that there is little risk of sanctions for doing so. Consequently, it has been argued, the system will never be fully effective unless the custody officer role is performed by independent civilians rather than serving police officers.

At a more general level, it has to be asked whether PACE has solved the central problem that led to the Royal Commission which preceded the Act: how to prevent the use of unfair and oppressive techniques of questioning, including threats or improper inducements designed to obtain 'confessions'. Undoubtedly, the Act has brought about some progress in these respects, especially in relation to categories of people thought to be particularly vulnerable to making 'false confessions'. The protection of juvenile suspects—one of the key issues in the Confait case, which was crucial in bringing the whole subject to public attention—has been significantly increased by the requirement to have an 'appropriate adult' present at their interviews. Mentally handicapped suspects, too, are now better protected by similar rules, although there are still serious doubts about the ability of custody officers to recognize cases in which they should be applied. More generally, however, there remain some major obstacles to a truly effective set of safeguards against unfair or oppressive interviewing across the whole range of suspects.

First of all, as discussed in the previous section, there are no clear definitions of these terms in either the Act or the Codes of Practice. The identification of abuses of the interrogation process is left to police supervisors, to lawyers attending interviews, or to the courts. As all interviews now have to be tape-recorded—potentially the most significant development arising from PACE—and all the above parties have access to the tapes, one might think that this is a sufficiently robust system to prevent any serious abuses by interviewers. However, it is clear from research that police supervisors rarely monitor interviewers on a systematic basis (Maguire and Norris 1992). It is also clear that many lawyers attending interviews (and it must be remembered that lawyers are still present in only a minority of all interviews) are not effective in recognizing and preventing unfair or oppressive questioning (Baldwin 1992, 1992a; Hodgson 1994). Furthermore, courts rarely hear the full transcript of interviews, large parts of which are simply summarized by the interviewer: this makes it difficult for them to identify abuses of the process. Perhaps the most dramatic example of how the system can fail, even when all the correct procedures appear to have been followed, is the 'Cardiff Three' case, mentioned above—a murder case in which the lengthy and shockingly oppressive questioning of a mentally impaired suspect was supervised by senior officers, observed throughout by a lawyer, and remained unquestioned in court, being identified only in the appeal court at a later date when the conviction was quashed as unsafe and unsatisfactory. It is quite likely that major miscarriages of justice of this kind are considerably less frequent post-PACE than pre-PACE, but the Cardiff Three events give a strong warning that, in the absence of constant vigilance, an apparently sound system of safeguards can still fail disastrously with major consequences for a suspect's life.

Finally, it is important to note that the system of regulation we have been discussing covers only those events which occur inside police stations, but that these events can be closely linked to, and affected by, events *outside* police stations. In particular, the elaborate arrangements to ensure that all interviews in custody following a person's arrest are recorded and properly regulated can be rendered less effective by 'informal' interviews which take place before s/he arrives at the police station. In theory, police officers should take an arrested person directly to a designated police station for formal interview after arrest, and not discuss the circumstances of the offence until that point. However, there is some evidence that unrecorded conversations sometimes take place in police cars (which may take the 'scenic route' to the station), in which negotiations take place and 'deals' are made, whereby the suspect agrees to make certain admissions on tape in response to (perhaps improper) inducements (see, for example, Moston and Stephenson 1993; Maguire and Norris 1992). The lesson of this phenomenon may be that it is impossible to regulate formally every aspect of the complex process of interaction between suspects and the police, and that stricter regulation of one part of it (here, events within the police station) may simply 'displace' certain types of activity to another part (here, the police car). As this, as well as many of the other research findings on PACE discussed above, illustrates, police officers (whose work in almost every arena inevitably allows them a great deal of discretion) belong to a highly adaptable culture, and if they feel that new regulations unreasonably inhibit their 'crime-control' activity, they are likely to find ways around them. Successful regulation, therefore, requires not only the specification of rules, but an understanding of the views, attitudes, and practices of ordinary officers. Ultimately, it is only through changes in these basic views—which may take many years to take hold—that significant and lasting change in practice on the ground, as opposed to simply on paper, can be achieved.

Bibliography and Further Reading

BALDWIN, J. (1992), *Video Taping Police Interviews with Suspects: A National Evaluation*, Police Research Series, Paper 1 (London: Home Office).

—— (1992a), *The Role of Legal Representatives at the Police Station*, Research Study No. 3 (London: Royal Commission on Criminal Justice).

—— and BEDWARD, J. (1991), 'Summarizing Tape Recordings of Police Interviewing' [1991] *Criminal Law Review* 671–9.

BOTTOMLEY, A. K., COLEMAN, C., DIXON, D., GILL, M., and WALL, D. (1991), *The Impact of PACE: Policing in a Northern Force* (Hull: Centre for Criminology and Criminal Justice).

BROWN, D. (1989), *Detention at the Police Station under the Police and Criminal Evidence Act 1984*, Home Office Research Study No. 104 (London: HMSO).

—— (1991), *Investigating Burglary: The Effects of PACE*, Home Office Research Study No. 123 (London: HMSO).

—— (1992), *Changing the Code: Police Detention under the Revised PACE Codes of Practice*, Home Office Research Study No. 129 (London: HMSO).

—— (1997), *PACE Ten Years On: A Review of the Research*, Home Office Research Study No. 155 (London: Home Office).

DIXON, D. (1992), 'Legal Regulation and Policing Practice' (1992) 1 *Social and Legal Studies* 515–41.

—— (1995), 'New Left Pessimism' in L. Noaks, M. Levi, and M. Maguire (eds.), *Contemporary Issues in Criminology* (Cardiff: University of Wales Press).

ERICSON, R. (1981), *Making Crime: A Study of Detective Work* (Toronto: Butterworth).

EVANS, D., and MORGAN, R. (1999), *Preventing Torture: A Study of the European Convention for the Prevention of Torture and Inhuman or Degrading Treatment or Punishment* (Oxford: Clarendon Press).

FISHER, SIR H. (1977), *The Confait Case: Report* (London: HMSO).

GUDJONSSON, G., CLARE, I., RUTTER, S., and PEARSE, J. (1992), *Persons at Risk During Interviews in Police Custody: The Identification of Vulnerabilities*, Research Study No. 12. (London: Royal Commission on Criminal Justice).

HARDING, R. (1995), *Aboriginal Contact with the Criminal Justice System and the Impact of the Royal Commission into Aboriginal Deaths in Custody* (Sydney: Hawkins Press).

HODGSON, J. (1994), 'Adding Injury to Injustice: The Suspect at the Police Station' in S. Field and P. Thomas (eds.), *Justice and Efficiency? The Royal Commission on Criminal Justice* (Oxford: Blackwell).

Home Office (1985), *Code of Practice for the Detention, Treatment and Questioning of Persons by Police Officers* (London: Home Office).

—— (1991), *Revised Code of Practice for the Detention, Treatment and Questioning of Persons by Police Officers* (London: Home Office).

—— (1995), *Revised Code of Practice for the Detention, Treatment and Questioning of Persons by Police Officers* (London: Home Office).

IRVING, B., and HILGENDORF, L. (1980), *Police Interrogation: A Case Study of Current Practice* Royal Commission on Criminal Procedure, Research Study No. 2 (London: HMSO).

—— and McKENZIE, I. (1989), *Police Interrogation* (London: Police Foundation).

McBARNET, D. (1981), *Conviction* (London: Macmillan).

McCONVILLE, M. (1993), *Corroboration and Confessions: The Impact of a Rule Requiring that no Conviction can be Sustained on the Basis of Confession Evidence Alone*, Research Study No. 13, Royal Commission on Criminal Justice (London: HMSO).

—— and HODGSON, J. (1993), *Custodial Legal Advice and the Right to Silence*, Research Study No. 16 (London: Royal Commission on Criminal Justice).

—— SANDERS, A., and LENG, R. (1991), *The Case for the Prosecution: Police Suspects and the Construction of Criminality* (London: Routledge).

McGURK, B., CARR, M., and McGURK, D. (1993), *Investigative Interviewing Courses for Police Officers: An Evaluation*, Police Research Series Paper 4 (London: Home Office).

MAGUIRE, M. (1988) 'Effects of the "P.A.C.E." Provisions on Detention and Questioning: Some Preliminary Findings' (1988) 28 *British Journal of Criminology* 19–43.

—— (1994), 'The Wrong Message at the Wrong Time? The Present State of Investigative Practice' in D. Morgan and G. Stephenson (eds.), *Suspicion and Silence: The Right to Silence in Criminal Investigations* (Oxford: Blackstone).

—— and NORRIS, C. (1992), *The Conduct and Supervision of Criminal Investigations*, Research Study No. 5 (London: Royal Commission on Criminal Justice).

—— and—— (1994), 'Police Investigations: Practice and Malpractice' in S. Field and P. Thomas (eds.), *Justice and Efficiency? The Royal Commission on Criminal Justice* (Oxford: Blackwell).

MORGAN, D., and STEPHENSON, G. (eds.) (1994), *Suspicion and Silence: The Right to Silence in Criminal Investigations* (Oxford: Blackstone).

MORGAN, R. (1995), 'Authors Meet Critics: The Case for the Prosecution' in L. Noaks, M. Levi, and M. Maguire (eds.), *Contemporary Issues in Criminology* (Cardiff: University of Wales Press).

—— REINER, R., and McKENZIE, I. (1991), *Police Powers and Police: A Study of the Work of Custody Officers*, Report to Economic and Social Research Council (Swindon: ESRC).

—— and EVANS, D. (eds.) (1999), *Protecting Prisoners: The Standards of the European Committee for the Prevention of Torture in Context* (Oxford: Oxford University Press).

MOSTON, S., and STEPHENSON, G. (1993), *The Questioning and Interviewing of Suspects Outside the Police Station*, Research Study No. 22 (London: Royal Commission on Criminal Justice).

——, —— and WILLIAMSON, T. (1990), *Police Interrogation Styles and Suspect Behaviour*, Final Report to Home Office Police Requirements Support Unit (Canterbury: UK Institute of Social and Applied Psychology).

PACKER, H. (1969), *The Limits of the Criminal Sanction* (Stanford, Cal.: Stanford University Press).

Royal Commission on Criminal Justice (1993), *Report*, Cmnd 2263 (London: HMSO).

Royal Commission on Criminal Procedure (1981), *The Investigation and Prosecution of Criminal Offences in England and Wales: The Law and Procedure*, Cmnd 8092–1 (London: HMSO).

ROZENBERG, J. (1992), 'Miscarriages of Justice' in E. Stockdale and S. Casale (eds.), *Criminal Justice Under Stress* (London: Blackstone Press).

SANDERS, A. (2002), 'From Suspect to Trial' in M. Maguire, R. Morgan, and R. Reiner (eds.), *The Oxford Handbook of Criminology* (3rd edn., Oxford: Oxford University Press).

—— and YOUNG, R. (1994), *Criminal Justice* (London: Butterworth).

SKOLNICK, J. (1966), *Justice Without Trial* (New York: Wiley).

STOCKDALE, J. (1993), *Management and Supervision of Police Interviews*, Police Research Series Paper 5 (London: Home Office).

WILLIAMSON, T. (1996), 'Police Investigation: The Changing Criminal Justice Context' in F. Leishman, B. Loveday, and S. Savage (eds.), *Core Issues in Policing* (London: Longman).

ZANDER, M. (1990), *The Police and Criminal Evidence Act 1984* (2nd edn., London: Sweet & Maxwell).

—— and HENDERSON, P. (1993), *Crown Court Study*, Research Study No. 19, Royal Commission on Criminal Justice (London: HMSO).

6

ASSISTING AND ADVISING DEFENDANTS BEFORE TRIAL

Ed Cape

The right to a fair trial is enshrined in the Universal Declaration of Human Rights and in those human rights instruments that are modelled on it.[1] Most of those instruments explicitly recognize that the principle of equality of arms, which is a prerequisite of fair trial, requires States to permit persons accused of crime to defend themselves through the assistance of a lawyer of their own choosing. Furthermore, they provide that accused persons must have adequate time and facilities to prepare their defence. What is not explicit in most human rights instruments, including the European Convention on Human Rights (ECHR), is the stage at which the right to legal assistance crystallizes. The declaration of the *Basic Principles on the Role of Lawyers* does require States to 'ensure that all persons are immediately informed by the competent authority of their right to be assisted by a lawyer of their own choice upon arrest or detention or when charged with a criminal offence'.[2] It is arguable, therefore, that international standards require States to permit persons arrested and detained on suspicion of having committed a crime to consult a lawyer at that stage even though formal criminal proceedings have not commenced.

In England and Wales, the Police and Criminal Evidence Act 1984 (PACE) granted to suspects, for the first time, an unambiguous statutory right to legal advice at the investigative stage of criminal proceedings. This right may be exercised by anyone who is arrested on suspicion of committing a criminal offence and who is then held in custody at a police station. The right also extends to a person who voluntarily assists the police in the investigation of a crime without being arrested. As will be seen, PACE entitles suspects not only to consult a lawyer, but also to have the lawyer present with them when they are interviewed by the police. In this respect, PACE goes further than Article 6 of the ECHR (the right to fair trial) which, *inter alia*, provides that a person charged with a criminal offence is entitled to legal assistance. The European Court of Human Rights (ECtHR) held in *Murray* v. *United Kingdom* (1996) 22 EHRR 29 that

---

[1] In particular, the International Covenant on Civil and Political Rights and the European Convention on Human Rights.

[2] See Principle 5. The declaration was adopted by the Eighth UN Congress on the Prevention of Crime and the Treatment of Offenders in Havana, Cuba, on 7 Sept. 1990 and welcomed by the UN General Assembly in Resolution 45/121 on 14 Dec. 1990.

the right of access to a lawyer granted by Article 6 applies even before a person has been formally charged with a criminal offence if consequences for trial might flow from the attitude of the suspect during police questioning. However, the Court has not gone so far as to hold that Article 6 requires a suspect to be permitted the assistance of a lawyer during such questioning.

This chapter briefly explains the position prior to PACE, and the rationale for the introduction of a statutory right to legal advice at the investigative stage, before proceeding to examine that right. It then explains and analyses the response to what amounted to a fundamental change in criminal procedure by the police, defence lawyers, and the courts and, in so doing, demonstrates the critical value of research in assessing the efficacy of legislative change.

THE CHANGING PURPOSE OF ARREST AND DETENTION

Historically, the police power of arrest was primarily a mechanism for securing a person's appearance before a court. It was the role of magistrates (a judicial office), rather than the police, to decide whether someone should be prosecuted and, although the police did have limited summary arrest powers, arrests were normally made on the authority of a warrant issued by a magistrate. In theory at least, an arrest warrant would be issued only after an investigation had been conducted and a judicial decision to prosecute had been made. Under this approach a person, once arrested, would be detained by the police only for so long as was necessary to enable them to be brought before a court. It was not anticipated that the police would conduct an investigation, at least by interviewing the arrested person, between the time of the arrest and production before the court.

However, over the latter part of the nineteenth century and much of the twentieth century, as the police became increasingly professionalized and the investigative powers of magistrates diminished, the police came to use the period of detention between arrest and production in court as an opportunity to interview suspects and to carry out other inquiries. In effect, the purpose of arrest changed from a procedural mechanism for initiating court process to an investigative mechanism used by the police to create and strengthen the prosecution case. The law and the courts were slow to recognize this change and its implications. Prior to PACE the police in England and Wales had no explicit legal authority to detain arrested suspects for questioning and investigation. Although it became normal practice for the police to interrogate suspects between their arrest and their production in court, it was considered that there was no need to give suspects a right to legal advice since, in theory, any period in police detention was merely the consequence of the practical impossibility of producing the suspect in court immediately. During the twentieth century a body of judicial rules was developed governing the police treatment of suspects, including a qualified right of suspects to legal advice, but these rules did not have direct legal force and research demonstrated that few suspects requested legal advice (partly because many suspects could not afford it), and even fewer were permitted by the police to consult a lawyer. Thus prior to PACE, custodial legal advice was rare, even in serious cases such as murder.

THE STATUTORY RIGHT TO LEGAL ADVICE

The change in the purpose of arrest represented a constitutional shift in the relationship between citizens and the State. Rather than delaying arrest until a *prima facie* case had been established against the suspect, the police came to use arrest, and thus deny liberty, as a coercive mechanism for creating evidence sufficient to justify prosecution. However, this was not adequately recognized until the Royal Commission on Criminal Procedure (the Philips Commission), which was set up following the wrongful conviction for murder of three young people, reported in 1981.[3] The Philips Commission recommended that in order for there to be a 'fair, open, workable and efficient' criminal justice system a 'fundamental balance' was necessary between the rights of suspects and the powers of the police. It proposed that the police should have the statutory power to detain arrested suspects in order to gather evidence and to question them, but that this should be balanced by granting suspects protective rights, including the right to legal advice, during the period of police detention prior to charge. Recognizing that a statutory right to legal advice would be of little value to the majority of suspects who would not be able to afford a lawyer, the Philips Commission recommended that the State should provide funds to pay lawyers for giving such advice.

These recommendations were subsequently implemented by PACE, the relevant parts of which came into force in January 1986. Section 58 of PACE provides that a 'person arrested and held in custody in a police station or other premises shall be entitled, if he so requests, to consult a solicitor privately at any time'. Where a person has been arrested for a serious offence, section 58 does not confer an absolute right since a senior police officer may authorize delay in access to a lawyer if he or she is satisfied that exercising the right will lead to interference with the investigation. However, an early Court of Appeal decision made it clear that delaying access to a lawyer under this provision should rarely occur and, although research has established that the police do use informal 'ploys' to discourage suspects from seeking legal advice, in practice formal delay under section 58 is hardly ever authorized. The right under section 58 is primarily directed to persons arrested on suspicion of committing an offence, but it also extends to those arrested for other reasons, such as under mental health legislation where a person is temporarily held at a police station as a 'place of safety'. Although PACE refers to 'a solicitor', PACE Code of Practice C extends the meaning of 'solicitor' to include others who are not qualified as solicitors,

---

[3] Royal Commission on Criminal Procedure, *Report*, Cmnd 8092 (1981).

and in practice the use of non-solicitors to provide police station advice has been a significant issue (see further below).[4] The right to consult a solicitor 'privately' is absolute. The provision that suspects can consult with their lawyers 'at any time' is important because it permits suspects to seek legal advice during the course of a police interview, if necessary, by interrupting it. It is strengthened by Code of Practice C paragraph 6.8 which expressly provides that the solicitor must be allowed to be present in police interviews, a right that goes further than in most other jurisdictions.

In order to ensure that suspects are aware of their right to legal advice, Code of Practice C requires the police to inform them of their right when they first arrive at the police station and again at the beginning of each interview. Early research evidence suggested that, despite this requirement, many suspects remained unaware of the right to advice, and subsequent revisions of Code C have strengthened the requirement in a number of ways. This probably provides a partial explanation for the fact that the proportion of suspects requesting legal advice has risen significantly, from about 25 per cent shortly after the introduction of PACE, to about 40 per cent more recently. Nevertheless, a majority of suspects still refuse legal advice, and explanations for this include the use by police of 'ploys' that discourage suspects from exercising their rights, fear of delay, fatalism (and, conversely, confidence that suspects can deal with the situation on their own), and the negative attitude of some suspects to lawyers.

The cost of legal advice should not be a deterrent to the exercise of the right to advice since PACE introduced a free legal aid scheme that is neither means-tested nor merits-tested. The Philips Commission was concerned that there should be mechanisms to ensure that solicitors are available to provide legal advice, especially to suspects who have had no previous dealings with a lawyer. Thus whilst suspects may consult their 'own' lawyer if they have one (and if the lawyer is willing to be called out to the police station), a duty solicitor scheme was established to ensure that a solicitor is always available to provide legal advice, and both 'own' solicitors and duty solicitors are paid for under the legal aid scheme. The duty solicitor scheme, originally run by the Law Society but now administered by the Legal Services Commission (the government body responsible for administering the legal aid scheme), organizes defence lawyers in private practice in order to provide a twenty-four-hour service, and requires members of the scheme to undertake to provide advice, if necessary, outside normal office hours. In fact most law firms that provide a criminal defence service now employ at least one duty solicitor and are encouraged to do so by the structure of the contract with the Legal Services Commission under which they now operate.

In order to facilitate the provision of legal advice, PACE and Codes of Practice C and D give solicitors a limited number of rights, including the right to inspect the custody record (the written record that the police are required to compile, setting out all significant events concerning a suspect's detention) and certain rights in relation to

---

[4] See Code of Practice C, para. 6.12. This and other codes are issued by the Secretary of State under the authority of s. 66 of PACE, and although the Codes do not have direct legal force, police officers are required to comply with them, and by s. 67 they are admissible in evidence in civil and criminal proceedings to the extent that they are relevant.

identification procedures. They also impose an obligation on the police to seek the views of the lawyer when conducting a review of a suspect's detention. However, such rights are limited and the lawyer has no formal right to make representations about the need for detention of the suspect, nor regarding the charge or bail decisions, and there is no legal obligation on the police to take into account any representations made. Furthermore, it has been clearly established in a number of cases that the right to legal advice is the right of the suspect, and does not bestow any rights on the lawyer. The police may, therefore, exclude particular solicitors in certain circumstances, and, although in practice lawyers are rarely excluded, the threat of exclusion can be used by the police to encourage compliance.

Finally in this description of the right to legal advice, it should be noted that the mechanisms for enforcing the right to legal advice are very weak. A suspect who is improperly persuaded not to seek legal advice or who is denied access to a lawyer may make a formal complaint against the police under the Police Act 1996, but complaints against the police are currently investigated by the police, and only a tiny minority of complaints are upheld. The only other significant 'enforcement' mechanism is the exclusion of evidence obtained following the wrongful denial of a solicitor.[5] However, evidential mechanisms are directly applicable only where a suspect is prosecuted and pleads not guilty and, as is discussed further below, the approach of the courts to exclusion of evidence in such circumstances has not been consistent, and is generally concerned with substantive rather than procedural fairness.

THE POLICE RESPONSE TO PACE

The question whether PACE changed police behaviour in their treatment of suspects has been the subject of considerable debate, reflecting a wider debate about the potential of legal regulation to affect and control police conduct. Whilst most would reject the notion, put forward by some police commentators, that PACE led to a 'sea change' in police conduct, disagreement has centred on whether PACE did result in significant changes to police behaviour or whether, on the other hand, whilst changing certain procedures, it had little or no impact on the substance of police conduct.[6] The available evidence suggests that the police have largely complied with certain PACE requirements, such as the obligation to open a custody record in respect of each suspect and the requirement to tape-record most police interviews. Further, after some initial reluctance, it seems that suspects are now normally informed of their right to legal advice. However, the rules concerning authorization and review of detention, and supervision generally, have turned out to be largely presentational and, as noted earlier, there is evidence that the police do sometimes actively discourage suspects from exercising their right to legal advice.

---

[5] Under s. 76 or 78 of PACE.

[6] See, in particular, D. Dixon, *Law in Policing* (Oxford: Clarendon Press, 1997) and M. McConville, A. Sanders, and R. Leng, *The Case for the Prosecution* (London: Routledge, 1991).

Code of Practice C regulates the physical conditions in which interviews in police stations may be conducted. For example, there must be breaks at intervals of about two hours and at recognized meal times, suspects must be given at least eight hours' respite from interviewing in any twenty-four-hour period, and interviews must be conducted in adequately lit, ventilated, and heated rooms (Code C, paragraph 12). However, the rules regarding the way in which interviews may be conducted are minimal, going little further than requiring them to be contemporaneously recorded (Code C, paragraph 11 and Code E), and prohibiting the police from acting oppressively or from offering the suspect any inducements (Code C, paragraph 11.3). Nevertheless, the police reacted to the increased regulation of interviews, and particularly the presence of lawyers, in a number of ways.

There is strong evidence that the police continued the pre-PACE practice of conducting some interviews away from the police station or informally at the police station, thereby avoiding the protective provisions set out above, although there is little reliable evidence of the extent of this practice. Police officers conducting interviews also sought to control interviews in a number of ways. First, the police are in a position to, and do, control the release of information about the investigation to suspects and to their lawyers, a technique implicitly supported by the courts which continue to hold that the police are under no legal obligation to disclose information at the pre-charge stage.[7] Secondly, there is research and anecdotal evidence that the police sometimes resort to undermining the position of lawyers by challenging the advice given and by seeking to marginalize them by, for example, manipulating the seating arrangements in interview rooms. Thirdly, there is extensive evidence that questioning techniques designed to trap the unwary, and particularly the suggestible, suspect are used with some frequency.

It is clear that even before the introduction of PACE the significant events in terms of determining the outcome of most criminal cases were taking place at the police station rather than at court. This was an inevitable consequence of the change in the purpose of arrest and detention identified earlier. According to McConville and Baldwin, writing in 1982:

. . . the really crucial exchanges in the criminal process have shifted from courts into police interrogation rooms. It is these exchanges that, in a majority of cases, colour what happens at later stages in the criminal process. Indeed, they often determine the outcome of cases at trial.[8]

Given the adversarial nature of the criminal justice system, it is hardly surprising that the primary objective of police investigations, particularly by the time a suspect is arrested and detained at a police station, is to 'construct' a case against the suspect.[9] This entails the use of police interrogation to try to secure a confession or, failing that, to secure material that will be of use in the prosecution of the suspect. During the

---

[7] See *R. v. Imran and Hussain* [1997] *Crim. LR* 754.

[8] M. McConville and J. Baldwin, 'The Role of Interrogation in Crime Discovery and Conviction' (1982) 22 *BJ Crim.* 165 at 174.

[9] See, in particular, McConville *et al.*, n. 6 above.

1990s, however, the police publicly sought to portray the purpose of interviews as being a 'search for the truth', and this was reflected in the official police interview training material.[10] This was an important rhetorical strategy since characterizing police interviews as a search for the truth rather than a search for proof would justify the increasing inquisitorial powers being claimed by the police, would encourage the notion that suspects were at least under a moral duty to account for their actions to the police, and would cast doubt on the legitimacy of defence lawyers' advice to their clients not to answer police questions. It is in this context that the pressure to 'abolish' the 'right to silence' must be seen.

Soon after the introduction of PACE some elements in the police wanted to turn the clock back and remove the right of suspects to legal advice. However, it was clear that this was not politically possible, and police attention turned to the so-called 'right to silence'. The common law position was, broadly, that the failure or refusal of suspects to answer police questions or to inform the police of the nature of their defence was of no evidential value in determining guilt or innocence. The Philips Commission had expressly recommended that the rule should be retained. The government, however, embarked on a process of 'abolition' by setting up a Home Office working party in 1987 to make recommendations on precisely how this should be achieved, but, although the 'right to silence' was abolished in Northern Ireland in 1988, a series of highly publicized miscarriage of justice cases delayed action in England and Wales. The Royal Commission on Criminal Justice (the Runciman Commission), itself established in the wake of a notorious miscarriage of justice case (the 'Birmingham Six' case), recommended, like its counterpart a decade earlier, that the rule should be retained. In its view:

> ... the possibility of an increase in the convictions of the guilty [resulting from 'abolition' of the 'right to silence'] is outweighed by the risk that the extra pressure on suspects to talk in the police station and the adverse inferences invited if they do not may result in more convictions of the innocent ... There are too many cases of improper pressures being brought to bear on suspects in police custody, even where the safeguards of PACE and the codes of practice have been supposedly in force, for the majority [of the Commission] to regard this with equanimity.[11]

The government ignored this recommendation and, shortly after the Runciman Commission reported, introduced legislation—the Criminal Justice and Public Order Act 1994 (CJPOA)—abolishing the common law rule. The evidential effect of the CJPOA is that, whilst a defendant cannot be convicted on the basis of 'silence' alone, a court can draw adverse inferences where defendants rely on facts at their trial that they did not tell the police about when being interviewed. Similarly, provided certain conditions are satisfied, inferences can be drawn if defendants failed to account to the police for incriminating marks or substances found on or near their person at the time of arrest or failed to give an explanation for being at the location where they were when they were arrested.

---

[10] See *A Practical Guide to Investigative Interviewing* (Bramshill: National Crime Faculty, 1998).
[11] N. 3 above, 54 and 55.

The 'silence' provisions of the CJPOA had a number of profound implications for the relationship between the individual and the State and for the police approach to interviewing suspects. The shift which had already taken place prior to PACE, which permitted the police to arrest and detain in order to gather evidence, was taken a stage further. Arrested persons are now required to account for themselves to the police since if they do not, they risk their failure or unwillingness to do so being used as evidence against them. Furthermore, it enables the police to justify detention for questioning even if a suspect clearly indicates that they have no intention of answering questions. This is so because in order to persuade a court that adverse inferences should be drawn, the police will want to ensure that they have put appropriate questions to the suspect. As Sanders and Young have pointed out, this has the ironic effect that a suspect who remains silent may be detained without charge for a longer period of time than a suspect who confesses their guilt.[12] Also, simply by repeating the caution, which warns suspects that although they do not have to answer questions it may harm the defence that they put forward in court if they do not do so, pressure can be put on a suspect who is reluctant to speak.[13] There is some evidence that the rate of 'silence' in police interviews has decreased, although it was exercised in a relatively small minority of cases even prior to the CJPOA. The rate of confessions does not appear to have increased, but there is evidence that more suspects are lying, or at least giving a different version of events to the police from that they give in evidence at court, either of which can be used by the prosecution to their advantage at trial.[14]

The 'right to silence' provisions have also had significant implications for legal advice to defendants when they are in custody, and the available evidence suggests that suspects who receive advice at the police station are also remaining silent less frequently than prior to CJPOA. Under section 34 of CJPOA inferences may be drawn only if defendants rely on facts at trial which they could *reasonably* have been expected to mention to the police when interviewed. In the first Court of Appeal case on the CJPOA, *R. v. Condron and Condron*,[15] the defence argument that inferences should not be drawn where the suspect was acting on legal advice was rejected. The court decided that the reasonableness of acting on legal advice was a matter of fact to be decided by the jury. The accused pursued the case to the ECtHR, arguing that the drawing of inferences in such circumstances interfered with their right to a fair trial under Article 6 of the ECHR. This argument was rejected by the ECtHR.[16] Although accepting that where a defendant remains silent on legal advice, inferences should be drawn only if the court is satisfied that the defendant had no innocent explanation or

---

[12] A. Sanders and R. Young, *Criminal Justice* (2nd edn., London: Butterworths, 2000) 255.

[13] There is evidence from Northern Ireland that the police use the 'silence' provisions of legislation similar to the CJPOA to put 'considerable pressure' on suspects to speak. See J. Jackson, M. Wolfe, and K. Quinn, *Legislating Against Silence: The Northern Ireland Experience*, Northern Ireland Office Research And Statistical Series: Report No. 1 (Belfast: Queen's University, 2000) esp. chap. 7.

[14] For research evidence on the impact of the 'silence' provisions of the CJPOA see T. Bucke, R. Street, and D. Brown, *The Right of Silence: The Impact of the Criminal Justice and Public Order Act 1994*, Home Office Research Study 199 (London: Home Office, 2000).

[15] [1997] 1WLR 827.

[16] *Condron* v. *UK* (2001) 30 EHRR 1.

none that would stand up to cross-examination, it did not accept the argument that it must necessarily be reasonable to remain silent if advised by a lawyer to do so.

The result is that a lawyer advising a client at the police station can never be sure what the consequences of advising silence will be. Likewise, suspects can never be sure whether they should rely on the advice of their lawyer. Whilst the right to legal advice at the police station has come to be recognized as a human right under Article 6 of the ECHR, a defendant can actually be penalized for exercising that right by enabling the prosecution to use the consequence of relying on the advice as evidence against them. The 'right to silence' provisions of the CJPOA have, therefore, seriously undermined the value of legal advice at the pre-charge stage.

THE LEGAL PROFESSION AND CUSTODIAL LEGAL ADVICE

The introduction of the right to legal advice at the police station coincided with a period of sustained growth in the size of the legal profession, and sustained growth in the criminal legal aid budget. The cost of custodial legal advice formed a significant part of this growth, reaching £50 million in 1991, and £100 million by the late 1990s. Advice at the police station rapidly came to make up a very significant proportion of the income of criminal defence solicitors. Its effect was to create a whole new dimension, both professionally and financially, to the work of defence lawyers, a dimension that had hardly existed prior to 1986. Yet early research on the impact of PACE demonstrated that the response of the legal profession to the new statutory right to legal advice was inadequate in many ways. Criminal defence lawyers failed to grasp the significance of the role they could, and should, play in advising clients at police stations, and the firms within which they worked failed to make the structural and organizational changes necessary to offer a high standard of service to suspects detained by the police.

A significant minority of suspects who ask for legal advice subsequently withdraw their requests. In part this may be attributed to delay by the police in contacting the chosen lawyer, but it can also be partly explained by the fact that in some cases solicitors either do not respond, or are slow to respond, to the request for advice. There is evidence that in recent years the performance of solicitors in this respect has improved, but it is of particular importance, given that most suspects hate delay and want to get out of the police station as quickly as possible. If the solicitor contacted fails to respond to the request or is slow to respond, such suspects will be susceptible to suggestions by the police that they proceed with the police interview without having obtained legal advice. There are various explanations for solicitors' failure to provide advice or failure to provide it quickly, including the fact that they may be engaged on other cases (although this is, in part at least, a consequence of inadequate organization of their work by solicitors' firms) and a reluctance on the part of many solicitors to attend the police station until the police are ready to interview the client.

Related to the issue of delay is the method by which advice is provided, that is, whether on the telephone or in person. Estimates of the proportion of suspects advised only on the telephone have varied, both as between different areas of the country, and over time. It is clear that the pattern varies as between duty solicitors and defendants' 'own' solicitors. Approximately one third of police station legal advice claims of the former are for telephone-only advice, compared to about one sixth of claims by the latter. Advice given on the telephone, without visiting the client in person, is not necessarily inappropriate, particularly in the case of less serious offences, although in view of the possibility of telephone surveillance by the police a lawyer can never be sure that a telephone conversation is confidential. However, the major concern has been that the decision whether to attend the client in person has been determined by reference to the needs of the lawyer rather than the needs of the client.

A further issue identified by research has been the use made of non-qualified staff to provide legal advice. Although section 58 of PACE refers to the right of suspects to consult with a solicitor, Code of Practice C permits a solicitor to send a representative to the police station on their behalf. It was clear soon after the introduction of PACE that some solicitors were routinely using non-legally qualified staff who were often poorly trained or completely untrained. Estimates of the proportion of cases in which advice was being provided by non-solicitors have varied greatly, partly because of sampling methodology, but again there is a clear distinction between duty solicitor and defendants' 'own' solicitor cases, with the latter making much greater use of non-solicitors than the former. Until recently duty solicitors were largely prevented from sending non-qualified personnel to the police station, a restriction that did not apply in 'own' solicitor cases. Using non-lawyers for police station work does not necessarily result in the provision of a lower standard of advice. A key issue is the level of training and competence of those who provide the legal advice. More recent research has tended to show that, with appropriate training, specialist non-lawyers can provide a service that is just as good, and sometimes better, than that provided by fully qualified lawyers.

The quality of advice and assistance provided to suspects at the police station, that is, the standard and correctness of the advice given to clients and the actions taken by lawyers on their behalf, has been perhaps the most important and most controversial issue. It is important because, as noted earlier, the right to a lawyer is regarded as a fundamental feature of the right to fair trial. It is controversial because of the contested, and contestable, nature of the role of defence lawyers. Whilst adversarial principles imply that defence lawyers should act, and only act, in their clients' best interests, such a role may be regarded by the police and other state agencies as inimical both to their interests and to the interests of justice.

Adversarial principles and the professional obligation to act in a client's best interests would lead to the expectation that defence lawyers acting for clients during the investigative stage would attempt to obtain information from the police about the case, would spend adequate time in consultation with clients advising them of their legal position and on the strategy to adopt in police interviews, would attend police interviews with their clients, and would intervene in interviews if necessary to protect their clients' interests. To the surprise of some, early research on the impact of PACE established that many defence lawyers were not acting adversarially, nor did they appear to be acting in the best interests of their clients. In as many as half of all cases lawyers were making no inquiries of the police officers investigating the case against their clients, and therefore were in possession of very little information about the nature and strength of the police case prior to the police interview. Nearly half of the private consultations between lawyers and their clients were found to take less than ten minutes, and in a significant minority of cases lawyers did not consult with their clients at all prior to the police interview. Advice to clients to co-operate with the police by answering questions was found to be the norm, irrespective of the strength of the evidence in the hands of the police, and in as many as a third of cases clients were given no real advice at all by their lawyers.

The most surprising findings were in relation to the conduct of defence lawyers during police interviews. As noted earlier, suspects are legally entitled to have their solicitors with them in police interviews and the power of the police to exclude them is limited to circumstances where the lawyer misbehaves. It is well established that the prosecution can make evidential use of what suspects say during the course of an interview, most obviously if suspects makes admissions but also if they demonstrably lie or, following the enactment of CJPOA, if they unreasonably fail to mention facts that they rely on in their defence at trial. Thus there are many reasons why defence lawyers should continue to advise their clients and, if necessary, intervene during the course of police interviews. However, the main research finding was that defence lawyers generally said little or nothing in police interviews and rarely intervened to protect their clients' interests. In those cases where defence lawyers did intervene, it was frequently in order to obtain clarification of what was being said, but on occasions this had the effect of facilitating the police questioning, and one research study even found that in one in ten interventions by defence lawyers actually had the effect of assisting the police rather than the client.

Why is it that so many defence lawyers were acting contrary to their adversarial role and professional obligations? Confusion on the part of lawyers about their proper role provides a partial explanation. The principal professional obligation of all lawyers is to act in the best interests of their clients. However, as with all statements of general principle, this is capable of being interpreted in different ways, allowing scope for lawyers legitimately to act in different ways in similar circumstances. As a result, mechanisms for enforcing this kind of professional rule are relatively weak. At the same time, there were a number of contrary pressures on solicitors. Following the introduction of the statutory right to legal advice, the Law Society had issued detailed guidance to defence lawyers on advising clients at police stations. This guidance was markedly non-adversarial in tone. It emphasized the need for co-operation with the police and identified the lawyer's primary role as being to ensure fairness. Furthermore, it tended to stress the role of the lawyer in providing advice before the commencement of police interviews rather than assistance during the course of interviews. This approach was reinforced by Code of Practice C which, whilst providing no positive description of the defence lawyer's role, emphasized the circumstances in which a lawyer might be excluded from police interviews. Thus, in official terms, the defence lawyer's role was represented in non-adversarial and negative terms.

The police, on the other hand, were generally quite clear about their adversarial role and its legitimacy. Most suspects are interviewed at police stations where the police are on their own, familiar, and secure territory. Defence solicitors were used to appearing in court, where their role and its legitimacy were well established, but were unused to acting in the unfamiliar surroundings of police stations. Furthermore, as many of those actually providing legal advice were not solicitors at all but unqualified staff, who were often untrained and inexperienced, they were susceptible to pressure to identify with police values and objectives, especially since a sizeable proportion of them were former police officers. Finally, as 'repeat players', defence lawyers had a direct interest in being seen by the police as co-operative. Ironically, the police themselves could, by directing suspects to particular solicitors and firms, be an important source of work for defence lawyers. Even if this was not a consideration for any particular lawyer, acting adversarially on behalf of one client could affect the way in which the police treated other clients of the same firm on future occasions.

The notion of defence lawyers as 'repeat players' underlines the importance of recognizing that solicitors operate within the context of law firms which share many of the characteristics of commercial enterprises. Whilst the primary objective of the partners may not be to make a profit, they operate in a business environment in which it is necessary to make sufficient money to pay wages and overheads and to provide for capital investment, whilst delivering a sufficient surplus for the partners to live on. Police station work, particularly for specialist criminal defence firms, represents high turnover, low value, business. In this context, it is economically rational in an environment which permits non-solicitors to be used for police station work, to allocate such work to relatively low paid staff and to routinize procedures so that they are economically efficient. This does not necessarily have adverse consequences for the quality of work done, but if it is not to do so it does require good management, adequate supervision of staff, and appropriate training. Some of the problems concerning the quality of the work of defence lawyers resulted from the failure of lawyers to recognize such business imperatives. Traditionally, criminal defence work was largely court-based and was largely conducted by solicitors working within relatively small firms. The major fee-earners were partners of the firm[17] who could appear in magistrates' courts in the morning, see clients in the afternoon, and for whom management tasks were minimal. Many such lawyers failed to understand that changes in work patterns, an important element of which was a higher level of police station work, required them to make structural and organizational changes in their firms if they were to provide a high standard of service. Whilst providing a twenty-four-hour police station service and spending adequate time with clients at the police station may make economic sense, many firms had not developed the organizational structures to enable them to deliver such a service.

Socio-legal research into the implementation of PACE and the right to legal advice

---

[17] Until recently, solicitors' firms could not be constituted as companies, and solicitors would either work as (or for) sole principals or partnerships.

led to a number of significant changes. The PACE Codes of Practice were revised a number of times in an attempt to encourage more suspects to make use of their right to advice. For example, custody officers are now required to tell suspects that legal advice is free, that a solicitor can be requested at any time during the suspect's detention, and, if suspects refuse legal advice, the custody officer must ask them why. The request rate went up steadily during the 1990s, although part of this increase can be attributed to other developments such as the increasing knowledge of the right to advice and, probably, an increased perception of the need for advice following the right to silence changes introduced by the CJPOA. The government also acceded to pressure to change the way in which Code of Practice C characterized defence lawyers and their role, so that it is now set out in positive and unequivocal terms:[18]

The solicitor's only role in the police station is to protect and advance the legal rights of his client. On occasions this may require the solicitor to give advice which has the effect of his client avoiding giving evidence which strengthens a prosecution case. The solicitor may intervene in order to seek clarification or to challenge an improper question to his client or the manner in which it is put, or to advise his client not to reply to particular questions, or if he wishes to give his client further legal advice.[19]

It is difficult to establish what result this has had, but it confirms the legitimacy of the defence lawyer's obligation to act in a client's best interests and the importance of legal advice in contributing to fair trial.

The discovery that a large proportion of suspects were being advised, not by solicitors, but by unqualified representatives led to the creation of an accreditation scheme which is designed to ensure, through a system of testing, that all non-solicitors who give legal advice at police stations can demonstrate a minimum level of competence. Research on the impact of this accreditation scheme has shown that it has had a significant impact on the quality of police station advice and, interestingly, that the improvement extends to solicitors as well. It is likely that one reason for this improvement is that, in devising the scheme, the Law Society had to develop and articulate standards of competence by which candidates for accreditation could be judged. The standards confirmed the adversarial role of defence lawyers, set out in detail both the knowledge and skills required to perform the role effectively and articulated the steps to be taken by defence lawyers in advising clients at the police station. The accreditation scheme has now been adopted in a modified form for determining whether solicitors are sufficiently competent to become duty solicitors. Furthermore, since the accreditation scheme is, in effect, run jointly by the Law Society and the Legal Service Commission (the government body responsible for administering legal aid), it has helped to legitimize the adversarial role of defence lawyers, making it less vulnerable to challenge by the police and other law enforcement agencies, and by the government itself.

---

[18] Code of Practice C.
[19] Code of Practice C, Note for Guidance 6D. This was inserted following pressure from the Law Society.

THE RESPONSE OF THE COURTS

An important component in the development of pre-trial defence has been the attitude of the courts to police denial of legal advice and in respect of the role and professional standards of defence lawyers. Whilst exclusion of evidence is directly relevant only where a suspect is charged and pleads not guilty, a strong indication by the courts that they will not admit evidence obtained following a breach of a suspect's rights will, arguably, lead to greater respect for those rights by the police in all cases. Broadly, the tradition of English common law is that the courts are concerned with the relevance of evidence rather than the method by which it was obtained, but section 76 of PACE provides for exclusion of confession evidence if it was obtained as a result of oppression or in circumstances likely to render it unreliable, and section 78 of PACE gives courts a wide discretion to exclude any prosecution evidence by reference to principles of fairness.

The attitude of the courts to denial of legal advice has been both equivocal and contradictory. In an early post-PACE case, *R.* v. *Samuel*,[20] the Court of Appeal described the right to legal advice as a fundamental right of every citizen. This approach was followed some years later by the ECtHR in *Murray* v. *UK*[21] in which it was held that the right of suspects detained by the police prior to charge to legal advice was guaranteed by Article 6 of the ECHR. However, unlawful denial of legal advice has not automatically led to the exclusion of evidence obtained in consequence. Whilst in *Samuel* the court did hold that a confession obtained following the wrongful denial of legal advice should have been excluded at trial, this was not followed in *R.* v. *Alladice*[22] which was decided by the Court of Appeal shortly afterwards.

One reason for this is that the primary exclusionary rule, section 78 of PACE, places emphasis on substantive, as opposed to procedural, fairness. Underlying this is a tension between due-process and crime-control values and, in this context, an equivocal attitude by the courts to the role of the defence lawyer. Thus in *Alladice* the Court of Appeal held that a confession obtained following an unlawful denial of advice need not be excluded, since the defendant was well aware of his rights (in this case, not to answer police questions—a case decided before the CJPOA came into force). In other words, the role of the defence lawyer was largely confined to giving legal information to clients. In other cases, however, where the police have breached other requirements of PACE and the Codes of Practice in the presence of a defence lawyer, the court has approved the admission of a confession so obtained on the ground that the presence of the lawyer was sufficient to ameliorate the breach by the police. In other words, the role of the lawyer was to protect the rights of the client. It is unlikely that this tension will be resolved decisively in the foreseeable future. A further question that has yet to be authoritatively determined is whether evidence of police interviews should be excluded where it can be demonstrated that the defence lawyer advised the client incorrectly, or in circumstances where the lawyer's standard of conduct fell well below the accepted standards of professional competence.

---

[20] [1988] QB 615.   [21] (1996) 22 EHRR 29.   [22] (1988) 87 Cr. App. R 380.

CONCLUSIONS

In most, if not all, jurisdictions the police and other law enforcement agencies are permitted to detain persons suspected of crime in order to interrogate them before deciding whether and when to initiate criminal proceedings and to produce them before a court. Whether the jurisdiction is based on inquisitorial or accusatorial principles, unless the prosecution is prevented from using the product of custodial interrogation as evidence, the police are likely to regard such interrogation as an important opportunity to obtain evidence to be used to encourage suspects to plead guilty or, failing that, to be used against the suspect at their trial. Such evidence may be in the form of a confession, but may alternatively be in the form of an inconsistent account given by the suspect, demonstrable lies told by the suspect, or even failure to answer questions put by the police. Irrespective of the rhetorical position regarding the presumption of innocence and the burden of proof, citizens are expected in practice to provide an account of their actions or a response to an accusation by state law enforcement agencies. The process of determining guilt or innocence therefore commences at the point of arrest and detention (if not before), rather than at the post-charge stage.

Fair-trial rights embodied in international human rights conventions generally recognize the importance of giving those accused of crime the right to legal assistance, but most do not explicitly guarantee a right to custodial legal advice. However, if the prosecution is to be permitted to use the product of custodial interrogation as evidence against the accused, it must follow that the right to fair trial requires States to facilitate access to a lawyer at the pre-charge stage. Furthermore, since custodial interrogation is, by its nature, coercive, the right to legal advice should extend to a right to have a lawyer present during interrogation, and to give the lawyer the right to intervene in order to prevent oppressive or unfair conduct on the part of the police or to give advice and support to the suspect.

To a large extent this was given statutory recognition in England and Wales by the Police and Criminal Evidence Act 1984. However, experience demonstrates that creating a statutory right to custodial legal advice, though necessary, is not a sufficient mechanism for securing fair-trial rights. Structures must be put in place to ensure that legal advice is available to all of those suspects who want it. This involves ensuring that suspects are aware of their right and are not discouraged by the police or by other considerations from exercising it. It also requires some kind of funding to be available to pay for legal advice to those unable to afford it and mechanisms to ensure not only that lawyers are available to attend police stations at short notice, but that they are willing to do so.

It must also be recognized, given the objectives of the police, that they may seek to undermine the right by conducting interrogations away from the police station, by withholding information, or by trying to undermine the advice given by lawyers. This requires effective supervisory and accountability mechanisms in respect of police conduct and also evidential mechanisms designed to discourage such conduct, perhaps by way of a *prima facie* exclusionary rule applicable where a suspect has been interrogated in the absence of a lawyer. It also requires a willingness on the part of the judiciary to hold the police to account for their conduct.

It is equally important that the legal profession recognize the fact that inadequate or incompetent legal advice may interfere with the right to fair trial just as much as oppressive or inappropriate conduct on the part of the police. The legal profession must, therefore, take responsibility for clearly articulating the role of defence lawyers in respect of custodial legal advice, for introducing training and other mechanisms for ensuring a high standard of professional conduct, and procedures for preventing incompetent lawyers from acting for clients at police stations.

Further Reading

ASHWORTH, A., *The Criminal Process: An Evaluative Study* (Oxford: Oxford University Press, 1998).

BRIDGES, L., CAPE, E., ABUBAKER, A., and BENNETT, C., *Quality in Criminal Defence Services* (London: Legal Services Commission, 2000).

—— and CHOONGH, S., *Improving Police Station Advice: The Impact of the Accreditation Scheme for Police Station Legal Advisers*, Research Study No. 31 (London: The Law Society, 1998).

BROWN, D., *PACE Ten Years On: A Review of Research*, Research Study No. 155 (London: Home Office, 1997).

—— and BUCKE, T., *In Police Custody: Police Powers and Suspects' Rights under the Revised PACE Codes of Practice*, Research Study No. 174 (London: Home Office, 1997).

——, ——, and STREET, R., *The Right of Silence: The Impact of the Criminal Justice and Public Order Act 1994*, Research Study 199 (London: Home Office, 2000).

CAPE, E., *Defending Suspects at Police Stations* (3rd edn., London: Legal Action Group, 1999).

DIXON, D., *Law in Policing: Legal Regulation and Police Practices* (Oxford: Clarendon Press, 1997).

EDE, R., and EDWARDS, A., *Criminal Defence: The Good Practice Guide* (London: The Law Society, 2000).

—— and SHEPHERD, E., *Active Defence* (2nd edn., London: The Law Society, 2000).

JACKSON, J., WOLFE, M., and QUINN, K., *Legislating Against Silence: The Northern Ireland Experience*, NIO Research and Statistical Series Report No. 1, (Belfast: Northern Ireland Office, 2000).

McCONVILLE, M., HODGSON, J., BRIDGES, L., and PAVLOVIC, A., *Standing Accused* (Oxford: Clarendon Press, 1994).

—— SANDERS, A., and LENG, R., *The Case for the Prosecution* (London: Routledge, 1991).

PALMER, A., and HART, M., *A PACE in the Right Direction?* (Sheffield: Institute for the Study of the Legal Profession, 1996).

SANDERS, A., and YOUNG, R., *Criminal Justice* (2nd edn., London: Butterworths, 2000).

7

BAIL IN CRIMINAL CASES

Anthea Hucklesby

INTRODUCTION

This chapter discusses some of the issues which arise from the question of what to do with defendants who have been accused of committing an offence but who are awaiting trial and, thus, are legally innocent. In England and Wales, as in many other jurisdictions, people can either be granted 'bail' during this time, i.e. allowed to go free, or remanded (detained) in custody. Remanding in custody legally innocent people requires justification as it contravenes fundamental human rights. There is a presumption in favour of bail in England and Wales which is based on two fundamental premises: that people are innocent until proven guilty and that innocent people have a right to freedom. In reality, however, the rights of victims and the public must also be considered. They have a right to be protected from harm, and it is for this reason that two out of the three main grounds on which bail can be refused in England and Wales relate to the possibility of the accused further offending and the protection of witnesses. Prioritizing these often competing rights makes bail decisions difficult.

This chapter demonstrates how the right to bail in England and Wales has been eroded since the early 1980s. The impetus for this shift has been two-fold: the increasing importance of the protection of the public and victims' rights and the need to save money. It will suggest that the present system of bail decision-making in England and Wales fails to fulfil the requirements of a system of pre-trial detention based on adherence to human rights, in particular the right to liberty, the right to a fair trial, and the right not to be punished without lawful authority. It will argue that people are unnecessarily remanded in custody or their lives are overly restricted by too many and/or inappropriate conditions being attached to their bail. These situations arise partly because of the way in which the law is drafted and partly because the operation of the remand process in practice bears little resemblance to the relevant principles of law.

The question of bail may arise at several stages during criminal cases. First, the police have the power to bail suspects before they are charged in order for further inquiries to be undertaken and to compel them to return to the police station on a specified date. Secondly, the police make bail decisions after suspects have been charged with an offence which take effect until defendants appear in court. Thirdly, bail decisions are made by courts when cases are adjourned to a later date. In many cases, this means that bail decisions relate to defendants who are unconvicted and awaiting trial, although bail decisions are also taken by courts after conviction but prior to a sentence being imposed. Fourthly, persons may be bailed while awaiting the outcome of appeals. It is the police bail decision after a charge and the court bail decision which are the main focus of this chapter.

The first section of the chapter discusses the significance of the bail decision. The second section scrutinizes police bail/detention decisions and demonstrates the crucial role the police play in the bail process. The rest of the chapter concentrates on issues relating to the court bail process. It identifies trends in bail policy and outlines the law on bail in England and Wales. It then focuses on how the bail process operates in practice before discussing the important issues raised by the increasing use of conditional bail. In the final section, recent moves to restrict the right to bail are reviewed.

THE SIGNIFICANCE OF THE BAIL/CUSTODY DECISION

The limited research on and debate about the bail process could lead to the conclusion that it is not a very important part of the criminal justice process. It could be argued that most people are remanded in custody because they are in fact guilty and are simply waiting for the criminal justice process to confirm their legal guilt. In a similar vein, it is often said that defendants 'prefer' to spend time on remand in prison where conditions are better and where they have more privileges than sentenced prisoners.[1] These comments undermine the fundamental tenet of the criminal justice process in England and Wales. Defendants are innocent until proven guilty, and the remand process, in the main, deals with legally innocent people. On this basis alone we should be concerned about how the process operates. As Lord Hailsham succinctly argued, the refusal of bail is 'the only example, in peace time, where a man can be kept in confinement without a proper sentence following conviction after a proper trial. It is, therefore, the solitary exception to the Magna Carta'.[2]

Another reason bail decisions are important is that they are related to later decisions taken by both defendants and courts. It is not, however, clear whether or not the relationship is a direct one, and the relationship of cause and effect has not been established. Nonetheless, in practice, defendants remanded in custody are more likely to plead guilty, less likely to be acquitted, and more likely to have custodial sentences imposed.[3] There is also some evidence that the threat of being remanded in custody is

---

[1] Time spent on remand in prison is deducted from any sentence received on conviction.

[2] Quoted in P. Cavadino and B. Gibson, *Bail: The Law, Best Practice and the Debate* (Winchester: Waterside Press, 1993) 69.

[3] A. K. Bottomley, *Prison Before Trial*, Occasional Paper in Social Administration, No. 39 (London: Bell and Son, 1970); M King, *Bail or Custody* (London: Cobden Trust, 1971); Home Office, n. 45 below, at 195.

used as a bargaining tool to put pressure on suspects and defendants to confess or plead guilty.[4]

Defendants remanded in custody end up in the remand sector of the prison system, which has some of the worst overcrowding and conditions in the whole of the prison system. Many remand prisoners are housed in very old nineteenth-century prisons, locked up in their cells for long periods, and have very limited access to facilities and services in the prisons. A thematic review recently undertaken by HM Inspector of Prisons highlighted the inadequacy of the treatment of unsentenced prisoners.[5] It concluded that some remand prisoners 'barely see the light of day outside their cells' and that there was a 'significant . . . gap between official provision for remand prisoners and their legitimate needs [which included] access to due process and reasonable opportunities to sustain mental and physical health'.[6] Of particular note was the reported lack of access to legal advisors, which it said 'constitute[s] an obstacle to the fair and just treatment of unsentenced prisoners'.[7] Being remanded in custody may impede the preparation of the defence case and make it more likely that defendants are convicted. Further, although remand prisoners should be housed separately from sentenced prisoners and have a number of additional rights, includ-ing daily visits and being able to wear their own clothes, the continuing problems facing the prison service mean that these principles are not always adhered to.[8]

Being remanded in custody may also have significant and long-lasting effects on defendants and their families. Defendants may lose their jobs or their future employ-ment prospects may be jeopardized. It may have considerable economic consequences which may result in the loss of the family home, and problems with the repayment of other loans. Emotional problems for both defendants and their families and friends may arise, as well as the time and expense of relatives visiting the remand prisoner.

The living conditions and consequences of being remanded in custody are all the more significant if defendants are later acquitted or given non-custodial sentences. In England and Wales, the majority of defendants held on remand in prison do not receive a custodial sentence. In 2000 under half (44 per cent) of those remanded in custody received custodial sentences. Around a quarter (23 per cent) were either acquitted or had their proceedings terminated. Eight per cent were given a discharge or a fine and 15 per cent received a community sentence.[9] These figures show that many defendants are probably remanded in custody unnecessarily, although it is possible that some of these defendants were given non-custodial sentences because they have already spent time in custody.[10] If defendants are remanded in custody yet are later acquitted or receive non-custodial sentences, it suggests that custodial

---

[4] A. Bottoms and J. McClean, *Defendants in the Criminal Process* (London: Routledge, 1976); M. McConville, A. Sanders, and R. Leng, *The Case for the Prosecution* (London: Routledge, 1991); M. McConville, J. Hodgson, L. Bridges, and A. Pavlovic, *Standing Accused* (Oxford: Clarendon Press, 1994).

[5] HM Inspector of Prisons, *Unjust Deserts: A Thematic Review by the Chief Inspector of Prisons of the Treatment and Conditions for Unsentenced Prisoners in England and Wales* (London: Home Office, 2000).

[6] *Ibid.* at 119.   [7] *Ibid.* at 52.   [8] *Ibid.*

[9] Home Office, *Criminal Statistics England and Wales 2000*, Cmnd 5312 (2001), Table 8.8.

[10] R. Morgan and S. Jones, 'Bail or Jail' in E. Stockdale and S. Casale (eds.), *Criminal Justice Under Stress* (London: Blackstone, 1992) 39.

remands may be used as a form of pre-trial punishment, giving defendants a 'taste of prison' even when they are unlikely to be sentenced to a period of imprisonment. This practice is expressly forbidden by the courts.[11] There is no compensation available for those remanded in custody who are later acquitted or have their cases dropped, despite the devastating effect this may have on their lives. There have been periodic calls for compensation to be paid to defendants wrongly remanded in custody.[12] Some other European countries have compensation schemes, but the cost of such a provision is probably prohibitive.[13]

POLICE BAIL

Recent legislation in England and Wales has assimilated police and court bail decision-making to one another.[14] When a person is charged with an offence, it is for the custody officer to decide whether the accused should be detained in police custody, to appear before the next available court, or released on bail. Since 1994, the police have been able to attach conditions to defendants' bail and may use any conditions they feel are appropriate, with the exception of residing at a bail hostel.[15] According to official statistics the police detain in custody 15 per cent of those arrested and charged.[16] Some research studies have found somewhat higher figures of between 20 and 28 per cent.[17] No official figures are available on the use of police conditional bail, but research findings suggest that the use of conditional bail by the police may have increased recently. Burke and Brown found that 17 per cent of defendants were conditionally bailed, whereas Hucklesby found that just under a third (32 per cent) of defendants were conditionally bailed by the police.[18]

Very little research has been conducted into the use of police bail, but what has been done raises a number of issues. First, variations between stations and forces have been found in detention/bail rates and the use of conditional as opposed to unconditional bail.[19] Secondly, the number and type of conditions attached to police bail vary between stations.[20] Neither of these variations can be fully accounted for by differences in the type of cases. This suggests that whether or not defendants are detained in police custody depends, in part at least, on which station they are detained in. The third issue relates to the way in which the police justify their decisions. The

---

[11] R. v. Brentford Justices, ex parte Muirhead (1941) 106 JP 4.

[12] Cavadino and Gibson, n. 2 above, at 74.   [13] Ibid. at 74.

[14] Criminal Justice and Public Order Act 1994.

[15] Criminal Justice and Public Order Act 1994, s.27.

[16] Home Office, n. 9 above, at Table 8.3.

[17] T. Burke and D. Brown, In Police Custody: Police Powers and Suspects' Rights under the Revised Codes of Practice, Home Office Research Study No. 174 (London: Home Office, 1997) 61; C. Phillips and D. Brown, Entry into the Criminal Justice System: A Survey of Police Arrests and their Outcomes, Home Office Research Study No. 185 (London: Home Office, 1998) p. xv.

[18] Burke and Brown, n. 17 above, at 61; A. Hucklesby, 'Police Bail and the Use of Conditions' (2001) 1 Criminal Justice 441.

[19] Phillips and Brown, n. 17 above, at p. xv; Hucklesby, n. 18 above.   [20] Ibid.

police simply tick boxes on a *pro forma* which indicate which exceptions to bail they believe apply. As we see later, this may not constitute adequate justification for their decisions to withhold unconditional bail in terms of human rights legislation. Further, while the police always ensure that these boxes are completed when defendants are detained, they are less meticulous when defendants are subject to conditional bail.[21]

The police were given the power to attach conditions to bail in order to reduce the number of defendants detained in police custody.[22] The research evidence suggests that this objective has not been universally achieved. There is evidence of a 'net-widening' effect, with defendants being subject to conditions when they would have been released unconditionally prior to the introduction of the police conditional bail.[23] One of the possible explanations for problems in the police's interpretation of the legislation may be the lack of training which they receive on how to make these important decisions. Most custody officers receive a very brief introduction on bail decision-making as part of their custody officer training and no special training was undertaken when the 1994 legislative changes were introduced.[24]

The police bail/detention decision is important not simply because it restricts the liberty of the individual, but because it affects similar decisions made later on in the process. First, the police provide a recommendation to the Crown Prosecution Service (CPS) about the bail status of defendants. Again, very little is known about how the CPS uses this recommendation although what little research there is suggests that the police recommendation is very influential. Phillips and Brown found in their study that the CPS followed the police recommendations in 85 per cent of cases.[25] The CPS was least likely to do this when the police believed that bail should be opposed, but even in these cases the recommendations were followed in nearly three-quarters of cases (71 per cent). The correlation increased to 89 per cent of cases where conditional bail was recommended and 96 per cent of cases where the recommendation was for unconditional bail.[26] Although some of reasons given for the CPS disagreeing with the police recommendation seemed to be simply differing opinions of bail risk, others were explained by new information coming to light, such as a verifiable address or evidence of past breaches of bail.[27] This implies that the correlation between police and CPS decisions is higher than the data first suggest. This raises the issue of how independent CPS decisions relating to bail are and how much they rely on information from the police.

Secondly, research has found a high correlation between the police bail/detention decision and whether or not the CPS opposes court bail. In cases where defendants are bailed by the police, the CPS is very unlikely to object to bail.[28] The picture is more

---

[21] *Ibid.*

[22] Royal Commission on Criminal Justice, Report, Cmnd 2263 (1993) para. 22.

[23] Burke and Brown, n. 17 above, at 67; Hucklesby, n. 18 above.

[24] J. Burrows, P. Henderson, and P. Morgan, *Improving Bail Decisions: The Bail Process Project, Phase I*, Research and Planning Unit Paper 90 (London: Home Office, 1994) 54; Hucklesby, n. 18 above.

[25] Phillips and Brown, n. 17 above, at 135.   [26] *Ibid.* at 135.   [27] *Ibid.*

[28] Burrows, Henderson, and Morgan, n. 24 above, at 24; A. Hucklesby, 'Remand Decision Makers' [1997] *Crim. LR* 269.

complicated when defendants have been detained by the police. In these cases, the CPS almost always objects to unconditional bail by requesting either a remand in custody or conditional bail. Prior to the introduction of police conditional bail, defendants to whose bail the police believed conditions should be attached were routinely detained in custody only for the CPS to request conditional bail.[29] There is some evidence that this still occurs, and this makes the research evidence in this area inconclusive.[30]

Thirdly, there is a high correlation between the police bail/custody decision and the court remand decision.[31] Research has found that if the police released defendants on bail they were very unlikely to be remanded in custody by the courts.[32] Conversely, if the police detained defendants, they were more often than not remanded in custody by the courts. It has been argued that one of the effects of the new power of the police to attach conditions to bail is that this makes the police bail/detention decision more visible and precise to the courts. Courts now clearly know whether the police believe that defendants should be remanded in custody or bailed, and what, if any, conditions are appropriate because they have already made a similar decision of which the court is aware. This arguably heightens the potential police influence on court decision-making, and may partially account for the rise in the use of conditional bail by the courts which will be discussed later in the chapter.[33]

Before going on to look in more depth at how court remand decisions are made, it is worth mentioning briefly another type of police bail decision. The police are able to release defendants on bail prior to charge and require them to return to the police station for further inquiries.[34] A person who fails to return to the police station can be rearrested.[35] Phillips and Brown found that 17 per cent of suspects were bailed by the police for further inquiries.[36] They also found considerable variations in the use of pre-charge bail between stations. It appears that the use of this type of bail has increased in recent years. A study by Brown found that only 12 per cent of suspects were bailed in these circumstances.[37] Phillips and Brown explain this trend by reference to the police's need to maximize the time available to them to conduct inquiries and the direct effect of the introduction of time limits for detention in order for this process to take place.[38] If this is indeed the explanation, then it can be surmised that the introduction of measures to reduce delay introduced in 1999 as a result of the Narey Report[39] will increase the use of this type of bail still further.

---

[29] A. Hucklesby, 'Bail or Jail? The Practical Operation of the Bail Act 1976' (1996) 23 *Journal of Law and Society* 213.

[30] A. Hucklesby and E. Marshall, 'Tackling Offending on Bail' (2000) 39 *Howard Journal* 150.

[31] Hucklesby, nn. 28 and 29 above; P. Morgan and P. Henderson, *Remand Decisions and Offending on Bail: Evaluation of the Bail Process Project*, Home Office Research Study No. 184 (London: Home Office, 1998) 37.

[32] Morgan and Henderson, n. 31 above, at 135.   [33] Hucklesby, n. 28 above, at 274.

[34] Police and Criminal Evidence Act 1984, s.47(3).

[35] Police and Criminal Evidence Act 1984, s.46A.   [36] Phillips and Brown, n. 17 above, at 82.

[37] D. Brown, *Detention at the Police Station under the Police and Criminal Evidence Act 1984*, Home Office Research Study No. 104 (London: Home Office, 1989).

[38] Phillips and Brown, n. 17 above, at 83.

[39] Narey, *Review of Delay in the Criminal Justice System* (London: Home Office, 1997).

The existence of pre-charge bail may encourage the police to arrest suspects without enough initial evidence, knowing that time limits on detention can be by-passed. This may have been one of the factors which facilitated the use of arrests as a way of collecting evidence rather than as the end-point of investigations.[40] Phillips and Brown state that the police may use pre-charge bail in the hope that further evidence will come to light.[41] They also speculate that the police rarely have the resources to pursue cases once suspects have been bailed. These factors help us to understand why in over two-fifths of cases where suspects were subject to pre-charge bail no further action is taken.[42]

COURT BAIL POLICY

The origins of bail can be traced back many centuries, but the present bail system in England and Wales is based on the Bail Act 1976.[43] For the first time, this legislation provided for a right to bail and laid down the justifications for the removal of that right. The preceding Criminal Justice Act 1967 had already started this process. It had introduced conditional bail and a weak presumption of bail by setting out circumstances in which bail should be granted. Both these pieces of legislation resulted from pressure from various quarters to alter fundamentally the way the process was operating. The first of these was the inexorable rise in the prison remand population, which was expensive and contributed to the problems experienced by the prison system. The second was several research reports which highlighted the high number of unnecessary remands in custody, variations in bail and custody rates between courts, the injustice produced by the widespread use of sureties as a system of money bail, and the lack of information available to magistrates on which to base their decisions.[44]

The 1970s saw wide agreement that the number of defendants on bail should be increased. For example, the Working Party (1974) set up to review the bail decision-making process stated that its main aim was to consider strategies to enable courts to release more defendants on bail.[45] Very soon after the report was published, a Home Office circular stated that courts should operate in the spirit of the report, thus introducing a presumption of bail.[46] As a result of these moves, there was a rise in the proportion and numbers of defendants granted bail even before the Bail Act was enacted. By the end of the 1970s, the custody rate had dropped to around 13 per cent of those remanded.[47]

---

[40] A. Sanders and R. Young, *Criminal Justice* (London: Butterworths, 2000) 136.
[41] Phillips and Brown, n. 17 above, at 84.   [42] *Ibid.*
[43] A. K. Bottomley, 'The Granting of Bail: Principles and Practice' (1968) 31 *Modern Law Review* 40.
[44] Bottomley, n. 3 above; King, n. 3 above.
[45] Home Office, *Bail Proceedings in Magistrates' Courts: A Report of the Working Party* (London: HMSO, 1974).
[46] Home Office Circular 155/1975.
[47] Home Office, *Criminal Statistics England and Wales 1979*, Cmnd 8098 (1980).

The increase in the proportion of defendants granted bail continued after the Bail Act was introduced and was briefly translated into a fall in the prison remand population in the late 1970s. This was not sustained, however, with the prison remand population rising relentlessly throughout the 1980s. A major contributory factor in this rise was the acute delays being experienced in the criminal justice process, which increased the length of time defendants spent on remand awaiting trial.[48] In order to deal with this problem, Custody Time Limits were introduced in 1985 which, as the name suggests, limit the time defendants can spend in custody awaiting trial.[49] The direct effect of these limits has been minimal, because they are routinely extended and were generously set to begin with.[50] The indirect effect on the time taken for case preparation is less clear. It is also unclear what effect, if any, their introduction had on the time taken to prepare the cases of defendants on bail.

The concern over defendants' rights and the optimism that more defendants could be safely released on bail, seen in the 1970s, did not last long. Although courts were expected to release ordinary run-of-the-mill defendants on bail, the policy towards more serious offenders hardened in line with the broader strategy of 'bifurcation'.[51] By the late 1980s, amendments to the Bail Act 1976 had, arguably, overturned the presumption of bail for some defendants charged with serious offences. This trend to restrict the right to bail for certain defendants deemed as 'dangerous' continued in the 1990s. The Criminal Justice and Public Order Act 1994 completely removed the right to bail for those accused of committing a second grave offence.[52] A major shift in policy which occurred in this Act was the introduction of restrictions to the right to bail for allegedly 'persistent' offenders accused of committing offences on bail. The offences in question did not have to be particularly serious. It was their alleged repetition that was the justification for defendants' freedom being restricted.

The Bail Act 1976 had also introduced a system which enabled defendants to apply for bail on each and every occasion they appeared in court. During the 1980s, however, this began to be seen as wasteful of resources, particularly when the defendants' circumstances had not changed and magistrates were unlikely to overturn a previous court's decision in any event. As a consequence, several policy changes in the 1980s made it more difficult for those remanded in custody to apply for bail. The Criminal Justice Act 1988 codified a practice, already widespread, of limiting the number of bail applications defendants could make as of right to two.[53] It also reduced the frequency of routine appearances in court from seven days to twenty-eight days after the defendant's second court appearance. In practice, this means that defendants can be remanded in custody after two court appearances for up to twenty-eight days, albeit with the right of appeal.

The number of defendants remanded in custody by magistrates has nearly doubled in the last decade from 48,000 in 1990 to 84,000 in 2000 in England and Wales.[54] This

---

[48] Home Office, *Criminal Statistics England and Wales 1992*, Cmnd 2410 (1993).

[49] Prosecution of Offenders Act 1985, s. 22.

[50] A. Samuels, 'Custody Time Limits' [1997] *Crim. LR* 260.

[51] M. Cavadino and J. Dignan, *The Penal System: An Introduction* (London: Sage, 1997) 23.

[52] Criminal Justice and Public Order Act 1994 s. 25.

[53] Criminal Justice Act 1988, s. 154.   [54] Home Office, n. 9 above, at Table 8.4.

represents a percentage increase in the use of custodial remands from 10 per cent of defendants in 1990 to 14 per cent of defendants in 2000, and means that the proportion of defendants remanded in custody has returned to levels last seen in the late 1970s. The increased use of custodial remands during the 1990s translated into a steady rise in the prison remand population. In 2000, the average prison remand population in England and Wales was 11,270, 63 per cent of which were unconvicted.[55] However, the prison population has not risen in line with the larger number of defendants being remanded in custody, as the length of time defendants spend awaiting trial has reduced during this time. The average time spent on remand in prison has decreased from fifty-four days for men and forty-four days for women in 1989 to forty-nine days for males and thirty-six days for females in 2000.

THE LAW ON BAIL

The question of bail arises when criminal courts adjourn cases. In England and Wales, the bail decision can take three forms. Defendants can be remanded on unconditional bail, conditional bail, or in custody. Defendants granted bail are released into the community to appear at court on a specified date. Those granted conditional bail have additional requirements to fulfil, such as residing at a specified address or keeping away from specific people or places. Defendants remanded in custody are detained in a local prison or remand centre to await their next court appearance.

The Bail Act 1976 is the major piece of legislation governing court bail decisions. Under this Act, defendants have a right to bail.[56] As a consequence, defendants must be released on unconditional bail unless certain exceptions apply.[57] For offences for which imprisonment is a possible punishment, defendants need not be granted bail if there are *substantial grounds for believing* that they will:

- fail to return to court when they should;
- commit an offence on bail;
- interfere with witnesses or otherwise obstruct the course of justice, whether in relation to themselves or another person.[58]

Section 26 of the Criminal Justice and Public Order Act 1994 added a further exception by inserting paragraph 2A, stating that the defendant need not be granted bail if:

- the offence is an indictable offence or an offence triable either way; and
- it appears to the court that he was on bail in criminal proceedings on the date of the offence.

---

[55] Home Office, *Prison Statistics England and Wales 2000*, Cmnd 5250 (2001) 40.
[56] Bail Act 1976, s. 4.
[57] Different exceptions apply for imprisonable and non-imprisonable offences.
[58] Bail Act 1976, Sch. 1, Part 1, para. 2.

Other exceptions to the right to bail are also given in the Act. The most important are that bail may be refused for the defendant's own protection or there is insufficient information available to make a decision.[59]

The Act also sets out a number of factors which courts should consider when deciding whether or not any exceptions apply.[60] These *reasons* include: the nature and seriousness of the offence; the probable method of disposal; previous bail and offending history; the strength of the evidence against the defendant; and the character, associations, and community ties of the defendant.[61] So, in making a decision to revoke the right to unconditional bail, a court must have *reasons*, such as the seriousness of the offence, which lead it to believe that at least one of the *grounds* or *exceptions* for the removal of the right to unconditional bail exists, such as that the defendant may commit further offences. There is some confusion over the relationship between *exceptions* or *grounds* and *reasons* for the refusal of bail. Magistrates and other bail decision-makers often cite *reasons* as exceptions to the right to bail.[62] Research highlights, for example, the use of the nature and seriousness of the offence as a *ground* for the removal of the right to bail rather than a *reason* which may result in a ground being found to exist. The problem is further illustrated by a Home Office Research Study which presents *grounds* as *reasons* and *reasons* as *grounds* for the refusal of bail.[63] This was highlighted by a recent Law Commission report as an area where the current bail procedure may breach the Human Rights Act 1998.[64]

The law on bail provides only a basic framework for criminal justice decision-makers to work with. As a result, they have considerable discretion when making their decisions, and it is difficult for defendants to challenge decisions because it is unclear how they were arrived at. For example, the phrases *substantial grounds for believing* or *necessary* can have broad and/or different interpretations. One of the consequences of this is that considerable variations and inconsistencies occur in bail decision-making, both between and within courts. Research has found variations in custody rates and conditional bail rates between courts which cannot be explained by differences in the types of cases dealt with.[65] There is also some evidence of discrimination. Research suggests that black defendants are more likely to be remanded in custody.[66]

The bail/custody decision is a difficult one, as it necessitates the weighing-up of competing rights. On the one hand, defendants; have the right to bail while on the other the public has the right to be protected from serious harm. This weighing-up of

[59] Bail Act 1976, Sch. 1, Part 1, paras. 3–7.

[60] Exceptions to bail are often referred to as grounds for the refusal of bail although this is not legally defined.

[61] Bail Act 1976, Sch. 1, Part 1, para. 9.

[62] A. Hucklesby, *Bail or Jail? The Magistrates' Decision* (unpublished: 1994).

[63] J. Airs, R Elliott, and E. Conrad, *Electronically Monitored Curfew as a Condition of Bail—Report of a Pilot* (London: Home Office, 2000) 11.

[64] Law Commission, *Bail and Human Rights* (London: TSO, 1999) 43.

[65] P. Jones, 'Remand Decisions in Magistrates' Court', in D. Moxon (ed.), *Managing Criminal Justice* (London: HMSO, 1985); A. Hucklesby, 'Court Culture: An Explanation of Variations in the Use of Bail in Magistrates' Courts' (1997) 36 *Howard Journal* 129; Morgan and Henderson, n. 31 above.

[66] I. Brown and R. Hullin, 'Contested Bail Applications: The Treatment of Ethnic Minority and White Offenders' [1993] *Crim. LR* 107.

rights is made more difficult when the decision-makers are predicting future behaviour. This is usually done on the basis of past behaviour. It is well documented that such predictions are flawed and are likely to be 'more wrong than right', resulting in a large number of erroneous decisions.[67] Such decisions may result in a self-perpetuating cycle of increases in the number of defendants remanded in custody as the only errors which come to light are those where defendants are released on bail only to commit further offences or abscond.[68] In short, remand decisions always include an element of guesswork on the part of the courts.

The usual way of assessing bail risk is to consider the offending and bail history of the defendant, the nature and seriousness of the offence, and community ties.[69] These factors have been shown to influence bail decisions.[70] The research has also shown the dominant importance of offending-related factors in the bail decisions.[71] One explanation for this may be that this information is perceived as factual and unchallengeable by the majority of decision-makers.[72] This may arise partly from its source, which is most likely to be the CPS which is assumed to play an independent and neutral role in the process, whereas defence solicitors are seen as working in the interest of their clients.[73] As a result, any information provided by defence solicitors is more likely to be seen by magistrates as subjective and a particular interpretation of events, and, therefore, not as reliable as information from the prosecution.[74]

Despite the difficulties posed to decision-makers, the majority of bail decisions are taken in a few minutes.[75] Many are taken on very limited information where relevant information is either missing or incomplete. This is especially true with cases where defendants have been detained in police custody overnight.[76] It is difficult to see in such cases how a considered and informed remand decision can be always made.

The grounds for the decision by a court to withhold unconditional bail must be stated in open court and formally recorded.[77] In most instances, decisions are recorded on pre-printed bail forms.[78] The record of grounds means, in theory at least, that courts sitting later on in the proceedings or an appeal court have access to the rationale for bail decisions and that defendants know why they have been refused unconditional bail. Research evidence suggests that reasons are not always stated in open court.[79] This is most likely to occur when defendants are granted bail with conditions. Even when reasons are recorded, most courts simply require a court clerk to tick boxes indicating which of the exceptions to bail have been found to exist.[80] In

---

[67] N. Walker (ed.), *Dangerous People* (London: Blackstone, 1996).

[68] Von Hirsch *et al.*, *Criminal Deterrence and Sentencing Severity: An Analysis of Recent Research* (Oxford: Hart, 1999).

[69] These include whether or not the defendant is in employment, has a stable address, has a stable relationship, family, and children.

[70] Burrows, Henderson, and Morgan, n. 24 above; Hucklesby, n. 29 above; Airs *et al.*, n. 63 above.

[71] Hucklesby, n. 29 above; Hucklesby and Marshall, n. 30 above.

[72] Hucklesby, n. 29 above.   [73] Hucklesby, n. 28 above.   [74] *Ibid.*

[75] R. East and M. Doherty, 'The Practical Operation of Bail' (1985) *Legal Action* 12.

[76] Burrows, Henderson, and Morgan, n. 24 above; Hucklesby, n. 29 above; Hucklesby and Marshall, n. 30 above.

[77] Bail Act 1976, s. 5(3) and (4).   [78] Law Commission, n. 64 above; Airs *et al.*, n. 63 above.

[79] Hucklesby, n. 29 above.   [80] Law Commission, n. 64 above, at para. 4.20.

these circumstances, it is not unsurprising to find that in the majority of cases all three boxes representing the three main exceptions to bail are ticked routinely.[81] There is also evidence that magistrates habitually use the main exceptions to bail in most cases, rather than tailor their reasoning to the particular circumstances of the case.[82]

The use of a formalized form of words such as is found on bail forms was highlighted by the Law Commission as a possible breach of the Human Rights Act 1998. It believed that such an approach might be challenged and upheld as being 'abstract' or stereotyped, thus indicating faulty reasoning.[83] The report also pointed out that the reasoning must be *continuously* sustained, which suggests that simply reiterating reasons in subsequent remand hearings does not satisfy human rights legislation.[84]

THE COURT BAIL PROCESS

In common with other aspects of our court process, the bail process is an adversarial process. In theory, the prosecution and the defence make their representations to the court, and the magistrates or the judge make an independent decision on the basis of that information. In the majority of cases, however, the reality is far from this image. The majority of bail decisions are uncontested because the prosecution and defence agree on the decision to be taken.

In most cases, the CPS does not oppose bail. In these circumstances, the courts almost always grant defendants bail.[85] In such cases, also, the court agrees with the CPS's assessment of whether or not conditions are appropriate and, if so, what specific conditions are to be imposed. This occurs even when defendants appear in court from police custody. Defence solicitors do not tend to question the use of conditions as they are aware that this may result in defendants being remanded in custody.[86]

The cases where the CPS opposes bail can be split into two—those where the defence applies for bail and those where it does not. The terminology here is interesting. Despite the law requiring that there be a presumption of bail, as soon as the CPS opposes bail, a *bail application* has to be made. It is almost as if the presumption of bail is reversed in such circumstances. Unsurprisingly, where the defence does not oppose bail, defendants are normally remanded in custody.[87] In cases where a bail application is made, the majority of defendants are still remanded in custody.[88] In some respects this is to be expected, as the information available to the court would be similar to that on which the CPS decided to oppose bail. However, the issue is more complex than this explanation suggests.

---

[81] Hucklesby, n. 29 above.   [82] Hucklesby, n. 62 above.

[83] Law Commission, n. 64 above, at paras. 4.10, 4.20.   [84] *Ibid.* at para. 4.14.

[85] Burrows, Henderson, and Morgan, n. 24 above; Hucklesby, n. 28 above.

[86] A. Hucklesby, 'The Use and Abuse of Bail Conditions' (1994) 33 *Howard Journal* 258.

[87] Hucklesby, nn. 28 and 29 above; Morgan and Henderson, n. 31 above.

[88] Hucklesby, nn. 28 and 29 above; Morgan and Henderson, n. 31 above.

What the above evidence indicates is the dominance of the prosecution assessment of the bail risk the defendant poses. Research has found that the courts follow the CPS recommendation with regard to bail in the majority of cases.[89] But this raises the question of how the CPS makes its assessment. The information available to the CPS comes almost exclusively from police files. The information in these files, especially for those detained in police custody, is limited and often assessed by the CPS as inadequate.[90] The information is inevitably going to be the police view of the case, and evidence to support this view is likely to be incomplete at this stage, with little, if any, forensic evidence and few witnesses statements. Detailed information about previous offending and bail history is often incomplete.[91] The lack of information available, coupled with the source of this information, raises issues about how well-informed the CPS assessment of bail risk is, as well as the influence the police have on CPS decisions.

The research evidence which suggests that the prosecution view is dominant in bail/custody decisions makes it difficult to come to any conclusion other than that in the majority of cases the magistrates simply rubber stamp decisions made earlier in the process. But this explanation is too simple. Research evidence suggests that magistrates have an important influence on how the court operates and the expectations and working practices of practitioners.[92] Observations of the remand process and interviews with practitioners have suggested that both the prosecution and defence tailor their decisions and the way in which they present their cases to the magistrates before whom they are appearing.[93] The contrast is starkest between district judges and lay magistrates, but it also occurs between lay benches.[94] Decisions and behaviour seem to be tailored around assessments of how harsh or lenient the magistrates are assessed to be, but also what the practitioners believe they can get away with. For example, members of the CPS stated that they were more likely to recommend that defendants were remanded in custody when they appeared before district judges, and defence solicitors stated that they kept their bail applications shorter and more to the point when appearing before district judges.[95]

These differing practices of members of the CPS and defence solicitors in front of different benches of magistrates were explained by them in terms of their reputations and credibility within the courtroom workgroup.[96] This is illustrated most obviously by defence solicitors who explained that they used particular forms of words, such as 'I'm instructed to . . .', in bail applications where they were required to make the application by their client but did not believe that the defendant should be released on bail. This signalled to the court that they realized that their application should be turned down.[97] Similar conclusions were drawn by McConville *et al.* in their study of defence solicitors.[98]

---

[89] Hucklesby, nn. 28 and n. 29 above.

[90] Burrows, Henderson, and Morgan, n. 24 above; Hucklesby and Marshall, n. 30 above.

[91] Burrows, Henderson, and Morgan, n. 24 above; Hucklesby and Marshall, n. 30 above.

[92] A. Hucklesby, 'Court Culture: An Explanation of Variations in the Use of Bail by Magistrates' Courts' (1997) 36 *Howard Journal* 129.

[93] *Ibid.* [94] District judges were formerly known as stipendiary magistrates.

[95] Hucklesby, n. 92 above. [96] *Ibid.*

[97] *Ibid.* [98] McConville, Hodgson, Bridges, and Pavlovic, n. 4 above.

Several important changes have recently been introduced in relation to who makes remand decisions. One of the principal concerns of the measures introduced by the Crime and Disorder Act 1998 was to reduce delay in the criminal justice process. In order to do this, it provided that bail could be granted but not denied by a single magistrate. Conditions can be imposed and varied as well. It was argued by the Narey Report that benches of three magistrates are not conducive to decisive action.[99] However, benches of magistrates provide an important mechanism to offset differences in philosophy. The same Act enables court clerks, the legal advisors of magistrates, to impose and vary conditions of bail as long as the prosecutor and defendant consent. It also enables bail proceedings to be conducted by lay prosecutors. All of these measures can be criticized singly but it is as a package that they raise the most fundamental issue. Bail decisions are arguably downplayed and trivialized by these measures and are not seen as central, important decisions in the criminal justice process. They are perceived to be so unimportant that they require only lay prosecutors, one lay magistrate, or a clerk to deal with them. Yet, they restrict the liberty of unconvicted and therefore presumptively innocent people.

CONDITIONAL BAIL

Conditional bail was introduced in an attempt to reduce the number of defendants remanded in custody. It was originally set up to provide an alternative to a custodial remand, whereby the conditions attached to bail directly were intended to counteract the exceptions to the grant of bail which the court believed existed. Conditional bail aimed to strengthen the control over defendants on bail, therefore increasing the credibility of bail in the eyes of the decision-makers.

The court can impose any conditions it believes are *necessary* in order to invalidate exceptions to bail it believes exist, as well as to make defendants available for inquiries or reports.[100] The most commonly used conditions include, *inter alia*, conditions as regards residence, curfew, reporting to the police station, and keeping away from prosecution witnesses.[101] Several new conditions of bail are likely to be made available to courts shortly, including electronic monitoring and drug testing.[102] If conditions are breached defendants are brought back to the court, which then reconsiders the bail decision. Courts are regularly criticized for re-bailing defendants after breaches of conditions.[103] However, there are potentially many reasons why this may occur, including the relative triviality of the breach, good reasons being presented about why the breach occurred, limited evidence about the breach, or the fact that the original alleged offence does not warrant a remand in custody.

---

[99] Home Office, *A Review of Delay in the Criminal Justice System* (London: Home Office, 1997) 25.

[100] Bail Act 1976, s. 6.

[101] Hucklesby, n. 86 above; J. Raine and M. Willson, 'The Imposition of Conditions in Bail Decisions' (1996) 35 *Howard Journal* 256.

[102] See Airs *et al.*, n. 63 above; Criminal Justice and Court Services Act 2000.

[103] Hucklesby, n. 86 above.

Since its introduction in the Criminal Justice Act 1967, the use of conditional bail has increased significantly. No statistical information is collected nationally on the use of conditions, so research studies are the only source of such information. Studies in the 1980s and early 1990s suggested that between a quarter and a third of defendants were granted bail with conditions.[104] Some more recent studies have suggested that this proportion may have risen to just over 50 per cent, so that the use of bail with conditions rather than unconditional bail has become the norm.[105] One reason for this may be the introduction of police conditional bail. While this increase may mean that conditional bail is successfully diverting defendants from custody, it may also mean that a process of net-widening is occurring, whereby defendants are subject to conditions when they could be safely granted unconditional bail.

Critical comment on the use of conditions of bail is rare.[106] This is because it provides an alternative to remands in custody. However, it is an important issue for a number of reasons. Conditional bail restricts the liberty of defendants who are legally innocent. Defendants can be subject to the conditions imposed for considerable lengths of time. Conditions, whether singly or as a package, can be unjustly restrictive and would not be imposed as part of a sentence on conviction.[107] Packages of conditions may be overly restrictive, making defendants' lives impossible. The more conditions imposed, the more restricted defendants are, and arguably the more likely they are to breach their bail.

Several concerns with the use of conditions have been highlighted. First, that the conditions imposed have very little relevance to the exceptions to bail in individual cases,[108] for example, a night-time curfew attached to the bail of a defendant who is known to commit all her offences of shoplifting in daylight hours. This problem is worsened by defence solicitors who propose packages of conditions in an attempt to persuade magistrates to release defendants on bail. If bail is then granted, magistrates impose all the proposed conditions without checking their relevance to the exceptions.[109] In these circumstances, the specific conditions are unlikely to be challenged because of the relief that defendants have avoided being remanded in custody and from fear of being so remanded. Secondly, conditions do not necessarily prevent absconding, offending, or witness intimidation.[110] For example, a curfew may simply result in defendants changing their hours of operation. Other conditions, such as reporting to the police station, simply seem to miss the point entirely, as defendants can abscond immediately after reporting and have several days to abscond before their next reporting session. Finally, many of the conditions cannot be enforced effectively.[111] This partly reflects the lack of resources of the police and the low priority which checking compliance with conditions necessarily has. However, just as important is that some conditions, such as a requirement to keep out of the city centre, are

---

[104] M. Doherty and R. East, 'Bail Decisions in Magistrates' Courts' (1984) 25 *British Journal of Criminology* 251; Hucklesby, n. 86 above; Morgan and Henderson, n. 31 above.

[105] Airs *et al.*, n. 63 above.

[106] For exceptions see B. Block, 'Bail Conditions: Neither Logical or Lawful' [1990] *Justice of the Peace* 83 and Hucklesby, n. 86 above.

[107] *Ibid.*   [108] *Ibid.*   [109] *Ibid.*   [110] Block, n. 106 above; Hucklesby, n. 85 above.

[111] *Ibid.*

practically impossible to enforce. Enforcement is an important part of the deterrence value of conditions. If defendants perceive that the likelihood of getting caught is negligible then they are less likely to abide by the conditions imposed.

Unsurprisingly, the longer defendants are on bail the more likely they are to breach conditions.[112] There is no evidence available to indicate why this occurs. Defendants may simply forget what conditions they are required to observe, or they may realize that conditions are not enforced as no checks have been conducted. Breaches may be made all the more likely by the practice of not restating every single condition attached to bail on each court appearance, but simply stating that defendants are subject to the same conditions as previously imposed.[113] This is a further practice, highlighted by the Law Commission's review of bail law, which may be in a breach of human rights legislation.[114]

Delays in the criminal justice process have arguably made breaches more likely, although there are no statistics on the length of time that defendants spend on bail awaiting trial. However, requiring legally innocent people to abide by restrictive conditions over a period of months raises civil liberties issues. One way of limiting these problems would be to introduce time limits for defendants on bail. The result of this would be that if cases were not completed within a specific time the case would be discontinued. Despite concerns over the operation of custody time limits, there is some evidence that such restrictions influence the minds of practitioners and reduce delays in some cases.[115]

Recent legal changes have increased the importance of the financial circumstances of defendants in relation to bail. The Crime and Disorder Act 1998 provided for the extension of court powers to require securities before releasing defendants on bail. Securities involve the defendants or their representatives being required to deposit a sum of money with the court before the defendants can be released in order to ensure their attendance at court.[116] Where the defendants fail to turn up for a court appearance the money is forfeited unless there is reasonable cause. The provision was enacted as a result of a perceived increase in the number of defendants who failed to appear at bail hearings. Despite this, official figures show that around 12 per cent of defendants do not answer bail.[117] This figure has remained relatively constant over time.

The effect of this provision is to bring in a form of money bail for all. Prior to the Bail Act 1976 requirements for sureties[118] and securities were regularly imposed by courts but the reliance on money bail was heavily criticized for being unjust and resulting in unnecessary remands in custody.[119] Common practice included setting securities and sureties so high that defendants could not possibly raise the sums involved, thus facilitating remands in custody by the 'back door'. Further, in the case

---

[112] Morgan and Henderson, n. 31 above.   [113] Hucklesby, n. 86 above.

[114] Law Commission, n. 64 above.   [115] Hucklesby, n. 86 above.

[116] N. Corre and D. Wolchover, *Bail in Criminal Proceedings* (London: Blackstone, 1999).

[117] Home Office, n. 9 above at 195.

[118] These differ from securities in that they require payment of the specified sum if and when defendants abscond, not before they are released on bail.

[119] Bottomley, n. 3 above; King, n. 3 above.

of securities, defendants must have the cash to deposit with the court. It is not enough that the money is, for example, in a building society account. Defendants or someone they know must have the cash or equivalent available immediately. There are, also, no limits on the amount of time the security may be kept or on the amount set.

Requiring the lodging of money with a court prior to release on bail is not a new idea. It was discussed and rejected by the 1974 Working Party on bail procedures.[120] The subsequent report acknowledged the additional leverage which securities could provide but also pointed out important disadvantages. First, it discriminates against the less well-off and less well-connected defendants. Secondly, it links the grant of bail to the possession of money, therefore giving the impression that getting bail is reliant on the financial resources of defendants. Thirdly, there could be problems limiting the use of the power to those cases where it was appropriate. Fourthly, there might be difficulties with fixing the amount of money required in order to balance the need to ensure the defendants' appearance and their means. Finally, it recognized the problem of raising money in a short time period and the consequent danger that defendants could be kept in custody simply because they could not raise the money required.

Another noteworthy initiative is the use of electronic tagging to monitor compliance with bail conditions, in particular curfews.[121] The intention is that this should provide an alternative to remands in custody. The first set of trials was abandoned in the late 1980s because of poor take-up by the courts, high failure rates, and problems with the equipment.[122] A second pilot was undertaken in the late 1990s, which raised similar issues to the previous trials. Take-up by magistrates was low, partly because magistrates did not use the option but also because many defendants did not fulfil the residence requirement or were not deemed trustworthy.[123] In all, 198 curfews were made on 173 defendants. The failure rate was high, with two-thirds of defendants violating their curfews, but only around half of these had action for breach of the condition taken against them.[124] The study also highlights other problems with the scheme. Inconsistencies were found in the application and use of the curfew with electronic monitoring and in procedures in case of breach and their outcomes. The police were concerned about reoffending and the fact that they have no right of access to a defendant's home to monitor compliance. Some evidence of aggression and increased tension within the family was noted, as was the important role of women in ensuring compliance. Technical difficulties again affected the trials.[125] The trials found evidence of possible net-widening as curfews were used both as an alternative to custody and as an additional bail condition. This contributed to the conclusion that the costs of bail curfews were greater than the savings produced by subsequent reductions in the prison population.[126]

This section has suggested that the use of conditional bail has increased since it was introduced in the late 1960s, so that it is now the most frequent bail outcome. While conditional bail has probably reduced the use of custodial remands, it has also been

---

[120] Home Office, n. 45 above.   [121] Airs *et al.*, n. 63 above.
[122] G. Mair and C. Nee, *Electronic Monitoring: The Trials and Their Results* (London: Home Office, 1990).
[123] Airs *et al.*, n. 63 above.   [124] *Ibid.*
[125] *Ibid.*   [126] *Ibid.*

used for defendants who would otherwise have been released on unconditional bail. The range of new conditions available to courts and increasing frequency of use also raise important issues about civil liberties, enforcement, and the feasibility of attaching ever more restrictive conditions to the lives of defendants who are still legally innocent.

RESTRICTING THE USE OF BAIL

During the 1970s and 1980s the emphasis of policy was on reducing custodial remands. Measures such as the introduction of the duty solicitor scheme and the extension of legal aid provision indirectly contributed to achieving this goal. Other initiatives were introduced specifically to further this aim. The first of these were special bail hostels, which were set up to provide an alternative to a remand in custody. Defendants can be required to reside at hostels as a condition of bail. Hostels provide not only an address for defendants but structured activities and a set of rules. A recent HM Inspector of Probation inspection report concluded that 'hostels . . . demonstrated their ability to accommodate and work successfully with some of the most difficult, damaged and potentially dangerous defendants . . . in a manner which gave due regard to public safety'.[127] Yet, bail hostels may facilitate 'net-widening', as many of those sent there have not been remanded in custody.[128] This may occur partly because high-risk offenders, including those accused of serious offences and those with drug and/or alcohol problems, are often excluded.[129] There are, also, inconsistencies in the provision of hostel places across the country and a lack of provision for women.

The second initiative was Bail Information Schemes. These schemes eventually covered most of the country. They are run by the probation service and provide verified information to the CPS, particularly about defendants' community ties. The original rationale for their creation was to provide information which countered police recommendations to remand defendants in custody, in an attempt to persuade the CPS to recommend that bail could be granted safely. In recent years schemes have been required to provide negative as well as positive information about defendants in order to enhance public safety. Research has suggested that bail information schemes were successful in reducing the number of cases where the CPS recommended remands in custody.[130] However, the ring-fenced budgets for such schemes were removed in the early 1990s, which resulted in a gradual running down of many of the

[127] HM Inspector of Probation, *Delivering an Enhanced Level of Community Supervision, Report of a Thematic Inspection on the Work of Approved Probation and Bail Hostels* (London: Home Office, 1998).

[128] H. Lewis and G. Mair, *Bail and Probation Work II: The Use of London Probation/Bail Hostels for Bailees*, Research and Planning Unit Paper No. 50 (London: Home Office, 1988).

[129] Hucklesby, n. 62 above; Corre and Wolchover, n. 115 above.

[130] C. Lloyd, *Bail Information Schemes: Practice and Effect*, Research and Planning Unit Paper No. 69 (London: Home Office, 1992); D. Godson and C. Mitchell, *Bail Information Schemes in English Magistrates' Courts: A Review of the Data* (London: Inner London Probation Service, 1991).

schemes throughout the 1990s. More recently, the importance of bail information schemes has been recognized, and further resources are now being made available.

While these initiatives continued to exist, by the late 1980s important changes were being made to the law on bail, restricting the right to bail for those accused of committing serious offences. This followed a number of cases in which defendants released on bail by the courts allegedly committed further serious offences whilst awaiting trial. The Criminal Justice Act 1988 provided that reasons had to be given by courts when they released on bail defendants who had been charged with certain serious offences, namely murder, rape, and manslaughter.[131] In practice, this meant that the right to bail was reversed for certain categories of defendants. This clearly overturns the presumption of bail, as courts had to justify why such defendants were being released. After several further cases in which defendants on bail were alleged to have committed further serious offences, the Criminal Justice and Public Order Act 1994 completely overturned the right to bail by providing that defendants charged with certain serious offences who had been convicted of other serious offences in the past could not be granted bail.[132] In short, for the first time since the enactment of the Bail Act 1976, the grant of bail was prohibited for certain categories of defendants. The Act was passed as a result of a number of cases in which defendants had been released on bail only allegedly to commit another serious offence whilst on bail.[133] It was argued that this section was unnecessary, as the courts were unlikely to grant bail in these circumstances.[134] The section was also challenged under the European Convention on Human Rights but was repealed by the Crime and Disorder Act before a ruling was made.[135] Although these provisions had little practical effect, as it is unlikely that courts would release such defendants in any event, they signalled an important transformation in remand policy away from attempts to reduce the number of defendants remanded in custody.

In the early 1990s the emphasis shifted again towards restricting the use of bail for defendants who, it was alleged, persistently offended on bail. During the early 1990s, a moral panic occurred in relation to offenders, particularly young offenders, being out of control and committing large amounts of crime.[136] Newspapers regularly carried headlines about young offenders on 'crime sprees' and concern about 'joy-riding' was at its height. One group of offenders highlighted as a particular problem were the 'Bail Bandits'—defendants who allegedly committed large numbers of offences whilst on bail, contributing to a large proportion of the crime problem.[137] The official response to the problem was perceived to be inadequate. The criminal justice process was

---

[131] Criminal Justice Act 1988, s. 153.

[132] Criminal Justice and Public Order Act, s. 25.

[133] The best known is that of Winston Silcott who was on bail for murder when he was alleged to have committed a second.

[134] Hucklesby, n. 28 above.

[135] Art. 5(3) of the European Convention for the Protection of Human Rights and Fundamental Freedoms (1950), which requires that a person charged with an offence must be released pending trial unless the State can show that there are relevant and sufficient reasons to justify continued detention.

[136] M. Hinchcliffe, 'Beating the Bail Bandits' (1992) 25 *Law Society Gazette* 19; B. Goldson, *Youth Justice: Contemporary Policy and Practice* (Aldershot: Ashgate, 1999).

[137] Hucklesby and Marshall, n. 30 above.

portrayed as powerless to tackle this problem, as there was no power to remand such offenders in custody, primarily because they were juveniles.

Contemporaneously, police forces published two research studies which high-lighted the problem of offending on bail.[138] As a result of this, ACPO lobbied the government for a change in the law. Instead, the government asked the Home Office to review the relevant research. The subsequent report argued that the two police studies had overestimated the problem due to the way in which they measured offend-ing on bail.[139] Difficulties in measuring the extent of the problem and actually defin-ing offending on bail continue as different measures are used by different studies and agencies and include those arrested, charged, as well as those convicted of offences allegedly committed on bail.[140] The Home Office report estimated that between 10 and 17 per cent of defendants offended on bail, which meant that the vast majority did not. More recent research studies have confirmed that around 17 per cent of offenders are convicted of committing offences while on court bail, with the figure rising to 21 per cent for defendants charged with an offence committed while on bail.[141]

The considered position of the Home Office review was overtaken by events, how-ever. A Private Member's Bill[142] was introduced in Parliament which aimed to tackle the problem. It consisted of two clauses. One proposed that the presumption in favour of bail should be overturned if a defendant had been convicted of committing an offence on bail in certain circumstances. The second proposed that the CPS should be given the right to appeal against magistrates' decisions to grant bail in the face of CPS objections. While such an appeal was being processed, defendants would be remanded in custody. The first of these clauses was dropped in return for government support, which resulted in the remaining clause becoming law.[143] In practice, the CPS's right to appeal is not often used. This is not surprising in light of the fact that in the vast majority of cases the magistrates agree with the CPS assessment of bail risk.[144] How-ever, its existence means that the CPS has increased its potential influence over the decision-making process.

Meanwhile, ACPO continued to call for offending on bail to be made a criminal offence.[145] The government decided, after taking advice, that this was probably unlaw-ful and certainly unworkable. Instead, legislation made the fact that an offence had been committed on bail an aggravating factor for sentencing purposes.[146] This still did not satisfy demands for the problem of offending on bail to be tackled. As a con-sequence, the Criminal Justice and Public Order Act 1994 included a number of measures to deal with the problem. This included the introduction of a further excep-tion to bail, so that bail can now be refused if the court believes that the offence was

---

[138] Northumbria Police, *Bail and Multiple Offending* (Newcastle: Northumbria Police, 1991); Avon and Somerset Constabulary, *The Effect of Re-Offending on Bail on Crime in Avon and Somerset* (Bristol: Avon and Somerset Constabulary, 1991).

[139] P. Morgan, *Offending on Bail: A Survey of Recent Research*, Research and Plannning Unit Paper 65 (London: Home Office, 1994); Hucklesby and Marshall, n. 30 above.

[140] Hucklesby and Marshall, n. 30 above.   [141] Morgan and Henderson, n. 31 above.

[142] Bail (Amendment) Bill 1992.   [143] Bail (Amendment) Act 1993.

[144] Hucklesby, n. 28 above; Morgan and Henderson, n. 31 above.

[145] A. Hucklesby, 'The Problem with Bail Bandits' (1992) 142 *New Law Journal* 558.

[146] Criminal Justice Act 1993, s. 66(6).

committed on bail, provided that the offence in question is an offence which is indictable or triable either way.[147]

At the time of its introduction, it was argued that this provision was unnecessary, as the existing law enabled magistrates to remand in custody defendants who had allegedly committed offences on bail.[148] They could do this by using the exception of the risk of further offences being committed which could be substantiated with the reason that the court believed that the offence was committed on bail. Risk of further offending was already the most frequently used exception to bail.[149] Research into the effect of this new exception to bail has supported this early concern, and has shown that its impact has been limited on the number remanded in custody, and that it is not used by courts to any great extent.[150] This study, however, highlighted an increase in the use of conditional bail for such defendants. This could be explained, however, by the introduction of police conditional bail at the same time.[151]

CONCLUSIONS

This chapter has shown that while, in theory, all defendants have a right to unconditional bail, in practice an increasing number are denied that right. While it is accepted the risks involved in releasing some defendants on bail are too great, there is evidence that some defendants are unnecessarily remanded in custody. In addition, increasing numbers of defendants have their liberty restricted in the community through the imposition of conditions. The courts are also being given a greater range of conditions of bail which they may impose. Critically, these moves are not an attempt to reduce the prison population, but rather further to restrict the liberty of defendants while awaiting trial in the community. While being remanded on conditional bail does not have the same acute consequences for defendants as being remanded in custody, it raises issues about whether the restrictions on their liberty are necessary, and also whether or not it is realistic to expect defendants to abide by the conditions imposed.

The way in which the remand procedure operates makes it difficult to conclude that informed, considered decisions are made. A large proportion of decisions are uncontested. Many hearings last for only a few minutes and the information available to decision-makers is often limited. This has the effect of accentuating the roles played by the police and the prosecution in the decision-making, as the courts rely heavily on their version of events and often agree with their recommendations. Defence solicitors acquiesce in the view of the prosecution or negotiate a position with it prior to the court hearing. One result of this is hearings in which the professionals and the

---

[147] Criminal Justice and Public Order Act 1994, s. 26.
[148] Hucklesby, n. 29 above; Hucklesby and Marshall, n. 30 above.
[149] Hucklesby, n. 29 above.
[150] Morgan and Henderson, n. 31 above; Hucklesby and Marshall, n. 30 above.
[151] Criminal Justice and Public Order Act 1994, s. 27.

magistrates invariably agree with the proposed decision, and where there is little need for justification in terms of information or reasoning presented in open court. While this may reduce delays, it fails to live up to the principle of justice being seen to be done.

As remand decisions attempt to weigh up probabilities of what defendants may do in the future it is impossible for each and every decision to be correct. However, accurate decisions are more likely to be taken if the court receives all the necessary information and takes a considered approach to its decision-making. This would improve the legitimacy as well as the accuracy of the decisions taken.

It seems clear that in the current climate remand policy will continue to focus on restricting the use of bail, by either remanding more defendants in custody or restricting their liberty whilst in the community by increasing the number of defendants subject to conditional bail and/or strengthening the conditions imposed. It is inevitable that offending on bail will continue to be the catalyst for change. This is exemplified by the perennial headlines and political comment about 'Bail Bandits' which, at the time of writing, have again hit the headlines, particularly in relation to juveniles. The present government has signalled its intention to facilitate greater use of custody for these defendants. In such a climate it is unsurprising that magistrates are making greater use of remands in custody and conditions of bail in an attempt to ward off criticism of their decision-making.

Further Reading

CAVADINO, P., and GIBSON, B., *Bail: The Law, Best Practice and the Debate* (Winchester: Waterside Press, 1993).

CORRE, N., and WOLCHOVER, D., *Bail in Criminal Proceedings* (London: Blackstone, 1999).

HUCKLESBY, A., 'The Use and Abuse of Bail Conditions' (1994) 33 *Howard Journal* 258.

—— 'Bail or Jail? The Practical Operation of the Bail Act 1976' (1996) 23 *Journal of Law and Society* 213.

—— 'Court Culture: An Explanation of Variations in the Use of Bail in Magistrates' Courts' (1997) 36 *Howard Journal* 129.

—— 'Remand Decision Makers' [1997] *Crim. LR* 269.

—— and MARSHALL, E., 'Tackling Offending on Bail' (2000) 39 *Howard Journal* 150.

MORGAN, P., and HENDERSON, P., *Remand Decisions and Offending on Bail: Evaluation of the Bail Process Project*, Home Office Research Study No. 184 (London: Home Office, 1998).

MORGAN, R., and JONES, S., 'Bail or Jail' in E. Stockdale and S. Casale (eds.), *Criminal Justice Under Stress* (London: Blackstone, 1992) 39.

RAINE, J., and WILLSON, M., 'The Imposition of Conditions in Bail Decisions' (1996) 35 *Howard Journal* 256.

8

THE RIGHT TO REPRESENTATION AND LEGAL AID

Lee Bridges

The principle of equality of arms between the prosecution and defence is one of the cornerstones of the adversarial system of criminal justice, and the rights to legal representation and to legal aid may be regarded as essential to guarantee such equality. Today Britain—or to be more precise, England and Wales—can be said to have one of the most comprehensive systems of criminal legal representation and legal aid in the world. This system covers a range of state-funded services to those suspected or accused of crime, from advice and representation for those held for questioning by the police, through to representation at the various levels of court at which those accused of crime are tried, to assistance in preparing appeals against criminal convictions and challenges to miscarriages of justice.

Yet, this system of legal representation and legal aid for criminal suspects and defendants is of relatively recent historical origin, with the main developments in this field taking place since the 1960s. Indeed, it is interesting to note that prior to this the costs of providing legal representation for those accused of the most serious and notorious crimes was often borne not by the State but rather by the proprietors of national newspapers, whose sales would be increased by sensational revelations arising during criminal trials. Ironically, such media interventions in criminal justice, whether in the form of pre-trial publicity or payments to potential witnesses for their stories, is now regarded as undermining the integrity of the process,[1] whereas in an earlier era it served to provide at least some minimal protection for the rights of the accused.

Nor can it be said, even today, that the rights to legal representation and legal aid are fully guaranteed, even if in practice they have increasingly been recognized in decisions relating to individual cases. Consideration of this subject raises a number of subsidiary issues and questions. At what stage in the criminal justice process are the rights to representation and legal aid to become effective? Do they apply only to the criminal trial itself or to earlier parts of the process, such as preliminary court

---

[1] See, e.g., Lord Chancellor's Advisory Committee on Legal Education and Conduct, *Lawyers' Comments to the Media* (London: Lord Chancellor's Department, 1997).

hearings dealing with such matters as bail for the accused or to judicial or police questioning of suspects prior to formal charges being laid? Is it only those who are suspected or accused of the most serious offences, or those most at risk of losing their liberty if convicted, who should be afforded these rights, or should they be available to a much wider group of defendants? Should the rights to legal representation and legal aid be limited to those who wish to challenge the charges against them or also extend to those who intend or are likely to plead guilty? What are the criteria by which such decisions about the availability of criminal legal aid are to be made, and who is best placed to make such decisions? Does the right to representation also imply a right of the accused to choose his or her own lawyer, and, if so, does this right extend to those who must rely on the State to pay for such services through legal aid? And what is the best system for providing representation in criminal cases—through charitable or 'pro bono' services by private lawyers or state subsidies to them, by the State directly employing defence lawyers, or by some combination of these methods? Should such services be provided only by lawyers, or is there a role for lay or paralegal advisers.

While legal representation and legal aid may be essential to protecting the interests of those accused of criminal offences and to underpinning the integrity of adversarial criminal justice, they may also serve other functions. Recently in Britain there has been considerable debate over the suggestion that those accused of certain offences should be compelled to be represented in court by lawyers, rather than acting in their own defence, in order to protect others involved in the process. For example, it has been argued that to allow a man accused of rape personally to cross-examine his accuser in court is to violate the victim's rights, in effect subjecting her to a further and more public personal assault by him, and that such defendants should be required to be represented by lawyers. Similar considerations may apply to trials involving child witnesses. The provision of legal representation and legal aid to defendants may also help to promote the smooth-running of the courts in various ways. Indeed, many of the advances in state funding for criminal defence services in Britain over recent years have been linked to administrative reforms of the courts and other criminal justice agencies designed, for example, to speed up or streamline the process.

THE HISTORICAL GROWTH OF CRIMINAL LEGAL AID[2]

Historically the rights of the accused in Britain to legal representation have been restricted in various ways. Although defendants in misdemeanour cases have long had a right to representation (if not necessarily the means to pay for it), it was not until 1836 in the Trials for Felony Act that counsel could appear on behalf of a person charged with a serious offence, and then only to argue points of law. In practice, few

---

[2] For a fuller discussion of the historical developments outlined here see T. Goriely, 'The Development of Criminal Legal Aid in England and Wales' in R. Young and D. Wall, *Access to Criminal Justice: Legal Aid, Lawyers and the Defence of Liberty* (London: Blackstone Press, 1996).

defendants were represented in court, and they were not even afforded the right to give evidence on their behalf before 1898. It was not until the Poor Prisoners' Defence Act of 1903 that any form of legal aid was made available to fund such representation, and this was limited to those of insufficient means who were on trial on indictment for serious offences, and then only in cases where it appeared to the court 'desirable in the interest of justice' that they should be legally represented. It was also required that the defendant disclose his or her defence in advance in order to obtain such assistance. Although this latter provision was removed and the scope of the poor persons' defence somewhat widened in 1930, a major failing of these provisions was the inadequacy of the remuneration paid to lawyers acting in such cases. This even led at times to private lawyers refusing to continue to act for such 'poor persons' in some parts of the country.

No effective provision for legal aid in what are now magistrates' courts, where the vast majority of criminal defendants are tried, was made until well into the middle of the twentieth century. In this respect the key legislation was the Legal Advice and Assistance Act 1949, which established the principle that legal aid should be available to persons with limited means in all criminal cases where the court considered it was in 'the interest of justice' for legal representation to be provided. This principle was to apply not only to the very poorest defendants but to those of more substantial but still modest means, although in some cases they would be required to make some financial contribution to the costs of their defence. In effect, the State was to provide a subsidy to meet the costs of lawyers undertaking legal aid cases. The 1949 Act also provided for these lawyers to receive 'reasonable' remuneration, to be determined through the assessment of bills undertaken either by the courts or by the solicitors' professional body, the Law Society, which were given responsibility for administering legal aid on behalf of the government.

Perhaps the most important feature of this scheme was that the decision on who should be granted legal aid rested with the courts, while the responsibility for paying for it fell to the government under a legal aid budget administered separately from other court costs. This had two effects. First, the courts could make decisions on granting legal aid without regard to the costs of doing so, while the government had little control over expenditure in this field. In other words, legal aid was 'demand-led', with the government at any one time being obliged to meet the costs of whatever cases the courts decided required legal aid 'in the interest of justice'. Perhaps not surprisingly, therefore, successive governments were slow to implement fully the provisions of the Legal Advice and Assistance Act, and it was not until the 1960s that it was brought into effect for all criminal courts, including magistrates' courts. Up to this time the norm in most magistrates' court cases was for defendants to be un-represented, with the court through its clerk attempting to assist them to understand the proceedings but not being able to advise them confidentially or to speak on their behalf.

Secondly, even when the 1949 Act was implemented, there was a pattern of inconsistent decision-making as between different local courts, so that defendants appearing on similar charges might be granted legal aid in some courts but refused it in others. This was one of the main issues which led to the establishment of the

Departmental Committee on Legal Aid in Criminal Proceedings (the Widgery Com-mittee),[3] which reported in 1966. This Committee rejected both the idea of setting up an American-style public defender service, with lawyers directly employed by the State, and the more limited proposals for 'duty lawyers' to attend court each day in order to provide legal 'first aid', to assist defendants in making applications for bail and for legal aid. Rather, it supported a continuation of the existing system under which legal aid in criminal cases was provided solely though lawyers in private prac-tice whose costs would be subsidized on a case-by-case basis by the State. The Widgery Committee also recommended that the practice of courts assigning lawyers off a list to represent defendants in legal aid cases should be replaced by one where the choice of representative lay with the client.

Most importantly, while the Widgery Committee accepted that the granting of legal aid should be the norm for cases that were to be committed and tried in the higher criminal courts, it proposed more restrictive criteria to govern the grant of legal aid in magistrates' courts. Thus, legal aid would be made available only where the defend-ant was in 'real danger' of imprisonment or loss of employment or reputation if convicted; where the defence involved substantial questions of law or tracing and interviewing witnesses; or because representation of the defendant was necessary to conduct cross-examination of prosecution witnesses or in the interest of someone other than the defendant. On the other hand, the Widgery Committee suggested that legal representation and legal aid should not normally be required where the defendant was pleading guilty.

These criteria—known as the Widgery criteria—for granting criminal legal aid have remained virtually unchanged since they were first formulated in the mid-1960s.[4] Yet, in that period there has been a major expansion in both the numbers and the proportions of defendants appearing before the criminal courts who are granted legal aid for representation. At the time of the Widgery Report, only one in nine defendants appearing in magistrates' courts on the more serious indictable/either-way offences[5] received legal aid. Implementation of the Widgery Report was one factor that led to an expansion in the numbers receiving legal aid. Another was procedural changes introduced under the Criminal Justice Act 1967 allowing for defendants to be sent or committed to the higher courts for trial on the basis of the prosecution papers alone, without the necessity of an oral hearing to test the evidence, but only where the defendant was legally represented. By 1970 the number of defendants receiving legal aid in magistrates' courts had increased four-fold from the pre-Widgery level,

---

[3] Named after its Chairman, who later became Lord Chief Justice of England and Wales.

[4] These are now contained in Sch. 3 to the Access to Justice Act 1999.

[5] Criminal cases in England and Wales fall into three categories. The most serious are *indictable* offences (e.g. murder, rape, etc.) which are required to be tried in the Crown Court before a judge and jury (unless there is a guilty plea, in which case they are dealt with by a Crown Court judge sitting without a jury). The least serious are *summary only* offences, which must be tried before magistrates' courts consisting either of one professional judge or three lay justices. The third category is *either-way* offences (e.g. burglary, theft) where the defendant has a right to be tried at Crown Court before a judge and jury but can consent to be tried in the magistrates' court. There are currently between 25,000 and 30,000 indictable only cases each year, around 500,000 either-way cases, and between 700,000 and 800,000 summary only cases (excluding motoring offences).

although this still represented only a third of the numbers charged with indictable/ either-way offences.

The 1970s were a period when the numbers charged with criminal offences increased dramatically, by as much as 30 per cent over the decade, but when the rise in grants of legal aid was even greater, increasing three-fold from just over 100,000 to in excess of 300,000. There are a number of factors that might explain the increase in demand for criminal legal aid. One was the growth in the legal profession itself. Indeed, prior to this it was a relatively small minority of solicitors who were involved in criminal legal aid, which was widely regarded as low status and poorly remunerated work. However, as rates of remuneration improved and the numbers of solicitors grew, more of them looked to criminal legal aid as a source of work. Local law societies around the country set up 'duty solicitor' schemes, in which their members in private practice would take it in turn to be available to unrepresented defendants in magistrates' courts who might need their assistance. The incentive for such solicitors lay in the possibility that at least some of the defendants who sought the services of the 'duty solicitor' would eventually require and receive grants of legal aid to meet the costs of their lawyers. In fact, in some courts a grant of legal aid for defendants represented by the 'duty solicitor' became virtually automatic as a means of funding these schemes.

But if it is easy to see why demand for criminal legal aid rose in this period, what is the explanation for the increased supply by the courts in their decisions on granting legal aid? As noted, the criteria by which courts were intended to assess applications for legal aid remained unchanged, yet increasing numbers of such applications were successful. The answer probably lies in the pressures on the courts in dealing with greater volumes of criminal cases and the way in which professional representation of the accused actually facilitated the processing of cases through the courts. Having lawyers available to advise, assist, and speak for defendants in court could be less time-consuming than the court itself having to carry out these functions through the clerk. Also, where both the defence and prosecution were represented by lawyers, they could often meet beforehand to negotiate and resolve points of difference between them, such as the conditions under which bail might be granted to a particular defendant or the terms of a guilty plea. This process was further facilitated by the creation, in the mid-1980s, of the Crown Prosecution Service, a national organization responsible for the conduct of all criminal prosecutions, which employed a staff of several thousand professional lawyers.

During the 1980s the growth in criminal prosecutions levelled off, while grants of criminal legal aid continued to expand, so that by the end of the decade over 500,000 defendants were represented under legal aid. This was a similar number to the total of prosecutions for indictable/either-way offences. The level of prosecutions and of grants of legal aid remained at a similar level during most of the 1990s, although there was some evidence toward the end of the decade that these numbers were again continuing to grow. Indeed, it is current government policy to increase the number of criminal convictions by at least 100,000 as part of a drive against 'persistent offenders'.

In summary, the current position in England and Wales is that legal representation for court proceedings under criminal legal aid is very widely available for those charged with relatively serious criminal offences, whether in the Crown Court or before magistrates. This applies both to those defendants who may be contesting the charges against them and to those pleading guilty. The latter constitute a large majority of criminal cases at both levels of court, and the Widgery Committee idea that they would normally not require legal aid has long since been abandoned in practice. Although until recently those receiving criminal legal aid could formally be liable to make a financial contribution, in practice this has applied to only a very small minority of cases. In fact, the formal requirement for applicants to be means-tested has actually served as a barrier to effective administration, with grants of legal aid often having to be delayed for this purpose. Under the Access to Justice Act 1999 the grant of legal aid for proceedings in magistrates' courts has been made free, and it is only defendants who are eventually convicted in the Crown Court who remain liable for the payment of a financial contribution to their legal costs in legal aid cases.

WIDENING SCOPE OF CRIMINAL LEGAL AID

The growth of criminal legal aid in England and Wales has by no means been confined to an increased number of defendants receiving it for representation at trials. During the last two decades there has been an even more significant expansion in the scope of advice and representation provided under legal aid. This began in 1982 with the 'nationalization' of duty solicitor schemes that had previously been organized on a voluntary basis by local law societies. A national network of local and regional duty solicitor committees was established for the purpose of selecting duty solicitors from among local solicitors in private practice and organizing them into 'rotas' to be available to assist unrepresented defendants in each magistrates' court. In larger courts, these duty solicitors were required to be physically present in court each day, while in less busy courts they had to be available to be called into court when the need for emergency representation arose in particular cases. A national system of payment for duty solicitors, separate from that available under grants of legal aid, was also established.

The principle of client choice of representative was recognized in the rules of duty solicitor schemes, which required that the duty solicitors should offer each defendant referred to them the opportunity to name another solicitor they would wish to have represent them. In practice, the establishment of duty solicitor schemes did involve some limitation on clients' freedom to choose their own legal representatives, although it remained open to them to change to another lawyer even when they had been assisted at a preliminary hearing by the duty solicitor.[6] At the same time, the setting up of official duty solicitors' schemes implied some approval by the government for the lawyers acting in this capacity, and to be

---

[6] This principle has recently been confirmed by the government in detailed rules put forward under the Access to Justice Act relating to client choice of representative in legal aid cases.

selected as a duty solicitor it was necessary to demonstrate some minimum experience of magistrates' court proceedings as well as accessibility to clients from the local area.

No sooner had the national network of duty solicitor schemes been established to provide emergency representation in magistrates' courts than they were given the much more onerous and complex task of ensuring the availability of legal advice for suspects arrested and held in custody for questioning by the police. This was the result of the Police and Criminal Evidence Act 1984 (PACE), a major piece of legislation reforming the whole range of police powers and procedures for dealing with criminal suspects. In particular, this Act for the first time provided a statutory basis for the police to arrest and detain suspects for the purpose of questioning them. Previously, such questioning did take place, but supposedly on the basis that the suspect had 'volunteered' for it. At the same time, suspects were given a statutory right to receive legal advice both prior to and during the course of police interrogations, and (unlike many other countries where such a right exists) PACE also provided for lawyers to be paid through legal aid for providing such advice. The suspects could choose to be advised by lawyers of their choice (who would also be paid under legal aid) or by duty solicitors, who now had to be organized to be available to attend police stations on a twenty-four-hour a day basis.

QUALITY IN CRIMINAL DEFENCE SERVICES

The extension of legal aid to police station advice, perhaps more than any other development, raised serious issues about the quality of services provided by lawyers under criminal legal aid. Solicitors were found to be ill-prepared, both individually and in terms of their organization into relatively small firms, to undertake police station legal advice. In part, this was a problem of not having sufficient qualified staff to be available both to represent defendants in court in the day and to attend police stations to advise suspects at night. To meet these demands, many solicitors turned to trainees and unqualified staff as a means of providing police station legal advice. But the problems were by no means confined to logistics and the inexperience of the staff often sent to police stations to advise. There were also weaknesses in the professional standards of the service provided to suspects by solicitors and unqualified 'representatives' alike. Suspects might receive advice only over the telephone, being left on their own to deal with the police interview; legal advisers arriving at police stations might rush their clients into police interrogations without advising them confidentially beforehand or seeking to obtain information from the police about the circumstances of the arrest and the evidence against the suspect; and in police interrogations advisers often failed to offer advice to clients or intervene to prevent improper questioning or treatment of them.

These failings in the provision of police station legal advice subsequently led to a more critical examination of the practices of criminal defence lawyers more generally,[7] and eventually to recommendations by the Royal Commission on Criminal Justice, in their 1993 report, that the Law Society and the legal aid authorities introduce stricter controls on non-lawyers advising in police stations. This did not take the form of seeking to ban the use of non-lawyers for such work but of providing them with better training and formal accreditation for it. Under these arrangements, non-lawyers seeking to be accredited as police station legal representatives were required to prepare a portfolio of cases in which they had either observed others providing advice or had themselves advised; pass an examination in criminal law and procedure as it relates specifically to arrest and detention of suspects; and undertake a 'critical incidents test' in which they would listen to an audio tape of situations arising in police stations and be required to respond to them. By the mid-1990s several thousand non-lawyers have been accredited under this scheme, thereby creating a 'sub-profession' within criminal defence practice. The accreditation scheme for non-lawyers also appears to have had a 'knock-on' effect in forcing lawyers to re-examine their own police station and wider defence practices,[8] and recently the accreditation scheme itself has been extended to new solicitors seeking to become either police station or magistrates' court duty solicitors.

Another development that has had a critical bearing on the drive to improve quality in criminal defence services was the transfer in 1988 of the administration of legal aid from the Law Society to a Legal Aid Board (LAB), directly appointed by the government although operating at 'arm's length' from it. The creation of the LAB raised concerns that the government might use its more direct control of criminal legal aid to diminish the scope and quality of services. Arguably, however, the Law Society, as the body looking after the interests of its members, has tended to be more cautious in seeking to impose quality-control measures than the LAB. Nor is there evidence that the LAB, although more vigorous in its promotion of cost control and administrative efficiency, has yet sought to limit the scope or availability of criminal legal aid.

Initially, the LAB was not empowered to employ its own lawyers to provide advice and representation to the public, but continued to operate through providing subsidies to meet the costs of private lawyers. It did, however, seek in various ways to re-define its relationship with such lawyers. In particular, it sought to move away from a system of payment based on the detailed assessment of costs in each individual case and toward a more 'corporate' relationship with private solicitors as providers of legal aid. Two aspects of this were the introduction of 'standard fees' in place of hourly-based rates of remuneration and the awarding of 'franchises' to selected firms of solicitors on the basis of their adopting improved procedures for case management and information-recording on cases. At first, 'franchising' was voluntary. However, under the Access to Justice Act 1998 the Legal Aid Board was replaced by the Legal Services Commission (LSC) and solicitors are now required to enter into contracts for the provision of legal aid services in order to continue to receive state subsidy for this

---

[7] See M. McConville *et al.*, *Standing Accused: The Organisation and Practices of Criminal Defence Lawyers in Britain* (Oxford: Clarendon Press, 1994).

[8] See L. Bridges and S. Choongh, *Improving Police Station Legal Advice* (London: Law Society and Legal Aid Board, 1998).

work. Contracting has resulted in a significant reduction in the number of small solicitors' firms eligible to provide advice and representation under criminal legal aid, although as yet this does not appear to have adversely affected the accessibility of such services for clients.

An interesting aspect of the recent reforms of criminal legal aid under the auspices of the LAB/LSC is that they have largely left the criminal Bar (as distinct from solicitors) untouched. This is because legal aid in the higher criminal courts (the Crown Court) remains separately administered by the Lord Chancellor's Department, although it is due to be transferred to the Legal Services Commission in 2003. There have been some parallel moves to make barristers' work under criminal legal aid in the Crown Court subject to standard fees, and the traditional monopoly that this branch of the profession has enjoyed to appear as advocates in the higher courts has now been formally ended,[9] although to date this latter change has had limited practical effect. However, once Crown Court legal aid is transferred to the LSC, it can be anticipated that barristers will also be subjected to greater external scrutiny of the quality of their services. There are also proposals for a major re-organization of the criminal courts and the creation of a middle-level tribunal (consisting of a single judge sitting with two lay magistrates) to hear many of the cases currently tried in the Crown Court,[10] and this is likely to reduce substantially the role of the criminal Bar and enhance that of solicitors in acting as advocates in these cases.

CURRENT DEVELOPMENTS IN CRIMINAL LEGAL AID

The most recent developments in criminal legal aid in England and Wales relate to a further major expansion in the scope of provision in connection with those pleading guilty at initial or 'early' hearings in magistrates' courts, and to government initiatives to experiment with salaried defence lawyers employed directly by the Legal Services Commission. The first of these developments provides a classic example of a situation in which the State's objectives to promote the efficient administration of the criminal courts can lead directly to the expansion of legal representation under legal aid. In an attempt to reduce delays in the processing of criminal cases through the courts, it was decided to abandon a practice of the police releasing those who had been charged with criminal offences on bail and requiring them to appear in court for the first time several weeks later. The theory had been that in this intervening period both the prosecution and the defence would complete their preparations for the court case. In fact, experience showed that such pre-court preparatory work frequently failed to happen. The police might delay passing their file on the case to the Crown Prosecution Service, which in turn would often leave its examination and decision-

---

[9] Under the Courts and Legal Services Act 1990, as amended by the Access to Justice Act 1999.

[10] See *A Review of the Criminal Courts of England and Wales by The Right Hon. Lord Justice Auld* (London: Lord Chancellor's Department, 2001).

making[11] until shortly before the scheduled court appearance. Equally, defendants bailed from the police station would often fail to contact their lawyers, and the lawyers themselves were reluctant to undertake substantial preparation on cases without an assurance that legal aid would be granted. Indeed, although legal aid was available for advising and representing suspects while they were being held in custody by the police, this form of legal aid did not extend to the period when they had been released from custody and were awaiting their first court appearance. Rather, a further application was required to be made to the court.

Under the new system implemented nationally in 1999, all persons charged with criminal offences are now required by statute to be scheduled to appear before the relevant court at its next sitting, usually the next day,[12] and courts are encouraged to dispose of as many of these cases as possible at this initial hearing through guilty pleas. In order to facilitate this process, a new form of legal aid was made available, in which defendants appearing for the first time in court on criminal charges could automatically be represented by a lawyer of their choice, without prior application to or the sanction of the court. In other words, it was left to defendants' lawyers to determine whether such representation was 'in the interest of justice' and their own eligibility to receive legal aid for providing it. It is not surprising that this has resulted in a further large increase in the numbers of criminal defendants being represented in court under legal aid and in the costs to the public purse in providing this service. In particular, many defendants on relatively minor criminal charges, who previously might have appeared before magistrates unrepresented and entered guilty pleas, are now being represented by lawyers at 'early' hearings for the same purpose, as a means of facilitating the expedition of cases through the courts.

A second recent innovation in criminal legal aid has been the setting up of experiments in Scotland[13] and in England and Wales[14] for the use of public defenders directly employed by the State. In Scotland this experiment initially involved a system under which some defendants, selected by reference to the month of their birth, were 'directed' to the public defender and thereby effectively denied their choice of lawyer to represent them under legal aid.[15] This system proved highly unpopular with defendants (as well as their normal lawyers) and undermined their confidence in the public defender to such an extent that it was eventually dropped. By contrast, the

[11] This process is known as review, and the Crown Prosecution Service has the power to alter the charges originally laid against the defendant by the police or to drop them altogether. In fact, in about a quarter of all indictable/either-way cases the charges are eventually dropped or the case otherwise terminated by the prosecution, and in many others there are significant reductions in the original charges.

[12] Under s. 46 of the Crime and Disorder Act 1998. Previously, it was only when defendants were refused bail by the police and held in custody awaiting their first court appearance that there was a requirement that they should be brought before the next available sitting of the relevant court. For a discussion of this and other measures to reduce delay in the criminal courts see L. Bridges and M. Jacobs, *Reducing Delay in the Criminal Justice System—The Views of Defence Lawyers* (London: Lord Chancellor's Department, 1999).

[13] This consisted of one public defender office in Edinburgh.

[14] To date, 4 public defender offices have been established in Birmingham, Liverpool, Middlesborough, and Swansea, and two further offices are due to start before Apr. 2002. The pilot project is due to last for 4 years.

[15] In fact, a number of such defendants continued to be represented by their lawyer of choice on a *pro bono* basis.

public defender experiment in England and Wales has been introduced without any compulsion on defendants to use it rather than their own lawyers, who will continue to be paid for providing representation in both police stations and at court under their contracts with the LSC. The Government's stated intention is not to replace the present system of contracting with private solicitors for such services with a monopoly public defender service consisting of lawyers and other legal advisers directly employed by the LSC. Rather, the aim is to create a 'mixed system' under which private solicitors with contracts will work in competition with the public defenders. Such a system may well lead to a segmentation of the criminal defence market, with public defenders specializing in certain types of case and contracted lawyers in others. For example, in Scotland it was found that the public defender tended to deal with cases more quickly, with their clients entering guilty pleas more often and at an earlier appearance in court than the clients of other lawyers. This result may have reflected different types of case being handled by the two types of lawyer respectively and also the fact that private lawyers would have to seek adjournments in order to process applications for legal aid.

CONCLUSION

In summary, the right to criminal legal aid has become increasingly entrenched in England and Wales, not only covering the representation of defendants on most criminal charges throughout the course of court proceedings (including preliminary hearings and guilty pleas) but also widely available for advice and representation of suspects held in police stations (including during the course of police interrogations). The latter is perhaps a unique feature of the criminal legal aid system in England and Wales (now also extending to Northern Ireland but not Scotland). While many other jurisdictions provide suspects with a theoretical right to receive custodial legal advice, very few make state funding available to pay lawyers and other forms of legal advisers to provide this service. Another feature of criminal legal aid in England and Wales is the primacy given to the right of defendants receiving legal aid to choose their own legal representative rather than being assigned or 'directed' to use particular lawyers. Some erosion of this principle has taken place in recent years, particularly as solicitors can perform legal aid work only if contracted to the Legal Services Commission for this purpose and must conform to minimum quality standards to be eligible for such contracts. If the number of contracts awarded in a given locality were to be severely restricted in future, either on quality or economic grounds, this could have an adverse effect on defendants' choice of representative. On the other hand, there is no indication to date of England and Wales adopting a practice, initially used in the public defender experiment in Scotland and commonplace elsewhere, of restricting those defendants requiring legal aid solely to lawyers directly employed by the State.

The entrenchment of the right to legal aid in England and Wales can be related to a number of factors. As indicated, expansions in the scope of legal aid have often been linked to changes designed to speed up or otherwise improve the efficiency of the criminal courts and criminal justice process. In other instances it has been related to restrictions on the substantive rights of defendants. For example, the restrictions that have now been introduced on a suspect's right to silence[16] when questioned by the police may have proven less politically acceptable had not provision already been made for the provision of custodial legal advice as of right under legal aid. Similarly, defendants in criminal cases in England and Wales may now be required to disclose details of their defence in advance of trial, and it is difficult to see how such a provision could be workable without most defendants being legally represented. These changes can also be said to have made the job of defence lawyers more complex and difficult. It is one thing to advise a suspect in the police station to exercise his right to silence and refuse to answer police questions; it is another to have to advise that person when it would be regarded as reasonable during subsequent court proceedings that the defendant withhold information from the police. This in turn has placed a greater emphasis on the quality of criminal defence services as an objective of the criminal legal aid system and its administration, as reflected in the 'franchising', contracting, and the accreditation of both duty solicitors and non-lawyer police station representatives.

Further Reading

BRIDGES, L., 'The Royal Commission's Approach to Criminal Defence Services—A Case of Professional Incompetence' in M. McConville and L. Bridges, *Criminal Justice in Crisis* (Cheltenham: Edward Elgar, 1994).

—— and ABUBAKER, A., *Work Patterns and Costs under Criminal Legal Aid* (London: Legal Services Commission, 2000).

—— CAPE, E., ABUBAKER, A., and BENNETT, C., *Quality in Criminal Defence Services* (London: Legal Services Commission, 2000).

—— and CHOONGH, S., *Improving Police Station Legal Advice: The Impact of the Accreditation Scheme for Police Station Legal Advisers* (London: The Law Society, 1998).

McCONVILLE, M., HODGSON, J., BRIDGES, L., and PAVLOVIC, A., *Standing Accused: The Organisation and Practices of Criminal Defence Lawyers in Britain* (Oxford: Oxford University Press, 1994).

Justice Report, *Public Defenders: Learning for the US Experience* (London: Justice, 2001).

YOUNG, R., and WALL, D., *Access to Criminal Justice: Legal Aid, Lawyers and the Defence of Liberty* (London: Blackstone Press, 1996).

[16] Under the Criminal Justice and Public Order Act 1994.

9

PROSECUTIONS SYSTEMS

Andrew Sanders

INTRODUCTION

Earlier chapters of this book have shown that the police in England and Wales have gradually increased their powers over the last 150 years or so but that, at times of public concern over miscarriages of justice or abuse of power, these powers have occasionally been curbed to some extent. This pattern reflects the tension highlighted by Choongh (Chapter 3 of this volume) between the 'ideals of liberal legalism' that seek to protect citizens from state power, and the view that the police need substantial power if they are to enforce the law effectively. In this chapter we shall see how these changes and tensions apply to prosecution decisions.

The English system, like other common law systems, is typically characterized as adversarial and discretionary. By comparison, Roman Law-based systems, including many in the rest of Europe, are in principle inquisitorial and non-discretionary. In practice, all systems are both inquisitorial and adversarial to some degree, and all allow some discretion that is, to a greater or lesser extent, structured.[1] Despite this convergence, however, we shall see that the roots and underlying principles of the English system are important in shaping its key features.

Choongh shows that the police claimed the dominant role in prosecutions in the mid-nineteenth century. This was done largely by developing policy and practice rather than by changing the law. In keeping with the idea of complete discretion, no-one was given a specific prosecution role in relation to most crimes. Thus the police could prosecute or not, as they wished, as could the victim. In practice, victims rarely had the ability, power, or resources to investigate or prosecute, nor do they now. Victims and society in general rely upon the police, a substantial part of whose organization is devoted to the administration of prosecutions. Nonetheless, the principle of private prosecution remains, and is still used from time to time.[2] For many years, victims who complained that the police did not prosecute were told that the remedy was for them to prosecute, a classically formalistic response. As we shall

---

[1] For a discussion of two inquisitorial systems with significant differences see L. Leigh and L. Zedner, *A Report on the Administration of Criminal Justice in the Pre-Trial Phase in France and Germany*, Royal Commission on Criminal Justice Research Study No. 1 (London: HMSO, 1992).

[2] G. Slapper, *Organisational Prosecutions* (Aldershot: Ashgate, 2001).

see later, this has in recent years been recognized as inadequate, although changes to the system have been typically *ad hoc*.

An important exception to the *laisez faire* 'anyone can prosecute' attitude is that of so-called 'regulatory offences', which are generally investigated and prosecuted (if at all) by specialized agencies. These are, in effect, specialist police forces. They include the Health and Safety Executive (for accidents and criminal dangers at work), local authorities (for a range of offences including some pollution offences), the Inland Revenue (income tax), Customs and Excise (other tax and drug imports), and various fraud agencies for different kinds of fraud and company offences. Neither the 'regular' police nor victims can prosecute most of these offences. Slapper estimates that there are some thirty of these organizations, and that they account for around 20 per cent of the activity of the magistrates' courts, that is, around 400,000 cases a year (the police, by comparison, prosecute around 1.5 million cases each year, although many of these are road traffic prosecutions where defendants do not usually appear in court).[3]

The principle of discretion applies equally to police and non-police organizations. Following investigation (which is, itself, an entirely discretionary matter for the organization) there are three main choices: no formal action; a formal alternative to prosecution in the form of some kind of warning; or prosecution. The courts reserve the right to review any non-prosecution policy decision that they consider fundamentally wrong,[4] but we shall see that very few challenges to prosecution decisions have been successful.[5] In the next two sections we shall examine the basis on which the police and the prosecution agency, the Crown Prosecution Service (CPS), makes these decisions. We shall then look at non-police agencies and, finally, at accountability in order to identify what organizing principles underlie the prosecution system, and how far these principles accord with legal ideals. Those ideals correspond with Packer's idea of 'due process', while largely unfettered discretion for state agencies is a characteristic of what he called the 'crime-control' ideology.[6] Whilst these polarities are problematic we will see that they are useful ways of characterizing conflicting tendencies within the system.

POLICE DISPOSITIONS

It would be wrong in any system for someone to be prosecuted if there was little evidence of guilt. At one time in England and Wales all that was needed was a *prima facie* case: that is, sufficient evidence to require an answer from the defendant. One

---

[3] Slapper, n. 2 above.

[4] *Metropolitan Police Commissioner, ex parte Blackburn* [1968] 2 QB 118.

[5] E.g. *R. v. Chief Constable of Devon and Cornwall, ex parte CEGB* [1981] 3 All ER 826; *R. v. Chief Constable of Sussex, ex parte ITF* [1999] 1 All ER 129. However, the decisions not to prosecute in *R. v. DPP, ex parte Treadaway* (Legal Action Oct. 1997, p. 15) and *R. v. DPP, ex parte Jones* (DC, 23 Mar. 2000, unreported) were quashed. See later discussion.

[6] H. Packer, *The Limits of the Criminal Sanction* (Stanford, Cal.: Stanford UP, 1968). The applicability of these models is considered in A. Sanders and R. Young, *Criminal Justice* (2nd edn., London: Butterworths, 2000), chap. 1.

result of this low evidential threshold was a high acquittal rate. As a result, in the mid-1980s the Royal Commission on Criminal Procedure prompted the government to establish a 'realistic prospect of conviction' threshold.[7] Whether, in any particular case, that evidential threshold is satisfied is for the police to judge. Common law systems are not unusual in this respect, but where they do differ from many others is that even if there is sufficient evidence to prosecute, a further test—that of the 'public interest'—needs to be satisfied. Again unusually in England and Wales it is the police who make this decision too.

NO FURTHER ACTION (NFA)

As Choongh shows in his chapter, over the last century and a half arrest has turned into a tool for (rather than the culmination of) investigation. The process of arrest, detention, and charge (by contrast with the summons procedure which does not involve detention in the police station) is now used to initiate almost all prosecutions apart from 'regulatory' and road traffic offences. However, suspects who are arrested and detained are not necessarily prosecuted. Rather like whales taking in water to filter plankton, a lot of suspects are taken in one side and ejected from the other. Despite ostensible controls to protect suspects, the Police and Criminal Evidence Act 1994 made it easier than previously to arrest and detain on flimsy grounds with little risk attaching to the police.[8] Arrests have therefore been rising over the last ten to fifteen years and so have the numbers of suspects released with no further action (NFA) (about 400,000: that is, 20–25 per cent of all annual arrests).[9]

It follows that many NFAs are a product of largely speculative arrests. Often the police accept that the suspect did not commit the offence or, at least, that it cannot be proved: for instance, where the police 'trawl' local people with relevant previous convictions simply to eliminate them from a major inquiry; where suspects are arrested so that they can be held pending their questioning as witnesses; and where *all* inhabitants of, and visitors to, a building where there has been a police raid (for drugs, for example) are arrested. Some NFAs, of course, are cases in which the police would have liked to prosecute had they acquired more evidence. The obstacle here is rarely physical or legal. The police rarely seek evidence other than from eye witnesses, the victim, and the suspect himself. They could often investigate further but choose not to because of limited resources. Cases are a product of police work, and so the absence of a prosecution case is also a police product. In the most serious cases, such as murder, the police devote very substantial resources to investigation, and the prosecution rate is correspondingly high. However, even in murder cases mistakes are sometimes

---

[7] Royal Commission on Criminal Procedure, *Report*, Cmnd 8092-1 (1981). The new guidelines were issued by the Attorney-General. See A. Sanders 'Prosecution Decisions and the Attorney-General's Guidelines' [1985] *Crim. LR* 4.

[8] A. Sanders and R. Young, 'The Rule of Law, Due Process and Pre-Trial Criminal Justice' (1994) 47 *Current Legal Problems* 125.

[9] M. McConville *et al.*, *The Case for the Prosecution* (London: Routledge, 1991); C. Phillips and D. Brown, *Entry into the Criminal Justice System*, Home Office Research Study, No. 185 (London: Home Office, 1998); P. Hillyard and D. Gordon, 'Arresting Statistics' (1999) 26 *Jo. Law and Society* 502.

made, as in the Stephen Lawrence case, in which a black teenage youth was murdered. Investigative mistakes, made at the start of the investigation, led to a weak case, which led the police to take no further action, rightly in terms of the lack of evidence—a police product—but possibly wrongly in terms of the truth.[10]

The many other reasons for NFAs include the fact that some arrests are a result of pressure from the public. When the police arrest reluctantly they usually decide not to prosecute, often after consultation with the victim, regardless of the strength of evidence.[11] This used to be a major problem in domestic violence cases, and to some extent still is.[12] As a result, the most recent government guidance to the police is that there should be a presumption in favour of arrest and prosecution in all domestic violence cases.[13] Other reasons for NFA in cases where the police have (or might be able to find) evidence include the doing of 'deals' with suspects, especially informants. And just as prosecution is sometimes used to protect the police against allegations of malpractice, so in some circumstances NFA prevents the airing in public of events about which the police prefer to keep quiet. In all these cases, the decision not to prosecute is taken on 'public interest' grounds even though it would often be difficult to justify on those grounds. But since the police alone take these decisions with no supervision from other agencies, they rarely need to justify them.

POLICE WARNINGS

It follows from the near-complete discretion that the police possess that they have been able to develop their own system of warnings (known as 'cautions') to people they believe to have committed crimes but for whom they do not think prosecution is appropriate. Resources have to be used with care in all systems, and every police force tends to develop, formally or informally, scales of seriousness in which something short of a full prosecution might be thought more appropriate. Initially used only for juveniles and road traffic cases, by the late 1970s some police forces in England and Wales were giving cautions to 4–5 per cent of adult offenders, although others did this hardly at all. As with arrest policies, each of the forty-three English and Welsh police forces had their own cautioning policies. The Home Office responded in 1985 with new guidelines that established clearer criteria for prosecution and caution. These criteria included offence seriousness, previous convictions, dramatic mitigating circumstances, wishes of the victim, and so forth. However, both inter-force and intra-force disparity continued, partly because prosecution and caution decisions are taken by fairly junior officers without supervision.

The guidelines themselves are also at fault. They are vague (how serious an offence

---

[10] This case was the subject of a major investigation by a judge, who concluded that many of the errors were a product of police institutional racism. See W. Macpherson, *The Stephen Lawrence Inquiry*, Cm 4262-I (1999).

[11] McConville *et al.*, n. 9 above.

[12] C. Hoyle, *Negotiating Domestic Violence* (Oxford: Clarendon, 1998); Sanders and Young, n. 6 above, 382–7.

[13] Home Office, *Domestic Violence* (Circular 19/2000). This 'pro-prosecution' approach, based on American mandatory arrest and prosecution domestic violence policies, is discussed further at p. 157 below.

or record? what kinds of personal circumstance should be taken into account?), manipulable (the police themselves sometimes influence the wishes of victims), and non-prioritized (are victims' wishes, suspect's circumstances, or offence seriousness to predominate?). New guidelines were produced in 1990 and again in 1994, and cautioning for youths was put on a statutory basis by the Crime and Disorder Act 1998. The 1994 and 1998 changes reversed the trend of increasing cautions because, the government stated (on the basis of no criminological evidence), this 'lenient' approach encouraged continued crime.[14]

Diversion is nonetheless still encouraged in many cases that would once have been prosecuted, because it is cheaper than prosecution and because it is thought to avoid stigmatizing offenders. Drawing on criminological 'labelling theory', it was generally accepted in the 1980s and early 1990s that prosecution and punishment can exaggerate criminal self-identity. The 1990 caution guidelines exhorted cautioning as 'reducing the risk that [offenders] will re-offend . . . courts should only be used as a last resort, particularly for juveniles and young adults'. Many juveniles, and even some adults, were thus repeatedly cautioned for relatively minor offences. The Crime and Disorder Act marks a distinct change in philosophy, in that a maximum of two cautions (save in exceptional circumstances) can now be offered to youths (in the form of 'reprimands' for minor offences, or 'warnings' for more serious or repeat offending). However, cost-reduction and stigma-avoidance aims are still important. The latter can be seen in the fact that the new referral orders created under the Youth Justice and Criminal Evidence Act 1999 require youths who are prosecuted for the first time (and who plead guilty) to be referred back out of the court to a Youth Offender Panel (made up of trained volunteers) with responsibility for devising an agreed programme of rehabilitative and reparative work for the young person. If this 'contract' is fulfilled, the conviction is regarded as 'spent' for most purposes.[15]

The Crime and Disorder Act is significant also for its endorsement of the idea of restorative justice. Warnings (although not reprimands, which are essentially informal warnings with no further action) are supposed to be accompanied by 'action plans' drawn up by the multi-agency Youth Offender Teams created under the 1998 Act. The idea is that 'early intervention' will 'nip crime in the bud'. The team assesses each offender for a rehabilitative programme. The programmes should vary according to types of offender and types of offence. But participation is neither a legal obligation nor a condition of receiving a warning, although non-participation (and any reasons given for non-participation) will be recorded and can be cited in future court proceedings. The essence of restorative justice is to make offenders ashamed of their behaviour in ways that promote their reintegration into their community. This is often done, in the first instance, by convening a 'restorative conference' in which offenders, victims, and their respective supporters are invited to participate. Offenders and victims (and their families and friends, if appropriate) tell their side of things, and

[14] R. Evans, 'Cautioning: Counting the Cost of Retrenchment' [1994] *Crim. LR* 566. See T. Newburn, 'Youth, Crime and Justice' in M. Maguire *et al.* (eds.), *Oxford Handbook of Criminology* (Oxford: OUP, 1997), in relation to juveniles.

[15] So that if asked by a prospective employer whether he or she had a criminal record, the youth could lawfully answer 'No'.

are asked what harm they think they caused (or, in the case of victims and the families of offenders, were caused). Restorative justice, while progressive in principle, does not necessarily work as intended when transplanted into the police context as it can be more punitive than necessary. However, it is at least an attempt to intervene positively in ways that could be beneficial for offenders and victims alike.[16]

Cautions, reprimands, and warnings are sometimes used in cases that would not otherwise be prosecuted. The Home Office guidelines try to reduce this 'net-widening' by requiring some preconditions for caution: that there is sufficient evidence to prosecute and that the suspect admits the offence and accepts the caution (although the requirement of consent was removed in the case of youths by the 1998 Act). However, these preconditions are sometimes ignored. Indeed, some suspects are cautioned precisely *because* there is insufficient evidence to prosecute, while others are cautioned in exchange for a favour, such as the provision of information about other offences or offenders.[17] In other words, cautioning is sometimes used by the police to further their policing gaols, and should not be seen as necessarily a progressive restorative process. As in all policing systems, it should not be assumed that the intention of law-makers is consistent with the goals of the police.

POLICE CHARGING

Suspects in some cases are charged (prosecuted) despite the evidence being weak. Is this oversight, deliberate flouting of the rules, or the pursuit of a policy that predominates over the rules? Just as the police sometimes use cautions as tools of broader enforcement polices, this is true of charging too. Whilst decisions to charge cases that are weak and to fail to charge cases that are strong appear inconsistent and incomprehensible in terms of the official guidelines, they are perfectly rational in terms of police 'working rules'.[18] This is clearly contrary to the due-process ideology, and also, at first sight, undermines the crime-control ideology as it increases the acquittal rate. But convictions are only one dimension on the crime-control scale. Acquisition of information (through interrogation which is then justified by charge), assertion of authority, and protection of an officer against whom a complaint is expected are all reasons which officers have given to researchers for instituting a prosecution with little or no regard for the rules of evidence. Pressure to meet the expectations of vulnerable victims (such as children, victims of rape, or victims with disabilities) is another reason for prosecuting weak cases.[19]

Unlike cautions, which are usually decided by inspectors or more senior officers,

---

[16] R. Young and B. Goold, 'Restorative Police Cautioning in Aylesbury: From Degrading to Reintegrative Shaming Ceremonies?' [1999] *Crim. LR* 126; A. Morris and G. Maxwell (eds.), *Restorative Justice for Juveniles* (Hart: Oxford, 2001). The limited role of restorative justice has been criticized by A. Morris and L. Gelsthorpe, 'Something Old, Something Borrowed, Something Blue, but Something New? A Comment on the Prospects for Restorative Justice under the Crime and Disorder Act 1999' [2000] *Crim. LR* 18.

[17] McConville *et al.*, n. 9 above.   [18] *Ibid.*

[19] A. Sanders *et al.*, *Victims with Learning Disabilities: Negotiating the Criminal Justice System* (Oxford: Centre for Criminological Research, Occasional Paper No. 17, 1997).

charges are a matter for the arresting officer and custody officer. Very rarely do custody officers caution or NFA when the arresting officer wants a prosecution, or vice versa, for custody officers are in a weak position in inquiring into evidential strength. If they try to evaluate arresting officers' evidence they have only one source of information on which to draw (apart from the suspect): that same arresting officer. As one custody officer told McConville *et al.*, 'I would go along with what the arresting officers have to say'. According to another, 'I accept that [the officer's] got no cause to be telling lies and the other chap [suspect] has'. As an arresting officer said: 'Perhaps by the book. . . . "The custody officer will decide" sort of thing, but in practice it's different. He trusts your judgement'.[20] Arresting officers sometimes 'gild the lily' and even if custody officers do want to hear suspects' accounts, the PACE rules on interviewing (discussed in Choongh's chapter) make this legally almost impossible. Custody officers could read interview transcripts, but these are rarely immediately available, and suspects do not always have lawyers in attendance, those that were in the station usually leave before the charging decision is made, and few are adversarial enough to challenge the police anyway.[21]

Even if custody officers were inclined to question what arresting officers wanted, the latter can, in many cases, 'construct' their cases to achieve the results they want. Case construction involves selection, interpretation, and creation of facts. Cases are constructed deliberately to appear strong in accordance with adversarial principles. The 'facts' that are created sometimes bear little relation to any reality that the suspect might recognize, sometimes through exaggeration (so that a 'serious assault' turns out to have caused no injury), sometimes through interrogation techniques that 'put words in suspects' mouths', and sometimes through sheer fabrication.[22] The existence of this 'noble cause corruption' has even been admitted by the Metropolitan Police Commissioner,[23] although of course the reasons for, and extent of, it remains contested. It follows that, just as officers can secure cautions when NFA would be more in keeping with the rules, so they can secure charges when cautions or NFAs would be more appropriate (and vice versa).

The patterns of bias identified in street policing (race, class, and so forth) are also evident in prosecution and diversion decisions. Once arrested, Afro-Caribbeans are less likely to be cautioned than whites and may be less likely than Asians to have no further action taken against them. This is largely because Afro-Caribbeans are less likely to admit the offence (thus disqualifying themselves from a caution or warning), are more likely to be disadvantaged by the ethno-centric application of social criteria

[20] McConville *et al.*, n. 9 above, 119–20. Later research suggests that little had changed by the mid-1990s: J. Baldwin and A. Hunt, 'Prosecutors Advising in Police Stations' [1998] *Crim. LR* 521; Phillips and Brown, n. 9 above.

[21] A. Sanders, 'Access to Justice in the Police Station' in R. Young, and D. Wall (eds.), *Access to Criminal Justice* (London: Blackstone, 1996).

[22] D. McBarnet, *Conviction* (London: Macmillan, 1981); R. Ericson, *Making Crime* (London: Butterworths, 1981); M. Maguire and C. Norris, *The Conduct and Supervision of Criminal Investigations*, Royal Commission on Criminal Justice Research Study No. 5 (London: HMSO, 1992), P. Waddington, *Policing Citizens* (London: UCL Press, 1999) 135.

[23] *Guardian*, 11 Mar. 1995. For a recent example see Sanders and Young, n. 6 above, 337–8.

(such as domestic circumstances), and tend to have more previous convictions and cautions, possibly because of earlier biased decisions.[24]

THE CPS

In 1981 the Royal Commission on Criminal Procedure, mentioned earlier, realized that, left to their own devices, the police would not consistently apply the guidelines on evidential sufficiency and cautioning when to do so would conflict with their own informal working rules. To secure consistency, and to counterbalance the extra police powers it recommended (and which were legislated in PACE 1984), it proposed the establishment of the Crown Prosecution Service (CPS). Counterbalancing strong police powers is now not just a policy objective, but a legal requirement under Article 6 of the European Convention on Human Rights (ECHR), which requires 'equality of arms' between prosecution and defence.

Prior to the establishment of the CPS, prosecutions in each police force were organized in one of three ways. Some forces (or their local political authorities) employed lawyers who prosecuted all cases. Some employed lawyers who prosecuted the most difficult and serious cases and who handled most cases in the busiest courts; in such areas, the remaining cases were prosecuted by police officers, either specialists in that role or the officer in the case. In the remaining force areas, lawyers in private practice were used in an *ad hoc* fashion in serious and complex cases, while the rest were prosecuted by police officers.

The police were initially resistant to reform of these arrangements. Although the police soon conceded that all police forces should use prosecuting lawyers in all or most cases, they were reluctant to lose the principle that the police *instruct* 'their' lawyers. In other words, the police wanted to retain control of all decision-making powers in prosecutions. By contrast, prosecution lawyers argued forcefully that not only should all cases be handled by lawyers but also that they should have independent decision-making powers because, they said, the police were sometimes too close to the case to make objective decisions.

The Royal Commission agreed with the prosecution lawyers. However, rather than giving prosecutors power to decide whether or not to prosecute, it recommended that the police retain this power. It further recommended, however, that prosecutors should be independent of the police and that they should have the power to terminate cases in which the police initially decided to prosecute. Once it decided that prosecutors should be independent of the police, all that was left to decide was whether prosecutors should be organized nationally or locally. Because the police were themselves organized on a local basis, it was thought logical that each police force and its corresponding prosecution agency should be accountable to the same local political authority. But in this respect (and only in this respect) the government disagreed and

---

[24] M. Fitzgerald, *Ethnic Minorities and the Criminal Justice System*, Royal Commission on Criminal Justice Research Study No. 20 (London: HMSO, 1993); Phillips and Brown, n. 9 above.

decided on a national system, with the CPS being accountable to the government through the Attorney-General.

The result was the Prosecution of Offences Act 1985 which built the CPS around the pre-existing system. The police continue to charge, summons, caution, and NFA as before. Once charged or summonsed, however, the accused becomes the responsibility of the CPS, which decides whether to continue the prosecution. The Director of Public Prosecutions (DPP), whose office had previously been responsible for national prosecutions of particular gravity and for the prosecution of police officers, was made head of the CPS. In principle, the CPS need not consult the police in any decision it takes. Although it is good practice to consult if the intention is to drop a case, the final decision should be taken entirely independently in accordance with the Code for Crown Prosecutors, which is produced by the DPP. The Code provides guidance on prosecution decisions in almost identical terms to the guidance discussed above on evidential sufficiency and cautionability, so that poor police decisions can be reviewed by the CPS.

McConville *et al.* found, from research in three police-force areas, that the CPS rarely dropped cases that were evidentially weak, and that when they did so this was usually on the initiative of the police and/or only after several court appearances. There were three main reasons for this: policy (the furtherance of police working rules, shared by both prosecutors and police officers); the chance of a freak conviction (because verdicts are so hard to predict); and guilty pleas (just because a case is evidentially weak it does not follow that the defendant will contest the case; weak cases are continued in the often correct expectation of a guilty plea).[25] Later research confirms that many weak cases continue to be prosecuted by the CPS. This is particularly so when there are strong 'public-interest' reasons for prosecuting (such as in domestic violence cases or when the victim is vulnerable), even though cases should be prosecuted only if they pass *both* the evidential *and* the public interest test.[26] If the CPS is passive in relation to weak cases where case failure is a measure of institutional efficiency, it is not surprising to discover that it is even more passive in relation to cautionable cases. McConville *et al.* found no cases being dropped on grounds of cautionability alone, despite many similar cases being cautioned by the police. Again, where police working rules point to prosecution, the CPS is reluctant to stop the case.

If the police charge, the CPS may stop the prosecution going further by 'discontinuing' the case. In recent years there has been a rise in discontinuances, both on evidential and 'public-interest' grounds, although the former outnumber the latter by two to one. However, many 'public-interest' discontinuances are of trivial cases, and are made on cost grounds. That there is scope for far more diversion by the CPS has been confirmed by research that found that cases that went through experimental 'Public Interest Case Assessment' schemes were far more likely to be discontinued than

---

[25] McConville *et al.*, n. 9 above.

[26] B. Block *et al.*, *Ordered and Directed Acquittals in the Crown Court*, Royal Commission on Criminal Justice Research Study No. 15 (London: HMSO, 1993); J. Baldwin, 'Understanding Judge Ordered and Directed Acquittals in the Crown Court' [1997] *Crim. LR* 536; A. Cretney and G. Davis, 'Prosecuting Domestic Assault' [1996] *Crim. LR* 162; A. Sanders *et al.*, *Victims with Learning Disabilities: Negotiating the Criminal Justice System* (Oxford: Centre for Criminological Research, Occasional Paper No. 17, 1997).

otherwise. Despite this, many cases that were assessed as cautionable were not discontinued and yet received nominal penalties.[27] Ethnic minority defendants have their cases disproportionately discontinued by the CPS *and* dismissed in court, suggesting that the CPS counters some of the race bias produced by the police discussed earlier in this chapter, but not all.[28]

The CPS is in a structurally weak position to carry out its ostensible aims primarily because of police case construction. The CPS reviews the quality of police cases on the basis of evidence provided solely by the police. This is like the problem of written records, where those who are being evaluated write their own reports. Cases being prosecuted are usually shaped to appear as prosecutable; the facts to support this are selected, and those that do not are ignored, hidden, or undermined. Thus weaknesses or cautionable factors, whether known by the police or not, often emerge only in or after trial: 'prosecutors have no way of knowing what gaps there are in the information they receive'.[29] This situation is exacerbated when the CPS relies on police summaries, which are very selective indeed, rather than upon a review of all the evidence in the police file. The CPS has long realized this and, as part of its striving for independence managed, some ten years after its establishment, to virtually eradicate the use of summaries. No sooner had this been achieved than reforms to the magistrates' courts set everything back again by encouraging the disposal of relatively simple, non-serious cases at the first hearing, which is before a full file can be prepared by the police and only a summary exists.[30]

Attempts to resolve problems of due process and disparity in cautioning by using the CPS suffer another structural problem. Although cautionable cases that are prosecuted are in theory reviewable by the CPS, prosecutable (and NFA-able) cases that are cautioned are not. If the police decide to caution, the case ends with them. However able or willing the CPS may be to deal with cases that should be cautioned, it cannot deal with cases which should *not* have been cautioned. This means that disparity will continue, and the violations of due process inherent in police cautioning procedures remain untouched by the CPS.

That the CPS is often viewed as a police prosecution agency is hardly surprising in an adversarial system, but it does suggest that suspects cannot rely on the CPS, as presently constituted, to protect them. Prosecutors could become adequate reviewers of either evidence or public interest only if placed in an entirely different structural relationship with the police. At present, the CPS is not so much a decision-*maker* (such as exists in inquisitorial systems[31]) as a decision-*reverser*. Reversing the decisions made by another body with which one needs a co-operative relationship is difficult

---

[27] D. Crisp and D. Moxon, *Case Screening by the Crown Prosecution Service*, Home Office Research Study No. 137 (London: HMSO, 1994).

[28] B. Mhlanga, *Race and the CPS* (London: TSO, 2000).

[29] D. Crisp, 'Standardising Prosecutions' (1993) 34 *Home Office Research Bulletin* 13.

[30] These 'Narey' reforms are discussed in Sanders and Young, n. 6 above, 339, 539–60.

[31] J. Hodgson, 'The Police, the Prosecutor and the Juge d'Instruction: Judicial Supervision in France, Theory and Practice' (2001) 41 *British Journal of Criminology* 342. On the Netherlands see C. Brants and S. Field, 'Discretion and Accountability in Prosecution' in C. Harding *et al.*, *Criminal Justice in Europe: A Comparative Study* (Oxford: Clarendon, 1995).

and will always be subject to tensions. It is therefore not surprising that 'prosecution momentum' develops, undermining the independence of the CPS and the 'equality of arms' principle in practice, so that cases which ought not to continue nevertheless go to court.

NON-POLICE PROSECUTIONS

The evidential and public interest tests applied by the police and CPS in deciding whether to prosecute, are also applied by non-police agencies. The difference is that, whereas the police and CPS usually prosecute, other agencies share a propensity *not* to prosecute. There are three exceptions to this: the drugs section of Customs and Excise, the Department of Social Security (DSS) (dealing with social welfare fraud), and the TV Licence Authority (TV licence evasion). The offences, and offenders, that they deal with are similar to those dealt with by the police. One might easily compare benefits fraud with income tax evasion, which involves similar offences (albeit that tax evasion usually involves larger sums and hence is more socially harmful) but dissimilar offenders. The DSS mounted 8,090 prosecutions in 1986–7, compared to the Inland Revenue's 459 in the same year, despite the far greater number of tax offences.[32]

The Inland Revenue is not the only non-police agency dealing with serious offences that rarely prosecutes. Take the Health and Safety Executive (HSE), for example, which deals with work-place safety. Some 500 people die at work every year (by comparison, there are fewer than 1,000 official homicides each year), thousands die each year from occupational diseases, and there are some 18,000 major work–related injuries annually. The HSE estimates that in most of these incidents the employer was in breach of the criminal provisions of the Health and Safety at Work Act 1974. Thus, most of these incidents give rise to potential criminal, as well as civil, liability. Yet not only does the HSE investigate little over 10 per cent of all major injuries reported to it (even though it believes most of those reported to involve criminal offences), but it prosecutes only 10 per cent of those it does investigate. Even the treatment of people who are unlawfully killed is completely different, for non-police agencies hardly ever ask the police and CPS to consider prosecuting for manslaughter in circumstances where this would be viable and, arguably, desirable.[33] There are government plans to change the law of corporate manslaughter in order to facilitate work-place homicide prosecutions, but even if there is legislation, the ethos of the DPP and HSE will not necessarily change.[34]

When these non-police agencies discover offences, they usually warn the offenders informally. Enforcement notices (formal warning letters) are rare; prohibition notices (stopping work until the law is complied with) are rarer still; and prosecution is the

---

[32] D. Cook, *Rich Law, Poor Law* (Milton Keynes: Open University Press, 1989).

[33] See generally G. Slapper, *Blood in the Bank* (Aldershot: Ashgate, 1999); G. Slapper and S. Tombs, *Corporate Crime* (Harlow: Longman, 1999); Sanders and Young, n. 6 above, 364–77.

[34] C. Wells, *Corporations and Criminal Responsibility* (2nd edn., Oxford: OUP, 2001).

last resort. Since most non-police agencies cannot usually arrest, neither can they charge or detain suspects. Instead they report for summons. Prosecution decisions are taken in the cold light of day, on the basis of full written files, by senior officials. In this atmosphere, these agencies tend to develop a philosophy which attempts to get the offender to obey the law in the future through a policy of persuasion rather than coercion. This 'compliance approach' is an elaborate version of the police system of warnings. As with police warnings, questions of retribution or deterrence are over-ridden by other considerations.

Whilst the compliance approach may be justifiable, there is evidence that it does not work well, at least judging by the volume of offending. *Jones*, discussed in the next section below, is a typical example. Here, a company used procedures that were dangerous. The HSE issued improvement and prohibition notices, but did not pros-ecute. The company continued to break the law, leading to the death of Jones, one of its employees. At a more general level, even if the compliance approach did work well, the more lenient treatment of 'regulatory' offenders, whose crimes are often more serious than those of other offenders, would still be difficult to justify.

Why do most non-police agencies differ from the police in their approach? First, there is the question of resources. The police budget, like the whole 'Law and Order' budget, always rises. But non-police crime (again with the exceptions noted earlier) is not seen as a Law and Order issue. In most years, the budget for most non-police agencies falls. For example, it has been found that waste operators dump tons of hazardous waste in unauthorized sites (including next to shopping centres) in order to evade tax. The Environment Agency, which is supposed to inspect sites, has admitted that it lacks the resources to discharge its responsibilities effectively.[35]

Secondly, there is the problem of 'corporate capture', whereby regulatory agencies become collusive as a result of their dependence on their suspects/clients. This dependence is often a product of such limited resources that the agencies need the co-operation of the firms in their industrial sector in order to do their job at all. A captured agency no longer mediates between the interests of the public, which is to be protected through regulation, and the interests of the regulated industry. Instead it uses its discretion to advance the goals of regulation only so far as industry interests permit.

The problem is that the HSE, Environment Agency, Inland Revenue, and so forth all regulate crime that is a by-product of legitimate economic activity. If these laws are enforced too rigorously, production costs will rise and firms may fail to thrive or they may re-locate. Every society is potentially vulnerable to the same dilemma. No such considerations arise with drugs, benefit evasion, or TV licence evasion, so the agencies that deal with these offences behave more like the police than do other non-police agencies. In the enforcement of most regulatory criminal laws, there is, or there is perceived to be, a need to preserve a fragile balance between the interests of economic activity on the one hand and the public welfare on the other. 'Don't rock the economic boat' is, in crude terms, the main working rule of these

---

[35] *Guardian*, 5 Apr. 2000.

agencies.[36] It is the unfortunate lot of the poor, the main target group for the police and TV licence authority, that their economic activity has increasingly become non-existent through unemployment or replaceable through de-skilling.

Police and non-police agencies use prosecution policy to further their particular working rules. But whereas, as we have seen, the police have working rules that aim to control crime and disorder, and to promote their authority, the working rules of most other agencies require a co-operative relationship with 'their' criminals. The result is that the stigmatizing and exclusionary process of prosecution is used routinely against the poor but rarely against the wealthy.

ACCOUNTABILITY AND THE VICTIM

In any criminal justice system, it is vital that state agencies—including police, other investigative bodies, and prosecution agencies—be accountable. This is to ensure, first, that the rule of law is upheld; secondly, that they operate in a non-discriminatory manner; thirdly, that (within these parameters) they carry out the policies set by law-makers. The political accountability of the police to local authorities has been in decline for many years and there has never been any such accountability for the other prosecution agencies. Although it is often said that this is of no consequence as the police are accountable to the courts, this is too complacent a view. We have seen that police and non-police agencies alike NFA and give warnings (or their equivalent) in large quantities. These decisions are never scrutinized by courts or any other bodies at all, except on the rare occasions when a warning is judicially reviewed (see below). This is a matter of concern where there should be a prosecution, as (many would believe) in many individual cases dealt with by non-police agencies, and also in terms of the different treatment of offence and offender type by the different agencies. On the other hand, the non-scrutiny of police NFAs and warnings means that the police are, in practice, not accountable for arrest decisions that end in NFA. It is possible to sue for wrongful arrest, but this is very difficult, and expensive, to do in practice. Consequently, arrests made on flimsy grounds are very difficult to challenge, giving the police great freedom to operate on the basis of crime-control, rather than due-process, principles.

The main group concerned about non-prosecution decisions are victims. Their 'stake' in official prosecutions is not formally recognized by the common law. But it is unrealistic to deny that victims have an interest in 'their' cases, and in recent years this has been increasingly recognized in the policy and practice of government and criminal justice agencies. Thus the caution guidelines and Code for Crown Prosecutors require the police and CPS to take into account the wishes and interests of victims (albeit balanced against the other considerations). A more recent requirement still is that, when the CPS considers dropping or significantly reducing charges in an

---

[36] See for an example in another area D. Cowan and A. Marsh, 'There's Regulatory Crime and There's Landlord Crime: From "Rachmanites" to "Partners"' (2001) 64 *Modern Law Review* 831.

on-going case, the victims should be consulted.[37] As we have seen, there are types of crime where the police and CPS take the victims' interests and views so seriously that prosecutions are sometimes based on little evidence. On the other hand, when the police and prosecution do not wish to prosecute they need only listen to the victims, not be influenced by them.

In theory, victims can privately prosecute most offences, although this is hardly ever successful, because private individuals do not have the material resources and legal powers possessed by the police. Thus the family of the murdered Stephen Lawrence unsuccessfully prosecuted privately after the police declined to do so. The CPS even has the power, under the Prosecution of Offences Act, to take over any private prosecution it wishes, and then (if it wishes) to drop the case. Ironically, however, 'regulatory' offences—which are prosecuted so rarely—are not capable of being prosecuted privately. Nor do non-prosecution agencies consult with victims.

We should not assume that all victims want prosecutions or that prosecution is always in their interest. We saw earlier that 'pro-charge' policies have developed for domestic violence cases. In other words, all domestic violence arrests should be prosecuted if they pass the evidential test. The idea is that the police would then not be able to manipulate victims into dropping their complaints and victims would not be exposed to the wrath of the violent perpetrator. However, many victims do not welcome the police deciding what is to happen. Most victims make decisions that are rational for them, given the very difficult circumstances in which they find themselves. If prosecution is likely to help them, they generally make and press their complaints, but if it is not (if, for example, they are still living with the perpetrator and do not wish to leave him) then they do not do this. Calling the police but not prosecuting is rational for women who want perpetrators to be taken away until their anger or drunkenness, for example, subsides. This is no guarantee that there will not be repeated violence in future—far from it. But prosecution provides no guarantee either. Acting against the wishes of victims, but in the supposed best interests of them or of society as a whole, would therefore often be counter-productive for those victims. Victims need to be helped into situations where they do not have to choose between the violence of their partners or other degrading situations such as the hardship of single parenthood on state welfare benefits. Domestic violence victims need to be reassured that they can be re-housed, given adequate benefits, and protected from further violence, if prosecution is to be of much value to them.[38] One of the major unresolved problems of prosecution policy in all jurisdictions is how far the interests of the individual victim in the particular case should override the interests of victims in general in deciding whether or not to prosecute.

The main way in which prosecution agencies in England and Wales, especially non-police agencies, are accountable to the law is through judicial review. For many years it has been possible in principle to seek judicial review of prosecution (and

[37] Attorney-General's Guidelines on the Acceptance of Pleas, 2000, discussed in A. Sanders and R. Young, 'Discontinuances, The Rights of Victims and the Remedy of Freedom' [2001] *New LJ* 44.

[38] C. Hoyle and A. Sanders, 'Police Response to Domestic Violence: From Victim Choice to Victim Empowerment' (2000) 40 *British Journal of Criminology* 14.

non-prosecution) decisions, and in recent years it has become more common. Decisions appear to be based on three principles. First, prosecution must not be made in bad faith. Secondly, decisions must not be unreasonable. These are both well-established principles of administrative law. So, for example, in *Manning*[39] a suspect in police custody was asphyxiated by police officers 'restraining' him. In *Jones*,[40] discussed earlier, a man died as a result of the negligence of his employers. The decisions not to prosecute for manslaughter were successfully challenged in both cases because the law of manslaughter had been applied wrongly.

Finally, prosecution decisions must be taken only after consideration and application of a consistent policy. Thus in *R. v. Commissioner of Police for the Metropolis, ex parte P*, a caution was successfully challenged on the grounds that the caution guidelines were not followed.[41] And in *R. v. DPP, ex parte C*[42] a decision to drop the prosecution of a man accused of non-consensual buggery of his wife on public interest grounds was successfully challenged because the prosecutor had not considered all the possibilities laid down in the Code for Crown Prosecutors before the decision was taken. The same principle applies to non-police agencies. However, the courts exercise a light touch in the control of prosecution policy and practice in relation to all agencies. So, in *R. v. Inland Revenue Commissioner, ex parte Mead*[43] the applicants, who were being prosecuted for tax offences, objected on the ground that similar offenders were not being prosecuted. Although the court stressed that agencies that prosecute selectively should ensure that all decisions should be in accordance with a stated policy, it was held that, as long as this was done, it was not necessarily wrong for apparently similar cases to be dealt with differently.

Although prosecution policies are public, the way that they are applied in individual cases is not. This makes it difficult to challenge decisions in practice. Even when a judicial review succeeds, the eventual decision may be no different. Thus, when the DPP reconsidered his decisions in the *Manning* and *Jones* cases, he decided again not to prosecute for manslaughter. The decision of the DPP in *Jones* reflects the general attitude relating to deaths at work discussed earlier, while *Manning* is one of many cases of deaths in police custody where the attitude of the DPP (who is responsible for taking prosecution decisions in relation to police officers) is similar. This is perhaps not surprising, as deaths in custody are particular instances of deaths at work, and the DPP and police have a close working relationship. The reluctance of the DPP to prosecute police officers in general has been criticized by the courts in several cases[44] and, less robustly, by an official inquiry.[45]

The case law shows that judges will correct grossly unfair decisions, but they will not do the legislature's job of establishing prosecution policy. This leaves a vacuum

---

[39] [2000] 3 WLR 463. [40] DC, 23 Mar. 2000, unreported.

[41] (1995) 160 JP 367. [42] [1995] 1 Cr. App. R 136.

[43] [1993] 1 All ER 772.

[44] See, especially, *Treadaway, Legal Action*, Oct. 1997, 15, where a man was given civil damages for the injuries he received at the hands of the police, who were nonetheless not prosecuted.

[45] G. Butler, *Inquiry into CPS Decision Making in Relation to Deaths in Custody and Related Matters* (London: TSO, 1999). For general discussion see M. Burton, 'Reviewing CPS Decisions not to Prosecute' [2001] *Crim. LR* 374.

that, as we have seen, agencies fill by establishing their own policies that may be inconsistent (in due-process terms) with each other. Moreover, sensitive issues such as deaths at work and in custody are subject to 'unofficial' policies that are unstated—as if it is thought that it would not be in the public interest to prosecute in such cases and equally not in the public interest to give that as the reason for not prosecuting! There is a clear need for an accountability mechanism that is less cumbersome, and more capable of probing the real reasons for decisions and the facts on which they are based, than the judicial review procedure. This was recognized in the Crown Prosecution Service Inspectorate Act 2000 by the establishment of an independent CPS Inspectorate, which scrutinizes CPS decisions and the more general operating policies and practices of the CPS. Its reports are public, and are often critical. Remarkably, however, there is no equivalent body to oversee the work of the non-police agencies. If the CPS Inspectorate were given a wider role as a Prosecutions Inspectorate, covering all prosecution agencies, the goal of a consistent and justifiable range of prosecution policies might be achievable.

CONCLUSION

We have seen that prosecutions (and non-prosecutions) by all agencies are tools of law enforcement. There would, in principle, be nothing wrong with this if enforcement policy was fair, though we would have to accept that the idea of 'independent' prosecutors is perhaps more of a myth except in relation to the conduct of those prosecutions that go ahead. Even police cautioning can serve crime-control objectives, and non-police agencies certainly use a range of measures to further economic and social policy, of which law enforcement is only one element. Accountability for all these decisions is minimal.

The most important police decisions—to arrest and then to prosecute or take less serious action—are taken without any supervision from the CPS or courts. Even senior officers are hardly involved. By contrast, report-and-summons—the method used in most cases by most non-police agencies—is less coercive (as it need not require detention of suspects) and offers scope for senior officers and/or the CPS to review a file of written evidence, allowing for more accountability and objectivity. The 1981 Royal Commission advocated the greater use of this procedure for these very reasons, but it has, instead, declined as the police themselves now decide to arrest and charge in most non-trivial cases (a tendency exacerbated by PACE which makes questioning outside the police station legally problematic). This is a major example of the tension between the due-process ideals of liberal legalism and the view that the police need substantial power if they are to enforce the law effectively. All systems are potentially subject to this tension.

One important conclusion to be drawn is that the CPS is not, in most important ways, independent of the police. Transforming the CPS from a police prosecution agency into an independent and quasi-judicial prosecution decision-making body would require fundamental changes in the adversarial system. Even then, it might well be unsuccessful, if the evidence of continental systems is anything to go by.[46] It might be better to strengthen the position of the defence in the adversarial system, but the political will to achieve this is singularly lacking. Until that time, prosecutions will continue to resemble a crime control system, far more than a due process one, and the Article 6 ECHR principle of 'equality of arms' will continue to be violated.

Finally, it is worth asking why the police do not adopt the 'compliance' approach of most non-police agencies, and why 'restorative justice' is confined largely to non-serious juvenile offences. Action short of prosecution for substantial proportions of offences and offenders might be as effective, or more effective, than the current approach. It would certainly be cheaper, which would release resources for improving the rehabilitative potential of custodial and non-custodial sentences when there are prosecutions, and for improving the social conditions that breed crime in the first place. If society can accommodate the crimes of the wealthy in order to foster broad socio-economic goals, why should it not adopt a similar attitude to crimes committed by those who are less fortunate?

Further Reading

BURTON, M., 'Reviewing CPS Decisions not to Prosecute' [2001] *Crim. LR* 374.

HAWKINS, K., *Law as Last Resort: Prosecution Decision Making in a Regulatory Agency* (Oxford: OUP, 2002).

HODGSON, J., 'The Police, the Prosecutor and the Juge d'Instruction: Judicial Supervision in France, Theory and Practice' (2001) 41 *British Journal of Criminology* 342.

McCONVILLE, M., *et al.*, *The Case for the Prosecution* (London: Routledge, 1991).

MHLANGA, B., *Race and the CPS* (London: TSO, 2000).

SANDERS, A. (ed.), *Prosecutions in Common Law Jurisdictions* (Dartmouth: Ashgate, 1996).

—— and YOUNG, R., *Criminal Justice* (2nd edn., London: Butterworths, 2000), chap. 6.

SLAPPER, G., *Blood in the Bank* (Aldershot: Ashgate, 1999).

---

[46] Hodgson, n. 31 above, in relation to France. A more positive view, from the Netherlands, is provided by Brants and Field, n. 31 above.

10

ALTERNATIVES TO PROSECUTION

Rob Allen[1]

INTRODUCTION

'It has never been the rule in this country—I hope it never will be—that suspected criminal offences must automatically be the subject of prosecution'. So the then Attorney-General, Lord Shawcross, told Parliament in 1951, in a statement which has been supported by Attorneys-General ever since.[2] Indeed the words are quoted with approval in the latest Code for Crown Prosecutors published in 2000, which gives guidance on the general principles to be applied when making decisions about prosecutions. The Code makes it clear that 'when deciding whether a case should be prosecuted in the courts, Crown prosecutors should consider the alternatives to prosecution'.[3] In addition, in England and Wales there is a strong tradition of police discretion in deciding how to deal with people who break the criminal law. No branch of the government or judiciary can direct a police officer or the CPS to bring proceedings or not to do so in a particular case. It is in fact police cautioning (and its equivalents for juveniles) which is the most important mechanism for dealing with offenders outside the courts. The aim of this chapter is to describe what alternatives are available to police and prosecutors in England and Wales, how these work in practice, and some of the key issues involved in their use. It is worth noting that a recent review of the criminal courts undertaken by Auld LJ (the Auld Review)[4] has given considerable support to an overall and principled reform aimed at removing from the courts matters for which they are not appropriate and necessary, while leaving them, in the main, to deal with matters for which they are well suited, in particular marking society's disapproval and safeguarding public and private safety.

The review makes specific recommendations that fixed penalties for minor offences be extended, that consideration be given to the development of 'conditional caution-

---

[1] Project Director, Esmee Fairbairn Foundation

[2] House of Commons Debates, vol. 483, col. 681, 29 Jan. 1951.

[3] Crown Prosecution Service Code for Crown Prosecutors, para. 6.12.

[4] Auld LJ, *A Review of the Criminal Courts of England and Wales* (London: Lord Chancellor's Department, 2001).

ing' arrangements, and that a national strategy for restorative justice be devised. If accepted by the government, these proposals will give substantial impetus to alternatives to prosecution.

CONTEXT

At the outset, it is worth considering the role which prosecution plays in different jurisdictions. A distinction is often drawn between jurisdictions based on the legality principle and those based on the opportunity or expediency principle. The former requires that all cases in which there is sufficient evidence be prosecuted in the courts. Such a system is seen to provide equality of treatment and prevent the danger of abuse of official power. On the other hand, the opportunity principle, which has always applied in England and Wales, deliberately allows discretion about whether to bring cases to court. This gives flexibility to the system and avoids courts being over-burdened with trivial cases and those where the public interest is best served by an alternative course of action. Minors, people with mental health problems, and drug addicts are particular groups of offenders for whom alternatives can be much more appropriate than prosecution.

In fact even systems based on the legality principle have moved to introduce more discretion. A review of European systems in the mid-1980s concluded that:

Jurisdictions requiring compulsory prosecution of all detected and investigated offences have vested the prosecution service with rights to waive prosecutions in cases involving minor crimes, or cases where the offender has become the victim of his own offence or the jurisdictions have introduced new ways of dealing with offences which circumvent the formal court procedure applied to criminal acts in general or to specific crimes such as those related to drug abuse.[5]

ALTERNATIVES TO PROSECUTION IN ENGLAND AND WALES

In England and Wales, there is a variety of alternatives to prosecution. Unlike in many countries most of the alternatives to prosecution are available *before* the case reaches a prosecutor.

For the most minor offences, there is a system of fixed penalties or on-the-spot fines. These currently apply to a range of motoring offences. The police, or other authorities such as traffic wardens, can issue penalty notices on the spot or at a police station. Such notices provide an opportunity to discharge any liability to

---

[5] P. J. P. Tak, *The Legal Scope of Non Prosecution in Europe*, HEUNI Publications No. 8 (Helsinki: HEUNI Publications, 1986).

conviction for the offence by payment of a sum of money. There is no criminal conviction or admission of guilt associated with payment, although the alleged offender has the right to opt for trial by a court and risk conviction if he so chooses. Failure to pay the penalty or opting for trial may lead to the imposition of a fine substantially higher than the amount of the penalty. In 1998, 3.4 million fixed penalty notices were issued in England and Wales, of which 78 per cent resulted in payment, 14 per cent were registered as fines, and less than 1 per cent were referred for court proceedings.

Very recently, legislation has expanded substantially the range of offences which can be dealt with in this way. The government considers fixed penalty notices as a simple and swift way of addressing a range of low-level anti-social offending associated with disorderly conduct, though the provisions have been controversial, not least because of the high level of discretion allowed to the police in applying them.[6] The Auld Review has recommended a presumption in favour of fixed penalty notices in all eligible road traffic cases and a systematic review of other kinds of infringements which might be suitably dealt with in this way. It also recommends that the use of a television without a licence be dealt with in the first instance by a fixed penalty—there are currently about 160,000 prosecutions a year for the offence.[7] An analogous system already applies in cases of vehicle excise duty evasion, when people use motor vehicles without registering them or paying tax. There are about 1,000,000 cases a year which could be prosecuted. The Driver Vehicle Licensing Authority (DVLA) operates an out-of-court settlement scheme for those who pay what they owe plus a penalty. Despite this, there are still about 300,000 prosecutions a year, of which 98 per cent result in a guilty plea. A discount for early payment is to be introduced shortly in order to encourage more offenders to pay up prior to prosecution.

In more serious cases, the police enjoy considerable discretion in how to respond to crime. It is the police who usually start proceedings when this is the course of action which is pursued. A survey of what happens to people arrested by the police found that 52 per cent of suspects were charged, 20 per cent had no further action taken against them, 17 per cent were cautioned, and the remaining 13 per cent were dealt with in other ways.[8]

When the police do start proceedings, the case is passed to the Crown Prosecution Service (CPS) which reviews it and decides whether to continue or discontinue it. How it makes that decision is described in a later section. The next section will concentrate on the options open to the police.

---

[6] Criminal Justice and Police Act 2001, Pt. 1.   [7] Auld, n. 4 above.

[8] *Entry into the Criminal Justice System*, Home Office Research Study 185 (London: Home Office, 1998).

DIVERSION BY THE POLICE

The police are responsible for much of what is sometimes called 'diversion'—the diverting of mainly low-level cases out of the criminal process. The main way of doing this is by the administration of an informal warning or a police caution, which is a formal warning given by an officer of the rank of inspector or above to an offender who admits to having committed a criminal offence which could have led to prosecution. Since 1998, cautioning has been replaced for juveniles by a new system of reprimands and final warnings (see below). But the most recent government guidance makes it clear that 'properly used cautioning continues to be regarded as an effective form of disposal and one which may be used for offenders of any age'.[9] Cautions are, in effect, administrative measures taken by the police. They can be accompanied by referral to social, health, or welfare agencies better able to deal with the matter. They do not, however, involve any element of punishment, although the Auld Review has suggested there might in future be a role for 'conditional cautioning' in which specified conditions could be attached, not by the police but by the prosecutor. (See the section on 'Discrimination by the Prosecution', below.)

CAUTIONING

The government has produced national standards for cautioning, which define the purposes of a formal caution as being to:

- deal quickly and simply with less serious offenders;
- divert them from unnecessary appearance in court;
- reduce the chances of their re-offending.[10]

A caution is not a form of sentence. Neither may it be made conditional upon the satisfactory completion of a specific task, such as reparation or the payment of compensation to the victim. A formal caution is a serious matter. It is recorded by the police and influences a decision whether or not to institute proceedings in the event of future offending. It may be cited in subsequent court proceedings, i.e. it can be taken into account by a court at the sentencing stage.

The following conditions must be met before a caution can be administered:

- There must be evidence of the offender's guilt sufficient to give a realistic prospect of conviction;
- The offender must make a clear and reliable admission of the offence;
- The offender must give his or her informed consent to being cautioned (in practice consent to the caution is not sought until it has been decided that cautioning is the correct course);

---

[9] Home Office Circular 18/1994, *The Cautioning of Offenders.*
[10] *Ibid.*

- The significance of the caution must be explained, i.e. that while a caution does not give the offender a criminal record in the same way as a conviction, a record will be kept and it can be cited in any future proceedings. A caution is not currently covered by the Rehabilitation of Offenders Act 1974, which allows the record of most convictions to lapse after a certain period, depending on the sentence.[11]

If the first two conditions are met, the police must consider whether a caution is in the public interest. The police take account of the public interest principles set out in the Code for Crown Prosecutors (see below).

The national standards draw attention to three particular points of importance when deciding whether to caution or not. First is the presumption that certain categories of offender should not be prosecuted. These include elderly people, and those suffering mental illness or impairment, or a severe physical illness. Membership of these groups does not offer absolute protection against prosecution, which may be justified if the offence is a serious one. But in reaching a decision the police will start off with the idea that these offenders should not be prosecuted.

Second is the question of the offender's attitude to his offence. If the offence was committed deliberately and wilfully and the offender shows little or no remorse a caution is less likely to be suitable. A practical demonstration of regret, such as apologizing to the victim or offering to put matters right, may support the use of a caution.

Third is the question of how to deal with offenders involved in 'group' offences where the experience and circumstances of individuals can vary greatly, as can their degree of involvement. While consistency and equity are considered important principles, the standards make it clear that each offender should be dealt with separately, and different disposals may be justified.

The national standards also suggest that it is desirable that the victim be contacted before a caution is administered. The aim of this contact is to establish his or her views about the offence, the nature of any harm or loss and its significance relative to the victim's circumstances, and whether any form of reparation has been made or compensation paid. The significance of a caution should be explained to the victim. The victim's view about whether or not a caution is appropriate will not normally be taken into account, although the standards suggest that in some cases where cautioning might otherwise be appropriate prosecution may be required in order to protect the victim from further attention from the offender.

Cautioning decisions are entirely a matter of police discretion, but that discretion is constrained by guidance from the Home Office. The most recent guidance, Circular 18 of 1994, set out in particular to discourage the use of cautions in inappropriate cases, to seek greater consistency between police force areas, and to promote the better recording of cautions.[12] We shall see below how far these objectives have been met.

At this point it is worth noting the main factors which the police are supposed to

---

[11] A consultation paper was issued in 2000 about whether cautions should be brought within the scope of the Rehabilitation of Offenders Act.

[12] Home Office Circular 18/1994, n. 9 above.

take into account in exercising their discretion. The guidance describes the proper use of discretion as a matter of common sense. The questions to be asked in each case are:

- Whether the circumstances are such that the caution is likely to be effective; and
- Whether the caution is appropriate to the offence.

Two key elements are the seriousness of the offence and the offender's previous record. The 1994 guidance on cautioning sought to discourage the use of cautions in inappropriate cases, 'for example for offences which are triable on indictment only'.[13] The guidance makes it clear that cautions should never be used for the most serious 'indictable only' offences, such as attempted murder and rape, because this undermines the credibility of the disposal. Cautions should be used only for other 'indictable only' offences in exceptional cases. A child taking another's pocket money by force (which in law counts as robbery) is given as an example of such a case.

The guidance lists the kinds of factors which are relevant to an assessment of seriousness. They include the nature and extent of harm or loss relative to the victim's age and means; whether the offence was racially motivated; whether it involved a breach of trust; and whether it was carried out in a systematic and organized way. Not surprisingly these are among the factors listed in the Code for Crown Prosecutors as being relevant to decisions to discontinue cases on public interest grounds, something which is discussed below.

As for the offender's record, the guidance makes it clear that multiple cautioning brings this form of disposal of a case into disrepute and that cautions should not be administered in circumstances where there can be no reasonable expectation that this will curb his offending. Multiple cautioning refers to the practice of giving a caution to an offender on more than one occasion for more than one offence. More than one caution should be considered only where the subsequent offence is trivial or where there has been a sufficient lapse of time since the first caution to suggest that it had some effect.

Cautioning in practice

In 2000, in England and Wales a total of 239,000 offenders were cautioned for all offences, excluding motoring offences.[14] That number represents a third of all those offenders cautioned or found guilty in that year—the so-called cautioning rate. The rate varies for different offences and different age groups. Girls and women are more likely to be cautioned than boys and men. There are also markedly different rates in different police force areas.

Table 10.1, overleaf, shows the cautioning rate for the main types of crime.

Most of the offences that attract a caution are minor ones. Two-thirds in the theft category, for example, were cases of shoplifting. It would be wrong, however, to suppose that it is only trivial cases that are diverted in this way. In 2000, 1,700

---

[13] Home Office Circular 18/1994, n. 9 above.

[14] All statistics are from *Cautions Court Proceedings and Sentencing 2000*, Home Office Statistical Bulletin 20/01 Nov. 2001 and *Criminal Statistics in England and Wales* (London: Home Office, 1999).

Table 10.1 Offenders cautioned as a percentage of those cautioned or found guilty

Offence Type	Cautioning Rate
Violence	15%
Sexual offences	25%
Burglary	21%
Theft	39%
Drug offences	50%

offenders were cautioned for the most serious offences—'indictable only' crimes like rape, robbery, and attempted murder which, if prosecuted, would have been tried in the Crown Court and for which there is available a maximum sentence of life imprisonment. Clearly the particular offences for which a caution was given are likely to have been among the least serious examples within the offence category. It is also possible that, notwithstanding the Home Office guidelines, the evidence in these cases was in fact relatively weak. Had proceedings been started, the cases might well have been discontinued by the CPS. In these circumstances the police may have effectively come to an agreement with the suspect under which the suspect received a caution if he admitted to the offence. This is attractive to the suspect because the matter will, in effect, not be taken further. It is attractive to the police because the offence is cleared up.

The relatively high cautioning rate is also explained by the fact that the offenders cautioned for these serious offences are likely to fall into the categories deemed most suitable for diversion—young or old people, those with physical or mental health problems, etc.

The cautioning rate for 'summary offences' (those less serious offences that if prosecuted have to be tried in the first tier magistrates' courts) stood in 2000 at 15 per cent. This is lower than the rate for more serious 'indictable' offences (those which can be tried either in the magistrates' or Crown Court or have to be tried in the Crown Court). The latter rate is 32 per cent. This is on the face of it surprising, as one would expect minor cases to be diverted more often than serious ones, whereas the reverse happens.

One reason for the difference is that large proportions of summary non-motoring offences are offences relating to social security, revenue law, and other offences such as television licence evasion. Police cautions are not generally available for these offences, largely because the police are rarely involved.

Table 10.2, overleaf, shows the cautioning rate by age and gender.

Cautioning rates vary substantially between police force areas. In 1999 more than half of offenders cautioned or found guilty in Surrey were cautioned whereas the proportion in West Yorkshire was less than a quarter. Among young offenders rates varied by as much as 35 per cent.

The use of cautioning has declined somewhat in recent years from a peak of 40 per cent in 1994.

Table 10.2 Offenders cautioned as a percentage of those cautioned or found guilty (Indictable offences)

Age Group	Males	Females
10–11	87%	96%
12–14	69%	87%
15–17	45%	64%
18–20	31%	43%
21+	22%	36%

MENTALLY DISTURBED OFFENDERS

Government policy has long held that, wherever possible, mentally disturbed offenders should be diverted from the criminal justice system and treated instead by the health and social services. There are various ways in which the police and the courts can deal with such offenders without resort to prosecution.

For example, the Mental Health Act 1983 gives the police specific powers to detain mentally disordered persons who are in a public place, in need of care and control, and must be removed in their own interests or for the protection of others. An assessment follows which may lead to admission to a hospital. In these circumstances, a prosecution does not normally follow even if an offence has been committed.[15]

DRUGS OFFENCES

In England and Wales, about half of drugs offences are dealt with by a police caution. These are mainly offences of possession of cannabis. In most areas of the country, arrest referral schemes have been developed. These enable the police to refer people under arrest who have drug or alcohol problems to agencies which can address those problems. While referral does not automatically mean that criminal proceedings are dropped, in more minor cases the willingness of an offender to attend a programme of treatment makes a diversion more likely. Under the current system, there is, however, no way that the police or prosecutors can ensure that the offender does complete or even attend the programme.[16]

---

[15] Mental Health Act s. 136.
[16] In the event of conviction, the court can do so by making a Drug Treatment and Testing Order.

JUVENILES

During the 1970s and 1980s there was a strong policy objective of keeping the youngest offenders in particular out of the criminal justice system, on the ground that involvement in the system could be an expensive way of labelling them as delinquents and confirming their criminal identities. There was, and is, a good deal of empirical evidence in favour of keeping young people out of the courts as far as possible. Some eight out of ten first-time offenders filtered out of the system at an early stage are not convicted of a further offence within two years.[17] International instruments encourage alternatives to prosecution; the UN Convention on the Rights of the Child requires States to promote measures for dealing with juvenile offenders 'without resort to judicial proceedings'.[18]

The practice of police cautioning of juveniles was encouraged by a series of government circulars to Chief Constables that made clear a presumption that juveniles should be diverted from courts.[19] A shift in policy in the early 1990s led to guidance which sought to restrict the use of cautions for serious offenders and for repeat offenders. At that time rates of cautioning varied substantially from one part of the country to another. The Crime and Disorder Act 1998 put this filtering system for offenders under the age of 18 on a statutory basis by introducing a 'final warning' scheme. The scheme is designed to:

- end repeat cautioning and provide a progressive and meaningful response to offending behaviour;
- ensure appropriate and effective action to help prevent re-offending;
- ensure that juveniles who do re-offend after a warning are dealt with quickly and effectively by the courts.[20]

The scheme enables the police to deal with children who have not previously been convicted of an offence by way of a reprimand in the most minor cases.[21] A final warning is available for those who have previously been reprimanded or who have committed an offence which is too serious for a reprimand but not considered so serious that a charge must result. A final warning is recorded and provides the opportunity for one officially recorded intervention for offending prior to a young person going to court for subsequent offences. The 1998 Act does allow a limited option of a second final warning where a minor offence is committed at least two years after the first warning has been given. To assist in securing the good behaviour of the young person, the police are required to refer the names of those given a final warning to the local Youth Offending Team (YOT) for an assessment of whether a rehabilitation programme is required.

Prosecution remains available for the most serious cases. Young people who

---

[17] See e.g. *Home Office Criminal Statistics*, Cm 5001 (1999) Table 5C.

[18] Art. 40.3.b.   [19] In 1978, 1985, and 1990.

[20] The *Final Warning Scheme Revised Guidance*, Home Office/Youth Justice Board, Mar. 2000.

[21] Informal warnings which are not recorded are still available, but they should be used only in exceptional circumstances.

re-offend after a reprimand can be given a final warning, but a final warning generally says what it means. If a young person offends after having received a final warning, proceedings will be started unless there are exceptional circumstances.

Decisions to give reprimands and final warnings are made by the police in accordance with guidelines produced by the Home Office and the Youth Justice Board. The current guidelines are in many respects similar to the guidelines and standards for cautioning, discussed above, which in respect of under 18s they have replaced.

The first step involves assessing eligibility. Before a reprimand or final warning can be given there must be sufficient evidence to give a realistic prospect of conviction if the juvenile were to be prosecuted and the juvenile must admit the offence. In addition, the police should check that the juvenile has not previously been convicted and must take the view that it is not in the public interest for the offender to be prosecuted. In reaching a view about the public interest, the police are expected to consider 'gravity factors' developed by the Association of Chief Police Officers. The Guidance contains tables of common offences, which are allocated a gravity score of between one (low gravity) and four (high gravity). Factors which can make an offence more or less serious are listed. These can upgrade or downgrade an offence by one point. Particular action is then recommended as an alternative to prosecution, as set out in Table 10.3 below.

Table 10.3 Non-prosecution alternatives

Final Score	Action
4	Always charge
3	Normally warn for first offence
2	Normally reprimand for first offence
1	Always the minimum response applicable

The second step involves assessing the options. As with cautioning the key factors influencing the choice are the young person's offending history and the seriousness of the offence. If an initial assessment suggests that either a warning or a charge is appropriate, a further key factor in the choice between them is whether a warning is sufficient to prevent re-offending.

As far as previous offending is concerned, the Guidance says that:

- first-time offenders should normally receive a reprimand for a less serious offence;

- second-time offenders who have been reprimanded cannot be given a further reprimand—they should either be warned or, if the circumstances warrant it, charged. Second-time offenders who have already received a warning cannot be given a reprimand and should not receive a further warning. They should be charged. The only exception is where the new offence has been committed more than two years since the previous warning and its circumstances are not so serious as to require a charge;

- third-time offenders who have already received a reprimand and a warning should usually be charged unless the new offence is not so serious as to require a charge and is committed at least two years after the final warning;
- those offending for the fourth time or more who have previously received a reprimand or warning must be charged.

As for the seriousness of the offence, the Guidance emphasizes the importance of the impact of the offence on the victim, suggesting that a police officer trained in victim awareness should make contact, and help with the preparation of a victim statement. The victim's view will be influential but should not be conclusive.

So far the final warning scheme does not look substantially different from the cautioning arrangements which preceded it. Research comparing juveniles receiving final warnings with those receiving cautions found that the final warning sample had statistically better outcomes, with fewer than a third involved in further criminal proceedings.[22] The key difference is the expectation that the majority of those receiving a final warning will be expected to participate in a rehabilitation programme. Prior to making a warning the police need to be satisfied that the offender is likely to engage in such a programme and that the programme is likely to be effective in preventing further offending.

In deciding these issues, the police should ask the YOT to undertake an assessment to:

- explore the young offender's attitude to intervention and likely engagement with a programme;
- consider the nature and content of the rehabilitation programme;
- explore with the young offender and victim the possibility of setting up a restorative process.

Participation in a rehabilitation programme is voluntary, and the Guidance makes it clear that there must be *no* suggestion that the warning is conditional on agreement to participate in the programme. 'This is an important point: the person will not have been tried and found guilty in a court of law, and therefore cannot be pressurised to undertake a programme.'[23] The same is true in respect of participation in a restorative conference.

The assessment is normally carried out at the young offender's home. Some YOTs use an assessment tool developed by the Youth Justice Board called Asset which systematically identifies the needs and problems experienced by the young person and the risks which they may pose.

Once the decision to warn has been made, the police must decide how to deliver the warning. Home Office guidance encourages the use of restorative principles whose aims have been described as encouraging:

---

[22] J. Hine and A. Celnick, *A One Year Reconviction Study of Final Warnings*, Home Office Research Study (London: Home Office, 2001).

[23] *The Final Warning Scheme Revised Guidance*, n. 20 above.

- responsibility—the young offenders take responsibility for the consequences of their offending;
- restoration—the young offenders apologize or give something back to the person or community they have offended against;
- re-integration—the young offenders are reintegrated into the law-abiding community.

The fullest way of putting these principles into practice is through a restorative conference in which young offenders meet the victims and hear first hand about the impact of their crime before being warned. The parents and other influential adults should also be present. Based on models developed in Australia and New Zealand, the conference must be set up by a trained police officer or other suitable person. Preliminary evidence suggests that young people who go through such a restorative process may be less likely to re-offend than those who simply receive a warning, but the results are not conclusive. Indeed, more generally, the research on final warnings surprisingly found no difference in criminal proceeding rates between those assessed as appropriate for a rehabilitation programme and those not seen by the YOT.[24]

There are, of course, costs attached to establishing rehabilitation schemes at this stage in the process, and particularly restorative schemes. Not everyone agrees that this is the most effective use of police resources, although early intervention which succeeds in averting a criminal career is likely to pay for itself several times over. There is also the question of delay. Current policy stresses the importance of swift processing of young offenders through the system. There is sometimes a tension between the need to deal quickly with a youngster and the preparation needed to ensure an effective conference. Experience shows that if the victims of crime are to be invited, they should be given time to consider and think through whether they wish to attend. There is growing interest in restorative justice across the UK. The Auld Review recommends the development and implementation of a national strategy to ensure consistent, appropriate, and effective use of restorative justice techniques.[25] It sees particular promise for restorative justice as an alternative to prosecution, albeit overseen by 'symbolic and practical involvement of the courts'.[26]

DISCONTINUANCE BY THE PROSECUTION

Compared with those of many countries the alternatives available to the official Crown Prosecution Service (CPS) in England and Wales are somewhat limited. Waiver of prosecution on grounds other than the insufficiency of evidence has become widespread in Europe. In Scotland, a separate jurisdiction, the Procurator Fiscal, has a range of options, including giving the accused a personal warning. The Procurator can also impose a fixed fine of £25 with the offender's agreement for a

---

[24] Hine and Celnick, n. 22 above.   [25] Auld, n. 4 above.   [26] *Ibid.*

common law offence including theft. The prosecutorial fine is a common option for dealing with less serious cases in many countries, particularly in Northern Europe. In Germany, prosecutors have broad powers to dismiss cases and impose sanctions such as community work. In Belgium, where there has always been the possibility of a conditional waiver of prosecution, there is a system of so-called penal mediation. If the prosecutor decides that an offence is unlikely to merit more than two years' imprisonment, the offender can agree to undertake a programme of reparation, of medical treatment, of training or community service. These options can be combined.[27]

There are some fundamental issues involved in expanding pre-court decision-making. While court time may be saved, there is a danger that defendants may be pressurised into admitting offences of which they are not guilty. There may also be a perception that the prosecution is 'copping out' of prosecuting cases or of the rich buying their way out of court. It is perhaps for these reasons that the CPS is effectively limited to discontinuing cases and, where appropriate, referring them back to the police for a caution. The 1993 Royal Commission on Criminal Justice recommended the introduction of prosecutorial fines in England, but the proposal has not been adopted.[28]

The Auld Review recommends that consideration be given to introducing a conditional cautioning scheme covering a wide range of minor offences. This would enable the prosecutor (not the police), with the consent of the offender and, where appropriate, with the approval of the court, (a) to caution the offender subject to him complying with specified conditions and (b) to bring him to court if he fails to comply.[29]

There are two clear stages in the decision made by the CPS whether to prosecute.[30] First is the evidential test. The CPS must be satisfied that there is enough evidence to produce a realistic prospect of conviction. The Code requires that prosecutors address two particular questions in making this assessment. Can the evidence be used in court? Is the evidence reliable?

The second stage is the public interest test. Where the evidential test is met, a prosecution will normally continue unless there are public interest factors tending against prosecution which clearly outweigh those tending in favour. The most important public interest factor is the seriousness of the offence. In addition, a prosecution is likely to be needed if:

- a conviction is likely to result in a significant sentence;
- a weapon was used or violence threatened;
- the victim was a public servant;
- the defendant was in a position of trust;

---

[27] International examples are summarized in a report on prosecution systems prepared for the review of the Criminal Justice System in Northern Ireland (2000).

[28] Royal Commission on Criminal Justice, Cm 2263 (1993).

[29] Auld, n. 4 above.

[30] The rest of this section is based on the Code for Crown Prosecutors, n. 2 above.

- the offence was premeditated;
- the offender was the organizer;
- the offence was committed by a group;
- the victim was vulnerable;
- the offence was motivated by discrimination on grounds of ethnicity, nationality, sex, religion, politics, or sexual orientation;
- the victim and defendant were different ages or there was any element of corruption;
- the defendant has relevant previous convictions or cautions;
- the offence was committed while the defendant was under a court order;
- the offence formed part of a pattern of conduct;
- the offence, although not serious in itself, is widespread in the area it was committed.

On the other hand, a prosecution is less likely if:

- the court is likely to impose a nominal penalty;
- the defendant is already under an order and any further conviction would be unlikely to add a penalty;
- the offence was committed as the result of a genuine mistake;
- the loss or harm is minor;
- there has been a long delay since the offence;
- the prosecution is likely to have a bad effect on the victim's health;
- the defendant is elderly or is or was at the time of the offence suffering from serious physical or mental ill health;
- the defendant has put right the loss or harm;
- details may be made public that could harm sources of information, international relations, or national security.

In 1999, the CPS discontinued about 165,000 cases. It is not known what proportion of these were discontinued for evidential and for public interest reasons.

CONCLUSIONS

Although the English system operates on the 'opportunity' principle, the range of alternatives to prosecution are, *prima facie*, limited compared to those in some European countries. A fixed penalty scheme operates for motoring offences and is being extended to cover a wider range of minor matters of disorder. By far the most important alternative is diversion, e.g. by way of police cautioning, and, in the case of under 18s, the reprimand and final warning scheme. Decisions are made by the police on the basis of the seriousness of the offence and the offender's record. Diversion can involve referral to measures designed to address the causes of offending. These are undertaken on a voluntary basis. Restorative justice principles are being introduced into the reprimand and final warning scheme to ensure that the juvenile understands the consequences of their offending.

The key issues about alternatives to prosecution relate to:

- fairness. Is it right for the police to exercise so much discretion? Can defendants be pressured into accepting a caution or warning?

- effectiveness. Evidence is strong for the effectiveness of diverting young and first-time offenders from the system, most of whom do not re-offend. It is less clear in respect of other offenders. While referral can be made to treatment agencies, diversion is not conditional on completion or attendance, as it might be if it were under the auspices of the Prosecutor.

- public confidence. If it is not properly explained or understood, diversion or discontinuance can be controversial, particularly in serious cases.

- inconsistency. Statistics suggest that despite guidance from government, there is considerable variation in the use of alternatives across the country.

- lack of legislative basis. While the reprimand and final warning scheme operates on the basis laid down by the Crime and Disorder Act 1998, the cautioning arrangements for adults have no basis in criminal law.

- expense. Alternatives to prosecution filter out minor cases in a swift and economical way. Yet some developments such as restorative conferencing incur expense. It is not clear whether these are outweighed by increased benefits in terms of reduced re-offending.

Further Reading

ASHWORTH, A., *Sentencing and Penal Policy* (London: Weidenfeld and Nicholson, 1983).

—— *Sentencing and Criminal Justice* (London: Butterworths, 1997).

CRAWFORD, A., 'Alternatives to Prosecution: Access to, or Exits from, Criminal Justice?' in R. Young and D. Wall (eds.), *Access to Criminal Justice: Legal Aid, Lawyers and the Defence of Liberty* (London: Blackstone Press, 1996).

EVANS, R., 'Police Cautioning and the Young Offender' [1991] *Crim. LR* 598.

—— 'Comparing Young Adult and Juvenile Cautioning in the Metropolitan Police District' [1993] *Crim. LR* 572.

HOYLE, C., YOUNG, R., and HILL, R., *Proceed with Caution: An Evaluation of the Thames Valley Police Initiative in Restorative Cautioning* (London: Joseph Rowntree Foundation, 2001).

LAYCOCK, G., and TARLING, R., 'Police Force Cautioning: Policy and Practice' [1985] 24 *Howard Journal of Justice* 81.

McCONVILLE, M., SANDERS, A., and LENG, R., *The Case for the Prosecution* (London: Routledge, 1991).

11

EVIDENCE IN CRIMINAL CASES

Sir John Smith QC

AN ACCUSATORIAL SYSTEM

The criminal justice system of England and Wales is an accusatorial, not an inquisitorial, system. In an inquisitorial system the judge calls and examines the defendant and the witnesses. An accusatorial system resembles a contest between the prosecution and defence, with the judge acting like an umpire. The prosecution calls the witnesses whose evidence, it claims, proves the guilt of the defendant beyond reasonable doubt. The defence may cross-examine those witnesses to destroy or diminish the effect of their evidence. The defendant may, if he chooses, give evidence in his own defence or in defence of a co-defendant. Though there are now controversial rules which encourage him to do so, there is no obligation and he may, if he chooses, remain a silent spectator of the whole proceedings. Whether he gives evidence or not, he may call witnesses in his defence, who will be cross-examined by the prosecution.

The question for the court or jury is whether the prosecution has proved beyond reasonable doubt that the defendant is guilty. A jury may think it probable, even highly probable, that the defendant is guilty but, if they are not sure, it is their duty to acquit.[1] Of course this must result in the acquittal of some persons who are in fact guilty. This is justified on the ground that the consequences of a criminal conviction are so serious that no one should be convicted unless his guilt is proved beyond reasonable doubt. A person who has been acquitted cannot be tried again for the same offence, except in very exceptional circumstances, but this does not prevent his guilt being proved in other proceedings when it is relevant and there is sufficient evidence to prove it.

---

[1] The specimen direction approved by the Judicial Studies Board is: 'How does the prosecution succeed in proving the defendant's guilt? The answer is—by making you sure of it. Nothing less than that will do. If after considering all the evidence you are sure that the defendant is guilty you must return a verdict of "Guilty". If you are not sure, your verdict must be "Not Guilty"'.

COMMON LAW AND STATUTE

We have no code of evidence in criminal cases. The basic law is common law, that is law made by decisions of the courts, establishing precedents for future cases. In modern times Parliament has passed many statutes modifying or adding to the common law, but it is the common law which must supply the answer when there is no statutory rule in point. The common law was created in jury trials where there is a division of functions between judge and jury. This had a profound effect on the nature of the law. The judges believed that certain matters, though relevant to the question to be decided, would have too great an effect on the untrained minds of jurors and so they excluded them. These rules of exclusion have been greatly reduced in effect by statutes over the last 200 years. There is now much more faith in the ability of jurors to give proper weight to evidence, but the exclusionary rules are still a large and very important part of the modern law. Though the gravest cases are all tried by juries, more than 90 per cent of cases today are tried by magistrates sitting without a jury. The same rules of evidence apply in these cases where, consequently, the magistrates may have to exclude from their minds evidence of which they are in fact aware but which, in a jury trial, the judge would withhold from the jury.

THE ROLES OF JUDGE AND JURY

In a trial in the Crown Court, all questions of law are decided by the judge and questions of fact by the jury. The distinction between fact and law is notoriously difficult. What appears to be a simple question of fact sometimes ends by becoming a question of law. Whether A has 'supplied' drugs to B looks like a straightforward question of fact. If A, being unlawfully in possession of cannabis, hands it to B to look after for an hour or two, and B then returns it to A as agreed, has A 'supplied' B with cannabis? Has B 'supplied' A? Is it open to a jury to find there was a supply in either case? Lower courts took different views about this and the matter had to be settled by the House of Lords.[2] It held that a transfer of possession is not a 'supply' unless it is done for the purposes of the transferee; so A has not supplied B, but B has supplied A. Generally, the question whether an ordinary non-technical word of the English language applies to a particular situation is a question of fact but there are many cases where it has been necessary to determine it as a question of law, as in this example.

WHERE THE JUDGE DECIDES FACTS

There are some exceptions to the general rule. Where the admissibility of evidence depends on the existence of certain facts, it is for the judge to decide whether those facts existed or exist. There are many such cases. An important example concerns confessions. When a confession by the defendant is tendered in evidence by the prosecution the defence may represent to the judge, in the absence of the jury, that it was obtained by oppression or by something said or done which was likely to render

---

[2] *R. v. Maginnis* (1987) 85 Cr. App. R 127 (HL).

any confession unreliable. When this is done, the confession is inadmissible unless the prosecution satisfies the judge that it was not so obtained. The decision necessarily falls to the judge so that, if the confession is inadmissible, the jury will never hear of it. Whether a witness is competent to testify is a question of fact but, if his competence is questioned, is also a question for the judge to decide. Foreign law is treated as a question of fact to be proved by witnesses, but it is decided by the judge because he is so much better fitted by his training and experience than the jury to decide such a matter.

FORMS OF EVIDENCE

Evidence may be testimonial (i.e., given orally in the witness box), documentary, or 'real'. Testimony is the most common form of evidence. A notable feature of the common law is its insistence on the evidence of a witness being presented orally in court and subject to cross-examination in the presence of the jury. This is thought to be the best way to enable the jury to determine whether the evidence is true and what weight to attribute to it. Because of the insistence on oral testimony the common law admitted documents as evidence of the facts stated in them only in exceptional cases, but this is often very inconvenient and Parliament has created many exceptions to the general rule in recent years. These are examined later. Sometimes a thing—for example, a weapon—is produced for the inspection of the court, or the court will 'view' a place, such as a crossroad where a collision has taken place. The court informs itself about relevant facts relating to the thing or place by looking at it. This is called 'real evidence'.

FACTS IN ISSUE AND RELEVANT FACTS

No fact is admissible in evidence unless it is 'a fact in issue' or is relevant to a fact in issue. The facts in issue are those facts which must be proved by the prosecution to establish the commission of the offence and those facts which are the essential elements of any defence that the defendant has raised. What facts are in issue depends on the substantive law defining the elements of the crime and the elements of any defence which has been put in issue. If the substantive law is changed, evidence which was inadmissible may become admissible, or vice versa. In R. v. Gosney[3] G was charged with dangerous driving. She drove along the fast lane of a dual carriageway in the wrong direction. She tendered in evidence maps and plans of the junction at which she entered the dual carriageway to prove that a competent and careful driver might have turned into the wrong lane as she had done. The judge excluded the evidence. It was relevant evidence that she was not at fault but fault was not in issue because in R. v. Ball[4] it had been decided that dangerous driving was an 'absolute' offence, not requiring the prosecution to prove any fault. The Court of Appeal allowed G's appeal, overruling Ball. It held that the offence did require proof of fault and the excluded evidence was therefore relevant to an issue in the case.

[3] [1971] 3 All ER 220.   [4] (1966) 50 Cr. App. R 266.

Relevance generally is determined by the application of logic, common sense, and experience rather than any rule of law. If the evidence would have a tendency to convince a reasonable person of the existence or non-existence of a fact in issue, then it is relevant. Such evidence is known as 'circumstantial' as distinct from the 'direct' evidence of a witness who testifies to the existence of a fact in issue. Circumstantial evidence may be admissible although its relevance is slight because, if it is one of many items of such evidence, the sum may be very cogent, sometimes overwhelm- ingly so. Suppose the issue is the identity of the offender. The fact that the offender was bald and the accused is also bald is of some, but very slight, relevance. If there is evidence of other shared characteristics, e.g., both walk with a limp and so on, they may be enough to convince a reasonable jury that the accused was the offender. Where the characteristic is discreditable, the judge should not admit it unless he is satisfied that the prejudice it might create in the minds of the jury is outweighed by its relevance. There is nothing discreditable about being bald or walking with a limp, so the evidence is admissible notwithstanding the slight relevance of each individual item.

Circumstantial evidence involves the trier of fact in drawing an inference. This may involve several steps. Where the issue was whether a confession had been obtained by torture or inhuman or degrading treatment, as D alleged, his own testimony that he had been a member of a terrorist organization for six years was held admissible.[5] If he had been a member, (i), it was probable that the police knew that it was so; and (ii), if they knew or even suspected that fact, they would be more likely to have been hostile to him and expect him to have received instruction in resistance to normal techniques of interrogation.

THE PRESUMPTION OF INNOCENCE AND THE BURDEN OF PROOF

The practical effect of the presumption of innocence is that the onus is on the prosecution to prove the defendant's guilt beyond reasonable doubt. This was not always so and it is subject to many exceptions today. The starting point for the modern law is the great case of *Woolmington* v. *DPP*[6] in 1935. Before that decision it is probable that the general rule was that the onus of proving defences, such as self-defence, was on the defendant. Woolmington (W) shot and killed his wife (V) who had left him. His defence to a charge of murder was that it was an accident, that he was carrying a loaded shotgun under his coat for the purpose of threatening to shoot himself if she would not return to him. The gun went off as he was getting it out. The judge directed the jury in accordance with previous authority that, once it was proved that V had died at his hands, the killing was presumed to be murder unless W satisfied them that it was an accident. The House of Lords held that this was a misdirection. Once W had given evidence that the killing was an accident, the onus was on the Crown to prove that it was not. An intention to kill or cause really serious bodily harm is an essential element of murder which they must prove. The House stated the law in general terms:

---

[5] *R. v. Brophy* [1982] AC 476 (HL).   [6] [1935] AC 462 (HL).

No matter what the charge or where the trial, the principle that the prosecution must prove the guilt of the prisoner is part of the common law of England and no attempt to whittle it down can be entertained.

The same principle applies where other defences such as provocation, duress, or self-defence are raised. *Woolmington* recognized two exceptions: the defence of insanity, and any statutory exception. Insanity, anomalously, is treated differently, probably because it was a common law doctrine, stated with unique precision, completeness, and authority by all the judges answering questions put to them by the House of Lords, at a time when, probably, the onus of proving defences generally was thought to be on the defendant.

At the time of *Woolmington* there were many statutory offences where it was expressly provided that the onus of proving certain matters (a 'reverse onus'), usually defences, was on the defendant. Today there are many more. In addition, the courts sometimes profess to discern an intention, which is not expressly stated in a statute, to impose a reverse onus.[7] There is one general provision, originating in the Summary Jurisdiction Act 1848, re-enacted in the Magistrates' Courts Act 1981, section 101, which provides that the burden of proving any 'exception, exemption, proviso, excuse or qualification' is on the defendant. This section applies only to magistrates' courts, but the House of Lords accepted in *R. v. Hunt*[8] that it would be absurd that the allocation of the burden of proof of an offence triable either way should differ according to whether it was tried summarily or on indictment. The effect seems to be that section 101 is a statement of the common law, applicable in all courts. It is probable that, like the defence of insanity, this provision was based on a now outdated view of the common law on proving defences. The courts have been inconsistent in their application of section 101. The law is by no means clear or satisfactory. There is an unimplemented recommendation of the Criminal Law Revision Committee to abolish all reverse onus provisions, leaving only an evidential burden (*infra*) on the defendant. The House of Lords has now ruled, obiter, that the Human Rights Act 1998 may require that a provision expressly imposing a reverse onus of proof must be 'read down', so that the defendant bears only an evidential burden and does not have to 'prove' anything. It is sufficient that he raises a reasonable doubt. It is not clear how far this ruling goes. The law is developing and, consequently, uncertain.[9]

THE EVIDENTIAL BURDEN

A jury need not, and should not, be directed to consider a defence unless there is some evidence of it. Where there is nothing in the prosecution's case which might persuade a reasonable jury that the defendant *may have been* acting, e.g., in self-defence, that defence will not be left to them, unless the defendant tenders evidence of it. This is not a burden of *proof*. He does not have to satisfy the jury that he was acting in self-defence, only that he may have been, because, if he may have been, the case against

---

[7] A recent example is *Gibson* [2000] *Crim. LR* 479.
[8] [1987] AC 352.   [9] *Lambert* [2001] 1 All ER 1014.

him has not been proved beyond reasonable doubt. This burden of introducing evidence is known as the 'evidential burden'.

STANDARDS OF PROOF

There are two recognized standards—(i) proof beyond reasonable doubt and (ii) proof on the balance of probabilities. The former is required of the prosecution but the latter suffices where the burden is on the defence—as where D raises the defence of insanity or where Parliament has imposed a reverse onus by statute. Juries are always directed that they must be 'satisfied so as to be sure' that the prosecution has proved its case. Only then are they satisfied beyond reasonable doubt.[10] Where the burden is on the defendant he must satisfy the jury that it is at least a little more likely than not that the conditions of the defence existed. If the jury thinks there is only an even chance that those conditions existed, the defence is not made out and they should convict. If the conditions did exist, the defendant was not guilty so, in such a situation, the jury may properly convict although they are not sure of the defendant's guilt.

Some legal systems, e.g. Scotland, do not allow conviction on the uncorroborated evidence of a single witness. There was never any such general rule in English law and the number of particular cases in which corroboration is required has been greatly reduced by the Criminal Justice and Public Order Act 1994. One variety of treason (unimportant in practice), perjury, and road traffic speeding offences are the surviving exceptions. Generally, a jury which is satisfied so as to be sure that a single prosecution witness is speaking the truth is entitled to act on his evidence and convict.

THE EFFECT OF AN ACQUITTAL

A person cannot be tried a second time for an offence of which he has been acquitted, except where the acquittal is 'tainted'; i.e., when a person has been convicted of an administration of justice offence involving interference with or intimidation of a juror or a witness or potential witness in any proceedings which led to the acquittal. An application may then be made to the High Court which, provided certain conditions are satisfied, may make an order quashing a tainted acquittal and the person can be retried for the same offence.[11]

Until recently there was high authority[12] that, not only was an acquitted person immune from further prosecution for that offence, but the prosecution was precluded from adducing any evidence that he committed it in any subsequent proceedings against him. Now, however, it has been decided by *R. v. Z*[13] that relevant evidence is not inadmissible merely because it shows, or tends to show, that the defendant was in fact guilty of an offence of which he has been acquitted. Z, who was charged with rape, claimed that V consented and that he believed she consented. The prosecution wished

---

[10] See n. 1 above.   [11] Criminal Procedure and Investigations Act 1996, s. 54(1).

[12] The Privy Council, *Sambasivam* v. *Public Prosecutor, Malaya* [1950] AC 458 (PC).

[13] [2000] 3 All ER 385 (HL).

to adduce the testimony of four other women who claimed they had been raped by Z. Their evidence was relevant to rebut the defence and would have been admissible under the 'similar facts' rule, but in three of the cases Z had been acquitted. The trial judge and the Court of Appeal therefore held that the women's evidence was inadmissible. The House of Lords disagreed. Z could not be tried again for the offences of which he had been acquitted, but the prosecution was not precluded from adducing evidence in other proceedings that he was in fact guilty. It is instructive to compare a variation of the facts of *Smith*, which are given below.[14] Suppose that S had been tried for the murder, first of A and then of B, and had been acquitted on each occasion. That would not have been in the least surprising as the evidence in each case, considered separately, would have been far from convincing. But when he is tried for the murder of C, the circumstances of the deaths of A and B have come to the attention of the prosecutor. They are, of course, no less relevant and compelling than they were in the actual circumstances of *Smith*, and it seems right that they should be, as they now would be, admissible in evidence.[15]

PRESUMPTIONS

The proof of facts is sometimes facilitated by the use of presumptions. These are rules that, on proof of a certain fact or facts, say A and B, the trier of fact either must or may presume the existence of a further fact, C. English law has traditionally divided presumptions into three categories. (i) *Conclusive presumptions:* on proof of A and B the trier must find C and no evidence is admissible to disprove C. These truly have nothing to do with proof, but are rules of substantive law which, traditionally, have been stated in this form. The only significant example surviving in the criminal law is section 50 of the Children and Young Persons Act 1933: '[i]t shall be conclusively presumed that no child under the age of ten years can be guilty of an offence'. There may be the most compelling evidence that the child did in fact commit a crime but the court may not act on it. (ii) *Rebuttable presumptions of law:* on proof of A and B, C must be presumed to exist until evidence is given to prove that it does not.[16] Examples are the presumption of 'regularity', that public and official acts have been properly performed. A person who acts in a public office as, e.g., a constable or public health inspector is presumed to have been properly appointed to that office until evidence is given to the contrary. When a motor patrol officer produced a 'breathalyser' to measure the alcohol in a motorist's breath, it was presumed to be the only type then authorized for use. The presumption may apply to physical things. Traffic lights are presumed to have been in working order. Proof that a nocturnal act was done as 'Big Ben' (the great clock at the Houses of Parliament) struck twelve would be sufficient to prove that the act was done at midnight. There is no closed list of these presumptions, but the courts are cautious about expanding them. (iii) *Presumptions of fact:* on proof

---

[14] See below.

[15] McEwan 'Law Commission Dodges the Nettles in Consultation Paper No. 14' [1997] *Crim. LR* 93 at 94.

[16] This category is, in fact, rather more complicated. For a simple explanation see J. C. Smith, *Criminal Evidence* (London: Sweet & Maxwell, 1995) 48–9.

of A and B, the court *may* infer the existence of C but will do so only if actually satisfied to the required standard of the existence of C. A and B amount to circumstantial evidence of C sufficient to justify the inference. This is nothing more than the general rule of evidence, but the term 'presumption' has been used (perhaps unfortunately) in respect of certain commonly recurring situations. The most conspicuous example is the so-called 'doctrine of recent possession'. Where D is found to be in possession of, or dealing with, property which has been recently stolen, and he offers no explanation, or an explanation which the court disbelieves, then it *may* infer that he is guilty of stealing the goods or handling them knowing them to be stolen (a different offence). It should do so only if sure that D was in fact guilty of the particular crime.

JUDICIALLY NOTICED FACTS

A further essential supplement to the means of proof is the doctrine of judicial notice. Certain matters do not require proof because they are taken to be known to the court. If the jury were to be treated as visitors from outer space, intelligent beings knowing nothing of life on earth, trials would be impossible. It must be assumed that the judge and jury are aware of that very large body of knowledge possessed by all ordinary citizens. In addition to that knowledge which people generally do have, notice is also taken of facts which are capable of immediate and accurate determination by resort to sources of indisputable accuracy. Not many people know that 15 January 1922 was a Sunday, but that fact is readily ascertainable from an almanac and, if it were relevant, it could be looked up and noticed without evidence.

JUDICIAL NOTICE; LAW

Judges and magistrates are taken to know the law of England and Wales. Of course, no one has all the law in his head. Judges are 'reminded' of it by the citation of the relevant statutes and cases by counsel and by their own reference to law books. They do not receive evidence as to the state of the law. It is different with foreign law, including the law of Scotland and Northern Ireland. Foreign law, unless agreed, must be proved as a fact by witnesses, expert in that law, who may be cross-examined.

HEARSAY

The general rule that all relevant evidence is admissible is subject to many exceptions on grounds of policy. Far the most important of these is the rule against hearsay. The meaning of hearsay is not completely straightforward. When a witness says, 'I heard X say . . .', it does not necessarily follow that he is about to give hearsay evidence. This depends on the purpose for which X's statement is offered in evidence. If it is to prove a fact asserted by X, it is hearsay, but if it is for some other relevant purpose, it is not.

Sometimes the mere fact that a statement was made is relevant, irrespective of its truth or falsity. The fact that the statement was made is then no different from any other relevant fact. If, however, X's statement is offered to prove a fact asserted by X, the question must arise whether X, who is not present in court, was speaking the truth. X cannot be cross-examined to test the reliability of the statement, his means of knowledge, and his credibility, etc. This is the most important reason for the general exclusion of hearsay evidence.

Some examples may clarify the rule. D, who is charged with the murder of X, raises the defence that he was provoked by X to lose his self control and testifies, 'X said to me, "You are a ruthless adulterer"'. D is not tendering this evidence to prove that he is a ruthless adulterer. It is an accusation he would hotly deny. The fact that the statement was made is relevant because of its provocative nature. Or D, pleading the defence of duress, testifies, 'X (a terrorist) said to me, "carry the ammunition or you will be shot"'. This is not hearsay. It does not matter whether the terrorist in fact intended to shoot D or not. If the statement was made and D believed X meant it, that amounted to duress. In these examples, no question of X's credibility arises. D's credibility, of course, matters. Was he accurately and truthfully reporting what X said? But D is present in the witness box and can be cross-examined.

If, on the other hand, the purpose is to identify a car used in a bank robbery as D's car and W says 'Y [a bystander who cannot now be found] told me, "I saw the car quite clearly. The number was AB12"'. Everything depends on whether what X said was true. W's evidence is inadmissible unless it falls within one of the exceptions to the rule against hearsay.

The judge decides whether evidence is hearsay or not, so usually, the jury need not be troubled by this distinction. Occasionally, juries may have to grapple with it. Where D is charged with handling stolen goods the prosecution has to prove (a) that the goods were stolen and (b) that the accused handled them, knowing or believing them to be stolen. If a witness, W, overheard X tell D, 'I stole the jewellery from Z', W's testimony is hearsay evidence that the jewellery was stolen (because its relevance depends on whether the absent X was speaking the truth) but it is not hearsay and is admissible (though not conclusive) evidence that D believed the goods to be stolen. Whether X's statement was true or false, D may have believed it to be true. The jury must be directed that W's testimony is relevant to issue (b) above, but that they must ignore it when deciding issue (a). Clearly juries and magistrates may have difficulty in understanding and applying this distinction.

DOCUMENTARY HEARSAY

The term, 'hearsay' is misleading, in that the rule against hearsay applies equally to written statements. The test is the same as for oral evidence. If the witness of the bank robbery, Y (above), had written down 'The robber's car number was AB12' and handed the note to the officer, the writing would be hearsay evidence of the car number and inadmissible, unless an exception to the hearsay rule were applicable. Where D declared to customs officials that the origin of certain seed was India but the inner bags containing the seed were found to bear the legend, 'Produce of Morocco', it was held that this was inadmissible as evidence that D's declaration was false. It was a statement by some unknown person offered to prove the fact asserted by him.[17] In the case of a written statement, there is no doubt about what the writer 'said'; but the vice of hearsay is exactly the same as in the case of the oral statement. We cannot test by cross-examination whether he was lying or mistaken. In the leading case, *Myers* v. *DPP*[18] the prosecution wanted to prove that a car in D's possession was the same vehicle as one that had been stolen. In order to do so it needed to prove that, when the stolen car was built, its engine number was, say, 123. A witness from the makers produced a form filled in by some unknown and now undiscoverable workman stating (in substance) 'I installed engine 123 in chassis 456'. That was exactly what the prosecution needed to prove. The workman's statement was hearsay. There was no reason to doubt that the workman had made an accurate record, a routine matter, and it was obviously very cogent evidence. But it did not fall within any of the exceptions to the hearsay rule, and the House of Lords declared that it was not open to them to create any new ones, so the statement was inadmissible.[19]

This decision led immediately to the enactment of the Criminal Evidence Act 1965, the predecessor of the current provisions for the admission of documentary hearsay in certain circumstances. So *Myers* would be decided differently today, but it remains authority for the proposition that a document is inadmissible to prove a fact asserted in it, unless it comes within some exception to the hearsay rule, no matter how attractive and reliable the evidence may be.

CONDUCT AS HEARSAY

Where conduct, other than speaking or writing, is intended by the actor to assert a fact, clearly it may be hearsay. A statement may be made, e.g., in morse code or by the use of flags or any pre-arranged signal. Different arrangements of flags have been used for centuries to convey messages by ships at sea. There is no difference in principle between statements so made and ordinary written or spoken statements.

More controversially, it has been decided that conduct which is not intended to assert, but merely assumes, the existence of a fact is hearsay. It is a matter which has been hotly debated since the case of *Wright* v. *Doe d. Tatham* in 1834.[20] In that civil case, the question was whether a deceased testator had been competent to make his will. The fact that his acquaintances had treated him, in his absence, as a person competent to do business was held to be inadmissible. By doing business with him, they were not, of course, intending to assert his competence, but presumably they would not have dealt with him if they had not believed him to be competent. His competence was an assumption underlying their conduct. If they had said he was competent, that statement would have been hearsay; and their conduct showed only that they believed him to be competent, just as a statement would have done. Only recently, the House of Lords confirmed in *R.* v. *Kearley*[21] that such conduct is hearsay

---

17 *Patel* v. *Comptroller of Customs* [1965] AC 356 (PC).   18 [1965] AC 1001 (HL).
19 But see *R.* v. *Ward* [2001] *Crim. LR* 316.   20 7 Ad. and El. 313 at 388.
21 [1992] 2 AC 228.

and inadmissible in criminal as well as in civil cases. D was charged with possession of prohibited drugs with intent to supply them. Only a small quantity of drugs was found at his flat, but, while he was in custody at a police station, ten telephone calls were received at the flat and seven people arrived personally, all asking for drugs. Clearly, many people believed D was a drug dealer. The trial judge and Court of Appeal held that this evidence was admissible but the House of Lords, by a majority of three to two, that it was not. The fact that the callers believed D to be a supplier of drugs was irrelevant, unless it was evidence that their belief was true. And if it was evidence that the belief was true, then it was hearsay.

The logic is impeccable but the effect is to exclude highly cogent evidence. In *Kearley* it was highly cogent because so many people were acting, apparently independently, on the same assumption. If there had been just one inquirer for drugs, the cogency would have been slight. It seems unlikely that so many were mistaken, though not impossible. An unfounded rumour may have circulated in the neighbour-hood that drugs were available from D. If the justification for excluding hearsay is that an uncross-examined person may have been lying or mistaken, it is weaker in a case such as *Kearley*. It is not credible that all the callers were acting in order to 'frame' him, so there was no question of their telling lies. But they may have been mistaken. The Law Commission has recommended the reversal of *Kearley*, but it still represents the law.

In the *Wright* case the acts in question were done in the absence of the testator and in *Kearley* in the absence of the defendant. If those acts had been done in his presence, his response, if relevant, would have been admissible against him. Wright's intelligent response to a proposed business deal would have demonstrated his competence. In *Warner and Jones*[22] D was present in his house when, over a period of eight days, great numbers of people called briefly, eight of them being known heroin users. *Kearley* was distinguished, i.e. the court said the situations were different. The implication was that the callers were seeking heroin from D, just as in *Kearley*. But the evidence against him was his own conduct in associating with heroin users.

STATEMENTS BY MACHINES

Hearsay is excluded because of the danger of human untruthfulness and inaccuracy of observation and recollection. Some statements by machines are not subject to these risks. A maximum and minimum thermometer states the maximum and minimum temperature in a period of twenty-four hours and the reading it provides is admissible to prove what those temperatures were. Photographs of a bank robbery while it is taking place are admissible evidence of the facts recorded. A tape-recording of a conversation is admissible to prove what was said, if that (as distinct from the truth of what was said) is in issue. The radar speedometer and the breathalyser are admissible evidence of the facts they observe. After some hesitation, it is now recognized that statements by computers are frequently of the same character as statements by other machines.

---

[22] (1992) 96 Cr. App. R 324.

DRAWINGS AND PHOTOFIT PICTURES

It has been held that a drawing of the offender by, or under the direction of, a person (W) who saw the offence committed is admissible in evidence to identify the defendant as the offender. Similarly with a photofit picture assembled under W's direction.[23] The courts have denied that this is hearsay, saying that the photofit is analogous to a photograph. This seems fallacious because the result is no less a description by a person than his written statement to the same effect; but, while these decisions stand, it must be accepted that such drawings and photofit pictures are admissible as an anomalous exception to the hearsay rule.

EXCEPTIONS TO THE RULE AGAINST HEARSAY

There are many exceptions to the hearsay rule at common law. No general principle satisfactorily explains all of them. They were created in a haphazard way at different periods in English legal history. Two characteristics are generally present. (i) There is some special need to admit the evidence. Many exceptions apply only when the declarant is dead. (ii) Some factor is present which tends to give the statement a degree of trustworthiness not generally found in hearsay evidence. Where a statement has been made in writing, any common law exception which would justify its admission is likely to be covered by the much broader exceptions (discussed below) created by modern statutes. The common law exceptions, however, remain in force and may still be invoked where no statute applies. Three of them are worth consideration.

(1) A statement by a person, now deceased, which is against his financial or proprietary interests is admissible provided that he knew it was against his interest at the time he made it. The theory is that he would be unlikely to make such a settlement unless it were true. An entry by a midwife of the fact that her fee had been paid was against her pecuniary interest because, if she had subsequently sued for the fee, it would have been evidence against her that she had received it.[24] The declaration is evidence of connected facts stated by the declarant, in that case the date of birth of the child, provided that they explain the nature of the transaction.

(2) Where a person, now deceased, was under a duty to do an act and to record or report it, the record or report is admissible provided that it was made at the time of, or immediately after, the act and he had no incentive to misrepresent the facts. An entry in a ship's log by the deceased first mate was held inadmissible because (i) being made two days after the event, it was not sufficiently contemporaneous, (ii) the mate had an interest to misrepresent the facts, and (iii) the entries referred not only to his acts but also to those of the crew.[25]

(3) In a homicide trial a statement by the alleged victim as to the cause of the fatal injury is admissible, provided it was made when he had a 'settled, hopeless

---

[23] *Percy Smith* [1976] *Crim. LR* 511; *Cook* [1987] *Crim. LR* 402.

[24] *Higham* v. *Ridgway* (1808) 1 East 109.   [25] *The Henry Coxon* (1878) 3 PD 156.

expectation of death', a test that was strictly applied. Where the victim, being asked to sign a statement containing the words 'with no hope of my recovery', required the words 'at present' to be inserted, the statement was held inadmissible.[26] The theory was that a person would be unlikely to be willing to go before his maker with a lie on his lips, somewhat unrealistic today in view of the widespread decline in religious belief in England and Wales. But the rule is still applied. When the judge has ruled that the deceased had the necessary expectation of death and admitted the declaration, the jury must be directed that they may reconsider that issue in deciding what weight to give to the statement.

Other common law exceptions, where admissibility is not conditional on the declarant's death are:

(4) *Res Gestae.* This term, literally meaning 'the things done', is used in various senses in the law of evidence, but particularly to justify or explain the admission in certain circumstances of the use of words by way of exception to the hearsay rule. In the criminal law the usual case is one of an exclamation made spontaneously on the occurrence of a disaster or emergency, and therefore unlikely to be concocted. Long ago the statement of the victim of an assault was admitted because it was made immediately 'before she had time to devise or contrive anything for her own advantage'.[27] Where there was a sudden loud bang at a window and a boy 'hooted "There's Butcher"', his 'hoot' was admissible as evidence that Butcher was there at the window.[28]

(5) A person's declaration as to the present state of his body or mind is admissible to prove that that state existed. 'I have a headache' is admissible to prove that the declarant had a headache. A person's declaration of his intention to include certain provisions in his will is evidence that he did so intend, and, if he made his will shortly afterwards, it is circumstantial evidence (the will being lost) that he did include those provisions.

(6) Declarations made in pursuance of a conspiracy or joint enterprise. A statement made by one conspirator, A, for the purpose of carrying out the conspiracy is admissible against another, B, to prove the facts stated and to establish that they had indeed conspired. There is an obvious logical difficulty here. The rule seems to assume the existence of that which it is sought to prove. But the courts contrive to apply it in practice.

STATUTORY EXCEPTIONS TO THE RULE AGAINST HEARSAY

Following the decision in *Myers*[29] a succession of statutes has established wide-ranging exceptions to the hearsay rule in respect of documentary evidence. The fact that the statement was made in a document leaves no doubt about what was 'said'. The other weakness, that the declarant is not available for cross-examination which might show that he was lying or mistaken, remains. The Criminal Justice Act 1988

---

[26] *Jenkins* (1869) LR 1 CCR 187.

[27] *Thompson v. Trevanion* (1693) Skin. 402, *per* Holt CJ. The leading case is now *Andrews* [1987] AC 281.

[28] *Fowkes, The Times,* 8 Mar. 1856.   [29] See above.

therefore confers a wide discretion on the court to exclude a document which that statute makes admissible in law, where the court is of the opinion that, in the interests of justice, it ought not to be admitted. Statements prepared for criminal proceedings or investigation are treated with particular suspicion. These may not be given in evidence without leave, and leave is not to be given unless the court is satisfied that the document ought to be admitted in the interests of justice. The Act specifies matters which the court must take into account in deciding to exercise its discretion whether to exclude or to admit documents.

The two principal provisions are sections 23 and 24 of the 1988 Act. 'Document' is widely defined and section 23 applies to any document. A document is admissible as evidence of any fact of which 'direct oral evidence' by the maker (M) would be admissible if he had been called as a witness. This appears to limit admissibility to first-hand hearsay. M would not be allowed to testify, 'X told me that ... ' for the purpose of proving the fact asserted by X. M could not give 'direct oral evidence' of that fact; so his statement in the document is inadmissible. The condition of admissibility is that M is not available for one of the reasons specified, that he is dead, or unfit, or outside the United Kingdom and it is not reasonably practicable to secure his attendance, or he cannot be found. Where the statement was made to a police officer or other person investigating offences or charging offenders, there is another alternative. M does not give evidence through fear or because he is kept out of the way.

Section 24 applies only to what the Act calls 'business documents', any document 'created or received by a person in the course of a trade, business profession or other occupation or as the holder of a paid or unpaid office'. It is not limited to first-hand hearsay. The document is admissible although the information in it was supplied through an unlimited number of intermediaries, but only if each intermediary was acting in a trade, business, etc. Clearly the justification is that the routine of business supplies some assurance of truth and accuracy not found in documents generally. These provisions have given rise to numerous problems of interpretation which it would not be appropriate to discuss here, and to one decision[30] which appears to contravene the limitation of section 23 to first-hand hearsay.

Many documents are now produced by computers. They may be put in evidence for various purposes. (i) The printout may be offered as evidence of some fact 'observed' by the computer and recorded by it. No statement by a person is involved and there is no question of its being hearsay. If the fact recorded is relevant, the printout is admissible evidence of it. The automatic record of the timing and destination of telephone calls made in a hotel is evidence that those calls were made at those times. The record of alcohol level by a breathalyser or of speed by a radar speedometer is admissible whether or not these instruments are computers. (ii) The printout may be the fact to be proved. When a bank clerk operates the keys of a computer so as to record the crediting of £100 to a client's account, the record *is* the crediting of the account, the fact to be proved. It is not offered as evidence of some other fact. (iii) If, however, that record were tendered as evidence that someone had paid a cheque for £100 into the account, then it would be hearsay and admissible only if some exception

---

[30] *Derodra* [2000] 1 Cr. App. R 39, criticized by the writer in [1999] *New Law Journal* 1550.

to the rule against hearsay applied. In such a case, it is offered as evidence of a fact *stated by a person*, the bank clerk, that he had received that cheque. When a document is so tendered it must be shown that it comes within the terms of section 23 or 24 or some other exception to the hearsay rule.

At first legislators were suspicious of computers and, in cases (ii) and (iii) above, statute required evidence that the computer was operating properly. That provision has now been repealed and, as with other instruments,[31] it will be presumed that the computer was functioning properly, unless evidence is tendered that it was not.

ADMISSIONS AND CONFESSIONS

A very important exception to the hearsay rule is that which admits a confession by the defendant that he committed the offence or an admission by him of one or more of the facts alleged against him. This exception is commonly said to depend on the notion that a person is unlikely to say something so contrary to his interests unless it were true.[32] This evidence has always been treated with special caution. A confession was not admissible at common law unless the prosecution proved that it was 'voluntary'; and, if it was induced by any threat or promise, it was not voluntary. The common law rules have now been replaced by PACE.[33] Under section 76, a confession is now admissible unless it is represented that it was obtained (a) by oppression of the confessor, or (b) in consequence of anything said or done which was likely to render unreliable any confession which he might make in consequence. If it is represented that it was so obtained, the confession is inadmissible unless the prosecution satisfies the judge beyond reasonable doubt that it was not. Even when the judge is so satisfied, he may exclude the confession by the exercise of his discretion under section 78 of PACE because of the adverse effect which he thinks its admission would have upon the fairness of the trial. If the confession is admitted, the prosecution must satisfy the jury that it is true. In deciding that question, the jury may take into account the evidence of the circumstances in which the confession was made, which have already been considered by the judge alone in deciding whether the confession was obtained by oppression, etc. Additional safeguards apply where the defendant is mentally handicapped or a child. In spite of all these precautions, convictions based on confessions are sometimes found to be unsafe and quashed.

THE RIGHT TO SILENCE

The 'right to silence' is every citizen's general right (for it is subject to exceptions) not to answer questions by the police or anyone else. The problem is whether the defendant's silence in the face of accusations made in his presence may be used

---

[31] See above.

[32] There is, however, another view about this. See J. C. Smith, n. 15 above, 97.

[33] The abbreviation generally used for the Police and Criminal Evidence Act 1984.

against him, as amounting to an admission of the facts alleged. The common law rule is that where an accusation is made against a person in such circumstances that it would be natural to expect a denial and he says nothing, his silence may be evidence from which a jury can infer that he admitted the truth of the accusation. This rule applies where a defendant offers no specific defence at his trial but simply pleads not guilty. But, where he sets up a defence relying on any fact, his failure to mention that fact may be used against him under the Criminal Justice and Public Order Act 1994. This applies (a) at any time before he was charged, when he was questioned by an officer investigating the offence and (b) when he was charged or informed by the officer that he might be prosecuted for it. This may put considerable pressure on the suspected person to speak. The provisions of the Act have been much criticized and remain controversial.

THE DEFENDANT'S CHARACTER

The defendant (D) has always been allowed to call witnesses to give evidence of his good character for the purpose of showing that he is a person unlikely to have committed the offence charged. The prosecution however is not permitted to adduce evidence of his bad character for the purpose of showing that he is likely to have done so. They are limited to rebutting evidence of good character produced by the defendant. Since 1898 D can testify in his own defence and give evidence himself of his good character. Nowadays it is accepted that the mere fact that D has no previous convictions is evidence of good character.

Whenever there is evidence of good character, the judge must direct the jury as to its relevance to the issue whether D committed the crime. When D gives evidence, or when his exculpatory pre-trial answers or statements have been admitted in evidence, good character is relevant also to D's credibility as a witness; and the judge must so advise the jury.[34] D is not to be deprived of his right to have his good character taken into account because he is charged jointly with a person of bad character, E. The judge then has a discretion to say nothing about E's character or to tell the jury that there is no evidence of his character and they must not speculate about it. Whatever the judge does, it seems inevitable that the jury will assume—rightly—that E's character is bad. So ensuring that D gets a fair trial may well mean that E does not get one. However, there is no rule requiring separate trials for defendants of good and bad character.

The fact that D has committed crimes on other occasions is generally inadmissible, not because it is irrelevant, but because its probative value is likely to be outweighed by its prejudicial effect. The effect is 'prejudicial' because it is considered that the jury may attribute to it too much probative value. But, if the wrongful acts done on other occasions have very high probative value, the jury would be right to attribute that value to them. The effect would no longer be 'prejudicial'. The most common source

---

[34] *Vye* (1992) 97 Cr. App. R 134.

of the high probative value required is 'similar facts', best explained by an example. In *Smith*,[35] D was charged with the murder of a woman, A. Evidence was admitted of the deaths of two other women, B and C, which had occurred after the death of A. D had gone through a ceremony of marriage with each woman, using a different name on each occasion, and each had drowned in her bath in similar circumstances. Each had made a will in his favour and he had insured their lives. He had taken each woman to a doctor, describing the symptoms of epileptic fits. There was no direct evidence of killing in any case. The coroners' juries returned verdicts of accidental death. Smith was convicted of the murder of A, and it was held that the evidence relating to B and C had been rightly admitted. Each case, looked at in isolation, is quite consistent with accidental death; but, when the evidence was looked at as a whole, it became overwhelming that Smith intentionally killed the women.

WITNESSES

(1) Competence. The law has been reformed by the Youth Justice and Criminal Evidence Act 1999 (hereafter YJCE 1999).[36] All persons are now competent to give evidence in criminal proceedings (whatever their age) unless it appears to the court that the particular person is not able to understand questions put to him as a witness and to give answers which can be understood. The only exception is that defendants are not competent for the prosecution. Where competence is challenged, the party calling the witness must satisfy the judge, in the absence of the jury, that, on the balance of probabilities, he is competent. Any questioning which the judge considers necessary must be conducted in the presence of the parties; and expert evidence may be received.

Where a witness is suffering from one of a number of specified handicaps, or where the quality of the evidence of a witness (other than the accused) is likely to be diminished by fear or distress, the court may give a 'special measures' direction to assist him. Special measures include, among others, screening the witness from the accused in court, or enabling him to give evidence by means of a live television link, or the exclusion of certain persons, but not the accused and legal representatives, from the court while he is giving evidence. The YJCE Act contains elaborate procedural provisions.

Competent witnesses can be compelled to give evidence; except that the accused's spouse may be compelled to give evidence for the prosecution only in exceptional circumstances.[37]

(2) The oath. At common law all witnesses had to be sworn but that rule has been modified by a series of statutes.[38] Now a witness may not give sworn evidence unless

---

[35] (1915) 11 Cr. App. R 229.

[36] The following is written as if the provisions of that Act had been brought into force which, at the time of writing, is not so.

[37] Stated in PACE, s. 80.   [38] See now YJCE Act 1999, ss. 55–57.

he has attained the age of 14 and has a sufficient appreciation of the solemnity of the occasion and of the particular responsibility to tell the truth which is involved in the taking of an oath. Competent persons who may not be sworn give unsworn evidence. Anyone who objects to being sworn (whatever his reason—usually, no doubt, because he has no religious belief) may affirm, making no reference to a deity.

(3) Examination of witnesses. The party calling the witness (W) examines him first (examination in chief) to elicit from him by a series of questions evidence supporting that party's case. The examiner may not ask 'leading questions'— questions suggesting a particular answer—unless the matter is undisputed.

The other side then cross-examines W with the object of destroying or diminishing the effect of his evidence in chief and, if possible, of extracting further evidence in support of that party's case. The cross-examiner may ask leading questions and questions which are not directly relevant to the issue but which tend to undermine W's credibility. Where a question is relevant only to credibility, W's denial of the matter put to him is generally final. Evidence may not be called to contradict him. This is thought to be necessary to prevent the trial from being led into byways, distracting the jury from the matters in issue. There are exceptions. W's denial may be contradicted where the question alleges a reason for bias in favour of the party calling him. If W denies he is a close friend of that party, he may be contradicted by witnesses who say he is. Where he is asked if he has committed an offence—say perjury—and he does not admit it, the conviction may be proved by the production of a certificate. Where he denies that he once made a statement inconsistent with his present testimony, that statement may be put in evidence—but only for the purpose of showing that his present testimony is unreliable.

The first party may re-examine for the limited purpose of diminishing the effect of the cross-examination.

English law has always insisted on oral evidence. W may refresh his memory before going into the witness box by referring to any earlier written statement, but he is not permitted to read a statement from the witness box. He may be allowed to 'refresh his memory' in the box by reference to an earlier written statement. This rule used to be restricted to 'contemporaneous' statements—statements made by W at the time, or immediately after, the event in question. It has recently been relaxed to include a statement made 'much nearer to the time of the events'—i.e., it is significantly fresher than the witness's present recollection can be expected to be.[39]

Generally, W's credibility has to be judged by his performance in the witness box and may not be enhanced by calling evidence to prove what an upright character he is or that he has previously made statements consistent with his present testimony. There are exceptional cases where such statements may be proved, e.g., to disprove an allegation that his present testimony was recently fabricated. A prompt complaint made by the victim of an alleged sexual offence, which is consistent with her testimony, may be proved; and, where W has given identification evidence, it may be proved that he identified the same person on an earlier occasion—making it more likely that his testimony is true.

---

[39] R. v. *South Ribble Magistrates' Court* [1996] 2 Cr. App. R 544 (DC).

The cross-examiner has great freedom, subject only to the discretion of the judge, to put to a witness discreditable aspects of his past life which cast doubt on his present credibility. This has caused particular problems in cases of rape and other sexual offences. The cross-examiner was once allowed to put to the complainant sexual incidents in her past life, theoretically to undermine her credibility, but which were more likely in practice to be regarded by a jury as more relevant to the issue of consent than to her credibility. Statute now requires that questions about a complainant's sexual behaviour can be put only with the leave of the judge, who may not give leave unless the evidence satisfies certain criteria and where 'a refusal of leave might render unsafe' a conclusion of the jury.[40]

(4) The accused as a witness. The general principle of the common law, gradually whittled away during the nineteenth century, was that persons with an interest in the outcome of the case were incompetent to testify because they could not be expected to tell the truth. That rule is now gone completely though it was not until 1898 that the accused in a criminal case was made a competent witness for the defence.[41] He may, however, be called only on his own application. Where two persons are jointly charged and tried together, one is not competent to give evidence for the prosecution against the other—but, in giving evidence in his own defence, he may, incidentally, incriminate the other. Where persons are jointly indicted, but the proceedings against one have been concluded, he is then competent for the prosecution on the trial of the other.

In 1898 it was thought necessary to protect him from the continuing rule of the common law allowing wide-ranging cross-examination as to credit, while leaving him open to cross-examination to show that he committed the offence presently charged. If D goes into the witness box and denies that he committed a murder, saying that he was 100 miles away at the time, it must be possible to put to him the question that he was present and did the fatal act. So the Act provided that D might be asked any question tending to show that he committed the offence charged, but that he should not be asked whether he had committed or been convicted of, or even been charged with, any other offence, or that he was of bad character, though this was subject to four exceptions. (i) Where the commission or conviction of another offence is admissible evidence to show that he committed an offence now charged. This refers to cases like *Smith*[42] where evidence tending to show that D murdered B and C was admissible to show that he murdered A. (ii) Where D has cross-examined prosecution witnesses or called evidence to establish his own good character. That seems a sound common-sense principle. (iii) Where D has made imputations on the character of the prosecutor, the prosecution witnesses or (a recent addition) the deceased victim of the alleged crime. The rationale is that if D says that the prosecution is not to be believed because of bad character, the jury, in deciding whom to believe, should know that D too has a bad character. This does not apply if D does not testify because then there is no question of weighing his testimony against that of the prosecution. (iv) Where D has

[40] YJCEA, s. 41, replacing Sexual Offences (Amendment) Act 1976, s. 2.

[41] The provisions of the 1898 Act have now been incorporated, with some minor amendments, into the YJCEA.

[42] See above.

given evidence against any other person charged in the same proceedings. D is not a competent witness for the prosecution, but in testifying in his own defence he may incidentally incriminate a co-defendant, thus giving evidence 'against' him. In these four cases, D loses the shield protecting him from cross-examination as to his own character. These provisions have generated far too much case law to be considered here.[43]

(5) Illegally obtained evidence. Relevant evidence is admissible even though it has been obtained illegally. Evidence that D was unlawfully in possession of ammunition has been admitted although it was obtained by an illegal search by police. In *Khan*[44] the police attached an aural surveillance device to B's home without his consent or knowledge and so obtained a recording of a conversation which confirmed that K was involved in the importation of drugs. The attachment of the device was an unlawful act, a civil trespass, and probably an offence of criminal damage. But the House of Lords held that the evidence was admissible in law and the judge was right not to exclude it in the exercise of his discretion. The judge has always had discretion to exclude admissible evidence tendered by the prosecution if in his opinion it would operate unfairly against an accused. This is supplemented by section 78 of PACE which provides that the court may exclude prosecution evidence where, having regard to all the circumstances including the circumstances in which the evidence was obtained, its admission would have such an adverse effect on the fairness of the proceedings that the court ought not to admit it. In *Khan* it was held that the judge was fully justified in holding that the admission of the illegally obtained evidence would not have such an effect.

Further Reading

For general principles and historical background

DEVLIN, P., *Trial by Jury* (London: Methuen & Co., 1966).
WILLIAMS, G., *The Proof of Guilt* (3rd edn., London: Stevens & Sons, 1963).

Student textbooks: introductory work

SMITH, J.C., *Criminal Evidence* (London: Sweet & Maxwell, 1999).

Student textbooks: more detailed works

DENNIS, I.H., *The New Law of Evidence* (London: Sweet & Maxwell, 1999).
MURPHY, P., *Murphy on Evidence* (7th edn., London: Blackstone, 2000).
TAPPER, C., *Cross & Tapper on Evidence* (9th edn., London: Butterworths, 1999).

---

[43] P. Murphy (ed.), *Archbold's Criminal Pleading, Evidence and Practice* (London: Sweet & Maxwell, 2001 edn.), 8–161 – 8–218.

[44] [1997] AC 558 (HL). The ECtHR held that the admission of the evidence did not violate the Convention on Human Rights: *Khan* v. *United Kingdom* App. no. (35394/97) [2000] *Crim. LR* 684.

Detailed practitioners' works

HOWARD, M., HOCHBERG, D., MIRFIELD, P., GREVLING, K., HOLLANDER, C., and PATTENDEN, R., *Phipson on Evidence* (15th edn., London: Sweet & Maxwell, 2000).

MURPHY, P., *Blackstone's Criminal Practice 2002* (Oxford: Oxford University Press, 2002) Part F.

12

THE EXCHANGE OF INFORMATION AND DISCLOSURE

*Roger Leng**

The Royal Commission on Criminal Justice which reported in 1993 described the adversarial model of criminal justice operating in England and Wales in the following terms:

. . . a system which has the judge as an umpire, who leaves the presentation of the case to the parties (prosecution and defence) on each side. They separately prepare their case and call, examine and cross-examine witnesses.[1]

This simple description, which might adequately describe a criminal proceeding 200 years ago, however, fails to do justice to the complexity of the modern criminal justice system. In particular, by emphasizing the relative freedom of the parties, the model fails to acknowledge the extent to which, under modern law, the parties have continuing mutual obligations to provide or exchange information, and the importance of such duties in principle and practice if justice is to be done.

The purpose of the present chapter is to outline the mutual obligations imposed upon the prosecution and defence in England and Wales to provide and exchange information during the course of criminal proceedings, and to consider where the proper balance of such obligations should lie. As will become apparent, this is an area in which the English criminal justice process has been subject to extensive change during the past twenty years, and it seems probable that the law and practice in this area have yet to reach a settled state. What is described, therefore, is a system in a state of development in which various competing interests of the police, prosecutors, defendants, and the community must be balanced to produce a result which not only meets domestic expectations of fairness and justice but also satisfies the defendant's right to a fair trial as guaranteed by Article 6 of the European Convention on Human Rights.

In order to put procedures for the exchange and disclosure of information in perspective it is necessary also to consider the extent to which the defendant or

---

* Full citations for all books and articles cited in this chapter can be found in the Bibliography and Further Reading section.

[1] Royal Commission on Criminal Justice, *Report* (London: HMSO, 1993), para. 10.

defence lawyers gain information by virtue of participation in, or observation of, the processes of evidence construction for the prosecution. This occurs in particular in relation to formal police interviews, post-arrest searches of the person or premises, and identification parades (or other formal identification procedures) (Murphy *et al.* 2001; Cape 1999). The suspect has a right to have a lawyer present during each of these procedures and record-keeping requirements (which include tape-recording of interviews and photographic or video-recording or identification procedures) ensure that the evidential products of these procedures are available equally to both prosecution and defence.

For convenience the obligations to disclose and exchange information will be considered at the following successive stages of the criminal process: where a citizen has fallen under suspicion but has not been arrested; when a person has been arrested but prior to charge; and, finally, the period after charge leading up to the trial.

WHEN THE CITIZEN FALLS UNDER SUSPICION

Generally speaking, the citizen is under no duty to provide information to the police or other official criminal investigators (*Rice* v. *Connolly*[2]) and commits no offence in refusing to do so. This rule is viewed as embodying an important constitutional principle restricting the power of the State to interfere with the individual. This broad principle is now subject to numerous exceptions created by statute which attach duties to provide information when called upon to do so in relation to a wide range of activities or circumstances such as driving vehicles, acting as company director, or being insolvent. Similar duties apply in areas in which it is necessary for the State to collect information from all citizens, for instance in relation to taxation or the national census. These exceptions are justified on the ground of the national interest. However, although the citizen may not generally be required to answer questions put by the police or other official investigators, he may be required to submit to searches of the person, or his vehicle, or his premises, and consequent seizure by the State of material of apparent evidential value where there are reasonable grounds for suspecting involvement in a criminal offence (see generally Lidstone and Palmer 1996).

When a citizen is searched or arrested he must be provided with specific information. In particular, he must be told: (i) that a search or arrest is to be carried out under legal powers; and (ii) the nature of the suspected offence or the object of the search. The primary reason for requiring this information to be given is the constitutional principle that a citizen should not be required to submit to the coercive power of the State without first being told the lawful basis for the exercise of such power. However, the information provided at this stage may also assist the suspect in defending himself. Thus, if a suspect is made aware of the offence which he is suspected of committing he may be able to offer an immediate explanation which may negate the

[2] [1966] 2 QB 414.

grounds for suspicion against him. It is also important that he is given sufficient information to enable him to offer an explanation at this stage since an explanation given spontaneously at an early stage in the process is likely to be more credible than one which is proffered later.

Following arrest, the suspect may be detained for questioning (for a maximum period of twenty-four hours or up to ninety-six hours for more serious cases) where this is believed to be necessary in order to secure or preserve evidence. During questioning, the suspect remains free to remain silent or not to answer particular questions and must be reminded of this before questioning commences. This rule embodies both the defendant's privilege against self-incrimination and the broader right to silence, which applies to any information and not simply to material which might incriminate the person being interrogated. Similarly, the police enjoy a 'right to silence' (although it is rarely described as such), in that they are under no obligation to inform the suspect of the existence or nature of evidence against him. The right to silence both of the suspect and of the police has been criticized. The suspect's right has been criticized on the ground that the right is useful only to a guilty suspect but serves no purpose for the innocent suspect who would wish to speak to prove his innocence. It has also been argued that it should be the duty of all citizens to answer police questions in the course of investigations. The right of the police to remain silent about the ground for their suspicions and evidence available to them has been criticized on the basis that the defendant should be entitled to know the case against him and to be able to defend himself at every stage in the proceedings (Toney 2001).

Notwithstanding the formal position that there are generally no disclosure duties during the investigative stage, recent changes in the law have created a position in which a suspect is under considerable pressure to provide information during police interview, and in which there may be considerable incentives for the police to do so also. The Criminal Justice and Public Order Act 1994 attenuated the accused's right to silence during police interrogation by providing: (i) that evidential inferences might be drawn against an accused person who raised a defence in the course of the proceedings but had failed to mention the factual basis for the defence having had a reasonable opportunity to do so during police interview (section 34); (ii) that evidential inferences might also be drawn against an accused person who had failed to account for specific types of incriminating evidence (such as marks on clothing or presence near the scene of a crime) when asked to do so during police interview (sections 36 and 37) (see generally Wolchover 2001). In both cases the suspect must be given either a 'caution' or a 'special warning' during the police interview to inform him of the risk that his failure to provide certain information may be treated as evidence against him. Although it is arguable that the accused's right to silence remains, it is clear that, because exercising the right may involve a considerable risk, many accused persons, who might otherwise have remained silent, will now provide information to the police (Bucke et al., 2000; Jackson 2001).

An interesting side-effect of the 1994 legislation is that in many circumstances it also provides incentives for the police to disclose information to the accused during interview. Thus, if a suspect fails, during police interview, to mention the factual basis for a defence, this may be treated as evidence against him only if he had a reasonable opportunity to mention the relevant facts. This may not arise unless the police put specific factual allegations to the suspect during interview. Thus, in one case no evidential inference could be drawn from the defendant's failure to give an explanation for a semen stain on a nightdress because the police had failed to disclose in interview that they had evidence of the semen stain (*Nickolson* [1998] *Crim. LR* 61). Similarly, it will not be possible to treat as evidence a failure to explain a particular incriminating fact unless the police have fully disclosed the incriminating evidence in their possession.

DISCLOSURE OF THE PROSECUTION CASE

The requirement that an accused person must be informed of the case against him in order to answer it has long been recognized as one of the central principles of natural justice. This principle is expressed in Article 6.3(a) of the European Convention on Human Rights which provides that everyone charged with a criminal offence has the right 'to be informed promptly, in a language which he understands and in detail, of the nature and cause of the accusation against him'. This is supplemented by paragraph (b) which confers a right 'to have adequate time and facilities for the preparation of his defence'. As will be seen, English law respects the broad principle of the defendant's right to be informed of the case against him, but in certain circumstances it may be considered inadequate in respect of the requirements that disclosure should be made promptly. Consequently it may be doubted whether in all cases the defendant is given adequate time and facilities as required by Article 6.

For the most serious cases which are tried before a judge and jury in the Crown Court, disclosure of the prosecution case takes place when the case is transferred or committed from a local magistrates' court to the Crown Court (Murphy *et al.* 2001, paragraphs D.7, D.8). Disclosure is made of written versions of all witness statements or other evidence which the prosecution intends to adduce at court.

For less serious cases, in which a choice is made to hold the trial in the local magistrates' court, the prosecution must disclose its case but may choose whether to provide full copies of the evidence or a summary of the case. For the least serious category of offences which may be tried only in the magistrates' court, there is no duty on the prosecution to disclose the case prior to trial. The High Court has held that this rule does not breach either the common law principle of natural justice or the right to a fair trial under the European Convention on Human Rights, since the prosecution case must necessarily be disclosed at trial and the court would have a power to adjourn the trial in any case in which it appeared that the defence were prejudiced by not being given notice of the prosecution evidence (*R. v. Stratford Justices, ex parte Imbert*).[3] Notwithstanding this decision, it seems clear that cases may arise in which a failure to give the defendant advance notice of the case against him may prevent a trial

---

[3] *The Times*, 25 Feb. 1999.

being fair. Accordingly, it is the general practice for the Crown Prosecution Service to disclose at least a summary of the prosecution evidence, although this is not required by law.

The practice of disclosing only a summary of the evidence for less serious cases is efficient and avoids wasteful duplication of paperwork. However, the summary itself may have a significant impact on the proceedings, particularly if a defence lawyer relies upon the summary when advising his client whether or not to plead guilty. Thus, where the prosecution fulfils its disclosure duties by providing a summary, considerable trust is placed in the impartiality and competence of the person whose task it is to prepare the summary. There is evidence that such trust is misplaced. Although the summary is provided by the Crown Prosecution Service it is normal to rely upon summaries prepared by the police at the culmination of the investigation. Research has indicated that investigators do not simply collect evidence but are actively involved in constructing or moulding evidence. The prosecution case as a whole tends to be selective, over-emphasizing evidence consistent with the prosecution hypothesis whilst ignoring or under-emphasizing contrary evidence (McConville *et al.* 1991, Sanders 1987). It seems probable that this tendency would be exaggerated in the process of selection, interpretation, and description for the purpose of summarizing the evidence. This has been shown to be the case in relation to police summaries of tape-recorded interviews with suspects which were found to suffer from inaccuracy, incompleteness, and partiality (Baldwin and Bedward, 1991).

The Attorney-General has now addressed criticisms of the practice of disclosing only a summary of the evidence in minor cases. Under a new guideline, the prosecutor is now required to provide to the defence all evidence on which the prosecution proposes to rely at summary trial and to allow the accused and his advisers sufficient time to consider the evidence (Attorney-General, 2001, para. 43). The guideline applies only where a trial will be held, i.e. after the accused has indicated a not guilty plea. It will certainly enhance the fairness of trials. However, the guideline does not meet the criticism made above that misleading summaries may have a powerful influence on the way in which cases are conducted and may lead to guilty pleas being made in cases in which privately the accused asserts his innocence.

DISCLOSURE OF UNUSED MATERIAL— DEVELOPMENTS AT COMMON LAW

Over the last twenty years there has been a significant development of the prosecution's duty to disclose 'unused' material, which has been collected in the course of an investigation but which does not form part of the prosecution's case against the defendant. Examples of unused material might be, fingerprints collected at the scene of crime but which do not match any suspect, and interviews with persons present at a crime who said that they could not describe the criminal. Whereas generally unused material is of minimal value, cases have arisen in which the unused material included important evidence, the significance of which had been apparently overlooked. In some such cases there are grounds for believing that important evidence was deliberately suppressed in order to avoid the risk that it might lead to the acquittal of the defendant.

An example of a case in which significant unused evidence was never disclosed was that of Stefan Kiszko, who was convicted of the murder of an 11-year-old girl in 1976. The main evidence against Kiszko, who had a mental age of 12, was an alleged confession which he denied in court. His conviction was quashed in 1991 after it was discovered that evidence stored by the police included the child's underwear which was stained with semen containing sperm. This proved conclusively that Kiszko could not have been the killer because he suffered from a medical condition as a result of which he was incapable of producing sperm (Niblett 1997, 21–2).

An equally serious miscarriage of justice in the case of Judith Ward prompted the Court of Appeal to extend the common law disclosure duties of the police and prosecution. Judith Ward was convicted of twelve murders arising from a bomb exploding on a bus carrying servicemen and their families on a motorway. She was also convicted of causing explosions and injuries in relation to two other incidents. Ward was convicted on the basis of her own confessions to the police, supported by scientific evidence of traces of explosives found on her hands and in a caravan in which she had lived. When her case was reviewed in 1993 it was discovered that police files contained undisclosed transcripts of interviews with Ward which indicated a tendency to fantasize and that a forensic scientist had originally recorded a 'faint trace' of nitro-glycerine on her hands but had misleadingly described this finding as 'positive' in court. In quashing Judith Ward's convictions, the Court of Appeal laid down new rules, binding on investigators, prosecutors, and expert witnesses, to disclose all material relevant to the case, including such matters as experimental notes or findings which might contradict or undermine the expert evidence ultimately presented to the court (*Ward*).[4] Although the decision in *Ward* has now been superseded by the disclosure scheme set out in the Criminal Procedure and Investigations Act 1996, the case was important historically in drawing attention to the link between lack of disclosure and miscarriages of justice and in prompting government action to legislate on the issue.

DISCLOSURE BY THE DEFENCE PRE-TRIAL

Under the traditional adversarial model of criminal procedure, the prosecution bore the burden of proving the guilt of the accused beyond reasonable doubt. The accused was at liberty to decide to what extent he would play an active part in the proceedings. This was advantageous to the accused, who was able to reserve disclosing his defence until the day of trial. This practice was inconvenient for prosecutors and it was subject to statutory modification in relation to alibi defences and expert evidence.

[4] (1993) 96 Cr. App. R 1.

An alibi defence is a factual plea by the defendant that he did not commit the crime and could demonstrate that he was somewhere else when it was allegedly committed. It was thought that some defendants would gain unmerited acquittals by raising alibi defences for the first time on the day of trial, thereby depriving the prosecution of the opportunity of investigating and disproving the defence. As a result, in 1967 the law was changed to require accused persons to give advance notice of any proposed alibi defence, subject to the sanction that if the notice was not given the judge could refuse to admit the evidence on which the alibi defence was based.[5] In fact this provision was not a success because, where advance notice was not provided, judges proved to be unwilling to penalize defendants by denying them the opportunity of raising their alibi defence. A requirement for advance disclosure of expert evidence was created in 1987 (Crown Court (Advance Notice of Expert Evidence) Rules 1987). This was considered necessary because notice would be required if the prosecution was to have an opportunity to commission its own expert to evaluate or challenge the accused's evidence.

As discussed above, as a consequence of legislation in 1994 for the purpose of attenuating the accused's right to silence, the accused was placed under considerable pressure to disclose during police interview the factual basis of any defence which he intended to raise in the proceedings. At about the same time the judges began to encourage substantial defence disclosure in the period between charge and trial, and laid the foundations for the creation of a reciprocal disclosure scheme. This was achieved by indicating that the extent to which unused prosecution material would be relevant (and hence disclosable) would depend upon the extent of disclosure made by the accused, and hence to the extent to which the prosecution had been alerted to the range of issues to be raised at trial (*Keane*).[6]

PUBLIC INTEREST IMMUNITY—LIMITS ON DISCLOSURE IN THE PUBLIC INTEREST

Public interest immunity is the name given to the principle that the courts may not require the disclosure of evidence which it is in the public interest to keep secret. The principle is well established in relation to civil litigation and has been applied, for instance, in order to protect the secret design of a submarine and to preserve the anonymity of persons who report the abuse of children to child welfare organizations. The principle was also well established in criminal cases in relation to the protection of the identity of informants who had provided information to the police but who were not subsequently used as witnesses. For a long time however it was not clear to what extent public interest immunity could apply to evidence or other information which might be vital in order for the defendant properly to pursue his case.

The relevant principles to be applied in balancing these conflicting interests have

---

[5] Criminal Justice Act 1967 s. 11.   [6] [1994] 1 WLR 746.

now become apparent. The prosecution may apply to the court secretly (*ex parte*) where there is material which should normally be disclosed to the defence but in relation to which it is asserted that there is a public interest in non-disclosure. The court must then consider the relevance of the material and balance this against the asserted public interest in non-disclosure. If the court accepts that there is such a public interest and that the evidence would not be very significant for the defence, then the evidence may be withheld. However, if the court determines that 'the disputed material might prove a defendant's innocence or avoid a miscarriage of justice, then the balance comes down resoundingly in favour of disclosure' (Lord Taylor CJ in *Keane*). In substance, this ruling elevates the interest in the defendant receiving a fair trial over whatever public interest is claimed in favour of secrecy. Although this honours the United Kingdom's obligation to guarantee an accused person a fair trial under Article 6 of the European Convention on Human Rights, it remains controversial. A particular criticism has been that in some cases where disclosure is ordered, the prosecution has felt compelled to discontinue the prosecution rather than compromise the public interest. This has typically occurred in relation to large-scale drug-dealing prosecutions in which the courts have ordered the disclosure of the names of informants. In such cases, the case will often be dropped, motivated by a realistic fear that the informant will be murdered if his identity is disclosed. The result is that long-running investigations are aborted, public funds are squandered, and serious criminals walk free. These consequences are unwelcome to many members of the community, particularly those involved in investigating or prosecuting crime.

THE IMPETUS FOR CHANGE

Following public and political disquiet about the exposure of a number of infamous miscarriage of justice cases, the government appointed the Royal Commission on Criminal Justice, which reported in 1993 (see generally McConville and Bridges 1994). Amongst the recommendations of the Commission were proposals to restrict the duties of prosecution disclosure which had been so recently developed by the courts, and to place a new obligation on the accused to disclose his defence, in general terms, in advance of trial. This proposal coincided with an increased interest in the whole issue of pre-trial disclosure, and as a result the government produced its own set of proposals in a Consultation Paper which developed further the scheme suggested by the Royal Commission (Home Office 1995).

   The Consultation Paper voiced a number of criticisms of the legal arrangements for disclosure then current. It was said that the law was unbalanced as requiring substantial disclosure from the prosecution in return for minimal disclosure from the defence. The prosecution duty to disclose unused material was claimed to be wastefully burdensome on the police and prosecution authorities because they had to hunt through large amounts of material to determine what must be disclosed. It was said that the defence would demand large-scale disclosure of material from police files in order to conduct 'fishing expeditions' in the hope of finding some basis for fabricating a defence. Disquiet was expressed that the requirement to disclose information some-times forced prosecuting authorities to choose between breaching the public interest or discontinuing a viable prosecution. Finally, it was argued that to allow the defence to reserve its case until the day of trial was bad judicial administration because it meant that the judge and the parties embarked upon the trial without a clear idea of what the issues would be.

The Consultation Paper concluded by recommending a scheme of mutual dis-closure, based on that proposed earlier by the Royal Commission on Criminal Justice. These proposals were quickly translated into legislation but did not find favour in all quarters. Professor Zander, writing a note of dissent to the report of the Royal Com-mission on Criminal Justice, had argued against similar proposals on the ground that, by forcing the defendant to provide information to the prosecution, the proposals would undermine the defendant's right to devote his energies to defending himself. The human rights organization JUSTICE argued that to reduce the prosecution's duties of disclosure would reduce the availability of relevant evidence to defendants and would run the risk of generating miscarriages of justice (JUSTICE 1995). Finally, it was argued that the proposed scheme focused on the work to be carried out by professionals on both sides, but lost sight of the defendant, who might be seriously prejudiced by any incompetence in operating the scheme (Leng 1995).

THE CRIMINAL PROCEDURE AND INVESTIGATIONS ACT 1996

The Criminal Procedure and Investigations Act 1996 introduced a new statutory scheme of disclosure and a complementary Code of Practice governing the conduct of investigations. During its first three years, considerable concerns were expressed by judges, prosecutors, defence lawyers, and commentators about the operation of the Act. In order to allay these concerns, the government took two measures: first it commissioned research into the disclosure scheme, which has now been completed (Plotnikoff and Wolfson 2001); secondly, the Attorney-General issued guidelines. These are described as 'clarifying' the disclosure responsibilities of various actors in the criminal process. However, in reality the Guidelines, if followed, will involve a substantial modification of such responsibilities.

The aims of the legislation were: to improve judicial administration by enabling the issues in dispute to be ascertained in advance of the trial; to encourage early disposals either by guilty pleas or discontinuances by the prosecution; to secure the early dis-closure of defences in order that these might be investigated, and to avoid ambush defences; and to ensure that accused persons receive all material available to the prosecution which might assist them in defending themselves.

A particularly important feature of the scheme is the Code of Practice. This Code does not form part of the legislation but is prepared by the Home Secretary under powers given to him by the Act. The rationale for the Code is that it would be futile to place prosecutors under duties to disclose unused material if such material is not available. Accordingly, the Code imposes upon police and other investigators duties to pursue all reasonable lines of inquiry; to record evidence in various ways; to retain evidence, and to reveal any such retained material to the prosecutor if required.

The requirement that investigators should pursue all reasonable lines of inquiry represents a significant challenge to the practices of the police. Studies of investigative work and case construction have suggested that once the police have identified a suspect there is a tendency to collect evidence pointing to that suspect, whilst ignoring alternative hypotheses and the lines of inquiry which these might suggest (McConville *et al.* 1991). The result may be that evidence which might suggest another culprit, or which might be used by the accused as the basis of a defence, was not routinely collected in the past. The new duty, to pursue all reasonable lines of inquiry, is designed to stimulate the seeking and collection of evidence which might assist the defendant. Whether the creation of the duty will have such an effect may be doubted. The Code does not prescribe a sanction for breach of the duty and, historically, legislation has not been successful in changing entrenched police culture and practices. In any event, the duty applies only in relation to reasonable lines of inquiry and it might be easy to argue that it was not reasonable to expend scarce resources to pursue an alternative speculative investigation when the police had already identified a suspect and amassed evidence against him.

A key figure in the disclosure scheme is the police disclosure officer, whose job it is to retain all material gathered during an investigation (described as 'prosecution material'); to inspect such material, to record its existence, and to make a preliminary evaluation of what material should be shown to the prosecutor and what material may need to be disclosed to the accused. The prosecution material collected for a particular case is recorded and described in documents known as 'schedules'. Two schedules are prepared: the 'sensitive schedule' will include any material in relation to which, in the view of the disclosure officer, there is a case for withholding in the public interest. The 'non-sensitive' schedule should record the existence of the remainder of the collected material. These two documents will have a significant influence on subsequent disclosure between prosecution and defence. The non-sensitive schedule must be passed to the prosecutor and will later be disclosed to the defence. This schedule is therefore the main source of information about the collected unused material on which later decisions of both the prosecutor and the defence lawyer will be based. It is disturbing, therefore, that official studies of the operation of the disclosure scheme during its early years indicate that items are frequently omitted from the schedules, and the manner in which items are described on the schedules is frequently inadequate to permit a reasoned judgement to be made about the significance of that item (Crown Prosecution Service Inspectorate 2000; Plotnikoff and Wolfson 2001).

The 'sensitive' schedule must also be sent to the prosecutor. It will not however be made available to the defence lawyer. This means that the existence of material classified as sensitive may never be known to the defence, and that accordingly the defence can play no role in any future decisions about whether it should be disclosed or applications to the court to keep the item secret. Concern has been expressed in many quarters about the influence and lack of accountability of the disclosure officer in the statutory scheme. The Attorney-General's guidelines repeatedly emphasize that prosecutors should review the work of disclosure officers. However, it is not clear what may motivate them to do this in cases where, for instance, an item has been omitted from a schedule or described in a way which misrepresents its significance.

Disclosure between prosecution and defence takes place in three stages, subject to a continuing duty on the prosecutor to consider whether further disclosure should be made, and subject also to the possibility of an application to court by the defence if it is believed that material is being improperly withheld (see generally Leng and Taylor 1996, Corker 1996, Niblett 1997). Primary prosecution disclosure is required in summary cases where a not guilty plea is indicated, and in all of the more serious cases which are sent to be tried in the Crown Court. The test which the prosecutor must apply for primary disclosure is whether the material in question 'might undermine the case for the prosecution'(section 3). The next stage is defence disclosure, which is compulsory in cases to be tried in the Crown Court (section 5) and voluntary in cases to be tried summarily (section 6). This is followed by secondary prosecution disclosure of material 'which might reasonably be expected to assist the accused's defence as disclosed by the defence statement'.

It was probably the intention of the government that the test of undermining the prosecution case should be interpreted narrowly, so that in some cases material which might assist the accused would be withheld from primary disclosure. This would then provide an incentive for the accused to disclose his defence in order to gain access to any further material which might assist him. This interpretation of the legislation was strongly criticized on the ground that it invited prosecutors to play a tactical game with justice and also on the ground that it might prejudice some defendants who might be genuinely unaware of matters which might support their defence. This would be the case where the prosecutor held material, of which the accused was unaware, which could support a hypothesis alternative to that offered by the prosecution (Leng 2000). As a result of criticisms of this sort, the practice of withholding material which could assist the accused was discredited. As a consequence, prosecutors are now advised that primary disclosure should include any material which might have an adverse effect on the prosecution case, and this is widely interpreted to include not only material going directly to the substantive issues in the case, such as material which might point to the involvement of another person, but also material that might assist in procedural applications to exclude evidence or to halt the proceedings (Attorney-General 2001, paras. 36, 37, and 38). If the test for primary disclosure is widely interpreted this reduces the function of secondary prosecution disclosure to simply making available any material the relevance of which has emerged only as a result of any defences raised by the accused.

The new approach under the Attorney-General's Guidelines of 2001 should ensure that no material is withheld at primary disclosure which in the judgement of the prosecutor might assist the defence. Unfortunately, it does not follow that failure to disclose will not continue to be a cause of injustice in the future. The potential for such injustice lies because the accused does not have free access to *all* material kept by the prosecution side. Instead, access depends upon a judgement of relevance made by the prosecutor. This is problematic. First, in an adversarial system, it is the function of the defence lawyer to select evidence for the defence case. By placing this responsibility on the prosecutor, the Act denies the accused the opportunity to have an important defence function performed by his own legal adviser. This is arguably a breach of the right of an accused person to defend himself through legal assistance of his own choosing (European Convention on Human Rights, Article 6(3)(c)). A second and related criticism is that it is not clear what will motivate the prosecutor to do a good job of vetting evidence on behalf of the defence. Thirdly, the procedure may be criticized on the ground that in the great majority of cases the task of vetting for the defence will be left to the non-legally-trained police disclosure officer.

In drafting the Criminal Procedure and Investigations Act, the government wished to create an efficient administrative process which would operate between the parties without the need for applications to court. Under the scheme (except in cases involving sensitive material) the court would play a role only after the three stages of disclosure had been completed. The role of the court would be: (i) to comment on any alleged failure to disclose by the defence and to permit adverse inferences to be drawn from such failure if appropriate (section 11); and (ii) to hear applications for further disclosure where the defendant complained that prosecution material had been wrongly withheld (section 8). It is important that the court has an ultimate role in adjudicating disclosure disputes in order to ensure compliance with the defendant's right to have a fair trial under Article 6 of the European Convention on Human Rights. However, it may be doubted whether the limited role accorded to the courts would satisfy the fair trial obligation. Two areas of difficulty can be identified. First, the Act seeks to exclude the possibility of judicial review of primary prosecution disclosure by holding that it is sufficient if the prosecutor merely 'purports' to comply with his disclosure duties at this stage (section 3). Thus, where a prosecutor has made inadequate primary disclosure, the defendant has no recourse but may nevertheless be required to make defence disclosure subject to the sanction that any failure to do so may be treated as evidence against him. This appears to be a clear breach of the principle of equality of arms which underlies the notion of a fair trial. Secondly, the procedure which permits the accused to apply to court for further disclosure under section 8 is of little practical value. Under section 8, the accused must satisfy the court that he has reasonable cause to believe that there is undisclosed prosecution material which might reasonably be expected to assist his defence. In most cases the very fact that the accused has been denied access to prosecution material will make it impossible to satisfy this test.

In view of the modern acceptance that defence-relevant material should not knowingly be withheld there seems to be a strong argument for simply allowing the defence access to all non-sensitive material held by the prosecution. Such a procedure would avoid wasting police time in examining material for disclosure purposes and would also avoid the arguments, in or out of court, which the current procedures generate. This open-access option is favoured in the recent review of the criminal courts by Auld LJ, who points out that modern technology should allow documents to be made available electronically without any need to transport large quantities of paper (Auld 2001, 449–54).

The requirement that the accused should provide a defence statement represents a substantial departure from the tradition that it is 'not the job of the defendant to be helpful either to the system or to the prosecution' (Zander 1993). Under section 5, the accused is required to provide a 'defence statement' indicating the nature of his defence in general terms, the matters on which he takes issue with the prosecution, why he takes issue with those matters, and particulars of any alibi and any witnesses relied upon to support such an alibi. The provision has been criticized on the basis that by requiring the accused to disclose precise areas of dispute he will be deprived of the benefit of surprise when testing prosecution witnesses in cross-examination. In fact, empirical studies and anecdotal evidence suggest that generally defence statements rarely involve much more than a simple denial (Crown Prosecution Service Inspectorate 2000, Plotnikoff and Wolfson 2001).

It is clear that currently defence statements are ineffective in helping to clarify issues, encouraging early guilty pleas, or in shortening trials. Although, many commentators lay the blame for this at the door of defendants and defence lawyers, the disclosure scheme itself may militate against full and frank disclosure in defence statements. By section 11, various types of fault in defence statements may be the subject of comment by a judge and may be treated as evidence supporting the prosecution by the jury. Thus, adverse evidential inferences may be drawn against a defendant who in the course of trial departs significantly from his original statement, or who fails to pursue a defence earlier notified in the statement. Thus, drafting a defence statement is a process fraught with danger, and it is no surprise that defence lawyers adopt a minimalist approach to avoid committing their clients to a position which it might be difficult to resile from in court.

The theory that deviation from a defence statement may be treated as evidence against a defendant has also not found favour with judges. The studies referred to above have found a reluctance amongst judges to direct juries that adverse inferences may be drawn in such circumstances. This may be because judges recognize that the process of drafting defence statements is lawyers' work and has little evidential relevance for the purpose of proving involvement in a criminal offence. Judges have also been motivated by a concern that by focusing on defence statements, juries might be distracted from the main issues in the case, and have wished to avoid lengthy arguments in court and the possibility of future appeals over a piece of evidence of, at best, marginal evidential value.

In one respect, the Criminal Procedure and Investigations Act has failed in achieving its objectives. It was intended that the Act would create a complete Code to replace the former procedures developed at common law. Whether this might be achieved or not was always doubtful: the common law exists in rules (which can be abolished) but also in principles (which cannot). Experience since the Act came into force has demonstrated that the vigour of the common law remains undiminished in this area. For instance, the courts have held that a prosecutor has a duty, additional to those set out in the Act, to disclose material which might assist a defendant to make a bail application or some other application in the early stages of a proceeding (*R. v. DPP, ex parte Lee*).[7] The recently promulgated Attorney-General's Guidelines, which responded to wide-ranging and disparate dissatisfaction with the strict legal rules of the Act, which sought to reflect a consensus of opinion amongst legal professionals, may also be understood as a vehicle for the expression of common law principles in practice.

CONCLUSION

Procedures for exchanging and sharing information between prosecution and defence are vital if the criminal process is to achieve both justice and efficiency. Over the last decade the courts and the legal professions, government, Parliament, and academic commentators have expended considerable effort in seeking to achieve a process which is both workable and fair. The results of these efforts has attracted the admiration of observers from elsewhere in the common law world (Fisher 1999).

However, a study of the recent history of the disclosure issue and an examination of the procedures currently in place indicate the complexity of the issues raised and the difficulty of balancing the competing interests. Predictably, a number of problems persist: because of the limited role for judicial supervision, police officers and prosecutors are unaccountable for important decisions; to vest the function of vetting prosecution material for materiality and sensitivity in relatively junior police officers without legal training is not acceptable; nor is it acceptable to corrupt the process of proof by treating disclosure failures by defence lawyers as evidence against the accused.

However, a number of positive lessons emerge from the English experience: state investigators best serve the community by not only collecting evidence against their selected suspect but also by collecting evidence favourable to him; it is important to regulate the collection and retention of evidence; the decision to withhold evidence in the public interest should be taken by a court not by the prosecution or the executive; adherence to statutory rules may need to be tempered by prosecutorial discretion if unfairness and miscarriages of justice are to be avoided. Perhaps the most important lesson to be learned from the recent history of disclosure in England is that as much has been achieved by the dynamic engagement of those working in criminal justice in debating the disclosure issue, as by legislation imposed from above.

Bibliography and Further Reading

ATTORNEY-GENERAL, *Disclosure of Information in Criminal Proceedings*, www.lslo.gov.uk/pdf/guidelines.pdf.

AULD, R., *A Review of the Criminal Courts of England and Wales*, www.criminal-courts-review.org.uk.

BALDWIN, J., and BEDWARD, J., 'Summarizing Tape Recordings of Police Interviews' [1991] *Crim. LR* 671.

BUCKE, T., STREET, R., and BROWN, D., *The Right to Silence: The Impact of the Criminal Justice and Public Order Act*

---

[7] [1999] 2 All ER 737.

1994, Home Office Research Study 1999 (London: HMSO, 2000).

CAPE, E., *Defending Suspects at Police Stations* (3rd edn., London: Legal Action Group, 1999).

CORKER, D., *Disclosure in Criminal Proceedings* (London: Sweet & Maxwell, 1996).

CROWN PROSECUTION SERVICE INSPECTORATE, *Report on the Thematic Review of the Disclosure of Unused Material* (London: TSO, 2000).

FISHER, S. Z., 'The Prosecutor's Ethical Duty to Seek Exculpatory Evidence in Police Hands: Lessons from England' (2000) 68 *Fordham L. Rev.* 1379.

HOME OFFICE, *Disclosure: A Consultation Document*, Cm 2864 (1993).

JACKSON, J., 'Silence and Proof: Extending the Boundaries of Criminal Proceedings in the United Kingdom' (2001) 5 *International Journal of Evidence and Proof* 145.

JUSTICE, *Disclosure: A Consultation Paper. The Justice Response* (London: JUSTICE, 1995).

LENG, R., 'Losing Sight of the Defendant: The Government's Proposals on Pre-trial Disclosure' [1995] *Crim. LR* 704.

—— 'Defence Strategies for Information Deficit: Negotiating the CPIA' (1997) 1 *International Journal of Evidence and Proof* 215.

—— 'Disclosure: A Flawed Procedure' in K. Akester (ed.), *Papers Submitted to the Auld Review of Criminal Justice* (London: JUSTICE, 2000), **www.justice.org.uk/ publications/listofpublications/ index.html**.

—— and TAYLOR, R., *Blackstone's Guide to the Criminal Procedure and Investigations Act 1996* (London: Blackstone Press, 1996).

LIDSTONE, K., and PALMER, C., *The Investigation of Crime: A Guide to Police Powers* (2nd edn., London: Butterworths, 1996).

McCONVILLE, M., and BRIDGES, L., *Criminal Justice in Crisis* (Aldershot: Edward Elgar, 1994).

——, SANDERS, A., and LENG, R., *The Case for the Prosecution: Police Suspects and the Construction of Criminality* (London: Routledge, 1991).

MURPHY, P., *et al.*, *Blackstone's Criminal Practice 2001* (London: Blackstone Press, 2001).

NIBLETT, J., *Disclosure in Criminal Proceedings* (London: Blackstone Press, 1997).

PLOTNIKOFF, J., and WOLFSON, R., *A Fair Balance? Evaluation of the Operation of Disclosure Law* (London: Home Office, 2001).

ROYAL COMMISSION ON CRIMINAL JUSTICE, *Report*, Cm 2262 (London: HMSO, 1993).

SANDERS, A., 'Constructing the Case for the Prosecution' (1987) 14 *Journal of Law and Society* 229.

TONEY, R., 'Disclosure of Evidence and Legal Assistance at Custodial Interrogation: What does the European Convention on Human Rights Require?' (2001) 5 *International Journal of Evidence and Proof* 39.

WOLCHOVER, D., *Silence and Guilt* (London: Lion Court Lawyers, 2001).

ZANDER, M., 'A Note of Dissent' in *Report of the Royal Commission on Criminal Justice*, Cm 2263 (London: HMSO, 1993), 221.

13

PUBLICITY SURROUNDING THE TRIAL

John Sprack

Above all else, the criminal trial must be fair. The notion of fairness has at its core the need for an impartial fact-finder, acting according to the law. At the same time, a free press, reporting freely on matters of public interest, plays a central role in the functioning of democracy. Is there a clash between the fair trial and freedom of the press?

Certainly, they can be reconciled at the level of theory. Society wishes to encourage the reporting of crime, its investigation, and the way in which cases are dealt with, for the ultimate health of the criminal justice system. In the direct sense, investigative journalism may bring crime to the attention of the authorities. More indirectly, the fact that the public is aware of what goes on in pursuing and trying someone accused of criminal behaviour is an incentive to all concerned to act both efficiently and with propriety. In most cases, the victim, the accused, and the State all have an interest in a trial which is public as well as fair.

Yet the theory and the practice do not always coincide. From the accused's point of view, there is a risk of unfavourable publicity which leads to prejudice in the finder of fact. In extreme circumstances, such prejudice may result in a miscarriage of justice. This risk is perceived as more prevalent in a system which relies on jury trial to deal with the more serious crimes,[1] but there is no reason in principle why lay magistrates should be regarded as immune from its effects. Further, although the training of lawyers helps equip them to deal with such factors, it would perhaps be naïve to suggest that members of the judiciary are totally unaffected by a hostile media campaign. Indeed, some of the leading cases in the jurisprudence of the European Court of Human Rights deal with the infringement of a fair trial which inevitably follows when the authorities identify with prejudicial material.[2]

There is another conflict of fundamental rights which needs to be considered when looking at pre-trial publicity. The participants in a trial have the right to privacy, particularly if they are the victims of crime or witnesses who have come forward to give evidence in order to help the courts to do justice. How does that right square with

---

[1] See, e.g., *Crociani* v. *Italy* (1980) 22 D&R 147, where the European Commission on Human Rights indicated that prejudice would be harder to establish in a case tried by a judge than in one tried by a jury.

[2] *Allenet de Ribemont* v. *France* (1995) 20 EHRR 557 (ECtHR).

the intrusion which the media's freedom of expression and the public's right to information may constitute?

In describing the main features of the English approach to these problems, I will deal first with the rules relating to pre-trial publicity, and then with the trial itself. Three particular areas are then looked at: how the courts deal with prejudice to the defendant resulting from adverse publicity; the position of juveniles (those under 18); and the protection of the victim and the witness from publicity.

THE LAW RELATING TO PRE-TRIAL PUBLICITY

The duty to ensure that the law relating to pre-trial publicity is respected lies with the Attorney-General and the law officers of the government. In other words, it is the responsibility of the executive, rather than the judiciary.

The law governing this area is contained primarily in the Contempt of Court Act 1981. There is strict liability, without the need to prove mens rea in relation only to:

- publications (communications addressed to the public);
- which create a substantial risk that the course of justice in the proceedings in question will be seriously impeded or prejudiced;
- if those proceedings are active.

Proceedings are active for these purposes from the time when an arrest is made or a warrant or summons is issued, and until acquittal, discontinuance, withdrawal, or sentence. In other cases strict liability does not apply and the prosecution needs to prove a specific intent, i.e. intention to interfere with the course of justice.

There is an important defence available under the Contempt of Court Act 1981: '[a] person is not guilty of contempt of court under the strict liability rule in respect of a fair and accurate report of legal proceedings held in public, published contemporaneously and in good faith'.[3] The proceedings in question can of course take place prior to the trial itself, subject to what is said later in this section about committal proceedings.

Contempt of court is a serious offence and could result in a custodial sentence of up to two years' imprisonment, although a fine is more usual in the case of publication by the media of material in contempt of court. The last editor to be imprisoned for publishing an article in contempt of court was Sylvester Bolam. He was jailed for three months in 1949 over an article regarding the arrest of John Haigh, the acid-bath murderer. Although a fine is the usual punishment, the amount can be quite large. In 1998 the murder trial of James McArdle was stopped after the *Sun* published an article while the jury was considering its verdict. The *Sun* was fined £35,000 for what the judge described as 'a dreadful error' and 'a serious contempt'.

Although there is a defence relating to fair and accurate reports of legal proceed-

---

[3] Contempt of Court Act 1981, s. 2.

ings, there is an important exception in practice where the magistrates' court is deciding whether to commit a defendant to the Crown Court for trial.[4] In these preliminary proceedings only the prosecution is allowed to present evidence and the defence role is confined to arguing (in appropriate circumstances) that there is not sufficient evidence to justify a trial in the Crown Court. As a result, any report of the evidence will inevitably be biased in favour of the prosecution. The law therefore forbids the media to publish a report of committal proceedings, other than the bare details about names, ages, addresses, and occupations of the accused, witnesses, and legal representatives, together with the decisions about whether to commit, the charges, venue, dates, and arrangements as to bail, legal aid, and the like. The prohibition is for the protection of the defendant, who is entitled to waive it, e.g. in the hope that a witness favourable to the defence will come forward as a result of any publicity which is generated. If co-defendants differ on whether the rule should be lifted, then the magistrates must decide what is in the interests of justice.

PUBLICITY DURING THE TRIAL ITSELF

The general principle in our criminal justice system is that justice should be open.[5] Hence proceedings should be held in a court which is open and accessible to the public. As mentioned in the preceding section, the media have power to report on contemporaneous court proceedings, using the defence under the Contempt of Court Act. This aspect of freedom of expression is better protected than comment on matters which are still to come to trial, and hence are regarded as *sub judice*.

The courts do, however, have power to derogate from the general principle of open justice. The most radical departure from that principle is the power to sit *in camera* (in private). This power may be exercised only within well-defined circumstances, however, such as:

- where there is the possibility of disorder;
- where a witness would refuse to testify publicly;
- where a public hearing would prejudice the possibility of future prosecutions;
- in cases under the Official Secrets Acts.

One common reason for a request to sit *in camera* is the need to communicate evidence confidentially, e.g. on the part of the victim in a blackmail case. The fact that the witness will be embarrassed by giving evidence in public is not, however, sufficient reason to breach the principle of open justice. A real risk to the administration of justice is required to override that principle.

---

[4] The restrictions on publicity relating to committal proceedings are contained in the Magistrates' Court Act 1980.

[5] For a detailed account of the case law and statutes relating to the principle of open justice see P. Murphy (ed.), *Blackstone's Criminal Practice* (London: Blackstone, 2001), D2.47 to 53.

An alternative to sitting *in camera* is an order by the court that a witness should remain anonymous. There can also be a ban on publication of the witness's evidence, or identity, without the necessity for the court to sit in private.

Certain specific acts relating to the trial itself are covered by the law of contempt of court, and hence prohibited.[6] In particular, disclosure of the deliberations of the jury is a contempt of court. Not only are the media prevented from probing into what went on in the jury room—even the lawyers are unable to do so, with the result that an appeal based on the proceedings in the jury room is virtually impossible to mount. The use of a tape-recorder in court is prohibited, as is the taking or publication of photographs of the court proceedings. In addition, where the judge has ordered restrictions on the reporting of a case heard in public, it is contempt for the media to contravene that order. Similarly, where there is publication of matter exempted from disclosure in court, e.g. the identity of a rape victim, or of a child, that will constitute contempt.

Generally, then, the trial itself is open to the public and the media are entitled to report upon it freely, provided that their reports are fair and accurate. There are, however, other restrictions placed on the media, as problems in securing a fair trial for the accused may result from reports other than those about the trial itself. There are also problems about making any restrictions effective. It is on those problems that we now ought to focus.

THE PROBLEM OF PREJUDICE TO THE DEFENDANT

The law relating to contempt of court aims to stop the publication of material prejudicial to the defendant, with the object of protecting the impartiality of the jury, and ensuring a fair trial. This can be done either by obtaining an injunction in advance prohibiting publication or by prosecuting after the event, in the hope that the punishment inflicted on the publisher will discourage others from similar wrongdoing in the future. If a newspaper or broadcaster is intent on publishing regardless of the consequences, however, then it has only to keep its intentions secret to escape the possibility of prior restraint by means of an injunction. Any penalty imposed by the courts after the event is then part of a calculated risk.

Even where the authorities know about the publication in advance, they have a formidable obstacle to overcome. What the Attorney-General has to prove in order to succeed under the Contempt of Court Act 1981 is that a particular article or broadcast in itself, in isolation from any other media report, has created a substantial risk of serious prejudice. The usual risk, however, is from the cumulative effect of coverage over a period, often by a number of separate newspapers and broadcasters. By the time that the trial takes place some months later, the chances of the jury remembering

---

[6] See *ibid.*, B14.82 ff. for an account of these various particular restrictions on publicity during the trial.

any specific article will be slim, but that does not necessarily mean that the overall effect of media coverage has had no prejudicial effect.

Inevitably, these factors mean that the trial judge must deal with allegations of biased media coverage. There are a number of judicial strategies available to cope with such a situation. The most radical step which the judge may take is to stay proceedings, on the basis that they could not be fair, given the extent of prejudicial media coverage. For understandable reasons, this is a course of action which is extremely rare, although it is not entirely without precedent. One case where it was done was that of *Reade*,[7] where the trial of the police officers prosecuted following the successful appeals of those convicted of the Birmingham bombing ('the Birmingham Six') was stopped. Garland J granted a stay of proceedings against the officers in question, partly on the basis of the publicity which had surrounded the case, which he characterized as 'a powerful factor'. He said that prejudice engendered by publicity is usually local and temporary, but if the impossibility of having a fair trial becomes national and continuing then there is 'quite literally nowhere to go'. He ordered a stay of proceedings on two bases:

(a) 'The Birmingham Six' has become a synonym for 'forced confessions';

(b) publicity attending the 1991 appeal gave the impression that the court was finding the defendants (i.e. the police officers now on trial) guilty of conspiracy and perjury.

A somewhat less radical approach is for the judge to discharge a particular jury on the basis of prejudicial publicity. That does not shut out the option of a retrial. One recent such case is that of two well-known Leeds United footballers, Lee Bowyer and Jonathan Woodgate, accused of beating an Asian student unconscious. Their trial was halted, after it had lasted ten weeks at a cost of £8 million, because of the publication of an interview with the father of the alleged victim. He claimed in the *Sunday Mirror* that the attack was racially motivated. The trial judge, Poole J, held that this constituted a serious prejudicial threat to the trial and ordered that the newspaper be reported to the Attorney-General.[8] A few days later, the editor of the *Sunday Mirror* resigned. Unlike Garland J in the *Reade* case, however, Poole J ordered a retrial. The article was held to have been prejudicial to this particular trial, but this did not mean that a future trial would be unfair.

Although *Reade* stands somewhat in isolation as a case where a decision to stay proceedings was made largely on the basis of adverse publicity, there are several cases where the Court of Appeal has, by holding that a conviction was unsafe, in effect held that the trial ought not to have been held, or that the jury should have been discharged during the course of the trial. Generally, these decisions appear to be confined to cases where the adverse publicity appears during the trial.

In *Taylor and Taylor*[9] the prosecution case was that the appellant sisters had stabbed

---

[7] See the news report in *The Times*, 16 Oct. 1993, of the proceedings at the Central Criminal Court (Old Bailey), and the judgment of Garland J.

[8] See news report in *The Times*, 10 Apr. 2001.

[9] (1993) 98 Cr. App. R 361.

the victim to death because one of them was jealous, having had a sexual relationship with the victim's husband, and the other had disliked the way in which her sister was treated. The main ground of appeal related to the prosecution's failure to disclose certain important material to the defence. An important additional ground, however, was that the press coverage was 'unremitting, extensive, sensational, inaccurate and misleading' and consisted of 'comment which assumed guilt on the part of the girls'. The Court of Appeal said, 'We find it quite impossible to say that the jury were not influenced in their decision by what they read in the press'.[10] They were 'satisfied that the press coverage of this trial did create a real risk of prejudice against the defendants'. They quashed the convictions for both reasons, and refused to order a retrial because a fair trial could not take place. They further ordered that the papers in the case should be sent to the Attorney-General to consider whether action should be taken against any of the newspapers concerned.

In *McCann*[11] M and others were tried for conspiracy to murder Mr King, who was then the Secretary of State for Northern Ireland. They elected not to give evidence. At the time the law was that no comment could be made about their silence in court and no inference could be drawn from it. During the closing stages of the trial, the Home Secretary announced in the House of Commons the government's intention to change the law on the right to silence, so that inferences could be drawn against those who elected not to give evidence. That night interviews were televised with Mr King and with Lord Denning, a former very senior and well-known judge. Both expressed in strong terms their view that in terrorist cases a failure to give evidence was tantamount to guilt. The trial judge refused to dismiss the jury and the defendants were convicted. The Court of Appeal held that there was a real risk that the jury had been influenced by the statement. The judge should have discharged the jury and ordered a retrial.

In *Wood*,[12] the appellant was convicted of possessing Semtex with intent to cause explosions and endanger life. His appeal was upheld, partly on the basis of prejudicial material appearing in the press during the trial and partly because of an unfair summing up on the part of the trial judge. As far as the press coverage is concerned, during the course of the trial there had been a number of articles indicating discontent with the criminal justice system in general, the tenor of which was that it was very difficult to obtain convictions of terrorists, that the police were hampered in their job by restrictions which the law imposed, and that some jurors were determined not to convict, whatever the weight of the evidence. The Court of Appeal was most concerned, however, with an article which appeared in the *Daily Star* which said:

We do not wish to prejudice the trial of the latest man to be arrested but the fact is that he was caught red-handed with a bag full of Semtex. If this man is not tried, convicted and sentenced to spend the rest of his life in jail justice will not have been done and the already shaky morale of the police will be even further eroded and the nation will have been betrayed.

---

[10] N. 9 above, at 369.   [11] (1991) 92 Cr. App. R 239.   [12] [1996] 1 Cr. App. R 207.

In fact, the article arguably referred, not to Wood, but to another man who had been caught with a Semtex bag earlier in the week. But jurors could well have concluded, in the view of the Court of Appeal, that there was evidence of Wood's guilt which could not be produced in court, and that they had a duty to the nation to make sure that he was convicted. The Court of Appeal commented:[13]

If we are to have a free and independent press, we must allow and welcome general comment on the faults of our system of criminal justice and on the errors that are sometimes made in one direction or the other. But fairness demands that pressure should not be put on jurors in a particular case by the press or anyone else. Newspaper editors and their readers rightly require that those guilty of serious crime should be convicted and punished. That objective may be endangered by the very measures taken to achieve it, if they result in an unfair trial.

The conviction was quashed, and a retrial ordered.

On the other hand, there are a great many cases where adverse publicity has been held, both by the trial judge and the Court of Appeal, to be insufficient reason to stay proceedings, discharge the jury, or (on appeal) hold that the conviction was unsafe: see, for example, the cases of *Malik*,[14] *Savundra*,[15] *Kray*,[16] *Ex parte The Telegraph plc*,[17] *Bow Street Metropolitan Stipendiary Magistrate, ex parte DPP*,[18] *West*,[19] and *Stone*.[20] The reason usually given for holding that it is proper to proceed in such circumstances is that the jury is capable of ignoring prejudicial coverage, provided that a clear direction is given by the judge that they should make their decision solely upon the evidence in the case. As Lawton LJ put it in *Ex parte The Telegraph plc*:[21] 'A court should credit the jury with the will and ability to abide by the judge's direction to decide the case only on the evidence before them'. In *Kray*,[22] the same judge at first instance said: 'The drama of the trial almost always has the effect of excluding from recollection that which went before'. Appellate courts seem to be particularly confident in the jury's ability to ignore adverse publicity where some time has elapsed between its publication and the trial. As Scott-Baker J put it in *Ex parte B*:[23]

In most cases, one day's headline news is the next day's firelighter. Most members of the public do not remember in any detail what they have seen on television, heard on the radio or read in the newspaper except for a very short period of time.

The Court of Appeal has been particularly anxious to ensure that the most notorious criminals should not escape justice because of hostile media coverage. In *West*[24] the appellant had been convicted of ten counts of murder, the prosecution case being that she had committed them with her husband, who killed himself while in prison awaiting trial. She appealed on the basis, *inter alia*, that press coverage prior to the jury being sworn was so hostile and extensive that it prejudiced a fair trial. In dismissing the appeal, Lord Taylor CJ said:[25]

---

[13] *Ibid.*, at 214.
[14] (1968) 52 Cr. App. R 140.
[15] (1968) 52 Cr. App. R 637.
[16] (1969) 53 Cr. App. R 412.
[17] [1993] 1 WLR 980 at 987.
[18] (1992) 95 Cr. App. R 9.
[19] [1996] 2 Cr. App. R 374.
[20] *The Times*, 22 Feb. 2001.
[21] N. 17 above, at 987.
[22] N. 16 above, at 414–5.
[23] Unreported, 17 Feb. 1994.
[24] [1996] Cr. App. R 374.
[25] N. 24 above, at 386.

there can scarcely ever have been a case more calculated to shock the public who were entitled to know the facts. The question raised on behalf of the defence is whether a fair trial could be held after such intensive publicity adverse to the accused. In our view it could. To hold otherwise would mean that if allegations of murder are sufficiently horrendous so as inevitably to shock the nation, the accused cannot be tried. That would be absurd. Moreover, providing the judge effectively warns the jury to act only on the evidence given in court, there is no reason to suppose that they would do otherwise.

It is clear, then, that there is a great reluctance on the part of the Court of Appeal to hold that a judge at first instance should have stopped proceedings, or even a particular trial, on the basis of adverse publicity, however sustained and hostile it was. An alternative strategy which a trial judge may adopt is to inquire, before the trial begins, about the extent to which prospective members of the jury have been exposed to prejudicial publicity about the accused. The high-water mark of this approach was the serious fraud trial of *Kevin Maxwell*,[26] where the trial judge, Philips J, adopted a procedure which meant that:

- the jury empanelment took several days;
- potential jurors filled in a forty-item questionnaire;
- some jurors were then sifted out by agreement between prosecution and defence;
- the judge questioned those remaining in open court;
- the final jury was then drawn by lot from the survivors.

In *Andrews*,[27] however, some doubt was cast upon the adoption of the *Maxwell* approach in all but the most exceptional cases. Tracey Andrews was convicted of murdering her boyfriend by stabbing. Her defence was that another motorist had killed him in a fit of road rage. There was extensive press coverage, which included a number of false stories, one being that a knife had been found in the petrol tank of the car driven by the appellant and the victim. At a contested bail application in the magistrates' court prior to trial, evidence was given and reported of the appellant's violence towards others, especially a former boyfriend. This evidence was not admitted at the trial. At the trial, the defence argued that all jurors should answer a questionnaire on the lines of that used in the *Maxwell*[28] case. The judge rejected this and directed the jury on several occasions to put all pre-trial publicity out of their minds. He also required the prosecution to refute the 'knife in the petrol tank' story in its opening speech and it did so. The defendant was convicted, and appealed on the basis that the judge should have put a questionnaire to the jury and that the trial was unfair because of the pre-trial publicity. The Court of Appeal rejected the appeal, endorsing the approach of the trial judge. Several months had elapsed between the inaccurate reports and the trial. The random jury principle meant that there should be no jury

---

[26] Central Criminal Court, 25 May 1995; unreported but quoted from in numerous appellate judgments since, e.g. *Stone, The Times,* 22 Feb. 2001.

[27] [1999] *Crim. LR* 156.

[28] N. 26 above.

vetting or questioning in our jurisdiction unless there was a real risk of bias, in accordance with the test in *Gough*.[29] Only in exceptional cases could the jury be questioned, e.g. where they might have lost money due to the alleged offences which were the subject of the trial. Questioning might remind jurors of the very matters which it was sought to exclude. The trial judge was the one in the best position to assess whether questioning was appropriate. The reports of A's previous violence would not have had an impact on the jury, because the judge had directed them to ignore matters not in evidence before them.

The test for determining whether there should be a retrial after a successful appeal, in circumstances where there has been publicity adverse to the accused, was recently set out in *Stone*.[30] The appellant was convicted of two offences of murder and one of attempted murder, arising from an attack with a hammer on a mother and her two daughters. There was substantial publicity in the months immediately after the verdict was returned in October 1998, when many matters were revealed which had properly been kept away from the jury. There was then a trickle of publicity, which erupted again immediately prior to and during the appeal in early 2001. The Court of Appeal upheld the appeal, quashing the convictions because a crucial prosecution witness had retracted his evidence the day after the jury returned their verdicts, telling journalists that he had given false evidence. There was then argument about whether there should be a retrial, in the light of the publicity generated by the trial and appeal. The court endorsed the test put forward by Phillips J in the *Maxwell*[31] trial when he said:

No stay should be imposed unless the defendant shows on the balance of probabilities that owing to the extent and nature of the pre-trial publicity he will suffer serious prejudice to the extent that no fair trial can be held.

The Court of Appeal said that this was a case where, but for the publicity, a retrial would certainly be ordered. They took the view that a retrial should be ordered unless they were satisfied on a balance of probabilities that, if at the retrial the jury returned one or more verdicts of guilty, the effect of the publicity would be such as to render any such verdicts unsafe. They accepted that the early publicity was sensational and extended far beyond what a jury in 2001 might normally be told. But the retrial would not start until nearly three years after the 1998 publicity which was the main target of complaint. People did forget. Even if they did not forget entirely, the passage of time made it easier for them to set aside that which they were told to disregard.

---

[29] [1993] AC 646.   [30] N. 20 above.   [31] N. 26 above.

JUVENILES: SPECIAL CONSIDERATIONS

In England and Wales, there are special rules governing publicity relating to young defendants and witnesses. Generally, juveniles (aged under 18) are tried in a Youth Court, which is not open to the public, although representatives of the media can attend. The media may not, however, reveal the name, address or other identifying details of any juvenile, whether a defendant or a witness.[32] This ban can be lifted by the court to avoid injustice to a juvenile, or to enable the apprehension and return to custody of a juvenile charged with certain serious offences. Further, the court can allow publication of the juvenile's name and other details if he or she has been convicted of an offence and it is in the public interest to allow publication.

Juveniles may also appear in an adult magistrates' court or the Crown Court on occasion as witnesses or defendants. In those circumstances, reports in the media may be subject to restrictions similar to those which apply in the Youth Court, if the court makes an order restricting reporting.

Although the rules relating to juveniles provide better protection than that for adults, they do not go nearly as far as the standards laid down internationally. The United Nations Convention on the Rights of the Child[33] states that '[e]very child alleged as or accused of having infringed the penal law has at least the following guarantees ... to have his or her privacy fully respected at all stages of the proceedings'.

The Standard Minimum Rules for the Administration of Juvenile Justice[34] state that:

8.1 The juvenile's right to privacy shall be respected at all stages in order to avoid harm being caused to her or him by undue publicity or by the process of labelling

8.2 In principle, no information that may lead to the identification of a juvenile offender shall be published.

The International Covenant on Civil and Political Rights, which sets out a general rule that judgments should be made public, makes an exception when the interests of juveniles so require.

Publicity surrounding a trial may be prejudicial to the interests of an accused, whatever his or her age. But in the case of a juvenile defendant, its effect may be particularly powerful. In *T* v. *UK*, *V* v. *UK*,[35] the British government was held by the European Court of Human Rights to have violated the right to a fair trial of two defendants, aged 11, on the charge of murdering James Bulger, a child aged two. The adverse finding was largely due to the frenzy of media attention which surrounded court proceedings. The Strasbourg Court held that the criminal justice system must be adapted when children are on trial, particularly if there is considerable media attention:[36]

---

[32] See *Blackstone's Criminal Practice*, n. 3 above, D21.17 ff. for details.
[33] 1989, Art. 40.2(b)(vii).
[34] The Beijing Rules, adopted by the UN General Assembly in 1985.
[35] (1999) 30 EHRR 121 (ECtHR).   [36] *Ibid.*, paras. 87–89.

in respect of a young child charged with a grave offence attracting high levels of media and public interest, it would be necessary to conduct the hearing in such a way as to reduce as far as possible his or her feelings of intimidation and inhibition.

Further, where press and public interest intensified the atmosphere in court and the defendant was:

suffering the post–traumatic effects of what he or she has done and unable to even think about the events in question without extreme distress, such that he or she cannot give instruction or evidence, Article 6 [the right to a fair trial] is likely to be breached.

As a result of the Strasbourg judgment in *T* v. *UK*, *V* v. *UK*, the *Practice Direction (Crown Court: Young Defendants)*[37] was issued by the Lord Chief Justice for the guidance of the Crown Court. It was aimed at ensuring that '[t]he trial process should not itself expose the young defendant to avoidable intimidation, humiliation or distress'. As far as publicity is concerned, the *Practice Direction* states:

If any case against a young defendant has attracted or may attract widespread public or media interest, the assistance of the police should be enlisted to try and ensure that a young defendant is not, when attending for the trial, exposed to intimidation, vilification or abuse . . . [T]he court may restrict the number of those attending in the courtroom to report the trial to such number as is judged practicable and desirable.

When the defendants T and V were released later in 2001, they were given new identities, so that they could begin new lives in different parts of the country, with carefully manufactured histories designed to obliterate their past. The High Court has imposed an injunction which prohibits the media from revealing any details about their whereabouts, or their new identities, which would enable them to be identified. It is perhaps worth emphasizing that if the international rules summarized above had been part of English law, their identities ought never to have been in the public domain in the first place.

The Youth Justice and Criminal Evidence Act 1999, section 44, extends the scope of the protection from publicity for young people under the age of 18. When it is brought into force, it will prohibit the publication of material which might lead to the public identification of a young person under the age of 18 who is involved in a criminal investigation as suspect, victim, or witness. There is a power to dispense with the restriction in the interests of justice. There are, however, no current plans to implement section 44 in so far as it relates to investigations involving juvenile victims or witnesses. The reason is that this provision might hinder the assistance which the press can provide to police investigations. As a result, it appears that the government is content, for the time being at any rate, to rely on the press to regulate itself in this field.

In so far as it applies to juvenile suspects, however, section 44 constitutes an important restriction on publicity. It augments the separate provisions which cover proceedings in the Youth Courts on the one hand, and the Crown Court and adult

---

[37] [2000] 1 WLR 659.

magistrates' courts on the other.[38] It also represents an important extension of the restriction on publicity for the juvenile suspect or accused, since it applies from the start of the investigation, rather than from the commencement of court proceedings.

PROTECTION OF VICTIMS AND WITNESSES

Dealing now with those who are aged 18 or over, there are various measures which aim to ensure that witnesses who are vulnerable for one reason or another receive a measure of protection. The best established of those measures is the statutory guarantee of anonymity afforded to rape complainants by the Sexual Offences (Amendment) Act 1976. The restriction aims to protect the witness from harmful publicity, but also has the policy objective of encouraging victims who might be reluctant to report the crime against themselves. In 1992, it was extended so that it takes effect from the time that the allegation is made and, also, so that it covers not just rape, but a broad range of sexual offences.

The Youth Justice and Criminal Evidence Act 1999 provides the criminal courts with the power to restrict publicity in order to protect the identity of vulnerable witnesses. A reporting direction can be made when:

- the witness is eligible for protection,
- a reporting direction would be likely to improve the quality of a witness's evidence, or the level to which the witness co-operates with a party,
- the court decides to make such a direction in the interests of justice and after taking into account the public interest in avoiding the imposition of a substantial and unreasonable restriction on the reporting of proceedings.

A reporting direction will order that no matter relating to the witness shall, during his or her lifetime, be published if it is likely to lead members of the public to identify him or her as a witness in the proceedings. Identifying factors which are mentioned by the statute as likely to have this effect are the witness's:

- name
- address
- school or other educational establishment
- place of work
- a still or moving picture.

The YJCEA creates new offences of breaching reporting restrictions relating to juveniles and vulnerable witnesses. It also provides certain defences in respect of those offences, e.g. proof that the defendant lacked awareness, suspicion or grounds for

---

[38] S. 45 of the Youth Justice and Criminal Evidence Act 1999 and s. 49 of the Children and Young Persons Act 1933, respectively.

suspicion, in relation to a relevant matter and, in certain limited circumstances, proof that publication was in the public interest or was made with the consent of the affected party.

CONCLUSION

There have in practice been two major areas of potential conflict in relation to publicity surrounding the criminal trial. The first relates to the rights of victims and witnesses, particularly those perceived as vulnerable. The conflict here is between the freedom of the media to report and the right of the public to receive information about matters of public interest, on the one hand, and the right to be protected from potentially harmful intrusion, on the other. To put it in terms of the rights contained in the European Convention on Human Rights, the conflict is between Article 10 (freedom of expression) and Article 8 (right to a private life).

Generally, the approach in our courts to this conflict has been to favour a system of open justice. Freedom of expression and information have been perceived as more important in the context of the criminal justice system than the right to privacy of the participants in proceedings. There are crucial exceptions in relation to certain vulnerable groups of witnesses, including for example the victims of sexual offences and juveniles. In these cases, the protection of the privacy of the vulnerable person has been given priority by the law. In the future, this trend may well be extended, in line with the increasing recognition by the European Court of Human Rights that the right to privacy of witnesses and victims should be taken into account in criminal proceedings.[39]

As far as juveniles are concerned, this regard for privacy extends to defendants, as well as victims and witnesses. It therefore overlaps, in terms of the beneficiaries, with the safeguards afforded to the right to a fair trial. But the reason juveniles are given this particular protection stems not primarily from their right to a fair trial, but from the enhanced right to privacy which the law believes that they ought to receive. The right to a fair trial enters into the equation only in the limited sense that hostile media coverage may provide particular difficulties for a juvenile defendant who needs to focus on the issues in the trial and give instructions and evidence (as was emphasized in *T* v. *UK*, *V* v. *UK*).[40]

The second major area of potential conflict relates to the difficulty of holding a fair trial against a background of adverse media publicity. In terms of the European Convention on Human Rights, the tension here is between Article 10 (freedom of expression) and Article 6 (right to a fair trial).

At times, this dilemma seems particularly acute in England and Wales, because of the power of the popular press, and its influence upon the public and the law-makers.

---

[39] See, e.g., *Z* v. *Finland* (1997) 25 EHRR 371 (ECtHR), paras. 95–97; *Doorson* v. *Netherlands* (1996) 22 EHRR 33 (ECtHR), para. 70.

[40] N. 35 above.

In principle, where there is a conflict between press freedom and the danger of prejudice to the jury, the criminal justice system ought to come down in favour of preserving the impartiality of its appointed finders of fact, the jury. This priority is reflected in the terms of Article 10(2) of the European Convention on Human Rights:

The exercise of [freedom of expression], since it carries with it duties and responsibilities, may be subject to such formalities, conditions, restrictions or penalties as are prescribed by law and are necessary in a democratic society, in the interests of national security, territorial integrity or public safety, for the prevention of disorder or crime, for the protection of health or morals, for the protection of the reputation or rights of others, for preventing the disclosure of information received in confidence, *or for maintaining the authority and impartiality of the judiciary* [emphasis added].

The restrictions relating to contempt of court can therefore be seen as necessary in order to maintain 'the authority and impartiality of the judiciary'. Provided that they are lawful, legitimate, necessary, and proportionate they can be justified. It is submitted that they do broadly fulfil these criteria. The difficulty which the criminal justice system faces is in the opposite direction. The controls upon the media are, in practice, imperfect. To prevent publicity prejudicial to the defendant in a high-profile case requires a degree of prescience which the authorities are not able to command. Further, the law is geared to prevent or punish individual instances of outrageously prejudicial publicity. The problem rather is the steady drip-feed of adverse publicity about a particular defendant. Inevitably, then, the trial judge and the appellate courts have to deal with an irreducible hard core of cases where the jury will have been subjected to such adverse publicity. How do they deal with these potential miscarriages of justice?

There are certain principles which have emerged from the cases. The test which seems to have received general approval is that set out by Phillips J in *Maxwell*:[41]

No stay should be imposed unless the defendant shows on the balance of probabilities that owing to the extent and nature of the pre-trial publicity he will suffer serious prejudice to the extent that no fair trial can be held.

This is a more stringent test for the defendant seeking to show prejudicial publicity than that which is current in Canada, for example, where the test is whether there is a realistic *potential* for partiality.[42] It is at least arguable that the stringency of our test means that there is the risk of miscarriages of justice in certain high-profile cases.

In assessing whether there is likely to be 'serious prejudice', the judiciary appears to have a firm belief in the inability of the jury to remember adverse media coverage. This is coupled with a considerable confidence in the ability of the jury to exclude whatever they can remember, once clearly directed to do so by the judge. It is submitted that this view of the jury's strengths and weaknesses is out of tune with reality. Some commentators have consequently remarked that there is a greater reluctance to recognize jury prejudice after the event. In other words, a judge hearing argument in favour of an injunction to restrict publication in advance of a trial might be prepared

---

[41] N. 26 above.   [42] *R. v. Sherratt* [1991] 1 SCR 509.

to agree that a press article, for example, would contaminate the jury. The trial judge would be much more reluctant to grant a stay of proceedings on the basis of the same article. The Court of Appeal would perhaps be even more unlikely to hold that the publicity in question made the conviction unsafe or the trial unfair. Some commentators have suggested that this is because the remedies available after the publicity has taken place (discharge of the jury, perhaps after a long trial, or even a stay of any future proceedings) may seem too extreme both to the trial judge and to the Court of Appeal.[43]

The reported appellate cases emphasize this judicial unwillingness to recognize the prejudicial effect of adverse media coverage. Of those which are dealt with above, the majority refuse to recognize that the jury could be irremediably prejudiced in the case before them. The minority of appellate cases which recognize such prejudice relate to publicity during the trial itself, rather than to pre-trial publicity. The 'fade factor' is therefore seen as determinative, and the jury are trusted to put the offending material out of their minds as a result of judicial urging. The only cases which can properly be regarded as authority for the proposition that adverse *pre-trial* publicity may make a fair trial impossible are *Reade*[44] (an unreported first instance case about allegedly criminal behaviour by police officers), and *Taylor and Taylor*,[45] which was said in *Stone*[46] 'to be regarded as a decision on its own facts'. It is submitted that the view of the powers of the jury to resist prejudice which this weight of judicial opinion represents is so optimistic as to be unrealistic. Clearly, any decision that the media had contaminated the trial process would invoke the wrath of the media themselves. In the current clamour for convictions, such a conclusion would in any event be unpopular. But a principled concern for human rights and for the underlying philosophy of Article 6 ought to encourage an independent judiciary, charged with the protection of the right to a fair trial, to resist such populist pressures.

In any event, careful scrutiny should be given to the selection of the jury. At the heart of the English jury system is the notion that it must be randomly chosen. Often, as here, that principle runs counter to the principle that it must be an instrument of impartiality. In circumstances where there has been pre-trial coverage which is hostile to the defendant, more attention should be given to securing that impartiality. The strategy adopted in *Maxwell* for jury selection surely deserves a prominence equal to the rather stringent test for prejudice which emerged from that case.

Finally, the relationship between hostile pre-trial coverage and jury trial needs to be recognized. It is right that for any serious criminal matter the defendant should be able to elect jury trial. That is a central tenet of our criminal justice system and is worth preserving for reasons related to both individual and collective rights. But that right to jury trial should not be taken to exclude the defendant, in appropriate circumstances, from choosing to be tried solely by a professional judge or a judge sitting with magistrates. Such 'bench trials' could provide a useful avenue for the provision of a fair trial in circumstances in which it might otherwise be impossible.

[43] D. Corker and M. Levi, 'Pre-Trial Publicity and its Treatment in the English Courts' [1996] *Crim. LR* 622 at 625.

[44] N. 7 above.   [45] N. 9 above.   [46] N. 26 above.

By a combination of these measures, it should be possible to reduce the number of trials where media hostility creates the suspicion that the jury will be prejudiced, perhaps unconsciously, thus ensuring that the accused receives the fair trial which is the primary goal of our system.

Further Reading

For details relating to the law of contempt, see *Blackstone's Criminal Practice*, sections B14.59 to 98 (London: Blackstone Press, published annually, references to 2001 edition).

For the principle of open justice and derogations from it, see *Blackstone's Criminal Practice* D2.47 to 57.

A critical analysis of the issues relating to adverse publicity and its effect on a fair trial is provided by D. Corker and M. Levi in 'Pre-Trial Publicity and its Treatment in the English Courts' [1996] *Crim. LR* 622.

The recent legislation aimed at protecting vulnerable witnesses is dealt with in D. Birch and R. Leng, *Blackstone's Guide to the Youth Justice and Criminal Evidence Act 1999* (London: Blackstone Press, 2000), 107–36.

14

SPECIAL MEASURES FOR WITNESSES AND VICTIMS

Jenny McEwan

In the adversarial trial, evidence is adduced by one of the parties and is challenged by the other. In practical terms using oral evidence best achieves this. Hence trials tend to be oral, and to depend heavily on witness testimony. The finder of fact, when choosing between disputed versions of events, is therefore forced to decide which of the various witnesses called is not telling the truth. To this end, magistrates and juries tend to examine not only the content of oral testimony, but also the appearance and demeanour of witnesses. It may be relevant that a witness is tall or heavily built. The demeanour of the witness whilst actually giving evidence is also thought to be significant. The more confidently the witness performs, the more likely he or she is to be believed. Hence a witness who struggles to comprehend the questions asked, or whose powers of self-expression are very weak, either as a permanent matter or temporarily in the context of the courtroom, is at considerable disadvantage. Where this witness is the victim of a crime, there is a danger that the criminal will be acquitted and go unpunished only because fluent, convincing oral evidence is not forthcoming at the trial.

Public concern about these issues, particularly where children are the victims of alleged offences, has led to the introduction of special measures to assist vulnerable witnesses in giving their evidence to the court. The first group of witnesses to receive these advantages was children. However, there are categories of adult witness who may be at least as vulnerable in the context of a criminal trial as children, or whose unwillingness to participate severely handicaps the criminal justice system. Fear of reprisals by the defendant or of humiliation in court in some, or even in many, cases may prevent potential witnesses from giving evidence for the prosecution, thus depriving the criminal justice system of crucial evidence. Over the last twenty years or so, considerable thought has gone into identifying who these vulnerable witnesses are. In 1999 a new statute, the Youth Justice and Criminal Evidence Act, extended the category of vulnerable witness beyond children, and provided a wide variety of special measures to make it easier for them to give evidence in court. The object has been to retain the orality of proceedings so far as is possible. At the same time, the Act recognizes that for some witnesses oral communication is particularly difficult, and the courtroom a particularly difficult place in which to communicate.

WITNESSES IN NEED OF SPECIAL TREATMENT

CHILDREN

Children have suffered from two disadvantages as potential witnesses. First, historically there have been doubts about their reliability. Secondly, the experience of giving evidence in court is particularly stressful for children, and the conditions in which they have been required to give evidence do not assist coherence in their testimony. Fear of unreliable child witnesses led the common law for many years to require corroborative evidence to support their credibility, or at least a warning to the jury in the absence of corroborative evidence, before a defendant could be convicted upon that testimony alone. This requirement was abolished in 1988[1] as a result of increasing faith in children's reliability. To some extent this was a response to evidence from psychologists suggesting that even small children can give a coherent account of abuse committed against them. The same reasoning contributed to the recent relaxation of the rules on competence so as to include younger children (see below), although another factor almost certainly was the reform that allowed children to give evidence through live link (closed-circuit television). There was some opposition to this from those who felt that it would make it easier for a child to tell lies in court, but expert opinion is divided on whether children are more likely to lie than adults. There does seem to be general agreement that over time a child's memory fades faster than that of an adult. This means that it is vital that evidence be obtained as soon after the event as possible. Since, in general, the court requires sworn oral testimony from a witness physically present in court at the time of trial, so that he or she may be challenged by cross-examination by the opposing party, children are clearly at a disadvantage where the trial takes place long after the event. In fact, society as a whole suffers where the criminal justice system is deprived of accurate testimony if delay in the case coming to trial means that a vital witness, who happens to be a child, has forgotten many details. Reformers therefore have advocated the introduction into evidence of a more contemporaneous statement of the facts by a child witness, either in writing or on videotape. The hearsay rule would exclude such a statement, and therefore legislative intervention would be required to permit such a procedure.

There can be no doubt that children are particularly vulnerable witnesses. In many cases where they are called upon to give evidence they have been the victims of crime. A case of suspected child abuse may involve them in a potentially harrowing investigative process, although this is now in the hands of specialist, inter-agency teams from the police and social services. Once in court few children are likely to comprehend the exact nature and purpose of the proceedings. Some children think they are there to prove their own innocence. The ordeal of a child victim giving evidence in court is exacerbated by such potentially distressing features as having to face the accused; the imposing atmosphere of a crowded court; the fact that in a jury trial they must speak loud enough to be heard over some distance; having to relate intimate and

---

[1] Criminal Justice Act 1988.

embarrassing details, if the case involves sexual abuse; in some cases, the child is afraid of the accused; or the child may be forced to condemn a loved parent, who may be removed from the family. Also, the defence will cross-examine the child in relation to evidence that is disputed, potentially exposing the child to allegations of dishonesty.

Where child victims of sexual abuse have given evidence in court, they have been found to suffer greater psychological damage than victims who have not. Nevertheless, it has been recognized that not all child witnesses are victims, and some, such as bystanders at a road traffic accident, may not require special measures to help them give evidence. And some children resent special measures being used when they give evidence. The Government Working Group which investigated the position of vulnerable witnesses in 1998 concluded that, although special measures should be generally available for child witnesses, they should not be used automatically whenever a child gives evidence in a criminal trial. The Working Group was also anxious that a vulnerable or intimidated witness should be given any emotional support and counselling needed. This is a complicated question, however. Witnesses who discuss the offence before trial run the risk of accusations that their evidence has been tainted. Official prosecution agencies have recently tried to devise guidelines on the kind of counselling which would not adversely affect any subsequent trial.

WITNESSES WITH LEARNING DISABILITY OR MENTAL ILLNESS

Problems of credibility and recall, difficulties of comprehension of court processes, and psychological stress may be as great for those with a learning disability as for children. But not all those with a disability will be vulnerable as witnesses or would wish to be regarded as such. The appropriateness of any special measure would depend on the nature of the disability. Lay people often assume (wrongly) that an adult with a low mental age thinks like a child and that the difficulties are therefore the same as those facing a child witness. The appropriateness of any special measure in fact depends on the nature of the disability. Courts therefore need the most accurate information possible about a particular witness. For example, the videotaped interview (see below) has obvious advantages for witnesses whose recollection may quickly fade. Using the witness's written statement to refresh his or her memory prior to trial may not solve the problem, as there may be reading difficulties. This is not necessarily solved by having the statement read aloud to the witness, who may have problems with concentration. Such statements also tend to be written in police language and may be confusing.

Producing a workable and enlightened statutory definition of the disabled vulnerable witness has not been a simple matter. A test based on IQ levels ignores a range of factors that are relevant to the capacity to give evidence in court, such as cognitive capacity, the ability to concentrate, and speech development. Also, a low IQ is unlikely to amount to an accurate indicator of the level of stress a witness will experience. A definition must obviously also encompass any mental illness that makes communication by the witness difficult. The definition employed in the Youth Justice and Criminal Evidence Act 1999 includes the witnesses who suffer from mental disorder within the meaning of the mental health legislation, or otherwise have a significant impairment of intelligence and social functioning; or witnesses who have a physical disability or are suffering from a physical disorder. The court must consult the witness as to his or her wishes before making a special order. If the witness falls within the statutory definition, the court may, if satisfied that a special measure would enhance the quality of the evidence, choose from the range of special measures discussed below. In this decision, the court is heavily dependent on the prosecution agencies to raise the issue of vulnerability and to provide relevant information. It is hoped that the police and the Crown Prosecution Service will make joint evaluation of the need for special treatment. A preliminary problem is whether the police are able accurately to identify vulnerable witnesses at the investigation stage. There have been cases where officers have erroneously thought a person with communication difficulties was drunk, and others where he or she appeared to be simply obstructive. Some police forces have appointed specialist officers responsible for identifying vulnerable witnesses. The Victim Support Service[2] may wish to alert the court to the need for a special measures direction.

INTIMIDATED WITNESSES

The actual scale of witness intimidation is difficult to assess, despite recent claims that it is increasing alarmingly. If a witness is afraid of retaliation, the criminal justice system is able to provide little in the way of reassurance. In extreme cases the police may be able to offer the witness a change of identity and police protection, but this is relatively rare. A witness with a learning disability may be especially vulnerable to intimidation. It has been suggested that the best solution to the problem is to involve citizens in crime prevention and detection at community level, but this is difficult to achieve. A more realistic alternative is to devise ways of protecting the anonymity of witnesses. Courts may allow witnesses to give evidence anonymously if it appears that they will otherwise be exposed to danger, but not if this operates seriously to the disadvantage of the defence. However, it has recently become the practice to remove the address of a witness from his or her statement prior to its disclosure by the prosecution to the defence. In many cases where genuine fears exist, such as cases of domestic violence or local rivalries, anonymity is impossible. Where witnesses are too afraid to give evidence, their written statements may be admissible under statutory exceptions to the hearsay rule introduced by the Criminal Justice Act 1988. However, the court has a discretion to exclude such statements in the interests of justice, if not to do so would be unfair to the defendant. In 1999 the government decided to allow the use of other special measures for this category of witness in order to ensure that the criminal justice system is not deprived of witnesses' testimony. These measures have been introduced by the Youth Justice and Criminal Evidence Act 1999. This provides for special treatment where a witness requires assistance on the grounds of fear or distress in relation to giving evidence. The definition here is so wide that it deals not only with the intimidated witness, but also the anxious witness. The court must take account of various factors in order to assess whether this is the case. These

---

[2] A voluntary organization which offers counselling and support for the victims of crime.

include: the nature and alleged circumstances of the offence to which the proceedings relate; the age of the witness; the social and cultural background and ethnic origins of the witness, the domestic and employment circumstances of the witness, and the religious beliefs or political opinions of the witness; the behaviour towards the witness on the part of the accused, members of the family, or associates of the accused or any other person who is likely to be an accused or a witness in the proceedings. The witness's own views must also be considered.

COMPLAINANTS IN SEXUAL CASES

There has been a significant fall in the number of convictions in rape cases, from 24 per cent in 1985 to 9 per cent in 1996. A large number of rape offences never come to trial at all, because victims are reluctant to appear as witnesses for the prosecution. Meanwhile a traditional controversy continues to rage between those who stress the risk to defendants of false accusations of rape from malevolent females, and those who emphasize that the trial procedure is intimidating and unfair to complainants in sexual cases, who are frequently compelled to answer questions on matters of an intimate nature. Parliament has decided that the latter problem is the greater. The 1999 Act creates a rebuttable presumption that special measures must be used for complainants in sexual cases. The kinds of measures available will be discussed below. But the main problem facing complainants in sexual cases will not be solved by technological aids to testimony. The gravest humiliation they will face in court lies in the nature of the defence cross-examination they will have to undergo (see below).

LEGAL COMPETENCE

The first question to arise in the case of a witness with poor comprehension or oral expression is whether he or she will be allowed to give evidence. The issue of competency has arisen chiefly in the case of child witnesses. Historically, they could give sworn evidence on oath (if they understood the religious significance of the oath) or unsworn evidence, not on oath (if they did not understand the religious significance of the oath, but did understand the normal social obligation to tell the truth). Judges used to question all child witnesses as a preliminary matter in order to ascertain whether they understood the difference between truth and lies. In practice, this tended to mean that evidence from children younger than 8 years old (unsworn), or 10 years old (sworn) was rejected. The law has now been altered so that all children under the age of 14 will give evidence unsworn. The test for competence has become more general, and demands only comprehension and coherence.[3] The law now sets no minimum age for child witnesses, although it is rare for a child aged less than 5 to give evidence.

---

[3] Youth Justice and Criminal Evidence Act 1999.

All witnesses, including children, are presumed competent. However, if it appears that an adult person is not able to understand questions put to him as a witness, or give comprehensible answers to them, he or she is not competent. When determining this issue the court must bear in mind that the witness's problems may be satisfactorily resolved by allowing a special measure to assist him or her in giving evidence.[4] Thus, if a witness may be understood only with the aid of an intermediary, for instance, someone interpreting for a deaf witness in sign language, this should not affect the issue of his or her competency. In the past, police and prosecution agencies have been found to be reluctant to pursue cases where the victim of a crime had a learning disability, possibly because of anticipated difficulty in court. But the evidence of such witnesses is very important. Research for the charity Mencap indicates that people with learning disabilities are far more likely than other adults to be the victims of sexual offences, assault, robbery, or personal theft.

It is clearly important that the criminal justice system should not make it difficult to protect members of the community who are particularly likely to be the victims of crimes. Therefore it has been decided that an adult witness should be able to give evidence even though he or she does not understand the significance of the oath sufficiently in order to be sworn. The 1999 Youth Justice and Criminal Evidence Act allows adults to give evidence either unsworn or on oath. The court must decide which is the appropriate method for a particular witness. However, there is an obvious risk involved in creating a two-tiered hierarchy of witnesses, in that unsworn evidence may be given less weight by juries and magistrates.

It can be seen that there is a conflict here between the desire of the criminal justice system to ensure that the evidence before the courts is as reliable as possible and the need to protect the young and the vulnerable from abuse. Where the victim of a crime is deemed incompetent as a witness, a successful prosecution is rendered less likely. If the test for competency is too strict, potential offenders can protect themselves by choosing the youngest or weakest victims to abuse. A further problem arises where a vulnerable witness is competent to give evidence but unwilling to do so. Although competent adult witnesses may generally be compelled under the threat of a penalty for refusal to give evidence, it is not necessarily appropriate to compel young children who are competent but unwilling to give evidence. Where those children are aged less than 10 years, and so are under the age of criminal responsibility, it is not clear what penalty there could be. However, it appears that in strict law they can be compelled.[5]

WAYS OF REDUCING STRESS

It is clearly advisable to give potential witnesses the most extensive information possible about what will happen to them at court. The Victim Support Service is manned by volunteers who will liaise with the court on behalf of victim witnesses and

---

[4] Youth Justice and Criminal Evidence Act 1999.

[5] R. v. Liverpool City Magistrates' Court ex parte Pollock unreported, 14 Mar. 1997.

explain what is involved. Courts also have officials specifically responsible for liaising with children who are to give evidence. Child witnesses generally visit the court before the trial begins and meet the lawyers who will appear. They are given a booklet, illustrated with colourful drawings, to explain court procedures and the roles of those involved. This booklet has been produced by a children's charity. A similar witness pack is being produced for witnesses with learning disabilities by a welfare organization.

More controversial is the notion that vulnerable witnesses should not have to give evidence in the traditional formal court setting. Although modification of trial procedures may reduce the stress suffered by such witnesses and make their evidence more coherent and possibly more reliable, traditionalists fear that the task of the defence lawyer is made more difficult as a result. They argue that it is more difficult to challenge the veracity of key witnesses. There is also a risk that magistrates or juries could be prejudiced against the defendant by the mere fact that special measures are considered necessary in the case of a particular prosecution witness. It is argued that removal of the witness from the courtroom may confound his or her expectations: and that they should retain the right to confront the defendant in court. However, if the witness is willing and is eligible for a special measure, the court may select whichever of the following would be likely to improve the quality of the particular witness's evidence.

REDUCING FORMALITY

Barristers in England and Wales wear both wigs and gowns. These may be dispensed with while the vulnerable witness gives evidence. The judge may also order in certain cases that the court be cleared of representatives of the press and of the public, to provide more privacy. However, this places the principle of open justice at risk. As a compromise, the 1999 Act has provided that one media representative may remain in court even if it is cleared.

SCREENS

One of the simpler devices that can assist nervous witnesses is a screen that shields the witness from the defendant. The advocates and the jury can still see the witness, although often the press cannot. The practice of using screens evolved in cases featuring child witnesses, but they are now generally available for all categories of vulnerable witness.

INTERPRETERS AND AIDS TO COMMUNICATION

Over the last thirty years there has been a continuing debate about how best to assist witnesses who have not the requisite oral communication skills to deal with the questions put to them by lawyers in court. Lawyers characteristically do not tend to use language that can be readily understood by children or people with learning disabilities. Some witnesses may be completely unable to communicate orally, by reason of mental or physical disability. One suggested solution has been the use of an intermediary who could 'translate' the questions from the lawyer into a form of language the witness could understand, and relay the answers back to the lawyers. Opposition has been expressed on the grounds that the intermediary may distort or invent questions or answers, or even suggest answers to the witness undetected by the tribunal. Despite this fear, Parliament has decided to allow the use of intermediaries in court where appropriate. Their function would be similar to that of an interpreter translating into a foreign language. In terms of accuracy, the best intermediary for a child witness or an adult with learning disability would probably be someone who knows the witness well, but fear of dishonesty or incompetence has meant the introduction of a scheme for the use of officially recognized intermediaries accredited on the basis of agreed criteria. They will be trained in court procedures.

Interactive computer graphics may be a potential aid to communication for witnesses who are unable to express themselves orally. Researchers are currently working on projects in this area. These programmes would have to be simple to operate and would have to be devised in such a way that there is no element of suggestion or prejudice to the defendant in the graphic. Hence the depiction of a character representing the defendant would have to be carefully designed to avoid either a resemblance to the defendant where identity is in dispute or any characteristic that could induce hostility in the magistrates or jury.

LIVE LINK

For some years some child witnesses have been allowed to give their evidence in a side-room of the court through a closed-circuit television link. The child can be seen on screens in the court by the judge, jury, lawyers, and the defendant, but the child can see only the face of the person asking the question. The advantage of this is that although the child has to be present in the court building, he or she is spared the public ordeal of the courtroom itself, and does not have to face the defendant. However, lawyers have proved somewhat hostile to the live link. Some prosecutors have not asked for it, apparently because of a belief that the screen image of a child lacks the power of his or her actual presence, reducing the likelihood of conviction. Some prosecutors believe that a frightened child makes a more effective witness. It is not clear whether these views are correct. Certainly, the conviction rate in child abuse cases is low, standing at 16 per cent against a national average of 50 per cent.

The live link has reduced the levels of stress suffered by many child witnesses, who consequently have given their evidence more fluently. Children seem not to have found the technology intimidating. However, it has been difficult to determine who should be with them in the live link room. The concern to avoid any risk of interference has resulted in courts refusing to allow a parent or social worker to be present. A court official, the usher, is now generally required to sit with the child in the transmitting room, but most of these officers ensure that they have met the child beforehand.

This technology is in future to be available to all categories of vulnerable witnesses.[6]

---

[6] Youth Justice and Criminal Evidence Act 1999.

And judges may raise the matter irrespective of the views of prosecuting counsel. The expansion of the scheme to include vulnerable adults and trials in magistrates' courts will involve considerable capital expense.

VIDEOTAPED INTERVIEW

Also previously available to child witnesses, but now to be available to all vulnerable witnesses, is the videotaped interview. A full account of the witness's testimony is recorded on videotape before the trial begins. It is then played at the trial so that the witness does not have to give oral evidence in chief in the courtroom. The interview is conducted in a pleasant environment, and therefore under less stressful conditions than would be involved in a court appearance. If conducted close in time to the events concerned, the likelihood of accuracy is greatly increased. In the case of children, particularly, a contemporaneous account is frequently more accurate and detailed than one given much later in court. When it was introduced, it was partly in the hope that it would encourage more defendants to plead guilty, since they would see the videotape before the trial started and might decide that the child was sufficiently convincing to make contesting the charge pointless. Unfortunately, there is no evidence to date that it is having this effect.

Since the function of such a video in a criminal trial is to replace the witness's evidence in chief, where no prompting or leading questions from the advocate would be allowed, those who conduct these interviews are similarly restricted in terms of the kinds of questions they may ask. There is a government-produced Memorandum of Good Practice which explains how the interview should be conducted. The emphasis is on allowing children to be spontaneous and to avoid suggestions being made to them. The Memorandum does not entirely rule out the use of leading questions. It has been customary for many years to allow a little leading of a shy child during conventional evidence in chief in a court. However, extensive use of leading questions will result in the trial judge refusing to allow the videotape to be used. In that case, the child will have to give evidence in court (possibly by way of live link). As an alternative, the judge may simply direct the editing out of inadmissible parts of an otherwise acceptable interview. The video may also be rejected for poor technical quality, something that has happened in a disappointingly high number of cases. Although some judges have the opportunity to watch the video prior to the pre-trial hearing; others are unable to do so until the trial itself. The unfortunate consequence of this is that the child has to wait until the last minute to know whether the video will be used or whether he or she will have to give evidence after all.

In terms of the law of evidence, these videotapes are difficult to classify. Their evidential status affects issues such as how many times a jury should be allowed to see them. The same uncertainty attaches to the question how many times, if at all, the witness should be able to see the video before giving evidence. The answer may vary according to whether the video is to be used instead of evidence in chief or not. Another problem has been that over recent years the relevant legislation became over-complicated, creating different categories of eligible child witnesses according to their age and the type of offence. It is difficult to see why, if the view is that the defendant is not prejudiced by evidence of this kind, the facility should not be generally available for all child witnesses. If, on the other hand, its use genuinely disadvantages defendants, then it would not be justified whatever the age of the child or the nature of the offence.

The government is now proposing to make the videotaped interview available for all categories of child witnesses and for vulnerable witnesses generally. It appears that the intention is to have the interviewing of adults conducted by police officers, social workers, or 'those involved in the investigation of crime' and/or an appropriate defence representative. The assumption is that the training and experience appropriate to the interviewing of children will serve for this 'very different group', but this may be misplaced. Those who suffer from learning disability may present an entirely different set of problems in communication, comprehension, and anxiety. This group also, typically, includes victims of a wide variety of crimes. Training which relates in particular to sexual offences may not help with a variety of different offences.

Although a contemporaneous account in the form of a videorecorded interview may be desirable in the case of vulnerable adult witnesses, there are problems about how this would work in practice. There would need to be a procedure whereby investigators promptly refer potential witnesses with communication difficulties for interview by specialist teams. Alternatively, the probability is that the recording would be made very shortly before trial, after securing permission from a judge at a 'plea and directions' hearing. In such instances, the rationale for this special measure would lie entirely in the reduction of stress, rather than increased accuracy through contemporaneity. To some critics, this merely makes it easier for the witness to lie.[7] As with the live link, there is no evidence to suggest that the video interview increases or, indeed, decreases the prospects of conviction. It does appear to reduce the levels of stress suffered by children who gave evidence by that means. There is no evidence that it increases the number of guilty pleas.

VIDEORECORDED CROSS-EXAMINATION

The most revolutionary of the special measures features the videorecorded cross-examination. Provision for this has been included in the Youth Justice and Criminal Evidence Act range of reforms, but it has not yet been implemented. The idea is that the witness would be cross-examined in the absence of the jury, outside the oppressive atmosphere of the formal courtroom and in the absence of the defendant. However, the accused must be able to see and hear the examination and to communicate with his lawyer. Meanwhile the judge or magistrates and advocates will be able to see and hear the examination of the witness, and to communicate with the persons in whose presence the recording is being made. Conducted before the trial begins, and combined with the videotaped interview, the videorecording removes from the witness any need to attend court or worry about trial dates. Though it is not necessarily the case that the videorecorded cross-examination will spare the witness from a court

---

[7] It remains possible to adduce an intimidated witness's written statement or statement recorded on videotape as a hearsay exception under the 1988 Criminal Justice Act.

appearance. Further cross-examination may become necessary after the recording has been made, which could involve the witness being subjected to the process twice. The Youth Justice and Criminal Evidence Act 1999 creates a rebuttable presumption that no further cross-examination will be permitted unless new material comes to light which could not have been discovered by reasonable diligence at the time of the original cross-examination. However, in those cases where a second cross-examination is allowed, there is a risk that inconsistencies may be found between statements made in the two recordings. This would justify yet another cross-examination on those inconsistencies.

Since the new procedure has not yet been introduced, it is not yet clear what, if any, practical problems will arise. However, assuming that most videotaped cross-examinations would involve a witness for the prosecution, a real concern is that the defence could be severely prejudiced by having to cross-examine in advance of the trial, before it has heard other prosecution witnesses give evidence. Also, rightly or wrongly, defence advocates may feel disadvantaged by the absence of the jury. They will have to conduct cross-examinations without any indication of jury reaction. Meanwhile, the disadvantage for prosecution witnesses for whom the measure is employed is that a last-minute change of plea to guilty does not spare them the ordeal of cross-examination. A steering group has been set up to advise on the best way to handle this innovative new measure, and to consider the technical problems that might arise.

PROHIBITION ON CROSS-EXAMINATION BY THE DEFENDANT IN PERSON

Since some defendants would rather represent themselves than allow a lawyer to act as advocate in court, and others are unable to afford legal representation, it happens in some cases that the defendant carries out the cross-examination of witnesses for the prosecution, including the victim. This has sometimes proved a very unpleasant, and even harrowing, experience for a victim. In 1991 legislation was passed removing the right to cross-examine in person from defendants charged with sexual or violent offences against a child.[8] However, in some notorious rape trials that took place subsequent to this reform, it became apparent that some defendants acting in person were using the opportunity of cross-examination deliberately to intimidate the complainant. The 1999 Youth Justice and Criminal Evidence Act consequently removed the right of an unrepresented defendant to cross-examine a rape complainant, and certain other kinds of witness.

This presented the problem of how prosecution witnesses were to be challenged if the defendant was to have a fair trial. In earlier cases involving child witnesses, judges had dealt with this problem by cross-examining the child themselves. This solution was not universally favoured, as it brought the judge into the arena of the contest. If the judge were to cross-examine vigorously, impartiality was lost. If the cross-examination was restrained, the witness's evidence was not adequately tested. Indeed,

8 Criminal Justice Act 1988, as amended by the Criminal Justice Act 1991.

some defendants refused the judge's help, which meant that the witness was not cross-examined at all. To remedy this, the 1999 Act took the dramatic step of imposing legal representation on defendants, even if they do not want it.[9]

The 1999 Act retains the protection from cross-examination by a defendant in person for child witnesses, but extends the prohibition to include cases where the child is the complainant of, or witness to, an offence of kidnapping, false imprisonment, or abduction. Adult complainants in sexual cases are now to have the same protection. More radically, other witnesses may be given this immunity if it appears to the court that the quality of evidence given by the witness on cross-examination is likely to be diminished if the cross-examination (or further cross-examination) is conducted by the accused in person, unless such immunity would be contrary to the interests of justice. Any accused person who is subject to this prohibition may arrange for a legal representative to conduct the cross-examination. If he or she declines to do so, the court may appoint a legal representative, chosen by the court, to cross-examine the witness. The judge is required to give the jury such warning as is considered necessary to ensure that the accused is not prejudiced, either by the fact that the accused has been prevented from cross-examining the witness in person or by the fact that the cross-examination was carried out by a court-appointed legal representative.

This procedure presents a number of practical problems, since the representative would have to become involved at a late stage, possibly with no co-operation from the defendant. The government may find that these provisions rebound on them. Ironically, it is possible that the procedure could produce a wave of sympathy for the defendant. Juries may be reluctant to convict where aware that a lawyer has been called in, at short notice, to perform a task on which he or she may have had insufficient information because the defendant refused to discuss the case. There is also a danger that the procedure will be found to be unfair under Article 6 of the European Convention on Human Rights.[10] To some critics, the new provisions on cross-examination amount to nothing less than a reversal of the burden of proof, not justified merely by the nature of the charge.

CROSS-EXAMINATION OF SEXUAL COMPLAINANTS

The kinds of questions asked in cross-examination are subject to very little regulation. Trial judges should generally ensure that questions are relevant and courteously put, but seem unable to protect some witnesses from being hectored or humiliated. The problem is extreme in rape cases, where it appears to be thought legitimate to quiz complainants upon the way they care for their children, what underwear they were wearing at the time of the alleged rape, whether they use make-up and take trouble

[9] This is not entirely novel. Under the Criminal Procedure (Insanity) Act 1964, the court may appoint someone to put the defendant's case if the jury decides he is under a disability. Wilful refusal to have a lawyer in these cases amounts to placing oneself under a disability.

[10] Art. 6 of the European Convention for the Protection of Human Rights and Fundamental Freedoms describes the right to a fair trial. The provisions of the Convention are now to be regarded as law, under the Human Rights Act 1998.

with their hair, and upon the details of their menstrual cycles, for no apparent reason other than to embarrass them. In order to suggest that the complainant is mentally unstable, some defence lawyers seek to show that she was the victim of child sexual abuse or rape in the past. Some complainants are asked whether they have had abortions. It has become routine to include questions about the complainant's sexual experience. Government recognized that in consequence women were reluctant to report rapes and many were refusing to give evidence. Given prevailing confusion amongst lawyers about the relevance of this kind of questioning, legislative intervention was thought necessary.

Section 2 of the Sexual Offences (Amendment) Act 1976 provided that no question about any sexual experience of a rape complainant with a person other than that defendant could be asked without the leave of the trial judge, and leave should be given 'if and only if . . . it would be unfair to that defendant to refuse to allow the evidence to be adduced or the question to be asked'. Difficulties of interpretation of this provision arose because the issue of unfairness depended heavily on that of the relevance of the cross-examination. The statute did not make it clear when questions about sexual relationships, promiscuity, or even working as a prostitute might be permitted. The courts were left to decide how section 2 should operate. In a leading case, *R v. Viola*,[11] the Court of Appeal explained that advocates would not be permitted to question on sexual experience in order to invite the jury to disbelieve the complainant. The questions must be relevant to the issue of guilt. It is not open to the defendant to argue that the fact that a woman consented to have sexual intercourse with another man means that she gave consent to have sexual intercourse with him. That argument lacks logic. The difficulty is to identify those cases where there is a logical connection between the earlier sexual encounters and the alleged rape. The Court of Appeal suggested: '[e]vidence of sexual promiscuity may be so strong or so closely contemporaneous in time to the event in issue as to come near to, or indeed reach the border between mere credit and an issue in the case'.[12]

Despite this strict approach, it has become apparent that courts have been allowing questions about the complainant's sexual history in a great many cases (leave is requested in about 40 per cent of cases, and about 75 per cent of applications are successful). Most of the applications were on the basis that the previous sexual relationships were relevant to an issue in the trial, usually to the issue of consent. Certainly it must be the case that if the questions *are* relevant to an issue, to disallow them would inevitably be unfair to the accused, and therefore the judge ought to permit them. However, it can only rarely be the case that a woman's sexual history has such a bearing. The reality seems to be that the matter is raised in order to humiliate or discredit the witness.

The difficulty in obtaining convictions for rape led to the matter being reconsidered by the Government Working Group in 1998. It thought that a total ban on cross-examination about sexual behaviour would be unfair. In some contexts it is relevant, for example, where it is said to explain the defendant's belief in consent. In effect, it was unable to devise a more effective test than that articulated by the Court of

---

[11] [1982] 3 All ER 73.   [12] *Ibid.*, at 77, *per* Lord Lane CJ.

Appeal in *Viola*, and so the new statutory provision, in the 1999 Youth Justice and Criminal Evidence Act, follows it closely. One change, however is that the leave of the judge must be sought in every case where the defence seek to ask questions about the complainant's sexual behaviour with the defendant. Another is the extension of the prohibition beyond rape trials to those involving sexual offences generally. Under the statute judges may give leave only in the following cases: first, where the question concerns a relevant issue and the issue is not consent (although it could be the defendant's alleged belief in consent); secondly, leave may be given where the questions are relevant to consent and the sexual behaviour was close in time to the event; thirdly, leave may be given where the issue *is* consent and the sexual behaviour amounts to 'similar fact' evidence, resembling her alleged behaviour on the occasion in question; fourthly, leave may also be given if the issue is consent and the evidence effectively rebuts evidence called by the prosecution. All these exceptions are subject to the caveat that the court should be persuaded that to refuse leave would render the conviction unsafe. The legislation fails to offer protection from the other examples of humiliating and irrelevant cross-examinations of sexual complainants with which courts are familiar.

SACRIFICING THE DEFENDANT'S RIGHTS?

It should be noted that the defendant in the criminal trial is the one potential witness who may not take advantage of special measures. Yet the criminal trial is potentially a terrifying ordeal for an accused person. The case *T* v. *UK*[13] highlights the intimidating nature of court proceedings from the point of view of the person with most to lose. The case featured the trial for murder of two boys aged 11. The European Court of Human Rights considered that formal adversarial trial by jury was inappropriate for such young children. They are likely to be intimidated and unlikely to be able to follow the arguments. Effectively, they are deprived of a fair trial because of their inability to participate by instructing their lawyers.

Curiously, there does not appear to be much pressure to introduce measures to assist defendants to give evidence, whatever their communication difficulties might be. Yet one may sympathize with the inarticulate defendant who is afraid of giving evidence. Since the Criminal Justice and Public Order Act of 1994, if a defendant refuses to give evidence he runs the risk that the inference can be drawn that he or she must be guilty. Thus pressure is placed on defendants of all ages and abilities to give evidence and undergo cross-examination. This they must do in court in the conventional manner. Meanwhile, as we have seen, witnesses whose problems may be less severe and, in the case of juvenile crime, may in fact be older than the defendant, are eligible for a wide range of facilitative measures which, when fully implemented, will make giving evidence far easier. The very fact that a witness appears to be unable to

---

[13] App. No. 24724/94 (2000) 30 EHRR 373.

provide testimony without the aid of a camera, for example, may create the impression that the defendant is a person to be feared. The Youth Justice and Criminal Evidence Act 1999 directs judges to give the jury such warning (if any) as they consider necessary to ensure that the fact that evidence given by way of special measure does not prejudice the accused. Nevertheless, the emphasis on witness protection risks the possibility of miscarriages of justice.

Further Reading

ADLER, Z., 'Rape—the Intention of Parliament and the Practice of the Courts' (1982) 45 *Modern Law Review* 664.

—— 'The Relevance of Sexual History Evidence in Rape: Problems of Subjective Interpretation' [1985] *Crim. LR* 769.

BIRCH, D., 'A Better Deal for Vulnerable Witnesses' [2000] *Crim. LR* 223.

—— and LENG, R., *Blackstone's Guide to the Youth Justice and Criminal Evidence Act 1999* (London: Blackstone, 2000).

DAVIES, G., WILSON, C., MITCHELL, L., and MILSOM, J., *Videotaping Children's Evidence: An Evaluation* (London: Home Office, 1995).

HEILBRON, R., *Report of the Advisory Group on the Law of Rape*, Cmnd 6352 (1975).

Home Office, *Speaking Up for Justice: Report of the Interdepartmental Working Group on the treatment of Vulnerable or Intimidated Witnesses in the Criminal Justice System* (London: Home Office, 1998).

—— Department of Health, *Memorandum of Good Practice on Videorecorded Interviews with Child Witnesses for Criminal Proceedings* (London: Home Office, 1975).

HOYANO, L., 'Variations on a Theme by Pigot: Special Measures Directions for Child Witnesses' [2000] *Crim. LR* 250.

KIBBLE, N., 'The Sexual History Provisions' [2000] *Crim. LR* 274.

LEES, S., *Carnal Knowledge: Rape on Trial* (London: Hamish Hamilton, 1996).

McEWAN, J., *Evidence and the Adversarial Process* (Oxford: Hart Publishing, 1998).

—— 'In Defence of Vulnerable Witnesses: The Youth Justice and Criminal Evidence Act 1999' (2000) 4 *International Journal of Evidence and Proof* 1.

Mencap, *Barriers to Justice* (London: Mencap National Centre, 1997).

SANDERS, A., CREATON, J., BIRD, S., and WEBER, L., *Witnesses with Learning Disabilities: Negotiating the Criminal Justice System*, Occasional Paper No. 17 (Oxford: Centre for Criminological Research, Oxford University, 1997).

SPENCER, J. R., and FLIN, R., *The Evidence of Children: The Law and the Psychology* (2nd edn., London: Blackstone, 1993).

—— NICHOLSON, G., FLIN, R., and BULL, R. (eds.), *Children's Evidence in Legal Proceedings* (Cambridge: Faculty of Law, University of Cambridge, 1990).

TEMKIN, J., *Rape and the Legal Process* (London: Sweet & Maxwell, 1987).

16

SCIENCE, EXPERTS, AND CRIMINAL JUSTICE

Paul Roberts

COMMON SENSE, SCIENCE, SUPERSTITION, AND SCEPTICISM

English law has a longstanding tradition, stretching back into the sixteenth century and beyond, of consulting expert advice on 'scientific' or technical matters which are beyond the knowledge or expertise of lawyers, judges, and jurors. One of the earliest precedents is *Buckley* v. *Rice Thomas* (1554), in which Saunders J appeared to be describing an already well-established practice of receiving expert testimony:

[I]f matters arise in our law which concern other sciences or faculties, we commonly apply for the aid of that science or faculty which it concerns. Which is an honourable and commendable thing in our law. For thereby it appears that we do not despise all other sciences but our own, but we approve of them and encourage them as things worthy of commendation. And therefore . . . in a case that came before the Judges, which was determinable in our [common] law, and also touched upon the civil [Roman] law, they were well content to hear Huls, who was a batchelor of both laws, argue and discourse upon logic . . . as men that were not above being instructed and made wiser by him. And in an appeal of mayhem the Judges of our law have used to be informed by surgeons whether it be a mayhem or not, because their knowledge and skill can best discern it.[1]

The foundation of the modern rule governing the admissibility of expert evidence, is generally traced to a case of 1782, *Folkes* v. *Chadd,* in which the court relied on the evidence of 'an eminent engineer' regarding flood defences alleged to be silting up a harbour.[2] Other old cases invoke expert evidence on such various matters as trade customs, commercial practice, the translation of ancient manuscripts, the paternity of children, and points of foreign law. (The judges are, of course, confident in their own expertise regarding applicable domestic law, so that expert evidence of English law is neither required nor permitted.) There are also old reported cases in which expert witch-finders testified to the accused's involvement in witchcraft, by declaring that blemishes on the accused's body were the mark of the Devil. On the basis of such

---

[1] (1554) 1 Plowden 118, CB, at 124–5 (Saunders J).   [2] (1782) 3 Douglas 157 (KB).

superstitious nonsense, delivered with all the beguiling authority of the witch-finder's expert diagnosis, men and women were condemned to be burnt at the stake.

The history of English law's recourse to science and experts attests, therefore, both to the common sense of consulting experts on their specialist subjects, *and* to the potential dangers of such reliance. English people no longer believe in witchcraft in this modern age of enlightenment science.[3] As a society, however, we do sometimes place an exaggerated—even superstitious—faith in the power of science to resolve our social problems and to deliver us from evil. Yet recent experience provides ample warning that scientific evidence can be a potent cause of miscarriages of justice. Defendants in now-infamous 1970s cases like the Birmingham Six and Maguire Seven were convicted of heinous terrorist crimes, held up to public outrage and vilification, and sentenced to long terms of imprisonment, only to be released some fifteen years later, when it transpired that scientific evidence was nowhere near as conclusive as the court and the jury had been led to believe at the original trials.

Any informed evaluation of the relationship between science and justice must proceed from an appreciation of the double-edged nature of science. Like a knife that may be used with equal facility to perform a life-saving operation or to murder a child, science can be employed for good ends or for ill. Scientific knowledge is an instrument with a dazzling array of applications and effects, but scientific expertise *per se* (as opposed to the practice of science) is devoid of ethical insight or constraint. The challenge for all those involved in the administration of justice, including policy-makers and forensic scientists as much as criminal justice professionals like judges and lawyers, is to ensure that the application of scientific knowledge and expertise to the criminal process works to promote justice, not to frustrate it. Success in this project is far from assured and must never be taken for granted. It cannot be stressed too often that science is no panacea, and that complacency will be paid for in miscarriages of justice and damage to the legitimacy of criminal proceedings. Crime and criminal law enforcement are, alike, social practices with immense significance for collective and individual wellbeing. At the same time as people fear crime and may be seriously harmed by it, they are also at risk of wrongful conviction, mistreatment, or abuse of power at the hands of the State, which may be as bad as, or worse than, being a victim of crime. (Wrongful conviction and execution for murder is arguably worse than being murdered, for example, because it involves condemnation and disgrace in addition to the loss of life, often with further adverse consequences for one's family and estate.) Where so much is at stake, the State should surely proceed with circumspection, and citizens, for their part, must be vigilant and sensitive to the signs of official abuse or overreaching. Scientific expertise is no exception to this general rule. The uses of science in the criminal process should be approached with a healthy scepticism and subjected to on-going critical scrutiny.

This is not to deny that the expanding use of scientific expertise in criminal process is (in both senses) a progressive and irresistible fact of modern life, and that its impact is likely only to increase for the foreseeable future. Criminal proceedings inevitably

---

[3] Much less do we still immolate convicted 'witches'. The death penalty was effectively abolished in England and Wales in 1965.

reflect their broader social environment (as well as helping to shape that social context in some measure), so it is hardly surprising that, as science and technology have come to exert a pervasive influence on all aspects of modern society, their forensic applications have undergone a correspondingly rapid expansion. As society becomes more complex and knowledge is further compartmentalized into ever smaller arcane specialisms, reliance on experts grows in every feature of daily life. As well as the traditional professions, like doctors and lawyers, whose authority (and corresponding social status) is well-established in England, and the physicists and chemists who brought us cars, aeroplanes, the atom bomb, personal computers, and the internet, we now routinely defer to experts who tell us what (and how much) to eat, what to wear, how to bring up children ('parenting'), even how to lead a happy and successful life.[4] To this, we must add the new biological and life sciences, which have opened up new vistas of genetically-engineered possibility and 'bio-risk'. Governments, meanwhile, run national economies following the expert advice of economists and bankers, and call elections on the basis of forecasts by expert political analysts and advertising gurus. There are occasionally muffled voices of dissent questioning the rise of 'experts in everything': and Mary Shelley's *Frankenstein* remains a powerful cultural symbol of the dangers of misplaced trust in science.[5] But for the most part everybody goes along with the proliferation and increasing influence of scientific expertise, because the benefits of doing so are manifest and, in any case, there is really very little choice in the matter if one wants to be able to negotiate the complex realities of modern life.

Contemporary trends in scientific advancement and proliferating expertise have direct implications for criminal process, not least because criminal offenders are no less ingenious than scientists in their ability to innovate. As soon as a new scientific or technological development is pioneered, criminal minds set to work to exploit it. Thus, credit cards and new electronic banking systems are accompanied by novel forms of fraud. Mobile phones have been the best gift to drug dealers and petty crooks since the invention of the internal combustion engine. And the communications miracle that is the internet, also heralds a bewildering catalogue of cyber-crime, from hacking (a new crime) to child pornography, money laundering, illegal arms sales, and drug dealing (new ways of committing old crimes). Yet if police officers, lawyers, judges, magistrates, and jurors need all the expert help they can get to keep pace with modern forms of criminality, developments on the general law-enforcement side of the equation are no less rapid and profound. A raft of new investigative techniques, of which DNA 'fingerprinting' is the most renowned and spectacular, has greatly enhanced the capacity of criminal law enforcement in recent times. Of course police are not geneticists, any more than lawyers or judges are trained to know one end of an autoradiograph from the other. Scientific experts have to be relied upon to produce and interpret DNA evidence, just as experts predominate in other recently

---

[4] Cf. the analysis of 'self-help manuals' developed by A. Giddens, *Modernity and Self-Identity* (Oxford: Polity, 1991), esp. chap. 3.

[5] In the on-going moral panic surrounding genetically-modified crops, GM produce has been dubbed 'Frankenfood' by the popular press.

pioneered fields, including document and handwriting analysis (stylometry), voice identification, forensic psychology, offender profiling, and facial mapping. As the sophistication and sensitivity of analytical techniques have increased, it has become possible to extract highly probative evidence from material that would have been useless to a criminal investigation only a few years before. A DNA profile drawn from a handful of skin cells—possibly even a single hair follicle—can positively identify an offender with an exceptional level of certainty, far exceeding the older blood-grouping technology DNA profiling has superseded. There is also a far greater *volume* of evidential material to be collected than ever before. CCTV cameras positioned in car parks, shopping centres, and high streets daily record millions of images, which can later be retrieved and sent for expert analysis to identify alleged perpetrators of any crimes caught on film. Corneal mapping, whereby offenders are identified from close-up pictures of their eyes, is being touted—possibly with premature enthusiasm—as an imminent addition to the law enforcement armoury. Micro-computers have meanwhile delivered unimagined capacities for data-storage and retrieval ('data-mining'). If I understand the position correctly (though only experts know for sure), computer files are not really erased by the 'delete' key or wastepaper bin icon, but—like every e-mail that is sent—are permanently available to be retrieved by a person with appropriate computing expertise. Criminal gangs and others who are using e-mail or the internet to arrange, prepare, or actually commit offences may therefore be leaving an electronic trail behind them which, when exposed and unravelled by expert computer investigators, is as conclusive of guilt as a 'smoking gun' with their fingerprints all over it. This is why governments are taking such a keen interest in encryption devices: it is imperative, from a security perspective, that the best encryption tools are reserved for national intelligence agencies, and never allowed to fall into the hands of organized crime.

Technological advances have far-reaching implications for civil liberties, personal autonomy, and democratic accountability, as well as for crime-fighting effectiveness. In fact, every aspect of criminal process has been affected by the broad social trend towards 'experts in everything', from high constitutional issues and macro policy-making, to the prosaic, daily routines of criminal justice administration. Perhaps it could be 'only in America' (as we British say) that a lawyer would advertise for an expert on the movement of shopping-trolley wheels, but this—it should be emphasized—genuine, real-life example does serve as a vivid illustration of the extent to which modern legal processes have come to rely upon scientific expertise. Law is obliged to accommodate itself to the broad grain of social attitudes and expectations; and lawyers and judges, who share many of those same attitudes and expectations, readily effect the necessary accommodation. In an age of science, law will appear arrogant, ignorant, distant, and out of touch if it refuses to incorporate scientific wisdom. To prefer superstition to science would be, on a common-sense view, to embrace irrationality, and thereby imperil criminal proceedings' primary aspiration to render legitimate and authoritative verdicts. But reality is complex and conflicted. At certain points, common sense and science are in tension or even flat contradiction. Scientific knowledge is sometimes strongly counter-intuitive. Whenever this conflict breaks out in the forensic context, law must somehow arbitrate between scientific learning and common-sense understandings. There is no simple equation between doing justice and preferring science to common-sense.

As well as reflecting prevailing social understandings, expectations, and evaluations of science, forensic applications of scientific expertise are a function of particular legal cultures and procedural traditions. In order to grasp how, and with what success, criminal process incorporates scientific expertise in England, for example, it is necessary to understand the workings of a particular version of the common law adversary procedural system, as it operates in England and Wales, and to appreciate certain aspects of English legal practice and culture. Only in this broader compass can the particular strengths, weaknesses, and reform options pertinent to any given legal system be properly assessed. The following description of scientific expertise in English criminal proceedings therefore attempts to identify the role of procedural tradition and legal culture in shaping current practice and to suggest how these aspects of practice may differ in countries with different legal cultures and procedural traditions.

There are of course many similarities, as well as significant differences, between contemporary national criminal justice systems. At least at a normative and rhetorical level (practice may be another thing entirely), all modern systems are committed to respecting individual rights, human dignity, equality, and non-discrimination. These commitments are reflected in, and reinforced by, universal and regional international conventions and resolutions (UDHR, ICCPR, ECHR, African Charter, Inter-American Convention etc.), as well as being written into national constitutions, Bills of Rights, and codes of criminal procedure. One important implication is that criminal investigation, prosecution, and trial must respect individual rights and observe norms of due process and procedural propriety, including in particular the 'fair trial' norm as developed, for example, in the jurisprudence of the European Court of Human Rights. Criminal justice involves convicting the guilty *by due process of law*, not identifying and punishing perpetrators any-which-way, as might a lynch mob or kangaroo court.

Criminal proceedings have dual aspirations, reflecting the two, irreducible components of criminal justice:

(1) to establish proof of guilt (to the criminal standard, beyond reasonable doubt);

(2) with respect for due process, fair trial, individual rights, and other applicable standards and values.

This basic structure suggests a convenient framework for further investigating the role of science in criminal proceedings, focusing first on truth-finding, and then on broader considerations. The next section considers the contribution of scientific expertise to the proof of guilt. This is very much science's strong suit, though matters are not quite as straightforward as first appearances may suggest. In the third and final section of the chapter, the discussion broadens out to consider the impact of science on other aspects of criminal process and procedure. Science here may appear as an obstacle, or even as a threat, to the pursuit of criminal justice. Once more, however, the picture is complex and conflicted: sometimes it is the *absence* of scientific expertise that poses difficulties, whilst in other cases the presence of science can be said to enhance procedural propriety even where it has no material bearing on the factual accuracy of the verdict.

It must be emphasized that *both* sections address essential, indispensable, and irreducible aspects of criminal justice. Disaggregation is convenient for ease and clarity of exposition, but it implies neither that the two components of justice are severable for anything other than analytical purposes nor that there is any simple order of priority between them. A meticulously fair proceeding resulting in the conviction of an innocent accused fails to achieve justice, as does the conviction of a guilty defendant based on a confession procured by torture. Criminal justice requires conviction of the guilty according to law, and nothing less will do as an ideal or critical standard for practice to emulate.

SCIENCE AS PROOF

All systems of criminal justice, ancient and modern, have embraced accurate fact-finding as their central objective. Criminal proceedings are designed to ensure that the truly guilty, and only them, are convicted, and the innocent set free. This point is worth underlining. Even our benighted ancestors who tried cases by battle and ordeal, ducked suspected witches to see if they would use their diabolical powers to float on water, and tortured suspects for their confession were trying to discover the truth of the matter. Their error lay in superstitious beliefs in divine intervention and possession by the Devil incarnate, but their commitment to truth-seeking cannot be faulted. Modern procedural systems based on the *Code Napoléon*, including Chinese criminal process, adopt an explicit and overriding normative commitment to discovering the truth of the events under investigation, which also exerts a strong ideological influence on the culture and practice of criminal justice professionals in those countries. Civil lawyers are sometimes given to thinking that Anglo-American common law proceedings exhibit less concern for truth-finding than their own Continental process, but that is a proposition that must be treated with considerable circumspection. Adversarial procedure sometimes *appears* to relegate factual accuracy to an obsession with following technical rules of procedure, but that is largely because: (a) the adversary process is considered to be an especially effective, albeit indirect and necessarily rule-bound, way of discovering the truth; and (b) fact-finding is constrained by other values, as it is in every modern jurisdiction. So do not be fooled by appearances! Contrary to what cynical practitioners might say, or even believe, the English criminal process is centrally (though of course not *exclusively*) concerned with accurate fact-finding.

For more than a century, the English criminal process has been an avid consumer of the latest developments in forensic science. Fingerprinting was one of the first types of scientific expertise to emerge as a standard feature of police investigations after its adoption by Scotland Yard in 1902. Throughout the twentieth century, and into the twenty-first, the forensic sciences have become increasingly influential, as new specialisms have developed in medicine, dentistry, pathology, psychiatry, psychology, toxicology, biological sciences (blood, hair, and bodily fluids analysis), genetics, ballistics, narcotics, trace mark examination (paint, glass, fibres, toolmarks, and footprint inspection), and document and handwriting analysis, to mention only some of the most common fields of expertise to be found in contemporary criminal litigation. Above all, DNA 'fingerprinting', hailed as an almost miraculous tool of criminal detection and proof, has had an enormous impact, especially in the prosecution of violent and sexual offences. The Runciman Royal Commission's Crown Court Study estimated that around one third of all contested trials on indictment involve scientific evidence.[6] Though on any reckoning a significant figure, this probably underestimates the true prevalence of scientific expertise in criminal proceedings, since many experts make their most regular and significant contributions prior to the trial.

Any process organized around an historical inquiry will naturally be eager to enlist the assistance of scientific expertise in its attempts to reconstruct the past. It will, indeed, accept any genuine help it can get in discharging this difficult function. Some writers believe that English judges have historically been unreceptive to expert evidence. They argue that the judges perceived science as a threat to judicial authority, a usurper which the law must at least contain, if not repulse. But the historical record provides little support for this thesis. Though judges often refuse to allow experts to testify in court, this is generally because they have decided—rightly or wrongly—that a particular expert cannot provide assistance with any matter relevant to the case. The modern English rule of admissibility, which is notably under-developed by comparison with other common law jurisdictions, remains simply this; that expert evidence is admissible whenever—but only in so far as—it will help the jury to determine a question which is beyond the knowledge and experience of ordinary people.

TWO CHEERS FOR SCIENTIFIC EVIDENCE

The increasing use of science in the modern criminal process should be welcomed as an overwhelmingly positive development. Forensic science is good for justice in the same way that all modern science improves on the knowledge and technology of the past. Aeroplanes are more effective conveyances than hot-air balloons, key-hole surgery is preferable to treatment with leeches, and rape is easier to prove with DNA evidence than without it. Any fair evaluation of scientific evidence must, moreover, consider the merits of alternatives, and indeed, whether there *are* any viable alternatives, to particular forms of scientific proof.

All will agree that DNA evidence is a more reliable guide to the truth than combat, ordeals, torture, or other pre-modern fact-finding techniques. The principal alternatives to scientific evidence in modern criminal proceedings are witness testimony,

---

[6] M. Zander and P. Henderson, *Crown Court Study*, RCCJ Research Study No. 19 (London: HMSO, 1993), at 84. Moreover, scientific evidence was judged 'very important' in over two-fifths of such cases, and 'fairly important' in a further one-third (*ibid.*, at 85).

statements by the accused, documents, material objects (called 'real evidence' in England and Wales), courtroom demonstrations, arguments and submissions by the parties or their advocates, and the judge's directions in summing up the case to the jury at the end of the trial.[7] Over time, however, confidence in these evidentiary sources and techniques has declined. A series of troubling miscarriages of justice since the 1970s has demonstrated, in particular, that identification evidence is sometimes completely unreliable, even when the witness is certain and convincing, and that apparently damning confession evidence can be fabricated, coerced by intimidation or bribery, or be otherwise deficient as proof of guilt. In a predominantly secular society, in which few witnesses are deterred from perjury by the fear of eternal damnation in hellfire, the oath is no longer a reliable guarantor of testimonial veracity. It would appear that even the police regularly tell 'white lies' in court—so-called 'pious perjury' in which police officers exaggerate or modify the truth in order to facilitate the conviction of an accused they 'know', but cannot necessarily prove, is guilty. With increased awareness and growing dissatisfaction with the shortcomings of other types of proof, scientific evidence comes to appear all the more reliable, valuable, and trustworthy.

A second pertinent development in English criminal justice is the historical shift, over the last 150 years or so, away from basing criminal liability on 'objective' conduct criteria towards the modern focus on 'subjective' mental standards of culpability. Although there is lively on-going debate between English scholars about how far subjective culpability standards should extend, this development is generally endorsed as humane and morally enlightened. It is consistent with neo-Kantian ethics that insist on evaluating conduct, not only by reference to its consequences—which, from the actor's point of view, are often more or less matters of chance—but also in terms of the actor's interior mental life of purpose, motivation, foresight, knowledge, practical attitudes, and desires.

Expert evidence has played an important role in the proliferation of subjective culpability standards. In the normal case, fact-finders easily draw inferences from overt conduct to mental phenomena, in the manner postulated in Wittgenstein's aphorism that 'the human body is the best picture of the human soul'.[8] If Arnold produces a gun, takes careful aim, and shoots Brenda dead, the obvious inference from Arnold's conduct is that he intended to kill Brenda. This inference will usually be conclusive evidence of Arnold's intention, unless there is some rational explanation for Arnold's conduct consistent with his not intending to kill Brenda. There is a range of conceivable possibilities, some of which can be assessed competently by ordinary jurors or magistrates. If, for example, Arnold says that he honestly believed the gun to be a harmless replica water-pistol and that he only fired at Brenda as a joke, the factfinder would need to evaluate any evidence that might support such a belief. Perhaps the gun was given to Arnold by Charlie, as part of Charlie's plan to do away

---

[7] Strictly speaking, neither counsel's arguments and speeches nor the judge's summing up are 'evidence' in English law. But they are—and are designed to be—*information* that will influence the jury's fact-finding, and can therefore be treated as evidence in this looser, functional sense.

[8] L. Wittgenstein, *Philosophical Investigations* (Oxford: Blackwell, 1953) Pt. II, p. iv.

with his enemy Brenda. Or perhaps the gun came in misleading packaging which might fool somebody like Arnold, who has never seen a real gun, into believing that it was only a toy. The more fanciful the story, the less likely a factfinder would believe it. But in principle lay jurors or magistrates would be in as good a position as anybody else to assess the value of such evidence. There are other types of claim that lay people cannot competently evaluate, however. Suppose that Arnold claims to have a brain injury that prevents him from connecting his actions with their consequences. He understands perfectly well that he pulled the trigger, but cannot appreciate that this action caused Brenda's death. Or suppose, alternatively, that Arnold says he was insane or an automaton at the time of the killing, or—again—that he suffered from a delusional fantasy that Brenda was going to attack and kill *him* unless he launched a pre-emptive strike. These matters lie beyond the common-sense knowledge and experience of most ordinary people. Expert neurologists (or other 'head-doctor' specialists), psychiatrists, and psychologists would be needed to help the court to decide whether Arnold's claims have any grounding in science and whether, in consequence, they merit belief.

Along with the advent of DNA evidence, the growing prevalence and influence of 'psy-experts' must qualify as the late twentieth century's most significant development in forensic science. Mental health professionals have facilitated and reinforced criminal law's shift towards subjective culpability criteria, and in the process have helped to modernize legal doctrines of diminished responsibility, provocation, automatism, psychiatric harm, and intoxication, amongst others. As psy-experts have pushed these expanding doctrines further into the territory of subjective mental states, so the reliance of the criminal process on psy-professionals to provide expert evidence of the workings of the human mind has grown dramatically. The point has been reached in England and Wales at which some courts and commentators have begun to doubt whether justice is truly served by this trend. Syndrome evidence is a particular area of contention. New forms of psychological evidence involving Post-Traumatic Stress Disorder, Battered Woman Syndrome, Rape Trauma Syndrome, Child Abuse Accommodation Syndrome, Gulf War Syndrome, Recovered Memories, and the like are hailed by some observers as valuable and timely forensic tools for giving appropriate legal recognition to forms of victimization, especially 'domestic' violence (assault by a spouse) and child abuse, which have previously remained invisible or been marginalized by the criminal process. Other commentators have questioned the scientific credentials of syndrome evidence and warned that a too credulous approach exposes criminal proceedings to new risks of abuse and injustice. Extensive elaboration would be required to expound the merits of these debates. Suffice it here to observe that the role of expert scientific evidence in re-orienting English criminal law towards subjective mental standards, though generally celebrated as a civilizing influence, becomes controversial and contested if pressed beyond certain limits.

IMPERFECT SCIENCE MAKES INCONCLUSIVE PROOF

Brief reference to psychological syndrome evidence hints at a more general truth about forensic science. If the first task of a general evaluation is to establish science's overwhelmingly positive contribution to the administration of criminal justice in England and Wales, the second—equally important—point to emphasize is that scientific evidence has significant limitations, some of which it shares with other forms of evidence, some of which are peculiarly problems of forensic science. No evidence type can guarantee to supply unassailable proof, because uncertainty in fact-finding and judgement is an inescapable, irremediable feature of the human condition. Yet in less reflective moments this indisputable fact tends to be forgotten or overlooked. Scientific evidence, furthermore, seems to be especially prone to encouraging the fantasy of perfect proof. When, in the grip of this fantasy, forensic science is used naïvely or uncritically its potential for causing injustice is just as impressive as its positive achievements when employed appropriately as an ally of justice.

Scientific evidence has five principal limitations which merit further elaboration: (i) science never tells the whole story; (ii) forensic science is not pure science; (iii) some purported 'science' is not scientific; (iv) some purported 'experts' are not experts; and (v) science has to be presented to, and be evaluated by, non-scientists.

(i) *Science never tells the whole story.* There are at least two independent and potentially cumulative reasons why scientific evidence is always incomplete proof of criminal charges. The first reason is that scientific evidence rarely settles every material fact in criminal proceedings and never proves everything potentially at issue. In a rape trial, for example, it is conceivable that the identity of the perpetrator could be the only fact in issue. Imagine that the victim positively identifies the defendant as her assailant, but he categorically denies it and puts up an alibi. If DNA evidence were introduced to show that semen left at the scene matched the defendant's genetic profile, to a probability of many millions to one, that would probably be enough to convince a jury that the defendant must be guilty. But even in this, the most straightforward, case loose ends remain. What if the defendant's alibi is provided by a trustworthy independent third party, such as a priest or police officer, who has no reason to lie? What if the laboratory's instruments are found to be contaminated with genetic material from other investigations?

Complications lurk even in apparently 'open and shut' cases in which science appears to be conclusive. However, the majority of cases do not even *appear* to be this simple and straightforward. DNA evidence proves nothing if the defendant admits intercourse but alleges the complainant consented, for example. Burglary is another crime in which scientific evidence is frequently significant. Fingerprints, blood, shoeprints, tool marks, and glass fragments can help to identify a housebreaker. But they do not establish the precise intention or motivation for the burglary, the items taken (or other offences committed) after entry, or—in many cases—distinguish between a convicted offence and a mere attempt. In an assault or wounding case, medical evidence can explain the nature of the victim's injuries and even specify the type of weapon used to inflict them, but provides at best only limited guidance if the defendant says he acted under duress or in self-defence. The point, simply put, is that criminal cases typically require a range of facts to be proved, some of which are more amenable to scientific proof than others. Though science often furnishes extremely valuable and cogent evidence of certain facts in issue in the proceedings, it is less frequently conclusive and only rarely accepted as self-sufficient proof of guilt.

The second reason scientific evidence is never the whole story is that science, like any other body of knowledge, has inherent limitations. Some sciences, like physics and chemistry, are about as certain and reliable as anything in life ever is, but other sciences are less certain and possibly also more prone to error. Sciences of the mind, like psychiatry and psychology, lie towards the less certain end of the spectrum. How should the criminal process respond to the indubitable limitations of scientific knowledge? Surely not by rejecting science as forensic proof. The value and comparative superiority of scientific evidence have already been established. The appropriate response is to retain a healthy scepticism towards the claims of science, never forgetting that science is potentially fallible and that even well-settled scientific propositions can turn out to be wrong. Critical scrutiny is essential. Those sciences that have demonstrated their worth across the broad gamut of human activity naturally merit most trust in criminal proceedings. This applies to Newtonian physics and modern biological sciences, for example, which in principle should work just as well when applied to the administration of criminal justice as they do when performing their 'miracles of science' in other spheres of life. The fact that aeroplanes very occasionally crash is not a good reason for refusing to fly (given the advantages of flight over available alternatives), but it is an excellent reason—reinforced by the seriousness of the consequences should tragedy occur—for keeping aeroplanes well maintained and working to improve their performance and safety. A greater degree of scepticism may be appropriate with regard to scientific fields that are more speculative, contested, or less demonstrable. There are several competing schools of psychology with divergent approaches, for example. This inevitably poses the question whether any of them is sufficiently reliable as a basis for criminal proof and, if so, which? That psychology has never given us anything as impressive as aeroplanes or test-tube babies does not demonstrate *ipso facto* that psychology is an unreliable basis for criminal verdicts. But it does mean that there is less reason to rely on psychological expertise than on physics or the biological sciences in this important sphere of public decision-making.

An attitude of healthy scepticism is particularly appropriate with regard to novel scientific techniques and discoveries. Scientific knowledge is confirmed and improved, or—more often, and just as importantly—exposed and rejected, through a process of critical challenge, experimentation, and replication in the wider scientific community. Cutting-edge science is therefore generally less stable, reliable, uncontroversial, tried, or tested than scientific knowledge that has withstood the test of time. This makes new scientific discoveries especially problematic as the basis of criminal verdicts. As a rough guide, any scientific knowledge or theory that is likely to require material revision before a defendant has served his gaol sentence is unlikely to be considered an acceptable basis for criminal conviction and punishment. Yet this presents a dilemma for the criminal process. Investigators and prosecutors will naturally want to make use of the latest cutting-edge discoveries and techniques for detecting crime and bringing perpetrators to justice. But policy-makers should carefully consider whether novel science has yet progressed beyond the point of durability at which it can safely be relied on as criminal proof. Early experiences of DNA evidence in England and the USA illustrate the consequences of reacting too quickly to scientific progress. Numerous convictions have had to be quashed because DNA evidence was utilized before scientifically robust protocols had been devised for its transmission, generation, interpretation, and presentation.

(ii) *Forensic science is not pure science.* To this point discussion has focused on the inherent limitations of science, conceived in the abstract as a disinterested pursuit of the truth under ideal conditions of inquiry. Sociological accounts of how scientists actually behave suggest that this ideal is seldom fully realized in practice. It is sometimes even argued that the ideal is a complete myth, on the basis that scientists are *typically* partial, biased, secretive, and competitive, and basically behave in a manner exactly opposite to the popular image of pure scientific investigation producing unassailable knowledge. One should be wary of over-exaggerating the undoubted infirmities of scientific practice by generalizing from unusually problematic special cases. Whatever the practical realities of pure laboratory science, however, *forensic* science inevitably falls well short of the ideal model of scientific inquiry.

Forensic science is *applied* science. Crime does not occur in the controlled environment of a laboratory, and criminal proceedings are not disinterested inquiries. Forensic scientists have to contend from the start with depleted raw materials and limited information. They also need to develop effective working relationships with other criminal justice professionals. Both factors have important implications for the validity and reliability of scientific evidence. Much forensic science is derived from familiar scientific disciplines, but often involves extensions or unusual applications of scientific knowledge. Moreover, in adapting science to legal ends and in presenting their results in a usable form, forensic scientists draw heavily on more or less subjective judgements and interpretations, disciplinary conventions, and accumulated personal experience. The subjective, interpretative component of forensic science has often been obscured by reporting conventions. Fingerprint experts, for example, simply declare that a crime-scene fingerprint 'matches' the suspect's finger, or, as the case may be, that no match has been found. Yet behind this apparently objective, definitive conclusion lies a succession of more subjective and equivocal judgements about the criteria for establishing a match and whether those criteria are satisfied in the instant case. The point can be generalized in relation to many of the leading sub-disciplines within the forensic sciences, which have less in common with their parent disciplines than casual acquaintance might suggest. Superficial appearances are therefore potentially misleading: the forensic sciences are more like distant cousins than direct descendants of the harder physical sciences.

In practice forensic scientists frequently have to work with unsatisfactory material. Samples from crime scenes may be degraded, contaminated, or only recoverable in very small quantities barely sufficient for testing. Fingerprints, shoeprints, or toolmarks may be smudged or incomplete. Glass or fibre evidence can easily get mixed up with other material accidentally imported into the crime scene by witnesses, investigators, or onlookers. Essential evidential material is sometimes overlooked or lost. In England and Wales specialist Scenes of Crime Officers (SOCOs) help police investigators to identify and collect crucial evidence and ensure that exhibits are properly bagged, labelled, and stored so that a contamination-free 'chain of continuity' can later be demonstrated in court. However, SOCOs cannot be expected to be as effective in identifying and preserving exhibits as a trained forensic scientist would be. The scientists themselves visit crime scenes only infrequently, due to the cost and logistical difficulties of arranging their attendance. Moreover, in a significant number of cases the task of securing and collecting evidential material falls to the investigating constable who happens to be first on the crime scene. Most police officers have very little relevant training, and mistakes are bound to be made. For all these reasons forensic scientists regularly find themselves trying to 'make the best of a bad job'. Analogous difficulties confront experts in other specialisms. The quality of medical evidence, for example, is contingent on timely examination, before marks or injuries have had time to heal. Medical practice also raises ethical difficulties, which are perhaps at their most acute in the fields of psychiatry and psychology. Some forms of psychiatric examination and psychological assessment with important forensic applications can be undertaken only with the subject's consent, which may not be forthcoming in the case of witnesses or defendants in criminal proceedings.

The impact of depleted material resources on the quality of scientific evidence is compounded by the goal-orientated nature of criminal investigations. A particular problem of the adversary process is that investigators and prosecutors may be tempted to see themselves as part of a 'prosecution team' trying, above all else, to secure convictions. Whilst the practical consequences of an adversary culture for the conduct of criminal proceedings should not be underestimated, the strict legal position is that police and prosecutors must be impartial agents of justice. It is worth noting, in particular, that the police are under a duty to search for all potentially relevant evidence, whether it incriminates or exculpates a suspect. In this formal respect English criminal investigations are no different from investigations in continental systems which are structured around a search for the truth. But if the English criminal process shares more with the civilian legal tradition than is sometimes appreciated, civilian criminal proceedings also mirror the adversary norm to a greater extent than the formal legal position would suggest. For investigations are *by their very nature* goal-orientated and in both procedural systems this structural feature tends to combine with the practical and psychological realities of the criminal process to produce a situation in which investigators concentrate more on proving the guilt of a suspect than on finding exculpatory evidence. Suspects are chosen in the first instance because they have been identified by a victim or witness, observed during police surveillance, or appear on the list of 'usual suspects' (generally because they are logged on the police computer as having relevant previous convictions). Once a police hypothesis of guilt has been formulated, sometimes based on quite flimsy initial indications, the natural human tendency is to look for evidence that confirms rather than refutes that hypothesis. This is not to deny that police investigations are reasonably flexible and open-ended. The police can simultaneously investigate a range of hypotheses, which are later up-dated, refined, and re-focused as new evidence emerges. In this way some suspects will be eliminated from the inquiry and others will fall under suspicion as the investigation proceeds. Even where officers entertain a single 'theory of the case' and strongly believe in one suspect's guilt, they may later be forced to abandon their theory if convincing proof of innocence comes to light. (Scientific evidence can be the most effective exculpation, as where a DNA profile demonstrates that the suspect cannot have been the offender.) But the goal-orientated, hypothesis-confirming structure of investigations retains its influence throughout. There are notorious examples in British legal history where police officers have pressurized witnesses to change their statements in order to conform with the police theory of the case. These well-documented *causes célèbres* imply that similar pressures, in a range of more subtle and pervasive variations, are regularly exerted, though the mechanisms and strategies of case construction are normally hidden from view. Moreover, even where investigators do not set out with the express intention of confirming a particular hypothesis, the goal-orientated dynamic of criminal investigations continues to operate at a sub-conscious level. It is reasonable to assume that the same institutional pressure and psychological forces are at play in every criminal justice system, irrespective of formal legal requirements. Detailed empirical research has been able to demonstrate their significance in England and Wales. The reality of the position in other jurisdictions cannot be established either way until those systems, too, have undergone comparably intense empirical examination.

Forensic science evidence can be just as much a product of police case-building, structured by a hypothesized theory of the case, as any other type of evidence. The process has been documented in considerable detail in England and Wales, albeit on the basis of a small sample of cases. Research conducted for the Royal Commission on Criminal Justice identified nine key phases in the production of scientific evidence: (1) first, investigators must decide to utilise scientific expertise. The initial decision is made by the police and prosecutors and therefore answers to investigative, rather than strictly scientific, imperatives. This creates an observable tension between the investigators' needs and expectations and the ability of science to satisfy them. In recent times attempts have been made to educate investigators about the possibilities and limitations of scientific evidence. Police officers have been encouraged to turn to science in the investigation of 'routine' volume crimes such as burglary and theft, where the potential for scientific assistance has often been overlooked in the past, though progress is uneven across the regions. But it remains the case that scientific evidence is produced only when investigators think they need it, which is not necessarily when science may in fact be of most—or indeed, of any—assistance. (2) If police or prosecutors decide to utilize scientific evidence, their first task is to locate an appropriate expert. For most standard types of forensic science assistance the laboratories of the Forensic Science Service (FSS) are on hand to provide what is generally acknowledged to be a first-class service. These labs were formerly part of the Home Office but are now semi-autonomous agencies required to cover their operating costs on a quasi-commercial basis. Their services are available to the defence as well as to the prosecution, but police forces are the FSS's most frequent customers. For other types of expertise, including clinical, medical, and the more esoteric forensic sciences, investigators have to look to the hospitals, universities, research institutes, and a growing number of private consultancies to locate an appropriate expert. An expert is usually found without too much trouble, but the process of hiring experts is surprisingly informal and sometimes fails to produce the best evidence.

(3) Once an appropriate expert has been engaged, the next step is to supply the expert with relevant crime-scene material (or other raw data) for analysis. The difficulties of identifying, preserving, and transmitting evidential material free from degradation or contamination have already been mentioned. (4) Another crucial aspect of the hiring and transmission process concerns the nature of the instructions received by the expert. Needless to say, experts do not slavishly carry out investigators' instructions in formulating their general approach, conducting tests or examinations, analysing and interpreting data, and so forth. These are matters of scientific judgement in which the expert, not police or prosecutors, knows best. However, scientists are inevitably influenced by the type and extent of background information provided to them by investigators, and even possibly by the form and wording of the police request for assistance. One way to respond to the risk of 'contamination' by such extraneous influences would be to insist that items must be sent to the laboratory without any accompanying background information and with a request for assistance in scrupulously neutral terms. At one time the FSS considered this best practice. Yet that approach and the language employed in its justification betray a fundamental misconception about the nature of forensic science. Following from the essentially applied nature of their discipline, most forensic scientists prefer to be told as much background information as possible, in order to be able to tailor their approach to the needs of the investigation. There is, most obviously, little point in a scientist wasting time and energy on matters that are not in issue in the proceedings. Background information is not so much, on this view, an external source of 'contamination' or 'bias', but an essential part of the scientist's data for analysis (though the continued risk of inappropriate, and possibly unconscious, influence suggests that—if it can be identified as such—irrelevant and potentially prejudicial material should be filtered out of the scientific brief).

(5) The scientist next proceeds to conduct whatever testing or examinations are judged appropriate, and (6) the results of the scientific investigation are written up into a report. Both testing and reporting reflect the investigators' instructions and expectations within the broader framework of criminal proceedings and the conventions of forensic science. The rules of substantive criminal law structure police investigations, which in turn influence the questions scientific experts are asked to consider, the tests they undertake, and the nature and content of the reports they produce. A simple illustration should help to clarify the dynamics of this process (bearing in mind that there is considerable variation in matters of detail depending on the legal and scientific circumstances of the case). Suppose, for example, that the question in a murder case is whether the defendant intended to kill the deceased, and/or whether she might have acted in self defence. English criminal law makes a crucial distinction between unlawful killings constituting murder, the gravest crime of all for which life imprisonment is the prescribed mandatory penalty, and lawful killings in self-defence, to which no penal consequences whatever attach. In any case involving a shooting, ballistics experts might be instructed to confirm that particular bullets were fired from the defendant's gun. However, if self-defence appeared to investigators to

be a genuine possibility, forensic scientists might also be asked to consider whether the distribution of bullets and the range at which they were fired were consistent with self-defensive conduct. Experts would not routinely comment on a self-defence theory or any other conceivable hypothesis such as provocation, mistake, or accident. But if specifically invited to do so, the expert would consider the bearing of ballistics evidence (such as powder residues, positioning of shell cases, distribution of bullet holes, burns on the deceased's skin, etc.) on the self-defence theory and report any relevant findings or advice to the police. When producing reports detailing their results and conclusions, scientists are conscious of the instrumental role of science in criminal proceedings and of a report's intended audience. Investigators expect scientists to help them prove, or disprove, criminal charges against a suspect, and the style and language of expert reports is directed to that end. There are generalized pressures to work quickly and produce definite conclusions. Even if scientists were always paragons of the ideals of impartial and objective inquiry, which most of them espouse, their work product would still remain a highly selective, constrained, stylized, and instrumentally orientated form of science. In fact, another feature of the serious miscarriages of justice that came to light in the last decade is that some scientists have been seduced, or corrupted, by adversarial culture. In succumbing to the institutional pressures that in some measure all forensic scientists experience, these experts allowed themselves to become mere functionaries of the prosecution, rather than impartial seekers of truth and purveyors of robustly objective scientific knowledge.

The production of a scientific report is often the end of the matter.[9] If the expert's evidence strongly confirms guilt the defendant may plead guilty, as most English defendants in fact do. If, on the other hand, the expert fails to produce cogent inculpatory evidence the prosecution may have to be abandoned. One of the reasons investigators typically seek scientific assistance is that they have no other evidence to rely on and science is their last best hope. In a minority of cases, however, the production of scientific evidence proceeds through three further key stages.

(7) Defence lawyers sometimes appoint their own experts, occasionally to follow up exculpatory leads, but more often just to double-check the work already conducted by a prosecution expert. The appearance of a defence expert may present opportunities for communication, and even co-operation and the exchange of ideas, between experts on opposite sides of the adversarial divide. Forensic scientists seldom share the adversarial culture of the police and lawyers who hire them, and some scientists treat their notional adversaries as colleagues. On the occasions when scientists meet in the laboratory to review test results, defence experts sometimes persuade scientists working for the prosecution to undertake further tests or to reinterpret their results in the light of a different perspective or new information. Scientific investigations undertaken by the defence, in conjunction with prosecution scientists or independently, do occasionally produce significant exculpatory evidence. In the majority of

---

[9] In the financial year 1999–2000 the FSS dealt with a record total of 109,000 cases, but its scientists appeared as expert witnesses on (only) 3,300 occasions: Forensic Science Service, *Annual Report & Accounts 1999–2000*, HC Paper 655, 25 July 2000.

cases, however, the defence examiner simply confirms the prosecution expert's data and conclusions.

(8) In cases that proceed to trial the expert may attend a pre-trial conference with counsel. This is potentially an important meeting, at which counsel can review the expert's evidence and ensure that the expert is prepared to stand by the conclusions expressed in her report. However, the Royal Commission research found that pre-trial conferences between experts and counsel are frequently short or non-existent. Time pressures are reinforced by a deeply held aversion on the part of some barristers to meeting any witnesses prior to trial, for fear of attracting accusations of 'witness coaching'. But that fear seems misplaced with regard to expert witnesses, not because experts are immune to pressure and undue influence, but because counsel are unlikely to lead scientific evidence successfully if they do not themselves understand the expert's evidence. Lack of pre-trial communication between experts and counsel is said on occasion to have adversely affected the presentation of scientific evidence at trial.

(9) A very small percentage of criminal cases go to trial, but these are dis-proportionately serious and important cases. Scientific evidence is adduced in per-haps one-third of these contested trials, though the scientific evidence itself may be uncontroversial. In those circumstances the expert report can simply be read out to the court, and is likely to be accepted at face-value by the jury. Where the defence (or, more infrequently, the prosecution) wants to challenge scientific evidence, however, the expert will usually be called to testify in person. Experts give their evidence like any other witness, through a series of answers to questions put by counsel. The expert is first taken through examination-in-chief by the barrister calling the expert and then undergoes cross-examination by counsel for the other side. Should it be necessary to clear up any matter raised in cross-examination, a third phase of ques-tioning ('re-examination') may be conducted by the side calling the evidence. Need-less to say, this is a highly artificial way of presenting scientific evidence to the court. Its success depends in large part on the skill and scientific understanding of counsel, which cannot always be relied upon, especially where pre-trial preparation has been inadequate. It might be preferable, in order to communicate scientific evidence more effectively, if experts could present their evidence in a more direct and less constrained fashion. As it is, counsel may, through incompetence or as a deliberate strategy, distort the intended meaning of an expert's evidence; and the effect may be compounded where experts called by the prosecution and defence disagree, or appear to disagree, with each other. I will return to the problem of evaluating scientific evidence in a moment, after first mentioning two further, related complications.

(iii) *Some purported 'science' is not scientific.* It has been assumed to this point that forensic science is essentially valid science. The discussion has shown that forensic science, as an applied discipline, inevitably falls short of the purist scientific ideal of objective, impartial knowledge. Elements of uncertainty are necessarily introduced by the practical and institutional conditions under which forensic science is produced as part of a goal-orientated, case-building investigative process. But the potential difficulties do not end there. Some purported 'sciences' are not even scientific, judged by any robust criteria of testability, replicability, falsifiability, and the prospect of generating consensus over time. This is obvious in the case of discredited former 'sciences' like alchemy, phrenology, treatment with leeches, and witch-finding. Most people would agree that astrology and creationism are not sciences either, although this is patently controversial in some quarters. Even greater controversy surrounds the status of certain branches of psychology, with criminal-process applications such as recovered memories, syndrome diagnosis, and offender profiling. Some people consider these techniques scientific, whilst others denounce them as speculative and insubstantial.

Determining the legitimate boundaries of science presents the law with two kinds of problem (or two variants of the same problem). The first is to identify the proper boundaries of recognized scientific disciplines, to determine the point at which legitimate theories and techniques are being over-extended into areas which are, as yet, too speculative to be considered truly scientific. The second problem is be able to distinguish between real science and pseudo-science, 'junk science' as it is known in the USA. Crank theories, invalid data, and wholly unsubstantiated empirical claims have sometimes been accepted by judges or jurors, who have been hoodwinked by the terminology and trappings of legitimate science. Junk science is said to be especially prevalent in American personal injury litigation, but it is not limited either by subject matter or jurisdiction. In the Birmingham Six and Maguire Seven cases in England, for example, convictions of murder and bomb-making were based on scientific tests for nitroglycerine which years later were utterly discredited by an official inquiry. The scientists involved in these cases were found to have been mistaken about the validity of the tests they conducted, which, moreover, had been performed in a slipshod and selective manner which further undermined the credibility of their data. Yet none of this emerged at the defendants' trials, and long prison sentences were served before the errors were discovered and the defendants' convictions quashed. This episode is a powerful reminder that only *valid* science contributes to the pursuit of truth in criminal proceedings, whereas pseudo-science breeds falsehood and injustice. It follows that for science to contribute positively to the administration of criminal justice there must be some reliable institutional means of filtering junk science out of the criminal process.

(iv) *Some purported 'experts' are not experts.* Related to the problem of unscientific 'science' is the problem of 'experts' who are not genuinely expert. The straightforward case of the charlatan expert with fake qualifications peddling bogus testimony is hardly ever seen in English criminal proceedings. If such characters ever did appear, perhaps tempted by the fees that can be earned for forensic work, they would probably be quickly exposed and denounced by genuine experts in the field. In practice, charlatanism is more subtle and pervasive, because it typically involves *bona fide* experts overstepping the boundaries of their true expertise. This is much harder to detect and to neutralize than out and out quackery.

Pure science tends towards narrow specialization, but forensic scientists are often generalists at the more technological end of their disciplines. A forensic expert may be very experienced in the generation and interpretation of data, for example, without properly understanding the physical or chemical science underpinning those data or the properties of the laboratory instruments that produced them. At various points in the production of forensic science evidence, however, experts may come under pressure to say more than they know. An expert may (or may not) be robust in the face of pressures from police or lawyers to stray into unfamiliar territory when writing a report in the comparative leisure of her study or laboratory, but the situation is very different when the expert is unexpectedly put on the spot whilst testifying in court. The temptation to make over-confident assertions or ill-advised concessions in response to counsel's enticing invitations and probing challenges may be almost irresistible to all but the most experienced courtroom performer. One example that has recurred in decided cases and secondary literature since the 1960s is the pressure on pathologists to state a time of death with greater precision than could be sanctioned by medical science. Pathologists have sometimes strayed or been pressed to the point where their authoritative expert opinion becomes merely the personal opinion of an expert, shading over the line into pseudo-science. DNA evidence, which rests on complex statistical analyses as well as biological science, affords another important contemporary example. An expert biologist risks charges of charlatanism if she expresses views on aspects of population genetics without an adequate grounding in statistical method. This problem was particularly acute in the early days of DNA evidence, before the multi-disciplinarity of DNA technology was widely recognized, and helped to perpetuate the systematic statistical errors now known as the 'prosecutor's fallacy' and the 'defence attorney's fallacy'.

Charlatanism and pseudo-science are overlapping, but distinct, forms of the same vice. As forensic evidence they are worse than useless, because they appear with the imprimatur of science to be strong proof and yet are no proof at all. It makes sense for verdicts in criminal proceedings to draw strength from the body of knowledge that made planes fly, amongst many other wonders of science. But it is salutary to recall that unless science is approached with a cautious respect and utilized with care, aeroplanes drop out of the sky, with terrible human consequences. As with aviation, so in criminal process: whilst good science and genuine experts are invaluable, nothing is more dangerous than pseudo-science and charlatan experts.

(v) *Science is presented to, and evaluated by, non-scientists.* An immediate problem arises whenever science is introduced into criminal proceedings. How can experts effectively communicate their knowledge to criminal-process decision-makers who, almost by definition, lack scientific expertise (otherwise they would not need an expert to help them)? Any respectable answer to this question lies somewhere on the continuum between *deference* and *education.* That is to say, criminal-process decision-makers can either defer to the authority of an expert by simply adopting her conclusions (a 'black-box' approach to science) or else undergo crash course instruction in some relevant aspect of the expert's discipline in order to be able to arrive at scientifically well-informed judgements for themselves. Locating an appropriate point on the continuum between deference and education depends on the relevant stage of criminal proceedings and the type of expertise involved, as well as on the personalities, knowledge, and skills of particular experts and decision-makers.

A reasonable generalization (though one subject to important qualifications and counter-examples) is that expertise receives greater deference in the earlier stages of criminal process, whereas a contested, educational model of expertise is more likely to be encountered in the later phases of criminal proceedings, especially at trial. If the police instruct a forensic psychologist to assist in their investigations, by constructing an 'offender profile' of possible suspects or by directing an undercover operation with psychological dimensions, for example, the expert's advice will simply be followed or rejected on operational grounds. An expert would not be expected to teach police officers how to construct their own offender profile, handwriting analysis, or facial reconstruction, etc. Forensic science reports are likewise usually accepted by police and prosecutors at face value. The prosecution proceeds if there is scientific evidence of guilt, but if science has drawn a blank the case is likely to be abandoned. On the defence side, different approaches reflect the working philosophies and practices of particular defence solicitors. Some solicitors interviewed in the Royal Commission research were quite fatalistic about certain forms of scientific evidence, considering DNA evidence, for example, to be conclusive and beyond challenge. A defendant might then be advised by his solicitor to plead guilty, though no type of evidence, DNA included, is literally beyond challenge. Other solicitors, who appeared more proactive and adversarially-minded, were more likely to instruct a defence expert in an attempt to unearth a fatal flaw in the prosecution's case. Contact between defence lawyers and the expert scientific examiners they instruct seemed closer and more frequent than the corresponding, and comparatively distant, working relationships between prosecutors and experts. One of the defence examiner's main functions is to explain the scientific merits of the case to the instructing lawyer and to explore further possibilities and avenues for challenge. But even in these co-operative exchanges, in which lawyers ask questions and pose alternative scenarios, the expert's role is still essentially one of providing advice and instruction, as opposed to educating lawyers in the ways of science.

The education model of scientific evidence assumes its greatest prominence at trial. There is high authority for the proposition that the expert's principal function is to put the jury in a position to evaluate the evidence for itself. Moreover, the jury are entitled to reject even uncontested scientific evidence if they choose to do so, though trial judges try to steer juries into accepting expert evidence which is uncontested or otherwise apparently uncontroversial. For all that, the education model is predominantly a legal fiction, invented to bolster the primacy of juries in fact-finding. In the vast majority of cases juries almost certainly simply defer to the predominant scientific view, at least where they understand what it is. If there is a conflict of scientific evidence, then jurors obviously have to make a choice, though that choice may well be to treat the contest as a no-score draw and ignore the scientific evidence completely. Where jurors do decide to favour one expert's evidence rather than another's, it is difficult to see how that choice can ever be based on *scientific* considerations. Jurors more likely pick the expert who has the better qualifications, or who appeared to be the most effective witness, or seemed to be favoured by the judge in his summing up. It is possible to conceive of a limited role for genuine juror education, but considerable procedural innovation would be required to support it, and recent litigation supplies a cautionary tale. In *Adams*[10] part of the defence challenge to prosecution

---

[10] *R. v. Adams* [1996] 2 Cr. App. R 467 (CA); *R. v. Adams (No. 2)* [1998] 1 Cr. App. R 377 (CA).

DNA evidence involved calling an expert statistician to instruct jurors how to perform probability calculations using Bayes' Theorem. The defence argument was that the prosecution's match statistic of 200 million-to-one was wildly inflated, and that the jurors could see this for themselves by undertaking the necessary calculations, following the instructions provided by the defence expert. Bayes' Theorem involves complex formulae and calculations requiring a far greater than average level of mathematical competence, so it is not really surprising that the defence's education strategy turned out to be highly problematic. Adams was convicted, successfully appealed, was convicted again at a re-trial, and appealed once more, this time unsuccessfully. In dismissing Adams' second appeal the Court of Appeal was strongly critical of the defence's approach to challenging DNA evidence. It could not help the jury, said the court, to confuse them with abstruse mathematical formulae which highly educated judges, let alone the average juror, could barely understand! Such evidence should never be given again.

The court in *Adams* did *not* deny the existence of a genuine scientific dispute between the parties. Rather, *Adams* held that trying to turn the jury into an instant third expert, equipped to form their own independent view, would only confuse the issue, because the attempt was almost certainly bound to fail. Statistical evidence is doubtless a specially strong case, because many people lack ability, or at least confidence, in mathematics. But a more general moral might safely be drawn. Scientific experts are called upon because they bring to criminal proceedings knowledge, skill, and experience that nobody else in the process can provide. Deference to scientific expertise, not fact-finder education, will therefore be the norm.

REGULATING SCIENCE FOR JUSTICE

The main conclusion of the discussion so far is that science requires careful management and regulation if its forensic potential is to be realized, without generating new, and uniquely troublesome, risks of miscarriages of justice. Different legal systems respond to the limitations and deficiencies of forensic science, if they do, in different ways. The particular rules, procedures, and strategies adopted in each system will in some measure reflect a distinctive legal tradition and culture. There is therefore no simple, universal prescription for 'the right way' to address the particular challenges of scientific evidence. Each jurisdiction must devise its own approach, uniquely suited to its local juridical, social, and political environment. What can be said, however, is that the full potential of science to contribute to the realization of criminal justice will not be achieved unless each of the problems identified in the last section is, in some satisfactory manner, confronted and overcome. Science will not even contribute to reliable proof unless the production of scientific evidence is appropriately structured and regulated. But comprehensive evaluation cannot be confined to an assessment of truth-finding strategies. It must extend to the full range of values and interests in play in criminal proceedings.

SCIENCE IN THE ENGLISH ADVERSARY SYSTEM

The procedural arrangements for utilizing forensic science evidence in English criminal proceedings flow directly from the basic adversary model. First, the parties are permitted, and expected, to arrange their own scientific investigations, and present their own evidence to the court. Secondly, the main testing of scientific evidence is through cross-examination of expert witnesses at trial by counsel, with or without the assistance of their own scientific expert. Thirdly, the merits of the scientific case are determined by lay fact-finders: juries in serious cases, magistrates in summary proceedings. There are pressure points at each of these procedural stages.

Whereas police procedures for securing scientific assistance are routine, standardized, and—generally speaking—reliable, defence lawyers vary greatly in their knowledge and experience of instructing experts. Though FSS services are available to all paying customers, defence lawyers are not necessarily aware of the fact, and some that are continue to be suspicious of the 'police labs'. There is a bewildering array of private practitioners offering forensic services, from accountancy to zoology, but lawyers have no real way of judging whether an expert is truly competent. Most probably are, but stories continue to circulate about 'cowboys', 'instant experts', and 'liars-for-hire'. Formal schemes of accreditation are being introduced, following recommendations to this effect by the House of Lords Select Committee on Science and Technology and the Runciman Royal Commission on Criminal Justice[11] in the early 1990s, but it may be some time before these schemes are reasonably comprehensive and fully operational. In the meantime, quality control of forensic science is more important than ever, as police and prosecutors increasingly join defence lawyers in 'shopping around' for forensic science services in the new free market created by the partial privatization of the FSS. Cost considerations are also encouraging police forces to keep some scientific work 'in house' by training their SOCOs in new areas of expertise formerly provided by the FSS, raising further issues of quality and appropriate supervision.

Closely related to the availability of high quality forensic science services is the thorny issue of cost. Forensic expertise never comes cheap and is sometimes quite expensive. Part of the background to the reorganization of the FSS and the creation of a new forensic science 'market' in the 1990s was the perception in government circles, which took hold from the early 1980s onwards, that the cost of forensic science would spiral out of control unless some means of curbing demand could be devised. Under the old system there was no reason why the police should not take even greater advantage of FSS services, since they were free at the point of demand. The taxpayer had effectively written a blank cheque for forensic science services. The new system requires police forces to pay the unit cost for scientific assistance out of their own budgets, creating pressure towards 'efficiency' and 'value for money' in their purchasing decisions. One could take the view that the rising cost of forensic science services was simply an unavoidable demand on the public finances, which ought to have

---

[11] House of Lords Select Committee on Science and Technology (Chair: Lord Dainton), *Fifth Report: Forensic Science*, HL Paper 24, Session 1992–3 (London: HMSO, 1993); Royal Commission on Criminal Justice (Chair: Lord Runciman), *Report*, Cm 2263 (1993).

continued to be met as the price of achieving criminal justice. But this is probably unrealistic. In practice, the FSS would have remained under-funded and over-worked, as is the way with public services. The backlog of cases would have grown to the point where the Service's basic effectiveness would have been compromised through excessive delay and staff demoralization. The free-market experiment brings its own threats to justice, nonetheless. Some have warned that financial discipline will deter the police from requesting sufficiently thorough scientific investigations, drive down the quality of forensic science services in the race to undercut rival suppliers on price, and weaken the research base of forensic science (such as it is). It is too early to assess the long-run truth of these predictions, but they are certainly plausible concerns, and a modicum of confirmatory evidence can already be marshalled (though other indicators are more favourable).

On the defence side, the issue is whether legal aid is available to instruct a defence expert. When this question was investigated empirically in the early 1990s the general view appeared to be that legal aid was *usually* forthcoming to support reasonable requests for defence scientific assistance, especially in serious cases, but that practical obstacles and bureaucratic inefficiency sometimes created difficulties. Legal aid, along with defence legal services generally, have been subjected to increasing financial stringency through the 1990s, and it may be that provision of scientific assistance for defendants has consequently deteriorated. In a culture of cash-limited budgets and pressures to secure 'value for money', forensic science services for the defence may be especially vulnerable to cost-cutting. If defence scientific examiners often merely confirm the prosecution expert's results, it may be asked, is this not a needless reduplication of effort and a waste of resources? The question is naïve and simplistic, as accountants' questions often are. Without proper legal and scientific advice, defendants will be unable to test and challenge the prosecution's evidence, undermining the basic premise of the adversary process. However, all criminal justice systems, regardless of procedural models, must confront the question of resources. Scientific evidence is often cogent proof, usually of guilt, but occasionally also of innocence. Political communities, through their parliamentary representatives, need to decide how much public money they are prepared to spend on this commodity, since potential demand is virtually unlimited. In a sense this involves 'putting a price on justice', an idea that some will find distasteful, but a conscious, planned funding policy is more likely to promote justice than simply muddling along and hoping for the best.

When it comes to testing the prosecution's scientific evidence, and assuming that the defence has been able to locate, instruct, and pay for experts of its own, the crucial issues surround access to evidential material, exhibits, and information. Defence experts have to overcome the structural and practical disadvantages of arriving relatively late on the scene, after prosecution experts have already received items for analysis and conducted their tests (perhaps using up or degrading all the crime samples in the process). The co-operation of prosecution scientists is essential for defence examiners to operate effectively, and this is usually forthcoming. Scientists generally behave less adversarially than lawyers, even in an adversarial system, and relations between prosecution and defence experts are normally cordial, even friendly. Pre-trial meetings between scientists facilitate exchanges of information, which sometimes lead to the formation of scientific consensus, allow errors to be corrected, or clarify a point which forestalls later misunderstandings. This is a rational way of approaching, and if possible resolving, the scientific aspects of the case, and there may be greater scope for more regular pre-trial meetings between experts. Lawyers are generally wary of 'giving anything away' to the other side, however. The prosecution's duties of disclosure are quite extensive, and extend, by statute, to requiring full disclosure of scientific evidence in trials on indictment. Prosecutors normally comply with their disclosure obligations. The defence, on the other hand, is obliged to disclose only scientific evidence that it intends to adduce at trial. A report that merely confirms the prosecution's evidence or finds that the case against the defendant is even *stronger* than the prosecution expert suggested is likely to be suppressed. It is not known whether the more limited scheme of prosecution disclosure introduced by the Criminal Procedure and Investigations Act 1996 has specifically had an impact on scientific evidence, but there are broader concerns that the prosecution may sometimes fail to disclose potentially exculpatory 'unused material', that is, material that the prosecution does not intend to use as part of its own case. (Such failure could be entirely innocent: the prosecutor may not suspect any relevance to the defendant's case.) One thing is clear, however: the consequences of inadequate disclosure can be catastrophic. The failure of prosecution scientists to disclose information which cast doubt on the reliability of their evidence was a significant contributory factor in several of the serious miscarriages of justice which came to light in the 1990s.

If an expert's report is not contested the report itself can be put in evidence at trial, by way of a special exception to the hearsay rule. But if they are required to testify in person, scientific experts are essentially treated like any other witness. Their evidence is led in chief in answer to questions posed by 'their' barrister, and subjected to cross-examination by the barrister for the other side. The artificiality of this process, and the difficulties of effective communication—especially where counsel are ill prepared, as they sometimes are—have already been mentioned. Adversary trial is not well suited to scientific dispute. Experts are called in order to support each party's case, and their evidence will be tailored, through counsel's questions, to appear to do so to the maximum. Few experts are sufficiently skilled as witnesses to be able to withstand this subtle manipulation, and many find the experience of testifying frustrating. Experts frequently say that they were not given adequate opportunity to explain their evidence to the court. A minority of experts, on the other hand, appears to relish the adversary battle, yet this attitude arguably calls into question their objectivity and impartiality as scientists, as does the fact that they are paid for appearing as witnesses. In either case, there is no guarantee that the jury will be given a clear impression of the merits of a dispute. One scientist may be stating the orthodox position assented to by 99.9 per cent of experts in the field, whilst his opponent is spouting a crack-pot theory only credited by the remaining 0.1 per cent. But in court this could look to a jury like one scientist's word against another's. The most brilliant scientist in the land could be made to look foolish by a lawyer's tricky questions, whilst a fool with bravado and a pleasing court manner might appear to the layman to be a scientific genius. It is possible that defence lawyers, in particular, could try to confuse the issue by asking irrelevant questions and exaggerating the significance of residual doubt, though there is no evidence that such practices are widespread. The more likely scenario is that prosecution evidence is simply accepted at face value without being subjected to thorough critical scrutiny.

At this point the inadequacy of English law's regulatory mechanisms is exposed. There is no currently operative scheme of comprehensive and reliable accreditation for scientific experts, and the rules of admissibility are fairly lax. Scientific evidence will be rejected if it appears to the judge, on a broad common-sense view, to be 'unhelpful', and also if it seems to trespass on the jury's role as fact-finder (as does, for example, psychological evidence of witness credibility, which is usually ruled inadmissible). But otherwise scientific evidence is likely to be received. People putting themselves forward as experts do not need any special qualifications, if they can plausibly demonstrate relevant knowledge or experience. In these circumstances it is inevitable that the jury will sometimes be given a misleading impression of scientific knowledge, and that charlatanism and sharp practice will occasionally go undetected. Judges probably have the power to instruct their own scientific experts to advise the court, but there are no standard administrative arrangements for doing so, and court experts are virtually unknown in criminal proceedings. Adversary process being directed and dominated by the parties, there are strong cultural and legal inhibitions on excessive judicial intervention.

THE INQUISITORIAL ALTERNATIVE, FROM A COMMON LAW PERSPECTIVE

The primary objective of inquisitorial criminal process, organized around an official inquiry into past events on the model established by Napoleon's Code, is to discover the truth. In structure this mirrors scientific investigations, and—at least superficially—is more compatible with the precepts of science than adversary pro-ceedings. Criminal investigations are conducted by the police under the supervision of the prosecutor or examining magistrate. Forensic science assistance is organized by prosecutors or judges, as part of the State's investigative responsibility. Scientists and laboratories are likely to be part of the public sector, or at least formally accredited by the State to provide forensic science services. Court experts are the norm. In some systems the parties are not allowed to instruct their own experts. In others, party experts are permitted, but generally given less credence than the officially accredited, judicially-appointed court expert. If scientific evidence were always a matter of incontrovertible objective fact, this would be the perfectly rational system for maxi-mising the instrumental value of science in criminal proceedings. But, as was explained, forensic science evidence is not uniformly or straightforwardly 'objective', any more than criminal justice is a simple function of factual accuracy. In fact, the strengths of the inquisitorial system appear, from a different perspective, as potential weaknesses. They are the mirror image of the forces shaping the production of scientific evidence in adversary proceedings.

So long as government scientists are properly trained, laboratories adequately funded, and expert accreditation awarded on the basis of merit—not rank, respect-ability, or connections—inquisitorial process is well suited to providing courts with impartial, reliable, and conventional scientific advice. Expert evidence will generally be presented in a written report, but if the expert for some reason is required to testify in court, it is the judge who asks the questions, and few constraints will be placed on the scientist's narrative freedom. The communication problems experienced in England and Wales do not appear to arise. There is no risk of experts being corrupted by adversarial bias, and no need to worry about disclosing information or making provision for defence experts to undertake duplicate investigations. The State undertakes the necessary arrangements, and makes the fruits of scientific investigation freely available to both prosecutor and defence lawyer. Since, moreover, there is unlikely to be any dispute about the scientific aspects of the case, problems of interpretation and evaluation are also effectively pre-empted. Judges simply defer to scientists' advice and adopt their conclusions. If this official expert system were felt improperly to exclude less conventional or more *avant garde* varieties of science, it is always possible to broaden the flow of information into court by allowing the parties to call their own experts, in addition to the court's advisors. But the exclusion of *avant garde* science is not necessarily a defect of the court-expert system. At some level, the reception of science into criminal proceedings is *by design* conservatively conventional, because novel scientific discoveries and techniques are insufficiently tried and tested to be relied on as the basis for criminal adjudication.

This model seems to suit continental European jurisdictions, and English lawyers, too, have extolled its virtues. Yet there is a fundamental defect in these arrangements for utilizing forensic science, when viewed from a common law perspective: *scientific evidence is rarely, if ever, challenged or adequately tested*. There are two kinds of reason why it arguably ought to be. The first relates to the reliability of science and its contribution to accurate fact-finding. Scientific progress is made through conjecture and refutation, the testing of hypotheses to destruction, and the incremental evolution of consensus in the wider scientific community. This process requires openness and free debate (as well as a willingness to stick doggedly with apparently crazy theories on the off-chance of being proved right, a valuable trait for a research scientist, but a serious character flaw in an expert witness). To the extent that forensic sciences are typically estranged from the wider circles of scientific research and debate, they start at an immediate disadvantage. There is a danger of evolving forensic sciences as a kind of self-referential, self-validating scientific ghetto, in which bad practice and communal error proliferate. Without external reference points as reality checks on the insider-community of forensic scientists, criminal proceedings risk being exposed to collective delusions masquerading as science; and there is no reason to expect that lawyers, judges, or jurors will reliably distinguish one from the other. Anglo-American experience suggests certain warning signs. Disciplines with small numbers of practitioners, perhaps a handful of committed individuals or a single research group, are especially vulnerable to blind faith in systematic error. Governmental research facilities are similarly prone to bad practice and inferior science in the absence of proper protocols and rigorous external audit, and the more secretive their operation the greater the risk. The forensic work of police labs and military establishments therefore requires especially careful scrutiny. If it is sound to generalize from Anglo-American experience, the organization of forensic sciences in inquisitorial systems could be a breeding ground for complacency and poor-quality scientific evidence. As in the common law world, government labs and accredited scientists are unlikely to have to answer to the standards of the wider scientific community, but nor is their evidence rigorously tested in the course of inquisitorial criminal proceedings. In those jurisdictions that have begun to look harder at the provision and regulation of scientific expertise, such as the Netherlands, there is growing awareness that degenerate science could be a potent causal factor in emergent, as well as thus far undetected, miscarriages of justice.

The second set of reasons for subjecting scientific evidence to challenge and scrutiny is linked to a range of procedural and other values which, though reinforcing truth-finding, also make an independent contribution to the realization of criminal justice. Prominent amongst these concerns is that justice must not only be done but also *seen to be* done, as the saying goes. This is part of reaching legitimate verdicts in which citizens can trust. That criminal proceedings should, so far as possible, be public and transparent is essential. Equally important is that the moral integrity of the criminal process should be upheld by criminal justice professionals who represent the State. To the extent that trust is socially conditioned and culturally variable, so must the detailed prescription for legitimate criminal process vary between jurisdictions. But three general observations can be made with regard to forensic science evidence.

First, adversary process is more likely to be open and transparent than inquisitorial proceedings. Prosecution scientific evidence is re-checked by independent defence examiners, who are not state employees, any more than the defence lawyers who instruct them. Both lawyers and defence examiners should be motivated to scrutinize prosecution evidence carefully in search of weaknesses and potential avenues for challenge. A vigorous culture of defence, though in practice by no means universal, is a legal expectation. At court, prosecution experts are subjected to aggressive questioning in public. Though the truth-finding deficiencies of adversarial examination have been noted, this system of proof-taking is certainly well adapted to forcing the prosecution to provide a meticulous, public demonstration of the defendant's guilt before a conviction can be entered. It compares favourably in this regard with the absence of rigorous evidence-testing typical of inquisitorial process, in which the inner workings of scientific evidence production, and therefore the detailed basis of conviction, remain hidden from view and unavailable for inspection.

Secondly, lay participation, and lay *fact-finding* in particular, is generally speaking of greater significance in common law countries than in Continental inquisitorial jurisdictions. Quite apart from the accuracy of lay fact-finding (which is disputed), trial by jury for serious criminal charges plays an important symbolic role in legitimizing criminal verdicts. In convicting, or acquitting, criminal defendants the jury deliver the verdict of the people more directly than a professional judge or magistrate. English criminal process goes to quite extraordinary lengths to protect a jury's deliberations from scrutiny. Not only are the jury sent away to reach their decision in secret, but courts steadfastly refuse to inspect the evidentiary foundations of a jury's general verdict. 'Guilty' or 'not guilty' is all the judge wants to hear, and it is a contempt of court, itself punishable by imprisonment, to ask or tell what transpired in the jury-room. The rule that expert evidence is admissible only, and just in so far as, it is helpful to the jury is very much in keeping with the symbolic significance of lay participation (as was the older, probably now defunct rule that experts should not testify on 'ultimate issues'). English law cannot bring itself formally to embrace the deference model of receiving expert evidence, because the centrality of jury fact-finding must not be displaced. With no equivalent commitment to lay participation, inquisitorial jurisdictions are free to follow the logic of deference to science. Experts are not mere witnesses, as they are in common law proceedings, but criminal justice professionals with their own unique staus and function.

These first two considerations flow into a third, more general point of comparison. As Damaška first noticed, models of criminal process can be mapped onto discernible contrasts in the structure of political authority. Very crudely, common law countries adopt flat or 'co-ordinate' authority structures in which political power is diffuse, decision-makers have considerable discretion, the State is an object of suspicion, and individual liberty is placed at a premium. Inquisitorial jurisdictions diverge on every point. Authority is 'hierarchical', political power is centralized, decision-makers are (formally) denied discretion through close legal regulation, the State is conceived paternalistically as the repository and executive of the public good, and the overriding objective is effective policy implementation. Of course, these models can be endlessly refined and qualified, and the contrasts they illuminate can be overstated. Yet the models seem to capture something significant and real, not least with regard to forensic science evidence. In adversary proceedings the defendant is in some measure the architect of his own fortunes. If he wants to challenge prosecution evidence, the means are there—or should be provided—for him to do so. He can have his own lawyers and experts re-examine incriminating evidence, and undertake new lines of inquiry, including new scientific testing, in search of exculpation. Defendants in inquisitorial proceedings, by contrast, must place their faith in the competence and probity of state functionaries. Their own role in the production and utilization of scientific evidence is minimal, or non-existent. Citizens are expected to trust, and apparently do trust, that bureaucratic regularities and hierarchical supervision will ferret out the truth, including the scientific truth, of criminal charges. In this way is criminal policy thought most effectively implemented, and criminal justice best achieved.

The account of scientific evidence production developed in this chapter has emphasized the potential pitfalls, as well as the indubitable value, of science in the administration of criminal justice. Each jurisdiction must face up to the common challenges of scientific and other expert evidence in ways that are compatible with local conditions. Investigation of forensic science and expert witnesses inevitably leads one to reconsider the basic legal, political, social, cultural, and moral criteria of criminal justice. The problems of the former cannot be properly understood, let alone addressed, without serious reflection on foundational issues of procedure, process, and justice.

Further Reading

ALLDRIDGE, P., 'Recognising Novel Scientific Techniques: DNA as a Test Case' [1992] *Crim. LR* 687.

—— 'Forensic Science and Expert Evidence' (1994) 21 *Journal of Law and Society* 136.

—— 'Scientific Expertise and Comparative Criminal Procedure' (1999) 3 *Evidence & Proof* 141.

—— BERKHOUT-VAN POELGEEST, S., and WILLIAMS, K., 'DNA Profiling and the Use of Expert Scientific Witnesses in Criminal Proceedings' in P. Fennell, C. Harding, N. Jörg, and B. Swart (eds.), *Criminal Justice in Europe: A Comparative Study* (Oxford: OUP, 1995).

ALLEN, R. J., 'Expertise and the *Daubert* Decision' (1994) 84 *Journal of Criminal Law and Criminology* 1157.

—— and REDMAYNE, M. (eds.), *Bayesianism and Juridical Proof*, Vol .1(6) *Evidence & Proof* Special Issue (London: Blackstone, 1997).

BALDING, D. J., and DONNELLY, P., 'The Prosecutor's Fallacy and DNA Evidence' [1994] *Crim. LR* 711.

BERNSTEIN, D. E., 'Junk Science in the United States and the Commonwealth' (1996) 21 *Yale Journal of International Law* 123.

BLAKEY, D. C., 'Does Forensic Science Give Value for Money?' (1995) 35 *Science and Justice* 1.

CHESEBRO, K. J., 'Galileo's Retort: Peter Huber's Junk Scholarship' (1993) 42 *American University Law Review* 1637.

CONNORS, E., LUNDREGAN, T., MILLER, N., and McEWEN, T., *Convicted by Juries, Exonerated by Science: Case Studies in the Use of DNA Evidence to Establish Innocence After Trial*, NIJ Research Report (US Department of Justice, 1996), on-line via **www.ncjrs.org/**.

DAMAŠKA, M. R., 'Rational and Irrational Proof Revisited' (1997) 5 *Cardozo Journal of International and Comparative Law* 25.

—— *Evidence Law Adrift* (New Haven: Conn.: Yale UP, 1997).

DURSTON, G., *Witchcraft and Witch Trials: A History of English Witchcraft and its Legal Perspectives* (Chichester: Barry Rose, 2000), chaps. 10 and 12–15.

EDMOND, G., 'The Next Step or Moonwalking? Expert Evidence, the Public Understanding of Science and the Case Against Imwinkelried's Didactic Trial Procedures' (1998) 2 *Evidence & Proof* 13.

—— 'Azaria's Accessories: The Social (Legal-Scientific) Construction of the Chamberlains' Guilt and Innocence' (1998) 22 *Melbourne University Law Review* 396.

—— 'Judicial Representations of Scientific Evidence' (2000) 63 *Modern Law Review* 216.

FAIGMAN, D. L., 'To Have and Have Not: Assessing the Value of Social Science to the Law as Science and Policy' (1989) 38 *Emory Law Journal* 1005.

Federal Judicial Center, *Reference Manual on Scientific Evidence* (2nd edn., Washington, DC: FJC, 2000), on-line via **www.fjc.gov**.

Forensic Science Service, *Annual Reports*, on-line via **www.forensic.gov.uk**.

FOSTER, K. R., and HUBER, P. W., *Judging Science: Scientific Knowledge and the Federal Courts* (Cambridge, Mass.: MIT Press, 1999).

FRECKELTON, I. R., *The Trial of the Expert: A Study of Expert Evidence and Forensic Experts* (Melbourne: OUP, 1987).

—— 'Science and the Legal Culture' (1993) 2 *Expert Evidence* 107.

—— 'Contemporary Comment: When Plight Makes Right—The Forensic Abuse Syndrome' (1994) 18 *Criminal Law Journal* 29.

—— 'Repressed Memory Syndrome: Counterintuitive or Counterproductive?' (1996) 20 *Criminal Law Journal* 7.

FREEMAN, M., and REECE, H. (eds.), *Science in Court* (Aldershot: Ashgate, 1998).

FRIEDMAN, R. D., 'Assessing Evidence' (1996) 94 *Michigan Law Review* 1810.

GALLOP, A. M. C., 'Market Forensics' (1994) 34 *Journal of the Forensic Science Society* 121.

GEE, D. J., 'The Expert Witness in the Criminal Trial' [1987] *Crim. LR* 307.

GIANNELLI, P. C., '"Junk Science": The Criminal Cases' (1993) 84 *Journal of Criminal Law and Criminology* 105.

GRAHAM, L., 'Criminal Legal Aid and Expert Witnesses' (1993) 4 *Journal of Forensic Psychiatry* 9.

HODGKINSON, T., *Expert Evidence: Law & Practice* (London: Sweet & Maxwell, 1990).

House of Commons Home Affairs Committee (Chair: Sir John Wheeler), *The Forensic Science Service*, HC Paper 26-I, Session 1988–9 (London: HMSO, 1989).

House of Lords Select Committee on Science and Technology (Chair: Lord Dainton), *Fifth Report: Forensic Science*, HL Paper 24, Session 1992–3 (London: HMSO, 1993).

HOWARD, M. N., 'The Neutral Expert: A Plausible Threat to Justice' [1991] *Crim. LR* 98.

HUBER, P. W., *Galileo's Revenge: Junk Science in the Courtroom* (New York: Basic Books, 1991).

IMWINKELREID, E. J., 'The Next Step in Conceptualizing the Presentation of Expert Evidence as Education: The Case for Didactic Trial Procedures' (1997) 1 *Evidence & Proof* 128

IRVING, B., 'Independent Expert Advice' (1991) 2 *Journal of Forensic Psychiatry* 242.

JASANOFF, S., *Science at the Bar: Law, Science and Technology in America* (Cambridge, Mass.: Harvard UP, 1997).

JONES, C. A. G., *Expert Witnesses: Science, Medicine and the Practice of Law* (Oxford: OUP, 1994).

JUSTICE (Chair: Judge Christopher Oddie), *Science and the Administration of Justice* (London: JUSTICE, 1991).

KENNY, A., 'The Expert in Court' (1983) 99 *Law Quarterly Review* 197.

Learned Hand, 'Historical and Practical Considerations Regarding Expert Testimony' (1901) 15 *Harvard Law Review* 40.

LEWIN, J. L., 'Calabresi's Revenge? Junk Science in the Work of Peter Huber' (1992) 21 *Hofstra Law Review* 183.

MACKAY, R. D., and COLMAN, A. M., 'Equivocal Rulings on Expert Psychological and Psychiatric Evidence: Turning a Muddle into a Nonsense' [1996] *Crim. LR* 88.

—— 'Excluding Expert Evidence: A Tale of Ordinary Folk and Common Experience' [1991] *Crim. LR* 800.

MAY, SIR JOHN, *Second Report on the Maguire Case*, HC Paper 296, Session 1992–3 (London: HMSO, 1992).

MOENSSENS, A. A., 'Novel Scientific Evidence in Criminal Cases: Some Words of Caution' (1993) 84 *Journal of Criminal Law and Criminology* 1.

—— STARRS, J. E., HENDERSON, C. E., and INBAU, F., *Scientific Evidence in Civil and Criminal Cases* (4th edn., New York: Foundation Press, 1995).

MOSTELLER, R. P., 'Syndromes and Politics in Criminal Trials and Evidence Law' (1996) 46 *Duke Law Journal* 461.

NESSON, C., 'The Evidence or the Event? On Judicial Proof and the Acceptability of Verdicts' (1985) 98 *Harvard Law Review* 1357.

NORRIS, J., and EDWARDS, M., 'Myths, Hidden Facts and Common Sense: Expert Opinion Evidence and the Assessment of Credibility' (1995) 38 *Criminal Law Quarterly* 73.

Note, 'Developments in the Law: Confronting the New Challenges of Scientific Evidence' (1995) 108 *Harvard Law Review* 1481.

ORMEROD, D., 'The Evidential Implications of Psychological Profiling' [1996] *Crim. LR* 863.

ORMROD, SIR ROGER, 'Scientific Evidence in Court' [1968] *Crim. LR* 240.

PEREIRA, M., 'Forensic Sciences: Our Changing World' (1993) 33 *Journal of the Forensic Science Society* 117.

PHILLIPS, J. H., and BOWEN, J. K., *Forensic Science and the Expert Witness* (Sydney: Law Book Co., 1985).

RAITT, F. E., and ZEEDYK, M. S., 'Rape Trauma Syndrome: Its Corroborative and Educational Roles' (1997) 24 *Journal of Law and Society* 552.

RAMSAY, M., *The Effectiveness of the Forensic Science Service*, Home Office Research Study No. 92 (London: HMSO, 1987).

REDER, P., LUCEY, C., and FELLOW-SMITH, E., 'Surviving Cross-Examination in Court' (1993) 4 *Journal of Forensic Psychiatry* 489.

REDMAYNE, M., 'The Royal Commission's Proposals on Expert Evidence: A Critique' (1994) 2 *Expert Evidence* 157.

—— 'Doubts and Burdens: DNA Evidence, Probability and the Courts' [1995] *Crim. LR* 464.

—— 'Expert Evidence and Scientific Disagreement' (1997) 30 *UC Davis Law Review* 1027.

—— 'Presenting Probabilities in Court: The DNA Experience' (1997) 1 *Evidence & Proof* 187.

—— 'The DNA Database: Civil Liberty and Evidentiary Issues' [1998] *Crim. LR* 437.

—— *Expert Evidence and Criminal Justice* (Oxford: OUP, 2001).

REECE, H. (ed.), *Law and Science: Current Legal Issues Volume 1* (Oxford: OUP, 1998).

ROBERTS, P., 'Science in the Criminal Process' (1994) 14 *Oxford Journal of Legal Studies* 469.

—— 'Forensic Science Evidence After Runciman' [1994] *Crim. LR* 780.

—— '"Will You Stand Up in Court?" On the Admissibility of Psychiatric and Psychological Evidence' (1996) 7 *Journal of Forensic Psychiatry* 63.

—— 'What Price a Free Market in Forensic Science Services? The Organization and Regulation of Science in the Criminal Process' (1996) 36 *British Journal of Criminology* 37.

—— 'Tyres with a "Y": An English Perspective on *Kumho Tire* and Its Implications for the Admissibility of Expert Evidence' *International Commentary on Evidence*, www.law.qub.ac.uk/ice/, posted 2 July 1999.

—— and WILLMORE, C., *The Role of Forensic Science Evidence in Criminal Proceedings*, RCCJ Research Study No. 11 (London: HMSO, 1993).

ROBERTSON, B., and VIGNAUX, G. A., *Interpreting Evidence: Evaluating Forensic Science in the Courtroom* (Chichester: Wiley, 1995).

—— —— and EGERTON, I., 'Stylometric Evidence' [1994] *Crim. LR* 645.

Royal Commission on Criminal Justice (Chair: Lord Runciman), *Report*, Cm 2263 (1993), chap. 9.

SCHUCK, P. H., 'Multi-Culturalism Redux: Science, Law and Politics' (1993) 11 *Yale Law and Policy Review* 1.

SMITH, R., and WYNNE, B. (eds.), *Expert Evidence: Interpreting Science in the Law* (London: Routledge, 1989).

SPENCER, J. R., 'The Neutral Expert: An Implausible Bogey' [1991] *Crim. LR* 106.

—— 'Court Experts and Expert Witnesses: Have We A Lesson to Learn From the French?' [1992] *Current Legal Problems* 213.

STARRS, J. E., 'In the Land of Agog: An Allegory for the Expert Witness' (1985) 30 *Journal of Forensic Sciences* 289.

STEVENTON, B., *The Ability to Challenge DNA Evidence*, RCCJ Research Study No. 9 (London: HMSO, 1993).

—— 'Statistical Evidence and the Courts—Recent Developments' (1998) 62 *Journal of Criminal Law* 176.

THAYER, J. B., *A Preliminary Treatise on Evidence at the Common Law* (Boston, Mass.: Little, Brown & Co, 1898), chap. 1.

THOMPSON, W. C., 'Evaluating the Admissibility of New Genetic Identification Tests: Lessons from the "DNA War"' (1993) 84 *Journal of Criminal Law and Criminology* 22.

TILLEY, N., and FORD, A., *Forensic Science and Crime Investigation*, Crime Detection and Prevention Series Paper 73 (London: Home Office Police Research Group, 1996), on-line via **www.homeoffice.gov.uk/prgpubs.htm**.

TRIBE, L. H., 'Trial By Mathematics: Precision and Ritual in the Legal Process' (1971) 84 *Harvard Law Review* 1329 [and see, further (1971) 84 *Harvard Law Review* 1801].

VALVERDE, M., 'Social Facticity and the Law: A Social Expert's Eyewitness Account of Law' (1996) 5 *Social and Legal Studies* 201.

VAN KAMPEN, P., *Expert Evidence Compared: Rules and Practices in the Dutch and American Criminal Justice System* (Antwerp: Intersentia, 1998).

WALKER, C., and STOCKDALE, R., 'Forensic Evidence' in C. Walker and K. Starmer (eds.), *Miscarriages of Justice: A Review of Justice in Error* (London: Blackstone, 1999).

16

MAGISTRATES

*Penny Darbyshire**

The English legal system is unique, in that around 97 per cent[1] of defendants to criminal charges have their cases disposed of in courts where most cases are adjudicated upon by lay justices. They sit in twos or threes[2] and are also known as lay magistrates or Justices of the Peace. The minority of cases are dealt with by professional magistrates, now called district judges (magistrates' courts)[3] and formerly known as stipendiary magistrates (hereafter DJMCs). They sit alone or, occasionally, with two justices. As magistrates are judges of fact and law and they do the sentencing, they perform the functions of both judge and jury in the Crown Court, and this makes English lay magistrates uniquely powerful, when compared with lay decision-makers in other jurisdictions.

Additionally, most defendants disposed of by the Crown Court are committed there by magistrates. Virtually all young offenders are tried by magistrates in the youth court.[4] Magistrates also have a significant civil jurisdiction, especially in family cases and, in most areas, they administer liquor and entertainment licensing.

Lay people are used in many jurisdictions in various forms, as jurors, taking decisions of fact on the evidence alone, or lay assessors sitting in a mixed bench with one or more professional judges, where they are generally arbiters of fact.[5] The most obvious advantage of including lay people as decision-makers of fact is that they represent the community both symbolically and in fact. The advantages and disadvantages of lay and professional justice or a mixed bench are discussed at length below.

Issues raised in relation to magistrates are the importance of magistrates' case-loads; the desirability of having most cases adjudicated upon by laypeople; the problem of recruiting lay justices who are sufficiently representative of the community; determining an appropriate system of training; the role of the clerk; and the desirability of localized justice.

---

* Full citations for all books and articles cited in this chapter can be found in the Bibliography and Further Reading section.

[1] For discussion of this statistic and an expansion of the discussion of magistrates' importance raised below, see Darbyshire, 1997b.

[2] 1995 Rules.

[3] Renamed by the Access to Justice Act 1999.

[4] Explained in Chap. 13 of this book.

[5] For a brief outline of their use in many different jurisdictions, see Vogler, discussed below.

THE IMPORTANCE OF THE MAGISTRACY[6]

Despite the typification of the English criminal trial as by judge and jury, juries hear under 1 per cent of criminal cases. Only around 5 per cent of sentencing is done by judges. For centuries, criminal business has been shifting down from the higher courts, but that trend accelerated significantly in the twentieth century. When new offences are created, they may be made either 'summary' (i.e. they are to be dealt with by magistrates sitting without a jury) or are made triable either summarily or before a jury, thus guaranteeing they will mostly be heard by magistrates. Magistrates can now deal with causing death by aggravated vehicle taking, all but the most serious assaults, most sex offences, most burglaries, thefts, frauds, and forgeries, arson, all drugs offences, perjury, betting and gaming offences, and most firearms offences. Prosecutors prefer to bring cases in the magistrates' court because proceedings are much cheaper and the conviction rate is higher. Similar trends can be seen in other jurisdictions.[7] The result of all this is that some very serious cases are heard by magistrates but tend to be trivialized because professionals and the public think magistrates deal only with trivia.

THE IMAGE OF THE MAGISTRACY IN POPULAR RHETORIC AND THE LAW

The symbolic function of the jury far outweighs its practical use. In rhetorical descriptions it is portrayed as central to the English legal system and an essential guarantee of democracy. Jury trial, in the Anglo-American hyperbole, is the only fair means of trial.[8] Historically, jury trial was a much more common form of trial. Despite its factual decline, the jury is still portrayed as the normal way of dealing with criminal cases. The media concentrate on jury trials. They are much longer and more sensational and conducted in the melodramatic setting of the Crown Court. Not surprisingly, if members of the public are asked to describe a court, they will describe the Crown Court.[9] 'The public know little about how the magistracy works ... [and] hugely underestimate the proportion of cases heard in the lower courts'.[10] That they glean this image from the media is not surprising. It should be obvious, however, that 97 per cent of criminal cases includes some very serious matters.[11]

Lawyers and judges share this misapprehension. Textbooks concentrate on jury trial, so lawyers are educated in ignorance of magistrates' courts and mistakes in law and socio-legal books are legion. In developing criminal law and procedure, Royal

---

[6] For lengthy discussion see Darbyshire, n. 1 above.   [7] *Ibid.*

[8] See Darbyshire, 1991, for an examination of this rhetoric and its basis in fact.

[9] Genn, 1999.

[10] Sanders, 2001.

[11] Darbyshire, n. 1 above.

Commissions, Parliament, and the Law Commission[12] act as if jury trial were routine. Judges of the House of Lords, Court of Appeal, and High Court, in developing the common law, make the same mistake. Most of them are ex-barristers and have no experience of magistrates' courts. This causes two types of problem: first, when Parliament legislates to introduce new procedures such as statutory pre-trial disclosure or prosecution appeals on sentencing, it is unwittingly catering for only a tiny fraction of cases, and when judges develop the common law to apply to judge and jury, where the division of responsibilities is clear, the principles are not easy to apply in magistrates' courts, where the magistrates are judges of both fact and law, including the admissibility of evidence.[13]

LAY MAGISTRATES OR PROFESSIONALS?

Because the English legal system is so ancient and its institutions have evolved through piecemeal changes since before 1066, we seldom see the need to justify its institutions in comparison with alternatives. Justices have been commissioned to keep the monarch's peace in their locality since 1195, over five centuries before the rise of the legal professions and before the police were created. Stipendiary, professional, magistrates did not emerge until the eighteenth century. They were introduced into London because of corruption among Justices of the Peace and because of the lack of police force.[14] From 1964 until the 1990s they had the same jurisdiction as justices and this is still virtually the case. There is not a shred of logic in the division of work between them. Owing to its history, Inner London has most of its cases tried by professsionals, sitting alone and who have normally been advised by a professionally qualified clerk. By contrast, in Outer London and the provinces, most cases are still heard by lay justices, many of whom are advised by an unqualified clerk.[15] Stipendiaries were appointed to a particular area to meet perceived local need, normally in metropolitan areas with a large case-load but sometimes in rural areas, where they sat with two justices. Only after the Access to Justice Act 1999 were they made into a single stipendiary bench, each one having jurisdiction throughout England and Wales. At the time of writing (January 2002) there are ninety-eight fulltime professionals (DJMCs) and 166 lawyers who sit part-time, as deputies. All are lawyers of seven years' standing. Lay justices have for years expressed an anxiety that this move to a national bench, plus a recent growth in DJMC numbers, betrays a secret plot by the

---

[12] Darbyshire, 1997a.

[13] For a discussion of the problem that magistrates must rule on the admissibility of evidence that they must then hear or ignore at trial, and a general critique that the law of evidence was designed for jury trial, see *ibid*.

[14] Skyrme, 1979, p. 166, quoting R. M. Jackson, *The Machinery of Justice in England* (7th edn., Cambridge: Cambridge University Press, 1977). For a comprehensive examination of the history of magistrates see Skyrme, 1994.

[15] By unqualified I mean some court clerks have no academic qualifications whatsoever. For discussion of clerks' qualifications see below and Darbyshire, 1997c and 1999.

Lord Chancellor to replace them, despite repeated reassurances by him[16] and his predecessor, Lord Mackay, that no government could afford to replace lay justices with professionals, even if it wanted to. History shows that justices have articulated this fear since at least 1970.[17] The fear is probably fuelled by legal journalists and lawyers who would like to see them replaced,[18] but is unfounded, I suggest, for these reasons:

1. Justices point to the growing numbers of professional magistrates, forgetting that lay justices' numbers have also increased year upon year and forgetting that the numbers of stipendiaries went down between the 1940s and 1970s.

2. Each justice now sits far more often than before. Since 1949, justices are required to sit a minimum of twenty-six times a year but they sit, on average, around forty-one times a year.[19] In 1948, over 65 per cent of justices sat fewer than twenty-six times and 10 per cent did not sit at all.[20]

3. If only they had a sense of their own history, justices would realize that, far from declining in importance, over the last three centuries most criminal business has devolved onto their shoulders so that they and, latterly, a handful of professionals have taken over the role of judge and jury.[21]

4. As they have been told repeatedly by Lord Chancellors, and this is now confirmed by Morgan and Russell (2000), they are much cheaper to run than a fully professional bench.

5. Auld LJ's *Criminal Courts Review* (2001), dismissing this rumour of a hidden agenda, gives very firm support to the continued use of lay justices in their current jurisdiction and, indeed, suggests an additional role for them, in a mixed bench with professional judges with greater sentencing powers, to deal with criminal offences of medium seriousness.

The last time a Royal Commission articulated the value of lay justices as opposed to stipendiaries was 1948:

[L]ike that of trial by jury, it gives the citizen a part to play in the administration of the law. It emphasizes the fact that the principles of the common law, and even the language of statutes, ought to be . . . comprehensible by any intelligent person without specialized training. Its continuance prevents the growth of a suspicion in the ordinary man's mind that the law is a mystery which must be left to a professional caste and has little in common with justice as the layman understands it. Further, the cases in which decisions on questions of fact in criminal cases are left to one man ought to be, as they now are, exceptional.[22]

---

[16] E.g. speech to the Magistrates' Association, 30 Oct. 1999 and press releases 349/99 and 351/99, Nov. 1999, both on the LCD website, **www.open-gov.uk.**

[17] Skyrme, n. 14 above, 167. See a modern example, T. Skyrme, 'The Magistracy Under Threat' (1998) 162 *JP* 804.

[18] E.g. editorials (1991) 141 *NLJ* 409, (1998) 148 *NLJ* 541, many later editorials and lawyers cited in Darbyshire, n. 1 above.

[19] Morgan and Russell, 2000.

[20] Royal Commission on Justices of the Peace 1946–48, *Report*, at 7.

[21] Darbyshire, n. 1 above.   [22] At 55.

Four recent academic publications compared the role and function of professional and lay magistrates and/or their value as adjudicators.

Doran and Glenn, commissioned to examine *Lay Involvement in Adjudication* for the review of the criminal justice system in Northern Ireland, provide a very useful survey of issues raised in debate between supporters and detractors of the principle of lay participation which can, in turn, be summarized as follows:

1. *The right of participation in the adjudicative process.* Every person has an equal right to participate in matters of general concern. Lay participants are more representative of the local community than professionals, and establish a link between the courts and local affairs. On the other hand, it is sometimes pointed out that, in practice, some members of the community are excluded from participation and lay adjudicators are a social elite.

2. *The personality of the participants.* '[O]n a general level, it is argued that lay participants possess an informal and experiential body of knowledge gleaned from the local environs of the courtroom, whereas professional participants possess formal technical knowledge acquired through structured legal education and professional training.'[23] The problems with this are whether participants are truly local, whether 'local knowledge' sits happily with the concept of acting as a neutral arbiter, and whether participants will encounter defendants outside the courtroom in an embarrassing or dangerous context. The argument that the professionals' training makes them superior can be countered by training lay participants, but that causes difficulty if the fact that they lack the advantages of legal education lies at the heart of the rationale for lay participation.[24]

3. *The process of participation.* The first argument here relates to the issues being decided. It is said to be safe to entrust minor matters to lay participants because they are legally advised and because the guilty plea rate is high. The problem with this argument, however, is that it trivializes the work of the lower courts and, as I have pointed out above, English and Welsh magistrates are not confined to trivia, as are lay magistrates in other jurisdictions.[25] It is also argued that lay involvement injects realism and popular values into decision-making so that law and legal procedure become less mysterious. Further, lay people are said to be cheaper, more flexible, and less case-hardened and their reasoning based on reasonableness, equity, and fairness. There are problems with these arguments. There is no evidence that the law is kept less complex by the presence of lay persons on the bench. Those who sit regularly may become just as case-hardened as professionals. The vague form of reasoning of lay people produces inconsistent decisions and regional disparities that are less susceptible to review, create uncertainty, and diminish public confidence.

---

[23] Doran and Glenn, at 11.

[24] The phrase comes from Bankowski, Hutton, and McManus.

[25] For a contemporary survey of how lay justices are used in other jurisdictions, see Morgan and Russell, n. 19 above.

Professionals are said to be more consistent and procedurally correct. On the other hand, some say that professionals can be inflexible, legalistic, detached from the community, and less sympathetic with arguments raised before them.[26]

Auld LJ, in his 2001 *Review of the Criminal Courts of England and Wales*, outlined the value of the system of lay justices as he saw it:

As with juries, magistrates are not wholly reflective of the communities from which they are drawn, but nevertheless they have an important symbolic effect of lay participation in the system which should not be under-valued. Unlike juries, they are volunteers who bring to their work public spirited commitment and ever increasing legal and procedural knowledge and experience. Their vulnerability to case hardening—in a way that juries are not—is off-set by a number of factors, namely: the relative infrequency of their sitings; the discipline that comes from their training; their sitting in ever changing panels; the advantage of a clerk to advise them on the law; and their obligation to explain their decisions. However, there is scope for improvement, particularly in the manner of their recruitment, so as to achieve a better reflection, nationally and locally, of the community, and in their training, so as to develop fairer, more efficient and more consistent procedures and sentencing patterns.

On the other hand, he thought the value of District Judges lay in their legal expertise.[27]

In research reported in *The Role and Appointment of Stipendiary Magistrates* (1995), Seago, Walker, and Wall aimed to examine the function of stipendiaries. They found:

1. Very few courts had rules for allocating work to stipendiaries.

2. There was a striking difference between the work of stipendiaries on the one hand and acting stipendiaries on the other, who were kept away from more legally and evidentially complex cases allocated to the former, especially provincial ones.

3. Metropolitan stipendiaries (Inner London) appeared to hear contested cases almost twice as quickly as provincial stipendiaries.

4. Most of their judicial work was everyday cases but they also heard long trials (especially those lasting more than a day) or complex or highly publicized trials and they had a heavier case-load than lay justices.

5. Stipendiaries dealt with all types of work more speedily than lay justices. One provincial stipendiary could replace thirty-two justices and one metropolitan stipendiary could replace twenty-four justices.

In discussing the future role of stipendiaries, the authors suggested that pressure on the Crown Court could be relieved. 'Consideration could be given to an enhanced jurisdiction (up to two to three years' imprisonment) for a trial tribunal consisting of a stipendiary and two lay magistrates'.[28]

---

[26] For further interesting discussion on alternative models for justifying the lay magistracy, see Dignan and Wynne, 1997.

[27] At 98.   [28] At 145, and see their 2000 article.

In 2000, major research was undertaken for the Home Office and Lord Chancellor's Department. It is reported in *The Judiciary in Magistrates' Courts* by Morgan and Russell. Its aims were to investigate the balance of lay and professional magistrates and the arguments in favour of that balance. Apart from the findings on composition, below, they were:

1. Lay justices sat on 41.4 occasions per year on average. (The required minimum is twenty-six days.) Additionally, they spent a full working week on training and other duties. They sat in threes, except in 16 per cent of cases, when they sat in pairs.

2. All professionals sat in court around four days a week. They rarely sat with lay justices.

3. Work allocation was the same as found by Seago *et al*. Stipendiaries' time was concentrated on triable-either-way rather than summary cases.

4. Stipendiaries heard 22 per cent more appearances than lay justices. If their case-loads were identical, they could deal with 30 per cent more appearances.

5. Stipendiary hearings involved more questioning and challenging.

6. Stipendiaries showed more command over proceedings and would challenge parties responsible for delay. People applied for fewer adjournments and were less likely to be granted them.

7. Lay justices were less likely to refuse bail or use imprisonment as a sentence.

8. Court users had more confidence in stipendiaries. They were seen as more efficient, consistent in decisions, asking appropriate questions, and as giving clear reasons.

9. Lay justices were more often judged better at showing courtesy, using simple language, and showing concern to distressed victims. Lawyers admitted to preparing better for stipendiaries.

10. Few members of the public had heard there were different types of magistrate. Most thought lay justices would be better at representing the views of the community and sympathizing with defendants' circumstances but that stipendiaries were better at making decisions on guilt and innocence.

11. One stipendiary could replace thirty justices. Doubling stipendiary numbers would cut down court appearances but increase the prison population. The net cost would be about £23 million per year.

In 2000–1 the Institute for Public Policy Research commissioned a MORI public opinion poll on the magistracy and then asked Andrew Sanders to compare the skills and experience which lay and professional magistrates bring to the bench. His 2001 paper, *Community Justice—Modernising the Magistracy in England and Wales* reports the following:

The MORI poll found a third of respondents did not know that the majority of magistrates were lay people and hugely underestimated the proportion of cases heard by magistrates. Only 29 per cent thought magistrates did a good job and 61 per cent thought they were out of touch. 49 per cent were unhappy that magistrates were legally untrained. 42 per cent would be more confident in a mixed panel, and 52 per cent when dealing with more serious offences.

Sanders concludes that the skills of both professional and lay magistrates, sitting as a mixed bench, are needed in deciding complex cases, legal skills to apply the relevant law to the facts, social skills to assess character and judge honesty, and managerial and administrative skills. Panel decision-making is preferable to sole decision-making. Justice should be transparent and accountable. This is promoted by lay participation. Public confidence needs to be safeguarded and increased.

MIXED BENCHES

The Bar Council recommended to the 1948 Royal Commission that a number of itinerant stipendiaries be created to chair benches with lay justices on a circuit system. While the Royal Commission rejected this recommendation, much to the regret of Williams, in 1955, they found some stipendiaries already sat regularly with justices and this circuit system was adopted in certain localities. For instance, in the 1970s, six peripatetic stipendiaries were located in Cardiff and travelled around the South Wales courts sitting as a mixed bench with two justices.[29] The mixed bench is still in use, occasionally, in some magistrates' courts and especially in youth courts and family panels. As mentioned above, it was briefly suggested as a new middle tier of criminal court by Seago, Walker, and Wall and the introduction of such a tier, with enhanced sentencing powers, is favoured by Auld LJ who completed a review of the criminal process of England and Wales in October 2001. He recommended this mixed bench as the middle tier of a unified criminal court.[30] In 1997[31] I briefly examined the use of mixed tribunals in other contexts. I pointed out that they hear criminal cases in some foreign jurisdictions and that in England and Wales over 100 sets of specialist mixed tribunals hear civil cases and appeals from administrative decisions. Further, lay justices in England and Wales are used to sitting with circuit judges in the Crown Court to hear appeals from magistrates' courts. Morgan and Russell provide a list of the use of mixed benches worldwide but neither they nor I mentioned something very significant in contrasting them with English and Welsh lay justices: that the lay participants in most of these mixed benches are often much more like jurors than lay justices. For instance, in Germany, laypeople may be called to adjudicate for a period of years but may expect to sit on only three or four trials in, say, a two-year period. I warned, however, that there were two obvious problems with mixed benches. The lay justices may defer to the professional and, if such a tribunal is to deal with longer trials, this may present difficulties in recruiting justices, taking time out from their normal occupations to sit for over a day. Auld LJ considered some of the research available on

---

[29] I observed such sittings while studying the role of the clerk for *The Magistrates' Clerk*.

[30] *Report of the Review of the Criminal Courts of England and Wales*, 2001. Auld LJ quoted the items by me and Seago, Walker, and Wall and Sanders, n. 10 above, discussed here.

[31] P. Darbyshire, 'An Essay on the Importance and Neglect of the Magistracy' [1997] *Crim. LR* 623.

the functioning of such mixed tribunals, such as that of Ivkovic.[32] The functioning of mixed tribunals and the relationship between the participants was considered briefly by Doran and Glenn, who conclude:

The prevailing view is that the professional member typically wields a more powerful influence than the lay participants, in spite of the numerical advantage of the latter . . . in terms of interventions in the course of the proceedings and in terms of influence on decisions on both sentencing and guilt, the contribution of the lay members was clearly more limited in practice than the theory of equal participation would suggest.[33]

Morgan and Russell, however, conclude that there is no consistent pattern to be discerned from research on mixed tribunals. For instance Ivkovic's summary of research on Eastern bloc models shows varying levels of participation, and her own research in Croatia found lay members had some but little influence.[34] Anderson concluded lay assessors in Denmark were highly influential and were substantially influential in Finnish mixed tribunals. As I suggested in 1997, if the model is to be imported into the English legal system, then it will be necessary to guard against domination by the professional by fully training them in their proper roles and by ensuring they keep to the structured decision-making which magistrates are encouraged to employ. In 2001, the comparativist scholar Vogler produced a powerful argument against mixed benches. He argued that the mixed tribunal was the trial court of choice of authoritarian regimes around the world, for instance, in the British colonies, the Stalinist regime in Russia, Maoist China, and Nazi Germany, with lay decision-makers performing the function of legitimizing the decision of the state-appointed judge in a purely symbolic manner. He claims that the available research evidence from other jurisdictions is that the functional role of the lay participants in a mixed bench is virtually nil, because lay judges do not have access to the same pre-trial information as the judge and seldom ask questions. There is no evidence, he says, of genuine panel decision-making because lay participants are inevitably overawed by the superior knowledge of their professional colleague(s). While I bow to Vogler's superior knowledge of the literature, my instant response is that he is not comparing like with like. In all of the regimes he describes, the lay assessors are more like or are, effectively, jurors. Indeed he quotes a French juror as saying they defer to the judge because they are newcomers. By contrast, Auld LJ insists that only experienced lay justices should participate in mixed tribunals and, as I said before, the danger of lay domination by the judge is so obvious, it should be the focus of training for both types of participant. Vogler fails to acknowledge that, as demonstrated by the research discussed here, benches of mixed magistrates already sit habitually in certain parts of the country in the adult courts and the Youth Court, and the Crown Court is composed of a mixed bench when hearing appeals. Further, although he mentions the use of mixed benches in tribunals, he fails to acknowledge that there is no research finding and indeed no anecdotal evidence of lawyer domination in over 100 sets of tribunals.

[32] As cited by me in 1997b and by Doran and Glenn and Morgan and Russell.

[33] At 44. For further reading on mixed tribunals already in existence, see items listed in Doran and Glenn's footnotes, n. 23 above.

[34] Morgan and Russell, n. 19 above, give her the wrong gender.

Since Vogler wrote, the Leggatt Report 2001[35] on tribunals has been published and, given the thorough nature of the Review, it is striking that no hint of such a problem was exposed by it. Nevertheless, Vogler's point that laypeople will defer to the professional when the latter has more knowledge of the case must be taken seriously. Auld LJ has suggested that evidentiary issues be decided by the judge prior to trial and that the justices should take no part in sentencing. Both suggestions would, I suggest, carry the danger to which Vogler alludes and should therefore be resisted.[36]

The Justices' Clerks' Society provoked the wrath of the Magistrates' Association in 2000, when, in its submission to Auld's Criminal Courts Review, it criticized the weaknesses of the lay magistracy and suggested they (justices' clerks) chair benches. This suggestion is, I suggest, unrealistic, as there would be a conflict with their advisory role (see below) and as there are only 133 justices' clerks to supervise the legal advice given to over 30,000 justices.[37]

THE PROBLEM OF RECRUITING LAY JUSTICES WHO REPRESENT THE COMMUNITY[38]

Lay justices are appointed by the Crown on the advice of the Lord Chancellor (or the Chancellor of the Duchy of Lancaster, in Lancashire, Greater Manchester, and Merseyside). The country is divided into areas. Each area has a Commission from the Crown which gives authority to those appointed as magistrates.[39] Magistrates must live within fifteen miles of its boundaries. They must be adults under 65 on appointment but need not be British citizens, unlike jurors. The Lord Chancellor (LC) or Chancellor of the Duchy (CD) receive recommendations for appointment from 109 advisory committees. They are composed mainly of magistrates but the LC now requires that a third are non-magistrates. Any adult can apply to be a magistrate. Qualities required by the LC are 'good character, understanding and communication, social awareness, maturity and sound temperament, sound judgment and commitment and reliability'.[40]

All candidates undergo a two-stage interviewing process, which is meant to ascertain whether they possess these necessary qualities and judicial aptitude. The committee must have regard to the number of vacancies and the 'Lord Chancellor requires that each bench should broadly reflect the community it serves in terms of gender, ethnic origin, geographical spread, occupation and political affiliation'.[41]

---

[35] *Report of the Review of Tribunals*, 2001.   [36] Vogler, 2001.

[37] See editorial (2000) 150 *NLJ* 1251 and the letter from Kevin McCormac, JCS President (2000) 164 *JP* 800.

[38] For discussion see Darbyshire, 1997c.

[39] See 'How to Become a Magistrate' and *Judicial Appointments Annual Report 1999–2000*, LCD website, **www.open.gov.uk/lcd**, chap. 5, summarizing the Lord Chancellor's Directions for Advisory Committees on Justices of the Peace (1998).

[40] See detail on the website and *Lord Chancellor's Directions for Advisory Committees on Justices of the Peace*, n. 39 above.

[41] *Ibid.*, para. 8.1.

Lay justices receive no remuneration. They are, however, entitled to travelling expenses and to certain subsistence payments and a loss of earnings allowance, but this allowance by no means compensates those who operate small businesses. Few justices claim their allowances.[42]

CRITICISM OF THE APPOINTMENT SYSTEM

The overwhelming problem with the magistracy is its lack of diversity. District Judges are appointed directly by the Lord Chancellor, in an annual selection process. Like the rest of the professional judiciary, they are over-representative of white males, and the same criticisms are made of their system of selection as of the judiciary generally.[43] As for lack of diversity in the lay bench, some say that this is partly caused by the fact that magistrates select new magistrates, although the 2000 report of the Lord Chancellor's Equality Working Group contests this (see below). Even the Magistrates' Association called this appointment system a 'self-perpetuating oligarchy'.[44] Committees are given no advertising budget, and only now are they being systematically trained in interview techniques. They occasionally advertise for applicants in local media. They also circulate local political and community organizations.[45] In the light of some of these criticisms, the Lord Chancellor's Department ran the first national recruitment campaign in 1999. It aimed to destroy the stereotype that magistrates are white and middle class.

THE PROBLEM OF ACHIEVING A BALANCED BENCH

Successive Lord Chancellors have boasted that the magistracy represents the community. This is not the case. Like many before me, I have argued, using the support of statistics and research, that it is predominantly Conservative, white, and middle class.[46] Unlike others, I am also concerned that magistrates are too old. For the most modern analysis, see Morgan and Russell. The Lord Chancellor's Department is currently trying to computerize records of all lay justices, with the aim of giving a profile of their balance in terms of gender, ethnic origin, politics, geographical spread, and occupation. By the time of the *Judicial Appointments Annual Report of 2000–2001*, they had profiled most in terms only of gender, politics, and ethnic origin.

---

[42] Morgan and Russell, n. 19 above.

[43] For detailed examination of these criticisms, see P. Darbyshire, *Eddey and Darbyshire on the English Legal System* (London: Sweet & Maxwell, 2001).

[44] In its evidence to the House of Commons Home Affairs Committee for its Third Report 1995–6, *Judicial Appointments Procedures*, as cited in Darbyshire, n. 38 above.

[45] For an expansion of this critique see *ibid.*.

[46] *Ibid.*

AGE

'In theory, you can become a magistrate at 21. In practice nobody is ever appointed before 27', said the late Rosemary Thomson, then Chairman of the Magistrates' Association, in evidence to the Home Affairs Committee investigation of judicial appointment procedures, in 1995–6.[47] In 2000, Morgan and Russell found that only 4 per cent of justices were under 40, a third are in their 60s (they must retire at 70), and two-fifths have retired from full-time employment. They confirmed my 1997 argument that older justices sit on the bench more often than younger ones, thus further skewing the bench towards the elderly. I argued that since the peak age of offending is around 18 for males and 15 for females, this makes a double generation difference between the bench and the accused, and this is in stark contrast to the Scottish youth panels, where panel members may not be much older than offenders. Since I articulated this criticism in 1997, the Lord Chancellor has made it clear that the age imbalance of the bench does not concern him. Indeed, he has raised the maximum age for new magistrates from 60 to 65, in the hope of achieving a more socially balanced bench.[48] Maybe the only thing to be said of the present age distribution is that it is an improvement on 1948, when 65 per cent of male justices were over 60 and 28 per cent over 70.[49] DJMCs are younger, according to Morgan and Russell, with over half being 45–54. According to the 2000–2001 *Judicial Appointments Annual Report*, of the 24,771 lay justices outside the Duchy of Lancaster, only 4 per cent of justices are under 40 and almost 78 per cent are over 50 and 31 per cent over 60.

SOCIAL CLASS/OCCUPATION

In 1910, the Royal Commission on the Selection of Justices of the Peace declared 'it is in the public interest that persons of every social grade should be appointed Justices of the Peace',[50] and this was endorsed by the 1948 Royal Commission and by most twentieth-century Lord Chancellors. Despite such hopes, successive studies[51] have shown a bias towards the middle classes and certain occupational groups, and this was confirmed by Morgan and Russell, who found the magistracy to be 'overwhelmingly drawn from managerial and professional ranks'.[52] Various reasons have been identified for this. People who travel in their jobs may be unavailable to sit. People who run small businesses may find the loss of earnings allowance inadequate. Insufficient blue-collar workers are attracted to apply.[53] Despite the fact that their jobs are protected by

[47] Cited in Darbyshire, n. 38 above.

[48] See 'Older Magistrates Appointed', LCD Press Release 268/98, 4 Sept. 1998.

[49] Royal Commission on Justices of the Peace 1946–8, *Report*.

[50] Cited by Skyrme, n. 14 above at 57.

[51] Cited in Darbyshire, n. 38 above. See also Dignan and Wynne, 1997, who, in their examination of one bench, confirmed the evidence of the Magistrates' Association to the Home Affairs Select Committee that some wards (expensive housing areas) were over-represented on the bench, while other wards had no representatives.

[52] At p. viii.

[53] Evidence to the Home Affairs Committee, discussed in Darbyshire, n. 38 above.

statute, it may be that people fear they will be dismissed for taking time off to be a magistrate, or will irritate work colleagues. Skyrme thought that wage earners felt their peers were not qualified to be magistrates.[54] People in certain occupations find their jobs much more compatible with sitting on the bench than others. An example is those involved in education, as teachers or lecturers. The Lord Chancellor instructs advisory committees that no more than 15 per cent of any bench should consist of the same group. Lord Chancellor Irvine recognizes this problem of social imbalance. He has tried to replace the committees' obligation to select a politically balanced bench (see below) with a mechanism for establishing a socio-demographic mix but his 1998–9 consultation exercise to this effect was unsuccessful.[55] His *Judicial Appointments Annual Report 1999–2000*[56] expresses his continued endeavour to find ways of securing a socially balanced bench.

RACE[57]

The precise racial balance of the Bench is unknown, but it is obvious that, historically, it has under-recruited minorities. Of the 24,771 justices outside the Duchy of Lanceaster, in the 2000–1 statistics cited above, 2 per cent are black, 2.4 per cent Asian and 0.8 per cent 'other', although the ethnicity of 5 per cent is unknown.[58] There is a visible contrast in court, where non-whites are over-represented among defendants and victims. This is especially acute in areas of minority population concentration, such as London.[59] Recognizing this, Lord Mackay LC and then Lord Irvine LC, have tried to compensate by appointing more non-whites than there are in the population at large, culminating in the appointment of 8.6 per cent of new justices in 1999–2000 and 9.3 per cent in 2000–1.[60] Morgan and Russell estimated that the Bench was 'approaching ethnic representativeness' of the population at national level in 2000. Incidentally, employment tribunals have no power to hear accusations of racial discrimination made against advisory committees.[61]

DISABILITY

The Equality Working Group (below) reported a shortage of applications from disabled people.

---

[54] Skyrme, 1979, chap. 4.

[55] 'Political Balance in the Lay Magistracy', LCD consultation paper, on LCD website, n. 16 above and 'Irvine Fails to Devise a Better Way to Pick JPs', *The Independent*, 26 Oct. 1999.

[56] On the LCD website, n. 16 above.

[57] Unfortunately there is not the space here to review the findings of King and May in *Black Magistrates*. Hopefully, recruitment lessons have been learned in the 16 years since its publication.

[58] *Judicial Appointments Annual Report*, Annex G.

[59] For detail see Darbyshire, n. 38 above.

[60] *Judicial Appointments Annual Report 2000–2001*.

[61] *Arthur* v. *A-G*, *The Times*, 18 Mar. 1999.

GENDER

Many commentators have complained in the past that the magistracy is overwhelmingly male. This is patently not true, as I pointed out in 1997 and as can be seen at a glance from the statistics. As of April, there were 28,735 lay justices, of whom 14,639 were women. In 1997, I pointed out that, from the appearance of many benches, it seems that women probably sit more often than men, but this hypothesis was not tested by Morgan and Russell. It is true that most DJMCs, like other judges, are male.[62]

POLITICS

While steps are taken to ensure that superior judges in the English legal system take no active part in politics, to safeguard judicial independence, it has proven impossible to keep politics out of the magistracy. Historically, magistrates were the local politicians and performed governmental functions until local government was created in the late nineteenth century. By the middle of the twentieth century advisory committees were still recruiting justices by asking political parties to put names forward, so many people were appointed to the magistracy because they were political party activists. Skyrme described the bench then as 'overwhelmingly political'.[63] The 1948 Royal Commission on Justices of the Peace reported that advisory committees were composed mainly of persons chosen from the main political parties. In 1955, Williams cited a survey of forty benches which found that on thirty-six at least half the magistrates were politically active.[64] By the late 1970s, I noticed that in the benches of large metropolitan towns, it was often the case that most local councillors were also magistrates,[65] and Burney, in 1979 said it was 'simply not true', as one commentator had claimed, that politically involved or politically nominated magistrates formed a tiny minority of the bench.[66] Interestingly, Skyrme, who was the Lord Chancellor's Secretary of Commissions responsible for the appointments process, reports that many Lord Chancellors, like the present Chancellor, would have liked to 'grasp the nettle' and order that political views should be ignored in the selection of the magistracy but none succeeded. Similarly, the 1948 Royal Commission also thought that too much attention was paid to the politics of candidates, but did not think a better practice could be secured by ignoring politics. Instead, Lord Chancellors instructed advisory committees to inquire into the political persuasion of candidates in order to avoid an imbalance and to see that 'justices are appointed from different sections of the community'.[67] The present Lord Chancellor repeated history by expressing a desire to replace politics as a criterion for selection but, as described above, the exercise failed, because suggested alternatives were too cumbersome, unpopular, and difficult to operate.[68]

There seems to be a natural tendency for Advisory Committees to favour Conservatives, or, rather, for Conservatives to favour service as magistrates. Skyrme reported

---

[62] For current statistics see the Monthly Judicial Statistics on the LCD website, n. 16 above.
[63] Skyrme, 1979, at 52.   [64] 1955, 284.   [65] Darbyshire, 1984.   [66] At 58.
[67] Skyrme, 1979, n. 14 above, 54.
[68] Press notice 329/99, Oct. 1999, LCD website, n. 16 above.

that even when non-political organizations were asked to nominate candidates, the people they selected tended to support the Conservative party. I pointed out that, according to the 1995 statistics, by far the biggest group of known political persuasion in England and Wales were Conservatives. Strikingly, in Wales, where virtually all MPs were Labour, all but one bench were dominated by Conservatives. Still, according to the 2000–1 statistics, of the 24,000 justices in the table mentioned above, over 75 per cent declared a party affiliation by far the most popular party was the Conservatives, with over 36 per cent of the total being Conservative.[69] Political balance continues to be controversial. In 2001, Jane Kennedy, a junior minister in the Lord Chancellor's Department, had to deny politicization of the judiciary when those accusations were made against a local advisory committee, which had advertised for Labour supporters to join the Bench in an attempt to redress the political imbalance in favour of the Conservatives.[70] In 2001, a pilot exercise was conducted in a limited number of areas to see whether a mixture of occupational and social groupings would be a practical alternative to political balance. The Report was not available at the time of writing (January 2002).

THE LATEST EFFORTS TO SECURE DIVERSITY

Like the 1948 Royal Commission and his twentieth-century predecessors, whom Skyrme described as fascinated almost to the point of 'obsession' with Justices of the Peace,[71] the Lord Chancellor has repeatedly expressed an anxiety to recruit a more diverse bench. For instance, he has lifted the ban on blind magistrates and several blind people have now been recruited. In response to the report of the Stephen Lawrence Inquiry, the Lord Chancellor's Department set up an audit of its procedures to assess whether they provide equality of opportunity and support diversity. An Equality Working Group was established to seek ways of encouraging applications from all sections of society, eliminating discrimination and producing a diverse Bench.[72] Its 2000 report praised the efforts of the Lord Chancellor to foster a nationally co-ordinated approach to recruiting a diverse bench in a fair way but made various recommendations, including that the LCD should do the following:

> Explore ways of attracting media attention to raise the magistracy's profile among under-represented groups;
> Train committees to distinguish between positive action and positive discrimination;
> Make it clear that discrimination would not be tolerated;

[69] The politics of justices in office in 1995 were those declared at the time of appointment. The current politics of most justices appear in the statistical tables at Annex G of the *Judicial Appointments Annual Report 2000–2001*, n. 60 above.

[70] Press notice 98/01, Mar. 2001, LCD website, n. 16 above.

[71] 1979 at 21.

[72] See their 2000 report on the LCD website, n. 16 above.

Copy the Territorial Army model of presenting awards to local employers who allowed their staff time off to be magistrates;

Consider how to change people's attitudes to colleagues who took time off to serve as magistrates;

Guide committees in targeting recruitment campaigns to under-represented groups;

Develop an integrated national strategy to replace the present piecemeal one;

Make court buildings more accessible for disabled magistrates;

Find out why justices resign. It seems to be because they cannot attend the sittings required. Benches should be guided on how to be flexible to accommodate such justices;

Ensure dress codes are not culturally biased.

The LCD website contains a progress chart of its implementation. The Lord Chancellor is currently considering what action might ease the difficulties magistrates find in securing time off to sit on the bench, and he has enlisted the help of Operation Black Vote, a non-party campaign to get black people to vote and be involved in the democratic process. In 2001, a shadowing scheme commenced, encouraging ethnic-minority citizens to accompany magistrates on the bench and in speaking to community groups, to enable them to experience the work of a lay justice.

Magistrates themselves take an active part in publicizing their work and the demystifying of the magistracy to the public at large. The Magistrates' Association received funds from the LCD for the Magistrates in the Community project. Magistrates give up yet more of their own time to establish links with the media, organize court open days and Mock Trial Competitions, and deliver presentations to community groups and schools.

In his 2001 Report, Auld LJ quoted at length the findings of Morgan and Russell and my own (1997) concerns over the composition of the bench and scrutinized the selection and recruitment process. He noted that, while a budget of £4.7 million was used to recruit people to the Territorial Army, only £35,000 was spent on recruiting magistrates. He wondered what statistics were available to advisory committees on the composition of their local community to assist them in recommending appointments which would secure a bench reflecting it. He recommended that the LCD should compile statistics on the composition of the magistracy, and these have now been collected and published, in the same month as the Auld Report (October 2001) (see above). He recommended eight steps[73] to be taken to provide benches that reflect more broadly the communities they serve, including better informing the public to try to attract more suitable candidates; devising a National Recruitment Strategy aimed not just at candidates but, employers; reviewing the role and terms of service; and persisting with the search for occupational and/or social groupings as a substitute for political affiliations as a measure of local balance.

---

[73] At 129.

REMOVAL

The Lord Chancellor can remove any magistrate under the Justices of the Peace Act 1997. This is rarely done but is usually because a magistrate refuses to enforce a particular law, i.e. in prosecutions arising from public demonstrations, or for personal indiscretion, such as conducting an obvious extra-marital affair with another magistrate. Between 1997 and 2000, the LC dismissed thirty-eight magistrates. One was dismissed for 'mooning'[74] at a man who had annoyed her and another after being put on probation for slashing the car tyres of a love rival and sending poison pen letters. Magistrates are generally removed from the bench if they commit a serious criminal offence. In 2002, a lay justice was imprisoned for five years for planting eight bombs.

Magistrates retire at 70. Their names are placed on a supplemental list so they can no longer sit on the bench but can deal with minor matters and so retain the status of a Justice of the Peace.

TRAINING LAY JUSTICES

Lay justices need to be given enough training to understand basic court procedure and such devices as the quantum and burden of proof, but there are limits. They should not become amateur lawyers and, most importantly, since they already sit, on average, on forty-one occasions a year, they cannot be expected to give up a significant extra amount of time for training. Morgan and Russell in 2000 found justices already spent a week a year on training and other duties.

Under the Magistrates' New Training Initiative, developed centrally by the Judicial Studies Board since 1998, newly appointed magistrates are trained to achieve four basic competences: applied understanding of the framework within which magistrates operate, the ability to follow basic law and procedure, to think and act judicially, and to work effectively as team members. They are assisted by a mentor and appraised by a trained appraiser. During the first two years, this involves eleven mentored sittings and one appraised sitting. The technical content consists mainly of an introduction to practice and procedure, punishment, and treatment. This is the basic minimum. Justices wishing to sit in a youth court or on the family panel undergo extra specialist training. The Judicial Studies Board organizes special training for all justices, along with the rest of the judiciary, on certain topics from time to time. For instance, human awareness or equality training was undertaken as a national exercise, as was human rights training, before the Human Rights Act 1998 came into force in 2000. Other than these nationally organized exercises, training is organized and conducted locally by training officers, who are usually justices' clerks, justices' chief executives, or the legal advisers who assist them. Benches now have Bench Training and Development Committees.

---

[74] Displaying her naked bottom.

Training has been funded and organized on a local basis since 1966, following the recommendations of the 1948 Royal Commision. This was regretted as a big mistake by Skyrme in 1979 because '[if] it is accepted that justices need training it would be difficult to devise a less efficacious system for ensuring they get it than that provided by the 1949 Act. Responsibility rests primarily with the Magistrates' Courts Committees but there is no sanction compelling them to discharge this duty. The cost is borne by the local authorities but they have no say in the manner in which the committees spend the money.'[75] Consequently, I found, in the 1970s, that some magistrates received only the prescribed minimum training while others were funded to attended unlimited extra courses, organized by the Magistrates' Association or academic establishments. Some Committees, I was told, 'believed in' training for magistrates and their clerks and others did not.[76] Nowadays, some Magistrates' Courts Committees have grouped together to provide training on a regional basis, but there remains 'considerable variety' in the way the latest training scheme, the Magistrates' New Training Initiative, is being interpreted and implemented in different areas, according to the *Evaluation of the Magistrates New Training Initiative* (MNTI) (2000).[77] Tellingly, the report reflects Skyrme's sentiments, twenty-two years later. 'This evaluation shows that perhaps the variation is too great in some areas, but the opportunity for greater direction and control by the JSB is severely limited by the remit the JSB has in relation to MCCs'.[78] Considering the Board is run by judges for judges and is not an arm of the executive, this illustrates just how the local administration of magistrates' courts has caused diversity. The report's conclusions are generally favourable, but it identifies a need for national performance standards for competences. In his 2001 Report, Auld LJ expressed concern over the lack of consistency in magistrates' training from one MCC area to another and recommended that the Judicial Studies Board be made responsible for devising the content and manner of all magistrates' training. Training should continue to be conducted locally, but justices' clerks and legal advisers and district judges could be involved, to help break down the perceived barrier between them and the justices. He said the competences measured in the MTNI should be simplified, and work on this commenced immediately.

Apart from these criticisms of its local administration and consequent inconsistency, no recent criticisms have been made of the training of lay justices. Critics who generally attack them for being 'untrained' are probably in effect demanding they be replaced by professionals.

---

[75] Skyrme, 1979, 74.   [76] Darbyshire, 1984, n. 65 above.

[77] See the Judicial Studies Board website: **www.cix.co.uk/jsb**, especially for a review of progress in the Magistrates' New Training Initiative.

[78] At 2.

MAGISTRATES' CLERKS

In 1968, Justice Parker CJ described the magistrates' clerk as 'in many ways the most important person in the whole set-up of the administration of justice'.[79] In 1984, in *The Magistrates' Clerk*, I made a statement which remains virtually accurate:

The magistrates' clerk has no public image. Most adults in England and Wales have heard of magistrates[80] and their courts but few have heard or thought about magistrates' clerks. . . . In public debate on the work of the magistrates' courts, the clerks are seldom even mentioned. Few legal textbooks make the situation any clearer. If they mention the magistrates' legal adviser at all, this is usually said to be the justices' clerk, who will normally be a barrister or solicitor . . . what little research has been conducted has paid scant attention to the role of the clerk. . . .[81]

FACTUAL BACKGROUND

Lay justices, like DJMCs, are judges of both fact and law and sentencers, but are wholly dependent on their clerks, or legal advisers, for guidance on the law and available sentences. Clerks have no power to rule on the law and, ironically, a magistrates' court is legally constituted without a clerk. The roles of the various clerks are set out in the Justices of the Peace Act 1997, as amended by the Access to Justice Act 1999, a ministerial statement of 2000,[82] and two Practice Directions,[83] dating from 1954 and 2000. The justices' clerk (JC) is the chief adviser at each court. She is statutorily appointed by the local magistrates' courts committee. Her deputies and assistants are employees of the committee. Because of a massive reduction in justices' clerks' numbers, from over 400 in the 1970s to 133 now, some JCs are in charge of whole counties, so in practice most benches sitting in court are advised by a court clerk/deputy/legal adviser, acting under powers delegated by the justices' clerk. While justices' clerks are required to possess a five-year general qualification (as a barrister or solicitor), under the Courts and Legal Services Act 1990, many court clerks and deputies are not professionally qualified. A 2001 LCD survey showed that, of 1,800 advisers, only 1,200 were professionally qualified as barristers or solicitors.[84] Justices' clerks used to be responsible for administering magistrates' courts, but lost most of these functions to the justices' chief executives, a post created by the Police and Magistrates' Courts Act 1994.

---

[79] In the House of Lords debate on the Justices of the Peace Bill.

[80] Reaffirmed in 2000 by Morgan and Russell, at p. x.   [81] Darbyshire, 1984, 1.

[82] In 'The Future Role of the Justices' Clerk' (2000), LCD website, n. 16 above.

[83] Practice Direction (Justices: Clerk to Court) [1954] 1 WLR 1163; Practice Direction (Justices: Clerk to Court) (2000).

[84] I explain clerks' qualifications and my concerns over the lack of professionally qualified advisers in Darbyshire, 1997c. In 2001, a revised scheme of evaluating court clerks' competences was introduced, along the lines of the MNTI scheme for magistrates. It is explained by Baker and Harding (2001).

ISSUES

These are: the proper role of the clerk in court and her relationship with the magistrates; the growing judicial powers of clerks; the (lack of) qualifications of court clerks; the problematic role of the clerk in the defaulters' court; the erratic distribution of criminal legal aid/criminal defence by clerks and the division of functions between the justices' clerk and the justices' chief executive.[85]

THE CLERK'S ROLE IN COURT

In *The Magistrates' Clerk* I explained:

The legal position is even more anomalous—a lay bench is properly constituted without a clerk and, despite the fact that they are lay people, justices are themselves supposed to take all the legal decisions in summary procedings so they invariably rely on their clerk who effectively takes all legal decisions.[86]

Glanville Williams described the whole arrangement as 'peculiar':

whereas justices are entrusted with the duty of deciding points of law, all technical knowledge is possessed by their servant, on whose advice they must therefore rely. If legal argument takes place in court, the argument is addressed to the justices who may hardly follow a word of it; in reality, however, it is intended for the ears of the clerk. Rulings on points of procedure and evidence are supposed to be made by the justices, the clerk having no authority to control the proceedings of the court; in practice, however, the decisions must be taken by the clerk who is thus led or tempted to interfere in the proceedings in a way that is theoretically unwarrantable. The clerk, in a word, has power without acknowledged authority or responsibility.[87]

The JC's functions include, according to the Justices of the Peace Act 1979 as amended by the Access to Justice Act 1999, giving to justices, at their request, advice on 'matters of law (including procedure and sentencing) including questions arising when he is not personally attending on them (when one of his court clerks/legal advisers is attending)'. The statute also empowers him to bring to the justices' attention, at any time when he thinks he should do so, points of law (including procedure and practice) that may be involved in any question so arising. This includes sentencing powers and practice. It is noticeable that this statutory power is given to the JC personally, not to other court clerks. Nevertheless, there is no statutory obligation on magistrates to call for the clerk's advice, listen to it, or follow it. The more delicate areas of this relationship are set out in case law and in Practice Directions which lack the force of law and, since October 2000, the European Convention on Human Rights.

---

[85] There were some initial difficulties in allocating such functions as the scheduling of courts and cases, but these have largely been resolved by clarification in the Access to Justice Act 1999 and 'The Future Role of the Justices' Clerk—A Strategic Steer' (2000) LCD website, n. 16 above.

[86] At 1.

[87] *The Proof of Guilt* (1955), at 290. My research in *The Magistrates' Clerk* (1984) examines the behaviour of clerks at 7 magistrates' courts in England and Wales, as well as discussing the case law (which is still binding) in depth.

In *Jones* v. *Nicks*[88] the Divisional Court, led by the Lord Chief Justice, warned justices that they 'came close to the borderline of being ordered to pay costs' for ignoring their clerk's advice. There is also a body of case law which demonstrates that proceedings may be quashed for breach of the English common law rules of natural justice if the clerk is too active in controlling trial proceedings or asking questions, or if she appears to influence the justices in areas which are not her province, such as decisions of fact or the selection of a particular sentence.[89]

A new Practice Direction (Justices: Clerk to Court) 2000[90] was issued by the Lord Chief Justice to take account of the Human Rights Act 1998. It makes the JC responsible for legal advice, for the performance of advisory functions of any of his/her staff acting as legal adviser, for ensuring that competent advice is available to the justices, and for effective case management and reduction of delay. Legal advisers may consult the JC or other authorized superior. If the JC or that person then gives advice direct to the bench, advocates must be given the opportunity to repeat any relevant submissions. The legal adviser is given the responsibility 'to provide the justices with any advice they require to properly perform their functions whether or not the justices have requested that advice'. The adviser is responsible for helping the justices to formulate reasons for their decisions. This is a new duty which takes account of the new practice of magistrates to give reasoned decisions, consequent upon the perceived duty to do so under Article 6 of the European Convention.[91] The JC or legal adviser 'must not play any part in making findings of fact but may assist the bench by reminding them of the evidence using any notes of the proceedings for this purpose'. Clerks may ask questions of the parties or witnesses to clarify evidence and issues. Justices can request advice at any time, preferably in open court. If advice is given in the retiring room, it should be provisional. Its substance should be given in open court and the parties given an opportunity to comment on it. The method of tendering advice is quite controversial. Some would argue that Article 6 of the European Convention requires all advice to be given in open court. In the past clerks have been criticized for retiring uninvited with the justices, which has led to accusations of undue interference. The previous Practice Directions and case law have tried to guard against this,[92] and the new one says justices should openly request, in the presence of the parties, that the clerk retire with them. Advisers also have a duty to assist unrepresented parties. My observations in 1997 confirmed my 1984 research finding that practice in following the old Practice Directions was patchy.[93] Much depends on the knowledge, attitude, and personality of individual clerks. I am not confident that all legal advisers (including JCs) will be aware of the contents of this new Direction or will bother to practise in accordance with its sentiments.

---

[88] [1977] RTR 175.   [89] For discussion see Darbyshire, 1984, chap. II.

[90] The Court Service website, **www.courtservice.gov.uk**. A 1954 Direction remains in force: Practice Direction (Justices: Clerk in Court) [1954] 1 WLR 213.

[91] For discussion see B. Gibson, 'Reasons: The Hub of Human Rights' (2000) 164 *JP* 755.

[92] See Darbyshire 1984.   [93] Darbyshire 1999 and 2000.

ENHANCED JUDICIAL POWERS OF THE CLERKS

JCs may exercise the powers of a single justice, under the Justices of the Peace Act 1979. In the Crime and Disorder Act 1998 and the Justices' Clerks Rules 1999, they were given a long list of new pre-trial management powers. I argued[94] that this was undesirable, since these are judicial powers. Clerks are not selected and appointed as judges. They are servants of the judges (magistrates) and, more alarmingly, these powers will mainly be delegated to court clerks/legal advisers, under the 1999 Rules, many of whom are not legally qualified. It was, therefore, very gratifing to see that Auld LJ recommended, in 2001, that there should be no further extension of the clerks' powers and that DJMCs should normally sit without a legal adviser.

COURT CLERKS'/LEGAL ADVISERS' QUALIFICATIONS

In 1997 I complained that many court clerks and deputies were not professionally qualified lawyers and expressed my concern face to face with the Lord Chancellor. 'The public might consider it self-evident that lay people taking legal decisions should have a lawyer's advice. Indeed, most lawyers assume this to be so.'[95] Further, the alternative qualifications or training required of court clerks were no match for a professional qualification as barrister or solicitor, and with the number of justices' clerks dwindling (there were 200 then and are only 133 now), the clerk in court will not always have easy access to help from the JC, who is now often in charge of a whole county. In response to such concerns, the Lord Chancellor required that, as from 1999, all new court clerks and all existing clerks now under 40 must be barristers or solicitors.[96] Unfortunately, the over-40s were exempted because it was found that some counties were so dependent on unqualified clerks that there would no be time for them all to qualify by 1999. Worse, following threats of industrial action by legal advisers, further delegated legislation was passed exempting all those appointed before 1998 from the need to qualify professionally. It could be beyond 2040, therefore, before the magisterial service is fully professionalized.

THE ADMINISTRATION OF MAGISTRATES' COURTS

Because magistrates' courts have been locally administered by the MCC and the JC, and now the MCC and chief executive, problems have arisen from inconsistencies from court to court and area to area. For instance, even by 1998, MCCs had purchased incompatible computer systems which made it difficult to link them from court to court and from courts to other criminal justice agencies. For a discussion of idiosyncracies in administration, such as provision of training and efficiency of case management, see Darbyshire, 1984. For a very interesting explanation of how central

---

[94] [1997] *Crim. LR* 105.   [95] Darbyshire, n. 38 above.
[96] For explanation and discussion see Darbyshire at 382, n. 93 above.

control is growing by stealth, see Raine and Willson, 1993. The development of the Magistrates' Courts Inspectorate, the promulgation of codes of 'best practice', for instance in magistrates' and clerks' training, the discussion of legal issues within the Justices' Clerks' Society, and the dramatic amalgamation of clerkships and courts[97] (which I am not condoning) have all helped to reduce differences but some remain, as discussed in the context of training, above.

In his 2001 Report, Auld LJ recommended centralized administration, for the same reasons Le Vay had recommended it in 1989, in the *Efficiency Scrutiny of the Magistrates' Courts*.[98] The funding system of magistrates' courts was, he said, 'cumbrous and inefficient'. Management by MCCs had led to inconsistency in administering national policies, court practices, procedure, and, indirectly, in local sentencing levels and investment in incompatible IT systems. The separation of magistrates' courts from the Crown Court 'leads to much waste of court and other accommodation'. His radical solution was a unified court system, administered by a centrally funded executive agency and managed on the basis of the existing forty-two criminal justice areas established under the Access to Justice Act 1999.

In my submission to Auld LJ, however, I argued that a distinction must be drawn between local management of justice, which is, for the reasons set out above, undesirable, and local justice administered by people familiar with the locality, which is what magistrates represent and think they represent. Auld LJ noted the concern among magistrates and their clerks that court closures are destroying the connection between magistrates and 'their community' and making life inconvenient for court users, who now have to travel longer and more expensive distances. In December 2001, the Lord Chancellor acknowledged that over 100 magistrates' courts had closed in the last six years.[99]

Bibliography and Further Reading

AULD, THE RIGHT HONOURABLE LORD JUSTICE, *Report of the Review of the Criminal Courts of England and Wales* (London, TSO, 2001,) **www.criminal.courts.review.org.uk**.

BAKER, J., and HARDING, E., ' "Competent Clerk?" ', *The Magistrate*, Sept. 2001, 239.

BANKOWSKI, Z. K., HUTTON, N. R., and McMANUS, J. J., *Lay Justice* (Edinburgh: T & T Clark, 1987).

BROWN, S., *Magistrates at Work* (Buckingham: Open University, 1991).

BURNEY, E., *JP, Magistrate, Court & Community* (London: Hutchinson, 1979).

CARLEN, P., *Magistrates' Justice* (London: Martin Robertson, 1976).

DARBYSHIRE, P., *The Magistrates' Clerk* (Chichester: Barry Rose, 1984).

—— 'The Lamp That Shows That Freedom Lives—Is it Worth the Candle?' [1991] *Crim. LR* 740.

---

[97] In spring 2001, county councils have launched appeals against the closure of 9 courts in Devon and Cornwall: LCD Press Release, 104/01, LCD website, n. 16 above.

[98] Le Vay, J., *Review of the Criminal Courts of England and Wales* (London: HMSO, 1989), at 288 and 290.

[99] House of Lords' written answer, 10 Dec. 2001, HL Debs., WA 54.

—— 'Previous Conduct and Magistrates' Courts—Some Tales from the Real World' [1997] *Crim. LR* 105.

—— 'An Essay on the Importance and Neglect of the Magistracy' [1997] *Crim. LR* 627.

—— 'For the New Lord Chancellor—Some Causes for Concern About Magistrates [1997] *Crim. LR* 861.

—— 'A Comment on the Powers of Magistrates' Clerks [1999] *Crim. LR* 377.

—— 'Raising Concerns About Magistrates' Clerks' in S. Doran and J. Jackson (eds.), *The Judicial Role in Criminal Proceedings* (Oxford: Hart, 2000).

—— (ed.), *Eddey and Darbyshire on the English Legal System* (7th edn., London: Sweet & Maxwell, 2001).

DIGNAN J., and WYNNE, A., 'A Microcosm of the Local Community?' (1997) 37 *British Journal of Criminology* 184.

DORAN S., and GLENN, R., *Lay Involvement in Adjudication* (London: HMSO, 2000).

FERGUSON, J. '"Access to Justice?"', *The Magistrate*, May 2001, 140.

GENN, H., *Paths to Justice* (Oxford: Hart Publishing, 1999).

HENHAM, R. J., *Sentencing Principles and Magistrates' Sentencing Behaviour* (Aldershot: Avebury, 1990).

House of Commons Home Affairs Committee, *Third Report*, Session 1995–6, *Judicial Appointments Procedures Volume II* (London: House of Commons Select HC 52–I, Committee on House Affairs 1996).

IVKOVIC, S., 'Lay Participation in Decision Making: A Croatian Perspective on Mixed Tribunals' (1997) 36 *Howard Journal* 406.

Judicial Studies Board, **www.cix.co.uk/jsb**, items on Magistrates' New Training Initiative.

Justices' Clerks' Society, 'Pilot Legal Adviser Competences', 2001.

Justices' Clerks' Society, Magistrates' Association, Home Office, *Local Sentencing Patterns in Magistrates' Courts* (1998).

KING, M., *The Framework of Criminal Justice* (London: Croom Helm, 1981).

—— and MAY, C., *Black Magistrates* (London: The Cobden Trust, 1985).

LEGGATT, SIR ANDREW, *Tribunals for Users One System, One Service*, Report of the Review of Tribunals (London: TSO, 2001) **www.tribunals.review.org.uk**.

Lord Chancellor's Department, see generally website, **www.open.gov.uk**.

—— Consultation papers as listed in the footnotes and

—— 'The Future Role of the Justices' Clerk', 1998.

—— 'Professional Qualification of Court Clerks in the Magistrates' Courts', 1998. Press releases as cited.

—— 'The Future Role of the Justices' Clerk—A Strategic Steer', 2000.

—— *Lord Chancellor's Directions for Advisory Committees on Justices of the Peace*, (1998) *Judicial Appointments Annual Reports*.

—— *Report of the Equality Working Group—The Lay Magistracy and the General Commissioners of Income Tax*, 2000. Items under 'Magistrates'.

McCONVILLE, M., HODGSON, J., BRIDGES, L., and PAVLOVIC, A., *Standing Accused* (Oxford: OUP, 1994), chap. 9.

McLAUGHLIN, H., 'Court Clerks: Advisers or Decision-Makers?' (1990) 30 *British Journal of Criminology* 358.

MAWDSLEY, H., 'Court Closures', *The Magistrate*, October 2001, 270.

MORGAN R., and RUSSELL, N., *The Judiciary in the Magistrates' Courts* (London: Home Office and Lord Chancellor's Department, 2000).

PADFIELD, N., *Text and Materials on the Criminal Justice Process* (2nd edn., London: Butterworths, 2000) chap. 6.

PARKER, H., SUMNER M., and JARVIS, G., *Unmasking the Magistrates* (Milton Keynes: Open University Press, 1989).

RAINE, J. W., and WILLSON, M. J., *Managing Criminal Justice* (Hemel Hempstead: Harvester Wheatsheaf, 1993).

Royal Commission on Justice of the Peace, *1946–48 Report*, Cmd 7463 (1948).

SANDERS, A., *Community Justice* (London: IPPR, 2001).

—— and YOUNG, R., *Criminal Justice* (2nd edn., London: Butterworths, 2000) chap. 8.

SEAGO, P., WALKER, C., and WALL, D., 'The Development of the Professional Magistracy in England and Wales' [2000] *Crim. LR* 631.

——, ——, and ——, *The Role and Appointment of Stipendiary Magistrates* (Leeds: University of Leeds, 1995).

SKYRME, T., *The Changing Image of the Magistracy* (London: Macmillan, 1979).

—— *History of the Justices of the Peace* (Chichester: Barry Rose, 1994).

VOGLER, R., 'Mixed Messages on the Mixed Bench', *Legal Action*, May 2001, 8.

WASIK, M., *Criminal Justice Text and Materials* (Harlow: Addison Wesley Longman, 1999).

WILLIAMS, G., *The Proof of Guilt* (London: Stevens, 1955).

17

THE ROLE OF
THE ADVOCATE

Stephen Solley QC

INTRODUCTION

Advocacy is at the heart of the operation of the English legal system. Oral advocacy plays a more substantial part in the English legal system than in the Continental inquisitorial systems. Indeed advocacy in many other common law jurisdictions is fettered in ways that have yet to grace these shores. For example, there are in England no time limits on advocacy in any court, other than those self-imposed by the advocate. Even in the highest court, the House of Lords, where there are extensive written legal arguments set out in advance, the House requires full oral submissions. The arrival of more and more written submissions has had some effect upon the English courtroom, but it is still the case that the main medium for the resolution of issues both civil and criminal, both legal and factual, is oral advocacy.

Naturally, different skills and types of advocacy exist to play their part in different areas of law. The technique required for a hostile cross-examination of a senior police officer in a criminal case at the Crown Court is very different from the presentation of a case on the last will and testament of a landowner tried in the Chancery Division of the High Court.

But for the adversarial system to operate successfully, the advocate must follow the joint key principles of independence and fearlessness. They may and should have many other attributes, such as good judgement and a tactical sense, but none are so important to the working of the system as independence and fearlessness. These principles will be developed in more detail later in this chapter.

THE PURPOSE OF ADVOCACY

Fundamental to the working of this system is the proposition that any legal or factual problem that is capable of more than one interpretation is tested and resolved by the medium of advocacy. The theory is that if advocates on either side of the case approach the question from the polarity of their distinct positions, the tribunal deciding the issue will be able to appreciate more easily where the correct legal or factual position lies. If the question is centred upon, for example, a point of law, then the presentation of the arguments from opposite perspectives will assist the tribunal to be clear about the correct law. If the problem is what facts are to be believed, then the advocates for the parties will, through questions which reflect the opposing factual assertions of each side, reveal to the tribunal which witnesses can be relied upon and which can be cast aside.

The adversarial system is different from Continental inquisitorial systems because at the point of trial the State has no continuous overarching role in directing the inquiry into the facts. Each side must decide what facts it relies upon, what witnesses are to be called, and what legal points it wishes to pursue.

THE DIVIDED LEGAL PROFESSION: SOLICITORS AND BARRISTERS

The English legal system has two separate branches of the profession of lawyer, namely barristers and solicitors. In general terms the role of the barrister is to advise on the merits and preparation of a case and to present the case in court, whereas the role of a solicitor is to provide the legal advice and to prepare the case ready for trial. Whereas a solicitor is engaged directly by the client, the barrister is briefed by a solicitor on behalf of the client.

Historically only the barrister was permitted rights of audience to the higher courts. However in recent times this distinction has become blurred to a considerable extent by the new rules that permit solicitors to be advocates at all levels of court work, subject to their having special advocacy qualifications.

Thus both barristers and solicitors can be advocates within the modern English legal system. This section, however, on 'the role of advocacy' is written mainly from the position of barristers rather than solicitors, because it is still the case that the vast majority of the more serious criminal cases, namely those at the Crown Court, are conducted by barristers.

THE ART OF ADVOCACY

Many books have been written by distinguished advocates about the art they practise. All these have one thing in common. It is much easier to write about than achieve!

All of the preparation and hard work (which are essentials) will be of no use if budding advocates simply cannot find the confidence to express themselves in a crowded court. Even if the confidence is there, there must be added the key ingredients of presence and *gravitas*, a sense of stature within the individual advocate. And what if the witness in the middle of the cross-examination changes the story or goes into dangerous territory? The advocate must be able to adjust instantly and imperceptibly to the new factual scenario. The advocate must always be on top of the situation, even if the advocate may sometimes deliberately permit the witness to look as if s/he has the upper hand. Sometimes it is necessary to show up a witness as domineering and ruthless, and to do this the advocate may appear to be weak so as to permit the ruthlessness of the witness to shine through. On other occasions a confident and clever witness will have to be handled authoritatively so as to keep them within bounds.

All of these techniques need to be learnt and, more importantly, practised. It is vital that the advocate learns the art slowly, by many, many appearances in court, most of them in smaller, less important cases, so that confidence builds and techniques improve.

TRAINING OF ADVOCATES

Advocacy is a specialism that it is increasingly appreciated requires a good deal of formal training. Entrants to advocacy in England undergo two types of special education. First, they have special advocacy training as part of their academic course work in becoming barristers or solicitors. Secondly, those who choose to become barristers and full-time advocates become pupils to a senior barrister who guides and trains them in practical advocacy. After six months of observation of advocacy without participation, the young advocate becomes entitled to appear in court on their own. It is a professional rule that a case must not be accepted if it is clearly beyond the capabilities or experience of an advocate. Since the advocate will have been chosen to carry out the court work by a solicitor, the public is further protected by the factor of the solicitor's judgement on the advocate's capacity to take on the particular case.

WHY AN ADVOCATE?

Although the right of a person to be represented in court by an advocate has been recognized by English jurisprudence for over 800 years, the individual can represent him/herself at all levels of English legal proceedings. However it is recognized that, save in the simplest and most minor civil and criminal cases, the individual usually requires the mouthpiece of the advocate to represent the language and legal points that arise from that complexity of thoughts and words. The advocate then becomes the personification of the client in the courtroom.

WHAT IS AN 'INDEPENDENT' ADVOCATE?

The tradition within the English legal system that an advocate may on one day be prosecuting and on the next day defending is a very important part of the maintenance of independence. At a lower level of criminal work it is possible for there to be prosecutors employed as full-time by the Crown Prosecution Service, but in any more serious case tried in the Crown Court the prosecutor will be an independent practitioner. The advantage of the advocate both defending and prosecuting is that it teaches the discipline of advocacy from both perspectives and expresses the true independence of the advocate as a presenter of a case, rather than a full-time employee of one side or the other.

The activities of barristers are regulated by rules set out in their professional *Code of Conduct*.[1] Under the formal *Code of Conduct of the Bar* (6th edition),[2] a practising barrister must not (a) permit his absolute independence, integrity, and freedom from external pressures to be compromised; (b) do anything (for example accept a gift) in such circumstances as may lead to any inference that his independence may be compromised; (c) compromise his professional standards in order to please his client, the court, or a third party.

Advocates never give their own opinion. They always 'submit' an opinion. The advocate will not be pressing personal opinions, but only submissions based on the law and facts of the individual case, there will be no personal conflict. This is for the same reason that underpins the 'cab-rank' principle, namely that barristers are under a professional obligation to accept instructions in any case that may arrive on their desks, so long as it is of the type of work they normally undertake and matches their level of experience. By this rule no individual with an unpopular cause to fight will find himself without an advocate.

There are many occasions within the life of an advocate, whether representing the State or an individual, when either the power of the State or the power of an important client may cause a potential professional conflict for the advocate. Perhaps the advocate will not wish to press an argument that the State wishes to put forward with vigour, or an advocate may wish to criticize the State in robust terms, or the advocate may refuse to cover up for a wealthy client. In all these instances, and many more besides, the independence of the advocate must reign supreme and he must act according to proper professional standards.

---

[1] These are set by the two professional bodies representing the split English legal system, namely barristers and solicitors. Barristers, the Bar, are regulated by the Bar Council of England and Wales. Solicitors are regulated by the Law Society of England and Wales. Both organizations have considerable power to ensure proper standards of professional conduct and ethics.

[2] Reproduced in P. Murphy (ed.), *Archbold's Criminal Pleading, Evidence and Practice* (London: Sweet & Maxwell, 2000 edn.), App.B.

PROFESSIONAL ETHICS

Reference has already been made to the Bar's *Code of Conduct*. Other important rules in the Code provide that a practising barrister when conducting proceedings at court:

(a) is personally responsible for the conduct and presentation of his case and must exercise personal judgement upon the substance and purpose of statements made and questions asked;

(b) must not, unless invited to do so by the court or when appearing before a tribunal in a case in which it is his duty to do so, assert a personal opinion about the facts or the law;

(c) must ensure that the court is informed of all relevant decisions and legislative provisions of which he is aware, whether the effect is favourable or unfavourable to the contention for which he is arguing, and must bring any procedural irregularity to the attention of the court during the hearing and not reserve such matter to be raised on appeal;

(d) must not adduce evidence obtained otherwise than from or through his professional client or devise facts which will assist in advancing his lay client's case;

(e) must not make statements or ask questions which are merely scandalous or intended or calculated only to vilify, insult, or annoy either a witness or some other person;

(f) must, if possible, avoid the naming in open court of third parties whose character would thereby be impugned;

(g) must not by assertion in a speech impugn a witness whom he has had an opportunity to cross-examine unless in cross-examination he has given the witness an opportunity to answer the allegation;

(h) must not suggest that a victim, witness, or other person is guilty of crime, fraud, or misconduct or make any defamatory aspersion on the conduct of any other person or attribute to another person the crime or conduct of which his lay client is accused, unless such allegations are relevant to a matter which is in issue (including the credibility of the witness) and which is material to his lay client's case and which appear to him to be supported by reasonable grounds.

The State has no power to control advocates. Advocates are subject to limited control by the judge during the trial process itself. Even within the process, the judge can only report the alleged misconduct to the barrister's professional organization. He can take no more direct action, unless in an extreme case the advocate is disruptive of the proceedings, in which case he can be removed in the same way that any individual can be removed from court for disruptive behaviour.

PRE-TRIAL DUTIES OF ADVOCATES

As with an iceberg in the ocean, much more work is done out of court than in it. Perhaps as much as three-quarters of the work in any case is in the preparation, the pleadings, the pre-trial interlocutory proceedings, the advice given on evidence and tactics. Therefore the skills required to draft the preparatory documents, in criminal proceedings, are paramount, and as necessary as the skills required to present the case in court. At all times in the drafting of pre-trial documents, there is the knowledge that at some later stage, in court, the advocates may have to defend their judgements.

PREPARATION OF CASES

The operation of the English court system is dominated by the notion that a courtroom must never be left idle, and that judges must at all times have a continuum of cases to deal with.

What therefore happens if an advocate who is engaged to represent a client finds him/herself unavoidably detained elsewhere, for example, by a trial that has been prolonged by the illness of a juror? Unless there are exceptional circumstances, such as the gravity of the case, the advocate who is detained elsewhere must ensure that another advocate takes over the case. This may happen only a few days or the day before the hearing.

The position may be complicated by the fact that advocates in England and Wales provide their services over a much wider geographical area than their home town or city. On any particular day they may have to travel as much as 100 kilometres to a court where they have been briefed to appear. A typical week for a busy advocate may therefore take them many hundreds of kilometres around their region.

To accommodate the late returning of cases from one advocate to another—and this may apply to prosecuting advocates as much as defending advocates—it is necessary that all the pre-trial work on a case is prepared in advance ready for any advocate to take over the court work. This is usually achieved by the split system of solicitors who prepare the brief and barristers who do the court work.

It is then the professional obligation of the advocate to ensure that, however late they may receive the case, they will be ready for the court hearing. In some cases the court will grant extra time for the advocate to see the accused at greater length. In a simple case an advocate may see the client for only a relatively short time.

Although a client may be represented in the best possible way by an advocate who has only recently taken over the case, the perception of a client may be that the system has failed to deliver good advocacy and fair justice. Therefore it is a fundamental part of the training of advocates that they master detail and law rapidly, and the late returning of work may often make it necessary for the advocate to work into the night in preparation for the next day. The expertise that is gained in absorbing information with great rapidity and selecting the key points in a case is a key component of good advocacy.

DUTIES OF THE PROSECUTION

It is important that a prosecution advocate avoids the use of emotive language or any words which will inflame an already tense situation. Advocates 'ought not to struggle for the verdict against the prisoner, but they ought to bear themselves rather in the character of ministers of justice assisting in the administration of justice',[3] not seeming to become over-involved and taken up with the case, but be seen to be detached and calm. This even extends to such questions as where the advocates stand. In England the advocate is not permitted to walk in court during the case. Advocacy is delivered from the place in court where the advocate's papers are placed. No dramatic movements towards the bench, witness stand, or jury are permitted. No hectoring of witnesses or jury is permitted. It is the cogency of the argument that holds sway rather than the personality of the advocate.

DISCLOSURE: CRIMINAL

The prosecution authorities themselves are obliged to disclose not only the evidence they intend to rely upon, but also other evidence or information that could be of assistance in establishing the innocence of the individual. The process of disclosure is now complex and controlled by statute (the Criminal Procedure and Disclosure Act 1996). The aim of these provisions is that, before the commencement of a trial, the defence advocate is in possession of all the evidence to be called. This means that there is no element of surprise at the trial, and the defence advocate should have had sufficient time to prepare its case. It is a responsibility of the advocate representing the prosecution to ensure that all appropriate material has been disclosed. To fail to do so may give rise to a successful appeal where the matters not disclosed could have been important to the result of the case.

A key part of the preparation by the defence will be to prepare the defendant for the giving of evidence, and arrange for all witnesses to be at court. The prosecution is not permitted to call surprise witnesses. If a late witness is proposed to be called then a 'notice of further evidence' must be served on the defence, and, if more time is required by the defence to prepare to deal with this further evidence, then the judge has the discretion to permit an adjournment. It may however be that the application to call further evidence happens so late that the judge will not permit the prosecution

---

[3] *R. v. Banks* [1916] 2 KB 621, *per* Avory J.

to call the evidence. The advocate must be in a position to present arguments to the judge at short notice so as to permit him to decide upon the issue.

THE INDICTMENT

The actual offences with which a defendant is charged are set out in an 'indictment'. This is the list of the precise crime or crimes alleged by the prosecution. It will contain a 'statement of the offence': the statutory provision which it is alleged has been broken or the common law offence it is alleged the defendant has committed. Then will follow 'the particulars of offence', which will set out in a sentence or two what the specific allegation is, so that the defendant knows the date, the place, and the nature of the case alleged against him. It will be the duty of the prosecuting advocate to draw up this list of offences in such a way that the criminal offence is set out with clarity. It may be that an error of substance made in the drafting of the indictment will bring about the failure of a criminal prosecution.

BURDEN OF PROOF

The State (called the Crown in English proceedings) makes the assertion against an individual and the responsibility of proving the case rests entirely upon the State. The individual has no burden to discharge, no requirement to prove his innocence.

STANDARD OF PROOF

The degree of proof required by a tribunal is a high one. Before there can be a conviction the tribunal must be satisfied so that it is sure of the guilt of a defendant. Any state of mind less than 'sureness' will not suffice, and will lead to a not guilty verdict, however suspicious the tribunal may be.

THE ORDER OF A CRIMINAL TRIAL

THE PROSECUTION'S OPENING STATEMENT

The prosecution advocate begins by explaining to the jury, in simple clear language what the case is about and how the prosecution will endeavour to prove the case. If the case is complex or lengthy, then the advocate should try to have visual aids for the jury, from photographs to schedules of events, or lists of relevant telephone numbers, or other such facts.

CALLING THE PROSECUTION WITNESSES

The next stage involves examination of the witnesses called by the prosecution. When the prosecuting advocate calls a witness, they will have a written statement which will form the basis of their questioning. Such questions must not be in leading form, that is, they must not suggest the answer or point the witness's mind to an important fact which may be in dispute. The rule against leading applies to both prosecution and defence in calling their own witnesses, including the defendant himself. This examination of the party's own witness is called examination in chief.

CROSS-EXAMINATION BY THE DEFENCE ADVOCATE

Cross-examination is the right possessed by advocates on each side of the case to question the witnesses from the opposite camp. The advocate sets out so to undermine the truthfulness, accuracy, or credibility of the witness. Cross-examination is regarded as the key tool of the English adversarial system. It has been described as 'beyond any doubt the greatest legal engine ever invented for the discovery of the truth'.[4] It is thus to this day regarded as a technique which will, if properly controlled and regulated, be the best way to establish the truthfulness, reliability, accuracy, and believability of a witness. As the defence will have written statements from all witnesses the prosecution intends to call, cross-examination can be prepared in advance.

In cross-examination, as distinct from examination in chief, the advocate is allowed to ask leading questions. This is in fact one of the key devices at the fingertips of an advocate, for it can lead the witness to contradict what they may have hitherto said or cause them to retract a fact or simply reveal to the jury/tribunal that the witness is in fact not reliable. It may be that a witness has a grudge against the defendant or is even being paid money to give evidence or is telling lies about so many other matters not quite central to the case that they are disbelieved on the central part of the case. Considerable latitude is given to the advocate in the questions that may be permitted, but they must be relevant to a matter in issue and they must never be gratuitously offensive.

There are fairly rare cases where a witness admits under pressure of skilled cross-examination that they have lied as to an important fact. For every case like these, there are many others where the witness is confirmed in the tribunal's eyes as accurate and truthful, having withstood a difficult cross-examination. More often the issue is not truthfulness but accuracy. For example, a case may depend upon an identification of the accused by a witness. The defence will have had an opportunity to study in advance what the witness is expected to say. In preparation, the defence may prepare plans of the locality drawn accurately to scale and photographs of the locality. The witness can be tested by the surprise appearance of the plan and photographs which show that it was much more difficult to see than the witness at first had testified. Real doubt is suddenly thrown on the key part of the case against the accused.

---

[4] J. H. Wigmore, *Evidence* (3rd edn., Boston, Mass.: Little Brown & Co, 1940) para. 1367.

The rest of the trial is taken up by the defendant's opening speech if they wish to make one; the defendant's evidence in chief; the cross-examination of the defendant by the prosecution advocate; a closing speech by the prosecution (summarizing the key parts of the evidence that indicate guilt and its relevance to the law as set out in the indictment); and finally the defence advocate's closing speech (summarizing the weakness of the prosecution case and the reasons why the prosecution have not made out their case as set out in the indictment so that the tribunal cannot be sure of guilt).

CLOSING SPEECHES

Closing speeches are sometimes the critical moments of advocacy in the whole trial process. This is the time when an advocate can speak directly to the jury, knowing that all the evidence in the case has been given and that there are no hidden pitfalls. That directness with the jury gives an advocate power, but the jury must be treated with respect. The case may be hanging by a thread, but with the evidence seeming to point towards the inexorable guilt of the defendant. The closing speech by the defence advocate may well turn the case.

To be an effective advocate at this stage of the proceedings requires a good mixture of attributes. This is not a time to deliver a dry, written address to the jury. Nor is it a time for wild histrionic advocacy which will serve only to embarrass the jury. It is a question of achieving a balance that will capture the minds of the jury, focus their attention upon the points made on behalf of the defendant, and move them towards a view which expresses doubt about the correctness of the prosecution case.

THE SENTENCE

It is not for the prosecution to suggest a sentence. Sentencing is for the judge alone. If the defendant pleads guilty or is convicted, however, the defendant's advocate is given the opportunity to make a speech in favour of mitigating the sentence to be imposed. The advocate must not suggest that the decision of the jury was wrong, nor must he present further argument designed to show innocence. The advocacy is to ensure that the judge gives a sentence to the accused which is of the minimum possible given the gravity of the offences. The time for dramatic advocacy is over. The jury have convicted. A delicate touch is required.

THE APPEAL

The advocate's duty does not end at the conclusion of the trial. The client must be advised on the chances of a successful appeal either against the sentence or the conviction itself. Advocacy at the Court of Appeal is a very different style from that at the trial. It is more concentrated, as can be imagined in a tribunal of three senior judges. It will concentrate primarily upon errors of law during the trial, although it is frequently necessary to rehearse factual issues so that the appeal court can determine the safeness of the conviction. Flamboyance and excess are thoroughly out of place.

THE FUTURE OF ADVOCACY WITHIN THE ENGLISH LEGAL SYSTEM

It is undoubtably the case that better advocacy provides for clearer justice. The problem that may be faced in England is the reduction of opportunity to learn the varied techniques of advocacy. Advocacy, whilst still present at the lower court levels of magistrates' courts for minor criminal work, and county courts for civil work, flowers best in the High Court, the Court of Appeal, and the Crown Court. The existence of non-barrister advocates alongside barristers may mean that they are deprived of the possibility of learning the art of advocacy at this lower level, so that when, after a couple of years, the advocate begins to appear regularly in the Crown Court the necessary skills will not be honed.

The new millennium has coincided with the formal incorporation of the European Convention on Human Rights into our law. There was never a time when advocacy was more needed. Submissions on legal points take on a Europe-wide perspective. The jurisprudence of Europe must be placed into the melting pot of authorities to be considered in every case. Indeed, Article 6 of the Convention guarantees legal assistance in criminal cases to anyone without sufficient means to pay for it. It is the advocates who are responsible for constructing fresh arguments, new ways of approaching old law, ingenious but defensible submissions on these new problems as they arise. The expansion of public law, the growth of prisoners' law, mental health law, civil remedies for criminal wrongdoing, all require imaginative advocacy, changing with the profile of modern law in our society. The energy and drive are sourced by the advocates. Without their active involvement English law and practice would tend to fossilize, and not remain the dynamic force that they have become in recent times.

Further Reading

ABEL, R., *The Legal Profession in England and Wales* (Oxford: Oxford University Press, 1998).

COCKS, R., *Foundations of the Modern Bar* (London: Sweet & Maxwell, 1983).

FLOOD, J., *Barristers' Clerks* (Manchester: Manchester University Press, 1983).

HAZELL, R. (ed.), *The Bar on Trial* (London: Quartet Books, 1978).

MORRISON J., and LEITH, P., *The Barrister's World and the Nature of Law* (Milton Keynes: Open University Press, 1992).

18

THE ROLE OF THE JUDGE IN CRIMINAL CASES

Sir Philip Otton

PRE-TRIAL

IDENTIFYING AND NARROWING ISSUES FOR TRIAL

Each defendant who is to be tried on indictment is committed by the magistrates' court to appear before the Crown Court for trial on indictment on a specific date. On that date, unless given leave, the defendant and the prosecutor should attend a plea and directions hearing or 'PDH'. The main purpose of the hearing is to take a plea of guilty or not guilty from the defendant. If the plea is guilty then the judge will proceed to sentence the defendant, adjourning for pre-sentence reports if necessary. If the plea is not guilty, the judge will then proceed to ensure that any steps necessary for a trial to take place have been or will have been taken within a set period of time so that the judge is able to fix a trial date.

At the PDH the advocates for both the defence and the prosecution (who should be those to appear at the trial) will hand to the judge responses to questionnaires that set out the following matters:

1. the issues in the case,
2. any mental or medical problems affecting the defendant or any of the witnesses,
3. the number of witnesses whose evidence will be placed before the court,
4. any exhibits or schedules,
5. the order in which prosecution witnesses are likely to be called,
6. any point of law anticipated, any questions of admissibility of evidence, and any legal authorities relied upon,
7. any alibi which should already have been disclosed,
8. any applications for the evidence of children to be given by video or live TV link,
9. the estimated length of trial, and
10. the dates of availability of witnesses and lawyers.

For serious and/or lengthy cases, a case summary may be produced for use at the PDH.

From this information the judge should then fix a trial date and give directions so that by then both parties have served their evidence on each other and have done all that is required for the trial to go ahead. The PDH should itself be in a situation to clarify the issues and focus the parties' attention on them as they prepare for trial. The issues can also be narrowed by the judge ruling on questions of law or on the admissibility of evidence. It used to be the case that the trial judge would be willing to overturn such rulings. This led to lawyers not taking the PDH seriously and sending more junior advocates to deal with the PDH in the knowledge that any 'mistakes' could be rectified at trial. However under the current rules, laid down by the Criminal Procedure and Investigations Act 1996, the trial judge can discharge or vary a pre-trial ruling, either on his own motion or on the application of either party. However, the party making the application must show that there has been a material change of circumstances since the pre-trial ruling was made. This reform ensures that advocates who attend the PDH take it seriously and understand that rulings made at the PDH are important and may well win or lose a case.

At the PDH it may be decided that, as the case is either long and/or complex, a pre-trial review or preparatory hearing should be held. These hearings are not strictly 'pre-trial' but are part of the trial itself, albeit that the jury is yet to be sworn. The advantage of the hearings is that they avoid having to constantly break up the trial and send the jury out to allow counsel to present legal argument to the court. Judges will often order the prosecution to produce a statement of case for use at any pre-trial hearing that sets out the prosecution's case including its version of the evidence and any inferences it will be asking the jury to draw from that evidence. The defence will usually be asked to reply with its own statement setting out how it takes issue with the prosecution's case, together with any points on admissibility of evidence or the relevant law that it will be making. The defence statement cannot be referred to in front of the jury without the consent of the accused. If either side does not produce such a statement according to the judge's order then the penalty will be that adverse inferences can be drawn by the jury and adverse comments made by the judge. The same will apply if either party departs from its statement at trial.

Any ruling made at a preparatory hearing may be the subject of an appeal to the Court of Appeal or the House of Lords. In such a situation the preparatory hearing may continue, but the trial may not commence until the appeal has been heard.

Both the preparatory hearings and the PDH assist the parties to narrow and define the issues between them. The system of disclosure between the parties of used and unused material from the prosecution, the defence statement, and/or a notice of alibi by the defence assist each party to concentrate on the issues that are in dispute before the trial. This is far better than having no disclosure up to the moment of trial, a situation which forces the parties to cover every possible angle of the case in anticipation of the other side's tactics. Such 'trial by ambush' was inefficient and often unfair to the prosecution.

It used to be the case that lawyers in criminal proceedings could get away with putting every single possible point of law or admissibility before the court at trial.

This used to lead to long delays during the trial, including having the jury spend hours outside the courtroom waiting for the legal argument to finish. The justification was that someone's liberty was at stake, and hence it was not appropriate for the judge to force the parties to narrow the issues and confine the parties to points that had at least some prospect of success. Judges still do not have the power to limit the parties to certain issues unless an application to rule on a certain issue is made to the court by one of the parties. Therefore, active case management, in the sense of the trial judge of his own motion being able to control the points that the parties are seeking to raise, still does not occur in English criminal proceedings. However the ability to give binding pre-trial rulings and to force the disclosure or procurement of evidence within a specific period of time does allow the judge to force the parties to think about their case and to select the issues that they wish to pursue.

In the end, the ultimate sanctions of staying a prosecution because of wilful disregard of the orders of the court by the prosecution, or of punishing a defendant by ruling that adverse inferences may be drawn by the jury from his default, provide excellent incentives to the parties to co-operate with the court in defining and narrowing the issues that are to be put before the court.

TRIAL

SETTLING FACTS IN 'NEWTON' HEARINGS

The *Newton*[1] hearing is used by judges to identify the facts of a case where there is going to be no trial because the accused has pleaded guilty, but will not agree the facts of the case with the prosecution. The facts have to be determined so that the accused is sentenced on a proper basis. The finding of these facts is done without a jury except where the finding may well turn out to be that the accused has committed a more serious offence than that which he has pleaded to, or is in fact not guilty. Thus, it is a rare case of a Crown Court judge deciding issues of fact without the assistance of a jury. In a *Newton* hearing, usually the prosecution and the defence will call witnesses and other items of evidence. The judge will then accept the prosecution's version of the facts as being true only if satisfied beyond reasonable doubt that the defence version is wrong. The judge has to properly direct himself in exactly the same way as he would direct a jury at a trial. The rules of evidence apply just as they would in a trial. Where, however, the differences between the two accounts are so slight that they would not affect the sentence then the judge can dispense with the hearing and sentence on the basis of either version of events. Equally the judge can refuse to hold a *Newton* hearing where he thinks that the defendant's version of events is inherently incapable of being believed.

---

[1] See *R. v. Newton* (1982) 77 Cr. App. R 13.

OVERSEEING THE CHARGING PROCESS AND PLEA SETTLEMENTS

Unlike in many other European jurisdictions the English judges have no role to play in the actual investigation of crime and the charging of criminals with offences. It is for the Crown or private prosecutor to choose which offences it wishes to include in the indictment. A judge can remove a charge from an indictment if it does not disclose a criminal offence under the law or if it discloses more than one criminal offence (i.e. is duplicitous). The judge can also remove counts if they do not arise out of the same facts or do not disclose a series of offences of a similar character.

Usually the case has only advanced as far as the Crown Court after the magistrates' court has found that there is sufficient evidence to provide a case for the defendant to answer. In the absence of oppressive behaviour or an abuse of the process, a judge must allow the charges to be put to the defendant and allow the prosecution to proceed with its evidence, notwithstanding that the judge may feel that the magistrates should not have committed the case to the Crown Court, as he feels that there is no case for the defendant to answer. However, at the end of the prosecution case the judge can direct the jury to acquit where the prosecution has not adduced sufficient evidence to provide a case for the defendant to answer.

PLEA BARGAINING

This can take one of four forms:

(1) An agreement between the judge and the accused that if the accused pleads guilty to an offence the sentence will take a particular form (e.g. a fine or probation). This is not allowed in English law, and any guilty plea in such circumstances is a nullity.

(2) An agreement between the accused and the prosecution that if the accused pleads guilty to some offences the prosecution will leave others off the indictment or ask the judge for a more lenient sentence. This type of agreement should not be made as the indictment should not be drafted at a time that such an agreement can affect it, and in England and Wales the prosecution do not make submissions to the judge in relation to sentencing.

(3) An agreement between the prosecution and the defence in terms that they will accept a plea of guilty to a lesser offence than the offence charged. Although the prosecution can insist on a trial in the face of such a plea and ask that such a plea become a not guilty plea, very often *it* will accept the plea. The judge can direct that it should not, and the judge's consent should be sought before the prosecution makes such an agreement. Usually a judge does not object to such an agreement as it will save the costs of full jury trial and may have other ancillary benefits.

(4) An agreement that the accused will plead guilty to some of the counts upon the indictment but not to others, which the prosecution then agree not to proceed with.

It is important in dealing with the last two forms of permissible plea bargaining that the judge ensures that nothing underhand is occurring. It would be unusual to approve a bargain where the prosecution is accepting a plea to a lesser offence where the evidence before the magistrates' court clearly indicated guilt of the more serious offence.

PROTECTION OF WITNESSES AND JURORS AT TRIAL

The judge must always ensure that steps are taken to protect witnesses and jurors from intimidation at trials. Screens, different court exits and entrances, and general court layouts are all used to attempt to make sure that direct eye contact between the public, the accused, the jury, and the witnesses (with the obvious exception that the jury should be able to see the witnesses give their evidence) is avoided. The judge can also order the accused to stay behind after a day's hearing to lessen the chances of contact with the other parties. Any attempt to intimidate a witness or a juror by an accused will most probably amount to the offence of attempting to pervert the course of justice.

ADMISSIBILITY OF EVIDENCE

The general rule in English criminal law is that all evidence is admissible. Section 78 of the Police and Criminal Evidence Act 1984 allows the judge to exclude any evidence which he feels 'would have such an adverse effect on the fairness of the proceedings that the court ought not to admit it'. This is entirely a matter for the judge's discretion. The Court of Appeal will disturb the judge's determination of whether or not a piece of evidence was admissible only if it is a decision that is so unreasonable that no reasonable trial judge could have come to it. The Court of Appeal has said that it will be 'loathe to interfere' with a trial judge's decisions to exclude evidence. Just because evidence was obtained in bad faith, unfairly, by trick, entrapment, or even unlawfully will not automatically lead to it being excluded; the matter rests with the trial judge, to be judged on the merits of each individual case.

OVERSEEING THE EXAMINATION AND CROSS-EXAMINATION PROCESS

The judge has a complete discretion in how he or she conducts the case. The order that witnesses are called and the questions that they are asked are all within the judge's discretion. There are rules, such as the prohibition on leading questions during examination in chief and the rules that apply in cases of rape and these rules are to be respected and followed.

The judge has full authority to prevent irrelevant, bullying, or inappropriate questioning.

He can also intervene to compel a witness to answer a question whilst protecting people from self-incrimination with the use of warnings. The judge will also be ever mindful to ensure that witnesses are given breaks and will ensure that they fully understand the questions being put to them. This is often the case with elderly or young witnesses.

Another key matter in criminal proceedings is the defendant's so-called 'shield'. This is a reference to the rule that prevents the prosecution from mentioning or asking questions about the defendant's previous convictions or bad character. Although rules exist that set out the conditions under which the prosecution may ask such questions, they cannot do so without the leave of the judge. The decision to raise the shield, i.e. to allow the prosecution to reveal the defendant's convictions, is a crucial one; it may well have a serious effect on whether the defendant is found guilty by the jury. A judge must always think carefully about how to exercise his discretion to ensure that the defendant receives a fair trial but also that the prosecution is not unfairly deprived of the right to cross-examine the defendant in respect of his previous convictions where the law allows. A particularly difficult situation arises where the defendant alleges that police officers are lying, because in attacking their character the law allows the prosecution to reply by raising the 'shield'. It is for the judge to decide whether or not it is appropriate for him to raise the 'shield' in those circumstances. The Court of Appeal will interfere with the judge's ruling only if he has erred in principle or there was no material on which he could properly have exercised his discretion.

SUMMING UP EVIDENCE

The summing up of all the evidence in the case is the most important job of the criminal trial judge. Unlike the practice in the United States of America, judges in England and Wales are permitted to summarize and comment upon the evidence. The judge will review the evidence for the benefit of the jury, direct them on any questions of law, and set out the burden and standard of proof. The summing up must at all times be unbiased and fair; the judge must refrain from any perjorative or inappropriate comment about the case.

Many appeals against conviction are based upon the judge's misdirection of the jury. For this reason judges are given guidance by the Judicial Studies Board by way of 'Specimen Directions' that the judge can read to the jury. Failure to read the directions does not of itself constitute a ground of appeal and judges are free to be creative in what they say to the jury, as long as they do not depart from the principles outlined in the specimen directions. The judge must not fail to outline carefully both the prosecution's and the defence's cases. He may give his views on the evidence but must stress that they are his views alone and that they should be followed by the jury only if they agree with them.

The judge need not confine himself to the matters raised by the parties in the case; he may comment on matters that have not be raised in front of the jury. However, if he is going to do so he must first inform the parties of his intention and invite their comment in the absence of the jury. It is generally a good idea that the judge asks the parties to comment on any particularly contentious directions that the judge is thinking of making.

A recent innovation is for the judge to ask the parties to outline the way in which they think the jury should come to its verdict (in a document called a 'route to verdict') and to put such documents to the jury as a way of explaining how they can acquit or convict the defendant. Care must be taken in the wording of such documents, and the jury must be told that how they come to their verdict is entirely a matter for them alone. The judge should never unduly criticize or commend a witness in front of the jury.

If the defendant has chosen not to give evidence the judge must be very careful to inform the jury that they are not obliged to draw adverse inferences from his silence and can choose not so to do.

It is quite appropriate to point out a witness's possible ulterior motives and to point out to the jury that people often lie for innocent reasons. It is very unusual for a judge to direct a jury to convict a defendant. This can be done only where the defendant has admitted his guilt during the trial. Equally the judge should refrain from asking the jury to have mercy on the defendant.

Perhaps the role of the judge can be best summed up by Rt. Hon. Lord Hailsham of Marylebone LC in *R. v. Law*:[2]

The purpose of a direction to a jury is not best achieved by a disquisition on jurisprudence or philosophy or a universally applicable tour round the area of law affected by the case. The search for universally applicable definitions is often productive of more obscurity than light. A direction is seldom improved and may be considerably damaged by copious recitations from the total content of a judge's notebook. A direction to a jury should be custom-built to make the jury understand their task in relation to a particular case. Of course it must include references to the burden of proof and the respective roles of jury and judge. But it should also include a succinct but accurate summary of the issues of fact as to which a decision is required, a correct but concise summary of the evidence and arguments on both sides and a correct statement of the inferences that the jury are entitled to draw from their conclusions about the primary facts.

THE IMPACT OF THE HUMAN RIGHTS ACT

Since the coming into force of the Human Rights Act 1998 on 2 October 2000, judges have had to carry out all of the above judicial duties—be it granting bail, or merely granting an adjournment—with the European Convention on Human Rights very much in mind.

The Convention itself is not new, and dates back to the aftermath of the Second World War. It is a document based largely on the UN Universal Declaration of Human Rights (1948), and was intended to provide a minimum standard of protection for all citizens in Europe from the kind of state behaviour that had characterized the previous decade. It has been in force in international law since 1953, and since 1966 a significant number of Britons and other Europeans have had the opportunity to hold their governments to account in the European Court of Human Rights in Strasbourg, France.

Before October 2000 judges only rarely had to consider the Convention. Its

[2] [1982] AC 510, 519 (HL).

provisions did not have direct effect in UK law, and tended to be used mainly as an aid to interpretation of a domestic statute. That position has now changed. Whilst the Human Rights Act still falls short of wholesale incorporation, judges are now obliged to 'give further effect' (see below) to the Convention by ensuring that the existing laws, procedures, and practices are applied in a way that is compatible with its provisions. Petitioning the European Court in Strasbourg is still possible, but the 1998 Act now places squarely on litigants the onus of raising Convention points within the domestic courts of the United Kingdom.

The key sections of the Human Rights Act 1998 for our purposes are as follows:

Preamble

An Act to give further effect to rights and freedoms guaranteed under the European Convention on Human Rights; to make provision with respect to holders of certain judicial offices who become judges of the European Court of Human Rights; and for connected purposes. [9 Nov. 1998.]

Interpretation of Convention rights

2.(1) A court or tribunal determining a question which has arisen in connection with a Convention right must take into account any—

(a) judgment, decision, declaration or advisory opinion of the European Court of Human Rights,

(b) opinion of the Commission given in a report adopted under Article 31 of the Convention,

(c) decision of the Commission in connection with Article 26 or 27(2) of the Convention, whenever made or given, so far as, in the opinion of the court or tribunal, it is relevant to the proceedings in which that question has arisen.

Interpretation of legislation

3.(1) So far as it is possible to do so, primary legislation and subordinate legislation must be read and given effect in a way which is compatible with the Convention rights.

The two most significant Convention Articles relating to criminal proceedings are Article 5 and Article 6.

Article 5 *Right to liberty and security*

(1) Everyone has the right to liberty and security of person. No one shall be deprived of his liberty save in the following cases and in accordance with a procedure prescribed by law:

(a) the lawful detention of a person after conviction by a competent court;

(b) the lawful arrest or detention of a person for non-compliance with the lawful order of a court or in order to secure the fulfilment of any obligation prescribed by law;

(c) the lawful arrest or detention of a person effected for the purpose of bringing him before the competent legal authority on reasonable suspicion of having committed an offence or when it is reasonably considered necessary to prevent his committing an offence or fleeing after having done so;

(d) the detention of a minor by lawful order for the purpose of educational super-vision or his lawful detention for the purpose of bringing him before the competent legal authority;

(e) the lawful detention of persons for the spreading of infectious diseases, of persons of unsound mind, alcoholics or drug addicts;

(f) the lawful arrest or detention of a person to prevent his effecting an unauthorised entry into the country or of a person against whom action is being taken with a view to deportation or extradition.

(2) Everyone who is arrested shall be informed promptly, in a language which he understands, of the reasons for his arrest and of any charge against him.

(3) Everyone arrested or detained in accordance with paragraph 1(c) of this article shall be brought before a judge or other officer authorised by law to exercise judicial power and shall be entitled to trial within a reasonable time or to release pending trial. Release may be conditioned by guarantees to appear for trial.

(4) Everyone who is deprived of his liberty by arrest and detention shall be entitled to take proceedings by which the lawfulness of his detention shall be decided speedily by a court and his release ordered if the detention is not lawful.

(5) Everyone who has been the victim of arrest or detention in contravention of the provisions of this article shall have an exercisable right to compensation.

Article 6 *Right to a fair trial*

(1) In the determination of his civil rights and obligations or of any criminal charge against him, everyone is entitled to a fair and public hearing within a reasonable time by an independent and impartial tribunal established by law. Judgment shall be pronounced publicly but the press and public may be excluded from all or part of the trial in the interests of morals, public order or national security in a democratic society, where the interests of juveniles or the protection of the private life of the parties so require, or to the extent strictly necessary in the opinion of the court in special circumstances where publicity would prejudice the interests of justice.

(2) Everyone charged with a criminal offence shall be presumed innocent until proved guilty according to law.

(3) Everyone charged with a criminal offence has the following minimum rights:

(a) to be informed promptly, in a language he understands and in detail, of the nature and cause of the accusation against him;

(b) to have adequate time and facilities for the preparation of his defence;

(c) to defend himself in person or through legal assistance of his own choosing or, if he has not sufficient means to pay for legal assistance, to be given it free when the interests of justice so require;

(d) to examine or have examined witnesses against him and to obtain the attendance and examination of witnesses on his behalf under the same conditions as witnesses against him;

(e) to have the free assistance of an interpreter if he cannot understand or speak the language used in court.

At each stage of proceedings, judges can usually apply domestic law without fear that their decisions will be at odds with either of these provisions. For example, the tests under the Bail Act 1976 and Article 5(3) for granting bail are broadly similar; both assume a right to bail unless there are in the former case *substantial* grounds and in the latter *relevant and sufficient* grounds for refusing it (*Wemhoff v. Germany*).[3] Similarly, the domestic provisions relating to admissibility of evidence (under the Police and Criminal Evidence Act 1984) seem to sit easily with Article 6.

This broad conformity was to be expected, as much of the criminal legislation passed in the years leading up to 1998 was drafted with the Convention in mind. In addition, those statutory provisions which were thought to be potentially inconsistent were revised before the passage of the Act. For example, section 25 of the Criminal Justice and Public Order Act 1994, which imposed an absolute prohibition on the grant of bail on a charge of certain serious offences where the defendant had a prior conviction for any such offence, was thought to breach Article 5(3) and was repealed. As a result, most of what remains (even those more controversial developments, such as the abolition of the right to remain silent without giving rise to adverse inferences) is thought to satisfy the requirements of Article 6, so long as proper directions to the jury are given (*R. v. Birchall*).[4]

An interesting illustration of the effect of the Convention on English statutory law was provided by *R. v. A*[5] where the House of Lords ruled that the domestic legislation restricting cross-examination of complainants in a rape trial was inconsistent with the defendant's Convention right to a fair trial under Article 6. In a classic example of how domestic law must now be seen through the prism of the Convention, their Lordships held that judges should interpret section 41 of the Youth Justice and Criminal Evidence Act 1999 in a 'linguistically strained' (*per* Lord Steyn) manner: i.e., in conflict with its natural meaning. For English judges used to applying the strict letter of the law, this is a novel development.

Other aspects of the judicial process have also been affected. For despite the broad compatibility of the domestic bail regime noted above, the tone of the Convention case law dictates that judges must be slower to deny bail than they were previously (*R. v. Havering Magistrates, ex parte DPP*).[6] In another example, Convention case law has indicated that the judge should be even more zealous to ensure that the prosecution discloses any material in its possession which may assist the defendant (*Jespers v. Belgium*[7] and *Rowe and Davis v. UK*).[8] Failure to do so may infringe the Convention right to 'equality of arms', contained in Article 6, and any resulting conviction would ordinarily have to be quashed.

The Convention has also brought about certain structural changes, which have had a significant impact on the nature and appearance of English criminal trials. For example, magistrates sitting without a jury for the purpose of trying less serious offences must now give reasons for their decisions in order to comply with Article 6(1). It has also been held, following the trial of two boys aged 11 for the murder of a 3-year-old near Liverpool, that Article 6 requires a specially-adapted procedure to

---

[3] (1968) 1 EHRR 55.   [4] [1999] *Crim. LR* 311.   [5] [2001] UK HL 25.
[6] [2001] 1 WLR 805.   [7] 27 D & R 61.   [8] (2000) 30 EHRR 1.

promote the welfare of young defendants, adequately protecting their right to privacy, and enabling them to understand and participate fully in proceedings (*Venables* v. *UK*).[9] The British government immediately responded to that decision by invoking measures to make the process more informal and less intimidating; one obvious change is that, in such cases, wigs and gowns are no longer worn by either the judge or counsel.

Even after the trial process is essentially complete, the judge must continue to take account of the Convention for the purposes of passing judgment or sentence. In *Percy* v. *DPP*,[10] the decision of a district judge to convict a defendant for defacing an American flag outside a US air base was quashed on the ground that it was incompatible with rights contained in Article 10 (freedom of expression). In a second example, a judge's decision to exercise his statutory entitlement under the domestic law to impose a life sentence even though it was clear that the defendant was not in fact a danger to the public was found to amount to arbitrary detention within the meaning of Article 5(1) (*R.* v. *Offen*).[11]

It is clear then that the Human Rights Act has established a new legal climate in which modern British judges operate. That said, it is possible to exaggerate the extent of change to the judge's duties and the court process as a whole. In the nine months since 2 October 2000, human rights issues were raised in less than 0.5 per cent of the cases heard in the Crown Court.[12] Indeed, since the Human Rights Act 1998 came into force there has been little reason to suppose that the domestic law of the United Kingdom is fundamentally incompatible with the jurisprudence of the European Court of Human Rights.

Further Reading

ASHWORTH, A., *The Criminal Process: An Evaluative Study* (2nd edn., Oxford: Oxford University Press, 1998).

DEVLIN, P., *The Judge* (Oxford: Oxford University Press, 1979).

DU CANN, R., *The Art of the Advocate* (London: Penguin, 1993).

EVANS, K., *Advocacy at the Bar* (London: Blackstone, 1983).

JACKSON, J., 'Judicial Responsibility in Criminal Proceedings' [1996] *Current Legal Problems* 59.

JUSTICE, *The Judiciary* (London: JUSTICE, 1972).

MCCONVILLE, M., *et al.*, *Standing Accused: The Organisation and Practices of Criminal Defence Lawyers in Britain* (Oxford: Oxford University Press, 1994).

MUNRO, C., and WASIK, M. (eds.), *Sentencing, Judicial Discretion and Training* (London: Sweet & Maxwell, 1992).

NAPLEY, D., *The Technique of Persuasion* (4th edn., London: Sweet & Maxwell, 1991).

OLIVER, D., 'The Independence of the Judiciary' [1986] *Current Legal Problems* 237.

PANNICK, D., *Judges* (Oxford: Oxford University Press, 1987).

STEVENS, R., *The Independence of the Judiciary* (Oxford: Oxford University Press, 1993).

---

[9] (2000) 30 EHRR 121.   [10] [2001] EWHC Admin. 1123.

[11] [2001] 1 WLR 253 (CA).   [12] Lord Chancellor's Dept., Feb. 2002.

19

THE ADVERSARY TRIAL AND TRIAL BY JUDGE ALONE

John Jackson

The two features most commonly used to capture the essence of the English criminal trial are that it is adversarial in nature and that its outcome is determined by a jury of twelve persons rather than by a judge sitting alone. Yet in some respects it has always been misleading to characterize the English trial in these ways. Although the jury is typically presented as the fulcrum of the English adversarial trial, the part played by the jury in the criminal process is more limited than its popular depiction would suggest. We shall see that it is also misleading to describe the English mode of trial as purely adversarial, as this gives insufficient recognition to the pivotal role of the judge in the trial. These are nevertheless features of the English trial that have stood out in the last 200 years or so. But there are reasons to believe that they will feature less forcefully in years to come. Over the last thirty-five years the jury has been in more serious decline and, more recently, a number of developments seem to be moving in the direction of making the English trial less adversarial. Before we examine these developments we need to be clear about what we mean by the adversarial trial, and what are the special features of the English adversarial trial.

THE ADVERSARIAL TRIAL

The term 'adversarial' is often used rather misleadingly to describe common law or Anglo-American modes of trial in contrast to the non-adversarial or inquisitorial modes to be found in civil law or continental systems of justice. The difficulty with this is that a number of continental systems consider that they have systems that are a mixture of adversarial and inquisitorial features.[1] The attempt to portray adversarial and inquisitorial proceedings in terms of actual legal systems can then lead to rather sterile arguments about whether a particular system is best described as adversarial or inquisitorial.

---

[1] W. T. Pizzi, *Trials without Truth* (New York: New York University Press, 1999) 111. For the varied meanings given to the term 'adversarial' see M. Damaska, 'The Adversary System' in S. Kadish (ed.), *Encyclopedia of Crime and Justice* (London: Macmillan, 1983) i, 24.

Instead of associating adversariness with actual legal systems, another way to view it is as encapsulating a body of core rights to which individuals should be entitled in order to receive a fair trial. In its interpretation of Article 6 of the European Convention on Human Rights, which prescribes minimum standards for a fair trial for so-called adversarial and non-adversarial systems alike throughout Europe, the European Court of Human Rights has considered that it is a fundamental aspect of a fair trial that criminal proceedings should be adversarial and that there should be 'equality of arms' between prosecution and defence.[2] According to the Court, the right to an adversarial trial means that 'both prosecution and defence must be given the opportunity to have knowledge of and comment on the observations filed and the evidence adduced by the other party'.[3] This may be seen as part of a broader adversary ideology where the focus has been on the protection offered to the accused and on the position of the accused *vis-à-vis* the State.

Adversary ideology demands that the State proves its case against the accused before being subjected to sanctions and that the accused be given a meaningful opportunity to contest the case against him or her. To offset the considerable resources enjoyed by the State, the equality-of-arms principle requires that the parties have the same access to information that is relevant to the case and have equal opportunity to present evidence and contradict the evidence produced by the other. A number of rights specifically mentioned in Article 6 help to reflect this adversary ideology by providing for prompt notification of the charges, for adequate time for the preparation of the defence, for the right to legal assistance, for the right to cross-examination of witnesses, and for the free assistance of an interpreter. The European Court of Human Rights has also interpreted Article 6 to include certain other rights, not specifically mentioned in the Article, one of the most important of which has been the privilege against self-incrimination or the right of silence whereby defendants cannot be compelled to contribute to their own conviction.[4] Article 6 requires contracting states to organize their systems of criminal procedure in such a way as to guarantee these adversarial rights. But it does not prescribe precisely how these rights should be guaranteed.

Another meaning given to adversariness is to use it to describe an ideal type of adjudication in which these rights are not only guaranteed but also where the procedural action is controlled by the parties and the adjudicator remains essentially passive.[5] In this system the litigants and their counsel decide what facts shall be subject to proof, and they are entrusted with seeking the evidentiary material, preparing it for trial, and presenting it in court. Although such a system does not entail the contest taking place in one concentrated trial,[6] the adversarial trial is traditionally its focal point. The advantage of this is that the parties can devote their energies to preparing for one event at which all the relevant issues can be examined and adjudged

---

[2] See *Rowe and Davis* v. *United Kingdom*, App. No. 28901/95, (2000) 30 EHRR 1, para. 60.

[3] *Ibid.*

[4] This principle was first enunciated by the European Court of Human Rights in *Funke* v. *France* (1993) 16 EHRR 297.

[5] M. Damaska, *Evidence Law Adrift* (New Haven, Conn.: Yale University Press, 1997) 74.

[6] *Ibid.*, at 74–5.

all at once. Since it is essential that the parties persuade the adjudicator to decide in their favour, much energy is devoted to presenting their case in the best light, and this has meant a heavy reliance upon orality, as witnesses are called to testify to disputed facts, and upon advocacy, as skilful presentation of evidence becomes important in putting forward the case. In a criminal case the prosecutor will first present his or her case through a series of witnesses who are called and examined by the prosecutor about the relevant facts of the case, and then cross-examined by the defence. Assuming the prosecution case reaches a sufficiency of proof after it has been presented, the defence will then adduce its case, calling the witnesses of its choice, who will then be cross-examined by the prosecutor. At the end of the case the lawyers will put arguments to the tribunal deciding the case but there must be an evidential basis for what the lawyers say at this stage.

One of the problems with leaving control over evidence-gathering and presentation to the parties is that the factual material which is used may be distorted by them. In order to test the reliability of this material, it is necessary to have mechanisms which encourage those with the most direct knowledge of the evidence in dispute to be made available, and at the same time discourage or exclude unduly prejudicial or unreliable evidence. This function has been traditionally played by the rules of evidence. There is also a need to have rules to ensure that each party has an equal opportunity to participate. A major problem with structuring the criminal proof process in the form of a contest is that the balance of power and resources is inevitably weighted greatly in favour of the police and prosecution, and any attempt to structure the process in terms of a contest runs the risk of being extremely one-sided. To remedy this problem strong rules need to be put in place in the pre-trial investigative phase of the proceedings to protect defendants, and at the trial itself evidentiary barriers against conviction need to be erected to enable the defendant to confront and challenge the prosecution case, to prevent the prosecution relying on particularly prejudicial information, and to guard against governmental abuse in the earlier phases of the process.[7]

The adversarial trial is presided over by a judge whose role is confined largely to umpiring the contest and ensuring that the parties abide by the rules. Traditionally, the trial has also been associated with a jury sitting separately from the judge, whose task is to decide the case by entering a verdict of guilty or not guilty. The division of function between the judge and the jury is traditionally described in terms of a division between questions of law and questions of fact. It is the responsibility of the judge to charge or direct the jury on the law and the responsibility of the jury to apply the law to the facts as they find them. Whether a jury ultimately decide the case or this is left to the judge or to a panel of judges, the tribunal's opportunities for active inquiry during the trial and for generating new evidence on its own initiative are strictly limited. The fact-finding role of the tribunal is therefore restricted for the most part to weighing the evidence adduced by the various parties and deciding the issues on the basis of the burden of proof.

---

[7] See M. Damaska, 'Evidentiary Barriers to Conviction and Two Models of Criminal Procedure: A Comparative Study' (1973) 121 *University of Pennsylvania Law Review* 507.

Much ink has been spilt on the question of how effective this mode of trial is in obtaining the truth and in promoting other values such as defending the rights of the defendant.[8] The choice of procedure may depend upon particular ideological pre-conceptions such as the extent to which public officials are trusted, the degree to which it is considered necessary to provide safeguards from abuse within the proof process at the expense of truth-finding, and the importance of party participation.[9] Whatever the choices made, few actual systems adopt a pure adversarial mode of trial, and in the English system a number of distinctive features prevent the trial becoming wholly adversarial.

THE ENGLISH ADVERSARIAL TRIAL

Until recently all cases tried in the Crown Court were handled by a legal profession which was divided between solicitors, who prepared the case for trial, and barristers, who were briefed by solicitors to present the case in court. Only barristers had rights of audience in the Crown Court and the other higher courts, although this has now changed, with the result that certain solicitors, known as solicitor-advocates, may now present cases in these courts as well.[10] It might be thought that a small corps of lawyers dedicated almost exclusively to advocacy might provide the ideal condition for a pure adversarial trial, with each hired barrister trying to win his or her case at all costs. In fact there are a number of features of the English Bar which militate against extreme adversarialism.

The Bar has traditionally been composed of a small elite of advocates bound together by values and rituals which have set them apart from other lawyers and their clients.[11] One feature which has prevented the Bar becoming too closely aligned with particular types of client has been the 'cab-rank' rule whereby the barrister is required to accept the first brief given to him or her rather in the way that a taxi-cab driver must take the first person in the queue willing to pay the fare.[12] This means that barristers may be prosecuting in a case one day and defending in a case the next. Once the brief is accepted, the limited nature of the barrister's role means that he or she has to do the best with the instructions given by the solicitor. The barrister is the advocate of the brief, not of the client or, as it has been put, 'the bricks the barrister moulds can be no stronger than the straw supplied'.[13] The result is that a low priority has been put on establishing any kind of relationship between the barrister and the client. Briefs are

---

[8] For a useful synthesis of the arguments see D. Luban, *Lawyers and Justice: An Ethical Study* (Princeton, NJ: Princeton University Press, 1988) chap. 5.

[9] See M. Damaska, *The Faces of Justice and State Authority* (New Haven, Conn.: Yale University Press, 1986).

[10] The Bar's monopoly on advocacy in the higher courts was first broken by the enactment of the Courts and Legal Services Act 1990. These changes were taken further by the Access to Justice Act 1999.

[11] For an historical account see B. Hollander, *The English Bar: A Priesthood* (1964).

[12] See General Council of the Bar, *Code of Conduct of the Bar of England and Wales* (1990), para. 203.

[13] R. Du Cann, *The Art of the Advocate* (London: Penguin Press, 1980) 52.

often received very late in the day, and often the barrister does not speak with the defendant until the day of the trial.[14] This limited role has been reinforced by strict rules forbidding barristers from rehearsing or coaching witnesses and limiting the contact barristers have with clients and witnesses. Barristers are not supposed to speak with defendants except in the presence of a solicitor, and until recently they were not permitted to have any contact with witnesses (other than experts or the defendant).

This aloofness between the barrister and the defendant and witnesses carries on into the trial. Defendants are physically separated in the 'dock', a small box at the back or side of the courtroom, often quite a distance from the barrister, who stands in the 'well' of the courtroom. Barristers also wear wigs and gowns that appear to distance them from others in the courtroom. More significantly, barristers appear to offer little visible support for the witnesses they call during their examination of them, with the result that witnesses sometimes feel let down by their side.[15] Instead they appear more concerned to assist the judge, who often calls for assistance from them, and the jury during the course of the trial. This concern to assist the court is again reinforced by a strong rule demanding that they owe a duty to the court. Advocates, for example, are expected to offer dispassionate assistance to the court on legal issues whether the arguments support their side or not. Many trials admittedly take place in magistrates' courts where cases may be presented by solicitors or barristers and where the ritualistic formality of the Crown Court trial is notably absent. Nevertheless, even in them, the defendant still sits alone in the dock and many of the ethical rules governing barristers apply to advocates in the magistrates' courts as well.

Commentators have suggested that the English criminal adversarial trial is much less adversarial than its counterpart in the United States.[16] One study contrasting the style of advocacy in the USA with that in England concluded that in the USA the advocate takes every advantage legally and ethically possible. In England and Wales, by contrast, the advocate owes a strong loyalty to the court as well as to his or her client.[17] This does not mean that advocates are necessarily restrained in their cross-examination of witnesses for the opposing side. But in presenting the case for their own side either through the examination of witnesses or in arguments to the judge or jury, they appear to be more restrained than their American counterparts.

If one feature of the English adversarial trial is more restrained conduct on the part of counsel, another feature is that the trial judge has traditionally had much greater authority than his or her American counterpart. Lip service is often paid by judges to the umpireal role which they occupy in the adversarial trial. One example is Lord Denning's classic statement over forty years ago, in which he considered that the trial judge should intervene in limited circumstances:

[14] One study found that in 38% of cases in the English Crown Court the defendant had never spoken with the barrister before trial: see M. Zander and P. Henderson, *Crown Court Study*, Royal Commission on Criminal Justice Research Study No. 19 (London: HMSO, 1993) 52–5.

[15] J. Jackson, R. Kilpatrick, and C. Harvey, *Called to Court: A Public Review of Criminal Justice in Northern Ireland* (Belfast: SLS Publications, 1991) 106.

[16] See e.g. Pizzi, n. 1 above, chaps. 5 and 6.

[17] P. W. Tague, *Effective Advocacy for the Criminal Defendant: The Barrister vs the Lawyer* (Buffalo, NY: Hein & Co, 1996) 232–3.

only himself asking questions of witnesses when it is necessary to clear up any point that has been overlooked or left obscure; to see that the advocates behave themselves seemly and keep to the rules laid down by law; to exclude irrelevancies and discourage repetition; to make sure by wise intervention that he follows the points the advocates are making; and at the end to make up his mind where the truth lies.[18]

Although this statement of the adversary ideal was made in a civil case, it has been accepted as applying also to the judge in a criminal trial. Yet, historically, English judges played a much more dominant role in the trial process than one of simply seeing that the parties abide by the rules.[19] Even when lawyers came to occupy a significant role in the trial process in the nineteenth century, judges have never been inclined to give up their role as a 'director' of proceedings in favour of a purely umpireal role. Of course, judges are constantly reminded that they risk upsetting the adversarial balance between the parties if they 'descend' into the arena. But they have considerable freedom to stray beyond the umpireal boundaries and ask probing questions of witnesses.[20] Aside from their powers to question witnesses, they have always had powers to amend indictments or charges, to call witnesses, and to withdraw weak cases from the jury.

In reality, judges are not only empowered to undertake certain active fact-finding responsibilities, they have a duty to sum up the evidence before the jury whether they wish to or not. They also have duties to put before the jury any defence or defence issue which has arisen on the evidence, even if it has not been raised by the defence.[21] These duties appear to suggest that even in the traditional jury setting where juries bring in the final verdict, judges have always borne some responsibility for the outcome of the criminal trial beyond the merely umpireal concern to see that the parties abide by the rules. Hence the traditional view that judges have responsibility merely for the law and juries responsibility for the facts is a misleading one, and it is more apt to characterize the factual function as one in which responsibility is shared between the judge and the jury.[22] Until recently, however, the courts have not been prepared to be particularly open about acknowledging this role and about articulating its proper rationale and scope.[23] But new challenges are requiring judges to recognize that they have an expanding role within the criminal trial which will have considerable implications for the adversarial trial.

---

[18] Jones v. National Coal Board [1957] 2 QB 55 at 64.

[19] See J. Langbein, 'The Criminal Trial before the Lawyers' (1978) 45 University of Chicago Law Review 263; Wigmore on Evidence (Boston, Mass.: Little Brown, 1970) para. 784.

[20] J. Jackson and S. Doran, Judge without Jury: Diplock Trials in the Adversary System (Oxford: Clarendon Press, 1995) chap. 5.

[21] S. Doran, 'Alternative Defences: the "Invisible Burden" on the Trial Judge' [1991] Crim. LR 878.

[22] For discussion of the division of labour between judges and juries see J. Jackson and S. Doran, 'Judge and Jury: Towards a New Division of Labour in Criminal Trials' (1997) 60 MLR 759.

[23] See S. Doran, 'The Necessarily Expanding Role of the Criminal Trial Judge' in S. Doran and J. Jackson (eds.), The Judicial Role in Criminal Proceedings (Oxford: Hart Publishing, 2000) 3.

CURTAILING ADVERSARIALISM

We have seen that there have always been features of the English criminal trial which have inhibited the kind of adversarialism seen more evidently in the United States. Within the last thirty years, however, there has been a steady erosion of faith in even the more limited adversarial characteristics of the English trial. Three factors may be singled out as contributing to this decline in confidence. First of all, English criminal justice has been haunted by a series of miscarriages of justice during this period. Secondly, there has been concern at the way in which witnesses and victims have been treated in the adversarial trial, calling into question the entire adversarial mode of eliciting evidence. Thirdly, there have been increasing demands for the English criminal justice system to be more efficient and cost-effective, and the adversarial trial has become a target for those who consider that it is an inefficient and expensive way of resolving criminal disputes.

MISCARRIAGES OF JUSTICE

Confidence in English criminal justice declined to a very low point at the end of the 1980s when the Court of Appeal had to quash a number of high-profile convictions of Irish defendants charged with terrorist offences. Although many of these miscarriages were considered to be the result of flaws in police investigation that took place well before the trial stage, the lesson that some derived from this experience was that the miscarriages exposed the dangers of a zealous adversary system where partisan inquiries conducted by the police, and in some of the cases by government forensic scientists, could not be countered adequately by the defence at trial.[24] As the Court of Appeal recognized in a number of these miscarriage cases, a disadvantage of the adversarial nature of criminal proceedings is that the parties are not matched in terms of resources.[25]

The imbalance between prosecution and defence has been traditionally addressed by mounting evidential hurdles against the prosecution in the form of imposing a heavy burden of proof on the prosecution, and by strong exclusionary rules of evidence designed to protect the accused before trial and to enable the defence to cross-examine the primary sources of evidence against the defendant. But the miscarriage of justice cases showed that more was needed in the form of strong disclosure rules before trial to enable the defence to contest the prosecution case on a more equal basis, and the courts themselves began to develop rules requiring the prosecution to

---

[24] For discussion of the miscarriages of justice that blighted English criminal justice see B. Woffinden, *Miscarriages of Justice* (London: Hodder & Stoughton, 1989); C. Walker and K. Starmer, *Miscarriages of Justice* (London: Blackstone Press, 1999); R. Nobles and D. Schiff, *Understanding Miscarriages of Justice* (Oxford: Clarendon Press, 2000).

[25] *R. v. McIlkenny and others* [1992] 2 All ER 417; *R. v. Ward* [1993] 2 All ER 577.

disclose all material evidence to the defence.[26] As these rules were being developed, however, there was concern that they might give too great an advantage to the defence which has traditionally had to disclose very little information to the prosecution. One common complaint was that the defence was able to ambush the prosecution with surprise defences at trial which could not be properly investigated by the prosecution beforehand. As a result statutory measures were taken to put a greater onus on the accused to come forward with an explanation of events before and at trial. One important change has been to permit the court or jury to draw inferences against defendants when they rely upon facts at trial which could have been mentioned to the police before trial, or to draw inferences against them when they fail to give evidence after a case is made out against them.[27] Another change has been to require the defence to issue a defence statement disclosing its defence before trial after the prosecution has made initial disclosure to the defence, so that the prosecution is not taken by surprise at trial.[28]

Although these changes may be viewed as challenging the adversary ideology whereby the onus is on the prosecution to make its case without assistance from the defence,[29] they have not posed any fundamental challenge to the adversarial trial. The arguments have been over how the contest between prosecution and defence may be made fairer to both sides rather than about the nature of the adversarial trial itself. But another response to the miscarriages of justice in the late 1980s has been to recognize that it is not enough to depend on the adversarial trial itself to prevent miscarriages of justice and that more inquisitorial elements should be introduced into the criminal process before and at trial. The courts themselves have shown signs of being more open about the fact that they have a degree of responsibility for the outcome of criminal trials. A turning point came in the case of Judith Ward who was wrongly convicted of killing a number of people in an IRA bomb explosion in 1973. The Court of Appeal which quashed Ward's conviction in 1992 stated that trial judges had a responsibility to persevere in the task of ensuring that the law, practice, and methods of trial should be developed so as to reduce the risk of conviction of the innocent to an absolute minimum.[30] As a consequence it ruled that it was ultimately the responsibility of the judges and not just the prosecution to ensure that there was proper disclosure as it was the judges' responsibility to ensure that the accused received a fair trial.

Ward was the culmination of a long line of miscarriages of justice exposing weaknesses in the English criminal justice system and, after the notorious case of the Birmingham Six the year before, the government was compelled to appoint a Royal Commission on Criminal Justice to consider whether there was a need for more radical changes to the system.[31] Within its terms of reference the Commission had to

---

[26] See most importantly *R. v. Maguire and others* [1992] 2 All ER 433 and *R. v. Ward* [1993] 2 All ER 577.

[27] Criminal Justice and Public Order Act 1994, ss. 34–35.

[28] Criminal Procedure and Investigations Act 1996, s. 5.

[29] See G. W. O'Reilly, 'England Limits the Right of Silence and Moves Towards an Inquisitorial System of Justice' (1994) 85 *Journal of Criminology and Criminal Law* 402.

[30] [1993] 2 All ER 577 at 628.

[31] Royal Commission on Criminal Justice, *Report*, Cmnd 2263 (1993).

consider whether the courts should play a more investigative role before and during trial and move towards a more inquisitorial system of proof. Two reforms attracted particular attention. First of all, it was suggested that judicial officers should supervise the pre-trial investigation phase of criminal proceedings. The model most frequently cited was the *juge d'instruction* in France. The other suggestion was that with the increased reliance on forensic evidence in criminal trials, an independent forensic service should be established which would work for the courts, and court-appointed experts should be commissioned on behalf of the courts, as is the case in a number of Continental countries such as France, where judges commission experts from a list of official experts. One of the shocking revelations which emerged from a number of the miscarriage-of-justice cases was that supposedly neutral expert witnesses could come to see their function as helping the police and prosecution. In the *Ward* case, for example, three senior government scientists deliberately withheld scientific tests from the defence which threw doubt on the scientific evidence relied on by the prosecution. On the question how to prevent the kind of party allegiance bias on the part of experts which occurred in the *Ward* case happening again, the Commission recommended that there should be an independent Forensic Science Service but did not support a move toward a system of court-appointed experts. Some commentators have noted that such a system is not without its own defects.[32] Although court experts may not be so susceptible to party allegiance bias, they may nevertheless have their own biases, and there is a danger that although the parties should be able to cross-examine them, they might adopt an overly deferential stance towards them.

In the event the Royal Commission did not support the proposal for an English form of the *juge d'instruction*. It did not see how such an inquisitorial judge could fit into the established roles of the police, prosecution, and defence in an adversarial system and rejected the idea of court experts. But it did recognize that the English system had veered too far in the direction of a thoroughgoing adversarial system which seemed to turn the search for truth into a contest played between opposing lawyers and made certain proposals to make judges play a more active role during the trial. One recommendation was that judges should stop cases where they took the view that the prosecution evidence was demonstrably unsafe or unsatisfactory or too weak to be allowed to go to the jury. Another was that judges should be more prepared to call witnesses themselves, following a finding from research it commissioned that in 19 per cent of contested cases judges reported that they knew of one or more important witnesses who had not been called by either side.[33] On the other hand, although it was proposed that judges should take a more expansionist role in terms of asking questions and calling witnesses during the trial, the Commission considered that in summing up to the jury at the end of the trial they should be more restrained about the comments they made about the evidence. In a number of miscarriage cases the judges had made extremely damning and inaccurate observations before the jury on

---

[32] See the discussion in M. Redmayne, *Expert Evidence in Criminal Justice* (Oxford: Clarendon Press, 2000) at 205–13.

[33] N. 14 above at 111.

summation.[34] The Commission considered that judges should no longer comment on the credibility of witnesses and counsel should correct the judge on matters of fact.

THE TREATMENT OF WITNESSES AND VICTIMS

If the adversarial trial has proved wanting in guarding against miscarriages of justice, there have also been arguments that it has failed to offer enough protection to witnesses and victims of crime.[35] Attention has tended to focus chiefly on the difficulties which particularly vulnerable witnesses face in court, for example child witnesses and rape victims.[36] But there has also been a growing awareness of the ordeal that all kinds of witnesses can suffer in court, which can involve a fear of intimidation, a bruising attack on their character by counsel, and a difficulty in communicating effectively in the adversarial mode of trial.[37] This poses a challenge to the way in which witnesses are examined and cross-examined in the adversarial trial. We saw in the last section that counsel may be more restrained than their US counterparts in presenting their cases before the court. But this restraint has not prevented them exercising considerable control over the witnesses they examine and cross-examine. Too often it is said counsel try to intimidate or confuse witnesses, clouding the issues at trial and preventing witnesses telling events the way they wish to. One study conducted in Wood Green Crown Court in London found that almost as a matter of course counsel would so 'blackguard' witnesses that they were no longer believable.[38] Even when cross-examination appears more restrained as in the case of expert witnesses, counsel will attempt rigorously to control what they say.[39]

The Royal Commission did not propose any particularly radical solutions to these problems. It recommended that judges should be vigilant to check unfair cross-examination by counsel of witnesses who are likely to be distressed or vulnerable. But it did not face up to the fact that if the parties are to continue to control the presentation of evidence, as they must in an adversarial system, they must be given considerable freedom to develop their case as they wish. The dangers of judicial intervention

---

[34] For examples see Woffinden, n. 24 above, at 405 and J. Jackson, 'Trial Procedures' in Walker and Starmer, n. 24 above at 199.

[35] See e.g. J. R. Spencer, 'Court Experts and Expert Witnesses: Have We a Lesson to Learn from the French?' [1992] *Crim. LR* 213.

[36] See e.g. J. R. Spencer and R. Flin, *The Evidence of Children* (2nd edn., London: Blackstone Press, 1993); J. Temkin, *Rape and the Legal Process* (London: Sweet & Maxwell, 1987); J. McEwan, *Evidence and the Adversarial Process* (2nd edn., Oxford: Hart Publishing, 1998) chap. 4; L. Ellison, 'Cross-Examination in Rape Trials' [1998] *Crim. LR* 605.

[37] See Jackson *et al.*, n. 15 above, P. Rock, *The Social World of an English Crown Court* (Oxford: Clarendon Press, 1993); D. Brereton, 'How Different are Rape Trials? A Comparison of the Cross-Examination Of Complainants in Rape and Assault Trials' (1997) 37 *British Journal of Criminology* 242.

[38] Rock, n. 37 above at 34.

[39] P. Roberts and C. Willmore, *The Role of Forensic Science in Criminal Proceedings*, Royal Commission on Criminal Justice Research Study No. 11 (London: HMSO, 1993); C. A. G. Jones, *Expert Witnesses: Science, Medicine and the Practice of Law* (Oxford: Clarendon, 1994).

in the adversarial trial have been set out by a number of commentators.[40] Where there is a trial by jury there is the additional danger that jurors will become over-influenced by the judge's views of the facts. The Royal Commission did, however, suggest certain changes designed to free expert witnesses from the adversarial constraints of lawyers' control without handing over control to judges.[41] The Commission proposed that in cases where the defence is calling an expert the opposing experts should meet before trial to discuss the issues and draw up an agreed report. At the trial itself the Commission also proposed that, where the evidence was disputed, expert witnesses should be asked before they leave the witness box whether there is anything they wish to say.

These recommendations were designed to discourage excessive adversarialism, and thereby reduce the scope and effect of cross-examination by lawyers. But despite the criticisms made of it, cross-examination is likely to remain a crucial feature of the adversarial trial, especially since it has been given express recognition in Article 6(3)(d) of the European Convention on Human Rights, which states that one of the rights of the defendant is the right to examine or have examined witnesses against him or her.

In other respects, however, the Convention as interpreted by the European Court of Human Rights has come to pose certain challenges to the adversarial trial on behalf of victims and witnesses. Article 6 of the Convention makes no mention of the rights of witnesses, but a number of decisions have recognized that the principles of fair trial require that the interests of the defence are balanced against the interests of victims and of the witnesses who are called upon to give evidence. In *Doorson* v. *Netherlands*,[42] for example, the Court held that the trial was not unfair when two prosecution witnesses remained anonymous and were questioned by the judge in the presence of counsel but not the accused. There was a fear in this case that the witnesses and their families would be subjected to reprisals if their anonymity were not preserved. In a key passage the Court held that contracting States should organize their criminal proceedings in such a way that the interests of witnesses in their life, liberty, or security and their interests in privacy guaranteed under Article 8 of the Convention are not unjustifiably imperilled.

The adversarial trial has traditionally been structured with only two interests in mind, those of prosecution and defence, and in the polarized contest between these two interests the rights of victims and witnesses have been given little independent protection. Now that the Convention has been incorporated into United Kingdom law and the courts, as public authorities, must act in such a way as is compatible with Convention rights,[43] it seems that judges will in future be required to guarantee not only the rights of the individual accused but also the rights of witnesses and victims who become embroiled in the adversarial trial.[44] Already English legislation has begun

---

[40] See e.g. M. Frankel, 'The Search for Truth: An Umpireal View' (1975) 123 *University of Pennsylvania Law Review* 1031; S. Saltzburg, 'The Unnecessarily Expanding Role of the American Trial Judge' (1978) 63 *University of Virginia Law Review* 1.

[41] N. 31 above at 158, 160.   [42] (1996) 23 EHRR 330.   [43] Human Rights Act 1998, s. 6.

[44] For further discussion of the impact of the Human Rights Act upon the judicial role in the criminal trials see J. Jackson, 'The Impact of Human Rights on Judicial Decision Making' in Doran and Jackson, n. 23 above at 109.

to take account of the interests of particularly vulnerable victims and witnesses. Action has been taken to reduce the stress of child witnesses.[45] A child witness may not be cross-examined by the accused in person and may be permitted to give evidence through a live television link. Even more innovatively, the courts may also permit the admission into evidence of a videorecording of an interview with a child conducted before trial. Where the video is admitted the witness is not to be examined in chief on any matter dealt with adequately in the videorecording. These steps are to be extended to cover a range of vulnerable witnesses whose physical or mental disability or disorder or whose fear or distress in connection with giving evidence is likely to diminish the quality of their evidence.[46] Provision is also made for the first time in these new measures for videorecorded cross-examination and re-examination. In addition defendants are to be prohibited from cross-examining in person complainants of sexual offences, as well as children.[47]

INCREASING THE EFFICIENCY OF THE COURT SYSTEM

One interesting feature of these innovations is that they represent a movement away from regarding the adversarial trial as one concentrated hearing at which all the evidence is presented together. This is one example of an increasing tendency to hold preliminary hearings before trial in order to narrow down the evidence presented and contested in the adversarial trial. This narrowing down of the adversarial trial has been undertaken, not in the name of preventing miscarriages of justice or protecting victims and witnesses, but in order to increase the efficiency of the trial process, and it potentially presents the greatest challenge to the full-scale adversarial trial. A radical overhaul of civil trial procedure has already been undertaken over the last ten years in an attempt to shift the responsibility of civil litigation away from civil litigants and their legal advisers towards the courts.[48] The same process is now under way for criminal proceedings. Some steps such as the use of pre-trial reviews can be traced back a number of years but they were given further momentum by the Royal Commission on Criminal Justice, which recommended greater use of preparatory hearings before trial, more structured pre-trial disclosure, and sentence canvassing.

Since then the government has implemented a scheme for 'pleas and directions' under which all cases are to be initially listed for hearing after being transferred to the

---

[45] Criminal Justice Act 1988, ss. 32A and 34A.

[46] Youth Justice and Criminal Evidence Act 1999, ss. 16–33. A further provision, however (s. 41 of the 1999 Act) which clearly restricts the cross-examination of sexual complainants on their sexual history has had to be more broadly construed than intended by Parliament in order to ensure compatibility with Art. 6 of the European Convention on Human Rights: see, *R. v. A* [2001] 3 All ER 1.

[47] *Ibid.* at ss. 34–39.

[48] *Access to Justice: Final Report by Lord Woolf MR, to the Lord Chancellor on the Civil Justice System in England and Wales* (London: HMSO, 1996).

Crown Court.[49] Judges may order a pre-trial hearing in any case where an examination of the indictment suggests that the trial is likely to be long and complex and judges have powers to make binding rulings on issues of disclosure and admissibility.[50] More recently, a Criminal Courts Review was established in 1999 to determine how justice might be delivered 'by streamlining all their processes, increasing their efficiency and strengthening the effectiveness of their relationships with others across the whole of the criminal justice system'.[51] The Review has recommended that there should be a unified court structure, replacing the present dual structure of the Crown Court and magistrates' courts with a single court system in which professional judges and lay magistrates would sit at their different levels, all as judges of the same court.[52]

THE DECLINE OF TRIAL BY JURY

Greater managerialism has the potential to break up the concentrated nature of the adversarial trial into a number of stages at which particular issues can be examined in turn by the trial judge. But one constraining factor on this development is the fact that Crown Court trials are determined by a jury composed of lay persons who are summoned to hear cases for limited periods of time. Trial by jury continues to endure, but a number of steps have been taken to reduce the numbers of cases being tried by jury, and new steps such as the proposal to abolish the defendant's right to elect for jury trial in either-way cases would accelerate this trend.[53] Another issue which is likely to come to a head shortly is the longstanding question whether there should be an alternative to trial by jury in serious fraud cases.[54] The recent Criminal Courts Review considered that in such cases the trial judge should be empowered to direct trial by the judge sitting with lay members drawn from a panel of experts in various specialities, which would be maintained by the Lord Chancellor. The Review also proposed that all cases involving young defendants should be tried in the Youth Court consisting of a judge and lay magistrates. Another recommendation is that cases of middle-ranking seriousness, presently triable either in the magistrates' court or in the Crown Court, should be decided in a new court presided over by a district judge sitting with two lay magistrates. Such a court would not be a completely novel

---

[49] Practice Direction [1995] 1 WLR 1318.

[50] Criminal Procedure and Investigations Act 1996, s. 29.

[51] The review, conducted by Auld LJ, was announced by the Lord Chancellor on 14 Dec. 1999, and reported in Oct. 2001. See *Review of the Criminal Courts of England and Wales* (London: HMSO, 2001).

[52] This idea was previously endorsed in a recent government paper outlining the government's vision of the future of criminal justice. See *Criminal Justice: The Way Ahead*, Cm 5074 (2001).

[53] See S. Lloyd-Bostock and C. Thomas, 'The Continuing Decline of the English Jury' in N. Vidmar (ed.), *World Jury Systems* (Oxford: Oxford University Press, 2000). The proposal to abolish the defendant's right to elect for jury trial in either-way cases was originally made by the Royal Commission on Criminal Justice and was the subject of Mode of Trial Bills in 1999 and 2000.

[54] The proposal that complex fraud trials should no longer be tried by juries can be traced back as far as 1986: see *Report of the Fraud Trials Committee* (London: HMSO, 1986).

arrangement as currently appeals from the magistrates' court are heard by a Crown Court judge sitting with two magistrates. But one of the casualties of such a system would be the jury, with an estimated reduction of 40,000 jury trials per year.[55]

Apart from reducing the need for one concentrated oral hearing, the reduction in the number of jury trials would be likely to diminish the adversarial purity of the criminal trial in a number of ways, as was shown in a study which compared trials by jury with trials by judge alone in Northern Ireland where cases connected with political violence have been tried by judge alone in so-called 'Diplock trials' since 1973, primarily because of a fear of jury intimidation.[56] One of the hallmarks of the adversarial trial, judicial passivity, is encouraged by the jury since it is the jury and not the judge which makes the final decision. The study found that in jury trials judges were very conscious that while they had the *power* to interrupt the flow of counsel's presentation of the evidence, they lacked the *authority* to do so because they were not responsible for the final verdict. The absence of the jury, however, meant that judges became responsible for the outcome and this gave them greater authority to intervene. Although judges might not consciously intervene more in this situation, the study found that most judges admitted that they might take a more probing approach than if they were presiding over a jury trial. The conduct of the lawyers was also found to change in the absence of the jury. Before a jury the parties have to build up their case painstakingly, piece by piece, witness by witness, as juries do not have the benefit of knowing anything about the trial beforehand. Where judges preside alone, on the other hand, they have often read the statements of the witnesses before trial and they do not come nearly so cold to the trial. This means that there is more pressure on the parties to stick to the key contested issues. The basic adversarial structure of the trial is preserved, but the contest itself changes from an all-out forensic struggle between prosecution and defence towards a more focused skirmish on particular contested issues, with judges entering the fray of argument more readily, particularly in the closing stages. This led the authors of the study to conclude that the absence of the jury necessarily results in an adversarial deficit where there are pressures on the defence not to contest the prosecution case so fully as is usual in a jury trial.

There is no suggestion that English courts are going to go down the road of Diplock trials. England and Wales, with its tradition of jury trial in the Crown Court and lay magistrates in the magistrates' courts, has relied less upon trials by judge alone than possibly any other European jurisdiction. But there are signs that in the future there may be more reliance on the professional judge to determine the outcome of trials. Professional district magistrates are being deployed more readily in magistrates' courts and it is possible that judges may come to preside alone in fraud trials. The Criminal Courts Review also recommended the adoption of an idea which has found favour in a number of Commonwealth jurisdictions that defendants should be able to opt for a trial by judge alone in certain cases.[57] These trends along with greater

---

[55] 'Straw Condemns the Juries', *The Economist*, 13 Jan. 2001.
[56] See Jackson and Doran, n. 20 above.
[57] See S. Doran and J. Jackson, 'The Case for Jury Waiver' [1997] *Crim. LR* 155.

deployment of mixed tribunals, consisting of a professional judge and lay magistrates or lay members, are likely to dilute the quality of the adversarial trial.

Much may depend on the extent to which the norms associated with the classic adversarial jury trial will continue to influence an increasingly non-jury landscape. Although the absence of the jury in Diplock trials appeared to change the manner in which the adversarial trial was conducted by both counsel and judges, these changes were less dramatic than might otherwise have been the case, because judges and counsel were very aware that the Diplock trial represented a deviation from the ideal mode of trying a serious criminal case by jury. It was significant that judges and many counsel continued to appear in both Diplock and jury trials. Judges as a result regarded it as inappropriate to deviate too far from the umpireal role expected of them in the jury trial. Counsel similarly steeped in a jury culture did not deviate radically from the manner in which they would present evidence in a jury trial. It is also significant that in Scotland and the Republic of Ireland, where jury trials also feature in a small minority of contested criminal trials and where there is a greater tradition of trial by judge alone in criminal cases,[58] judges and advocates continue to operate an adversarial system in both jury and non-jury trials, and it is likely that they would look askance at any suggestion that the adversarial structure of the trial has been considerably diluted in the non-jury forum.

The danger for the adversarial trial, however, is that the tendencies which are likely to become prevalent in the non-jury context—a more pared-down trial, greater intervention from the bench, less open confrontation between prosecution and defence—will themselves assume a normality which the continuation of the jury in a much more attenuated state is unable to reverse. Indeed the extent to which the Diplock influence seemed to encourage smooth working practices between professionals both before and at trial led the authors of the Northern Ireland study to suggest that there may have been a Diplock influence on jury trials as well as a jury influence on Diplock trials.

THE FUTURE OF THE ADVERSARIAL TRIAL

This chapter has identified a number of features which appear to be curtailing adversarialism in the English criminal trial. As a result the character of the adversarial trial is likely to change from an all-out forensic struggle, albeit one which has always been kept within bounds by professional norms and ethics, towards a much more pared-down forensic contest. Moves towards greater managerialism and concern about exposing vulnerable witnesses to the full glare of cross-examination in open

---

[58] For the prevalence of criminal trials presided over by sheriffs without a jury in Scotland see G. Maher, 'Reforming the Criminal Process: A Scottish Perspective' in M. McConville and L. Bridges (eds.), *Criminal Justice in Crisis* (Aldershot: Edward Elgar, 1994) 59. For discussion of the erosion of jury trial in the Republic of Ireland see J. Jackson, K. Quinn, and T. O'Malley, 'The Jury System in Contemporary Ireland: In the Shadow of a Troubled Past' in Vidmar, n. 53 above.

court are likely to result in arguments and testimony being increasingly heard at pre-trial hearings. At the same time, the responsibilities of trial judges towards human rights may push them towards taking a more activist stance in what remains of the concentrated trial. Finally, the spectre of an attenuated jury is likely to result in less forensic combat and greater restraint on the part of lawyers.

The extent to which these moves away from traditional adversarial philosophy take hold will depend upon the willingness of the judiciary and the legal profession to embrace a more co-operative form of justice.[59] English judges have always taken a magisterial position within the adversarial trial and they may not find it so difficult to respond to the more activist responsibilities required of them by human rights obliga-tions. But they may prove more resistant to the managerial demands made of them by government. In his radical proposals for civil litigation Lord Woolf acknowledged that the new system of case management he was recommending would require a radical change of culture.[60] At the same time a new kind of judge appointed not merely from the ranks of the Bar but from a wider pool of legal talent may be less attached to the traditional advocacy skills inculcated by the Bar and more inclined to adopt the kind of managerial stance asked of them.

It is also uncertain how lawyers will respond to the changes which are being imposed by government. The traditional practices whereby barristers come to receive briefs very late in the day militate against the effectiveness of meaningful pre-trial hearings, and a significant cultural shift will be required within the legal profession to discard the 'gladiatorial tradition' of the adversarial trial.[61] However, the Bar is likely to undergo changes in the years ahead which may be just as significant as any changes within the Bench. The emergence of solicitor-advocates in the criminal courts is likely to upset the traditionally close relationship between barristers and judges.[62] Barristers may find that they have to adopt a more adversarial stance in the cases they present in order to compete for clients, and it is possible that the trend towards less adversarial-ism identified in this chapter may be reversed by a more openly adversarial atmosphere in court. At the same time an increase in solicitor-advocates able to provide continuity of service to clients throughout the case may result in a willingness to engage in pre-trial hearings with less emphasis placed on the concentrated adversarial trial.

Amid the changes likely to affect legal procedure and the legal profession, it will be important not to lose sight of the essential challenge facing all professsional partici-pants who work in the courts, which is how the criminal courts should be managed in the interests of justice. The adversarial tenets espoused by the European Convention on Human Rights mentioned at the beginning of this chapter help to underline the essential point that, however the criminal justice system organizes its procedures, the criminal trial is essentially about determining whether defendants are guilty of the

---

[59] J. McEwan, 'Cooperative Justice and the Adversarial Trial: Lessons from the Woolf Report' in Doran and Jackson, n. 23 above at 171.

[60] Lord Woolf, *Access to Justice: Interim Report to the Lord Chancellor on the Civil Justice System in England and Wales* (London: HMSO, 1995) 18.

[61] McEwan, n. 59 above at 180.

[62] G. Hanlon and J. Jackson, 'Last Orders at the Bar? Competition, Choice and Justice for All—The Impact of Solicitor Advocacy' (1999) 19 *OJLS* 555.

charges they face and the entitlement of defendants to certain minimum rights in order to defend themselves against these charges. Procedures also need to take account of other interests in the criminal trial, such as those of witnesses and victims, and it is, of course, important to ensure that procedures work as efficiently as possible. The English adversarial trial will no doubt change in character as these concerns are taken into account. But as changes are made, it is important that thought is given to how any adversarial deficit in the rights of the defence is filled by suitably compensatory measures.

Further Reading

DAMASKA, M., 'The Adversary System' in S. Kadish (ed.), *Encyclopedia of Crime and Justice* (London: Macmillan, 1983), 1: 24.

—— *The Faces of Justice and State Authority* (New Haven, Conn.: Yale University Press, 1986).

ELLISON, L., *The Adversarial Process and the Vulnerable Witness* (Oxford: Oxford University Press, 2001).

FRANKEL, M., 'The Search for Truth: An Umpireal View' (1975) 123 *University of Pennsylvania Law Review* 1031.

JACKSON, J., and DORAN, S., *Judge without Jury: Diplock Trials in the Adversary System* (Oxford: Oxford University Press, 1995).

LUBAN, D., *Lawyers and Justice: An Ethical Study* (Princeton: Princeton University Press, 1988), chap. 5.

McEWAN, J., *Evidence and the Adversarial Process* (Oxford: Hart, 1998).

PIZZI, W. T., *Trials without Truth* (New York: New York University Press, 1999).

REDMAYNE, M., *Expert Evidence and Criminal Justice* (Oxford: Oxford University Press, 2000), chap. 7.

TAGUE, P. W., *Effective Advocacy for the Criminal Defendant: The Barrister vs the Lawyer* (Buffalo, NY: Hein & Co.,1996).

20

PLEA BARGAINING

Mike McConville

INTRODUCTION

The administration of criminal justice in many countries has undergone dramatic changes in recent years as a result of the introduction of plea bargaining. Under plea bargaining, a formal or informal agreement is entered into, usually by the prosecutor and defence lawyer but sometimes involving the trial judge, under which, in return for a plea of guilty, the sentence that would otherwise be imposed on conviction after trial is replaced by a lesser sentence. Bargaining, though controversial, has become widespread practice in both codified and non-codified systems of law, and more and more experts, even when expressing varying degrees of concern, view this development as inevitable.

Whilst plea bargaining is conventionally associated with Anglo-American systems, having originated in the nineteenth century in the United States of America and being prevalent today in countries such as Australia, Canada, England, and South Africa, it is now becoming a prominent part of criminal justice in countries which have, or have historically enjoyed, an inquisitorial tradition, such as Germany, Italy, and Poland. It has been identified as a practice in lower courts, where crimes of the less serious variety are dealt with, as well as in higher courts which deal with more serious criminal offences.

Although plea bargaining is therefore widespread, it is at the same time controversial. For those responsible for the administration of criminal justice, the high rate of guilty pleas which plea bargaining produces offers an expeditious and cost-effective way of dealing with the large backlogs of cases that seem to be a feature of most modern systems. On the other hand, plea bargaining represents a direct challenge, not only to conventional understandings about the methods that are appropriate for deciding guilt, but also to the values that lie behind the system of criminal justice.

The criminal justice system in England and Wales, which is based upon adversarial principles, provides a good example of the basic tensions to which plea bargaining gives rise and of the difficult, perhaps intractable, nature of the problems of reconciling the competing demands of efficiency and fairness.

THE ADVERSARIAL SYSTEM OF JUSTICE: THEORY

In England and Wales criminal cases are resolved within an adversarial framework of justice that seeks both to operate and to promote a set of core principles involving the relationship between the State and its citizens. Under the adversarial system, the State (prosecution) and the defendant are opposed as adversaries. The central protective mechanism of the adversary system is the independent tribunal of fact. At trial, the State must convince a panel of independent individuals beyond a reasonable doubt of the truth of its case through the introduction of admissible and reliable evidence of guilt. Jurors, as triers of fact, have no connection with any of the parties and must be free to decide the question of legal guilt without knowledge of or responsibility for issues of punishment.

At trial, the State is viewed as an intrusive force which, because it seeks to limit the freedom of individuals, must justify its every act through the introduction of legally sufficient and admissible evidence which persuades to a very high degree of certainty. The State cannot convict defendants and inflict punishment on them without proving, at some cost to itself, that the defendant committed each and every element of the offence beyond a reasonable doubt, no matter how minor or inconsequential any component part of the offence may appear.

By contrast, under the adversary system there is no obligation whatsoever on the defendant to put forward any evidence in his defence. To secure an acquittal, it will be sufficient, for example, if the State has failed to produce enough evidence of guilt. The defendant does not have to produce any witnesses or say anything in his defence. It is for the State to bring forward enough evidence of guilt. If it does not do so, the court will be required to enter a verdict of not guilty.

The 'burden of proof', as it is called, is weighted in this way for a number of reasons. One of these is the enormous disparity of power and resources between the prosecution and the defence. No matter how rich or how mighty, no individual has access to the power and resources which are at the command of the State. Additionally, because it is the prosecution which makes the allegation and chooses the charge, it should be for the prosecution to prove what it alleges. Over and above all this, however, is the principle that, by initiating a prosecution, the State is claiming the right to punish one of its citizens and therefore should be required to justify its right to punish.

The adversary system not only places the burden of proof on the State, it also lays down rules about how that burden can be discharged. One of the key rules is the principle of orality. This principle means that in general the evidence upon which the prosecution can rely is that which is given in court through the live testimony of witnesses. It is not what the witness says to the police which finally matters but what the witness states in court when questioned by the prosecution and cross-examined by the defence.

Underpinning the adversary system is the further principle that the defendant has, with very few exceptions, a right to a public trial. In this way, citizens can participate in trials not only as jurors but also they may go into the public gallery of any court and see that justice is being done. The pressure of this external element is in itself a discipline on the legal actors—lawyers and judge—to respect the rules and procedures laid down in law for the conduct of criminal cases.

Whilst the adversary system described above guards against the possibility that a factually innocent person may be found legally guilty, by placing the burden of proof squarely and solely on the State, requiring it to conform to legal rules and to persuade a tribunal of fact which comes to the case with no preconceptions, this means that the system accepts some inefficiency. Occasionally, factually guilty persons may be found legally 'innocent', i.e. not guilty, when the State is unable to satisfy the standard of certainty required by the burden of proof. However, the distinction between factual and legal guilt is intended to ensure that the innocent are not wrongfully convicted and is at the very core of the adversary system's protections. All its procedures are designed to ensure that questionable assertions of factual guilt do not displace legal guilt as the test whether someone should be convicted of a criminal offence.

Seen in this way, the adversary system has both 'outcome values' and 'process values'. The outcome values focus upon ensuring that only the legally guilty are convicted and are convicted for the appropriate offence and that any who are *possibly* innocent are acquitted. The process values include promoting State accountability to the law and to its citizens, the involvement of ordinary citizens in their own governance and the fundamental human rights of all citizens, whether factually guilty or not, to be tried according to a procedure which is transparent and which respects the prevailing legal, evidential, and procedural rules.

It does not follow, it must be emphasized, that guilty pleas are inconsistent with adversary principles or that all criminal cases ought to go to trial. A plea of guilty, as a judicial confession, is regarded as the highest form of proof, and it is thus equivalent to conviction after a trial. Once such a plea is accepted by the court, the prosecution is relieved altogether of the normal responsibility to produce evidence and persuade the tribunal of fact that the accused person is guilty. Following the guilty plea, the only concern of the court is to decide upon the appropriate sentence.

Like the trial itself, this form of proof has its own underlying rationale. To protect defendants and to guard against incorrect outcomes, it has always been a cardinal principle that a guilty plea can be accepted by a court only if it is a genuinely 'voluntary' act of the accused, given of the accused's own free will and without external pressure or influence. If the guilty plea is a truly voluntary act of the defendant, it can be argued that courts should be entitled to reduce the sentence that otherwise would have been imposed in order to reflect the fact that through the plea the defendant has exhibited remorse and repentance, and has already gone some way towards meeting the rehabilitative ideals of sentencing. A contrary view is that any such reduction is incompatible with a just sentencing system, which should be based on the principle that the punishment should reflect what an offender has actually done.

THE ADVERSARY SYSTEM OF JUSTICE: PRACTICE

It is all too clear, however, that no criminal justice system can be described by theory alone. The rules, principles, and values outlined above have to confront the harsher realities of day-to-day practice. And a long line of research in criminal justice has demonstrated how important these real contexts are in shaping and re-shaping the living system by undercutting the commitment the legal actors have to the ideals of adversary justice.

Thus the prospect of a full-blown trial may not be attractive to the prosecution where it is not confident that it will be able successfully to discharge the burden of proof. Crucial evidence may have been illegally obtained by police officers through breach of procedural and evidential rules or by exerting improper pressure upon the suspect to make a confession in ways which contradict the prevailing legal regime. Police officers who know or believe the defendant to have committed the offence may have fabricated evidence to secure a conviction. Or, despite their best efforts, the prosecution may be lacking in the evidence it judges to be necessary in order to be confident of a successful outcome at trial.

For their part, defence lawyers may not wish to go to trial. There are very few, if any, jurisdictions in which the income defence lawyers obtain, usually from the State through a system of legal aid, allows them to devote the time they feel they need to prepare the case for trial. Generally, they can survive in the legal-aid market-place only by handling a large number of cases at any one time and disposing of cases by volume is best achieved through guilty pleas. Against this background and because many of their clients will have in fact committed the offence charged or some related crime, defence lawyers are prone to develop an occupational culture in which they form the view that their clients are guilty and do not deserve the expenditure of time and public money that a full trial necessarily involves.

Particularly against a background of rising crime, all the official actors—prosecution, defence, and judge—may look for ways which better enable them to manage the rising case-load that confronts them. Trials not only take up a great deal of time and resources, but it is also difficult to predict in advance exactly how much time and resources any given case will consume. Guilty pleas, by contrast, allow cost-effective management strategies to be applied thereby enabling a far greater volume of cases to be disposed of in the shortest time. Managing the case-load is also assisted by the fact that guilty pleas, unlike trials, have a predictable outcome.

For these and other reasons, no modern criminal justice system is immune from the pressures in favour of plea bargaining. The way in which a given system deals with plea bargaining and the tensions to which this gives rise, however, provide a useful insight into the problems of reconciling the 'law in the books' with the 'law in action' and the dilemmas and contradictions which beset any system. It is in this context that the English criminal justice system is illustrative of the more general challenges posed by plea bargaining.

THE *TURNER RULES*

Although the issue of plea bargaining had arisen in some earlier cases,[1] it was the case of *Turner*[2] in which the English courts first directly confronted the problems raised by plea bargaining and laid down general principles intended to guide the legal actors involved.

Turner was charged with the theft of a car, entered a plea of Not Guilty, and his trial commenced. In the course of the trial, the defence barrister suggested to Turner that he seriously consider changing his plea to one of 'Guilty'. This was done openly in the presence of the defence solicitor, with the barrister telling Turner, and 'putting it in strong words', that on a plea of Guilty there might well be a non-custodial sentence but if Turner was convicted after a full trial he ran the risk of a prison sentence. This advice was repeated after the barrister went to discuss the matter privately with the trial judge. Turner, however, stuck to his view that he was going to fight the case. Shortly afterwards, counsel again spoke to Turner in private, at the end of which Turner indicated that he would retract his Not Guilty plea. Accordingly, Turner entered a plea of Guilty and was sentenced on that basis.

On appeal against conviction, the Court of Appeal rejected the contention that the barrister had exercised undue pressure on Turner, thereby rendering his guilty plea involuntary but ordered a *venire de novo* (a new trial) because Turner might have gained the impression that counsel was merely echoing the words of the trial judge and, if so, it was 'really idle . . . to think that he really had a free choice in the matter [of plea]'. In short, the court concluded that Turner's plea had been involuntary. Whilst that was technically sufficient to dispose of the appeal, the Court of Appeal took the opportunity to make some 'observations' which were intended to help judges and lawyers in dealing with guilty pleas entered in such circumstances. It is these observations which have become known as the *Turner Rules*. With some slight modifications, these are set out below:

1. Counsel must be completely free to do what is his duty, namely to give the accused the best advice he can and, if need be, advice in strong terms. This will often include advice that a plea of Guilty, showing an element of remorse, is a mitigating factor which may well enable the court to give a lesser sentence than would otherwise be the case. Counsel, of course, will emphasize that the accused must not plead Guilty unless he has committed the acts constituting the offence charged.

2. The accused, having considered counsel's advice, must have a complete freedom of choice whether to plead Guilty or Not Guilty.

3. There must be freedom of access between counsel and judge. Any discussion, however, which takes place must be between the judge and both counsel for the defence and counsel for the prosecution. If a solicitor representing the accused is in the court, he should be allowed to attend the discussion, if he so desires.

---

[1] See, e.g., *Hall* (1968) 52 Cr. App. R 528.   [2] [1970] 2 QB 321.

4. This freedom of access is important because there may be matters calling for communication or discussion, which are of such a nature that counsel cannot in the interests of his client mention them in open court. Purely by way of example, counsel for the defence may by way of mitigation wish to tell the judge that the accused has not got long to live, is suffering maybe from cancer, of which he is and should remain ignorant.

5. Again, counsel on both sides may wish to discuss with the judge whether it would be proper, in a particular case, for the prosecution to accept a plea to a lesser offence.

6. It is of course imperative that so far as possible justice must be administered in open court. Counsel should, therefore, ask to see the judge only when it is felt to be really necessary and the judge must be careful to treat such communications as private only where, in terms of fairness to the accused person, this is necessary.

7. The judge should, subject to the one exception referred to hereafter, never indicate the sentence which he is minded to impose. A statement that on a plea of Guilty he would impose one sentence but that on a conviction following a plea of Not Guilty he would impose a severer sentence is one which should never be made. This could be taken to be undue pressure on the accused, thus depriving him of that complete freedom of choice which is essential. Such cases, however, are in the experience of the court happily rare. What on occasions does appear to happen however is that a judge will tell counsel that, having read the depositions and the antecedents, he can safely say that on a plea of Guilty he will, for instance, make a probation order, something which may be helpful to counsel in advising the accused. The judge in such a case is no doubt careful not to mention what he would do if the accused were convicted following a plea of Not Guilty. Even so, the accused may well get the impression that the judge is intimating that in that event a severer sentence, maybe a custodial sentence, would result, so that again he may feel under pressure. This accordingly must also not be done.

8. The only exception to this rule is that it should be permissible for a judge to say, if it be the case, that whatever happens, whether the accused pleads Guilty or Not Guilty, the sentence will or will not take a particular form, e.g. a probation order, a fine, or a custodial sentence.

9. Finally, where any such discussion on sentence has taken place between judge and counsel, counsel for the defence should disclose this to the accused and inform him of what took place.

Even accepting that this represented the first attempt by English judges to regulate the practice of plea bargaining, the *Turner Rules* are beset with contradictions and illustrate the difficulty of reconciling plea negotiations with ordinary adversary principles.

Whilst, for example, under Rule 1 the trial judge may (or must) give out a lesser sentence on a plea of Guilty than he would impose after conviction following a Not Guilty plea (sometimes called the 'discount principle'), under Rule 4 the judge must never disclose this, because to do so would constitute undue pressure and thereby destroy the defendant's complete freedom of choice over plea. By contrast, defence counsel must tell the accused that a plea of Guilty will attract a lighter sentence, but this will not amount to undue pressure even if the 'advice' is expressed, as Rule 1 permits, 'in strong terms'. Similarly, as the judges in *Turner* must have known, plea discussions initiated by both barristers and judges were common and were almost never based upon reasons relating to an extreme medical condition unknown to the defendant himself. And it would almost never happen that a judge would tell counsel that the sentence would be the same whatever the plea, since this would merely invite a Not Guilty plea in the hope of an acquittal without any risk of an enhanced sentence.

It is unlikely that these problems were attributable to inelegant drafting or to inadequate consideration of the issues by the judges. They appear, instead, to be an attempt to alleviate concern over the issue of plea bargaining, which had leaked into the public domain, by seeming to forbid the practice whilst at the same time creating a framework which would allow the practice to continue. And an even stronger indication of judicial support for the practice of plea bargaining was soon to come.

In the case of *Cain*,[3] the trial judge had sent for prosecution and defence counsel in advance of the trial, informed them that in his view the defendant had no defence and that if he persisted in a Not Guilty plea he would get a very severe sentence, but that a plea of Guilty would make a considerable difference. Once told of this, the defendant pleaded guilty but appealed against conviction on the ground that he had been denied a free choice of plea. Although the Court of Appeal accepted the defendant's argument and ordered a retrial, the Lord Chief Justice, Lord Widgery, threw the *Turner Rules* into chaos with the following observations:

[I]t was trite to say that a plea of guilty will generally attract a somewhat lighter sentence than a plea of not guilty after a full-dress contest on the issue. Every defendant should know that. If they did not know it they should be told, and the sooner the better. . . . It was not wrong for the judge to state the obvious.

This case plainly stated, contrary to the sentiments in *Turner*, that judges could after all make reference to the discount rule which, it seemed, no longer needed to be based on any sentencing principle such as reduction for remorse. Further confusion was caused by Lord Widgery's observation that judges could give counsel an indication about sentence on a *confidential* basis, qualifying the 'rule' in *Turner* that counsel for the defence should disclose to the defendant that a discussion with the judge had taken place and inform him or her of what the judge had said.

Following the reporting of *Cain*, legal practitioners were thrown into confusion and the Court of Appeal was forced to take corrective action. It took the unusual step of issuing a Practice Direction[4] which stated that in so far as *Cain* was inconsistent with the observations in *Turner*, the latter should prevail. In formal terms, this meant

---

[3] [1976] *Crim. LR* 464 (CA).

[4] [1976] *Crim. LR* 561. A Practice Direction is a statement giving formal guidance to judges and barristers on some aspect of law or procedure where there is uncertainty.

that the rules governing plea discussions were those set down in *Turner*, and any encouragement to bargaining which the remarks in *Cain* might have offered were to be disregarded by judges and lawyers.

PRACTICE IN THE COURTS

Whatever the formal intention behind the Practice Direction, however, the observation of the Lord Chief Justice in *Cain* much more closely reflected the views of barristers and trial judges, as research and reported cases were soon to show.

In the earliest comprehensive research study, Baldwin and McConville sought to identify why defendants had entered guilty pleas.[5] The results they presented are set out in Table 20.1.

Table 20.1   Reasons for entering guilty pleas

	No.	*%*
No deal or pressure—defendant guilty as pleaded	35	28.9
Plea bargain—an offer made and accepted by defendant	22	18.2
No explicit bargain but defendant thinks or assumes that a bargain has been made on his behalf	16	13.2
Pressure from defence barrister but no specific offer made to defendant	48	39.7
	121	100.0

Qualitative information obtained in interviews with defendants reinforced the view that plea bargaining was widespread, that few defendants entered pleas of guilty which were truly voluntary, and that most guilty pleas resulted either from bargain agreements ('explicit bargains'), or knowledge that there would be a reduced sentence without any formal agreement ('implicit bargains') or pressure from the defendant's own barrister, as the following examples illustrate:

> *Case 20* The defendant was initially charged with rape but after bargaining pleaded guilty to the reduced charge of indecent assault and the promise of a light sentence: 'the barrister intimated that I should plead guilty ... but I still said I wanted to fight it. Then he went away and had a [private] word with the Judge. He came back and said there wasn't sufficient evidence of rape and they would alter the charge to indecent assault. He suggested that I plead guilty to

---

[5] J. Baldwin and M. McConville, *Negotiated Justice* (London: Martin Robertson, 1977). See also S. McCabe, and R. Purves, *By-Passing the Jury* (Oxford: Oxford University Penal Research Unit, Blackwell, 1972); A. Bottoms and J. McClean, *Defendants in the Criminal Process* (London: Routledge, 1976); S. Dell, *Silent in Court* (London: Bell, 1971); M. McConville *et al.*, *Standing Accused* (Oxford: Clarendon Press, 1994).

that. He said they did not want [the victim] to have to go into the witness box [and give evidence]. I asked him if I would go to prison. He disappeared again and came back and said he had spoken to the judge who intimated that he would fine me. He said, "Are you agreeable to that?" I said, "Yes, I am." '

Case 61 'My solicitor and barrister were involved together. The solicitor contacted the barrister and they went to see the judge. They advised me to plead guilty . . . and I was actually given the choice of a fine or a suspended sentence. I chose the fine.'

The picture emerging from research was soon confirmed as cases flooded into the Court of Appeal. Judges and barristers were not only engaging in plea bargaining but also, and despite the guidelines issued in *Turner*, were openly acknowledging the practice. The Court of Appeal attempted to stop the practice by restating their opposition to plea bargaining, as can be seen in the extracts from two cases set out below:

Grice[6]

We find it astonishing that any [judge] should characterize what he is doing as 'plea bargaining' but even more so when it clearly was 'plea bargaining'. . . . He [the trial judge] indicated that he would not pass an immediate custodial sentence if the appellant pleaded guilty, and that had the effect of . . . making the appellant change his mind, having determined up to that point to plead not guilty. That was the clearest form of 'plea bargaining' and the clearest example of the very thing that should not be done.

Atkinson[7] (In this case the trial judge indicated that, in return for a guilty plea, he would impose a non-custodial sentence.)

Of course the trial judge was not striking any bargain with the defence. He was indicating the difference in sentence that a man can on occasion secure in his favour by a plea of guilty. But in this sensitive area, the appearance of justice is part of the substance of justice and it will not do if a [defendant] or the general public derive the impression that it is possible . . . to achieve a bargain with the court. Plea bargaining has no place in English criminal law.

The attractions of plea bargaining, however, proved much stronger than the repeated condemnations of the Court of Appeal. Indeed, even as the Court of Appeal was speaking in these cases, a trial judge, writing in a law journal, gave a contrasting defence of bargaining:[8]

Bargains between judges and defendants as to sentence happen every day. It is in the interests of all that they should. . . . The practice of . . . judges varies widely. Some see counsel in their rooms whenever they are asked. Some refuse to see counsel at all. . . . Some send for counsel before the case starts and virtually give directions [for a bargain]. . . . Some judges negotiate more subtly by sending and receiving messages through their clerks or the court-clerks.

That these sentiments more closely reflected the views of judges and lawyers soon

---

[6] (1977) 66 Cr. App. R 167.   [7] [1978] 2 All ER 460.
[8] HH Judge David, 'In the Crown Court' (1978) *The Magistrate* 74–5.

became clear as case after case involving plea bargaining came before the Court of Appeal. Moreover, when the Royal Commission on Criminal Justice[9] looked into this question, it quickly found widespread approval of bargaining among these groups. As part of the Crown Court Survey,[10] judges and barristers were asked whether the case of *Turner* should be reformed 'to permit full and realistic discussion between counsel and judge about plea and especially sentence'. Almost nine out of ten of barristers and two-thirds of judges answered 'Yes'.

FURTHER REGULATION

In an attempt to regulate what was clearly a common practice, the Royal Commission on Criminal Justice in 1993 recommended the introduction of what it called a 'sentence canvass' or discussion. This canvass or discussion would usually take place before the trial started and in advance of the jury being sworn in. Although it would be private, a record of the discussion would be made:[11]

The sentence 'canvass', as we have called it, should normally take place in the judge's chambers [private room] with both sides being represented by counsel. A shorthand writer should also be present. If none is available a member of the court staff should take a note to be agreed immediately by the judge and both counsel. The judge may give the answer to the question 'what would be the maximum sentence if my client were to plead guilty at this stage?' but to no other. The judge's indication should be based on brief statements from prosecution and defence of all the relevant circumstances, which should include details of the defendant's previous convictions if any and, if available, any pre-sentence report.

This proposal proved too controversial and was not accepted by the government. However, a provision in the Criminal Justice and Public Order Act 1994 tacitly recognized the practice of giving lesser sentences for a guilty plea by providing in section 48(1):

In determining what sentence to pass on an offender who has pleaded guilty to an offence in proceedings before that or another court a court shall take into account—

  (a) the stage in the proceedings for the offence at which the offender indicated his intention to plead guilty, and

  (b) the circumstances in which this indication was given.

  (2) If, as a result of taking into account any matter referred to in subsection (1) above, the court imposes a punishment on the offender which is less severe than the punishment it would otherwise have imposed, it shall state in open court that it has done so.

---

[9] Cm 2263 (1993).

[10] Research Study No. 19 for the Royal Commission on Criminal Justice (London: HMSO, 1993).

[11] Royal Commission on Criminal Justice, *Report* (London: HMSO, 1993), para. 51 at 113.

Following further controversy, the Attorney-General issued a set of *Guidelines on the Acceptance of Pleas* in December 2000 the substance of which is set out below:

(1) Justice in this jurisdiction, save in the most exceptional circumstances, is conducted in public. This includes the acceptance of pleas by the prosecution and sentencing.

(2) The Code for Crown Prosecutors sets out the circumstance in which pleas to a reduced number of charges, or less serious charges, can be accepted.[12]

(3) The Court of Appeal has said on many occasions that justice should be transparent. Only in the most exceptional circumstances should plea and sentence be discussed in the judge's chambers. Where there is such a discussion, the prosecution advocate should at the outset, if necessary, remind the judge of the principle that an independent record must always be kept of such discussions. The prosecution advocate should make a full note of such an event, recording all decisions and comments. This note should be made available to the prosecuting authority.

(4) Where there is to be a discussion on plea and sentence and the prosecution advocate takes the view that the circumstances are not exceptional, then it is the duty of that advocate to remind the judge of the relevant decisions of the Court of Appeal and dissociate himself or herself from involvement in any discussion on sentence. The advocate should not do or say anything which could be construed as expressly or impliedly agreeing to a particular sentence. If the offence is one to which section 35 of the Criminal Justice Act 1988 applies the advocate should make it clear that the Attorney-General may, if he thinks fit, seek the leave of the Court of Appeal to refer the case for review under section 37 of that Act.[13]

(5) When a case is listed for trial and the prosecution forms the view that the appropriate course is to accept a plea before the proceedings commence or continue or to offer no evidence on the indictment or any part of it, the prosecution should, whenever practicable, speak with the victim or the victim's family, so that the position can be explained and their views and interests can be taken into account as part of the decision-making process. The victim or victim's family should then be kept informed and decisions explained to them once they are made at court.

---

[12] The *Code For Crown Prosecutors* states the considerations that need to be taken into account in accepting pleas in these terms:

'Defendants may want to plead guilty to some, but not all, of the charges. Or they may want to plead guilty to a different, possibly less serious, charge because they are admitting only part of the crime. Crown Prosecutors should only accept the defendant's plea if they think the court is able to pass a sentence that matches the seriousness of the offending. Crown Prosecutors must never accept a guilty plea just because it is convenient.'

[13] The Criminal Justice Act 1988 ss. 35 and 36 empower the Court of Appeal to increase a convicted defendant's sentence where it considers that the sentence imposed by the Crown Court was unduly lenient. The referral of a case to the Court of Appeal is made by the Attorney-General.

This brief account of how the system has responded to the introduction of plea bargaining into England and Wales illustrates both the methods of the common law (a non-codified system) and the dilemmas posed by plea bargaining itself.

The common law method of developing the law is essentially pragmatic. The system of rules and guidance from judges is continually being adapted as new circumstances arise, with legislation taking a relatively subordinate role. The adversarial structure of the system ensures that little, if anything, can be kept private: one way or another, contentious issues will be brought into the public domain. In this way judges fashion more general propositions from individual cases that come before the courts. If new situations arise which are not covered by existing rules, the rules can be amended or new ones brought into existence, but only after the issues have been debated and forensically examined in open court.[14]

Establishing rules to deal with plea bargaining, however, is far from easy. The first instinct of the appeal court judges, that plea bargaining was contrary to the principles which animated the adversary system and must therefore be outlawed, has had to give way in the face of the powerful forces that appear to be driving practitioners towards informal settlement processes. But having allowed for the possibility of bargaining under certain conditions, the structural and, perhaps, intractable problems inherent in plea bargaining have made the formulation of a comprehensive regime of rules difficult and uncertain. It is to some of these inherent problems that we now turn, because they are ones which must be taken account of by every jurisdiction in which plea bargaining is permitted or being contemplated.

MANIPULATIVE DEFENDANTS

Underlying the impetus towards plea bargaining is the belief among legal personnel that the current, relatively unregulated, guilty plea system still imposes enormous and unwarranted costs on the administration of criminal justice through the decision-making of calculating defendants, and that a formal and open bargaining system would result in comparable or even greater savings. The experience in England, and elsewhere, suggests that these beliefs are less well supported by evidence than might be thought.

The most significant influence upon the popularity of plea bargaining in English courts and the primary reason why this practice has caused so little concern within the legal profession is the belief that enormous sums of public money are wasted in particular because of the decision by defendants to plead guilty at the very last

---

[14] By contrast, codified systems have to operate within the framework established by the words of the Code. The words of the Code can cover a variety of situations only by being drafted in the most general terms. In consequence, there is no real public debate on new fact situations and the principles which should apply and, in contrast to the common law, codified legal systems have little vitality, tend to be ossified, and render important debates untransparent rather than bringing them into the public domain.

moment, when the judge, jury, and witnesses have come to court and many of the costs have already been incurred. If a guilty plea is entered at this stage in the procedure, practitioners say that there is a 'cracked trial'. As the Royal Commission on Criminal Justice put it:[15]

'Cracked' trials create serious problems, principally for all the thousands of witnesses each year—police officers, experts and ordinary citizens—who come to court expecting a trial only to find that there is no trial because the defendant has decided to plead guilty at the last minute. This causes in particular unnecessary anxiety for victims whose evidence has up to that point been disputed.

The Royal Commission echoed the words of the Seabrook Committee, which had reported while the Commission was sitting, that 'the most common reason for defendants delaying a plea of guilty until the last minute is a reluctance to face the facts until they are at the door of the court'.[16] Delay in this context was stated to be the responsibility of defendants themselves. According to the Royal Commission:[17]

It is often said, too, that a defendant has a considerable incentive to behave in this way. The longer the delay, the more the likelihood of witnesses becoming intimidated or forgetting to turn up or disappearing. And, if the defendant is remanded in custody, he or she will continue to enjoy the privileges of an unconvicted remand prisoner whereas, once a guilty plea has been entered, the prisoner enters the category of convicted/unsentenced and loses those privileges.

The idea of manipulative defendants holding the system to ransom in order to turn it to their advantage is, on the face of it, plausible and a strong stimulus to reformers who seek a more cost-effective system for handling criminal cases. But is the image supported by the reality?

The principal evidence is found in research undertaken on behalf of the Royal Commission itself by Zander and Henderson.[18] In the survey, Zander and Henderson sought to discover from defence lawyers, in cases where the guilty plea was not notified to the court until the day of the hearing, why an earlier notification of the guilty plea had not been given. The answers in order of frequency were set out in Table 5.1 which is reproduced below as Table 20.2.

It is clear from these data that the facts do not support the widespread belief of lawyers. The occasions on which the collapse or 'cracking' of a trial at the last moment (usually on the day set for trial) results from a change of heart on the part of a calculating defendant are very rare indeed. Rather, trials 'crack' at the last moment

---

[15] Royal Commission on Criminal Justice (RCCP), *Report* (London: HMSO, 1993), at 111, para. 45.

[16] *Ibid.*, at 112, para. 48.   [17] *Ibid.*

[18] See n. 8 above. A survey was also undertaken by the Seabrook Committee, The Efficient Disposal of Business in the Crown Court (London: General Council at the Bar, 1992), but it has little empirical value because the methodological basis of the survey is not disclosed and it rests upon little more than opinion evidence. In so far as it reveals anything, however, it suggests that the vast majority of 'cracked' trials (70–75%) result from factors other than the defendant 'seeing the light' and are caused by a significant change in the prosecution case, judicial intervention, or the case being dropped altogether.

Table 20.2 Reasons for late notification of plea

	%
Earlier consultation with client impossible/did not take place	31
Change in prosecution's approach	28
Late consultation with counsel	19
Client changed mind	6
Plea bargaining	4
Miscellaneous	12
Total	100 n = 240

because the defendant is given advice for the first time on the day set for trial[19] or because the prosecution's case is significantly different from that with which it started. The 'waste' of resources so evident to practitioners is thus a result of dislocations in the criminal justice system itself, many of which are unavoidable, and not the product of cynical decision-making by defendants.

COSTS AND SAVINGS

Law reformers appear to be on safer ground in arguing for a plea-bargaining system on the basis that it would, by expediting the flow of cases through the courts, result in significant savings. The argument based on savings was forcefully advanced by an official committee of barristers which looked into this issue and gave evidence to the Royal Commission on Criminal Justice in these terms:[20]

The resource implications of early indications of guilty pleas are enormous. Listing becomes far more efficient. Subject to availability of counsel, cases could be listed as soon as the necessary case papers are received. . . . Not only would the whole process be quicker, but also the need for adjournments for [pre-sentence] reports would be greatly reduced and, in most cases, eliminated. All of this, particularly the reduction in the number of cracked trials, will save a lot of money. We believe that these facts are legitimate mitigation, quite as valid as the demonstration of remorse and contrition. The saving of public expenditure and relief of pressure on the Crown Court are matters of considerable public interest.

But the claims made by this committee are weakly supported by the evidence. To begin with, the overwhelming majority of Crown Court cases (at least 74 per cent)

[19] According to the Crown Court Study, barristers first met with defendants on the actual morning of the trial in half of the cases surveyed and in one-third of cases this meeting lasted less than 15 minutes. Against such a background it is unlikely that any barrister could establish that relationship of trust which is so essential to gain the confidence of the defendant and create a basis for meaningful and comprehensive advice.

[20] The Seabrook Committee, *The Efficient Disposal of Business in the Crown Court* (London: General Council of the Bar, 1992) 36.

do not involve any question of a 'cracked' trial.[21] In the Crown Court survey, when Crown Court judges were asked whether any of their time was wasted as a result of cases listed for trial turning into last-minute guilty pleas, the vast majority (81 per cent) said that no judicial time had been wasted, and in a further group of cases (9 per cent) the judges stated that less than two hours of their time had been wasted.[22] Similarly, according to those responsible for organizing court cases (court clerks), cracked trials caused no waste of time at all in the substantial majority of cases (69 per cent) and less than two hours in a further group of cases (20 per cent).[23] Other wasted resources are also far less than commonly claimed. In a substantial majority of cases (61 per cent) no police witnesses turn up at court for trials that do not go ahead[24] and no civilian witnesses' time is wasted in almost one-third of cases.[25]

Over the long term, it is arguable that systematic reliance on guilty pleas, far from saving court time and public expense, actually wastes time and increases the cost to the public purse. What must be taken into account is the fact that the negotiated guilty plea system becomes part of a vertical process: what will happen later in the court where the plea bargain is struck has a profound influence upon what happens at the police stage of the process. Routine case processing in court through guilty pleas reinforces the actions and expectations of the police who are, because of the comparative lack of court scrutiny, encouraged to engage in mass arrests and bring cases before the courts without respect to the sufficiency of evidence and without regard to whether any social objective may be achieved by the prosecution.[26] The predictable result is an unthoughtful, unreflective arrest process built around police (rather than justice) priorities, the hallmarks of which are commonly mass arrests, 'sweeps', and 'dragnets' of neighbourhoods often involving low-level offences.[27]

---

[21] Crown Court Study, n. 8 above, 149, para. 5.1.

[22] Ibid., 151, para. 5.5. Actually, judges most often saw a cracked trial as a way of using court resources economically. As one judge put it there: 'I do not regard cracked trials as wasting time. They save time.'

[23] Ibid., 151–2, para. 5.6.

[24] Ibid., 152, para. 5.7. Not all of this is wasted, of course, since officers may be required to give evidence in some guilty plea cases or may need to be consulted on the acceptability of a charge reduction which turns the case into a guilty plea.

[25] Ibid., 152–3, para. 5.8.

[26] Research points to the fact that many arrests are currently undertaken in circumstances where arresting officers do not consider the evidence on arrest to be sufficient to found a charge: C. Phillips and D. Brown, *Entry into the Criminal Justice System: A Survey of Police Arrests and their Outcomes*, Home Office Research Study No. 185 (London: Home Office, 1998). In this study, even though some officers felt that they could not risk saying that there was insufficient evidence, some 30% of arresting officers stated that there was insufficient evidence to charge suspects at the time of the arrest: ibid., 44.

[27] M. McConville and C. Mirsky, 'Guilty Plea Courts: A Social Disciplinary Model of Criminal Justice' (1995) 42 *Social Problems* 216.

THE SENTENCE DISCOUNT

Whilst there is no official 'sentence discount', as it is called, in England and Wales it is a common belief among practitioners that a plea of guilty should be rewarded with a one-third reduction in sentence.[28] A broadly similar principle of reduction exists in other plea-bargaining jurisdictions such as Australia, Canada, and the United States of America.[29] Any plea-bargaining system has to explain why it is acceptable to reduce sentences in return for guilty pleas.

Traditional justifications for the sentence discount involve entirely pragmatic considerations. By entering a guilty plea defendants are said to contribute to the smooth and efficient administration of justice through saving time and money which would otherwise be spent in a full trial. Consistently with this, in England and Wales the defendant who pleads guilty at the earliest stage in the process will be given the greatest reduction, whereas those who strategically delay a guilty plea until the last moment will get the least or no reduction.

Whilst there may appear to be an underlying rationale to this pragmatic response to the pressure on courts to expedite their business at minimum expense, the logic is not applied across the board. Thus, for example, in sentencing terms courts do not differentiate between defendants who do go on trial on the basis of the length of the trial itself or the proportion of trial time the defence case consumes, even though it is clear that the way in which a defendant chooses to conduct the trial can have a profound impact upon the court time and public expense thereby involved.

The underlying rationale of plea bargaining also raises serious questions relating to sentencing based on principles. Though there is no universally agreed grid on which to calculate sentences, most jurisdictions expect a sentence to reflect what the offender actually did in the light of the offender's personal characteristics. Added to this may be punitive, rehabilitative, or deterrent aims. A systemic difficulty with plea bargaining is that it may shift the offender from one offence category, and therefore one sentence category, to another: robbery to theft, burglary to theft, rape to indecent assault. When this happens, the judge, far from being able to address the accused's conduct in choosing a sentence, is actually prevented from doing so because the sentence must be based on the offence to which the accused has pleaded guilty, rather than on that which was actually committed. Broader sentencing aims may also be undercut if an offender sees a reduced sentence as a 'reward' or if the victim or the public (as appears to be the case) sees it as unjustified leniency.

The other side to this aspect of the debate is the impact plea bargaining has upon those who are sentenced after unsuccessfully contesting their guilt at trial. Research suggests that many defendants see the difference in sentence not as a reduction for those who plead guilty but rather as a coercive punishment inflicted on those who

---

[28] See also Royal Commission on Criminal Justice, *Report* (London: HMSO, 1993) at 110.

[29] See, e.g., Attorney-General's Advisory Committee, *Charge Screening, Disclosure, and Resolution Discussions* (Ontario: Law Reform Commission, 1993); K. Mack and S. R. Anleu, 'Guilty Pleas: Discussion and Agreements' (1996) 6 *Journal of Judicial Administration* 8.

exercise their right to go to trial. For these defendants, the sense of injustice they may feel in consequence can act only to inhibit reform and rehabilitation.

THE RISK TO THE INNOCENT

Lying behind the idea of 'wasted' public resources is the notion that they are wasted, not only because the defendant has delayed the decision to plead guilty, but also because a trial was never deserved. Defendants are thus viewed as both calculating and guilty; individuals who seek to gain what little advantage they can by exploiting the system when they know themselves to be guilty and when they have no prospects of avoiding conviction at trial. The Royal Commission on Criminal Justice put the point in this way:[30]

The primary reason for the sentence discount is to encourage defendants who know themselves to be guilty to plead accordingly and so enable the resources which would be expended in a contested case to be saved.

Once again, the image does not fit with the reality. Research which has focused upon the experience of defendants themselves consistently shows that defendants often change their pleas to guilty not because they have come to 'face the facts' but rather because they have succumbed to pressure, which they see as coercive and unfair, from their own lawyers.[31] Whilst it is always difficult to test claims of innocence, research also shows that plea bargaining distinguishes only crudely between those likely to be convicted at trial and those likely to be acquitted. Thus, in Baldwin and McConville's study[32] the prosecution files of evidence were given to two experts (a former Chief Constable of the police and a former solicitor and court clerk), who were asked to evaluate the likely outcome of the case. Although prosecution cases often look stronger on paper than transpires at court,[33] nonetheless the assessors were asked to assume that the prosecution case in court would be as strong as that on paper. Whilst the experts felt that there would be likely to be a conviction in some 79 per cent of these cases, they were uncertain about the likely outcome or expected an acquittal in the remaining 21 per cent. Two examples of the assessors' views in this latter category of case are given below:

There is a complete absence of evidence to support either charge. . . . There is a faint possibility that the jury will convict because of [the defendant's] statement but it is unlikely. I think that this case will not get off the ground. I have never read such inconsequential evidence. Taken in the context of the case as a whole, I do not consider that there was any

---

[30] N. 19 above, 110, para. 41.

[31] See, e.g., Baldwin and McConville, n. 5 above; Dell, n. 5 above.

[32] N. 5 above.

[33] Because, e.g., witnesses fail to appear or fail to give their evidence as clearly or as convincingly as on paper or because the witnesses' accounts do not stand up to cross-examination.

offence committed. . . . I consider that the time of the court should not be taken up with this rubbish.

That the assessors' views should be accorded weight is clear from the companion study that Baldwin and McConville undertook on contested cases. In that study the assessors examined the prosecution case papers of almost 1,000 defendants who pleaded not guilty in the Crown Court over a two-year period. The evaluations of the assessors were made in most cases in advance of trial and in all cases without knowledge of the actual outcome. Over 80 per cent of the cases in which the assessors said that the prosecution was not justified in putting the defendant on trial actually resulted in an acquittal. This is powerful evidence that in the plea-bargaining sample many of the cases they evaluated as weak or unjustified would have ended in acquittals had they gone to trial, and that the defendants ought not in such circumstances to have been persuaded to plead guilty.[34] There is other persuasive evidence that supports this conclusion.

In examining how to assess 'cracked' trials, the Royal Commission on Criminal Justice's Crown Court Study asked prosecutors how they viewed such cases. The response was overwhelmingly positive. Almost two-thirds (64 per cent) judged the outcome to be 'good', with virtually all the rest (34 per cent) believing the outcome to be 'satisfactory'.[35] The answers in order of frequency are reproduced here as Table 20.3.[36]

Table 20.3 Reason why cracked trial was good outcome

	%
The sentence would have been the same even if there had been a trial	35
The prosecution secured a conviction	23
Saved time/expense	21
It would have been difficult to get a conviction	13
Saved victim/witnesses an ordeal	7
Defendant pleaded guilty to the most serious charge	6
Total	100 n = 623

The findings disclosed here are the more surprising because prosecutors can hardly be expected to evaluate evidence with the same objectivity as independent assessors.[37] Yet, even so, in one in seven cases they conceded that it would have been difficult to

[34] See also M. Mileski, 'Courtroom Encounters: An Observational Study of the Lower Criminal Court' (1971) 5 *Law & Society Review* 473; R. Seifman, 'The Rise and Fall of Cain' [1976] *Crim. LR* 556.

[35] N. 16 above, at 156, para. 5.17.   [36] *Ibid.*, at 156.

[37] The table also suggests that the so-called 'sentence discount' might be more imaginary than real, given that the reason most often mentioned was that the sentence would have been the same even if the case had gone to trial. For an empirical demonstration of the uncertain nature of the discount see P. Robertshaw and A. Milne, 'The Guilty Plea Discount: Rule of Law or Role of Chance?' (1982) 31 *Howard Journal* 53. Courts have anyway always insisted that there is no rule on what the discount, if any, should be; everything is left to the discretion of the trial judge in each case: see, e.g. *Buffrey* (1993) 14 Cr. App. R (S) 511 (CA).

get a conviction had the case gone to trial. Indeed, when directly asked what would have been the chances of the defendant being acquitted if the case had gone to trial, prosecutors said the chances would have been 'good' in 8 per cent of cases, and 'fairly good' in a further 18 per cent of cases.[38]

In short, the evidence persuasively shows that there can be no confidence that plea bargaining operates only on the guilty and does not pose a threat to the innocent. Whilst the Seabrook Committee only dimly recognized the weakness of its argument that some defendants decide to take their chances before a jury even in an apparently hopeless case, hurriedly adding, '[i]n truth there is probably no such thing as [sic] "hopeless case"',[39] the Royal Commission on Criminal Justice conceded the point openly:[40]

Provided that the defendant is in fact guilty and has received competent legal advice about his or her position, there can be no serious objection to a system of inducements designed to encourage him or her so to plead. Such a system is, however, sometimes held to encourage defendants who are not guilty of the offence charged to plead guilty to it nevertheless. . . . This risk cannot be wholly avoided and, although there can be no certainty as to the precise numbers . . . it would be naïve to suppose that innocent persons never plead guilty because of the prospect of the sentence discount.

But having acknowledged this risk, the Royal Commission immediately set it aside for the perceived instrumental benefits bargaining would bring:[41]

Against the risk that defendants may be tempted to plead guilty to charges of which they are not guilty must be weighed the benefits to the system and to defendants of encouraging those who are in fact guilty to plead guilty. We believe that the system of sentence discounts should remain.

VOLUNTARINESS AND CHOICE

As in most other jurisdictions, it is a basic requirement that any guilty plea must be freely and voluntarily entered by the defendant and not be the product of pressure or coercion. Whilst, as we have seen, this fundamental principle is difficult to reconcile with a bargaining system in which all defendants (innocent and guilty alike) may be under pressure to plead guilty because of the promise of a lighter sentence, plea bargaining also potentially affects the basic rights that all defendants should enjoy. One of the rights which is relevant here is the right to a fair trial.

By giving effect in domestic law to the rights and freedoms guaranteed under the European Convention on Human Rights ('the Convention'), the Human Rights Act 1998 gives every defendant in England and Wales a right to a fair trial. Article 6 of the Convention provides:

---

[38] N. 16 above, 156–7, para. 5.18. These figures, on an aggregate basis, represent some 2,600 Crown Court cases each year.

[39] N. 16 above, at 36, para. 508.   [40] *Ibid.*, 110, para. 42.   [41] *Ibid.*, 111, para. 45.

In the determination of his civil rights or obligations or of any criminal charge against him, everyone is entitled to a fair and public hearing within a reasonable time by an independent and impartial tribunal established by law.

It is arguable that plea bargaining offends against the right to a fair trial set out in Article 6 because it acts to discourage all defendants from going to trial by the threat of more severe punishment if they do so and are convicted.[42] Indeed, it is arguable that the mere existence of a general policy offering reduced sentences for guilty pleas, without specific bargains being offered to individuals, has such a 'chilling' effect upon the decision-making of defendants as to amount to a violation of the right to a fair trial.

The more general point may be made that it is a fundamental right of all defendants to require the prosecution to prove the case against them, irrespective of whether they believe themselves to be guilty of the offence charged. On this view, there is simply a right to a trial in any event. It is this right which is jeopardized when defendants are made to pay (through additional sentences) for electing to go to trial. When this happens, trial by jury is no longer a right, but merely a privilege of which only the factually innocent can take advantage.

THE ROLE OF THE JUDGE

The practice of plea bargaining has a potentially significant impact upon the role of the judges and how they are perceived within an adversary system. Once indications of sentence are given in advance of the decision on the plea, the trial judge inevitably becomes a key factor in the decision-making of the defendant and, equally inevitably, the trial judge becomes identified with the outcome. There is a real risk, therefore, that the reputation of judges for independence and impartiality will be lost, and it is for this reason that the appellate courts were so hostile to any signs of bargaining.

VICTIMS' RIGHTS

The central notion of the system of criminal justice in England and Wales, that the State and the defendant are in a position of adversaries, graphically illustrates a feature that is common to many other criminal justice systems in the world—the lack

---

[42] A related question is whether the Convention requires the strict application of evidential rules in pre-trial hearings. The initial view of English law, considering bail applications, is that the strict rules of evidence are not necessary, and that what is more important is the quality of material forming the basis of the decision: *DPP* v. *Havering* [2001] 1 WLR 805. However, as David Ormerod has pointed out, this begs the question how rules guaranteeing quality in material adduced can be developed without reinventing the formal rules of evidence: *Case Note* on *Wildman* v. *DPP* [2001] *Crim. LR* 565.

of any formal role for the victim in the process.[43] Victims may appear as witnesses at trial, but they are otherwise accorded no part in the process. It is no surprise, therefore, that plea-bargain discussions involve only the prosecutor, the defence lawyer, and the trial judge, and not the victim.

The lack of direct involvement of the victim in the criminal justice process has, indeed, been often held out as a virtue, and one of the advantages of plea bargaining is sometimes said to be its ability to protect victims *from* the criminal justice process. It is very stressful for anyone to have to give evidence. It is much more upsetting for a victim, who will not only have to relive the crime but may have to suffer distressing cross-examination at the hands of the defence lawyer. And all of this, in England and Wales, has to occur in a public setting. It is hardly any wonder, therefore, that proponents of plea bargaining put forward the shielding of victims from the trial as one of its principal advantages.

For a number of reasons, however, this claimed advantage should not be taken simply at face value because this, together with several of plea bargaining's other features, may operate to the distinct disadvantage of victims. There is some evidence, for example, that women who give evidence against their attackers develop greater self-esteem than those who do not. Moreover, because plea bargaining commonly results in a reduction in the seriousness of the crime, the settlement of the case by a guilty plea may result in the victim's actual experience being contradicted by evidence in court. Thus, when a defendant's guilty plea to indecent assault is accepted by the prosecution on a charge of rape, the woman not only has to live with the fact that her attacker will receive a sentence far below what the crime deserved but also with the fact that the outcome of the court case amounts to a legal judgment that she has not been raped. It was precisely this kind of bargain that led to the Attorney-General's new guidelines on the acceptance of pleas in 2000.

The guidelines followed public concern over the case of Robin Peverett in October 2000.[44] Peverett was a private-school headmaster who had indecently assaulted young girls (aged 11–13) in his charge over a period of some eight years. In the course of pretrial discussions counsel for Peverett told prosecuting counsel that in his view the defendant might consider pleading guilty to some of the charges provided that he would not be sent to prison. Eventually, the prosecutor agreed to an arrangement under which Peverett would plead guilty to some charges in return for a suspended sentence of imprisonment which was to be supported on the basis that Peverett had sought by his actions to exert power over the girls rather than acting for the purpose of sexual gratification. On this basis the judge agreed to the bargain and imposed a suspended sentence of imprisonment.

The public outcry which greeted this outcome was increased by the subsequent

---

[43] China is an exception to this. Under the Criminal Procedure Law of China (1996), a victim (or near relatives) has, from the date on which the case is transferred for examination, the right to appoint agents *ad litem*. This right is rarely taken up in practice on grounds of cost. In some jurisdictions, as in the USA, victims are permitted to address the court before sentence is determined through 'victim impact statements'. See A. Ashworth, 'Victim Impact Statements and Sentencing' [1993] *Crim. LR* 498.

[44] See *Attorney-General's Reference No. 44 of 2000 (R. v. Peverett)* [2001] *Crim. LR* 60. See also, 'Making a pact with the devil', *The Guardian*, 30 Oct. 2000.

decision of the Court of Appeal to refuse the Attorney-General leave to appeal against the sentence on the ground that it was unduly lenient. Whilst recognizing that 'anguish on all hands' had been caused by the 'lamentable history' of the case, the court decided that, since the Crown Prosecution Service through counsel had made representations to Peverett on which he had relied in pleading guilty, the Attorney-General (the minister responsible for the Crown Prosecution Service) could not be permitted to go back on the bargain.

The anguish of victims points to a more general problem which plea bargaining presents, namely must all bargains be honoured later? Suppose, for example, that a bargain is entered into on the basis that there will not be a prison sentence but at the sentencing hearing facts emerge which require an immediate prison sentence. Is the trial judge bound to impose a non-custodial sentence? And if the judge does respect the bargain, is the Court of Appeal empowered to increase the sentence where it considers the punishment imposed by the trial judge inadequate? Victims and others require answers to such questions because they feel that those who obtain the benefit of a plea bargain always get, in sentencing terms, less than they deserve.

THE RESPONSIBILITIES OF DEFENCE ADVOCATES

Every system endorsing plea bargaining places substantial burdens upon defence lawyers in the discharge of their responsibilities. It is the defence lawyer who has the task of communicating the system's message—the sentence discount—to the defendant, managing the defendant's guilty plea and transmitting it to the court (and the public) in a manner which necessarily glosses over some vital facts.[45] This is most marked in situations in which the defendant continues to make a claim of innocence whilst agreeing to plead guilty, but it is a feature of almost all bargains in relation to 'the facts' which will be put before the courts. No system has yet been able to deal appropriately with the dilemmas thus created. In England and Wales, the problem is partially addressed in the ethical codes of barristers.

The principal duties of advocates in England and Wales are laid out in the *Code of Conduct for the Bar of England and Wales* as amended.[46] The Code addresses the problem of the 'inconsistent pleader' in these terms:

Where a defendant tells his counsel that he did not commit the offence with which [*sic*] is charged but nevertheless insists on pleading guilty to it for reasons of his own, counsel

---

[45] Many important questions relating to the defendant–lawyer relationship are raised by plea bargaining. One is the effect of discontinuous representation on the interrelationship and the quality of the defendant's decision-making. Another is the extent of the disadvantage in plea discussions of defendants who possess poor communication skills or, indeed, whose lawyers do, or who are the subject of wider disadvantage based on such things as race, class, or gender.

[46] Extracts from the Code of Conduct (5th edn.) are reproduced in (5th edn.) P. Murphy (ed.), *Blackstone's Criminal Practice* (London: Blackstone, 1997) at para. 12.5, Annex, App. 2, 2186 ff.; P. Richardson (ed.), *Archbold's, Criminal Pleading, Evidence and Practice*, (London: Sweet & Maxwell, 1998), App. B, 2517 ff.

must continue to represent him, but only after he has advised what the consequences will be and that what can be submitted in mitigation can only be on the basis that the client is guilty.

The Code of Conduct is based on two principles: that the plea is solely the responsibility of the defendant and that continued representation in these circumstances is permissible so long as counsel does not advance propositions in court which may be taken to imply that the defendant is innocent.

A moment's reflection will show, however, that counsel cannot help but be inconsistent in these situations. Counsel is not a mouthpiece of the client or a 'hired gun'. Counsel, as an officer of the court, has a concurrent duty to assist the court in the administration of justice and must not deceive or knowingly or recklessly mislead it.[47] Where, however, counsel allows or encourages a defendant who privately asserts innocence to plead guilty, counsel *is* allowing the court to be deceived or misled. And by arguing that the defendant deserves mitigation of sentence because guilt has been acknowledged counsel is knowingly misleading the court both as to the true quality of the plea and as to the grounds upon which the defendant 'deserves' a reduced sentence.

As counsel knows, a guilty plea is more than an act of recognition that a conviction is likely or an act of avoidance of the disagreeable consequences which a defendant fears may follow conviction at trial. A guilty plea is the highest form of confession to having *in fact* committed the prohibited act with the state of mind required by law. Indeed, so compelling is this confession that no evidence against the defendant need be put before the court, and the court is fully justified in proceeding immediately to sentencing. If, however, the defendant is asserting innocence in private whilst pleading guilty in public, counsel is put in the position of allowing the court to be misled because counsel knows that the client is asserting privately that the plea is false and counsel, in turn, also believes that it is or may be untrue.

The difficult situation in which defence counsel has been placed has resulted in counsel engaging in practices which amount to little more than taking out 'ethical insurance policies'. A classic illustration is the case of *Stephen Herbert*,[48] in which the defendant and his wife were charged with various drug offences. Stephen Herbert always maintained his innocence of the charges but, mid-way through the trial, changed his plea to guilty after learning from his barrister that the prosecution would drop all charges against his wife on condition that he pleaded guilty. Although Stephen Herbert continued to tell counsel that he was innocent, counsel allowed the guilty plea to be entered after drawing up a document, which he got Stephen Herbert to sign but which was never placed before the trial court, detailing Herbert's claim of innocence and the nature of the bargain which had led to the plea. This document, 'the ethical insurance policy', appears to be little more than a desperate attempt by counsel to act ethically in a situation in which ethical action was no longer possible. The endorsement of counsel's conduct by the Court of Appeal and its refutation of Stephen Herbert's complaints of unfair treatment simply reinforced

---

[47] Bar's Code of Conduct, n. 44 above, para. 202.   [48] (1992) 94 Cr. App. R 230 (CA).

the powerlessness of counsel in these situations without providing any justification for the action itself.[49]

PUBLIC INTERESTS

Plea bargaining raises important public-policy questions for any criminal justice system that go beyond the issues already discussed. All systems should be continuously engaged in self-improvement. Self-improvement, in turn, depends upon self-awareness. Before a system can improve, it needs to know *how* to improve, and this means that it needs to know where its weaknesses lie.

Whilst it has many other virtues, the trial provides an excellent opportunity to reveal and illuminate the workings of the system in all its aspects. During a public trial, failings of substantive and procedural law can be identified; police inefficiency or malpractice uncovered; prosecutorial wrong-headedness exposed; and defence lawyers' disorganization or lack of preparation brought to the surface. Any weaknesses thus exposed are exposed in a public domain and publicity brings its own pressure for reform.

By contrast, plea bargaining operates in the shadows. As a mechanism, it has no interest in exposing systemic failures and may, indeed, wish to suppress any that would otherwise come to light. By its very nature plea bargaining is subversive of the formal rules of the system and gives weight to political rather than legal values—the trade, the compromise, the deal. Experience in many jurisdictions has shown that where plea bargaining is rife, probity, rectitude, and fair dealing are at a disadvantage.

Any system, therefore, which chooses to adopt plea bargaining as a method of case disposition should be aware that bargaining is more than just another method of resolving cases or clearing a backlog of court cases. Plea bargaining contests values which any rational and fair system should protect and cherish, and any system which adopts bargaining should at least be aware of what it is losing when it degrades the idea of the trial.

CONCLUSION

However it is regarded—as an inevitable feature of modern systems of criminal justice, as a desirable way of doing business, or as a perversion of adversary ideals—plea bargaining has proved to be the most virulent virus ever to have invaded the criminal justice system's body. It has left no part of the process untouched. It has altered the language of the law. It has altered its capacity to treat like cases alike, its interest in and

---

[49] It is becoming increasingly common in England for defendants when entering a guilty plea to do so by means of a written statement in which the defendant admits only part of what the prosecution alleges: *Tolera* [1999] 1 Cr. App. R (S) 25; *R. v. Kester* [2001] *Crim. LR* 582.

concern with claims of innocence, its engagement with ethical professional practice and legal culture more generally, and it has spawned its own procedurres.

The question which any jurisdiction contemplating the introduction of plea bargaining will have to ask itself is whether it can reap the proclaimed benefits, principally the cost-effective processing of large numbers of cases, without also having to shoulder the burdens. The example of England and Wales strongly suggests that the benefits may be less than claimed and the burdens impossible to avoid.

Further Reading

BALDWIN, J., and McCONVILLE, M., *Negotiated Justice* (London: Martin Robertson, 1997).

BOTTOMS, A., and McCLEAN, J., *Defendants in the Criminal Process* (London: Routledge, 1976).

DELL, S., *Silent in Court* (London: Bell, 1971).

McCABE, S., and PURVES, R., *By-Passing the Jury* (Oxford: Oxford University Penal Research Unit: Blackwell, 1972).

McCONVILLE, M., *et al.*, *Standing Accused* (Oxford: Clarendon Press, 1994).

—— and MIRSKY, C., 'Guilty Plea Courts: A Social Disciplinary Model of Criminal Justice' (1995) 42 *Social Problems* 216.

MACK, K., and ANLEU, S., 'Guilty Pleas: Discussion and Agreements' (1996) 6 *Journal of Judicial Administration* 8.

21

TRIAL BY JURY

Sean Doran

INTRODUCTION

Trial by jury occupies a pivotal yet paradoxical position at the centre of the English criminal justice system. For many observers, particularly those looking in on the English trial process from overseas, it is the jury that stands out as its most striking and even most endearing feature. Moreover, arguably no other aspect of the system has attracted such widespread and intensive scrutiny. The paradox, however, is that in statistical terms trial by jury has undergone a steady decline over the years, and now accounts for a very limited proportion of cases that are dealt with in the criminal courts. More than 95 per cent of cases are dealt with in the magistrates' courts without a jury,[1] and a majority of cases heard in the Crown Court (approximately 60 per cent) involve the defendant pleading guilty without any jury being selected.[2] Even when a jury is sworn in to hear a case, the jury itself may not be called upon to adjudicate on the defendant's guilt, for in many cases the trial judge will actually direct the jury to acquit.[3] The ending of a case in this way is discussed further below, but it may happen, for example, where an important witness has refused to give evidence and the trial cannot proceed or where the prosecution evidence is too weak to justify a conviction.

This obvious gap between the number of cases disposed of by juries and the degree of attention given to the institution of jury trial has led some to conclude that the practical significance of the jury is clearly outweighed by its symbolic function.[4] Yet notwithstanding its relatively limited use in practice, the importance of jury trial ought not to be underestimated. Obviously, the cases that are heard by juries include the most serious offences, such as murder, manslaughter, serious sexual offences, and other serious offences against the person.[5] It is in such cases that the consequences for an accused person will be most severe in the event of a

[1] See P. Darbyshire, 'Magistrates' Courts' (Chap. 16 above).

[2] *Judicial Statistics for 1999*, Cm 4786 (2000), Table 6.8 and accompanying commentary.

[3] *Ibid.* at Table 6.10: 67% of jury acquittals were of this nature.

[4] For a very critical viewpoint see P. Darbyshire, 'The Lamp That Shows That Freedom Lives—Is it Worth the Candle?' [1991] *Crim. LR* 740.

[5] The classification of offences in English criminal procedure is explained below: see text accompanying n. 19 below.

wrongful conviction. Moreover, such cases will often tend to attract widespread publicity, sometimes gripping the attention of the public well beyond the locality in which the alleged crime was committed. Inevitably, therefore, the quality of justice dispensed by juries will often tend to form the basis of judgements made about the efficacy of the criminal justice system as a whole. In this regard, it is worth emphasizing that, even though the jury system is often portrayed as undergoing a crisis of confidence,[6] there remains strong support in the United Kingdom for the view that it provides the most appropriate method of dealing with the most serious cases. Significantly, the recent major review of the criminal court system in England and Wales, conducted by Auld LJ, accepted that trial by judge and jury should continue as the main form of trial of the most serious offences, albeit subject to certain exceptions.[7]

THE RATIONALE OF TRIAL BY JURY

The justifications that are advanced for maintaining a system of jury trial are manifold, but at their heart is the notion that the jury is the embodiment of participatory democracy.[8] Trial by jury, it is argued, brings the ordinary citizen into the professional world of the courtroom and gives representatives of the public a decisive voice at the very core of the legal process. Such participation is said to instil a sense of confidence in the system among those who serve on juries as well as among the general public. One writer illustrated this point very effectively with the powerful image of the jury injecting 'lay acid' into the legal system.[9] A significant corollary to this is that the legitimacy of the verdict—in the eyes both of defendants and of the public in general—will be enhanced by entrusting the defendant's fate to his or her 'peers', rather than to professional judges who may have a more limited insight into the community from which the accused is drawn. In extreme cases, the power that is invested in the jury may even extend to a decision to 'turn against' the strict application of the law, in order to do justice in an individual case. This notion of 'jury equity', as it is sometimes called, will be discussed in more detail below.

In conjunction with the arguments of principle that underpin the importation of community values into the legal system, it is also contended that the collective civilian common sense that jurors bring to their task equips them well for the basic job for

---

[6] The title of a collection of essays on the jury, published in 1988, is arguably just as pertinent today as it was then: M. Findlay and P. Duff (eds.), *The Jury Under Attack* (London: Butterworths, 1988).

[7] *Review of the Criminal Courts of England and Wales* (London: TSO, 2001) 26 and chap. 5. The reader should note that the present chap. was written prior to publication of the review and that it has not been possible to incorporate comprehensive references to all aspects of the review that relate to trial by jury. The website of the review is located at www.criminal-courts-review.org.uk.

[8] The most frequently cited exposition of this view is to be found in P. Devlin, *Trial by Jury* (London Stevens, 1956) at 64 (describing the jury as a 'little parliament').

[9] Z. Bankowski, 'The Jury and Reality' in Findlay and Duff (eds.), above nn. 6, 8 and 20.

which they are employed in the courtroom, namely the finding of fact. Unlike professional lawyers, who will become accustomed to hearing certain kinds of argument and evidence in the course of their daily contact with the courts, jurors come 'cold' to the evidence in each case, and as such are in a unique position to exercise a fresh judgement on the facts. As John Jackson has explained elsewhere in this book, this is why the jury is so well suited to an adversarial trial system.[10] This justification for jury trial is probably at its strongest when applied to the basic assessment of the credibility of witnesses. It is argued that, in the general run of cases, jurors' collective experience of everyday life ought to equip them to determine the plausibility of the respective stories of prosecution and defence. This argument runs into difficulty, however, when applied to the evaluation of more complex evidence such as forensic evidence, or even evidence that tends to be persuasive on its face but experience has shown frequently to be prone to error, such as evidence of eyewitness identification.[11] As we shall see, doubts have also been raised about whether juries are ever properly able to cope with the evidence in particular kinds of case, such as those involving serious fraud, and consideration has been given to new ways of handling such cases.[12]

This challenge to the effectiveness of the jury in certain classes of case is just one facet of a more widespread scepticism that has arisen about the merits of jury trial in recent years.[13] In particular, critics of jury trial have pointed out that a jury is rarely a truly representative selection of society, given the range of individuals who are either excused or disqualified from serving (see below). Moreover, the concept of trial by one's peers is an elusive one, particularly in the context of a multi-racial society. As for the image of the jury as a protector of the interests of the individual against the power of the State, this can be counteracted by concerns that have been expressed about various cases in which juries have convicted accused persons in questionable circumstances.[14] Certainly, even though acquittal rates by juries tend to remain at a fairly high level,[15] the image of the jury as a 'defence-friendly' institution is more open to question than it was in the past.

It is fair to say, however, that the decline in the number of cases in which juries are now used has been more attributable to matters of cost and administrative

---

[10] J. Jackson, 'The Adversary Trial and Trial by Judge Alone' (Chap. 19 above).

[11] See *R. v. Turnbull* [1977] QB 224, in which the Court of Appeal established guidelines for judges to follow in trials involving disputed identification evidence.

[12] *Report of the Fraud Trials Committee* (London: HMSO, 1986) ('The Roskill Report'); Juries in Serious Fraud Trials: A Consultation Document (London: Home Office, 1998).

[13] See Darbyshire, n. 4 above; L. Blom-Cooper, 'Article 6 and Modes of Trial' [2001] *European Human Rights Law Review* 1.

[14] See, e.g. the landmark study of jury trials in England conducted in the 1970s: J. Baldwin and M. McConville, *Jury Trials* (Oxford: Clarendon Press, 1979), chap. 5; and, more recently, M. Zander and P. Henderson, Royal Commission on Criminal Justice Research Study No. 19, *The Crown Court Study* (London: HMSO, 1993) 170–1.

[15] Crown Court statistics for 1999 show that 65% of the defendants who pleaded not guilty to all counts were acquitted. Of these, 33% were acquitted by a jury and 15% were acquitted by the jury at the direction of the judge; the other 52% were discharged by the judge: *Judicial Statistics for 1999*, n. 2 above, Tables 6.8–6.10 and accompanying text.

convenience than to matters of principle.[16] Jury trial is an expensive business,[17] and several attempts have been made by successive governments to whittle down its sphere of application and hence its demands on the public purse. Significantly, however, such attempts habitually meet with strong public and political resistance, which is illustrative of the strong esteem in which the jury continues to be held. This sentiment is captured most eloquently in the words of one prominent lawyer, who described the spirit of jury trial as 'burnt into the consciousness of every Englishman—to such an extent that the jury's detractors may as well attempt to do away with Parliamentary democracy as trial by jury'.[18] Nonetheless, although the future of jury trial for the most serious cases may appear to be secure, the battle over the proper extent of its scope looks set to continue, a theme that we now turn to address in the next section.

CASES SENT FOR JURY TRIAL

THE CLASSIFICATION OF CRIMINAL OFFENCES

As mentioned above, a jury will only be called upon to deal with a case where the defendant pleads not guilty in a case that is tried in the Crown Court. English criminal procedure groups criminal offences within three categories.[19] First, 'indictable only offences': these are the most serious offences which must be tried on 'indictment' in the Crown Court. Secondly, at the other end of the scale are the 'summary offences', the least serious offences which can be tried only in the magistrates' court, whether by lay justices or a professional district judge.[20] Thirdly, there is an intermediate band of offences that are 'triable either way': they may be tried in the magistrates' court if the magistrates are willing to hear the case and the defendant consents, but the defendant has the right to insist on being tried in the Crown Court. Around 80 per cent of cases tried in the Crown Court fall within this third category, which includes offences such as theft, burglary, criminal damage, and a range of serious offences against the person.

It is difficult to give a conclusive answer to the question why defendants opt for Crown Court trial, but research suggests that the most prominent reasons include the

[16] The cost factor has been a prominent feature in recent debates on the scope of jury trial: see C. Dyer, 'Why Straw plans to ditch defendants' right to choose', *The Guardian*, 19 Jan. 2000.

[17] Home Office figures suggest that the average cost of dealing with a not guilty plea in the Crown Court is over 10 times the average cost of dealing with a not guilty plea in the magistrates' court (£17,550 as compared to £1,700): R. Harries, *The Cost of Criminal Justice* (London: Home Office, 1999, Home Office Research Development and Statistics Directorate, Research Findings No. 103) 2.

[18] From a conference address by Roy Amlott QC in 1997 when he was Chairman of the Bar Council, cited in S. Lloyd-Bostock and C. Thomas, 'The Continuing Decline of the English Jury' in N. Vidmar (ed.), *World Jury Systems* (Oxford: OUP, 2000), at 57.

[19] For a detailed explanation of the system, see P. Murphy (ed.), *Blackstone's Criminal Practice 2001* (London: Blackstone Press, 2001), section D3.

[20] See P. Darbyshire, 'Magistrates' Courts' (Chap. 16, above).

advice of their solicitor and the perception that the chances of an acquittal are more favourable before a jury than before magistrates.[21] This perception is borne out by statistical evidence showing acquittal rates of approximately 40 per cent in jury trials as compared with 25 per cent in magistrates' courts.[22] It would be dangerous, however, to interpret these figures as proving that juries are more favourably disposed than magistrates to defendants, because there are other important variables involved in the comparison: for example, it may be that more cases in which there is a strong line of defence end up being heard in the Crown Court.

Whatever the motivation behind defendants' choices, it is this 'middle ground' of offences that has provided the main focus for debate on the right to jury trial over the last twenty-five years in England and Wales. A series of legislative enactments has reclassified several offences (for example, minor cases of criminal damage) so as to bring them within the 'summary only' category, the result being to deny the accused the opportunity of opting for jury trial in such cases.[23] More significantly, however, the government intends to remove from defendants generally their exisiting right to choose jury trial in 'either way' cases where the magistrates are willing to deal with the matter. The political sensitivity engendered by this plan is illustrated by the fact that the House of Lords in the last parliamentary session twice rejected proposed legislation to curtail the defendant's right to choose.[24]

It is not possible to explore in detail all strands of the debate in relation to 'either way' cases in the course of the present chapter. In brief, the arguments in favour of abolishing the right to choose include the reduction of delay; the saving that would be effected in terms of cost; the subsidiary point that a large number of defendants who opt for jury trial do so for purely tactical reasons (such as to delay the proceedings or to pressurize the prosecution into accepting a plea to a lesser charge), many of whom in turn end up pleading guilty, thereby entailing further unnecessary expense; and the contention that the decision on what form of trial should take place ought to be made by the court on an objective basis rather than by the defence on the basis of what kind of trial it thinks might work to its advantage.[25]

---

[21] C. Hedderman and D. Moxon, *Magistrates' Court or Crown Court? Mode of Trial Decisions and Sentencing*, Home Office Research Study No. 125 (London: HMSO, 1992) 18–21.

[22] *Determining Mode of Trial in Either-Way Cases: A Consultation Paper* (London: Home Office, 1998), para. 9. See also *Criminal Justice (Mode of Trial) Bill Briefing Note* (London: Home Office, 2000).

[23] Criminal Law Act 1977, s. 15; Criminal Justice Act 1988, ss. 37–39. The recommendation that a number of offences be transferred to the sole jurisdiction of the magistrates was initially made by the James Committee in 1975: *The Distribution of Business Between the Crown Court and the Magistrates' Courts: Report of the Interdepartmental Committee*, Cmnd 6323 (1975).

[24] See, most recently, HL Debs., vol. 616, cols. 961–1033; 28 Sept. 2000, 'Jury Bill heads for stand-off', *The Times*, 30 Sept. 2000. Auld LJ's review has recommended the removal of the defendant's right of election: *Review of the Criminal Courts*, n. 7 above at 181–200. See also text accompanying n. 33 below. The issue has been the subject of debate for some years now: see, in particular, *Report of the Royal Commission on Criminal Justice*, Cm 2263 (1993) 85–9; *Review of Delay in the Criminal Justice System: A Report* (London: Home Office, 1997), chap. 6; *Determining Mode of Trial in Either-Way Cases: A Consultation Paper* (London: Home Office, 1998).

[25] For a summary of the arguments for and against preservation of the right to elect, see *Determining Mode of Trial in Either-Way Cases*, n. 24 above, at paras. 10–20.

Those in favour of the retention of the right of choice claim that the projected savings in terms of cost and administrative convenience are over-inflated. They also challenge the assumption that a large number of defendants choosing jury trial necessarily do so for tactical reasons.[26] More significantly, they argue that the right to jury trial should be preserved as a matter of principle in respect of the offences falling within the 'either way' category, as the consequences of conviction in many cases will be of a serious nature for the individual concerned. It is argued that if it is accepted that trial by jury is the 'ideal' method for trying serious cases, then to curb it in this way will lead to a perception of injustice in individual cases as well as a loss of confidence in the system as a whole. Some research has indicated that the restriction of the right to choose might be perceived as particularly unfair by certain groups of ethnic minority defendants who have less confidence in magistrates' courts than in the Crown Court, as they regard the former as more inclined to take the side of the police.[27]

DIVERTING SERIOUS CASES FROM JURY TRIAL

We have seen that the range of cases sent for trial by jury can be limited in the future, first, by classifying offences as not being sufficiently serious for the Crown Court and, secondly, by withdrawing the right of defendants charged with 'either way' offences to have the final say on how their cases are dealt with. There are, however, other factors that have led to a reduction in the use of jury trial, even in cases of a very serious nature. In Northern Ireland, for example, cases connected with political violence are tried not by a jury but by a judge sitting alone in the Crown Court in what are known as 'Diplock courts'.[28] One reason for this has been the possibility that jurors dealing with such cases might be subjected to threats or intimidation.

Another argument for seeking an alternative method of trying a case might be its complexity. In particular, it has been questioned whether juries are effectively equipped to try complex fraud cases, and proposals have been made to divert such cases away from jury trial.[29] The most notable was the Roskill Committee's recommendation in 1986 that such cases should be tried by a judge sitting with two expert assessors.[30] Although this idea was not put into practice at the time, the debate over whether juries should continue to be used for complex fraud cases has resurfaced in recent years, and the present government would appear ready to consider reform of

---

[26] See, e.g. *Criminal Justice (Mode of Trial) Bill Counter Briefing Note*, located at www.law.warwick.ac.uk/lawschool/mot.html.

[27] L. Bridges, S. Choongh, and M. McConville, *Ethnic Minority Defendants and the Right to Elect Jury Trial* (London: Commission for Racial Equality, 2000). Note, however, that Home Office research suggests that white defendants are statistically more likely to be convicted than black defendants in both the magistrates' courts and the Crown Court: *Criminal Justice (Mode of Trial) Bill Counter Briefing Note*, n. 26 above.

[28] For a history of the Diplock court system see J. Jackson and S. Doran, *Judge Without Jury: Diplock Trials in the Adversary System* (Oxford: Oxford University Press, 1995), chap. 2.

[29] For detailed discussion see M. Levi, 'Economic Crime', Chap. 12 below.

[30] The Roskill Report, n. 12 above, at paras. 1.6 and 8.52–8.74.

the current position.[31] For defenders of jury trial, such a development would be seen as a further chink in the jury's armour: if juries are deemed unfit to deal with complex cases of this nature, then the fear is that their competence may be challenged in other cases too, not least in cases involving complex scientific evidence. An alternative to the *abolition* of jury trial in complex cases would be the development of measures to assist jurors to comprehend more effectively the evidence that is presented. As we shall see, this may have benefits for jury trial in general that are not confined to cases of particular complexity.

The discussion so far has centred on measures that restrict the defendant's ability to opt for a jury trial. Another measure that would have the effect of reducing the number of cases tried by jury, but arguably not to the defendant's disadvantage, would be to allow the defendant to waive jury trial in respect of 'indictable only' offences or 'either way' offences in respect of which the magistrates have declined jurisdiction, and be tried instead by a judge sitting alone in the Crown Court. This would provide a form of trial between that of the magistrates and the jury, but without limiting in any way the defendant's freedom to choose trial by jury. Other jurisdictions, such as the United States, Canada, and Australia, operate such a system, but it has not until recently been given serious consideration in the United Kingdom: a system of waiver has been recommended by Auld LJ in his review of the criminal courts, subject to the court consenting to the defendant's election.[32]

Finally, it is interesting to note that this review has also recommended a new system of 'intermediate' criminal court consisting of a district judge sitting with two experienced magistrates instead of a jury.[33] This would provide an alternative mode of trial for a range of offences falling within the 'either way' category. The idea, however, is unlikely to placate those who view the current tide of reform as placing the institution of the jury under threat.

SELECTING THE JURY

RULES AND PROCEDURES GOVERNING JURY SELECTION

If a case is to be tried by jury, the question then arises how the jury will be selected. The current legislation governing this matter is the Juries Act 1974. The general rule is that all persons between the ages of 18 and 70, who are registered as electors and who have been resident in the United Kingdom for a period of five years, are eligible for

---

[31] See *Juries in Serious Fraud Trials: A Consultation Document* (London: Home Office, 1998). Note also that Auld LJ has recommended that in serious and complex fraud cases, the trial judge should be empowered to direct trial himself or herself sitting with specialist lay members: *Review of Criminal Courts*, n. 7 above at 200–14.

[32] *Review of Criminal Courts*, n. 7 above, at 177–81. See C. Dyer, 'Accused may get right to trial by judge alone', *The Guardian*, 12 July 2001. For a comparative study of jury waiver and an assessment of the arguments for and against such a system see S. Doran and J. Jackson, 'The Case for Jury Waiver' [1997] *Crim. LR* 155.

[33] *Review of the Criminal Courts*, n. 7 above, at 275–81.

jury service. Lists of jurors are selected at random from the electoral register; panels of jurors are then summoned to attend particular court sittings over a period of time.

The general rule, however, needs to be qualified as follows. First, certain groups are *ineligible* for jury service for a variety of reasons. These include members of the legal profession and others working in the field of criminal justice, the clergy, and the mentally disordered. Secondly, certain categories of persons who have been convicted of criminal offences or who are currently on bail are *disqualified* from jury service. Thirdly, certain individuals are entitled to be *excused* as of right from serving on a jury if they so request. This includes persons who have been called for jury service within the past two years, those who have been specifically excused by the court on a previous occasion for a period that has not elapsed, Members of Parliament, members of the medical and related professions, serving members of the armed forces, and persons over the age of 65. Finally, persons summoned for jury service can apply to the court to be excused as a matter of discretion on the ground that there is 'good reason' why they should be excused. Examples of a good reason would be that the prospective juror is acquainted with the accused or a witness or that personal hardship would be caused, e.g. as where the individual has pressing business or family commitments.[34] The court also has power to defer jury service until a later date.

When it comes to the point at which a jury has to be sworn for an individual case, part of the panel is assembled in the courtroom and a process of selection takes place in order to appoint a jury of twelve persons. The selection is made on the basis of a random ballot,[35] but this does not mean that the first twelve jurors randomly called will end up serving on the jury. First, it is possible for the defence or prosecution to challenge a juror for 'cause', for example on the ground that a particular juror may suffer from prejudice against the accused. Secondly, the prosecution has an unrestricted right to 'stand by' a prospective juror. No reason need be given for the exercise of this right, the effect of which is to send the juror back to the panel (with the possibility of being recalled in the unlikely event of the panel being exhausted).[36] Thirdly, the judge has a residual discretion to exclude a person from the jury as part of his duty to ensure a fair trial for the accused. This discretion would be exercised, for example, in a situation where a juror was plainly incompetent or too infirm to carry out the functions of a juror properly.[37] The judge may also discharge individual jurors in the course of the trial, for example where a witness falls ill, and in extreme cases can discharge the entire jury, such as where evidence of the defendant's previous bad character has been inadvertently revealed to them.

---

[34] See *Practice Direction (Jury Service: Excusal)* [1988] 1 WLR 1162.

[35] On the need for the selection of the jury to be random see *R. v. Tarrant* [1998] *Crim. LR* 342.

[36] Whilst the right of stand by is in theory unrestricted, as the Attorney-General's Guidelines make clear, it has been customary for those instructed on behalf of the Crown 'to assert that right only sparingly and in exceptional circumstances. It is generally accepted that the prosecution should not use its right in order to influence the overall composition of a jury or with a view to tactical advantage': *Attorney-General's Guidelines: Exercise by the Crown of its Right of Stand By* (1989) 88 Cr. App. R 123 (para. 1).

[37] See *R. v. Mason* [1981] QB 881 at 887.

REVIEWING THE PRINCIPLES OF SELECTION

Following on from this brief explanation of the mechanics of jury selection, some important matters of principle need to be addressed. The idea of judgement by one's 'peers' was identified in an earlier section as an important aspect of the rationale for jury trial. This is fine in theory, but what precisely does the idea of judgement by one's peers mean in practice? The following passage illustrates effectively the difficulty to which the question gives rise:[38]

Does it imply the judgment of a body of fair minded people, the judgment of one's equals and neighbours, the judgment of an independent and impartial body, the judgment of a randomly selected tribunal, the judgment of representatives of the community, or the judgment of 12 clones of the accused? Towards which of these images is confidence directed?

It will have become obvious from the discussion of selection procedures that the notion of the jury being 'representative' is a qualified one, given the range of individuals who are ineligible, disqualified, or who may be excused for various reasons. Prior to 1972, jury service was restricted to an even more limited field, as one requirement of eligibility was that the individual had to be an owner of property above a certain value. This tended to have the effect of producing juries composed of predominantly middle-class and middle-aged men.[39]

The removal of the property qualifications and the subsequent extension of eligibility to a much wider range of individuals have certainly made juries more generally representative of the population as a whole, but there remain concerns that a proper balance of representation on juries has not yet been struck. First, some research has suggested that women and ethnic minorities tend to be under-represented on jury panels.[40] Secondly, a practical consequence of the selection arrangements—in particular the 'excusal' categories—is that many individuals who seem particularly well equipped to serve on juries are lost to the system. Recent government statistics also suggest that nearly 40 per cent of those summoned for jury service are excused on a discretionary basis.[41] One way of addressing the problem would be to make the list of individuals excused as of right a more restrictive one, and to make it more difficult for individuals to gain exemption on the basis of a 'good reason'.[42] There are of course difficult policy choices to be made here between the competing claims of civic duty and other interests. It is also worth noting that a juror who is caused genuine personal hardship or serious professional inconvenience through serving on a jury may not be in the proper frame of mind to discharge the role effectively.

When considering the general issue of how to ensure balanced representation on a jury, it is important to recognize that the notion of a jury being 'representative' can be difficult to reconcile with the practice of 'random' selection. For example, in a trial

---

[38] Findlay and Duff, n. 6 above, at 3.
[39] See Devlin, n. 8 above, at 20.
[40] See, e.g. Zander and Henderson, n. 14 above, at 234–5, 241–2.
[41] See the government's White Paper, *Criminal Justice: The Way Ahead*, Cm 5074 (2001) 66.
[42] See discussion in Lloyd-Bostock and Thomas, n. 18 above, at 71.

involving a black defendant from a racially mixed community, it is perfectly possible that random selection of jurors will produce twelve white jurors.[43] This does not, of course, mean that the jury would inevitably be prejudiced against the accused any more than a jury composed of twelve members from the *same* racial background as the accused would necessarily be free of prejudice. Each and every juror will bring to a trial an individual set of values and preconceptions. If, however, the composition of the jury is wholly different from the accused's personal background and circumstances, then the legitimacy of the proceedings may be devalued in the perception of the accused. The question arises, therefore, what mechanisms might be made available to the parties to ensure that random selection does not produce a jury whose composition raises serious concerns about the fairness of the accused's trial.

Mention was made above of the right of a party to challenge a juror 'for cause'. In theory this may seem to provide a means of guarding against specific bias or prejudice against the accused. There is, however, in the English system no general opportunity for the defence to question jurors about their suitability, for example about their backgrounds or political beliefs. Before such questioning is permitted, some evidence needs to be brought forward to justify the challenge, and since the only information revealed to the parties about jurors is their name and address, such evidence will rarely be forthcoming.[44] In any case, to allow a searching examination of individual jurors by the defence with a view to eliminating jurors that the defence deems 'unsuitable' would be seriously to undermine the principle of random selection. If defendants were routinely acquitted in circumstances where it appeared that the defence had a major influence on the composition of the jury, this would in turn lead to a loss of faith in the effectiveness of jury trial.

One way of addressing the particular problem of ensuring a racially balanced jury would be to permit the judge to intervene to ensure that the jury has representatives from the same ethnic background as that of the accused. This approach has been rejected in England, specifically on the basis that the responsibility for summoning jurors lies with the Lord Chancellor, and that it is not part of the judge's function to interfere with the composition of the jury in order to ensure racial balance, or to issue directions about the area from which a jury should be drawn.[45] In 1993, the Royal Commission on Criminal Justice recommended that measures should be adopted to ensure that in cases with 'unusual and special features' a jury would include at least three members from the accused's ethnic grouping, but this proposal has not been implemented.[46] One final argument that might be made in this context is that a racially unbalanced jury could contravene Article 6 of the European Convention on

[43] For detailed discussion of this dilemma in an American context see J. Abramson, *We, the Jury: The Jury System and the Ideal of Democracy* (Cambridge, Mass.: Harvard University Press, 2000), chap. 3.

[44] A. Sanders and R. Young, *Criminal Justice* (2nd edn., London: Butterworths, 2000), at 563. In *R.* v. *Chandler (No. 2)* [1964] 2 QB 322, it was stated that there has to be 'a foundation of fact creating a prima facie case before the juror can be cross-examined' (*per* Lord Parker CJ at 338).

[45] *R.* v. *Ford* [1989] QB 868.

[46] *Report of the Royal Commission on Criminal Justice*, n. 24 above, at 133–4. Auld LJ's review has also recommended the adoption of a scheme for ensuring selection of ethnic minority jurors in cases where the court considers that race is likely to be of relevance to an issue in the case: *Review of the Criminal Courts*, n. 7 above, at 156–9.

Human Rights, which protects the accused's right to a fair trial by an 'independent and impartial' tribunal. The argument is, however, unlikely to succeed if no *specific* prejudice is established on the part of an individual juror or jurors.[47]

The principle of random selection may also be modified by giving the defence the right to challenge a limited number of jurors without having to undertake the difficult task of showing specific cause why a juror is unsuitable: this is generally known as 'peremptory challenge'. In Northern Ireland, for example, each defendant retains the right to challenge up to twelve jurors without showing cause.[48] In England, however, the practice of peremptory challenging was gradually phased out until it was finally abolished in 1988.[49] The reasoning behind this change was that defendants could on some occasions use the system to their advantage to create a jury that was clearly more defence-oriented.[50] On the other hand, research has suggested that there is no necessary correlation between peremptory challenges and the likelihood of acquittal.[51] The main benefit of peremptory challenges may therefore have been that they increased the confidence of the defendants in the process by which they were being tried, rather than routinely offering them an enhanced prospect of acquittal. A potent argument *against* such challenges, however, is that they may be exercised on the basis of stereotypical views of how jurors of a particular age, class, race, or gender would react to the alleged offence and the particular defendant. This takes us back to the whole ethos of random selection, which is geared towards eradicating such subjective and impressionistic judgement from the process of choosing a jury.

As explained above, however, the prosecution retains the right to 'stand by' jurors without showing cause. Following on from the abolition of peremptory challenges for defendants, new guidelines were issued by the Attorney-General on the exercise of this right.[52] The guidelines seek to restrict the exercise of the right of stand by to two situations: first, where a juror is clearly unsuitable and the defence agrees that the juror should be excluded, for example where it becomes apparent that a juror selected to try a complex case is in fact illiterate; secondly, where jury checks reveal information justifying the exercise of the right of stand by.

It is this latter situation that occasionally causes some concern among defence lawyers. It is generally known that the practice of 'jury vetting', whereby the prosecution obtain information about the background of potential jurors from the police or security services, has taken place in certain kinds of case for many years.[53] The extent of its use, however, is less clear. This matter has also been dealt with by Attorney-General's guidelines, which make it clear that investigation of the jury panel should be allowed only, first, in cases in which national security is involved and part of the

---

[47] For discussion of this point see Sanders and Young, n. 44 above, at 566; see also *Gregory* v. *UK* (1997) 25 EHRR 577 and *Sander* v. *UK* (2000) 8 BHRC 279.

[48] Juries (Northern Ireland) Order 1996, art. 15(1)(a).

[49] Criminal Justice Act 1987, s. 118. See J. Gobert, 'The Peremptory Challenge—An Obituary' [1988] *Crim. LR* 528.

[50] *Criminal Justice, Plans for Legislation*, Cmnd 9658 (1986), para. 33.

[51] J. Vennard and D. Riley, 'The Use of Peremptory Challenge and Stand By of Jurors and their Relationship to Trial Outcome' [1988] *Crim. LR* 731.

[52] N. 36 above.

[53] See P. Duff and M. Findlay, 'Jury Vetting—The Jury under Attack' (1983) 3 *Legal Studies* 159.

evidence is likely to be heard 'in camera' and, secondly, in terrorist cases.[54] More routine checks by the police are also permitted in certain circumstances, for example to ensure that disqualified persons are not permitted to serve on a jury.[55] There are at least three specific concerns about the practice of jury vetting: first, it appears to run contrary to the notion of random selection that we discussed above;[56] secondly, it is conducted in secret, and the fact that a juror has been excluded because of information obtained through vetting will not become known, because no reasons need be given for the exercise of the right of stand by; thirdly, it has been argued that the practice may fall foul of the principle of 'equality of arms' between prosecution and defence, which is at the heart of Article 6 of the European Convention on Human Rights.[57]

To conclude, English jury-selection procedures are generally based on the principle of random selection. They provide a fairly 'rough and ready' mechanism for appointing a jury to do justice in an individual case, with minimum opportunity for the parties to influence its composition. For most cases, the selection process will not take up more than half an hour of the court's time. An alternative approach would be to permit fairly protracted questioning of prospective jurors with a view to testing their impartiality, as occurs in the United States.[58] The only parallel for this kind of practice in England has been the screening of jurors in certain high-profile cases to see whether their exposure to extensive pre-trial publicity about the defendant might lead to their judgement being clouded.[59] There is, however, no compelling evidence to suggest that such an approach produces juries that are more effectively equipped to discharge their allotted function in the trial process.

THE JURY IN THE COURSE OF THE TRIAL

ISSUES OF LAW AND FACT

The discussion so far has centred on the principle of trial by jury, the mechanisms for sending a case to trial by jury, and the process of jury selection. When we arrive at the trial itself, however, it becomes clear that the proceedings may be more accurately described as 'trial by judge *and* jury'.[60] No discussion of jury trial would be complete without a reference to the important function that the judge plays in the proceedings. More detailed consideration is given to the judge's role in criminal proceedings generally in Chapter 18 above.[61] What is important to emphasize here is that, although the

---

[54] N. 36 above, at 124.

[55] *Ibid.* at 125 (Recommendations of the Association of Chief Police Officers).

[56] But see *R. v. McCann, Cullen, and Shanahan* (1991) 92 Cr. App. R 239, in which the Court of Appeal did not accept this argument (at 246–7).

[57] G. Robertson, *Freedom, the Individual and the Law* (7th edn., London: Penguin, 1993) 358–9.

[58] See R. May, 'Jury Selection in the United States: Are there Lessons to be Learned?' [1998] *Crim. LR* 270.

[59] See D. Corker and M. Levi, 'Pre-trial Publicity and its Treatment in the English Courts' [1996] *Crim. LR* 622 at 628; Lloyd-Bostock and Thomas, n. 18 above, at 80.

[60] The point is well made by Sanders and Young, n. 44 above, at 552.

[61] P. Otton, 'The Role of the Judge' (Chap. 18 above).

trial is organized on the basis that the judge is responsible for issues of law and the jury for making decisions on the facts, this depiction of the respective roles of judge and jury can be misleadingly simple.

There are three points that need to be addressed. First, the judge is frequently called upon to make factual determinations. In the introduction we saw that the judge has the power to halt a weak prosecution case and direct the jury to acquit. The exercise of this power has at times given rise to some debate about where the dividing line between the judge's function and the jury's function should be fixed. In an important ruling in 1981, the Court of Appeal expressed concern that judges were too often usurping the jury's function and stated that the judge's power to intervene in this way should be confined to those cases where the judge arrives at the conclusion that the prosecution evidence, taken at its highest, is so weak that a properly directed jury could not properly convict on it.[62] Nonetheless, even since then empirical evidence has suggested that judges have been prepared to withdraw cases too readily, and that there is some disagreement among judges about the circumstances in which the power ought properly to be exercised.[63] The Royal Commission on Criminal Justice actually recommended that the Court of Appeal ruling should be reversed to allow judges to direct an acquittal if they subjectively regard the prosecution case to be clearly too weak to be left to the jury.[64] When a case ends prematurely, there are many possible explanations for this—for example, it may be attributable to an erroneous decision by the prosecution to proceed with a case in the first place or to a poor performance by witnesses at trial. But the judge's power to stop a case raises important matters of principle in the context of jury trial. This power is, on the one hand, an important safeguard against miscarriages of justice. On the other hand, excessive reliance on the power could be seen as implying a lack of faith in the jury itself to arrive at a satisfactory outcome.

Secondly, the judge has an important responsibility in the course of the trial to assist the jury in its determination of the facts. Perhaps the two most significant aspects of this responsibility are the judge's power to intervene during the course of the evidence and the judge's power to comment on the facts in the judicial summing-up at the end of a case. Even though the questioning of witnesses is generally left to the lawyers for each side, it is recognized that the judge may intervene where necessary to clear up points that have been overlooked or left unclear or to exclude irrelevant matters and discourage repetition.[65] In theory, therefore, the judge has an important part to play in ensuring that the evidence is presented to the jury in a comprehensive and an effective manner. Indeed, in practice, judges have an even wider discretion to intervene while witnesses are giving their evidence. It would be a very rare case

---

[62] R. v. *Galbraith* [1981] 2 All ER 1060.

[63] B. P. Block, C. Corbett, and J. Peay, *Ordered and Directed Acquittals in the Crown Court*, Royal Commission on Criminal Justice Research Study No. 15 (London: HMSO, 1993) 70–4. For a summary of the findings of the study see 'Ordered and Directed Acquittals in the Crown Court: A Time of Change?' [1993] *Crim. LR* 95 by the same authors.

[64] *Report of the Royal Commission on Criminal Justice*, n. 24 above, at 59.

[65] For the classic statement by Lord Denning of the trial judge's role in intervening during the evidence see *Jones* v. *National Coal Board* [1957] 2 QB 55 at 64.

indeed for a successful appeal to be based on the fact that the judge intervened excessively.[66] There are, however, potential difficulties that may arise when judges interrupt too frequently during the flow of the evidence, including the danger that the jury may be unduly influenced by the attitude that the judge adopts towards a witness.[67] On balance, however, the questioning of witnesses by the judge can play an important function in assisting the jury in its comprehension of the evidence. As a general proposition, such questioning is arguably most effective and least disruptive if carried out *after* the witness has been questioned by counsel for each side rather than in the course of counsel's questioning.[68]

As for the judge's power to comment on the facts, this has frequently led to controversy following cases in which judges have appeared to make strong comments in favour of the prosecution while disparaging the case for the defence.[69] One writer captured this problem very effectively when he referred to the danger of the judge's summing-up becoming a 'second prosecution speech from the bench'.[70] There is an interesting contrast here with the position in the United States, where the favoured approach is to prevent judges from commenting on the evidence in the case at all and to confine their role at this stage of the trial to legal directions to the jury on the law.[71] Of course, there is no guarantee that a jury will necessarily be swayed by the judge's opinion,[72] but regardless of this point, there is a fear that in putting forward a strong opinion in favour of the prosecution, a judge may compromise the jury's independence of judgement, which as we have seen is an important aspect of the very rationale for jury trial. On balance, the power to sum up on the facts can be justified as an aid to juror comprehension, but there is an argument for developing procedures to ensure that the parties, and in particular the defence, have an opportunity to have some input into the content of the judge's address.[73]

The third point to be made regarding the division of function between the judge and the jury is that there is a 'legal' dimension to the jury's decision-making task. The criminal law is an ever-developing field of considerable complexity, and the jury's decision on the facts of a case is predicated on the assumption that they have understood the legal concepts applicable to the crime for which the defendant is on

---

[66] The relevant authorities are summarized in S. Doran, 'Descent to Avernus' (1989) 139 *NLJ* 1147; see also *R. v. Sharp* [1994] QB 261.

[67] For a penetrating analysis of the issue see S. Saltzburg, 'The Unnecessarily Expanding Role of the Criminal Trial Judge' (1978) 64 *Virginia Law Review* 1 at 54–61.

[68] For discussion see Jackson and Doran, n. 28 above, at 140–2.

[69] For some examples see J. Jackson, 'Trial Procedures' in C. Walker and K. Starmer, *Justice in Error* (London: Blackstone Press, 1993) 130 at 144–6, 159–62. The Royal Commission on Criminal Justice suggested that 'judges should be wholly neutral in any comment that they make on the credibility of the evidence': n. 24 above at 124.

[70] D. Wolchover, 'Should Judges Sum up on the Facts?' [1989] *Crim. LR* 781 at 791.

[71] *Ibid.* at 784–6.

[72] For interesting research findings on this issue, see Zander and Henderson, n. 14 above at 217–18. Note, however, that caution needs to be exercised in interpreting these findings: see Lloyd-Bostock and Thomas, n. 18 above, at 85.

[73] For consideration of how greater accountability might be built into the process, see S. Doran, 'The Necessarily Expanding Role of the Criminal Trial Judge' in S. Doran and J. Jackson (eds.), *The Judicial Role in Criminal Proceedings* (Oxford: Hart Publishing, 2000) 3 at 16–17.

trial.[74] In many cases, this 'legal' dimension will not be particularly significant. If, for example, the defendant relies on a defence of alibi, the jury will be faced with a purely factual assessment of whether it has been established beyond doubt that the person accused was the person responsible for the commission of the crime. If, however, the question to be determined in a murder trial is whether the defendant 'intended' to kill the victim, or in a theft case whether the defendant was 'dishonest', the position is not quite so straightforward. These concepts have been the subject of intensive scrutiny by the higher courts, and their 'legal' meaning will have to be very carefully explained to the jury by the judge in summing up, and in turn applied by the jury in the course of its factual decision-making.[75] Therefore, to say that the jury is appointed only to arbitrate on factual disputes is to underestimate the complexity of its role in many cases.

EVIDENTIAL ISSUES

The judge's summing-up must guide the jury not only on the relevant law applicable to a case, but also on the burden and standard of proof in criminal cases and on particular evidential issues arising in the course of the trial. The rules of evidence in criminal cases are dealt with by Professor Smith in Chapter 11, but it is worth noting a couple of points in the present context.

First, many of the rules of evidence have been developed to ensure that juries are shielded from information that might prejudice them in their assessment of the case against the accused or that might affect the quality of their decision-making.[76] The rules that prevent the admissibility of evidence of the accused's bad character and of hearsay evidence, except in limited circumstances, are examples of how the rules of evidence reflect such concerns. Decisions concerning the admissibility of evidence are made by the trial judge, and it is often necessary to take special measures to ensure that the jury is prevented from hearing evidence that might 'taint' their decision-making. To take an obvious example, in order to determine whether a confession made by the accused should be admitted in evidence before the jury at the trial, it is necessary, first, for the judge to hold a 'trial within a trial' in the absence of the jury. If the confession is ruled out by the judge as a matter of law and the prosecution still proceeds with the case, care has to be taken to ensure that the jury remain unaware of the confession evidence.[77] The debate over what range of information it is 'safe' to

[74] For discussion of the jury's task in applying the law to the facts of a case see E. Griew, 'Summing Up the Law' [1989] *Crim. LR* 768, particularly at 775–6.

[75] As Zuckerman has commented, 'fact-finding and interpretation of law are so interwoven in the criminal procedure that it is sometimes difficult to discern where fact ends and law or morality begin': A. A. S. Zuckerman, *The Principles of Criminal Evidence* (Oxford: Clarendon Press, 1989) 32.

[76] Historically, there have been competing theories on whether the exclusionary rules of evidence are a product of the jury system or of the adversarial trial system: for the former view see J. B. Thayer, *A Preliminary Treatise on Evidence at the Common Law* (Boston, Mass.: Little Brown, 1898, reprinted 1969) 47, 266, 509 (describing the rules as the 'child of the jury'); for the latter see E. M. Morgan, 'The Jury and the Exclusionary Rules of Evidence' (1937) 4 *University of Chicago Law Review* 247.

[77] For details of the procedures to be followed in a trial within a trial or '*voir dire*' see *Blackstone's Criminal Practice*, n. 19 above, at paras. F.17.24–F.17.31.

allow the jury to hear is an ongoing feature of the development of the law of evidence. Considerable controversy has been provoked, for example, by the current government's consideration of whether the rules of evidence should be changed in order to allow a defendant's previous convictions to be revealed to the jury in a wider range of circumstances than at present.[78]

Secondly, the jury has to receive instructions in many cases on how it should approach certain kinds of evidential material in reaching its decision. Special advice has to be given, for example, in cases involving disputed identification evidence.[79] A warning is needed in cases where a prosecution witness may be prone to unreliability.[80] Particular instructions have been devised to guide the jury in situations where the accused has told a lie.[81] Perhaps most significantly of all, since legislation was introduced to permit inferences to be drawn from a suspect's failure to mention to the police facts that are later relied on by the defence at the trial and from the accused's failure to give evidence at the trial, much judicial effort has been devoted to developing appropriate advice for juries on the evidential significance of the defendant's silence.[82] The irony, as we shall see, is that for all the effort that is put into attempting to sum up the facts and the relevant legal issues and evidential principles which should inform the jury's deliberations, the verdict that is handed down by the jury offers no real clue about the impact this painstaking advice has had on its decision.

LINES OF COMMUNICATION

Despite the fact that jurors are appointed to determine the facts of a given dispute, they generally play a very passive role in the course of the trial. Questioning of witnesses is left to counsel for the prosecution and defence and, as we have seen, the judge too may engage in questioning from the bench. Jurors technically do have the power to ask questions, but there are no formal mechanisms for doing so. One possibility is for a note to be passed through the court usher to the judge, who will then deal with the questions as he or she sees fit. Open dialogue between the jury and the judge is not, however, generally encouraged, and the process of addressing questions posed by jurors can be a very cumbersome one.[83] In a survey of criminal trials carried out in Northern Ireland, one judge was quoted as remarking ironically, 'fortunately, we have been blessed with many silent juries'.[84] The point that he was

[78] See the government's White Paper, *Criminal Justice: The Way Ahead*, n. 41 above, at 58–9. For a critique of this and other proposals in the White Paper see J. Upton, 'Keep your Nose Clean' (2001) 23(12) *London Review of Books* 15.

[79] N. 11 above. Special instructions are also required in respect of voice identification: see, e.g. *R. v. Roberts* [2000] *Crim. LR* 183.

[80] *R. v. Makanjuola* [1995] 3 All ER 730.

[81] *R. v. Goodway* [1993] 4 All ER 894.

[82] Criminal Justice and Public Order Act 1994, ss. 34–38. For an analysis of some of the difficulties to which the legislation has given rise see D. Birch, 'Suffering in Silence: A Cost-Benefit Analysis of section 34 of the Criminal Justice and Public Order Act 1994' [1999] *Crim. LR* 769.

[83] For discussion of the difficulties involved see Jackson and Doran, n. 28 above, at 172–9.

[84] *Ibid.*, at 110.

making was not so much that the *principle* of jurors asking questions is wrong, but that the structure of jury trial is not really conducive to this practice. Questions put by jurors after the jury has retired are more easily accommodated, as they do not disrupt the course of the evidence in the case, but great care has to be taken by the trial judge in responding, particularly to avoid opening up new issues that have not been addressed during the trial.[85]

One avenue of reform in the future may be to develop more effective procedures for ensuring that juries can engage with the evidence as it unfolds. A number of American states have introduced reforms of this nature, for example, providing notebooks to jurors, granting opportunities to jurors to discuss the evidence among themselves during the proceedings, and providing the jury with written copies of the judge's instructions.[86] In England, the government has recently supported the wider use of non-spoken means of communication, such as video and computer graphics, to assist juries in following the evidence.[87] The introduction of innovative measures of this nature may go some way to addressing the particular concerns that have been expressed about the use of juries in unusually complex cases, such as cases of serious fraud. The argument that juries are *incapable* of processing complex information might prove more difficult to sustain if greater care were taken to assist jurors' comprehension of the evidence as a trial proceeds.[88]

THE JURY'S VERDICT

The discussion so far has revealed that a fairly intricate set of rules and procedures governs the allocation of cases to jury trial, the selection of the jury, and the conduct of the trial itself. By contrast, the verdict itself is a more straightforward affair, comprising a statement of guilty or not guilty, unaccompanied by reasons for the decision that has been taken. The jury's verdict raises a number of issues for discussion: first, the level of agreement required before a verdict can be returned; secondly, the question whether juries might be made more accountable for their decisions; thirdly, the concept of 'jury equity' which recognizes that the jury may return a verdict against the evidence in a case; and, finally, the question of how we can evaluate the process of decision-making that lies behind the verdict returned. Each of these issues will now be addressed in turn.

---

[85] See *Blackstone's Criminal Practice*, n. 19 above, at paras. D.16.5–D.16.6.

[86] See American Judicature Society, *Enhancing the Jury System: Guidebook for Jury Reform* (Chicago: American Judicature Society, 1999).

[87] *Criminal Justice: The Way Ahead*, n. 41 above, at 57. Auld LJ's review also contains a number of recommendations aimed at assisting jurors' comprehension of the evidence: *Review of the Criminal Courts*, n. 7 above, at 518–38.

[88] For discussion of this argument in the American context see R. D. Myers, R. S. Reinstein, and G. M. Griller, 'Complex Scientific Evidence and the Jury' (1999) 83 *Judicature* 150.

AGREEING ON A VERDICT

The traditional rule that a jury's decision had to be unanimous was changed by legislation in 1967, which made it possible for a verdict to be reached by a majority of ten to two.[89] At the end of the summing-up, the judge advises the jury to consider their verdict and to try to reach a unanimous decision. The jury then retire to the privacy of the jury room. The jurors are led to this room under the supervision of a court usher, but they are then left unaccompanied in the room for their deliberations. If, however, the jury cannot reach a unanimous decision, they are brought back into court and advised by the judge of the possibility of arriving at a majority verdict. Before this possibility arises, the jury must have been deliberating for such period as the court considers reasonable, given the nature and complexity of the case and in any case for at least two hours. The verdict is announced in open court by the juror who has been appointed as spokesperson or 'foreman' of the jury. If a verdict of guilty has been reached by a majority, then the size of the majority must also be stated. If ultimately, the jury cannot reach a verdict on a majority basis—i.e. if it is a 'hung' jury—the jury is discharged and the decision is then left to the prosecution whether to ask for a retrial.

The majority-verdict procedure has been justified on two main grounds: first, it prevents one or two individuals with 'extreme' or eccentric views from blocking the agreement of a clear majority; secondly, it prevents professional criminals from securing an acquittal by subjecting one or two jurors to intimidation or offering them bribes, a practice commonly referred to as 'jury nobbling'.[90] Against this, it has been argued that the majority-verdict procedure is difficult to reconcile with the requirement that the prosecution must prove the case against the accused beyond reasonable doubt.[91] This in turn may undermine the perceived legitimacy of the verdict, which we identified as an important element of the rationale for trial by jury. Further, a real risk of 'nobbling' is likely to arise in only a small minority of cases and, even then, the court has the power to order that measures be taken to protect jurors from the risk of intimidation. There is also a specific criminal offence of intimidating a juror or potential juror.[92] It is fair to say that the majority-verdict procedure provokes much less debate today than it did at the time of its introduction and that it is unlikely that a requirement of unanimity will be reintroduced in the future. It is also worth noting that a survey of jury systems worldwide reveals a considerable variety of approaches to the matter. In New Zealand, for example, the unanimity rule survives,[93] while in Scotland, a simple majority of the fifteen-member jury is required.[94]

---

[89] Criminal Justice Act 1967, s.13; see now Juries Act 1974, s.17.

[90] For a useful summary of the arguments for and against the majority verdict procedure see Sanders and Young, n. 44 above, 1 at 567–70.

[91] See, e.g., M. Freeman, 'The Jury on Trial' [1981] *Current Legal Problems* 65 at 69.

[92] Criminal Justice and Public Order Act 1994, s. 51.

[93] N. Cameron, S. Potter, and W. Young, 'The New Zealand Jury: Towards Reform' in N. Vidmar (ed.), *World Jury Systems* (Oxford: OUP, 2000), 167 at 201–3.

[94] P. Duff, 'The Scottish Jury: A Very Peculiar Institution' in *ibid.*, 249 at 269–72. Note, however, that other differences in Scottish procedure need to be considered carefully when making any comparison: see Sanders and Young, n. 44 above, at 569–70.

REASONING AND ACCOUNTABILITY

The jury is not required, indeed not permitted, to present reasons for its verdict. As an observer of the American jury system once remarked:[95]

Complicated and insoluble factual disputes have the appearance of being settled with ease when wrapped in the silent garb of a verdict returned in supposed compliance with strict legal rules.

For all the care that is taken in presenting a case before the jury, there is no guarantee that its verdict has been properly based on the evidence or that its reasoning has been in accordance with the relevant legal and evidential principles on which it has received instruction. The absence of a requirement for a jury to give reasons is not without justification.[96] There would be practical difficulties in requiring a body of twelve individuals to formulate an agreed set of reasons. In particular, it needs to be borne in mind that the process of communal decision-making by a jury is not necessarily reducible to the kind of logical statement that one might expect from the reasoned judgement of a professional lawyer. Moreover, a requirement to give reasons may not sit easily with the jury's freedom to depart from strict legal instructions to do justice in an individual case, which is often portrayed as an important aspect of its strength as an institution.

There are, however, practical methods of promoting greater accountability on the part of juries for their decision-making. For example, the jury may be presented with a specific list of questions and asked to return a 'special verdict' on them. It is interesting to note that this approach has been adopted in certain civil law countries that have only recently reintroduced a system of trial by jury.[97] In Spain, an additional requirement has been imposed that the jury give a 'succinct rationale' for the verdict, indicating the evidence on which it was based and the reasons for finding that particular propositions have been proved.[98] In England, a fresh debate on the desirability of reasons has been prompted by certain recent decisions of the European Court of Human Rights that have emphasized the importance of reasoned decision-making in the context of the accused's right to a fair trial under Article 6 of the European Convention.[99] In the specific context of jury trial, the Court has placed great emphasis on the need for careful instruction by the trial judge to the jury on matters such as the drawing of inferences from the accused's silence. Even if this does not go so far as to require a statement of reasons by the jury itself, it suggests the need to demonstrate that the jury's decision has been made on the basis of

---

[95] D. W. Broeder, 'The Functions of the Jury: Fact or Fictions?' (1954) 27 *University of Chicago Law Review* 386 at 417.

[96] For a thorough exploration of the debate on whether juries should be made more accountable see J. D. Jackson, 'Making Juries Accountable' (2002, forthcoming).

[97] See S. C. Thaman, 'Europe's New Jury Systems: The Cases of Spain and Russia' in Vidmar, n. 93 above, 319 at 338–47.

[98] *Ibid.*, at 344–5.

[99] See, in particular, *Murray* v. *UK* (1996) 22 EHRR 29; *Condron* v. *UK* (2000) 30 EHRR 1. For a consideration of the implications of Art. 6 for this aspect of jury trial see L. Blom-Cooper, 'Article 6 and Modes of Trial' [2001] *European Human Rights Law Review* 1 at 9–13.

carefully structured advice. Auld LJ's review has made quite far-reaching recommendations aimed at achieving this objective, including the formulation of a series of written factual questions by the trial judge, the answers to which could logically lead only to a guilty or not guilty verdict; in appropriate cases, the judge could require the jury to answer the questions publicly and declare a verdict in accordance with the answers.[100]

'JURY EQUITY'

The jury's freedom to decline to apply the rigours of the law in an individual case, in spite of apparently irrefutable evidence of the accused's guilt, was historically entrenched as an expression of the jury's independence from judicial authority.[101] There have been some high-profile examples of this 'jury equity' or 'jury nullification' at work, the most often mentioned being the acquittal of the civil servant Clive Ponting in 1985 of offences involving the leaking of certain secret documents in contravention of official secrets legislation.[102] He admitted passing on the documents, but argued that he was acting out of a sense of public duty that was more important than his duty to abide by the official secrets legislation. The jury's motivation in a case such as this may be to express dissatisfaction about a particular law or to resist the application of the law to a particular case.

Cases in which the jury can be said deliberately to have set its face against the law are, however, comparatively rare. A more pervasive form of 'jury equity', however, is central to the very nature of trial by jury itself. Unlike the professional lawyer, who will be trained to focus on whether the evidence matches the prescribed legal standards in a case, a jury is more likely to take a broader view of the 'merits' of a case. Consequently, factors such as sympathy for the defendant's personal circumstances or an understanding of the defendant's motivation may influence the jury in its assessment of the prosecution case. In other words, the jury is not constrained by the 'hard logic and reason' of the professional.[103] Of course, it should be noted that if juries at times take into account factors beyond the strict application of the law to the facts of the individual case, this will not necessarily work in the defendant's favour. Some research studies have pointed to a small yet not insignificant proportion of cases in which juries appear to have *convicted* in questionable circumstances.[104]

Critics of jury trial have denounced the power of juries to decline to apply the law strictly in an individual case. Juries, it is said, are there to apply the law in accordance with the evidence, not to determine whether its application to a particular accused conforms to a wider conception of 'justice'. Such non-legal considerations, it is

---

[100] *Review of the Criminal Courts*, n. 7 above, at 172 and 532–8.

[101] See P. Devlin, 'The Conscience of the Jury' (1991) 107 *LQR* 398.

[102] For a brief account of the case by Ponting himself see C. Ponting, *Secrecy in Britain* (Oxford: Basil Blackwell, 1990) 64–5.

[103] For further discussion of this issue see Jackson and Doran, n. 28 above, at 224–40.

[104] See references at n. 14 above.

argued, should have 'no place in a modern criminal justice system'.[105] The point has been put even more forcefully by one writer who describes the jury as 'an anti-democratic, irrational and haphazard legislator, whose erratic and secret decisions run counter to the rule of law'.[106] Taken to extremes, the refusal of juries to convict routinely in the face of the evidence could have serious implications for the administration of justice. It is fair to say, however, that the specific issue of jury nullification has aroused less controversy in recent times in England than in other jurisdictions such as the United States.[107] In this jurisdiction more debate has arisen over the quality of jury decision-making generally, and it is to this matter that we now turn.

ANALYSIS AND EVALUATION OF JURIES' DECISION-MAKING

Given the fact that the jury do not have to give reasons for their decision and that juries may in some cases return verdicts that do not appear to be in accordance with the evidence, the question arises how we can be satisfied that juries' methods of arriving at decisions are satisfactory. Are there methods for testing the quality of their decision-making?[108]

An obvious method of studying jury decision-making would be to ask jurors themselves about their deliberations. In England, however, there is a strict rule against this practice. Section 8 of the Contempt of Court Act 1981 makes it a contempt of court 'to obtain, disclose or solicit any particulars of statements made, opinions expressed, arguments advanced or votes cast by members of a jury in the course of their deliberations in any legal proceedings'.[109] One reason for this is that the whole system might be thrown into chaos if the deliberations leading to a particular decision were opened up to public scrutiny. Not only might this produce a flood of attempts to have cases reopened, but it might also inhibit individual jurors in their participation in the discussions. Moreover, revelation of the details of juror discussions might leave individual jury members open to retaliation. A more sceptical view is that public knowledge of what actually goes on in the jury room might damage the image of the jury so severely that it would struggle to survive as an institution.[110] It may be, however, that properly controlled research into jury decision-making could actually

---

[105] Blom-Cooper, n. 99 above, at 6. Aulds LJ's review comes down strongly against the right of juries to acquit defendants in defiance of the law or in disregard of the evidence and goes so far as to suggest that a statutory declaration to this effect should be made if need be: *Review of the Criminal Courts*, n. 7 above, at 173–6.

[106] Darbyshire, n. 4 above, at 750.

[107] See Abramson, n. 43 above, chap. 2; N. J. King, 'Silencing Nullification Advocacy Inside the Jury Room and Outside the Courtroom' (1998) 65 *University of Chicago Law Review* 433.

[108] For a comprehensive survey (conducted for the *Review of the Criminal Courts*) of research that has been carried out on jury decision-making see P. Darbyshire, A. Maughan, and A. Stewart, 'What Can the English Legal System Learn From Jury Research Published up to 2000' available on the review website at **www.criminal-courts-review.org.uk**.

[109] See J. Jaconelli, 'Some Thoughts on Jury Secrecy' (1990) 10 *Legal Studies* 91.

[110] For discussion of this issue, see J. C. Smith, 'Is Ignorance Bliss? Could Jury Trial Survive Investigation?' (1998) 38 *Medical Science and the Law* 98.

go some way to strengthening public faith in the jury system.[111] In the absence of such research, anecdotal evidence about jurors' behaviour in individual cases tends to assume greater prominence than is merited in public debate about the system. The Royal Commission on Criminal Justice in 1993 recommended that section 8 should be amended to enable research into juries' reasons for their verdicts, but this recommendation has not been implemented. A survey carried out for the Commission had indicated that jurors were fairly positive about their experiences, although the statutory restrictions meant that the questions put to the jurors involved had to be kept at a very general level.[112]

Aside from asking jurors directly about their experiences, there are two other general methods of analysing the performance of juries. The first is to ask other participants in the trial process, such as judges and prosecution and defence lawyers, whether they agreed with the verdict reached by the jury, as in the landmark study carried out by Baldwin and McConville in the 1970s.[113] The other method is to use either a 'shadow' jury, which hears the evidence at the same time as the real jury and can then be observed as it deliberates, or a 'mock jury', which listens to evidence in a simulated trial situation.[114]

It is not proposed to analyse in this chapter the various studies that have been carried out on the jury in England, but a few general points are worth making. Each kind of study is useful for improving our understanding of the jury. The 'professional' studies give us an insight into the views of those who work closely with juries in the day-to-day practice of the courtroom. The simulated studies enable us to study the patterns of behaviour and approaches to decision-making of a group of people deliberating under conditions similar to those faced by a jury. Each kind of study, however, has its limitations. It would be wrong to place too much emphasis on judgements made by professional lawyers about decisions made by juries, because part of the very rationale for having a system of trial by jury is, as we have seen, to enable non-lawyers to participate in the administration of criminal justice.[115] While a wide divergence of views between the jury and the professionals may give cause for concern,[116] some divergence can be expected—and even welcomed—as a reflection of the different approaches to decision-making adopted by the layman and the lawyer. Finally, the simulated studies can arguably never fully capture the dynamics and pressures that are at work in the 'real' jury room.

---

[111] The most ambitious research project of this nature in recent times was carried out in New Zealand: see W. Young, N. Cameron, and Y. Tinsley, *Juries in Criminal Trials: Part II* (Wellington: New Zealand Law Commission, 1999).

[112] See Zander and Henderson, n. 14 above, chap. 8.

[113] N. 14 above.

[114] For an example of the former, see S. McCabe and R. Purves, *The Shadow Jury at Work* (Oxford: Basil Blackwell, 1974) and of the latter, S. Lloyd-Bostock, 'The Effects on Juries of Hearing About the Defendant's Previous Criminal Record: A Simulation Study' [2000] *Crim. LR* 734.

[115] See Freeman, n. 91 above, at 85–8.

[116] See, e.g., Baldwin and McConville's 1970s study, n. 14 above, particularly at 66–7, 83–7.

CONCLUSION

This chapter has examined the English system of trial by jury from the standpoints of both principle and practice. Support for the principle of trial by jury remains strong, despite the gradual reduction over the years in the number of cases heard by juries. In the future it is likely that the trend of restricting the use of juries to an ever-narrowing band of trials will continue. The defendant's right to opt for jury trial in 'either way' cases and the deployment of juries in serious fraud cases are the most obvious short-term candidates for reform. Notwithstanding this trend, however, the principle of jury trial is an obdurate one, and it is likely that it will remain as a foundational feature of the English criminal justice system for many years to come. In tune with the broader criminal justice system of which it is a part, however, the actual process of trial by jury will continue to undergo reform. Measures to ensure wider participation in jury service, to encourage innovative ways of assisting jurors in their comprehension of the evidence, and to improve jury accountability are all likely to feature in the future development of the system. The challenge for jury trial will then be to adapt where necessary to the demands of a modern criminal justice system, but without losing its unique character as a lay institution playing a key role at the heart of the professional world of the criminal courts.

Further Reading

BALDWIN, J., and McCONVILLE, M., *Jury Trials* (Oxford: Clarendon Press, 1979).

BANKOWSKI, Z., HUTTON, N., and McMANUS, J., *Lay Justice?* (Edinburgh: T & T Clark, 1987).

CORNISH, W., *The Jury* (London: Penguin, 1968).

DEVLIN, P., *Trial by Jury* (London: Stevens, 1956).

FINDLAY, M., and DUFF, P. (eds.), *The Jury Under Attack* (London: Butterworths, 1988).

HASTIE, R. (ed.), *Inside the Juror* (Cambridge: Cambridge University Press, 1993).

KALVEN, H., and ZEISEL, H., *The American Jury* (Boston, Mass.: Little, Brown, 1966).

TONRY, M., and FRASE, R. (eds.), *Sentencing in Western Countries* (Oxford: Oxford University Press, 2001).

VON HIRSCH, A., and ASHWORTH, A., *Principled Sentencing: Readings in Theory and Practice* (2nd edn., Oxford: Hart Publishing, 1998).

22

JUVENILE JUSTICE

Nicola Padfield*

INTRODUCTION

Most of the chapters in this book concentrate on the criminal process as it is applied to adults (those over the age of 18). Yet a large proportion of crime is committed by young people. Statistics on crime are notoriously unreliable, but it seems likely that a quarter of all crime is committed by those under the age of 18. Changes in official processing and decision-making can mean that statistical changes are 'almost certainly an illusion' (Farington, 1992). The most recent youth lifestyle survey in England and Wales[1] states that almost a fifth of 12–30-year-olds admitted to one or more offence in the last twelve months. Men (26 per cent) were more likely to admit offending that women (11 per cent). Those aged 14–21 were the most likely to be offenders. Between 1992–3 and 1998–9, offending amongst boys aged 14–17 increased by 14 per cent. These figures clearly mask changes in specific offending (fighting increased among males, though it fell among females; buying and selling stolen goods fell, as did fraud amongst males). But the basic fact is clear. Young people commit a large amount of crime. How does the English criminal justice system respond to this?

This chapter allows us to consider ways in which children are treated differently within the criminal justice system in order to assess whether this different treatment is really appropriate. The most important point to note is that in England and Wales huge numbers of children are dealt with in the criminal justice system. Crimes committed by children may be both more troubling and paradoxically more understandable than those committed by adults, and the English criminal justice system has developed many features which make 'juvenile justice' a distinct topic. For the purposes of this chapter we will look exclusively at the criminal justice system applied to those aged from 10 until they reach 18. A child under the age of 10 is held not to be criminally responsible (many argue that this 'cut-off point' is too low. It is certainly considerably lower than most other European jurisdictions).

The English attitude to juvenile crime seems to shift at different times and places. This chapter concentrates on current concerns and pressures, but starts with a review

---

* Full citation for all books, and articles cited in this chapter are to be found in the Bibliography and Further Reading section.

[1] C. Flood-Page et al., *Youth Crime: Findings from the 1988/99 Youth Lifestyles Survey*, Home Office Research Study No. 209 (London: HMSO, 2000).

of some of the shifting priorities witnessed over the last century. Whilst there is widespread acceptance of the causes of juvenile crime (poor family relationships; school and peer pressure; drug use; as well as easy opportunities for criminal behaviour), the responses vary from tolerance/care/rehabilitation (based perhaps on the realization that most young people grow out of crime) to punishment (a concern that 'bad' young people should be punished firmly and should not be allowed to 'get away with it'). Many young offenders may never 'enter' the criminal justice system. Their crimes may be ignored or they may come to the attention of social services departments, or they may be informally cautioned by the police. However, some will find themselves within the formal criminal justice system, either as recipients of reprimands or final warnings from the police or being prosecuted in the Youth Court (or in the Crown Court for the most serious offences). The chapter concludes with a consideration of the extent to which the conflicting responses to juvenile crime mentioned above can and should co-exist within the criminal justice system.

HISTORICAL BACKGROUND[2]

This brief historical review starts in 1908, when Juvenile Courts were set up as separate courts, to deal with both civil and criminal matters concerning children (then defined as those aged between 7 and 16). Several of the features of the Juvenile Court at that time remain features today. They could deal with a wider range of offences than the adult magistrates' courts. They sat in a different place or at a different time from the adult magistrates' courts; and the public were excluded. A major review of juvenile justice was undertaken by a Departmental Committee (the Molony Committee), whose *Report on the Treatment of Young Offenders* (1927) argued for the 'welfarist principle' in the treatment of young offenders: that the welfare of a child was to be a priority in dealing with even 'criminal' children. This principle was incorporated into the Children and Young Persons Act 1933, section 44(1), which remains in force today:

Every court in dealing with a child or young person who is brought before it, either as an offender or otherwise, shall have regard to the welfare of the child or young person and shall in a proper case take steps . . . for securing that proper provision is made for his education and training.

The Malony Committee also suggested that the age of criminal responsibility be raised to 8, and that the jurisdiction of the Juvenile Courts be changed to deal with all those between their eighth and seventeenth birthday. They also recommended that special panels of magistrates should be selected to sit in the juvenile courts. These changes were introduced in the 1933 Act.

The next landmark change in the law was the Children and Young Persons Act

---

[2] This part of the chapter relies in particular on Bottoms (2001) and Newburn (1999), which should be consulted for more historical details.

1963, which raised the minimum age of criminal responsibility to 10. But it was the Children and Young Persons Act 1969 which marked the 'high water mark' of welfare priorities. The then Labour government considered abolishing Juvenile Courts, but instead simply abolished the power of courts to send juvenile offenders to approved schools,[3] replacing these orders with care orders. This had the effect of transferring the main decision-making power from the courts to social services departments, since under a care order the social services department had wide discretion whether or not, for example, to leave a child at home or to take him or her into local authority accommodation. However, the juvenile magistrates seemed reluctant to lose their control in this way, and it was perhaps not surprising that the use of care orders declined in the 1970s, whilst the use of detention centre orders[4] and orders for Borstal training[5] went up.

In 1970 a Conservative government was returned to power and many of the welfarist provisions of the 1969 Act were not implemented. After a brief Labour government from 1974–9, Mrs Thatcher became Prime Minister of a Conservative government, which remained in power until 1997. The 1980s produced an interesting mixture of punitive thinking ('short sharp shock' detention centres) and welfare priorities (increasing diversion and experiments with 'intermediate treatment'[6] as a community-based alternative for young offenders). This led to what Bottoms famously identified as bifurcation: a system which dealt harshly with those perceived as serious or persistent offenders and more leniently with those perceived to be merely a nuisance. This bifurcation also illustrates the tension which continues to this day, an uncertainty at the heart of the system between a desire both to punish the bad and at the same time to help the unfortunate. Bottoms *et al.* (1998) identify two conflicting tendencies in the 1980s. One concentrated on providing services for identified offenders with a policy of minimum interference. The other recognized that worried parents of children with behavioural problems were not getting enough support from social services departments. The 1980s also saw the beginnings of inter-agency co-operation, which became a recurrent theme of the 1990s and beyond. Another feature of the 1980s was a sharp reduction in the number of children in custody. Criminal Justice Acts in 1982 and 1988 made it harder to sentence juveniles to custody, which meant that the number of juveniles in custody halved between 1981 and 1987.

The next landmark was the Children Act 1989 (implemented in October 1991) which made major changes to Juvenile Courts. Most importantly, the courts lost their care (civil) jurisdiction, which was transferred to the Family Proceedings Courts of magistrates' courts, where likely harm to the child became the sole ground for compulsory care. At the same time, care orders were abolished in criminal proceedings. Shortly afterwards (in the Criminal Justice Act 1991, which came into force in

---

[3] Reformatory schools which provided juvenile offenders with education and training.

[4] A custodial order for those over the age of 14, first introduced in 1948.

[5] A custodial order for those over the age of 15, first introduced in 1908.

[6] This term was first used in the White Paper which preceded the Children and Young Persons Act 1969 to describe a possible requirement of a supervision order. Yet it was really in the 1980s that 'IT' came to be seen as a serious alternative to custody for juvenile offenders, with the government investing considerable sums of money in many IT projects (see White Paper, *Children in Trouble*, Cmnd 3601 (1997).

October 1992), Juvenile Courts were renamed Youth Courts; and the maximum age was raised to include offenders up to their eighteenth birthdays (though it left a curious overlapping jurisdiction for 16 and 17-year-olds). The Criminal Justice Act 1991 provided clear guidance to sentencers of adult and young offenders that proportionality and commensurability in sentences were required. The Act also sought to strengthen parents' responsibilities, with, for example, mandatory binding-over orders for parents of 10–15-years-olds. The early 1990s also saw a growth in 'managerialism', well documented elsewhere.[7]

In February 1993, a toddler, deliberately kidnapped in a shopping centre, was murdered by two 10-year-old boys. This shocking and extraordinary murder is widely recognized as a turning point in the hardening of public and political attitudes to young offenders. It has also led to a host of litigation which will be discussed later in this chapter, well illustrating the tensions apparent in juvenile justice: do 10-year-olds who kill deserve rehabilitation and care or severe punishment? But the immediate impact of the public shock at this murder was a significant decline in the diversion of minor offenders from the criminal justice system. The previous growth in formal cautioning of young offenders by the police, as an alternative to prosecution, was halted. This followed a Home Office Circular (No. 18/1994), which strongly discouraged repeat cautions, particularly of young people. The Criminal Justice Act 1993 also 'toughened up' the criminal justice system, weakening some of the desert-based criteria of the 1991 Act, allowing, for example, previous convictions to be taken into account when sentencing. The number of young people sentenced to Young Offenders' Institutions started to increase significantly. This hard-line approach was pursued in the Criminal Justice and Public Order Act 1994, which introduced secure training orders for repeat offenders aged 12–14. These were to be for between six months and two years, for one half of which the child was to be held in secure detention in a Secure Training Centre, the first of which, at Medway, developed some notoriety both because of its high costs and its tough regime. At the same time, the power to detain young offenders in a Young Offenders' Institution was extended from twelve months to two years.

Two other influential reports worth highlighting from this time were the Audit Commission's report on *Misspent Youth* 1996, which concluded that 'the current system for dealing with youth crime is inefficient and expensive', failing both young offenders and their victims. The Audit Commission's recommendations for speeding up the criminal justice process were echoed in an equally influential report on *Delays in the Criminal Justice System* (the Narey Report), published in February 1997. It is fair to conclude that the Labour government, elected in May 1997, came to power driven not only by a manifesto commitment to be 'tough on crime, tough on the causes of crime', but also by an 'efficiency' agenda which put great store by questions of managerial economy, efficiency, and effectiveness.

---

[7] See James and Raine (1997), for example.

CHANGES SINCE 1997

The Crime and Disorder Act 1998 was the first major piece of Labour legislation in this area. It followed from the White Paper, *No More Excuses—A New Approach to Tackling Youth Crime in England and Wales*: (Cm 3809) in which the government developed its manifesto commitment:

For too long there has been a lack of clear direction in the youth justice system. The Government will give the necessary leadership

This Act provides in section 37 that *'the principal aim'* of the youth justice system is to prevent offending by children and young persons. By section 37(2):

In addition to any other duty to which they are subject, it shall be the duty of all persons and bodies carrying out functions in relation to the youth justice system to have regard to that aim.

This new statutory aim is what Bottoms calls 'explicitly correctionalist' (Bottoms, 2001). How can this be reconciled with section 44 of the Children and Young Person Act 1933 (quoted above) which remains in force? In a recent case, *R. v. Inner London Crown Court, ex parte N and S*,[8] the Vice President, Rose LJ, stated that in the light of the principal aim of the criminal justice system to prevent offending, 'it may be that the need to impose a deterrent sentence in relation to an offender under 18 may take priority over the provisions of section 44 of the Children and Young Persons Act 1933'. This raises significant issues. First it suggests a worrying belief in the efficacy of deterrence.[9] Perhaps of even more concern is Rose LJ's response to the 1998 Act. There is no obvious reason why the provision of the 1998 Act should have to take priority over the welfare principle of the 1933 Act.

The Crime and Disorder Act 1998 also imposed a statutory duty on local authorities to secure the availability of youth justice services (see the consultation paper, *New National and Local Focus on Youth Crime* published in October 1997). Youth justice services are defined very widely.[10] Youth Offending Teams (YOTs) now co-ordinate

---

[8] [2000] *Crim. LR* 871.

[9] Yet, as A. Von Hirsch *et al.*, *Criminal Deterrence and Sentence Severity: An Analysis of Recent Research* (Oxford: Hart, 1998) pointed out so graphically in their review of the literature on sentence severity and general deterrence, five logical conditions must exist before an increase in the severity of sentences can work:

   (i)   Potential offenders must realize sentence levels have increased;

   (ii) Potential offenders must think about heavier sentence levels when contemplating their offences;

   (iii) Potential offenders must believe they have at least a reasonable chance of being caught;

   (iv) Potential offenders must believe that if caught the heavier sentencing policy will be applied to them;

   (v) Potential offenders must be prepared to desist where (i–iv) are present.

All these conditions must be present for general deterrence through heavier sentencing to work.

[10] Including the provision of persons to act as 'appropriate adults' at police stations after a young person has been arrested; assessment and rehabilitation work associated with a warning; bail support; placement in local authority accommodation of those committed under s. 23 of the Children and Young Persons Act 1969; the provision of reports etc. to criminal courts; the provision of responsible officers in relation to parenting orders, child safety orders, reparation orders, and action plan orders; the supervision of community sentences; post release supervision; the performance of functions carrying out detention and training orders.

the provision of youth justice services and carry out the functions assigned to the team in the youth justice plan. YOTs must include social workers, probation officers, police officers, and education and health authority staff, and are described by the Youth Justice Board as 'the one stop-shop for all young offenders'. The Youth Justice Board for England and Wales, also a creation of the Crime and Disorder Act, has between ten and twelve members, with 'extensive recent experience of the youth justice system'. Its functions are to:

- monitor the operation of the youth justice system and the provision of youth justice services;
- advise the Secretary of State on the operation of that system and the provision of such services; how the principal aim of that system might most effectively be pursued; the content of any national standards he may see fit to set; the steps which might be taken to prevent offending by children and young persons;
- to monitor the extent to which that aim is being achieved and such standards met;
- to obtain and publish relevant information;
- to identify, make known, and promote good practice in the operation of the youth justice system and the provision of youth justice services;
- to make grants, with the approval of the Secretary of State, to local authorities and other bodies to develop or commission research into good practice in working with young offenders;
- themselves to commission research.

Perhaps, given this wide remit, it is hardly surprising that the Youth Justice Board has come to play a dominant role in youth justice in England and Wales. Its powers were extended in April 2000 to include responsibility for commissioning and purchasing all places for 10–17-year-olds in custody.

The Labour Party in its election manifesto had also made a commitment to 'halve the time it takes to get persistent young offenders from arrest to sentencing'. Following its election, the government issued a consultation paper, *Tackling Delays in the Youth Justice System and Reducing Remand Delays*, with a Bill following swiftly afterwards. The Crime and Disorder Act 1998 restricted the court's discretion to grant extensions of time and allowed the Home Secretary to make regulations for young offenders which set time limits from arrest to first court appearance ('the initial stage') and from conviction to sentence. The Prosecution of Offences (Youth Court Time Limits) Regulations 1999[11] provide that:

- trial must commence within ninety-nine days of the first court appearance (this is known as the 'overall time limit');
- if the defendent is under 18, the first court appearance must be within thirty-six days of arrest (the 'initial stage time limit');
- sentencing must be within twenty-nine days of conviction (the 'sentencing stage limit').

[11] SI 1999 No. 2743.

The Act seeks to reduce delays in other ways. The youth court may remit to the adult court any person who reaches his eighteenth birthday before trial, or after conviction and before sentence (and there is no appeal from this). There is now a presumption against adjournments in the youth court, in effect reversing the decision in *Khan*.[12]

Does reducing delay reduce crime (which, as we saw, is now the 'principal aim' of the youth justice system)? Whilst undue delays clearly bring the system into disrepute, and delayed proceedings may have less impact than a speedier trial, especially in the case of children, this determination to speed up the process itself underlines the tensions evident in juvenile justice. There is a real danger that the 'process' may be so speeded up as to both undermine the due-process rights of suspects and to limit decision-makers' powers to make informed decisions based on the welfare needs of the child. It may achieve some other beneficial consequences, such as saving money (but only maybe in the long run and out of some budgets). The priority still given to reducing delays can be seen in the publication of national league tables, which are openly available on a website maintained by PA consulting group for the Youth Justice Board.[13] These league tables reveal the average number of days between arrest and sentence and the numbers of days off target for persistent young offenders in each police force area, and can be accessed in performance order, alphabetical order, or even improvement order.

The Crime and Disorder Act 1998 also abolished the system of police cautioning of young offenders. Cautioning had evolved in a piecemeal, non-statutory way, without any discussion in Parliament, yet by the 1970s it had become common for cautions to be cited in court as part of an offender's record. The Home Office had issued a number of circulars[14] to develop greater consistency of practice. Thus, an offender was not to be cautioned unless there was sufficient evidence to prosecute. The offender had to admit the offence. And he or she had to give an 'informed consent'. During the 1980s and 1990s there had been a growth in inter-agency police cautioning panels, with the development of informal 'caution plus schemes' in various parts of the country.[15] The Crime and Disorder Act 1998 introduced a new system of reprimands and warnings, which took effect nationwide in April 2000. 'Final warnings' involve a compulsory referral to the local YOT and compulsory participation in a rehabilitation or change programme. Early research[16] into the pilots of this new scheme suggests that these change programmes, which may include mediation and reparation, are evolving inconsistently around the country, some involving very mundane tasks bearing no relationship to the offence. However, this is not to suggest that attempts to bring greater meaning into the way minor offenders are treated are to be rejected: see the great interest in restorative justice, discussed below by Hoyle and Young in Chapter 28.

We are still in a time of great change. Part 1 of the Youth Justice and Criminal

---

[12] See *The Times*, 24 Mar. 1994.   [13] See www.youth-justice-board.gov.uk.

[14] In 1978, 1985 (which had warned against net-widening), 1990 (again stressing the dangers of repeat cautions), and 1994 (condemning multiple cautioning as bringing the process into disrepute).

[15] See Giller and Tutt (1987).

[16] J. Dignan, *Youth Justice Pilots Evaluation: Interim Report* (London: Home Office, 2000), S. Holdaway et al., *New Strategies to Address Youth Offending* (London: Home Office RDS Occasional Paper No. 69, 2001).

Evidence Act 1999 took forward many of the ideas of the Crime and Disorder Act 1998. Section 1(1) introduced a mandatory referral order for most young offenders pleading guilty on their first youth court appearance. Such offenders are to be referred to Youth Offender Panels, which will be made up of lay members and a member of the Youth Offending Team (see section 6). These panels will seek to reach a contractual agreement with the offender about a 'programme of behaviour' (see section 8) and will monitor compliance with the contract. The emphasis seems to be on 'restorative justice',[17] with reparation putting greater emphasis on the victim. The aim is to repair the harm caused by the crime as far as possible, and to involve a number of parties (victim, offender, families, communities, and professionals) in resolving the aftermath of the crime. Whether or not it works depends on what one would count as success. The government's principal aim of 'reducing offending' is particularly difficult to measure, given the huge unreliability of crime statistics, especially using reconviction rates.

Going one stage further are the new Intensive Supervision and Surveillance Programmes. Designed for hardcore persistent young offenders, these programmes are funded by the Youth Justice Board and run by local Youth Offending Teams (YOTs). As the name suggests, they have two elements. Each offender is intensively monitored by either electronic tagging, voice verification (a form of telephone monitoring), or the police or youth offending team staff. The programme takes account of the risks of offending outside regular 9.00 a.m. to 5 p.m. hours and is designed to ensure, where necessary, that young offenders are engaged during the late evening and at weekends. A structured programme is specifically designed for the individual to tackle the causes of their offending behaviour. This should include education and training, especially literacy and numeracy, reparation to the victims of their crimes, and family support and other programmes to address offending behaviour. Intensive Supervision and Surveillance Programmes (ISSPs) are available for those young offenders who are appearing in court either charged with or convicted of an offence, and who have been charged or warned for an imprisonable offence on four or more separate occasions within the last twelve months, and have previously received at least one community or custodial sentence.

Before we turn to a review of juvenile justice today, brief mention should be made of the impact of the European Convention on Human Rights. Whilst the British government was the first European government to ratify the European Convention on Human Rights in 1950, until 2000 British citizens could enforce their rights under the Convention only in the European Court of Human Rights in Strasbourg. However, the Human Rights Act 1998, which came into force only in October 2000, has incorporated the Convention into domestic law. It is too early to say what impact this may have on developments in juvenile justice, but it is worth raising the case of *T* v. *UK; V* v. *UK*[18] by way of example. The two children who had been convicted of the toddler's murder mentioned earlier challenged the legality of both their trial and their

---

[17] For additional reading on this, see in particular, Pollard (2000), Morris and Gelsthorpe (2000), Ball (2000).

[18] (1999) 30 EHRR 121, [2000] *Crim. LR* 187.

sentence. The trial had taken place in 1993 in an adult courtroom before a judge and jury. The European Court of Human Rights held, by twelve votes to five, that there had been no violation of Article 3 of the Convention (the right not to be subjected to torture or to inhuman or degrading treatment or punishment) but, by sixteen votes to one, that there had been a violation of Article 6 in respect of their trial. This was largely because the Court considered that, in the tense courtroom and under public scrutiny the boys were unable to participate effectively in the proceedings. Unanimously the Court held that there had been a violation of Article 6 in respect of the setting of the boys' 'tariffs', the period of time specified by the Home Secretary as the minimum number of years they should serve of their indeterminate sentence (known as 'Her Majesty's Pleasure'), before they could be considered for release by the Parole Board. This judgment has already caused a number of changes. First, in relation to the trial process, the then Lord Chief Justice, Lord Bingham, on 16 February 2000, issued a *Practice Direction (Crown Court: Trial of Children & Young Persons)*[19] which specified that there is an 'overriding principle' when it comes to the trial of young people in the Crown Court:

Some young defendants accused of committing serious crimes may be very young and very immature when standing trial in the Crown Court. The purpose of such a trial is to determine guilt (if that is in issue) and decide the appropriate sentence if the defendant pleads guilty or is convicted. The trial process should not itself expose the young defendant to avoidable intimidation, humiliation or distress. All possible steps should be taken to assist the young defendant to understand and participate in the proceedings. The ordinary trial process should so far as necessary be adapted to meet those ends. Regard should be had to the welfare of the young defendant as required by section 44 of the Children and Young Persons Act 1933.

The Practice Direction mentions other steps which should be taken to satisfy this overriding principle. Young defendants should ordinarily be tried on their own. A courtroom visit in advance may be appropriate. There may be restrictions on publicity or public attendance. All participants should sit at the same level in the court. There should be no robes/wigs or uniforms.

We will return later to the impact of this case on the sentencing of child murderers. It has also re-awoken the public debate about the sentencing and treatment of children who commit serious offences. It was clearly a key influence on Dame Elizabeth Butler-Sloss when she decided in early 2001 that the High Court had jurisdiction, in exceptional cases, to extend the protection of confidentiality of information, even to the extent of imposing significant restrictions on the press. In this case,[20] the President of the Family Division took the very unusual step of granting injunctions restraining the press from publishing any information leading to the identity or future whereabouts of Venables and Thompson, the two young killers of the toddler, now and once they were released. The considerable publicity and heated debate which have followed this decision reveal just how attitudes have polarized. Whilst much academic and

---

[19] [2000] 1 Cr. App. R 483.
[20] *Venables and another* v. *News Group Newspapers Ltd and others* [2001] 1 All ER 908.

professional opinion suggests that these two young people, now aged 18, have 'paid the price' for their crime committed when they were aged 10, others believe passionately, with the victims' family, that the criminal justice system should impose a much more severe punishment. We will return to this issue in the final section of this chapter.

JUVENILE JUSTICE TODAY

Children under the age of 10 cannot be guilty of any offence. Until 1998, there was also a rebuttable presumption of criminal law that a child aged between 10 and 14 was incapable of committing a crime. Thus it was established that until a child reached the age of 14, the prosecution had to prove that the child not only had the mens rea for the relevant crime, but also that she or he knew that what they did was a wrong act and not merely an act of simple naughtiness or mischief. However, the government decided that the presumption should be abolished. ('To respond effectively to youth crime, we must stop making excuses for children who offend.')[21] Section 34 of the Crime and Disorder Act 1998 provides simply that:

The rebuttable presumption of criminal law that a child aged 10 or over is incapable of committing an offence is hereby abolished.

Walker (1999) argues that this change does not abolish the presumption, but merely reverses the burden of proof. It may still be possible for a child to argue by way of defence that he or she did not know that what they were doing was wrong. However, this proposition has yet to be tested in court.

It is also worth noting at this stage that Youth Courts, the adult magistrates' courts, and the Crown Court have the power to order the parents of a juvenile defendant to attend. If the child is aged 15 or under, the court must order a parent or guardian to attend unless it would be unreasonable to do so.[22]

POLICE REPRIMANDS AND WARNINGS

As was noted earlier, formal cautions by the police grew enormously in the 1970s, and the police also began to make use of 'police juvenile liaison bureaux'.[23] Although the percentage of children formally cautioned dropped over the 1990s, the numbers remain huge. Thus the cautioning rate (i.e. the number cautioned as a proportion of those sentenced or cautioned) for 10–11 year old males was 87 per cent in 1999 (down from 95 per cent in 1994); for males aged 12–14 it was 69 per cent (down from 81 per cent in 1994); for males aged 15–17, 45 per cent. Girls aged 10–11 had a cautioning rate of 96 per cent aged 12–14, 87 per cent, and aged 15–17, 64 per cent. Figure 22.1

---

[21] Para. 4.1. of the White Paper, *No More Excuses* Cm 3809 (1997).

[22] S. 34 of the Children and Young Persons Act 1933.   [23] See Giller and Tutt, n. 15 above.

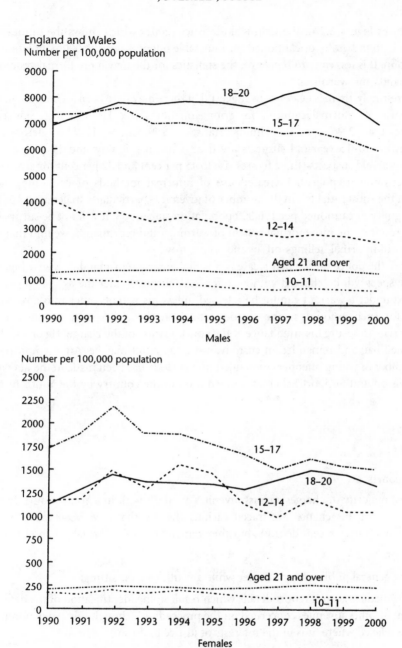

Fig. 22.1 Offenders found guilty of, or cautioned for, indictable offences per 100,000 population by age group 1990–2000.

reproduces Figure 5.2 of the Criminal Statistics (2001) which shows the number of offenders found guilty or cautioned for indictable offences per 100,000 population by age group. It is too early to report on the statistics for the new more formal system of reprimands and warnings.

Interestingly, there is evidence to suggest that there may have been an increase in the police use of informal cautions for young offenders (see Home Office Statistical Findings Issue 2/96, cited in Criminal Statistics 1999, Cm 5001). Thus, perhaps 37 per cent of 10–13-year-old suspects are dealt with in this way, and 19 per cent of 14–16-year-old suspects (these figures rise to 45 per cent and 32 per cent for arrests by the Metropolitan police). Increased use of informal methods of cautioning help explain the substantial fall in the number of juveniles (particularly males aged 10–14) found guilty or cautioned per 100,000 population since 1988. It will not be surprising if, as a result of the more formal system of warnings and reprimands, we find that the number of informal 'tellings-off' by the police grow.

Where the police decide that a case is unsuitable for a reprimand or a warning, the child suspect will be charged with an offence. A suspect under the age of 18 who is arrested under a warrant cannot be released unless his parents enter into a recognizance for such amount as the custody officer at the police station considers is appropriate to secure his attendance at the court hearing of the charge. He or she may be denied bail and remanded in custody, just as an adult may be. An attempt to cut the number of young offenders remanded into custody has been made in the new Bail Supervision and Support Schemes, funded around the country by the Youth Justice Board.

COURTS

Youth courts

The vast majority of charges against juveniles are dealt with in a Youth Court. In the earlier part of this chapter we traced various changes that have been made to the Youth Courts over recent decades, but they remain a more informal version of adult courts:

- the general public may not enter while a youth court is sitting;
- the media may not report details which result in the identification of the defendant or other juveniles concerned on the proceedings (though this restriction may be relaxed where 'it is in the interests of justice to do so');
- a Bench of lay magistrates should consist of those from a special panel, and should normally include a man and a woman (though increasingly cases are heard by District Judges (Magistrates' Courts)—professional judges who sit alone);
- there is no dock, so that the juvenile can sit in front of the magistrates, with his lawyer and parents.

It was noted above that a significant (over significant?) priority has been given to 'fast-tracking' procedures in the Youth Court, in particular by introducing time limits. The problems which arise from the introduction of rigid custody time limits were seen in a recent appeal from a Youth Court hearing. In *R. v. Croydon Youth Court, ex parte C*,[24] the gist of the complaint seems to have been that a 14-year-old was effectively forced into applying for an adjournment rather than have his trial start at 3 pm. This the Divisional Court held was a 'good and sufficient cause' for an extension of the overall time limit. The court suggested that good practice would dictate that, where two or more trials are listed at the same court on any one day, the court should be told of the time limit position for the different cases, so that if a choice has to be made about which case is adjourned, the court is aware of all the relevant facts.

One of the tensions noted in the summary of the history of juvenile justice above was the balance of power between magistrates and social workers. The latest swing is reflected in the referral orders, created in 1999 and being fully implemented in April 2002. The referral order is mandatory where the offender has pleaded guilty or where he/she has no previous convictions and has never been bound over to keep the peace or to be of good behaviour, or where the sentence is not fixed by law. It is also an option where the offender has not pleaded guilty to all offences. The court when making the referral order fixes the period, between three and twelve months, for which any 'youth offender contract' shall have effect. After that the Youth Offending Team is responsible for implementing the order. It is the YOT which will establish a youth offender panel and fix the date of the first meeting of the panel. It is too early to assess the referral order, but without doubt its introduction marks a swing away from traditional 'due process' justice imposed by magistrates towards inter-agency negotiated justice.

Adult magistrates' courts

Since a joint charge against a juvenile and an adult must be heard in an adult magistrates' court if it is to be heard summarily, some juveniles will find themselves tried in an adult court. However, if the adult pleads guilty and the juvenile does not, the juvenile may be remitted to a Youth Court for trial.

The Crown Court

Whilst a juvenile will usually be tried in a Youth Court, there are certain circumstances when he or she will instead be tried in the Crown Court.[25] These circumstances include all cases of homicide (normally murder and manslaughter, but also presumably causing death by dangerous driving), and cases where the juvenile is charged jointly with an adult and it is 'necessary in the interests of justice' for both the juvenile and the adult to be sent to the Crown Court for trial. Here the court has to weigh up the advantages of trying co-accuseds together against the advantage of a Youth Court for the trial of young offenders. Generally, the seriousness of the offence may tip the balance in favour of the Crown Court, whereas the youth of the child may tip the balance in favour of trial in a Youth Court. A Youth Court (or an adult magistrates'

---

[24] (13/07/2000).
[25] See s. 24(1) of the Magistrates' Courts Act 1980.

court) also has a discretion to send a juvenile for trial in the Crown Court where the offence charged is one which carries a maximum sentence of up to fourteen years or more in the case of an adult, or indecent assault.[26]

A report by PA Consulting Group on *Reducing Delays for Youth Cases Sentenced in the Crown Court* (2000), commissioned by the Court Service, reported that about 11 per cent of all persistent young offenders are sentenced in the Crown Court and that they make up about 6 per cent of all cases in the Crown Court. It is not surprising that the average time from arrest to sentence for those tried in the Crown Court is far longer than the average in Youth Courts (though committals for trial take only fractionally longer than committals for sentence). The conclusion of PA Consulting is that there is still scope to reduce delays by early guilty pleas, and by increasing the proportion of cases sentenced on the day a plea is entered.[27]

The Crown Court has the power and duty to remit young offenders to a Youth Court for sentencing unless satisfied that it would be undesirable to do so.[28] The possible reasons for not exercising this power to remit include the fact that the judge who presided over the trial would be better informed as regards the facts and circumstances of the matter or that the exercise of the power would create a risk of disparity between co-defendants sentenced on different occasions by different courts or would lead to delay or unnecessary duplication of proceedings or confuse the position in the event of an appeal. It may, however, be desirable to remit where the trial judge will be unable to sit, and a report is being obtained.[29] Unfortunately the Crown Court does not have the power to remit the case to a Youth Court for trial, but only for sentencing.

SENTENCING OPTIONS[30]

For convenience, sentencing options will be dealt with in the order followed by the Powers of the Criminal Court (Sentencing) Act 2000, although this codifying statute has already been modified in various ways by the Criminal Justice and Court Services Act 2000.

In 1999, 50,500 young people were sentenced for indictable offences. For an illustration of sentencing patterns, Figure 22.2, overleaf, reproduces Figure 7.9 of the Criminal Statistics 1999.

Community orders for offenders of any age. Curfew orders/electronic monitoring of curfew orders

The curfew order was introduced in 1991. It requires the offender to remain at a particular place (e.g. at home) for between two and twelve hours on any specified days, over a period of no more than six months. It may include a requirement as to

[26] See s. 91 of the Powers of the Criminal Courts Act 2000 (formerly s. 53(2) of the Children and Young Persons Act 1933).

[27] The author was astonished to learn at a series of lectures she gave to judges in the spring of 2001 that only a tiny percentage of judges had heard of this report which had been published more than 9 months earlier, despite the fact that it was designed to give advice to judges.

[28] See s. 8 of the Powers of the Criminal Courts (Sentencing) Act 2000, formally s. 56 of the CYPA 1933.

[29] See *Lewis* (1984) 6 Cr. App. R (S) 44.

[30] See D. A. Thomas's chapter for more details.

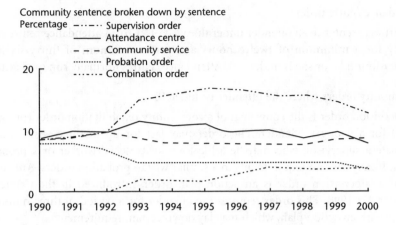

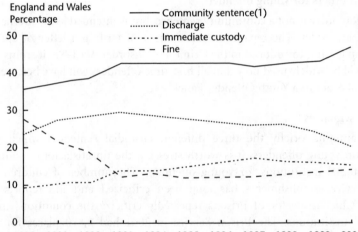

Fig. 22.2 Percentage of male offenders aged 15 to 17 sentenced for indictable offences who received various sentences or orders

electronic monitoring (the use of which the government intends to expand: see the references to ISSPs earlier).

Community orders available where the offender is aged 16 or over

These orders include community rehabilitation orders (until April 2000 known as probation orders); community punishment orders (previously known as community service orders or CSOs); community punishment and rehabilitation orders (previously combination orders); drug treatment and testing orders; and orders for petty persistent offenders. These are dealt with in Thomas's chapter in this book,[31] but it is worth mentioning the encouraging response of many professionals of the early drug treatment and testing orders.

---

[31] See Chap. 25 below.

Attendance centre orders

A court may sentence an offender under the aged of 21 to an attendance centre order, usually for a minimum of twelve hours and for a maximum of thirty-six hours (twenty-four if he or she is under 16). Attendance centres normally run on Saturdays.

Community orders where the offender is under 18

A supervision order is the equivalent of a community rehabilitation order (probation order) for a younger offender. The order may last for up to three years and will designate a supervisor, who may be a local authority social worker or a probation officer. It may contain requirements in a similar way to probation orders. An alternative to a supervision order is an action plan order, introduced in the Crime and Disorder Act 1998. This order requires the offender for a period of three months to comply with an action plan, which may lay down certain requirements.

Reparation orders for young offenders

A reparation order is not a community sentence, but is intended as an alternative to a compensation order. The reparation may consist of writing a letter of apology or cleaning up graffiti. Introduced in the Crime and Disorder Act 1998, it seems unlikely that this will be widely used now that all first-time offenders will have been sentenced to a referral order to a Youth Offender Panel.

Custodial sentences

Before examining briefly the three different custodial sentences which may be imposed on young offenders, it is worth stressing the unsatisfactory conditions of many custodial institutions for young offenders. The number of children held in Prison Service establishments has long been criticized and the reports of Her Majesty's Chief Inspector of Prisons repeatedly criticize the conditions in Young Offenders' Institutions. The Prison Service in 2001 had 2,870 places for boys in thirteen discrete juvenile units in Young Offenders' Institutes and 100 places for girls in adult prisons. Local Authority Secure Units have 300 places for boys and girls, and there are 130 places in three privately managed and owned secure training centres for sentenced boys and a few girls. A priority for the Youth Justice Board, which now buys in the necessary custodial provision for young offenders, is finding more places for girls and vulnerable 15- and 16-year-old boys outside Prison Service accommodation.[32]

The custodial sentences include detention during Her Majesty's Pleasure. This is imposed on any offender under the age of 18 who is convicted of murder. Until recently this indeterminate sentence was dealt with in a similar way to that imposed on adult murderers. The trial judge would not announce in open court the minimum period that the offender should serve. Instead, he would write a recommendation within a report for the Lord Chief Justice, who would add his recommendations to a report passed on to the Home Secretary, who would fix the 'tariff'. This is what happened after the trial of Thompson and Venables (the 10-year-olds who murdered

---

[32] See *Youth Justice Board News*, No. 7, Mar. 2001, 6.

the toddler, mentioned earlier) in 1993. The trial judge recommended a tariff of eight years, the Lord Chief Justice suggested an increase to ten years, but the Home Secretary fixed it at fifteen years. The House of Lords upheld the decision of both the Court of Appeal and the High Court to strike down this decision in *R. v. Secretary of State for the Home Department, ex parte Venables and Thompson*[33] on the ground that the Home Secretary had not taken into account the correct considerations. In subsequent proceedings, as we have seen, the European Court of Human Rights also held that the tariff-setting process infringed the young offenders' rights under the European Convention on Human Rights and the procedure has been changed. First, a Practice Statement from the Lord Chief Justice, Lord Woolf, was issued on 27 July 2000.[34] Lord Woolf explained the tariff as 'the amount of time actually to be served by a person convicted of murder in order to meet the requirements of retribution and general deterrence' and said that the usual length would be fourteen years. Whilst this statement implied (wrongly) that a prisoner is likely to serve only the tariff, it provided welcome guidance on the imposition of the tariff. Later on 26 October 2000, the Lord Chief Justice announced that the tariff in this particular case would be eight years.[35] Matters have moved on. Section 60 of the Criminal Justice and Court Services Act 2000 adds a new section 82A to the Powers of the Criminal Courts (Sentencing) Act 2000. Drafted in extraordinarily complex language, this appears to say that murderers under the age of 18 will in future have their tariffs fixed in open court in the same manner as discretionary life sentence prisoners.

Detention under section 91 of the Powers of the Criminal Courts (Sentencing) Act 2000. Any offender under the age of 18 who has been convicted of certain serious offences may be detained up to the possible statutory maximum for that offence, usually in a Young Offenders' Institution. Whilst it used to be thought that these provisions should be used only where a significantly longer sentence was required, this seems no longer to be the case. Thus in *Jenkins-Rowe and Glover*[36] two 14-year-olds chased and threatened another 14-year-old boy with a penknife demanding money and ended up stealing a pencil and a pencil sharpener. One pleaded guilty to, and the other was convicted of, robbery. Both had clean records and were sentenced to twenty months' and three years' detention under what is now section 91. The Court of Appeal, while upholding the principle of sentences under section 91, reduced the sentences to fifteen and thirty months.

Detention and training orders. Detention and training orders were introduced in 1998 to replace the secure training order for 12 to 14-year-olds and detention in a Young Offenders' Institution for 15 to 17-year-olds. In essence, these orders combine a period of detention and training in custody followed by a period of supervision in the community. Before such an order can be imposed, the court must be satisfied that the general criteria for a custodial sentence apply. In addition, if the offender is under 15, it must be proved that he or she is a persistent offender, and if he or she is under 12, that only a custodial sentence would be adequate to protect the public from serious harm. The main problems for sentencers when imposing these orders has

---

[33] [1998] AC 407.   [34] [2000] 4 All ER 831.
[35] [2001] 1 All ER 737.   [36] [2000] *Crim. LR* 1022.

proved to be, as was widely predicted, the fixed table of lengths to be found in section 100(2)(a). Detention and training orders can be imposed only in chunks of four, six, eight, ten, twelve, eighteen, and twenty-four months. Particularly difficult is the problem of taking into account time spent in custody on remand. The Court of Appeal in *R. v. Inner London Crown Court, ex parte N and S*[37] confirmed that the minimum period of four months raises the custody threshold. Nor, said the court, need the period in custody on remand be reflected precisely in the sentence imposed. (This was the case mentioned earlier in which the Vice President, Rose LJ, stated that in the light of the principal aim of the criminal justice system to prevent offending, 'it may be that the need to impose a deterrent sentence in relation to an offender under 18 may take priority over the provisions of section 44 of the CYPA 1933'.) Another case which well illustrates the difficulties with detention and training orders in practice is *Fieldhouse and Watts*[38]. F pleaded guilty to burglary, having acted as a look-out. W, on the other hand, pleaded guilty to two burglaries and a theft. W, who also had the longer record, received twenty-four-months' DTO as opposed to F's twelve months. A key question on appeal was the fact they had spent a weekend in custody on remand. The Court of Appeal upheld the twenty-four-month DTO but reduced the twelve months order to eight months. The periods in custody on remand could safely be ignored. It seems that the Court of Appeal believes that no clear guidance is needed and that common sense will prevail. But, as Thomas has repeatedly pointed out, it is not as easy as that. Consider the case of an 18-year-old convicted with a 17-year-old. Both receive a sentence of eighteen months. The 18-year-old will get the period served on remand reduced and the 17-year-old will not. Thomas poses many such problematic sentencing scenarios and concludes that 'there is something seriously wrong with a sentencing system which forces judges to spend time answering silly questions like these'.[39]

Financial penalties and young offenders

There are limits on fines imposed by magistrates' courts in respect of young offenders: £1,000 for those under 18, £250 for those under 14. The courts have powers to order statements as to the financial circumstances of parents or guardians and the power to order parents or guardians to pay fines, costs, or compensation.

CONCLUSION

In England we are faced with a statutory framework which states that the principal aim of the youth justice system is a reduction in offending. Few disagree with the aim, but it is easy to disagree over the appropriate routes to achieve the aim. Lyon *et al.* (2000) talked to marginalized young people in custody and reported their clear views on how to reduce offending. Whilst these children took full responsibility for their crimes and did not want, for example, to blame their mothers, they pointed out the

[37] [2000] *Crim. LR* 871.   [38] [2000] *Crim. LR* 1020.   [39] [2000] *Crim. LR* 1024.

need for early intervention and prevention, improved living conditions, and the need to take illegal drugs out of schools and colleges. Once within the criminal justice system they saw themselves as being processed by an unprofessional system with high staff turnover and ineffective practices. Judges were perceived as being out of touch and inconsistent. Surely if the aim of the criminal justice system is to reduce offending, more emphasis should be placed not only on the act done by the child, but also on the social circumstances surrounding it? Key questions concern the quality of residential care and the quality of the care available at home for all children, but another question is: when should the formal criminal justice system become involved?

Since 1970, the Scottish system of children's hearings has in effect diverted all children under the age of 16, except those who have committed the most serious offences, from the formal criminal justice system (see Scottish Executive, 2000). Children's hearings are a more informal and welfare-oriented system. Yet in England the proliferation of YOTs and YOPs still function within the context of the criminal courts. In the historical section of this chapter both the tension between courts and social workers and the shifting balance between care and punishment were highlighted; how, for example, at one stage (the 1950s and 1960s) young 'criminals' were more likely to be dealt with in a juvenile court which blurred crime and care, but by the 1990s, the care proceedings were removed from juvenile courts in order to avoid the criminal overtones of juvenile courts for 'genuine' care cases. 'Young offenders' were to be separated from 'children in need of protection'. Yet human rights and due process are just as important for those children who are detained under powers which lie outside the criminal justice system. A graphic example is provided by the recent case of Re K (a child)[40] in which the Court of Appeal addressed the human rights of a 15-year-old child who had been detained in secure accommodation for two years because of his non-criminal disruptive behaviour. A child who remains outside the formal criminal justice system still requires a system that protects his fundamental rights.

So why separate the 'criminal' child from the 'non-criminal'? A criminal court is not the only way to safeguard a child's due process rights. Another route is possible: to decide that children should not be brought within the criminal justice system until they are much older (16?) than at present. Then youth courts could concentrate on care and on reducing the chances of re-offending for all children. Child offenders would be seen as simply a sub-set of 'children in need', some of whom may well need and deserve[41] high levels of intervention. Suitable, humane, well-supervised, and constructive placements may be needed for many children. The English criminal justice system has not yet resolved the tensions apparent when dealing with juveniles: is there a correct age at which young persons need to be brought within the criminal system?

---

[40] [2001] 2 WLR 1141.

[41] Little mention has been made in this descriptive chapter of penal philosophy. Von Hirsch has recently explored why 'deserved' punishments for juveniles should be scaled well down below those applicable to adults: juveniles are less culpable (self-control is a learned capacity); punishment has greater bite when applied to adolescents; a principle of greater tolerance should be applied in the application of penal censure to juveniles: see (2001) 3 *Punishment and Society* 221. Any of these reasons could be used to justify removing juveniles from the criminal justice system altogether.

Are the priorities to be applied in a juvenile criminal justice system different from those applicable in adult courts? Perhaps the answers, towards which the government is edging as it experiments with reparation and referral orders, is to remove juveniles from the criminal justice system altogether. Putting the welfare and human rights of the child first is not incompatible with a desire to reduce offending, but attempting to achieve either within the criminal justice system may be inappropriate.

Bibliography and Further Reading

Audit Commission, *Misspent Youth: Young People and Crime* (Abingdon: Audit Commission Publications, 1996).

BALL, C., 'The Youth Justice and Criminal Evidence Act 1999. Part I: A Significant Move Towards Restorative Justice, or a Recipe for Unintended Consequences?' [2000] *Crim. LR* 211.

BOTTOMS, A. E., 'The Divergent Development of Juvenile Justice Policy and Practice in England and Scotland' in K. Rosenheim *et al.* (eds.), *The Juvenile Court at 100* (Chicago, Ill.: University of Chicago Press, 2001).

—— HAINES, K., and O'MAHONY, D., 'Youth Justice in England and Wales' in J. Mehlbye and L. Walgrave (eds.), *Confronting Youth in Europe* (Copenhagen: AKF, 1998).

CAMPBELL, S., and HARRINGTON, V., *Youth Crime: Findings from the 1998/99 Youth Lifestyles Survey*, Home Office Research Findings No. 126 (London: HMSO, 2000).

DIGNAN, J., 'The Crime and Disorder Act and the Prospects for Restorative Justice' [1999] *Crim. LR* 48.

EVANS, R., and ELLIS, R., *Police Cautioning in the 1990s*, Home Office Research Findings No. 52 (London: HMSO, 1997).

FARINGTON, D. P., 'Trends in English Juvenile Delinquency and their Explanation' (1992) 16 *IJ of Comparative and Applied Criminal Justice* 151.

GELSTHORPE, L., and MORRIS, A., 'Much Ado about Nothing—a Critical Comment on Key Provisions Relating to Children in the Crime and Disorder Act 1998' [1999] 2 *Child and Family Law Quarterly* 209.

GILLER, H., and TUTT, N., 'Police Cautioning of Juveniles: The Continuing Practice of Diversity' [1987] *Crim. LR* 367.

Home Office, *No More Excuses: A New Approach to Tackling Youth Crime in England and Wales*, Cm 3809 (1997).

JAMES, A., and RAINE, J., *The New Politics of Criminal Justice* (London: Longmans, 1998).

LYON, J., *et al.*, *'Tell them so they listen': Messages from Young People in Custody* (London: Home Office, 2000).

MORRIS, A., and GELSTHORPE, L., 'Something Old, Something Borrowed, Something Blue, But Something New? A Comment on the Prospects for Restorative Justice under the Crime and Disorder Act 1998' [2000] *Crim. LR* 18.

NEWBURN, T., 'Youth Crime and Justice' in M. Maguire, R. Morgan, and R. Reiner (eds.), *The Oxford Handbook of Criminology* (Oxford: OUP, 2002).

PADFIELD, N., *A Guide to the Crime and Disorder Act 1998* (London: Butterworths, 1998).

POLLARD, C., 'Victims and the Criminal Justice System: A New Vision' [2000] *Crim. LR* 5.

Scottish Executive, *The Evaluation of Children's Hearings in Scotland* (Edinburgh: Scottish Exceutive, 2000).

Also many relevant websites: for example, **www.homeoffice.gov.uk**

23

ECONOMIC CRIME

*Mike Levi**

INTRODUCTION

Each society has the kind of financial crime problems that reflect the form and organization of its commerce at different historical periods. Regulatory and criminal justice responses to those problems are the result of a combination of socio-legal traditions and political priorities that themselves have complex influences. These include the need to reassure outside investors that no-one will steal or make a secret profit from their capital, and that the legal system to which they can ultimately appeal will determine their cases fairly.

Offender mobility and economic openness in the era following the dissolution of the USSR and the changing trading and investment patterns in the People's Republic of China have created major risks for *all* economies, especially those less experienced in judging the merits of phoney deals. As an increasing proportion of the Western and other affluent populations directly or indirectly have an interest in the securities market and other savings and investment media, the *political* risks arising from some frauds and from popular and business fears about cyber crime increase. This also raises questions about how we should respond to such crimes, for most public security and criminal justice systems are oriented around (a) public order maintenance, and (b) street and household crime. Crimes committed both by and against business (whether owned by the people or by shareholders) are outside this routine area of policing and prosecutorial expertise. Whilst, for example, China has not so far been included in the International Victimization Surveys (which interview a representative sample of the population about their experiences of crime, whether reported or not), outside the advanced capitalist countries, consumer fraud and corruption are the two most commonly experienced crimes (Mayhew and van Dijk 1997). Hence, it is not surprising that anti-corruption has become a key component of the government's response to the crime and nation-building problem in the PRC (Levi and Fangmin 1996). Nevertheless, although our instincts may be in the direction of repression and ensuring 'just punishment for all', this may not be the most effective way of regulating harm, for enterprise culture is a delicate flower that

---

* Full citations for all books and articles cited in this chapter are to be found in the Bibliography and Further Reading section.

requires sophisticated nurturing rather than sudden lurches between drought and monsoon.

Some criminologists argue in favour of a forward-looking approach to negotiated change in business (and other) offending rather than a backward-looking retributive approach to dealing with offenders once offences have occurred (see, for example, Ayres and Braithwaite 1992; Fisse and Braithwaite 1993; Braithwaite and Drathos 2001). However many major frauds are committed by companies that—intentionally or not—go bust, so the *corporate* rehabilitation model cannot be applied *in those settings*. In large, complex societies (including, arguably, China and the USA) there is a felt need for symbolic punishment to emphasize the seriousness of the behaviour: an approach specifically rejected by the restorative-justice supporters whose views in many ways resemble the 'community re-education' model of traditional Chinese and Cuban sanctions.

Clarity of criminal justice purpose is also needed. Many victims understandably want to get back as much money as possible, but also to repair emotional injury which some of them suffer in terms of missed life opportunities and because they may feel ashamed at having been made a fool of, whether by strangers or friends (Levi and Pithouse, forthcoming). We should not therefore forget the *civil* law of compensation for tort, at least where the 'offender' has the means to repay and can be shown to be *able* to repay. (In practice, it may be hard to find out where the money has gone, especially if it has been laundered overseas.) But the State has the broader remit of deciding not only what to do *for* victims but also what to do *to* 'offenders', and the latter category is a highly contentious one in fraud. Where corruption scandals either directly implicate governing elites or reflect practices from which they may benefit, there is an ambivalence in how far investigators and prosecutors are allowed and should be allowed to go in following through the ramifications of individual investigations, and there are differences in the political accountability of these investigative and prosecution structures which have implications for how controllable the criminal justice process is. Thus in Italy and the USA, and to a lesser extent France, Germany, Hong Kong, the Philippines, and Russia, independent investigators and prosecutors have taken action against *current* senior politicians and businesspeople during the 1990s—thereby creating public confidence in the fairness of the justice system. In other countries, the passion for corruption investigations is considerably less, and prosecutions are much more readily controlled, especially where the media are tightly controlled or are passive. Contemporary Russia is an example, especially after the exile of the 'oligarch' Gusinsky, who owned the more critical press and television stations, and whom the Spanish authorities refused to extradite in 2001 because they considered his prosecution was politically motivated. In this context, we should appreciate the role that the internationalization of capital and business affairs and the push towards greater transparency of offshore finance centres through anti-money-laundering initiatives play in opening up national and international corruption and fraud to enhanced risks of exposure if *anyone wishes to do anything about the revelations* (Blum *et al.* 1998; Levi and Raphael 1999; Financial Action Task Force 2001). In particular, whistleblowers (given legal protection in the UK following the Public Interest Disclosure Act 1998)[1] or chance arrests of one of the parties can affect both legal and natural persons internationally.

In Britain most very serious offences are tried before juries drawn from the general public, who do not have to give reasons for their decisions. There are particular difficulties in recruiting jurors for lengthy trials, since many professional people are excused from jury service because of job commitments. There have been few trials and even fewer convictions for complex securities trading frauds. It is unlawful to interview jurors about their decision-making, so we cannot tell whether the lack of convictions is because jurors do not regard the *behaviour* as wrong or whether they simply cannot be *sure* that the defendants *in that particular case* on the evidence presented to them had the requisite level of criminal intent (see Levi 1993).[2] There is much disagreement over whether criminal or administrative measures should be taken against insider dealing and 'market offences' more subtle than those traditional 'confidence tricks' where crooks merely inflate the prices of shares with little underlying value. But irrespective of the (in)efficiency of the criminal law in this area, making insider trading criminal is a symbol of respectability for countries competing in the global securities business. Consequently, those countries that appear *not* to take market abuses seriously may be at a competitive global disadvantage.

THE INVESTIGATION AND PROSECUTION OF FRAUD

How is fraud policed in the UK? Where the victims are individuals, this is by a combination of:

(1) regulators (the Financial Services Authority) who scan the media and the internet for fraud risks (Financial Services Act 2001);

(2) public police who, except where 'organized crime' is involved, are mostly reactive, responding to complaints; and

(3) private civil action, such as freezing bank accounts, mostly reserved for the wealthy who can afford to pay for expensive legal help.

During 2000–1, the FSA (2001) formally investigated 226 suspected frauds, resulting in three criminal prosecutions for unauthorized banking and court orders for repayments of over £1.5 million to investors and depositors. Where the victims are government departments, the police or specialized tax or social security investigators deal with them, using reports of auditors to assist them. Where the victims are businesses, there is a mixture of public and private policing, with an increasing amount of

---

[1] Where the inside informant or whistleblower is victimized in breach of the Act, s/he can bring a claim to an employment tribunal for compensation. Awards will be uncapped and based on the losses suffered. Additionally where employees are sacked, they may apply for an interim order to keep their jobs.

[2] There are many other factors, not least whether jurors—in theory, a random sample of those permitted to vote—consider that the people in the dock are any more blameworthy than the prosecution witnesses or anyone else who is not before the court.

work being done (at the victim's expense) by large firms of corporate investigators or the forensic accounting arms of the major accounting firms. This has been formalized in the UK by an Authorized Investigators Scheme under which the police license private investigators as co-operative partners. Private policing develops further as British businesses operate in emerging markets, such as those of Eastern Europe, where the official police may not have the time or expertise or perceived integrity to investigate fraud allegations. Anywhere in the world, firms may want to know how the suspected fraud or error was committed, who is responsible, and whether they can get their money back. This may be done reactively, in response to a detected event, or proactively, as part of a risk-management strategy in dealing with markets known or believed to 'problem-prone'. For the most part, what is done to the 'offenders' is of very secondary concern.

In the UK, there have been continuous decentralizing pressures since the 1970s to divert scarce resources from central detective squads to uniformed 'sector policing'. There have also been changes in the number of serious frauds reported. In tune with these changes, the number of specialist Fraud Squad officers in England and Wales (who also deal with corruption) has fluctuated, from 588 in 1985 to 770 (of whom 238 were in London) in 1992, falling back to fewer than 700 in 2000 (Doig *et al.* 2001). (In areas such as corruption and fraud, where the police can turn down cases by defining them as 'no crime' and/or 'civil complaints', the resources available can also affect the official crime rate.) Moreover, a new regulatory apparatus has been created under the Financial Services and Markets Act 2000, one of whose specific core object-ives is 'to contribute to reducing financial crime'. If successful, this will reduce the number of 'City frauds' with which the police and Department of Trade and Industry (DTI, which has responsibility for company investigations) will be required to deal in future. Thus, the more effective the *preventive* apparatus, the less need there will be for criminal justice. Nevertheless, there always will be a need for formal policing, because it is inconceivable that any society will be able to suppress fraud without suppressing its entire economy, both official and 'hidden'. Demand for investigation of massive frauds is cyclical in nature. The late 1980s and early 1990s saw some massive corporate collapses in the UK, leading to revelations of fraud, but these have now disappeared and the frauds detected are less massive in nature, though still very big compared with other crimes.

It is important to understand where the current organization of fraud policing, prosecution, and trial has come from. Until 1988, these offences were dealt with in a manner similar to other crimes, with similar powers. However, in addition to the police, at the national level there was the Customs & Excise, the Inland Revenue (which deals with income tax), the Insolvency Service, the Department of Trade and Industry, and the Office of Fair Trading, all of which had some (sometimes overlap-ping) regulatory role and saw criminal prosecution only as a final resort, to be undertaken when conciliation/debt recovery had failed or seemed certain to fail, or to meet some deeper strategic objective, like showing particular categories of tax-payer or insolvent that they really meant business. There was also the Department of Social Security, which was more police-like in prosecuting social security fraud-sters. During the mid-1980s, there was growing dissatisfaction with the way that the criminal justice system was dealing with major frauds, and there was a political desire to show the rest of the world that Britain *could* deal with its frauds competently. This led to the review of the investigation, prosecution, and trial of fraud by Lord Roskill (1986), which in turn led to the establishment of the Serious Fraud Office (SFO) by the Criminal Justice Act 1987, which included lawyers, accountants, and police in the same investigative groups and in the same building. In the interests of effectiveness, the SFO deliberately violates the 'Philips principle' (in the Report of the Royal Commission on Criminal Procedure 1981) of separating the investigation from the prosecution process, on which the Prosecution of Offences Act 1985 and the Crown Prosecution Service (CPS) are founded (Wood 1989). On the other hand, like the tax fraud departments, the decisions to prosecute are taken by different persons in the department, to try to create *some* detachment in the process.

There is enormous disparity in the powers available to different agencies, the degree of judicial scrutiny to which those powers are subjected, and the conditions under which the results of the exercise of powers are admissible as evidence in subsequent criminal trials. (For a review of Serious Fraud Office powers, see Levi 1993 and Kirk and Woodcock 1996.) Let us first deal with the police, who undertake most fraud investigations.

INVESTIGATION POWERS OF THE POLICE

Many serious fraud inquiries—used here in the sense of the kind of things dealt with by fraud squads—start with a complaint from a businessperson, a private investigator, or a lawyer acting on behalf of private or corporate victims. They normally supply the police with an account of what happened to them, and some leads as to who might be responsible. It will often not be self-evident that what happened was a crime. It could be a civil debt which has been unpaid, or a victim's belief that he has been 'conned', which may not disclose the sort of deception covered by the criminal law. It is not uncommon for the officer to ask the victim or his representative to carry out some further investigation on his behalf. Where there are such co-operative victims, the police powers needed may not be very great, at least until the officer is in sight of his (or, more rarely, her) suspect.

Before the Police and Criminal Evidence Act 1984 (hereafter, PACE)—see Maguire, Chapter 5, this volume—the police had no power to require evidence prior to the institution of proceedings. However, under section 9 of and Schedule 1 to PACE, a circuit judge may issue the police with a warrant to search for evidence in relation to 'special procedure material' (such as information held in confidence by banks—section 14) if s/he is satisfied that there are reasonable grounds for believing, *inter alia*, that:

i.   a serious arrestable offence has been committed;[3]

---

[3] This being defined in s. 116 as an offence which has led, or is intended or likely to lead, to substantial financial gain or loss to any person.

ii. there is material likely to be of substantial value (whether by itself or together with other material) to the investigation;

iii. the material is likely to be relevant evidence;

iv. there is no prospect of the material being obtained without a Production Order; and

v. access to the information is overall in the public interest (whatever that may mean!).

Applications for orders under Schedule 1 paragraph 4 must be made *inter partes* (i.e. both parties are represented), though under section 8 of PACE 1984 search warrants are available *ex parte* (in the absence of the defence) where the holders of special procedure material themselves are clear suspects and/or service of notice may seriously prejudice an investigation. These search powers can now be exercised on behalf of overseas police forces, in relation to 'conduct which is an offence under the law of a country or territory outside the United Kingdom and would constitute a serious arrestable offence if it had occurred in any part of the United Kingdom'.[4]

Section 8(2) of PACE 1984 defines three categories of extraordinary material for which the police may wish to search: 'items subject to legal privilege', which cannot be subject to a search warrant from anyone at all; and 'excluded material' and 'special procedure material', for which warrants may be issued only by a circuit or a deputy circuit judge under section 9. A search warrant may be issued only for material that has evidentiary value in the legal sense, that is, it must be admissible and not hearsay. Banking and police sources state that where banking information is sought, there is very seldom any objection to Production Orders under Schedule 1 to PACE 1984 in *inter partes* hearings (though this may partly reflect pre-application agreement between the parties). It is contempt of court to breach a Production Order, with a potential sanction of imprisonment, though this has never yet had to be activated.

No warrant may ever be issued to search for evidence that is legally privileged. Such material is defined in section 10(1) as covering communications between a professional legal adviser and his client or his client's representative made in connection with the giving of legal advice;[5] communications made between the adviser and his client and any other person that have been made in connection with or in contempla-

---

[4] See s. 7 of the Criminal Justice (International Co-operation) Act 1990, and the Order in Council, 10 June 1991, which brought these powers into effect. S. 3 of this Act also provides reciprocal rights for UK prosecutors on the authority of a magistrate or judge to issue letters of request to obtain information from overseas, which represents a significant problem in the investigation of international frauds.

[5] This can cover in-house lawyers: a matter that—Law Society guidelines notwithstanding—can give rise to real concerns about cover-ups and conflicts of interest where a company which is itself under suspicion both marshals evidence and organizes (and pays for) the legal representation of its staff. Even in the *Guinness* inquiry, some lawyers sought to insist on being present during police interviews of 'their' witnesses, possibly inhibiting the latter from telling the truth. In the Blue Arrow investigation, one of the financial institutions tried to withdraw funds for legal representation of its former executive when his defence conflicted with the company's, and he had to resort to the courts to get it to continue paying for his lawyers.

tion of legal proceedings; and items enclosed with or referred to in such communications and made in connection with the giving of legal advice. Legal advisers include barristers, solicitors, and their clerks, and 'any other person', which might include an accountant or banker asked by a lawyer to prepare a report 'in connection with' legal proceedings. So all documents and other records in the possession of a lawyer—including a firm's legal department—in relation to the affairs of his clients are either legally privileged or special procedure material.

Section 10(2) states that 'items held with the intention of furthering a criminal purpose are not items subject to legal privilege'. But whose intention is included here? The House of Lords decided that legal privilege does not apply, first, where the criminal purpose is that of the client and, secondly, where the documents are said to further the criminal intentions of a third party.[6] This ruling applies to all serious arrestable offences, i.e. most frauds.

Where the solicitor is not under suspicion personally, an *inter partes* order is applied for and, normally, provided that access conditions are met, is made to take effect within seven days, during which time the solicitor can apply to the judge to discharge the order.

One problem that sometimes arises relates to how specific the request for documents has to be. In R v. *Central Criminal Court, ex parte Adegbesan & others*,[7] a politically sensitive case which concerned allegations of corruption in relation to the administration of funds by a trustee of the Youth Association on the riot-hit Broadwater Farm Estate in London, the Divisional Court quashed the 'special procedure' order made by the judge, stating that it was the duty of the police to set out a description of all the material that was to be produced. Otherwise, the person receiving the notice could unwittingly destroy the material and commit contempt of court, since it was impossible for him or her to know whether or not it was covered by the order. When the police did provide more specific requests, the defendants appealed once more, on the ground that the particulars were still inadequate. The Court of Appeal, however, held that orders could be granted against each or any of the parties, where the applicant does not know which party has which documents.[8]

These are characteristic problems in police fraud investigations. The police may not know precisely where they may be able to find documents which they suspect exist without inspecting them, but they cannot get an order requiring production until they know where the information can be found. The Court of Appeal held that in cases which involve a very large quantity of records, the police should be broadly selective, ruling out those documents that are 'clearly irrelevant' and taking away others that they reasonably believe to have evidential value.

---

[6] See R. v. *Central Criminal Court, ex parte Francis & Francis* [1988] 3 WLR 989.

[7] [1986] 3 All ER 113.

[8] The principal target in that case claimed that the documents had been taken away by her to Jamaica and had been swept away in a flood. She was found guilty of perverting the course of justice and was given a modest fine.

In 1991, in connection with allegations of corruption against former left-wing Liverpool councillor Derek Hatton *et al.*, the builders Wimpey complained not only that the police had misinformed the judge prior to the issue of the PACE search warrant by failing to disclose that Wimpey were co-operating fully with them (as they claimed), but also that 'the police seized a mass of irrelevant documents, which were not covered by the warrant, including all accounting records which were bringing the group "to a grinding halt"'.[9] The case subsequently went to judicial review, where it was held that, once granted, the issuing judge had no power to rescind a warrant:

Despite concern on the part of many victims, it was plain that some complaints were thoroughly investigated before being dropped, indicating that a good deal of in-house supervisory control is exercised before some cases are in practice submitted to CPS Branch or Headquarters.

INVESTIGATING SERIOUS FRAUD: PROSECUTION AGENCIES AND THE POLICE

When the Serious Fraud Office (SFO) was established in 1988, the number of cases was estimated at thirty to forty cases annually. In 2000, the SFO had sixty-five active cases, reflecting the larger number of cases that came to light in the 1990s and after, though at one time it predicted it would be dealing with 100 cases a year.[10] It had in 2000 a budget of £17 million (of which £8 million was spent directly on investigations and prosecutions). This SFO budget is tiny compared with (i) the size and complexity of the losses it is required to investigate (totalling an annual average of some £4.5 billion 'at risk' during the 1990s, though actual losses are much lower); and (ii) the funds available to some of the corporations and individuals it is investigating.

The SFO is an independent government department and its Director—two out of four Directors have been female—exercises her powers under the supervision of the Attorney-General. She maintains contact with government departments and regulatory bodies such as the Department of Trade and Industry, the Financial Services Authority, and others. These and other organizations such as the police, private investigation agencies, or sometimes victims report directly to the SFO allegations of serious or complex fraud. Thus, in 2001, when an insurance company came close to collapse and had to be closed down, there was a conference between the regulators

---

[9] *The Independent*, 27 Mar. 1991. S. 22 of PACE 1984 does give the suspect the right to obtain copies of documents seized, at his or her own expense, but this inevitably takes time, particularly given the volume of papers involved.

[10] *Results of SFO Completed Cases, 1999–2000*. In 8 trials where sentences were handed down, 5 defendants pleaded guilty and 7 were found guilty. Additionally, one defendant was found not guilty. (9 of these defendants received custodial sentences.) Appeals against conviction and/or sentence were heard in relation to 5 trials unvolving 7 defendants. In 2 cases, defendants had their sentences reduced; in all other cases, the appeals were rejected. During the year, it took on average 32 months to transfer or commit to the Crown Court 19 fraud cases.

and the SFO, and it was decided that the case was of sufficient public concern that, if there was sufficient evidence to prosecute, there should be prosecution rather than just a regulatory disciplinary process. Other cases of fraud—sometimes major ones— are mainly dealt with by the police and are prosecuted by the Crown Prosecution Service. Partly for historic reasons going back to the establishment of the Office of the Director of Public Prosecutions (DPP) in the nineteenth century, public-sector cor- ruption cases are dealt with by the police and CPS, since, by statute, prosecution for corruption requires the consent of the DPP. This is not always an easy demarcation, since fraud and corruption overlap.

When a case is referred to the SFO, there is a vetting process and the Director will institute an investigation only if it appears to her, on reasonable grounds, to involve serious or complex fraud. These are terms undefined by law but, in practice, the key criterion is that the suspected fraud's investigation requires direction by those responsible for the prosecution. In judging referrals, account is taken of the need to use the Office's section 2 powers and, normally, whether the value of the alleged fraud exceeds £1 million. Other factors include whether there is a significant international dimension; whether the case might give rise to widespread public concern; and/or whether the case requires highly specialized knowledge.

The distinctive feature of the SFO's approach to investigations is the use of multi- disciplinary teams. Section 1(4) of the Criminal Justice Act 1987 provides for the conduct of investigations by the SFO in conjunction with the police. The consti- tutional independence of the police, their accountability, and their command struc- ture remain unchanged by the establishment of the SFO or by the attachment of the police to it, though the Director would like to employ her own investigative officers rather than request the sometimes unwilling police for staff.

When a case is accepted, a case team of lawyers, accountants, police officers, and support staff is appointed. The team is headed by an in-house SFO lawyer who, as 'case controller', is responsible for ensuring a fast and effective investigation and for any ensuing prosecution. However, as in other English cases, the case controller does not prosecute personally. The case is actually presented by a senior independ- ent barrister, who normally is invited to participate in investigative decisions at an early stage. Though it costs the SFO a lot of money to bring in barristers early, the aim is to avoid time and money being wasted on pursuing aspects of the case that do not need to be analysed. Experience suggests that otherwise, when the barrister is introduced, s/he will discard some evidence and demand the investigation of other lines of inquiry. (In Crown Prosecution Service fraud and corruption investi- gations, to save money in less sensitive cases, they normally are brought in at a later stage.)

Unravelling major fraud often involves examining vast quantities of documents left in a deliberately obscure and fragmented form. A proper evaluation of such information means that the documents need to be seen by several people contributing different forms of expertise (police, accountants, lawyers, bankers, stockbrokers, and computer specialists among them) with a view to producing the information in a compact and coherent form for presentation in court.

Case conferences are held at regular intervals throughout the investigation and provide a forum for agreeing joint lines of action. They are attended by representatives from all the different disciplines from the case team, including prosecuting counsel. At the conclusion of each case a final conference is held to review the case and learn from the experience gained, though the level of self-criticism varies (Levi 1993), whether or not there is criticism of the Office in the media (see Levi and Pithouse, forthcoming).

One of the most controversial powers of the SFO is section 2 of the Criminal Justice Act 1997, which enables it to require information from third parties and suspects and to require them to answer its questions. It is a criminal offence to refuse or to lie to the SFO. In 1999–2000, 687 section 2 notices were issued in relation to the SFO's own investigations, and a further 109 section 2 notices were issued on behalf of overseas authorities. Many section 2 notices are issued to banking businesses, financial institutions, accountants, and other professionals who may, for completely innocent reasons, be in possession of information or documents relevant to a fraud. In most instances those institutions and persons owe duties of confidence to their clients. Many are willing to assist but cannot do so while such duties of confidence remain. A section 2 notice removes these difficulties for them. For those who do not wish to assist, the power involves compulsion, and in 1999–2000 one person was convicted of deliberately misleading the SFO when required under section 2 to give potential evidence.

Since February 1995 the SFO has been able to use its investigative section 2 powers on behalf of foreign authorities. International co-operation is a vitally important priority for the Office, since, of the core cases investigated, around two-thirds now have a foreign dimension. A greater ability to assist criminal justice authorities in other countries is the only way that fraud can be combatted on an international level. To receive SFO help, an overseas authority must first write to the Home Office Central Authority. If the Home Office thinks the case is appropriate for the SFO, it will refer the case to the Director, who will decide whether the case meets the SFO's criteria of seriousness or complexity. Giving assistance to overseas counterparts is now a vital part of the Office's work.

In some cases the mere existence of section 2 is used as a background threat to induce co-operation. When done with tact, a voluntary witness statement can be very useful to the prosecution, more so than a section 2 notice would be. In one case an accountant was examined patiently and eventually gave a good voluntary witness statement, and made a good witness in court, showing that later accountants could have been deceived by a forged letter. Yet without the threat of section 2, he would not have made the statement in the first place, since issues of professional negligence were lurking in the background. Even though it is a criminal offence to refuse to answer questions from the SFO without reasonable excuse,[11] some witnesses test the limits of what constitutes a 'reasonable excuse' for failing to answer, by stating that they cannot remember. Sometimes they actually may not remember what the purpose was of

---

[11] In 1992, despite the House of Lords ruling in *Wallace Smith*, Larry Trachtenberg, one of the principal accused in the Maxwell case, refused to answer the SFO's questions after charge because he considered they violated his civil rights. At his trial on this issue, his lawyers raised a variety of technical objections to the

documents or actions taken years earlier. The difficulty is proving whether or not they are having genuine problems of recall.

In one mortgage fraud which was a spin-off from a more major investigation, everyone exercised the right to silence and there was insufficient hard evidence to obtain warrants. A section 2 notice was issued against a solicitor who had refused to co-operate and, eventually, after two days of questioning (with appropriate refreshment breaks as per PACE), he admitted being part of a conspiracy. Having previously denied that he knew of any relevant files, he went to a pub car park where all the files were in a car. He pleaded guilty, as did an accountant. The principal, who exercised the right to silence under caution and, extraordinarily, introduced her own section 2 statement in evidence to explain her reasons for departing from it, was convicted and imprisoned for thirty months.

In short, section 2 powers are particularly useful where witnesses may be frightened to give information voluntarily or where the SFO is trying to trace funds and to enable better decisions to be made about who is telling the truth (particularly where someone has offered to give evidence for the Crown but does not want to make self-incriminating admissible statements). In CPS cases, where these powers are not available, the investigations are not only more difficult but also receive fewer expert resources.

Once the case has been investigated, before instituting any criminal proceedings, the SFO will consider whether, on the evidence against each potential defendant, there is a realistic prospect of securing a conviction and whether the public interest requires a prosecution.

In SFO prosecutions, where a Case Controller has had to lose detachment by conducting interviews, etc., the decision to prosecute (or not) is taken by someone senior (normally one grade above). A similar division has been forced upon the Financial Services Authority—which can prosecute investor fraud and money laundering—and on other investigating and prosecution agencies by the Financial Services and Markets Act 2000.

Contested fraud cases generally result in long trials when compared with other kinds of criminal prosecutions. This is because fraud trials face particular difficulties, such as vast paperwork, multiple defendants (and lawyers), and may require special accommodation and court facilities such as an ability to copy evidence using CD-ROMs which can be played before the court. Although such matters are generally for the Lord Chancellor's Department and circuit and court administrators to deal with, they need assistance from the prosecuting authorities.

One serious problem for both prosecutors and defendants is that there is a huge degree of overlap between the different investigative groups, both public and private sector, in parallel civil and criminal actions. Many serious fraud cases involve companies in liquidation or in administrative receivership. The work done by

authority of SFO investigating lawyers to use delegated powers. After charge, the Maxwell brothers also refused further SFO questioning on the ground that they were entitled to obtain disclosure from the 'prosecuting authority' of the case against them, and the SFO stated that it would grant disclosure only once the 'investigative stage' had been completed. The SFO's position was upheld by the courts.

liquidators in the course of their ordinary functions is very helpful to the SFO, but this can create enormous problems for the defence—which is uncertain what can be used for which purposes—and for the SFO itself, whose case controllers have to grapple with questions of privilege and of what can be passed on to various organizations, as well as the problem that admissions made under compulsion and/or without being cautioned are inadmissible in court proceedings.

SPECIAL PROBLEMS RELATING TO FRAUD CASES: THE DECISION TO PROSECUTE

It is formally proper for prosecutors to take into account 'the public interest' when deciding to prosecute or not to prosecute. Thus in 1978, when the state of Zimbabwe had already been formed, the DPP decided not to prosecute companies which broke sanctions at the time of the Rhodesian Unilateral Declaration of Independence on the grounds that 'no good would be served by raking over these almost dead coals'. On the other hand, a number of defendants have argued that they were the victims of politically motivated prosecutions: for example the illegal share-support operations on behalf of the Guinness takeover of Distillers, where defendants alleged to me that the government needed prior to the 1987 election to demonstrate that it was getting tough on white-collar criminals; and the illicit share-support operation for Blue Arrow, where the government was embarrassed by revelations in *The Economist* magazine, and—as in Guinness—was concerned about its reputation in the international market-place. However, just because a prosecution produced or was intended to produce a political benefit to a country and/or a party does not mean that it was unjustified. What it does is to highlight the legitimation problem caused by the accountability of both the DPP and the Director of the SFO to the Attorney-General—a government minister—within the UK's informal constitution.

Highly selective prosecutions have always been the policy of the Revenue Departments, largely because, with few resources and departmental objectives which avoid retribution in favour of maximizing revenue, they seek to spread a few prosecutions around the country, and to target high-profile persons and conduct with prosecutions that will maximize publicity and general deterrence. In a case in which two clients of an accused accountant sought judicial review of their own prosecution on the ground that, to be fair, all his 'suspected clients' should have been prosecuted, the Divisional Court held that the Inland Revenue is not required to treat in the same way all taxpayers alleged to have committed similar offences, and observed that it 'is inherent in such a [discretionary] policy that there may be inconsistency and unfairness as between one dishonest taxpayer and another who is guilty of a very similar offence'.[12]

Though almost never as hysterical as that which accompanies acts of terrorism or child murders and which adds to the pressure to charge and convict in such cases, media and political pressure during the late 1980s and early 1990s has acted to bring

---

[12] R. v. *Inland Revenue Commissioners, ex parte Mead and Cook* [1992] STC 482.

more people and more complex cases into the prosecutorial net. The growing numbers of financial journalists with an interest in exposures of fraud cases have played a significant role in this, with intensified competitive pressure to find not only new victims and 'scams' but also to reveal (or, as seen by some regulators, to invent) new examples of regulatory incompetence in allowing frauds to occur or continue. The clearest example of this is seen in the vastly greater number of journalists than SFO staff and police who were investigating the background to the collapse of the Maxwell empire, at least until the arrests created publicity restrictions (except in relation to the deceased Robert Maxwell) and thus made heavy investigative journalism cost-ineffective for editors. (See Corker and Levi 1996; Honess *et al.* 1998; and Levi and Pithouse, forthcoming, for a critical analysis of some of the media treatment in this case.)

Traditionally, whatever the arguments over the inherent seriousness of white-collar crimes or over public perceptions of them (Levi 1987; Levi and Pithouse, forthcoming), little active pressure has been exerted by the public or government to do much about them—particularly not to do much about them immediately, and the kind of people who commit white-collar offences are not normally those whom the police (and prosecutors) feel it is important to 'put away',[13] though there may be a temptation to arrest suspected fraudsters 'to let them know you are on to them'. However, those who investigate fraud, particularly fraud against the public, can use the weapon of media publicity to put an end to the profit of suspected fraudsters, whether by alarming those who are willing to listen or by pressurizing the regulators to close their businesses down. This preventive technique is not normally available with other serious crimes, for the distinguishing feature of credit and investment fraud—as opposed to the looting of company/state assets by senior or junior staff—is that people are induced to part with their money or goods voluntarily. If the media can stop people putting their money into fraudulent schemes, investment and 'advance fee' fraud is greatly reduced, if only by inhibiting the number of victims who are fleeced on any particular occasion. Defamation law does inhibit this fraud-prevention role of the media (see Bower 1996; Lever 1992): but in this respect the media sometimes offer an alternative to criminal justice control.

THE CHARGES: NARROWING DOWN CASES

Perhaps because the SFO is an elite organization dealing with a small number of very serious cases, there is a marked reluctance to take risks by focusing on relatively narrow charges which, if those chosen are unsuccessful, would allow the defendants to escape conviction.

The Code for Crown Prosecutors—which applies to all prosecution agencies—states that the counts in the indictment should reflect the complexity and gravity of

---

[13] Except, perhaps, through envy and resentment at the lifestyles of the rich and famous. Except in very 'political' or organized crime/money-laundering cases in which the proceeds of fraud are funnelled into narcotics trafficking or terrorism, white-collar 'offenders' are seldom targets for proactive surveillance or undercover work.

the offences, but should go no further than that. However, over-charging tendencies reflect, first, a desire to boost sentencing via conviction on major charges; and, secondly, personal and organizational performance indicators, whether explicit or simply part of the general culture of prosecutors, which stress high-profile convictions and sentences. There is also a strong sense in which, in order to justify, internally, the case having been taken on at all by the SFO rather than by the CPS, the charges have to reflect the scale of the malefaction. Another kind of problem encountered arises from SFO defensiveness about acquittals, given negative publicity about its competence that acquittals generate (Levi and Pithouse, forthcoming). The first half of the 1990s saw high-profile acquittals in the second, third, and fourth Guinness trials—where the case had to be broken up to make it manageable. At the beginning of the 1990s, excluding guilty pleas, half of those prosecuted by the SFO were not convicted.

CLARIFYING THE ISSUES

The establishment of the SFO was accompanied by attempts to 'modernize' the pre-trial and trial processes. This meant abolishing the right to have the prosecution case heard before magistrates and introducing a requirement for the defence to outline its case before the trial in answer to the prosecution's case outline. One reason this was particularly important was that jurors needed more simplified cases to be able to follow. In practice, to be effective, the judge may also have to bind subsequent counsel and litigants in person to the case outline he has set in the preparatory hearings.

However, transfers have not speeded up the processing of cases as much as had been hoped, because some preparatory hearings take so long. In the light of the three months that preparatory hearings took in *Guinness 1*, it is with a sense of profound irony that one notes Recommendation 48 in the Fraud Trials Committee Report (Roskill 1986): 'a full day should be set aside for preparatory hearings'.

In complex and serious fraud cases, the judge can order the prosecution to prepare, *inter alia*, a 'case statement'. Where the prosecution has done so, the judge (section 9(5)) may require each defendant to produce a case statement which must set out his defence 'in general terms'.[14]

Because it pressurizes the in-house legal team to prepare its cases with far greater rigour than is needed for committal, the working up of the Statement of the Evidence is an excellent discipline for the lawyers in assessing the evidential strengths and

---

[14] Under the Criminal Justice Act 1987 (as amended), the judge 'may order the defendant or, if there is more than one, each of them—

(i)   to give the court and the prosecution a statement in writing setting out *in general terms* [italics not in original] the nature of his defence and indicating the principal matters on which he takes issue with the prosecution;

(ii) to give the court and the prosecution notice of any objections he has to the case statement;

(iii) to inform the court and the prosecution of any point of law (including a point as to the admissibility of evidence) which he wishes to take, and any authority on which he intends to rely for that purpose;

(iv) to give the court and the prosecution a notice stating the extent to which he agrees with the prosecution as to documents and other matters to which a notice under subsection 4(c) above relates and the reason for any disagreement.'

Unfortunately, there is no ability to require cross-service of defence case statements among defendants.

weaknesses of their own cases, and in enabling case controllers to become full members of the legal team. Its very specificity, though very time-consuming and therefore expensive, sometimes gives defence counsel the ammunition to interrogate their clients thoroughly. One case was cited to me where this stopped the client bluffing and induced a guilty plea. The aim of narrowing the case statement and requiring a defence response has not been as successful as was hoped, first because the SFO presents a large amount of evidence to draw a defence response, and secondly because few judges have been able to pressurize or persuade defendants to present lengthy, detailed case statements. In large cases, there may be as many as twenty defence lawyers, and this can generate exhausting social dynamics for one judge and three prosecutors.

One response to this is to substitute multi-defendant trials by a series in which many defendants are prosecuted in small trials. But there everyone learns what the prosecution case is and can find out what defence 'works' and what does not, particularly if the cases are similar. In one police/CPS investigation into collusive retailers who were involved in helping the passing through of false credit card transactions, following on from the arrest of several Chinese on a train with Far Eastern counterfeit Gold Cards, some five couriers and twenty-seven alleged collusive retailers were prosecuted. The five couriers were convicted, one other trial having been discontinued for evidential reasons. Because they were in different parts of the country and had little obvious interconnection—being the 'spokes' of the wheel conspiracy—the seventeen English alleged collusives were split up by the CPS into nineteen separate trials and tried one after the other. All passed the half-way stage, though two were discharged at committal because the banking evidence was not available. The majority were convicted. Some collusives claimed that they were under duress, because people forced them to process transactions after hours at knifepoint. In two cases, this has worked, and so others will probably claim this also, whether it is true or false.

DEFENDING WHITE-COLLAR CRIME

Some wealthy individual and corporate defendants pay for their own defences, but otherwise, serious fraud defendants are eligible for public Legal Aid, at higher rates than in simpler cases but nevertheless well below the hourly fees charged in civil or privately funded cases. Representing legally aided clients in serious frauds requires huge resources for firms to carry until the conclusion of the case. In *Barlow Clowes*, the legal aid authorities paid the defence solicitors a substantial monthly sum, topped up periodically on the presentation of appropriate documentation, and with very large further sums at the end. In other cases, this does not happen. Although the fees for complex cases are higher than normal legal rates, there has been pressure for the defence to be paid a total fixed sum. One of the key problems in all serious cases is material that is not used by the prosecution, which can sometimes fill entire buildings in fraud cases. Sometimes, it is unreasonable to expect the prosecution to be able to discover material that will assist the defence, though the defence itself, if it has the funds, may be able to do so. The SFO has a document management and control system for use in investigations and for presentation of evidence in court, called

DOCMAN. It stands for Document Management System and scans in all the documentation that it gets in the course of an investigation so that every piece of paper scanned into the system will be available for the defence, the judge, and counsel on a CD-ROM. The same applies to unused materials. One example was the defence by Marconi and individual staff against allegations by the SFO that they had deliberately loaded all the costs of defence product development into their 'cost plus' contracts. The enormous resources of the defence enabled it to show that there were other areas of business where cost mis-allocations had not worked in its favour and that this was a mistake rather than a conspiracy by them. Had it not had the resources to comb through mountains of its own documentation, it might not have been acquitted. On the other hand, had a (probably undetected) miscarriage occurred, the investigators and prosecutors would not have been blameworthy for wilful non-disclosure in the same way that some other miscarriage cases have indicated blameworthiness.

PLEA-BARGAINING: THE FRAUDULENT SOLUTION?

Advocates of reducing costs and uncertainty in the criminal justice process sometimes display enthusiasm for a more formalized system of plea-bargaining or 'sentence canvassing' (see Baldwin and McConville 1977, for a research-led critique of this general proposition). A variety of lawyers and defendants who pleaded not guilty in serious fraud cases have suggested that guilty pleas would have been offered if they had simply been charged under the Companies Acts and/or where they would have admitted gross recklessness rather than 'dishonesty' and so minimized damage to their reputations. Several persons acquitted in serious fraud cases had offered pleas which were rejected by the prosecution, partly because it wanted the 'offenders' to get substantial sentences. So long as that remains the case, making plea-bargaining official will make no difference.

The general sentencing practices in white-collar crime are unclear, and this also discourages guilty pleas, since it is uncertain what the sentence would be if the defendant pleaded not guilty. The guideline judgment of *R. v. Barrick*[15] was not mentioned in mitigation or by the judge in the Blue Arrow case when imposing suspended prison sentences which are specified in that guideline judgment as inappropriate for professional persons. No sentencing cases were mentioned in mitigation in Guinness either, and in the sentencing appeal of *Saunders et al.*, the court made no attempt to give guidance on what, if former Chief Executive Saunders had not suffered from Alzheimer's (as was mistakenly believed), the correct sentence would have been. Sentences of fourteen years were upheld by the Court of Appeal in the case of Abbas Gokal, convicted of a massive fraud involving BCCI, and ten years for Peter Clowes in a massive investment fraud involving Barlow Clowes. In the UK, alone among the Western world, the prosecution does not play an active role in the sentencing process, making no sentence recommendations or arguments about offence and offender seriousness. If the trials were held before judges without juries,

---

[15] (1985) 7 Cr. App. R (S) 142. See the extensive discussion in M. Levi, 'Suite Justice: Sentencing for Fraud' [1989] *Crim. LR* 420.

as considered by the Home Office Consultation Paper (1998), then defendants might be more inclined to plead guilty to get reduced sentences, but this might be because they did not expect to get a fair trial before a judge alone. On the other hand, one should not forget that many acquittals are at the direction of trial judges (Levi 1993, though less so in the subsequent period) so defendants may still wish to gamble, especially if the abolition of jury trial leads the SFO and other agencies to go for more adventurous and complex prosecutions.

THE IMPACT OF PROSECUTION ON DEFENDANT AND VICTIMS

For most high-status individual and corporate defendants the opportunity cost of being prosecuted is enormous, almost irrespective of the outcome. The process is the punishment. *After* their business has 'failed' or after conviction, directors can be disqualified by criminal courts (following offences committed 'in connection with the management of a company') or by civil courts. 1,284 directors were disqualified thus in 1998–9, a very substantial rise since 262 in 1993–4. The period of disqualification may vary between two and fifteen years: in 1998–9, 3 per cent were disqualified for over ten years; 34 per cent for six to ten years; and the remainder for two to five years.

Finally, we should note that one objective of the justice system—compensation for victims—is achieved in Europe for those who lose money to banks, insurance companies, and investment funds that are authorized to conduct financial services business by the FSA. In the period from August 1988 to April 2000 when the Investor Compensation Scheme (ICS) has been in operation, 16,329 claims were compensated (of which a quarter were in the year to April 2000). In 1999–2000, £51.6 million was paid by the ICS to investors, out of a total of £193 million in the twelve-year period altogether. This is a burden on the industry which pays a levy to the Scheme. By sustaining investors' confidence, this brings it more business than it would otherwise receive, and it also does a measure of justice irrespective of whether 'offenders' are prosecuted or can be made to compensate personally.

HUMAN RIGHTS AND THE RISKS OF MISCARRIAGES OF JUSTICE

Prima facie, one would expect most violations of rights to occur (1) when the crime under investigation is viewed very seriously, encouraging investigators to feel that they must 'do justice' (the 'Dirty Harry' syndrome); (2) when great organizational pressure is exerted towards obtaining 'a quick result', perhaps to reassure the public that 'crime' (or a particular sort of crime) is under control; and (3) when the individual under suspicion has a character that is tainted in the eyes of the investigators, creating the sense either that such a person 'must have done it' or that his conviction is 'overdue' (for even if he did not commit this crime, he will have got away with other previous or subsequent ones). By those criteria, we would not expect to find many miscarriages of justice in the area of corruption and fraud in the UK.

Nonetheless there remains widespread concern about the powers exercised by some agencies that investigate white-collar crime and about prosecution decisions, the trial process, verdicts, and sentences. The investigator's notion of 'efficiency' may be what a defendant views as 'oppression'. In the sphere of serious fraud prosecutions, oppression as seen by defendants may arise as the result of:

(i)   the compulsion to answer questions, whether or not these are admissible in subsequent criminal proceedings, but especially where the evidence *is* so used;[16]

(ii) delays and consequential economic and emotional costs which frequently accompany major investigations, whether or not they lead to prosecutions and convictions, which may be summarized as 'the process is the punishment';

(iii) the improper use of prosecutorial discretion, so that the 'less guilty' are prosecuted while the 'more guilty' are not; and

(iv) convictions which 'fly in the face of the evidence', or which have been obtained by improper means.

The term 'miscarriage' is an emotive one. The typical police/prosecutor perspective is that most miscarriages are those in which, as a result of substantive and procedural technicalities of law, many people who are guilty of serious commercial misconduct in which victims have lost vast amounts of money have been allowed to get away without being convicted or even charged. So far as miscarriages by way of unjust convictions are concerned, the only case in which my interviews in 1992 suggested a significant number of lawyers were convinced that their white-collar clients had been convicted, though innocent, was Blue Arrow (DTI 1989).[17] As I write in 2001, the *Guinness* case of 1988 awaits its final hearing before the Criminal Appeals Review Commission, which will have to determine whether current human rights standards are applicable retrospectively to cases over a decade earlier. But the questions are less to do with substantive issues (did they do what was alleged?) than with procedural human rights, e.g. (a) whether statements made under compulsion to the Department of Trade Inspectors were admissible against the defendants in their subsequent criminal trials; and (b) whether the prosecution withheld information from the trial that might have

---

[16] It is important to separate out more clearly than is commonly done the 'right to silence' from the 'privilege against self-incrimination'. See, for analytic guidance, the House of Lords decision in *R. v. Director of the Serious Fraud Office, ex parte Smith*, 11 June 1992.

[17] Though the Court of Appeal quashed the convictions because of the unmanageability of the trial, this does not lead to the conclusion that the defendants were innocent. Some defendants to whom I spoke admit that what was done by them was a serious error of judgement, though this does not imply breach of regulations or criminal law on their part. Apart from the actual conduct of the trial, the main issue is whether their states of mind were dishonest or reckless enough to place them over the borderline into 'fraud'.

assisted the defendants.[18] More common is the claim that what was done was perhaps done to evade taxes or capital export controls rather than to commit the specific fraud offences charged. Whether conviction in these circumstances counts as a miscarriage of justice is questionable, but one can understand the reluctance to make this a principal line of defence, and it plainly reduces the attractiveness of the complainant.

Whether in a Department of Trade and Industry (hereafter, DTI) report or, often some years after the event, in a criminal courtroom, the reconstruction of complex

[18] *Saunders v. United Kingdom* (1996) 23 EHRR 313. Suspicion of an unlawful share-support operation in the shares of Guinness plc had led to the appointment of inspectors, who had found evidence of criminal conduct and had thereafter interviewed Mr Saunders, formerly a director and the chief executive of Guinness, on 9 occasions. He was charged with numerous offences, and the prosecution sought to rely on the transcript of his interviews by the inspectors. The admissibility of such transcripts was challenged, but the judge ruled that under the relevant statute the inspectors were entitled to ask witnesses questions that tended to incriminate them, that the witnesses were under a duty to answer such questions, and that the answers were admissible in criminal proceedings. The issue before the European Court of Human Rights did not concern the propriety of compelling answers to the inspectors' questions at the investigatory stage but the propriety of admitting the evidence of those answers, compulsorily obtained, in the criminal proceedings. The Court ruled in Mr Saunders' favour

'68. The Court recalls that, although not specifically mentioned in Article 6 of the Convention, the right to silence and the right not to incriminate oneself, are generally recognized international standards which lie at the heart of the notion of a fair procedure under Article 6. Their rationale lies, *inter alia*, in the protection of the accused against improper compulsion by the authorities thereby contributing to the avoidance of miscarriages of justice and to the fulfilment of the aims of Article 6. The right not to incriminate oneself, in particular, presupposes that the prosecution in a criminal case seek to prove their case against the accused without resort to evidence obtained through methods of coercion or oppression in defiance of the will of the accused. In this sense the right is closely linked to the presumption of innocence contained in Article 6(2) of the Convention.

The Court does not accept the Government's premise on this point since some of the applicant's answers were in fact of an incriminating nature in the sense that they contained admissions to knowledge of information which tended to incriminate him. In any event, bearing in mind the concept of fairness in Article 6, the right not to incriminate oneself cannot reasonably be confined to statements of admission of wrongdoing or to remarks which are directly incriminating. Testimony obtained under compulsion which appears on its face to be of a non-incriminating nature—such as exculpatory remarks or mere information on questions of fact—may later be deployed in criminal proceedings in support of the prosecution case, for example to contradict or cast doubt upon other statements of the accused or evidence given by him during the trial or to otherwise undermine his credibility. Where the credibility of an accused must be assessed by a jury the use of such testimony may be especially harmful. It follows that what is of the essence in this context is the use to which evidence obtained under compulsion is made in the course of the criminal trial.

74. Nor does the Court find it necessary, having regard to the above assessment as to the use of the interviews during the trial, to decide whether the right not to incriminate oneself is absolute or whether infringements of it may be justified in particular circumstances.

It does not accept the Government's argument that the complexity of corporate fraud and the vital public interest in the investigation of such fraud and the punishment of those responsible could justify such a marked departure as that which occurred in the present case from one of the basic principles of a fair procedure. Like the Commission, it considers that the general requirements of fairness contained in Article 6, including the right not to incriminate oneself, apply to criminal proceedings in respect of all types of criminal offences without distinction, from the most simple to the most complex. The public interest cannot be invoked to justify the use of answers compulsorily obtained in a non-judicial investigation to incriminate the accused during the trial proceedings. It is noteworthy in this respect that under the relevant legislation statements obtained under compulsory powers by the Serious Fraud Office cannot, as a general rule, be adduced in evidence at the subsequent trial of the person concerned. Moreover the fact that statements were made by the applicant prior to his being charged does not prevent their later use in criminal proceedings from constituting an infringement of the right.'

corporate events is an inherently difficult and subjective exercise, even with the aid of
the documentary evidence that is often lacking in other areas of criminality. In serious
fraud trials, given that the necessary ingredients of the offence occurred within the
jurisdiction, the key issues usually relate to the interpretation of some mental element
on the part of the defendants (and, sometimes, prosecution witnesses): e.g. who was
party to which agreements? Was anyone actually deceived by them? Was the defendant
director acting as the directing mind of the company, or was he acting on his own?
Did each defendant have enough awareness of 'the big picture' to found culpability?
And if they did see the overall picture, did each defendant appreciate that there was a
risk that ordinary people would regard their actions as dishonest, as is required by
fraud case law? Many witnesses in fraud cases have an interest in portraying events in
a way that minimizes their culpability, sometimes, in the case of professionals such as
accountants and lawyers, to mitigate professional insurance liability as well as damage
to their reputations or even personal criminal liability. Conversely, if someone has run
businesses that have gone bust in the past, or mixes with professional criminals,
assumptions may be made about his or her character which lead to prosecution
(though these prior commercial experiences may not be admissible evidence). Let us
take one illustration, whose precise formulation may not be agreed totally by all sides
but the facts are sufficiently argued to illuminate the central issues.

THE RISK OF MISCARRIAGE: A CASE STUDY

The Inland Revenue was looking at tax-avoidance schemes which shade into evasion.
It was particularly concerned about the abuse of charitable status, and—reinforced by
pressure on it from the Public Accounts Committee of the House of Commons—
believed that the Charity Commissioners were far too lax in stopping the use of
charities as an artificial tax-avoidance strategy. If it could prove widespread evasion,
this would strengthen their hand in seeking to regulate charities. In the course of its
inquiries it came across systematic practices in several public schools which indicated
to it that there was fraudulent use of covenants and charitable vouchers, principally by
reducing the fees paid by parents by getting them to make covenants to the schools on
which tax could be reclaimed. The unpaid treasurer of one school was someone who
in his professional capacity had been involved in some major tax-avoidance schemes
which the Revenue had attempted to close down and the Revenue assumed that he
was the driving force behind what it construed as evasion, though it has stated that his
prior activities had no bearing on the decision to prosecute, which was taken on the
basis that his was the case on which the evidence was strongest and that an exemplary
prosecution had to be brought. There was some evidence that previous and the
present accounting officers of the school understood that they were engaged on 'a
fiddle', which in common parlance does not necessarily imply that they believed it to
be a crime, but the investigators assumed (or, more charitably, concluded) that these
persons were middlemen and used them as witnesses to launch a prosecution against
the treasurer, a former headmaster, and the school. Crucially, perhaps, for the failure
of the prosecution, the former headmaster had not received any financial benefit from
the alleged frauds, while the treasurer allegedly benefited in a very minor way from

some of the charity voucher frauds, though this was trivial compared with the donations he had given to the school.

Unfortunately, perhaps, for the accused, legal advice restrained them in the early stages from approaching the Revenue with their interpretation of the tax manoeuvres advice which rested on the difficult judgement that it might adversely affect them by revealing their defence to the prosecution. Even had the accused gone to it, the Revenue policy is that where it is minded from the beginning to prosecute for strategic reasons, it will interview under caution rather than under its normal civilized terms.[19] Several sources stated that in this case the Revenue never asked the suspects for an explanation and refused at any time to discuss the allegations with any representatives of the school, perhaps because it was concerned about the admissibility of statements made in such discussions, perhaps because it was keen to preserve its political independence from 'the Jewish lobby',[20] but perhaps also because of the prosecutorial tunnel vision of certitude, i.e. that it must be right, that can easily set in, and which is responsible for many miscarriages in the non-fraud area. Due to problems of proving that the individuals concerned were acting as the 'directing mind' of the school, which make corporate criminal liability difficult to prove,[21] the school itself was acquitted at the committal stage, for the magistrate was persuaded that the individuals were 'on a frolic of their own'. The individuals' defence was essentially that the avoidance schemes may have been artificial but that they were not done with any criminal intent on the part of the defendants. The trial judge later directed acquittal on most charges at the end of the prosecution case and the jury acquitted the individuals on the rest. Many jurors came up afterwards to hug the defendants, expressing surprise that the prosecution was ever brought. The forewoman of the jury told the former headmaster 'my heart bled for you'. The treasurer was awarded £50,000 towards his costs, even though the judge stated that, on some charges, he had 'brought the prosecution upon his own head'.

Was this a 'miscarriage of justice' in that the guilty were acquitted, or a near-miss of what would have been an unjust conviction which, acquittal notwithstanding, severely blighted the subsequent life of the Rabbi/headmaster who was prosecuted and affected more subtly the prominent businessman whose friends and colleagues stood by him throughout? Should the defendants, as the presumed 'organizers' of the alleged fraud, have been in the dock, should other school officials have been there instead, or should no-one at all have been prosecuted, since the acknowledged 'fiddle' may well not have been a crime at all? This is far from being typical of white-collar crime trials conducted by the Serious Fraud Office (or even by the Inland Revenue, which brought the school case), but it does indicate the dangers involved when

---

[19] The typical Revenue approach is to issue suspected fraudsters, as well as less culpable underpayers, with 'the Hansard warning': if they make full and frank disclosure, they will not be prosecuted, though they may be liable for back tax and penalties.

[20] It was not suggested by anyone I interviewed that the prosecution was motivated by anti-Semitism, nor was this raised as an issue during the trial. Nevertheless, the decision to prosecute the only significant Jewish boarding school in England was open to misinterpretation.

[21] The Law Commission has subsequently recommended a law on corporate killing, which the government intends to introduce, but this still does not resolve issues in fraud, corruption, and money laundering.

strategic prosecutions are brought to criminalize previously tolerated or undetected practices. It also indicates the difficulty of working out whether a miscarriage did occur. There were no faulty scientific procedures for example, nor—apart from the absence in the prosecution case of at least one example where a tax inspector had approved a scheme similar to that used in this school—were there any non-disclosures of important counter-factual evidence.[22]

INTERNATIONAL CO-OPERATION

Since the 1970s especially, a key area of concern has been international co-operation. It might have been expected that enhanced globalization of asset confiscation provisions under, *inter alia*, the Vienna Convention 1988 and the Council of Europe Convention 1990, might lead to prosecutorial pursuit of booty to finance investigations. Furthermore, the more general pressures from the Financial Action Task Force and the European Union to enhance judicial co-operation produce a side benefit for fraud, even though their primary purpose tends to be combating drugs and organized crime. However, because the assets are forfeited where they are found, at least where there are no identifiable victims, this has not happened. Rather, there is a desire to be seen to be doing something or, to the more cynically inclined, not to be seen to be doing nothing about a case. The establishment in 2001 of Eurojust—a central group of lawyers from the EU Member States—is aimed primarily at organized crime and fraud against the European Union, but may also smooth fraud investigations within those countries. However, many offshore finance centres are outside the EU, and it takes only one to frustrate a prosecution as well as asset recovery. (Though wealthy individuals and governments can pursue civil action as well.)

The international dimension of many frauds—73 per cent of new frauds reported to the City of London police during 1991 had a foreign element, and the proportion has risen subsequently—causes particular problems because far less can be done to compel the production of evidence outside the jurisdiction, particularly the evidence of live persons. Some of these difficulties can be predicted before the trial, or even before the charge, while others arise only during the trial. (See, generally, Henry 1992.) In one Customs & Excise VAT and customs duty case in 1992, several witnesses were concerned that their jobs might suffer if they had to come to the UK to give evidence. The solution adopted was that twelve witnesses in Hong Kong were examined and cross-examined in Hong Kong following a request by the defence on the ground that their evidence was important. It asked the trial judge to issue a Letter of Request under section 3 of the Criminal Justice (International Co-operation) Act 1990 to have the evidence deposed. The Attorney-General's Chambers in Hong Kong obtained an Order of the High Court to have this done, and the witnesses were issued

---

[22] It is not suggested that the Inland Revenue knew about the other Inspector's decision, but the defendants claimed to know and used that to buttress their claim of honest belief that what they were doing was not wrong.

with local subpoenas. Counsel for both sides flew out to Hong Kong for three weeks, and each night the tapes were couriered back to London to receive instructions from clients. Counsel then had to turn these into agreed depositions to be read to the jury. Evidence can be presented by satellite television, though care has to be taken that the witnesses do not make statements that are not legally admissible (which can happen also with live evidence in court).

Bibliography and Further Reading

AYRES, J., and BRAITHWAITE, J., *Responsive Regulation* (Oxford: Clarendon Press, 1992).

BALDWIN, J., and McCONVILLE. M., *Negotiated Justice* (Oxford: Martin Robertson, 1977).

Bingham Report, *Inquiry into the Supervision of The Bank of Credit and Commerce International* (London: HMSO, 1992).

BLUM, J., LEVI, M., NAYLOR, R., and WILLIAMS, P., *Financial Havens, Banking Secrecy and Money-Laundering*, Issue 8, UNDCP Technical Series (New York: United Nations UN document V.98–55024, 1998).

BOWER, T., *Maxwell: the Final Verdict* (London: HarperCollins, 1996).

BRAITHWAITE, J., and DRATHOS, P., *Global Business Regulation* (Cambridge: Cambridge University Press, 2000).

CORKER, D., and LEVI, M., 'Pre-trial Publicity and its Treatment in the English Courts' [1996] *Crim. LR* 622.

Department of Trade and Industry, *County NatWest and County NatWest Securities*, Department of Trade and Industry Inspectors' Report (London: HMSO, 1989).

DOIG, A., JOHNSTON, S., and LEVI, M., 'New Public Management, Old Populism and the Policing of Fraud' (2001) 16 *Public Policy and Administration* 91.

FISSE, B., and BRAITHWAITE, J., *Corporations, Crime, and Accountability* (Cambridge: Cambridge University Press, 1993).

Fraud Trials Committee Report (Chairman: Lord Roskill) (London: HMSO, 1986).

HENRY, MR. JUSTICE, 'Serious Fraud, Long Trials, and Criminal Justice', The 1992 Child & Co. Lecture (London: unpublished, 1992).

HONESS, T., LEVI, M., and CHARMAN, E., 'Juror Competence in Processing Complex Information: Implications from a Simulation of the Maxwell Trial' [1998] *Crim. LR* 763.

KIRK, M., and WOODCOCK, A., *The Serious Fraud Office* (2nd edn., London: Butterworths, 1996).

LEVER, L., *The Barlow Clowes Affair* (London: Macmillan, 1992).

LEVI, M., *The Phantom Capitalists: The Organisation and Control of Long-Firm Fraud* (Aldershot: Gower, 1981).

—— *Regulating Fraud: White-collar Crime and the Criminal Process* (London: Routledge, 1987).

—— 'The Role of the Jury in Complex Cases' in M. Findlay and P. Duff (eds.), *The Jury under Attack* (London: Butterworth, 1988).

—— 'Suite Justice: Sentencing for Fraud' [1989] *Crim. LR* 420.

—— *The Investigation, Prosecution and Trial of Serious Fraud*, Royal Commission on Criminal Justice Research Study No. 14 (London: HMSO, 1993).

—— and FANGMIN, R., 'Corruption Legislation and Socio-economic Change in the People's Republic of China', *Journal of Financial Crime* 116.

—— and PITHOUSE, A., *White-Collar Crime and its Victims* (Oxford: Clarendon Press, forthcoming).

—— and RAPHAEL, M., 'Anti-corruption—a Signpost for Transactional Lawyers' (1999) *Business Law International* 80.

McCONVILLE, M., SANDERS, A., and LENG, R., *The Case for the Prosecution* (London: Routledge, 1991).

MAYHEW, P., and VAN DIJK, J., *Criminal Victimisation in Eleven Industrialised Countries* (The Hague: WODC, Ministry of Justice, 1997).

Royal Commission on Criminal Procedure, *Report* (London: HMSO, 1981).

Serious Fraud Office, *Serious Fraud Office, Annual Report* (London: HMSO, 2000).

WOOD, J., 'The Serious Fraud Office' [1989] *Crim. LR* 175.

24

MENTALLY ABNORMAL OFFENDERS
Disposal and criminal responsibility issues

R. D. Mackay

The issue of the criminal liability and the disposal of mentally abnormal offenders presents special problems for both criminal and mental health law. On the one hand there is the fundamental notion that some mentally disordered offenders should be excused, have their responsibility reduced, or at the very least be dealt with therapeutically rather than punished. On the other hand issues of public protection, social defence, and the perceived risks posed by the mentally disordered continue to loom large in the shaping of policy. The result has been a tension which the current English legal framework has found it difficult satisfactorily to resolve. This in turn has culminated in a government White Paper which proposes a new Mental Health Act[1] together with a new strategy for dealing with high-risk patients.[2] This chapter will attempt to show how the current system dealing with mentally disordered offenders has perpetuated this tension and how current reform proposals seek to resolve this. In doing so it will briefly outline the current law relating to sentencing and disposal options and will argue for a greater emphasis to be placed on the issue of criminal responsibility, which has been eclipsed by other developments favouring hospitalization and treatment.

MENTALLY DISORDERED OFFENDERS AND THE MENTAL HEALTH ACT 1983

A person who has committed a criminal offence and is also found to be mentally disordered may be hospitalized rather than punished. However, before this form of involuntary hospitalization is examined, it is first necessary to mention that

---

[1] White Paper, *Reforming the Mental Health Act, Part I: The New Legal Framework*, Cm 5016–I. (2000).
[2] White Paper, *Reforming the Mental Health Act, Part II: High Risk Patients*, Cm 5016–II (2000).

there are other methods of dealing with such persons. It is best to deal with this in chronological order, from before until after the trial process.

POLICE POWERS OUTSIDE THE CRIMINAL PROCESS

Section 136 of the Mental Health Act 1983 provides that a police officer may remove to 'a place of safety' any person found in a 'place to which the public have access' and who appears to be suffering from mental disorder[3] and in immediate need of care or control, provided the officer thinks the removal is necessary in the interests of the person concerned or for the protection of other persons. No formality is required and the police officer need not suspect that any offence has been or will be committed. A 'place to which the public have access' includes parks, railway stations, shops, public houses, but not private premises, such as a dwelling house or the garden path.[4] However, the landing of a block of flats has been held to be a public place on the grounds of public access, but this depends on the facts.[5] A place of safety means residential accommodation provided by the local authority for the mentally disordered such as private or voluntary residential or nursing homes, even though they are not obliged to admit such persons. It also includes a hospital, a police station, or any other suitable places which are willing to receive the patient (section 135(6)).

Once at a place of safety detention is for up to seventy-two hours 'for the purpose of enabling him to be examined by a doctor and to be interviewed by an Approved Social Worker and of making any necessary arrangement for his treatment and care' (section 136(2)). No treatment can be imposed without consent (section 56(1)(b)). Detention lapses once these interviews are over provided no further action concerning admission is taken.

Clearly, the person detained need not actually be suffering from mental disorder and the Department of Health's view is that detention arises most often 'where a person's abnormal behaviour is causing nuisance or offence'.[6]

Such statistics as there are suggest that section 136 is rarely used outside London. However, it is clear that the statistics must be treated with caution.[7]

---

[3] Mental disorder is defined in s. 1(2) of the Mental Health Act 1983 as 'mental illness, arrested or incomplete development of mind, psychopathic disorder and any other disorder or disability of mind'.

[4] See *Edwards* v. *Roberts* (1978) 67 Cr. App. R 228.

[5] See *Knox* v. *Anderton* [1983] *Crim. LR* 114.

[6] See *Carter* v. *MPC* [1975] 2 All ER 33.

[7] See P. Bartlett and R. Sandland, *Mental Health Law—Policy and Practice* (London: Blackstone Press, 2000) 110.

CURRENT DISPOSAL OPTIONS

The Mental Health Act 1983 contains a range of methods for dealing with mentally disordered offenders. These are outlined in Home Office Circular No. 66/90 entitled 'Provision for Mentally Disordered Offenders'. At the outset it summarizes government policy by making it clear that 'wherever possible, mentally disordered persons should receive care and treatment from the health and social services' and that in cases where there is 'sufficient evidence to show that a mentally disordered person has committed an offence, careful consideration should be given to whether prosecution is required by the public interest'.[8] On the face of it diversion[9] and treatment are the overriding considerations. However, in the light of recent concerns over the suggested failure of existing legislation the government has made it clear that there is now a need for a 'modern legal framework [which] must offer the flexibility to tackle unacceptable risk to personal or public safety wherever it occurs'.[10] In short 'public protection will remain our first priority at all times'.[11] It is clear therefore that this is now the overriding criterion.

With this in mind we can now examine the current disposal options under the existing Mental Health Act 1983.

HOSPITAL CARE WHILE AWAITING TRIAL

REMANDS TO HOSPITAL

Sections 35 and 36 adopt proposals recommended in the Report of the Committee on Mentally Abnormal Offenders[12] (hereafter referred to as the Butler Report) that defendants in criminal cases may be remanded to hospital for a medical report (section 35) or for treatment (section 36). These sections provide an opportunity for a person who has been brought before a court to be examined or treated in hospital for a limited period (twenty-eight days with further twenty-eight-day periods for not more than twelve weeks in all) before the court makes a final decision.

Section 35 requires the evidence of a *single* approved practitioner that there is 'reason to suspect' that the accused (D) is suffering from one of the four specified forms of mental disorder and that it would be 'impracticable' for a report to be made if he were remanded on bail. Section 36 requires evidence of two doctors (one

---

[8] Home Office Circular No. 66/90, 'Provision for Mentally Disordered Offenders', para. 2.

[9] For a full discussion of diversion see J. Laing, *Care or Custody? Mentally Disordered Offenders in the Criminal Justice System* (Oxford: Oxford University Press, 1999).

[10] Department of Health, *Modernising Mental Health Services* (London: Department of Health, 1998) para. 4.27.

[11] *Ibid.*, at para. 5.   [12] Cmnd 6244 (1975), chap. 12.

approved) that D is suffering from a major disorder which makes it appropriate for him to be detained in hospital for medical treatment.

Neither of these powers has been greatly used with recent statistics showing that in 1996–7 there were 267 section 35 and thirty-three section 36 remands.[13] Further, the recommendation of the Reed Committee[14] to extend these powers has not been implemented, with the result there continue to be a considerable number of mentally disordered offenders who are inappropriately remanded in custody.[15]

Under section 48 of the 1983 Act the Home Secretary can direct that any person who has already been remanded in custody be transferred to hospital in any case where at least two doctors, one approved, report that the person is suffering from mental illness or severe mental impairment[16] of a nature or degree which makes it appropriate for him to be detained in hospital for medical treatment, and that he is in urgent need of this treatment. The doctors must agree on the form of disorder (section 47(4)).

All such transfers have the same effect as hospital orders (section 47(3)) with restrictions (section 49(1)) in the case of remand prisoners. The effect of this is that both magistrates and Crown Courts may make a hospital order over a transferred remand prisoner without trying him, since if when the case comes up for trial the prisoner is still in hospital, the court may make a hospital order in his absence without convicting him (see section 51(5)). Whether this is more satisfactory than a finding of unfitness to plead (see below) is now debatable in view of the fact it does mean detention without even a 'trial of the facts'.[17] Further, since the enactment of the Criminal Procedure (Insanity and Unfitness to Plead) Act 1991 flexibility of disposal has been introduced for unfitness to plead cases (except where the charge is murder).

The number of transfers under section 48 has risen dramatically in recent years from ninety-eight in 1989 to a maximum of 535 in 1994, and it may well be that this in turn is inhibiting the number of cases of unfitness to plead. Indeed, recent research into the operation of section 48 found that of a total sample of 370 transfers in 1992,

---

[13] Department of Health, *Statistical Bulletin 1998/01* (London: Department of Health, 1998).

[14] Department of Health/Home Office, *Review of Health and Social Services for Mentally Disordered Offenders and Others Requiring Similar Services*, Cmnd (1992) 2088.

[15] See A. Maden *et al.*, 'Mental Disorder in Remand Prisoners', Report commissioned by the Home Office Research and Planning Unit (London: Institute of Psychiatry, 1995).

[16] The 1983 Act does not define mental illness but defines severe mental impairment in s. 1(2) as 'a state of arrested or incomplete development of mind which includes severe impairment of intelligence and social functioning and is associated with abnormally aggressive or seriously irresponsible conduct'. This is to be contrasted with mental impairment, which is defined in exactly the same way except that the word 'significant' replaces the word 'severe'. Finally, s. 1(2) also defines psychopathic disorder as 'a persistent disorder or disability of mind (whether or not including significant impairment of intelligence) which results in abnormally aggressive or seriously irresponsible conduct'. Both mental impairment and psychopathic disorder are subject to a treatability criterion which requires that the medical treatment in hospital must be 'likely to alleviate or prevent a deterioration in his condition' (s. 3(2)(b)) before the compulsory admission for treatment of patients suffering from such mental disorders can take place.

[17] See R. (on the application of Kenneally) v. Snaresbrook Crown Court (2002) WLR 1430 where the Court of Appeal stated that s. 51 was to be used only in exceptional circumstances, as to pass sentence without first convicting was a drastic step.

while 76 per cent were subsequently convicted, a mere 2 per cent were found unfit to plead or not guilty by reason of insanity.[18] With regard to unfitness this is hardly surprising in view of the fact that such cases will either be dealt with under section 51(5) or treatment will have been effective or will at least have improved the patient's condition to such an extent that he is now fit to plead.

The research referred to above indicates that section 48 transfers play an important role in ensuring that mentally ill remand prisoners receive the treatment they need. Although the number of transfers fell to 473 in 1995, they rose again slightly to 494 in 1997. However, most recently the number of transfers again fell in 2000 to 393, the lowest figure since 1992.[19] This reduction in numbers seems odd in view of the continued increase in prison numbers. However, an increased pressure on bed availability seems likely to have been a contributing factor. The Department of Health's proposal to create more beds is welcome in this connection. The research also indicates that transfers have increasingly been made in cases involving less serious offences, which strongly indicates that it would be desirable to remove the requirement in section 48 that the prisoner has to be in 'urgent need of treatment'. In this way the scope of the section could be extended easily rather than relying on the current practice which may vary according to the attitude of particular psychiatrists as to whether a case is 'urgent' or not.

SENTENCING

The law gives a wide range of 'therapeutic' disposal methods after the conviction of a mentally disordered offender.

PSYCHIATRIC PROBATION ORDERS

Requirements of psychiatric treatment are contained in section 3 Powers of Criminal Courts Act 1973, as substituted by Schedule 1 to the Criminal Justice Act 1991.

A court may when making a probation order impose a condition of psychiatric treatment, which means that the offender can remain in the community and be treated or enter hospital informally or be treated as an outpatient, but he cannot be treated without consent. Before sentencing a doctor must state to the court that D's mental condition 'requires and may be susceptible to treatment but is not such as to warrant his detention in pursuance of a hospital order'.

This has been a relatively popular form of psychiatric disposal.

---

[18] R. D. Mackay and D. Machin, 'The Operation of Section 48 of the Mental Health Act 1983—An Empirical Study of the Transfer of Remand Prisoners to Hospital' (2000) 40 *Brit. J Criminology* 727.

[19] See *Home Office Statistical Bulletin 22/01, Statistics of Mentally Disordered Offenders* (London: Home Office, 2000), at Table 3.

HOSPITAL ORDERS

A hospital order may be made under section 37 for any offence, apart from murder, provided the court could impose a custodial sentence. The Crown Court must actually convict D unless he has already been transferred to hospital under section 48. Magistrates do not actually have to hold a trial provided they are satisfied that D did the act charged (section 37(3)).[20]

The criteria for imposition of a hospital order are as follows:

> Two doctors (one approved) must state that D is suffering from one of four mental disorders (mental illness, severe mental impairment, mental impairment, or psychopathic disorder) which makes it appropriate for him to be detained for medical treatment, and that in the case of the minor disorders (mental impairment or psychopathic disorder) that such treatment is likely to alleviate or prevent a deterioration of his condition; and the court is of the opinion 'having regard to all the circumstances, including the nature of the offence and the character and antecedents of the offender and to the other available methods of dealing with him' that the hospital order is the most suitable method of disposal.

The requirement of treatability in relation to minor disorders is likely to have had the effect of reducing the use of hospital orders in such cases.

Another likely reason for the reduction in number of hospital orders is the scarcity of beds. A hospital order cannot be made unless the court has evidence, either from the doctor who will be in charge of D's treatment or a representative from the named hospital or hospital unit, that a bed will be available within twenty-eight days (section 37(4)). As a result hospital orders have fallen by over a third since the 1960s and currently average about 700 *per annum*.[21]

The effect of a hospital order is that the defendant can be detained for up to six months, renewable for a further six months and then for a year at a time (section 40). There are two main differences between the hospital order and civil admission for treatment. First, the patient cannot be discharged by his nearest relative—who must make an application to a Mental Health Review Tribunal (MHRT)—and secondly, the offender, although he can appeal against the order, has no right to apply to an MHRT within the first six months of admission.

INTERIM HOSPITAL ORDERS

Interim hospital orders can also be made (under section 38) for twelve weeks renewable for twenty-eight days at a time up to twelve months. Here the requirements are that two doctors (one approved) give evidence that D is suffering from one of the four mental disorders and that it *may* be appropriate for a hospital order to be made. The offence must be one for which a full hospital order could be made. The purpose of an

---

[20] See *R. v. Lincoln Magistrates' Court, ex parte O'Connor* [1983] 1 All ER 901.

[21] See Home Office Statistical Bulletin 22/01, at Table 18 which reveals a figure of 749 for 1999, which remains close to the average for the last 10 years.

interim hospital order is to give the doctors the chance to see how the patient will respond to treatment, especially important in view of the treatability condition which will apply if a full hospital order is made later. Alternatively some other form of disposal including punishment or discharge if he is cured may be appropriate. These orders are rarely used.

RESTRICTION ORDERS

Under section 41 the Crown Court can add to a hospital order special restrictions on the discharge of the offender. A restriction order can be made only by the Crown Court which, in addition to the evidence needed for an ordinary hospital order, requires one of the doctors to give evidence in person (section 41(2)) as a result of which the court considers that special restrictions are 'necessary for the protection of the public from *serious harm*', having regard to the nature of the offence, the offender's record, and the risk of his committing further offences if set at large.

In *R. v. Birch*[22] the Court of Appeal made it clear that the 1983 Act had fundamentally altered the criteria for imposing a restriction, as under section 41 a restriction order can now only be made if it is 'necessary for the protection of the public from serious harm' where previously it was enough that there was serious risk of harm. The court is now required to assess, not the seriousness of the risk that D would re-offend, but the risk that if he did so the public would suffer serious harm. The court also made it clear that a restriction order should not be regarded as a form of punishment and the length of such an order is not related to the gravity of the offence.

The restrictions may be imposed for a definite or indefinite period (section 41(1)). However, in *R. v. Birch* it was confirmed that, because the function of such an order is not punitive but is to protect the public and because definite predictions about future dangerousness can rarely be made by doctors, orders should normally be made without a time-limit. Recent Home Office research confirms that time-limited orders are indeed rare, with only 6 per cent (n = 23) of a sample of 372 attracting such an order.[23] The study's findings indicate that restriction orders play a valuable 'role in controlling or even negating risk' but also drew attention to possible shortcomings. In particular, it expressed concern that in some cases restriction orders may have been imposed too readily by judges or recommended too hastily by psychiatrists in a desire to ensure post-discharge treatment rather than on the basis of a real assessment of risk. This type of concern is likely to have prompted Mustill LJ in *R. v. Birch* to remark that:

It might have been better if the conflicting social policies of the Act had been expressed in terms which set less stringent conditions for a restriction order, with perhaps a more flexible regime for discharge. As it is, the choice between a disposal which risks being too severe and one which with hindsight might be shown to have been not severe enough is posed in the terms of section 41.

---

[22] (1989) 11 Cr. App. R (S) 202.

[23] See R. Street, 'The Restricted Hospital Order: From Court to Community', Home Office Research Study No. 186 (London: Home Office, 1998).

It seems likely that over-caution on the part of judges may be the reason for the imposition of unwarranted restriction orders. It may be time, therefore, to consider Mustill LJ's proposal and introduce some mid-way provision between an ordinary hospital order and one with restrictions.

An additional concern about the present regime under section 41 relates to the fact that, because the vast majority of restriction orders are without limit of time, many patients are likely to spend longer in hospital than they would have spent in prison. In addition, the conditional discharge regime, together with the prospect of recall, raises legitimate civil liberties concerns, especially in the light of the fact that the recent Home Office research reveals that 'once recalled, these patients spent an average of almost two years in hospital'.[24] A more flexible discharge regime would go some way to answering these latter concerns, although it does nothing to deal with the former. Should there not be some degree of proportionality in restriction order cases? Is it fair that they should invariably be without limit of time irrespective of the nature of the offence? A simple way forward would be to reverse current practice by requiring the sentencing judge to declare the term of imprisonment he would have imposed had he not considered the case an appropriate one for a restriction order. This sentence would then become the 'cap' beyond which the restrictions would cease to have effect. Only in cases where the judge considered that the offence merited a term of life imprisonment would restrictions for an indefinite period be available.

HOSPITAL AND LIMITATION DIRECTIONS

A new 'hybrid' order was created in 1997 by section 46 of the Crime (Sentences) Act, which introduced two new sections (45A and 45B), into the 1983 Act. Before making such an order the court must be satisfied on the evidence of two doctors (one of whom must be approved and one of whom must give oral evidence) that D is suffering from psychopathic disorder, that the disorder is of a nature or degree which makes it appropriate for him to be detained in a hospital for medical treatment, and that such treatment is likely to alleviate or prevent a deterioration in his condition. The court must also have considered making a hospital order, unless D qualifies for a new automatic life sentence. The order is made in addition to a sentence of imprisonment and places D in much the same position as under a restriction order. But if D ceases to be in need of treatment before the end of his sentence he will be returned to prison. If he is still in hospital at the end of his sentence he will remain in hospital as if detained under an ordinary hospital order. This provision has come in for much criticism[25] and its utility is certainly open to question. Why should it apply only to psychopaths and why are existing powers not sufficient? The rationale given in Home Office Circular 52/1997 is that the hospital direction 'is intended to give the courts greater flexibility in dealing with cases where they conclude that a prison sentence is the appropriate disposal in spite of evidence that the offender is mentally disordered' (paragraph 4).

---

[24] N. 23 above, at 103.

[25] See N. Eastman and J. Peay, 'Sentencing Psychopaths: Is the "Hospital and Limitation Direction" an Ill-considered Hybrid?' [1998] *Crim. LR* 93.

Later it is made clear that although 'initially, the power is available only where the offender is suffering from psychopathic disorder' (paragraph 6) it may be extended to other categories of mentally disordered offender by order of the Secretary of State.

The fundamental effect of the hospital direction is that for the first time it openly mixes culpability with treatment. No longer are the two to be kept separate. Hitherto hospital orders, although premised on guilt, have been purely concerned with therapy, combined with risk in the case of restriction orders. However, as already mentioned, what this has meant is a lack of proportionality in respect of restriction orders. So would it be such a bad thing to extend the hospital direction to other forms of mental disorder? The answer to this question can be given only after a brief consideration of the role of mental condition defences.

TRANSFERS FROM PRISON

Under Section 47 the Home Secretary can direct that offenders serving prison sentences be transferred to hospital. He must have two medical reports that the prisoner is suffering from one of the four types of mental disorder. The conditions are then identical to ordinary hospital orders except that the Home Secretary must consider the transfer 'expedient' having regard to the public interest and all the circumstances: section 47(1). The patient must arrive at hospital within fourteen days of the direction and the Home Office must have secured a bed.

If the transfer is without restrictions (which is rare) he may apply to MHRT even within the first six months. If restrictions are imposed they cease automatically at the end of the sentence. He can apply to MHRT within the first six months, but even if discharged he may still be transferred back to prison if there is still some of his sentence to run.

The number of transfers under section 47 has greatly increased in recent years from ninety-four in 1987 to 271 in 2000.[26]

GUARDIANSHIP ORDERS

Guardianship orders can be imposed under section 37 in the same way as a hospital order provided the condition 'warrants . . . reception into guardianship'. They are used very rarely in criminal proceedings. In 1999 there were only ten such orders.[27]

MENTAL CONDITION DEFENCES

A defendant may seek to use his abnormal or disordered mental condition in answer to a criminal charge. The law within this area is a complex mix of common law and statute law. It is policy-based and lacks coherence. On the one hand it has

---

[26] See *Statistical Bulletin* 22/01.
[27] *Statistics under the Mental Health Act 1963* (London: Dept. of Health, 1999), at Table 1.

developed a range of excuses which may result in the accused's acquittal, while on the other hand it continues to be deeply troubled by the risks presented by mentally abnormal offenders. As a result the courts and Parliament have adopted a range of measures which seek to ensure public protection.[28]

UNFITNESS TO PLEAD

All defendants at trial are required to enter a plea of guilty or not guilty. But a mentally disordered offender may be found unfit to plead. This is not an 'excuse' as such because if found unfit to plead, D is not subject to an ordinary trial for the alleged offence. It represents an attempt by the law to protect defendants who are mentally incapable of participating in the trial process. Accordingly, the primary concern is with D's state of mind at the *present time*, rather than at the time of the alleged offence. The crucial question is, according to the case of *R v. Pritchard*,[29] whether D is 'of sufficient intellect to comprehend the course of proceedings in the trial so as to make a proper defence'. Thus, an illiterate deaf mute who is incapable of communication may not be tried.[30] A severely subnormal or psychotic may be unfit, but as long as he has sufficient understanding, he will be tried even if he is not able to act in his own best interests.[31]

Similarly in *R. v. Podola*[32] the Court of Appeal held that someone who was suffering from amnesia for the offence but who was capable of understanding the trial was fit to plead. But how can he give instructions for his defence if he cannot remember the incident, which led to the charge? The answer is that if D's mental state at the time of the trial is otherwise normal then he is fit to plead. *Podola* also decides that if D raises the fitness issue the civil burden of proof is upon him. But if the issue is raised by the prosecution, or presumably the judge, the full burden of criminal proof is on the prosecution.[33]

Formerly unfitness to plead was rarely put forward by defendants, largely because it was inevitably followed by an order that D be compulsorily detained in a hospital specified by the Home Secretary under the Criminal Procedure (Insanity) Act 1964.[34] As it originally stood, the unfit person could be detained for much longer than was appropriate for either the alleged offence or his mental state. In addition although he might have had a good defence which, had he been tried, would have led to an unqualified acquittal, the 1964 Act contained no requirement on the part of the prosecution to prove that the accused had committed any offence. This and other criticisms led to calls for reform which were implemented in the Criminal Procedure (Insanity and Unfitness to Plead) Act 1991, which came into operation in January 1992.

Although the 1991 Act leaves the legal tests for both unfitness to plead and the

---

[28] For detailed discussion see R. D. Mackay, *Mental Condition Defences in the Criminal Law* (Oxford: Oxford University Press, 1995).

[29] (1836) 7 C & P 303. [30] *R. v. Sharp* (1957) 41 Cr. App. R 196.

[31] *R. v. Robertson* [1968] 3 All ER 557. [32] [1959] 3 All ER 418. [33] N. 18 above.

[34] R. D. Mackay, 'The Decline of Disability in Relation to the Trial' [1991] *Crim. LR* 87.

defence of insanity (see below) unchanged, it nonetheless enacted procedural reforms of fundamental importance.

The major changes introduced by the 1991 Act are as follows:

Trial of the facts

A completely new procedure has been introduced in all cases where the jury has decided that the accused is unfit to plead. In essence this procedure requires the jury to examine any evidence already given, together with any further evidence adduced by the prosecution and the defence, in order that it may be satisfied that the accused 'did the act or made the omission charged against him as the offence'. If the jury are so satisfied then they will make a finding to that effect. However, this 'finding' is not the equivalent of a conviction. On the other hand if the jury are not so satisfied then a verdict of acquittal will be returned.

This procedure, referred to as 'a trial of the facts' in the long title to the Act, is clearly designed to remedy the criticism that under the 1964 Act there was no automatic requirement which ensured that the case against an accused found unfit to plead was tested, with the result that it was possible for innocent but mentally unfit persons to be detained in hospital indefinitely. The provision is an important safeguard for mentally unfit defendants. However, there has been difficulty about its interpretation.

On the one hand the Home Office Circular dealing with the 1991 Act indicated that mens rea (i.e. the state of mind which would have to be shown to be present if the defendant were to be convicted in the ordinary way of the offence with which he has been charged) is 'a matter which is *not* intended to be taken into account during the trial of the facts',[35] while on the other the Court of Appeal in *Egan*[36] decided that the Crown was required to prove 'all the necessary ingredients'[37] of the offence, including the mental ingredient. The Court of Appeal seemed to have in effect endorsed the approach of the Butler Report which recommended that 'on the trial of the facts the judge should direct the jury that if they are not satisfied that the defendant did the act *with the necessary mental state* they must return a verdict of not guilty'.[38] However, more recently the Court of Appeal cast doubt on this aspect of *Egan* on two occasions. First, in *Attorney-General's Reference (No. 3 of 1998)*[39] Judge LJ made it clear that *Egan* had no application to section 2(1) of the Trial of Lunatics Act 1883 which also requires the jury to be satisfied that the defendant 'did the act or made the omission charged' before returning a verdict of 'not guilty by reason of insanity'. Rather, after the jury is satisfied that the accused was legally insane 'the Crown is required to prove the actus reus of the crime'[40] and not the mens rea. Secondly in *Antoine*[41] the House of Lords decided that the plea of diminished responsibility could not be relied on during

---

[35] Home Office Circular 93/1991 at para. 8, emphasis added.

[36] [1998] 1 Cr. App. R 121.   [37] *Ibid.*, 125.

[38] Report of the Committee on Mentally Abnormal Offenders, Cmnd 6244 (1975), para. 10.24, emphasis added.

[39] [1999] 3 All ER 40.   [40] *Ibid.*, at 49.

[41] [2000] 2 All ER 208. See also *R. v. Grant, The Times*, 10 Dec. 2001, where the Court of Appeal ruled that provocation cannot be relied upon in the trial of the facts.

a trial of the facts for murder and also overruled *Egan*. In giving the judgment of the court Lord Hutton said 'by using the word "act" and not "offence" in subsection (2), Parliament made it clear that the jury was not to consider the mental ingredients of the offence'.[42]

However, although this seems to resolve the issue about the scope of the word 'act' in the relevant statutory provision (section 4A(2)), Lord Hutton expressed concern about cases where the defendant has an arguable defence of accident, mistake, or self-defence, especially as 'such defences almost invariably involve some consideration of the mental state of the defendant'. He sought to resolve this problem as follows:

> If there is objective evidence which raises the issue of mistake or accident or self-defence, then the jury should not find that the defendant did the 'act' unless it is satisfied beyond reasonable doubt on all the evidence that the prosecution has negatived that defence. For example ... if a woman was charged with theft of a handbag and a witness gave evidence that on sitting down at a table in a restaurant the defendant had placed her own handbag on the floor and, on getting up to leave, picked up the handbag placed beside her by a woman at the next table, it would be open to the jury to acquit.[43]

Although such an acquittal clearly results from a lack of mens rea as the woman in question is not dishonest, what this approach apparently does not allow is to require the prosecution to prove mens rea in all cases where there is a 'trial of the facts'. However, apart from permitting the accused himself to deny mens rea, it is difficult to understand what other limitations Lord Hutton has in mind, and it remains to be seen how this apparent compromise will operate in practice.

The second point worthy of comment concerns the burden of proof in relation to the trial of the facts. The Act is silent on this matter. It merely states that the jury must be 'satisfied' that the accused 'did the act or made the omission charged'. However the 1991 Circular clearly states at paragraph 9 that 'the test in regard to burden of proof should be consistent with other criminal proceedings (beyond reasonable doubt)', which seems right in principle. Finally, in *Moor et al.*,[44] the Court of Appeal ruled that Article 6 of the European Convention on Human Rights does not apply to the trial of the facts as the proceedings in question are not criminal in nature as they cannot result in a conviction.

FLEXIBILITY OF DISPOSAL

The 1991 Act introduced a much more flexible range of disposals in cases of both unfitness to plead and the defence of insanity. In addition to the restriction order which inevitably resulted from a finding of unfitness or legal insanity under the 1964 Act the court has been given the discretion to order admission to hospital without restrictions, or to make a guardianship order under the Mental Health Act 1983, or a supervision and treatment order, or an order for the absolute discharge of the accused. However, with regard to a finding of unfitness to plead none of these powers will be available unless the jury has found that the accused did the act or omission charged.

---

[42] N. 41 above, at 221.   [43] *Ibid.*, 222.   [44] [2002] *Crim. LR* 57.

Admission orders

The provisions relating to admission to hospital (which are set out in Schedule 1 to the 1991 Act) make it clear that an admission order with or without restrictions will now be available for all offences charged, with the exception of murder, where the court will continue to be required to make a restriction order without limitation of time.

Guardianship orders

Section 37 of the Mental Health Act 1983 has been adapted by the 1991 Act for the purpose of enabling those found unfit to plead and legally insane to receive care and protection rather than medical treatment. The information set out in Home Office Circular 66/90 (Provision for Mentally Disordered Offenders) at paragraph 8(1v)(c) is applicable to the making of such orders.

Supervision and treatment orders

Schedule 2 to the 1991 Act contains detailed provisions relating to the operation of this new form of order which is modelled on psychiatric probation orders under the Powers of Criminal Courts Act 1973 (as amended by the Criminal Justice Act 1991). The order, which is not a punitive measure, will allow for supervision to be carried out by a social worker or a probation officer for a period of not more than two years. However an order cannot be made unless the court considers that this is the most suitable means of dealing with the accused and is in possession of the necessary evidence of at least two doctors, one of whom must be duly approved. The order requires the supervised person to submit to medical treatment with a view to the improvement of his mental condition. In this context it is interesting to note that although paragraph 4(1) of Schedule 2 to the 1991 Act uses the word 'submit', the 1991 Circular prefers the word 'undergo' (see paragraph 17(c)(vii)) in order to emphasize that 'in the final analysis the order should not be conditional on the willingness of the accused to comply [as] the court will have no power to enforce the order or otherwise intervene in cases of non-compliance'. Accordingly, if the supervisor considers that compulsory medical treatment has become necessary then the provisions of Part II of the Mental Health Act 1983 will have to be used.

Finally, Part III of Schedule 2 to the 1991 Act contains detailed provisions relating to the revocation and amendment of such orders upon application to the magistrates' court.

Absolute discharge

The new section 5(2)(b)(iii) of the 1991 Act gives the court the option to make an order for the absolute discharge of the accused, while section 5(4) of the 1991 Act expressly applies section 1(A)(1) of the Powers of Criminal Courts Act 1973 to cases of unfitness to plead and insanity. The 1991 Circular's comment on the form of order is brief and is to the effect it might be used 'where the alleged offence was trivial and the accused clearly does not require treatment and supervision in the community'.

Murder charges

It is important to note that the only restriction on these flexible disposal provisions is in relation to a charge of murder where the trial judge will continue to be required to impose a restriction order. On this point the only comment made by John Patten during Parliamentary debate was that the preservation of the mandatory hospital disposal was 'very important for public protection'.[45] It is abundantly clear, therefore, that this decision to retain restriction orders for murder charges is a pure policy decision and is a cause for concern, in that there seems little doubt that its effect will be to continue to 'force' those mentally ill defendants charged with murder to avoid the result of pleading unfitness and insanity by pleading guilty to manslaughter by reason of diminished responsibility, and thus to retain the very disadvantages for this group of offenders which the Act seeks to remedy.

Miscellaneous matters

Section 1 of the Act provides that a jury is not to acquit on the ground of insanity except on the evidence of two or more doctors, one of whom must have special experience in the field of mental disorder, while section 2(6) introduces a similar provision in respect of unfitness to plead.

Section 4 of the Act amends the Criminal Appeal Act 1968, thus making, with respect to appeals to the Court of Appeal, provision corresponding to that made in sections 1 to 3 of the 1991 Act.

Schedule 1 to the Act retains the Home Secretary's power to remit for trial those found unfit to plead, but only in respect of those who are detained in hospital with restrictions, provided he is satisfied that the patient can properly be tried. Further, the Schedule now gives the Home Secretary the option of remitting such persons direct to court rather than to prison.

The Act makes it clear (see Schedule 1 paragraph 4(2)) that remission for trial in respect of hospital orders without restrictions in now impossible but is silent in relation to other forms of disposal under the 1991 Act. However, since the Act does not expressly prevent proceedings being otherwise recommenced, one must assume that it will be legally permissible for the Crown Prosecution Service to revive proceedings against those who later regain fitness but were not subject to a restriction order. How often this is likely to happen is difficult to know, but as there is no specific legal machinery contained in the 1991 Act to deal with such 'revivals' it seems likely that they may be rare. In any event, the chances of it being in the public interest to remit those subject to Guardianship Orders or Supervision and Treatment Orders seem remote unless D himself is insisting on his right to a full trial of the issue which in any event will already have led to a finding that 'he did the act or made the omission charged'.

The new sections 4(5) and 4A of the Act deal with the question of when it is appropriate for a fresh jury to be empanelled to decide the issue of fitness to plead, or to deal with the trial proper, or to decide the 'trial of the facts'.

[45] HC Debs, Vol. 186 No. 67 at col. 1279, 1 Mar. 1991.

Comment

The primary importance of the 1991 Act lies in the much-needed flexibility of disposal, which it introduces. There seems little doubt that the mandatory disposal measure contained in the 1964 Act was a major reason both unfitness to plead and insanity were rarely used.[46] Accordingly, there was some reason to suppose that the numbers of such cases will increase, and while this did not happen in 1992—the first year of the Act's operation—there has been an increase in numbers in subsequent years. Indeed a comparison of the last five years of the 1964 Act with the first five years of the 1991 Act reveals that there were sixty-one insanity and 125 unfitness to plead cases.[47]

THE DEFENCE OF INSANITY

In the Crown Court the defence of insanity is based exclusively on the McNaghten Rules, which require D to prove that he 'was labouring under such a defect of reason, from disease of the mind, as not to know the nature and quality of the act he was doing, or, if he did know it, that he did not know he was doing what was wrong'.[48]

By way of contrast, in magistrates' courts it has been decided that the common law defence of insanity has not been removed by legislation and is still available to a defendant in a summary trial.[49] However, it remains unclear what form the defence takes if it is not governed by the McNaghten Rules.

The whole defence revolves around the phrase 'disease of the mind' (DOM) which the judges, when expounding the Rules, seem to have regarded as analogous to insanity. Neither 'DOM' nor 'insanity' is a recognized medical concept. To the psychiatrist they are not meaningful and are no longer used in a medical context. The most apt medical equivalent to DOM is probably 'mental disorder', and for 'insanity' perhaps 'functional psychoses', which include schizophrenia and the affective disorders such as manic-depression.

Clearly then, insanity and DOM are purely legal concepts which have nothing to do with current psychiatric thought. This is despite the fact that psychiatric evidence is essential if an insanity defence is to succeed.[50]

Instead, what has occurred is that the concept of DOM has developed in the light of two conflicting principles, each struggling for dominance. They are (1) the need to protect society from certain types of mentally abnormal offender whilst at the same time recognizing that if such a person is found insane then he is irresponsible and cannot be 'punished'—hence the inevitable 'special verdict', (2) the need to control the scope of DOM so that certain types of condition can be excluded where it would be 'an affront to common sense' to declare such a person 'insane'. This principle has

---

[46] See Mackay, n. 32 above.

[47] See R. D. Mackay and G. Kearns, 'An Upturn in Unfitness to Plead? Disability in Relation to the Trial under the 1991 Act' [2000] *Crim. LR* 532.

[48] (1843) 10 Cl. & F 200 at 210.

[49] R. v. *Horseferry Road Magistrates' Court, ex parte K* [1996] 3 All ER 719.

[50] Criminal Procedure (Insanity and Unfitness to Plead) Act 1991, s. 1(1).

of course led to the development of the automatism defence, and indeed it is the development of the latter which has regularly caused the judiciary to consider whether particular mental conditions should be classed as diseases of the mind. Thus in *R. v. Kemp*,[51] where D suffered from arteriosclerosis, Devlin J confirmed that such a condition could fall within 'disease of the mind' saying:

In my judgement the condition of the brain is irrelevant and so is the question of whether the condition of the mind is curable, incurable, transitory or permanent.[52]

This approach has since been followed by the House of Lords on two occasions. First, in *Bratty* v. *A-G for N. Ireland*,[53] D, in answer to a murder charge, put forward defences of insanity and automatism based on a black-out due to epilepsy. In the course of his judgment, Lord Denning said:

The major mental diseases which doctors call psychoses, such as schizophrenia, are clearly diseases of the mind. But in *Charlson* Barry J. seems to have assumed that other diseases such as epilepsy or cerebral tumours are not diseases of the mind, even when they are such as to manifest themselves in violence. I do not agree with this. It seems to me that any mental disorder which has manifested itself in violence and is prone to recur is a disease of the mind.

Secondly, in *Sullivan*,[54] D was a life-long sufferer from epilepsy who, in answer to an assault charge, claimed at the time he was in the final stage of recovery from a minor epileptic seizure. The trial judge ruled that if the jury accepted the unanimous medical evidence they must return an insanity verdict (whereupon D, in order to prevent this, changed his plea to guilty).

In deciding that D's epileptic seizure constituted a DOM, Lord Diplock said:

The nomenclature adopted by the medical profession may change from time to time . . . but the meaning of the expression 'disease of the mind', as a cause of a 'defect of reason' remains unchanged for the purposes of the application of the McNaghten Rules. I agree with what was said by Devlin J. in *Kemp* that 'mind' in the McNaghten Rules is used in the ordinary sense of mental faculties of reason, memory and understanding. If the effect of a disease is to impair these faculties so severely as to have either of the consequences referred to in the latter part of the rules, it matters not whether the aetiology is organic, as in epilepsy, or functional, or whether the impairment itself is permanent or is transient and intermittent, provided that it subsisted at the time of the commission of the act.[55]

Interestingly, neither of the expert witnesses was prepared to classify D's condition as a DOM, since loss of consciousness for such a brief period of time could not be regarded psychiatrically as a mental illness, which would require the disorder to last for a period of time (one doctor saying more than one day, the other saying a minimum of a month). Indeed psychiatrists would not normally classify epilepsy as a form of mental illness at all. Rejecting this distinction, Lord Diplock said:

---

[51] [1957] QB 399. Compare *R. v. Charlson* [1955] 1 All ER 859.
[52] N. 51 above, at 406.   [53] [1963] AC 386.
[54] [1983] 2 All ER 673.   [55] *Ibid.*, at 677–8.

The purpose of the legislation relating to the defence of insanity ... has been to protect society against the recurrence of dangerous conduct. The duration of a temporary suspension of the mental faculties of reason, memory and understanding ... cannot on any rational ground be relevant to the application by the courts of the McNaghten Rules.

Clearly, *Sullivan* favours an expansionary definition of DOM in order to ensure protection of the public. However, Lord Diplock did concede the existence of the automatism defence, as will be noted later. Despite this DOM remains a wide-ranging term which is capable of including all forms of mental illness, whether organic or functional. The factors which restrict the scope of the insanity defence are the other requirements contained in the McNaghten Rules. These are:

(i) The DOM must have caused a 'defect of reason', a concept which has been used to exclude those who through absentmindedness or confusion of thought merely fail to make full use of their reasoning powers. In *R. v. Clarke*[56] D in answer to a shoplifting charge put forward the defence of lack of mens rea owing to absentmindedness due to depression. The medical evidence described D's condition as 'a minor mental illness' but the trial judge ruled in favour of insanity. On appeal the Court of Appeal held that whilst there might have been evidence of DOM there was *no* defect of reason, as the McNaghten Rules did not apply 'to those who retain the power of reasoning but who in moments of confusion or absentmindedness fail to use their powers to the full'.[57]

(ii) *R. v. Clarke* makes it clear that the intellectual defect capable of supporting an insanity plea must be a major one, and this is emphasized by the need for either lack of knowledge about 'the nature or quality of the act' which, according to Lord Diplock in *R. v. Sullivan*, means 'he did not know what he was doing' or 'that he did not know he was doing what was *wrong*', which in *R. v. Windle*[58] was restricted to 'legal' wrong. This second limb seems in theory to add very little to the first, since the McNaghten Rules require such a major defect in intellectual capacity that in the majority of cases both limbs will be satisfied. In other words, if D fails to realize that the killing or arson, etc., is legally wrong, it is likely that he also did not realize what he was doing. However, in practice the wrongness limb appears to be used most frequently when the insanity defence is used.[59]

AUTOMATISM

This defence, which recognizes the need for a voluntary act before D can be convicted, may lead to an outright acquittal and its relationship with insanity has created a complex body of law.

---

[56] [1972] 1 All ER 219.   [57] *Ibid.*, at 221.   [58] [1952] 2 All ER 1.
[59] See R. D. Mackay and G. Kearns, 'Fact and Fiction about the Insanity Defence' [1990] *Crim. LR* 247 and 'More Fact(s) About the Insanity Defence' [1999] *Crim. LR* 714.

Automatism, which is defined in *Bratty* as 'unconscious involuntary action',[60] has given rise to problems stemming in the main from the unqualified acquittal which results if the defence succeeds. Because of this the courts have restricted the scope and availability of this defence. This has been achieved in the main by dividing automatism into insane and non-insane varieties. By using this dichotomy, the courts have been able to ensure compulsory detention in cases where the automatism is caused by a DOM. Here we have a wide gulf between the legal and medical professions which can be explored by considering some of the different conditions which may give rise to such a defence.

Preliminary points

First, it should be appreciated that in medical usage the term automatism is normally restricted to epilepsy. However, despite this it is well recognized amongst psychiatrists that a person's normal state of consciousness and awareness may be interfered with by a whole host of different factors.

Secondly, it must be remembered that whether D's condition is to be regarded as automatism is a question of law which is for the most part entirely dependent on psychiatric evidence. This means that for all practical purposes, before the evidential burden can be satisfied, psychiatric evidence must be adduced in order to 'lay a proper foundation' for the defence.

Thirdly, it must be realized that, when giving his expert evidence, the psychiatrist is required to testify to the mental condition as psychiatrically recognized, not to 'automatism' which is a legal concept, although not a term of art, and was described in *Watmore* v. *Jenkins*[61] as a mere 'catchword'.

From the medical perspective, automatism is often divided into four groups—Normal, Organic, Psychogenic, and Feigned. Each deserves examination.

(1) Normal automatism occurs where the patient is regarded as essentially normal, i.e., there is no disorder of the mind found. Sleepwalking is a common example which had until recently been used to support an automatism defence and an outright acquittal, e.g. in *Boshears*.[62] But such a result is no longer possible in the light of *Sullivan*, where Lord Diplock restricted automatism to temporary impairment from some external physical factor. There is no such external factor in sleepwalking. Yet it seems harsh, if there is no underlying pathology, to subject the sleepwalker to the special verdict. However, in *R.* v. *Burgess*[63] the Court of Appeal ruled that sleepwalking was automatism of the insane variety.

In arriving at its decision the Court of Appeal emphasized that the fundamental question was whether the accused was suffering from a disease of the mind within the McNaghten Rules 'rather than a defect or failure of the mind not due to disease' and that this was 'a distinction, by no means always easy to draw, on which the case depended'.

---

[60] [1963] AC 386 at 403.　　[61] [1962] 2 QB 572 at 586.

[62] *The Times*, 17 & 18 Feb. 1961.　　[63] [1991] 2 All ER 769.

(2) Organic automatism can be caused by a great many factors. Here the distinction between insane and sane automatism becomes all-important. The most well researched form of organic automatism is epilepsy. Psychomotor epilepsy is most associated with automatism. There are isolated cases where serious violence does occur, as in *Sullivan*. Here, it will be recalled, the fact that the episode was brief did not prevent epilepsy being classed as a DOM which caused D to change his plea to guilty. Such a position is of course quite untenable, as is the distinction between internal conditions such as epilepsy and external factors, as in the consumption of drugs which may lead to a sane automatism plea. This is admirably demonstrated by diabetes and hypo-glycaemic episodes, where in *Quick*[64] an imbalance in blood sugar causing dimming of normal consciousness was recognized as sane automatism. It is difficult to support this in view of the fact that D's condition here is linked to his organic pathology, i.e. the diabetes. The courts however lay emphasis on the external factor here, namely the insulin, etc. in the same way that they regard a blow on the head as an external factor giving rise to sane automatism.[65]

(3) Psychogenic automatism is caused by hysterical neurosis resulting in dissociation. Once again the major problem here is whether automatism based on psychological shock should be classed as sane or insane automatism. In *Rabey*[66] the Supreme Court of Canada held that the ordinary stresses and disappointments of life (such as being jilted by one's girlfriend) do not constitute an 'external cause'. Thus D was found legally insane despite the fact that (a) he was not found to be suffering from any underlying pathology, (b) the violence was unlikely to recur, and (c) no treatment was needed. In the light of *Sullivan*, it is possible that this approach would be followed in England, especially as the emotional blow does not seem to qualify as an 'external physical factor'.[67] However in this connection the first instance case of *R. v. T*[68] is interesting. There the judge ruled that automatism induced by post traumatic stress caused by a rape, to which D had been subjected three days before the alleged offence, was an 'external factor [as] such an incident could have an appalling effect on any young woman, however well balanced'.[69]

Feigned automatism and amnesia

The fact that D could easily feign automatism is a constant source of worry to the courts. Indeed, this is one reason why amnesia is not itself a defence to a criminal charge. Despite this amnesia is a prevalent factor in automatism. The medical profession recognizes that the remembering process may be disturbed in any one of three

---

[64] [1973] QB 922.

[65] See the problem of diabetes raised in *Hennessy* [1989] 2 All ER 9, where Lord Lane CJ said at 14: 'hyperglycaemia, high blood sugar, caused by an inherent defect and not corrected by insulin is a disease, and if, as the defendant was asserting here, it does cause a malfunction of the mind, then the case may fall within the McNaghten Rules'.

[66] (1978) 79 DLR 414.   [67] [1983] 2 All ER 673 at 678.   [68] [1990] *Crim. LR* 256.

[69] *Ibid.*, at 257.

ways. (1) Failure of registration is where the subject's attention is impaired and is caused by any condition which affects the normal level of consciousness. The extent of the amnesia depends on the degree of clouding. (2) Failure to retain material already registered, which is usually the result of organic brain damage as in senile dementia. (3) Failure to recall memories which have been registered and retained is psychogenic and is normally an unconscious repression of unpleasant memories.

As far as automatism is concerned, it is failure of registration which is important, since when this occurs amnesia for the crime will usually be complete. If D can recall the crime in detail, he is most unlikely to have been in a state of automatism. Only careful questioning can discover whether the amnesia is genuine. In recent research into amnesia after criminal offences it was found to be prevalent especially after homicide, but none of the amnesias were found to have any legal implications.

Comment

To the medical profession, the distinction between insane and sane automatism is arbitrary and absurd. The courts now seem to have ignored the recurrence problem and the question whether D needs treatment seems to be unimportant. In addition, the law fails to recognize that there are different levels of consciousness whilst the medical profession allow for at least *five* different levels, namely:

(1) Full awareness—normal consciousness;

(2) Clouded consciousness;

(3) Delirium causing disorientation and hallucination—usually the result of a toxic process;

(4) Stupor causing decreased mobility, which is usually of organic origin;

(5) Coma where there is no consciousness or normal activity of any kind.

Automatism may occur in (2), (3), and (4) and it is clear that when the law demands that D be unconscious, it cannot require coma, and hence the law ought to recognize that different levels of consciousness exist.

Finally, there is no doubt that the unqualified acquittal which sane automatism attracts presents a dilemma for the courts which has resulted in repeated attempts to curtail the scope of the defence. Indeed, some may argue that with public protection as a first priority, automatism sits uneasily in a contemporary mental health framework. Such considerations have led to proposals in Canada to create a new 'verdict of not criminally responsible on account of automatism'[70] which, if implemented, would be followed by a disposition hearing which could result in a hospital order or an absolute or conditional discharge. Such a development would take place instead of the unqualified acquittal which sane automatism attracts and would align the plea more closely with the insanity defence as well as satisfying policy concerns about social defence.

---

[70] For discussion see Mackay, n. 23 above, at 71.

DIMINISHED RESPONSIBILITY[71]

In cases of murder the mandatory penalty of life imprisonment poses problems when dealing with the mentally disordered offender. However, some flexibility has been introduced by section 2(1) of the Homicide Act 1957 which allows for the plea of diminished responsibility, which reduces murder to manslaughter, giving the judge discretion as to sentencing.

The scope of the defence

What different forms of mental disorder may be used to support a plea under section 2? Clearly, the crucial concept here is 'abnormality of mind', which has been interpreted much more widely than DOM in the McNaghten Rules. Although 'abnormality of mind' is not expressly defined, the words in brackets in section 2 restrict the defence to mental abnormality 'arising from a condition of arrested or retarded development of mind or any inherent causes or induced by disease or injury'.

In the case of *R. v. Dix*[72] the Court of Appeal made two important points. First, the part of section 2(1) in brackets is descriptive of all forms of mental abnormality within the section. Secondly, medical evidence is essential, and without psychiatric evidence a section 2 plea is impossible.

The leading authority on 'abnormality of mind' is *R. v. Byrne*[73] where it was defined as 'a state of mind so different from that of ordinary human beings that the reasonable man would term it abnormal. It appears to us to be wide enough to cover the mind's activities in all its aspects—[including] the ability to exercise will-power to control physical acts in accordance with rational judgement.'

Thus, irresistible impulse has been brought into English law through the plea of diminished responsibility.

So far as the words in brackets are concerned, they cater for a very wide variety of disorders. 'Arrested or retarded development of mind' clearly caters for mental handicap which in Dell's research[74] applied in only 10 per cent of diminished responsibility pleas during a ten-year period. Other than this the problem here is that the four specified categories in brackets 'have no defined or agreed psychiatric meaning'[75] and yet the report should stipulate the cause of the abnormality. Such lack of certainty is bound to give rise to disagreement in many cases. Dell's research reveals that in about one-third of all cases psychosis was the mental abnormality which brought section 2 into play and that in 90 per cent of these cases the condition was described as a 'disease'. Of the non-psychotic population, Dell found that the two largest groups were personality disorders and depression. Here there is considerable difficulty. For example, endogenous depression of an hereditary nature tends to be classified as due to 'inherent causes', but reactive depression due to emotional upset, etc., is not

---

[71] See R. D. Mackay 'Diminished Responsibility and Mentally Disordered Killers' in A. Ashworth and B. Mitchell (eds.), *Rethinking English Homicide Law* (Oxford: Oxford University Press, 2000) chap. 3.

[72] (1982) 74 Cr. App. R 306.   [73] [1960] 2 QB 396 at 403.

[74] S. Dell, *Murder into Manslaughter—The Diminished Responsibility Defence in Practice* (Oxford: Oxford University Press, 1984).

[75] *Ibid.*, at 39.

normally regarded as a disease entity and is sometimes attributable to 'psychological injury'. Similarly, doctors face real problems in trying to assess where abnormality of personality begins and how such a condition is to be classified. Is it properly regarded as an arrested development of mind or is it an inherent cause?[76]

In many cases the courts have been prepared to include a whole host of different types of less serious forms of mental condition within the scope of abnormality of mind in order that a lenient sentence or disposal may be achieved. Thus, killings motivated by morbid jealousy, a form of psychosis, have resulted in section 2 pleas where probation or suspended sentences were felt appropriate.[77] In addition, there have been a series of 'mercy-killing' cases where a parent kills a severely handicapped child[78] or where a terminally ill person is relieved of further suffering by a loved one,[79] which have stretched the idea of 'abnormality of mind' even further. The diagnosis in these cases is commonly reactive depression, but once again there is the obvious problem of distinguishing between normal and abnormal here. Thus whilst some doctors will classify this form of reactive depression as a form of mental illness, others regard it as a normal reaction to human misery and do not think of it in terms of mental illness and abnormality. In this way psychiatric concepts are stretched and pulled in the hope of achieving an acceptable result, and the truth seems to be that diminished responsibility 'is interpreted more in accordance with the morality of the case than in relation to an application of psychiatric ideas'.[80]

Although the words in brackets do not encompass a condition caused solely by drink or drugs, nevertheless if there is a combination of intoxicants with other matters such as depression, the jury must consider whether the depression without the intoxication would be enough substantially to impair his mental responsibility.[81]

In order to succeed the abnormality of mind must substantially impair D's 'mental responsibility'. This is certainly not a clinical fact relating to D; instead it seems to be that psychiatrists are being required to testify to D's moral responsibility; yet the psychiatrist is no better equipped to judge this than anyone else.

The problem is exacerbated by the word 'substantial' which psychiatrists are also asked to testify in relation to, and in *Lloyd*[82] it was held that '[s]ubstantial does not mean total . . . but at the other end of the scale it does not mean trivial or minimal'. Clearly, therefore, it is a question of degree which, if the medical evidence is conflicting, is properly one for the jury.

---

[76] For discussion see R. D. Mackay, 'The Abnormality of Mind Factor in Diminished Responsibility' [1999] *Crim. LR* 117.

[77] See *Miller, The Times*, 16 May 1972; *Asher, The Times*, 9 June 2000.

[78] See *Gray* (1965) 129 JPN 819; *Price, The Times*, 22 Dec. 1971.

[79] See *Jones, The Times*, 4 Dec. 1979.

[80] G. Williams, *Textbook of Criminal Law* (2nd edn., London: Stevens: 1983) 693.

[81] For the complexity involved here, see e.g. *R. v. Gittens* [1984] 3 All ER 252; *R. v. Tandy* (1987) 87 Cr. App. R 45, [1989] 1 All ER 267; *R. v. Inseal* [1992] *Crim. LR* 35; *R. v. Egan* [1992] 4 All ER 470.

[82] [1967] 1 QB 175.

DISCUSSION

Although the section above on mental condition defences presents a complex body of law what is immediately apparent is the paucity of cases in which the issue of the criminal responsibility of mentally abnormal defendants is fully litigated. Both the pleas of insanity and unfitness to plead continue to be rarely used and the same is likely to be true of automatism. Even in diminished responsibility, research by Dell indicates that over 90 per cent of cases are based on guilty pleas accepted by the prosecution.[83] Further, it also seems likely that a great many hospital orders are imposed after a guilty plea where psychiatrists have already decided that this is the appropriate form of disposal. In short, the issue of criminal responsibility is now rarely litigated fully in cases of mentally disordered offenders.

Has this withering away of testing the issue of criminal responsibility been a good thing? What it is likely to have led to is a perpetuation of both insanity and unfitness to plead being underused. Rather, defendants are advised instead to plead guilty, even in cases where an insanity defence might have been available. This certainly seems to be true in some diminished responsibility cases where it has been preferred to insanity. And if this is true in such cases then it is more than likely to have occurred in cases where guilty pleas have resulted in hospital orders. The result is that insanity and unfitness have been sidelined by a strategy which has favoured therapeutic disposal premised on guilt or, where the charge is murder, a diminished responsibility plea, which also requires a guilty plea to the lesser offence of manslaughter. The new hospital direction referred to above could alter this state of affairs by ensuring that the issue of criminal responsibility becomes more mainstream. Defendants who wish to avoid the prospect of a prison sentence, which is the inevitable result of a hospital direction, may more readily plead insanity. However, although the hospital direction—especially if it was extended to other forms of mental disorder—might add momentum to the insanity defence, this alone is insufficient, as the stigma attached to the special verdict continues to be a major obstacle to its use, despite the flexibility of disposal introduced by the Criminal Procedure (Insanity and Unfitness to Plead) Act 1991. An obvious but radical reform would be to abrogate the McNaghten Rules. In this connection it is of interest to note that a court in Jersey has recently ruled that the McNaghten Rules are in breach of the Human Rights Act 1998, as the 'disease of the mind' component is wide enough to include those who are not mentally disordered.[84] As a result the law of Jersey has accepted a completely new and wider insanity defence.[85] It now remains to be seen whether an English court would follow this approach.

[83] See Dell, n. 71 above.

[84] See R. D. Mackay and C. Gearty 'On Being Insane in Jersey—The Case of AG v Prior' [2001] *Crim. LR* 560.

[85] *Ibid.*

CONCLUSION

Finally, we return to the question of reform of the Mental Health Act. As already mentioned, it has become clear that, although there will be a new statutory framework, it will not encompass mental condition defences. Rather it concentrates on the issues of detention, treatment, and discharge. With regard to mentally disordered offenders the White Paper contains a brief chapter[86] which makes it clear that, although the existing framework will remain the same, there will be a simplified procedure 'for the Courts to obtain a medical assessment and order treatment at any stage of the trial when mental disorder becomes an issue'.[87] While this may help procedurally it does nothing to address some of the fundamental criticisms aimed at the existing law. In particular, the White Paper rejects the notion that detained mentally ill patients should in certain circumstances be permitted to refuse treatment, and instead focuses on the risk they pose and the need to protect the community. With this in mind the government has decided that a completely new regime is required to deal with patients who are dangerous and severely personality disordered (DSPD). Accordingly, the 'treatability' provision in the 1983 Act is to be abandoned, thus permitting the indefinite detention of those assessed as DSPD under a care plan 'designed to give therapeutic benefit to the patient or to manage behaviour associated with a mental disorder which might lead to serious harm to other people'.[88] Such individuals are to be held in a new service separately managed from mainstream prison and health services, and the new law will permit detention in civil cases without the need for the commission of an offence. This has been criticized as a form of preventive detention analogous to quarantine, and has been strongly opposed on civil liberty grounds.[89] It certainly reflects a preoccupation with risk and is indicative of a policy shift in favour of public protection. If implemented it remains to be seen whether this type of detention can withstand challenge under the Human Rights Act 1998. It is to be hoped that the government will drop this initiative and instead focus upon the need properly to resource existing facilities for the care and treatment of mentally disordered offenders as well as considering wholesale reform of the mental condition defences dealt with above.

Further Reading

BARTLETT, P., and SANDLAND, R., *Mental Health Law—Policy and Practice* (London: Blackstone Press, 2000).

Committee on Mentally Abnormal Offenders, *Report*, Cmnd 6244 (1975), chap. 12.

DELL, S., *Murder into Manslaughter—The Diminished Responsibility Defence in Practice* (Oxford: Oxford University Press, 1984).

---

[86] See *Reforming the Mental Health Act, Part I*, n. 1 above.

[87] *Ibid.*, at para. 4.4.   [88] N. 2 above, at 2.

[89] See A. McAlinden, 'Indeterminate Sentences for the Severely Personality Disordered' [2000] *Crim. LR* 108 at 115.

HOGGETT, B., *Mental Health Law* (4th edn., London: Sweet and Maxwell, 1996).

Home Office, Circular No. 66/90, 'Provision for Mentally Disordered Offenders'.

JONES, R., *Mental Health Act Manual* (6th edn., London: Sweet and Maxwell, 1999).

LAING, J., *Care or Custody? Mentally Disordered Offenders in the Criminal Justice System* (Oxford: Oxford University Press, 1999).

McALINDEN, A., 'Indeterminate Sentences for the Severely Personality Disordered' [2000] *Crim. LR* 108.

MACKAY, R. D., 'Fact and Fiction about the Insanity Defence' [1990] *Crim. LR* 247.

—— 'The Decline of Disability in Relation to the Trial' [1991] *Crim. LR* 87.

—— *Mental Condition Defences in the Criminal Law* (Oxford: Oxford University Press, 1995).

—— 'More Fact(s) About the Insanity Defence' [1999] *Crim. LR* 714.

—— 'The Abnormality of Mind Factor in Diminished Responsibility' [1999] *Crim. LR* 117.

—— 'Diminished Responsibility and Mentally Disordered Killers' in A. Ashworth and B. Mitchell (eds.), *Rethinking English Homicide Law* (Oxford: Oxford University Press, 2000).

—— and GEARTY, C., 'On Being Insane in Jersey—The Case of AG v Prior' [2001] *Crim. LR* 560.

—— and KEARNS, G., 'An Upturn in Unfitness to Plead? Disability in Relation to the Trial under the 1991 Act' [2000] *Crim. LR* 532.

—— and MACHIN, D., 'The Operation of Section 48 of the Mental Health Act 1983—An Empirical Study of the Transfer of Remand Prisoners to Hospital' (2000) 40 *Brit. J Criminology* 727.

PEAY, J., 'Mentally Disordered Offenders' in M. Maguire, R. Morgan, and R. Reiner (eds.), *The Oxford Handbook of Criminology* (3rd edn., Oxford: Oxford University Press, 2002).

White Paper, *Reforming the Mental Health Act, Part I: The New Legal Framework*, Cm 5016–I (2000).

White Paper, *Reforming the Mental Health Act, Part II: High Risk Patients*, Cm 5016–II (2000).

25

THE SENTENCING PROCESS

David Thomas QC

HISTORY

In early English criminal law sentencing was a simple matter. The penalty for felony was death; the penalty for a misdemeanour was unlimited imprisonment or an unlimited fine. Gradually the judiciary developed procedures to mitigate the severity of the law. During the seventeenth century the judges evolved the concept of 'benefit of clergy'. This concept depended on the principle that a priest should be punished by the Church courts rather than by the State. If a defendant convicted of felony and otherwise liable to be sentenced to death could show that he was a priest, he was released from the criminal court on the assumption that the bishop would deal with him in the ecclesiastical court. As there were no records of who was and was not a priest, the courts developed a simple test of literacy. The assumption was that anyone who could read was likely to be a priest. What happened in practice was that a defendant convicted of felony was given the chance to demonstrate his ability to read by reading a particular verse from Bible. If he could do so, or at least make a reasonable attempt to do so, it was assumed that he was a priest and he would be released. Many felons who were not priests and could not read took the trouble to learn the test verse off by heart so as to be able to recite it from memory when the time came.

The doctrine of benefit of clergy declined in importance during the eighteenth century, as Parliament enacted numerous statutes abolishing the doctrine in particular cases. It was replaced by the practice of transportation under conditional pardon. While the penalty fixed by law for many offences was still death, in practice the judge would grant the defendant a temporary reprieve, while his friends attempted to secure a royal pardon. A royal pardon would normally be granted on the condition that the offender submitted to being transported to what were then the royal colonies in America to work as a labourer for a specified period—seven years, fourteen years, or, in some cases, for life. At this time the fate of the prisoner was entirely in the hands of the sentencing judge. If the judge refused to grant a temporary reprieve, the prisoner would be executed shortly after the conclusion of the court session. Contemporary observers pointed out that the system was arbitrary in the extreme and resulted in what was described as 'a lottery of justice'. This period is however important in the history of English sentencing law because it was in this manner that the central principle of the English sentencing system, the discretion of the judge, was established.

The loss of the American colonies in the late eighteenth century did not put an end to transportation. Australia had recently been discovered, and transportation continued with Australia being substituted as the destination for transported convicts. Transportation continued until the middle years of the nineteenth century.

By the early nineteenth century public opinion in England had turned against the widespread use of the death penalty, which remained the penalty fixed by law for numerous offences, even though it was carried out in only a small proportion of cases. Between 1820 and 1860 most statutes providing for the death penalty were repealed. The death penalty was replaced by periods of transportation, to be fixed by the sentencing judge in the exercise of his discretion. This process was accomplished in a piecemeal manner, with the result that there was no particular logic or order in the duration of transportation, which was made the maximum sentence for particular offences. There was often disagreement in Parliament about the proper duration of transportation for a particular offence. Such disagreements usually resulted in a compromise; rather than transportation for a fixed period of seven years or perhaps life, the politicians would agree that the penalty should be transportation for any period between seven years and life. What had begun as a mandatory penalty for a fixed period in this way often became a discretionary penalty. The actual period would be set by the judge within the limit provided by statute.

Attempts to codify English criminal law in the 1850s failed, but in 1861 most of the criminal law was consolidated in a series of major statutes which provided the foundations of English criminal law for the next 100 years. By the time these statutes, the Consolidation Acts of 1861, were enacted, transportation had given way to a new sentence called 'penal servitude'; the principle of judicial discretion in determining the lengths of sentences had become fixed in the law; and the death penalty had been restricted to a very small number of offences—murder, high treason, piracy with violence, and, possibly by oversight, arson in a royal dockyard. In practice, with the exception of wartime, the death penalty was restricted to the offence of murder. It was eventually abolished for murder in 1965, and completely abolished for the remaining offences, including treason, in 1998.

During the later part of the nineteenth century debates on sentencing were concerned primarily with the problem of establishing a consistent approach on the part of the judges and magistrates who now had formal responsibility for deciding on sentences. There was much concern over disparity of sentences, particularly in the treatment of persistent but relatively minor offenders. Different judges adopted different policies. Eventually the solution which found favour with Parliament was the creation of a system of appeals against sentence. In 1907, a Court of Criminal Appeal was established. This court had authority to hear appeals from the higher criminal courts throughout the country, and it was hoped that through its decisions it would bring some measure of consistency to the sentencing of offenders.

A second important development which began at the turn of the twentieth century was the introduction of a wider range of sentencing powers. In the late nineteenth century judges had at their disposal few alternatives to custody in the form of imprisonment or penal servitude. From the beginning of the twentieth century, legislation expanded the number of sentencing options available to courts, starting with the probation order in 1908. This process has continued up to the present time and English judges now have available a large number of sentences which do not involve imprisonment or custody.

SENTENCING POWERS

A modern English judge dealing with an offender is now able to choose between so many different forms of penalty there is a risk that some will be overlooked. For any offence of any degree of seriousness, Parliament normally provides for a sentence of imprisonment. With the exception of the offence of murder, and certain very recent statutes which apply in extremely rare circumstances, imprisonment is always a sentence within the discretion of the court. The sentencing judge is not obliged to impose a sentence of imprisonment in any case other than the exceptional cases. The length of the sentence is also within the discretion of the judge. Parliament in legislation normally provides only for the maximum sentence which may not be exceeded.

The sentence imposed by the judge is not normally served in full. Since the nineteenth century, there have been a variety of systems under which an offender sentenced to custody could be released before the end of the sentence pronounced by the court. The present system was introduced in 1992. Offenders sentenced to imprisonment are divided into three categories. Those sentenced to less than twelve months serve one half of the sentence pronounced by the court. They are then released but, if they offend during the second half of the sentence, they are liable to be ordered to return to prison to serve an additional period equal to the period of the original sentence which remained on the day the offence was committed. Offenders sentenced to twelve months and less than four years are also released automatically having served one half of the sentence. If they offend again within the second half of the sentence, they are also liable to be ordered to return to prison to serve a period equal to the remaining period of the sentence. In their case however release is also subject to supervision on licence, and they remain on licence until the end of three-quarters of the original sentence. During the period of licence they can be recalled to prison if the Parole Board decides that it is appropriate to recall them, whether or not they have committed any further offence. An offender sentenced to four years' imprisonment or more must also serve at least half of the sentence pronounced by the court, but is not necessarily released at this stage. In his case the Parole Board will decide whether the defendant can be released or whether he should continue in custody until two-thirds of the sentence has been served. Whenever such an offender is released he will be released on licence and will be liable to recall until the end of the third quarter of sentence. If he offends before the end of the whole period of the sentence he may be ordered to serve a period equivalent to the remaining period of the sentence. There are other special provisions which apply only to sexual or violent offenders.

As alternatives to custody, the sentencing judge has at his disposal a wide range of what are now known as 'community orders'. The earliest of these, originally known as a probation order, has recently been renamed a 'community rehabilitation order'. An offender who is subject to a community rehabilitation order, which lasts for a period of between six months and three years, is under the supervision of a probation officer whose duty is to supervise and assist him with advice and guidance. A community rehabilitation order may also include specific requirements designed to ensure that the offender does not repeat his offence. These requirements cover a wide range of matters and the sentencing court can choose which requirements should be included in a community rehabilitation order in a particular case. It is possible, for instance, for the order to include a requirement that the offender should reside in a particular place, or that he should undergo psychiatric treatment or treatment for drug or alcohol dependency. An offender convicted of a sexual offence may be required to attend a rehabilitation centre and take part in a treatment programme designed for sexual offenders.

Another community order is the community punishment order, previously known as a community service order. Under this kind of order the offender is required to perform unpaid work on behalf of the community. The minimum number of hours he can be ordered to perform is normally forty, and the maximum is 240. It is also possible to combine a community rehabilitation order with a community punishment order in the form of a community punishment and rehabilitation order, under which the offender is subject to supervision, possibly with additional specific requirements, and must also carry out unpaid work on behalf of the community.

Another community order is known as a curfew order. An offender subject to a curfew order is required to remain in a specified place, normally his home, for a specified period, usually a period beginning in the early evening and continuing until the following morning. Such an offender is free to continue his employment but is required to remain at home at all other times. An offender subject to a curfew order is normally required to wear a bracelet which is capable of being monitored electronically. If he leaves the premises where he is required to be, an electronic record will be created.

Two new community orders deal with the problems of drug taking. One is known as the drug treatment and testing order. Under such an order the offender must take part in a treatment programme for drug users, and also provide, at intervals stipulated by the court, a sample, so that the presence of drugs in his bloodstream can be identified. An alternative and more limited version of this order is the drug abstinence order. This applies only in the case of offenders who misuse heroin and cocaine. A drug abstinence order requires the offender to provide samples at stipulated intervals so that the presence of heroin or cocaine in his bloodstream can be identified.

An offender who fails to comply with a community order will normally be brought back before the court by the probation service. If the court is satisfied that the offender has failed to comply with the order, the court has power to impose an additional punishment for the failure to comply with the order while allowing the order to continue. Alternatively, the court may revoke the order and impose in its place a new form of sentence, which may be imprisonment.

Another group of penalties are directed at the offender's financial resources. For any offence other than murder the court has power to impose a fine, which requires the offender to pay a sum of money. In the Crown Court there is no limit to the amount of a fine which can be imposed for any offence. In the magistrates' courts, fines are generally limited to specific amounts. Fines are by far the most common penalties, as they are widely used for the less serious offences. A court which imposes a fine is required to relate the amount of the fine to the seriousness of the offence, but at the same time to take into account the financial circumstances of the offender. The court can order the offender to give details of his financial circumstances for this purpose. If an offender fails to pay a fine which the court has ordered him to pay, he may eventually be ordered to serve a short term of imprisonment in default. Alternatively, the court can order the seizure and sale of his goods to raise the money needed to pay the fine.

In addition to or instead of a fine the court may order the offender to pay compensation for the loss, damage, or personal injury which his offence has caused to the victim. Again, in making such an order the court must have regard to the offender's financial circumstances. If the offender is unable to pay compensation, the court should not make a compensation order which will merely leave the victim disappointed. In practice compensation orders are made only in relatively simple cases and for relatively small amounts. In cases where very large amounts of compensation are involved the court prefers to leave the matter to be resolved in a civil court.

More recent legislation has been directed at the confiscation of the assets of the more serious type of offender. An offender convicted of a drug-trafficking offence may have his property confiscated up to the total value of all the money he has received from drug-trafficking. The provisions for confiscation are extremely complicated and frequently give rise to difficult arguments in court. Similar provision is made for the confiscation of the assets of offenders who have committed serious offences of dishonesty, although these operate at the present time on a more limited scale. In a drug trafficking case the court may investigate allegations which go beyond the offences of which the defendant has been convicted. In other cases the court is normally limited to the offences of which the defendant has been convicted on the particular occasion.

In addition to these penalties courts are empowered to make a wide variety of orders prohibiting offenders from taking part in particular activities. An offender convicted of offences in relation to the driving of motor vehicles or who has used a motor vehicle in the course of committing an offence, can be disqualified from driving. In some cases disqualification is obligatory. An offender who has committed offences in connection with the management of a company can be disqualified from acting as a director of any company for a specified period. Offenders who take part in violence at certain football matches, or in connection with football matches, can be subject to banning orders, which prevent them from attending football matches or travelling abroad when an international match involving an English team is being played. Property used in the course of committing an offence can be forfeited.

The law contains a number of special measures for offenders under the age of 18. Offenders under this age are normally dealt with in a Youth Court. The Youth Court has power to make a supervision order, which is similar to a community rehabilitation order, or a variety of less onerous orders which last for a relatively short period of time. Offenders under the age of 18 may be sentenced to custody but the powers of the courts to impose custodial sentences on offenders in this age group are very restricted by comparison with the powers which apply in the case of older offenders. Unless the offence is extremely serious, an offender under the age of 18 may not normally be sentenced to custody for more than a total of two years.

Special measures exist for sexual or violent offenders. In the case of extremely serious sexual or violent offenders, courts may impose sentences of life imprisonment, which require the offender to be detained in custody until the Parole Board decides that he is no longer a danger to the community. In other cases, the court may impose an extended sentence, under which the offender remains under supervision for an extended period following his release from custody. Alternatively, a court may impose a sentence of custody which is longer than the offender would normally receive for the offence in question. More recently, courts have been empowered to make restraining orders in respect of sexual offenders, under which the offender can be placed under restrictions for an indefinite period following his release from custody. An offender who commits an offence against a child must now be disqualified from any employment involving access to children.

SENTENCING PROCEDURE

English criminal law divides the sentencing process clearly from the process of determining whether the defendant is guilty or innocent of the crime with which he is charged. In the Crown Court, a defendant who contests his guilt is tried by a jury, but the sentence is wholly within the authority of the judge. In the magistrates' court the sentence is decided by the same magistrates who had decided whether the defendant is guilty or innocent, but the process falls into two distinct stages.

In a high proportion of cases in both the Crown Court and the magistrates' court there is no trial of guilt or innocence. The offender admits his guilt by entering a plea of guilty and the court is solely concerned with sentence. The entry of a guilty plea sometimes conceals a process of negotiation which has taken place outside the courtroom. This process, sometimes described as 'plea negotiation' or 'plea bargaining', is discussed in Chapter 20. It is subject to a number of well understood principles. The first principle, stated in many decisions of the courts and now expressed in statute, is that a defendant who pleads guilty may generally expect a lesser punishment than one who pleads not guilty and is convicted of the same offence. The 'discount' for pleading guilty as it is called is justified on a number of grounds. First, it is said that the offender who admits his guilt is expressing remorse and that should mitigate his punishment. Secondly, in many cases it is said that the offender is relieving the victim of the obligation to give evidence against him and to submit to cross-examination. This is also seen as a reason for passing a more lenient sentence. The third ground for granting a discount is the more pragmatic one that unless a high proportion of defendants plead guilty, the court system will be unable to deal with the large numbers of cases which come before it and delays in the disposal of cases will become unacceptably long. The discount is an incentive to plead guilty and thus expedite the processing of the case.

The restrictions on 'plea bargaining' are clearly laid down in case law. Negotiations do not normally involve the judge. The judge is permitted to see the lawyers on both sides of the case outside the courtroom, although this practice is discouraged by the higher courts. If the judge does agree to discuss the matter of sentence before the defendant has pleaded guilty, the judge may only say that he will or will not impose a particular type of penalty whether the defendant pleads guilty or is convicted by the jury. He must not indicate that a particular penalty will be imposed only if the defendant pleads guilty.

In practice most negotiation takes place between the lawyers for the prosecution and the lawyers for the defence. They are not in any position to negotiate the sentence, because sentencing is the province of the judge and the prosecution do not have any right to suggest a particular sentence to the judge. Negotiations between lawyers are usually concerned with the charges to which the defendant will plead guilty or the factual account of the offence which the defendant will admit. For instance, a defendant charged with robbery, which is an offence of theft committed with violence, may offer to plead guilty to theft but deny the allegation of violence. The prosecution lawyer will then decide whether to accept that plea or to carry on a trial to have the allegation of violence determined. In another case, a defendant may be charged with possession of drugs as a trafficker or dealer. He may offer to plead guilty on the basis that he was in possession not as a trafficker but simply as a user. The penalty for 'simple' possession is much less than the penalty for possession with intent to supply. Alternatively, the defendant may offer to plead guilty to the offence with which he is charged, but only if the prosecution agrees to give a particular account of the facts of the offence. The definitions of many offences in English law cover a very wide range of circumstances. A defendant charged with a particular offence may agree that he is guilty in law of the offence charged, but his account of what actually happened is much less serious than the account given by the prosecution witnesses. It is increasingly common for a defendant to plead guilty to a particular charge subject to what is known as a 'basis of plea'—which is a document setting out the defendant's account of the offence. The prosecution is not obliged to accept such a basis of plea and may decide that the case should go to trial. Equally, the judge is not obliged to accept a basis of plea, and may direct the prosecution to call witnesses so that the judge may decide what is the true version of the offence. If however the prosecution and the judge accept the basis of plea, the offender must be sentenced in accordance with that account of the incident.

All negotiation of pleas and accounts of the offence takes place subject to the overriding principle that an offender may not be sentenced for an offence other than the offence of which he has been formally convicted, unless he admits the other offences. If a defendant pleads guilty to simple possession of drugs on an indictment charging possession with intent to supply, and that plea is accepted, the judge must sentence him on the basis that he was in possession of drugs for his own use only, even though the judge privately believes that he was a dealer or trafficker. In some cases, a defendant who has pleaded guilty to one or more offences may wish to admit large numbers of other offences with which he has not been formally charged. This has led to the procedure of 'taking offences into consideration'. A list of offences will be prepared, and if the defendant is prepared to admit responsibility for those offences, the court can take them into account although they have not been the subject of a formal indictment. The sentencing powers available to the court are based on the powers which arise in connection with the offences which have been the subject of the formal indictment, but as these powers usually allow a generous margin of discretion, the court is able to impose a more severe penalty without exceeding those powers.

Until relatively recently it was the practice to allow the prosecution to prefer charges which were said to be 'specimen charges'. A defendant who was believed to have committed a large number of similar offences would be charged with a small representative number of offences. If he was convicted of those offences, then the judge was entitled to sentence him on the basis that he had committed the greater number of offences alleged by the prosecution. This practice has now been discontinued, as result of a decision of the Court of Appeal.[1]

There are frequently cases in which, despite the plea of guilty, the prosecution and defence do not agree on what precisely happened at the time of the offence. In these cases it is normal for the judge to hear evidence on the issue in dispute and to decide the matter himself. This procedure, known as a 'Newton hearing', takes the form of a trial but without a jury. The defendant has admitted his guilt and a conviction has been recorded. The Newton hearing is intended to clarify the precise details of the offence of which the defendant has been convicted. It follows that the Newton hearing is limited to elucidating the details of the offence admitted by the defendant. It cannot be used, for instance, to show that the defendant has committed other offences or that the offence which he actually committed was more serious than the offence of which he has been convicted. If a defendant has pleaded guilty to possession of drugs as a trafficker, a Newton hearing may be used to establish whether the defendant was himself a trafficker or merely a 'minder', who was in possession of the drugs on behalf of some other person, but if the defendant has been convicted of 'simple' possession, it is not possible for the prosecution to allege in a Newton hearing that he was actually in possession as a trafficker.

In the case of a contested trial, the finding of guilt will determine the basis for sentence. If the jury has acquitted the defendant of a more serious charge and convicted him of a less serious offence, the judge must sentence on the basis that the defendant is guilty only of the less serious offence, whatever his private belief may be. Sometimes the verdict of the jury leaves a question of fact unresolved. The prosecution case and the defence case are both consistent with the verdict. What version of the facts should the judge adopt as the basis of sentence? The law is that if the verdict of the jury can be explained only on one version of the facts, the judge must pass sentence on the basis that that is the true version, but if the verdict is consistent with either case, then the judge must make his own decision on the evidence, applying the same standards as the jury has applied. A jury may convict the defendant of inten-

---

[1] *Clark* (1996) 2 Cr. App. R (S).

tionally causing grievous bodily harm. The defendant may claim that he inflicted the injuries with his fist, the prosecution may allege that he used a weapon. As this question is not resolved by the jury's verdict of guilty, the judge must decide it himself.

The sequence of events which takes place when a defendant comes to be sentenced follows a regular pattern. The proceedings will be opened by the prosecuting lawyer. If the defendant has pleaded guilty to the charge, the prosecuting lawyer will provide the judge or magistrates with a summary of the facts of the offence as they are disclosed in the evidence of the prosecution witnesses. (The witnesses themselves will not attend court or give evidence unless there is to be a Newton hearing.) The prosecuting lawyer is not permitted to make any suggestion to the judge about what the sentence should be. The prosecuting lawyer is entitled to draw the judge's attention to any legal rules which affect the penalty and to any guidance from the higher courts which may be relevant to the judge's decision, but he is not permitted to argue that a particular sentence should or should not be imposed.

The prosecuting lawyer will normally also give the court details of the offender's previous convictions and sentences, if he has any. These are commonly known as the 'antecedents'. The antecedents statement, normally prepared by the police, sets out brief details of the offender's previous court appearances, the offences he has committed, the courts before which he has appeared, and the sentences which he has received. The antecedents statement will also normally indicate whether the offender is currently subject to any kind of community order.

In many cases a pre-sentence report will be presented by the probation service. The pre-sentence report is prepared in accordance with national guidelines. It will normally give an account of the offence based in part on an interview or interviews with the offender by a probation officer. The report will normally include a 'risk assessment' in which the probation officer attempts to predict whether the offender will commit further offences in the future. In many cases, the pre-sentence report will contain a suggestion as to the community order which would be most appropriate for the offender, if the sentencing court is minded to deal with the matter by means of a community order. Such recommendations have in the past been a source of controversy.

The next stage in the sentencing process is an address by the defence lawyer in mitigation of sentence. The defence lawyer can, if he chooses, call witnesses on behalf of the defendant, but this is relatively unusual. In most cases, the defence lawyer speaks for the defendant, possibly giving an explanation of why he committed the offence, expressing the offender's regrets, and inviting the court to deal with him as leniently as possible. The defence lawyer may draw the court's attention to mitigating circumstances, the offender's family circumstances, and any other information which may in his judgement help to persuade the court to be lenient.

In most cases, the judge or magistrates will pass sentence at the conclusion of this process, although they may adjourn either to allow time to consider the question, or to obtain further information about a particular aspect of the case. Sentence is always pronounced orally in the presence of the offender, except in rare cases in which the offender has misbehaved in court and been removed or has absconded and does not attend. It is increasingly the practice in both the Crown Court and the magistrates' court for the judge or magistrate who passes sentence to give an explanation of the reasoning which has led the court to the particular sentence which has been chosen. The judge will indicate, for instance, what view he has taken of the facts of the offence and what mitigating circumstances he has taken into account. He will normally indicate that he has given the defendant a discount for his plea of guilty and refer to any other relevant matters. There are now in addition many statutory requirements relating to the matters which must be stated by the judge in passing sentence. For instance, if the judge imposes a custodial sentence he must state which of the statutory criteria for a custodial sentence is the relevant one (in practice, it is always the same—that the offence is so serious that only a custodial sentence can be justified). If the court has power to make a compensation order but does not do so, the court must explain why it has not done so (usually the reason is that the defendant has no financial resources from which to pay compensation). In addition there are other specific statutory obligations which arise in particular circumstances. Judges frequently complain that the duty to make specific statements of this kind prevents them from communicating clearly with the offender and others involved in the case regarding the matters of importance in the particular case.

APPEALS

An offender who has been sentenced in the Crown Court may in general appeal to the Court of Appeal (Criminal Division) against his sentence. (There are a few exceptions to this principle.) The procedure for appeal begins with an application made in writing on behalf of the offender, which must normally be lodged within twenty-eight days of the sentence. The application is first considered by a single judge in private. The single judge may grant leave for the case to proceed to the Court of Appeal or he may refuse leave to appeal. If he refuses leave, he will give a short written statement of his reasons—two or three sentences in most cases—which is communicated to the defendant. The defendant may then decide whether he wishes to have the case argued before the full court of three judges or whether he will abandon the appeal at this stage. The vast majority of defendants who are refused leave by the single judge abandon their appeals at this point.

If a defendant is granted leave to appeal, either by a single judge or by the full court of three judges in the case where the single judge has initially refused leave, the case will be argued in open court before three judges, one of whom is normally a Lord Justice of Appeal. In most cases where questions of sentence only are involved only the defendant will present arguments to the court, invariably through his lawyer. The prosecution will not normally take any part in a sentence appeal, and prosecution lawyers will not attend the appeal, unless the court directs that they should, usually for some very specific reason. The hearing of a sentence appeal is usually relatively brief. The judges will have read all the papers in the case before coming into court, and in most cases the defence lawyer will have prepared a written submission, usually described as a 'skeleton argument', in which he sets out the main points of his argument. The proceedings in court will normally take the form of a brief address by the defendant's lawyer, a brief private consultation between the three judges, followed by the delivery of an oral judgment by one of the judges. The judgment will usually give an account of the facts of the offence, the reasons given by the judge in the Crown Court for choosing a particular sentence, and the reasons given by the appeal court for deciding that that sentence was correct or otherwise. In deciding whether to allow an appeal by a defendant, the court is guided by the principle that an appeal will not normally be allowed unless a defendant shows that the sentence imposed by the trial judge is 'wrong in principle' or 'manifestly excessive'. The judges who sit in the Court of Appeal are not entitled merely to substitute their own personal opinions for those of the trial judge. It has often been said that the fact that the judges sitting in the appeal court would have awarded a less severe sentence if they had been the judges of first instance is not in itself a ground for allowing an appeal. It must be shown that the sentencing judge in the Crown Court exceeded the proper limits of his discretion in imposing the sentence that he did.

If the defendant appeals the Court of Appeal is prohibited from increasing the sentence. The law states that the Court of Appeal must not deal with the defendant more severely than he was dealt with by the court below. This means that the Court of Appeal cannot on an appeal increase the length of a custodial sentence or substitute a custodial sentence for a sentence which does not involve custody, although, given the increasing complexity of the English sentencing system, it is sometimes difficult to be sure whether a particular variation in sentence does amount to an increase or not. The Court of Appeal does have power, however, to order that a defendant whose appeal is unsuccessful should not be allowed to count the time he has spent in custody waiting for the appeal to be heard as part of the sentence. This in effect amounts to a hidden increase in sentence and does serve to some extent to deter defendants from appealing against their sentences. It is however a power which is very rarely exercised.

There is a procedure under which the prosecution can in effect appeal against a sentence imposed in the Crown Court on the ground that it is 'unduly lenient'. This power applies only to a limited range of offences—for most part the most serious offences, which are capable of being tried only in the Crown Court, and to a limited number of other offences which are specifically identified by statute. Only the Attorney-General may make use of this procedure. If a sentence for an offence in respect of which the procedure is available appears unduly lenient, those responsible for the conduct of the case in the Crown Court must draw it to the attention of the Attorney-General through the Crown Prosecution Service, and the Attorney-General will then decide whether the case should be brought before the Court of Appeal. If the case is brought before the Court of Appeal on a reference by the Attorney-General, the court will apply much the same principles as in the case of an appeal. A sentence will not be considered 'unduly lenient' unless it falls outside the range or bracket of sentences which is properly open to the sentencing judge in the exercise of his discretion. It is not sufficient that the judges sitting in the Court of Appeal would themselves have imposed a more severe sentence if they had been the judges in the Crown Court. If the Court of Appeal finds that the sentence was unduly lenient, the court will substitute a more appropriate sentence, although normally the sentence will be less severe than the sentence which the court considers the judge in the Crown Court should have imposed. There is by convention a discount in the sentence imposed on the defendant for what the Court of Appeal describes as the 'element of double jeopardy' involved in a reference. Additionally, the Court of Appeal has a discretion whether or not to make any increase, even if it considers that the sentence imposed was unduly lenient. By the time a case comes to the Court of Appeal, some months will have gone by since the sentence was imposed, and the court may take the view that, even though the sentence was unduly lenient when imposed, it would not be just or appropriate at this late stage to vary the sentence, in particular if it involves requiring the offender to serve a custodial sentence in place of a community order.

The procedure for appeals against sentences imposed by the magistrates' court is different. The defendant may appeal to the local Crown Court. The appeal in the Crown Court takes the form of a complete re-hearing of the case. The Crown Court is not required to consider whether the sentence imposed by the magistrates' court was correct or not. It has a discretion to impose whatever sentence it considers appropriate on the facts which are presented to the Crown Court (which may not be exactly the same as those presented to the magistrates' court). Unlike the Court of Appeal the Crown Court has an unrestricted discretion in the sentence that it may impose on an appeal. It may impose any sentence which would have been legally open to the magistrates' court, whether or not that sentence is more severe than the sentence actually imposed by the magistrates' court in the particular case. An offender who has been ordered by the magistrates' court to pay a fine and who appeals to the Crown Court may find that the Crown Court takes a much more serious view of the offence than the magistrates' court and imposes a sentence of imprisonment in place of the fine. For this reason appeals by defendants from the magistrates' court to the Crown Court are relatively rare.

The prosecution may not appeal to the Crown Court against an unduly lenient sentence imposed by the magistrates' court, but may invoke other procedures known as 'appeal by case stated' and 'judicial review'. It is open to the prosecution to argue that the sentence was so lenient that it was in effect unlawful. Such cases, which are relatively rare, are decided by the High Court in London. The majority of such cases involve the failure of the magistrates' court to impose a mandatory penalty, such as a disqualification from driving. It is a serious deficiency of the English sentencing system that there is no effective national court with power or jurisdiction in respect of the decisions of magistrates' courts. Decisions of the local Crown Court in particular cases do not establish precedents, or necessarily give guidance on how a particular type of case is to be approached.

CONTROLLING DISPARITY

Since the nineteenth century, the control of disparity in sentencing has been a significant concern. Parliament's initial reaction was the creation of the Court of Criminal Appeal in 1907. One of the reasons for establishing this court was the hope that it would tend to harmonize the approach of different judges in sentencing matters. In fact, after a short initial period in which the court was reasonably active, this expectation was not fulfilled. Relatively few offenders appealed to the court against their sentences, and the court did what it could to discourage them from doing so. One important factor in discouraging potential appeals was the fact that at that time the Court of Criminal Appeal had the power to increase a sentence as well as to reduce it. Anyone appealing against his sentence took the risk that the Court of Criminal Appeal might decide that his sentence was too lenient and substitute a more severe sentence than the one he had originally received. Undoubtedly a second reason why the Court of Criminal Appeal failed in its early days to establish any significant body of guidance for judges was the absence of any systematic reporting or analysis of its decisions.

The Court of Criminal Appeal was renamed the Court of Appeal (Criminal Division) in 1964 and began to assume greater importance in relation to the control of disparity in sentences at about that time. In part this was the result of the efforts of the Lord Chief Justice of the day, Lord Parker. A second factor was the beginning of more academic analysis and discussion of the court's decisions as academics attempted to deduce from the court's practice more generalized principles. Reporting of the court's decisions on sentencing also began in the late 1970s, and by now a large body of reported decisions has grown up which give illustrations and guidance on how particular types of offence or offender should be dealt with.

This process has been supplemented in a variety of ways. In a limited number of contexts, the Court of Appeal has formalized its guidance in the shape of what are called 'guideline judgments'. A guideline judgment sets out the proper approach which is to be adopted by a judge in dealing with offences within a particular category. Examples are rape, incest, dealing in drugs, and causing death by dangerous driving. In each of these cases there is a judgment setting out in detail the considerations which should be borne in mind by the sentencing judge. These guideline judgments are not intended to be treated as totally prescriptive. They endeavour to respect the principle that the sentence in any given case is within the discretion of the sentencing judge, but they do provide a framework within which that discretion is to be exercised.

A second element in the system in recent years has been the growth of what is called 'Judicial Studies'. Since the mid-1970s, judicial seminars have been held at increasingly frequent intervals. Judges meet and discuss matters of mutual concern. Sentencing has always played an important part in these seminars. Normally the judges are given a number of hypothetical cases, based on real cases, and asked to indicate what sentence they would pass in the given case. This process leads to a discussion of the principles involved. This method has proved extremely useful in identifying differences of approach between different judges and in securing consensus about the factors which should be considered when sentence is passed. Seminars are now conducted by a body known as the Judicial Studies Board. The Board has as its chairman a senior Lord Justice of Appeal and it organizes a regular programme of seminars throughout the year. Any judge who sits in criminal cases will be expected to attend a residential seminar, lasting four or five days, once every four years, and in addition a one-day seminar each year. The seminars will seek to ensure that judges are reminded of recent developments in the law, and other relevant developments in adjacent fields of knowledge.

Most recently a new body has been created, the Sentencing Advisory Panel. This body consists of members drawn from different disciplines—some judges, some academics from universities, and others with experience of different aspects of the administration of criminal justice. Their task is to devise guidelines which are then submitted to the Court of Appeal for possible inclusion in a guideline judgment dealing with a particular topic. The Panel has been in existence for only two years, and at this stage it is still establishing its role in the system, but it is expected that the existence of the Panel will lead over a period of time to the development of more sophisticated and generalized guidelines for sentencing than exist at the present time.

So far as magistrates are concerned, the system lacks officially promulgated guidelines. The magistrates' own representative body, the Magistrates' Association, produces a set of sentencing guidelines for magistrates' courts, which are designed to provide a framework within which magistrates can deal with the sentencing problems which confront them. These guidelines however have no official or legal status and it is a matter entirely within the discretion of the magistrates whether they are utilized.

No one would claim that all problems of sentencing have been solved within the English criminal justice system. There are many criticisms. There is far too much legislation and far too many legal technicalities have to be observed. In recent years there have been too many changes and those who have to operate within the system complain that they cannot keep up with the new legislation which is introduced at frequent intervals, often without any obvious necessity. Most judges and practitioners would prefer a period of stability without significant change so that the practical operation of recent innovations could be assessed. It is unlikely that this will happen. Sentencing has become a topic of acute political interest, and politicians believe they have found that changing the sentencing process may enhance their political popularity. While this continues, new legislation will continue to be introduced at frequent intervals, whether or not it leads to improvements in the quality of the sentencing system.

Further Reading

ASHWORTH, A. J., *Sentencing and Criminal Justice* (London: Butterworths, 2000).

THOMAS, D. A. (ed.), *Current Sentencing Practice* (London: Sweet & Maxwell, continuing), also available in CD-ROM form as The Sentencing Service.

Articles and case summaries with commentaries are regularly published in the *Criminal Law Review*.

26

CRIMINAL APPEALS
The purpose of criminal appeals

Rosemary Pattenden

Criminal appeals made a relatively late appearance on the English legal scene. Nevertheless, the right of the defence to appeal an adverse decision of a criminal trial court is now a firmly entrenched feature of the English legal process. It is also a right guaranteed by Article 14(5) of the United Nations Covenant on Civil and Political Rights and by Protocol 7 of the European Convention on Human Rights, a protocol that the United Kingdom has yet to sign. Article 2 of the protocol provides:

Everyone convicted of a criminal offence by a tribunal shall have the right to have his conviction or sentence reviewed by a higher tribunal. (2) This right may be subject to exception in regard to offences of a minor character, as prescribed by law, or in cases in which the person concerned was tried in the first instance by the highest tribunal or was convicted following an appeal against acquittal.

Why is a criminal appeal so important? First and foremost, it provides a wrongly convicted person with a remedy. A wrongly convicted person is not necessarily someone who is innocent of the crime charged. It may be someone whose guilt has not been proven by the prosecution beyond reasonable doubt, the required standard of proof for conviction. A no less important function of the criminal appeal is to protect the defendant's right, guaranteed by Article 6 of the European Convention on Human Rights and the Human Rights Act 1998, to a fair trial. The defence right of appeal simultaneously deters and corrects unfairness. It could be described as a quality-control device. Unfairness in the way a trial is conducted not only exposes the defendant to the risk of being wrongly convicted, it threatens the integrity of the criminal trial which operates from the premise that means do not justify ends. A third function of the criminal appeal is to promote consistency, consistency in the way discretions are exercised by trial judges, including the all-important sentencing discretion, and consistency in the formulation and application of rules of law. This consistency is achieved through authoritative rulings by the appeal courts on the common law and on the way that statutes are to be interpreted and by the provision of guidance on the manner in which the exercise of discretions should be approached.

CATEGORIES OF ERROR AND APPEAL

TYPES OF ERROR

It helps to understand the appeal process to be aware of the way that errors are classified and appeals are categorized. A criminal trial may give rise to several types of error. The first possibility is an 'error of law'. When this happens the law that is applied by the judge is wrong in its formulation (common law), in its interpretation (statute law), or in the way that it is applied to the facts. The second possibility is an error of fact. The accused is convicted of something that he did not do or it has not been satisfactorily proven that he did. The converse is also possible. The defendant is acquitted when he ought to have been convicted. Many appeals by convicted defendants complain about a third type of error, an irregularity in the trial process as a result of which the accused lost a chance of acquittal. The possible causes of such irregularities are many. In a jury trial, the judge may be to blame. For example, he may have shown bias in his summing up or interrupted defence counsel excessively. It may be the fault of the prosecution. This happens when evidence that should have been disclosed to the defence is not disclosed. The jury may be to blame. In *R. v. Young*[1] the jury used a ouija board during an overnight adjournment of the trial to contact the deceased. The fault may lie with the media which, by publishing material during the trial, may prejudice the defence, as in *R. v. Taylor*.[2]

TYPES OF APPEAL

The English legal system recognizes four generic types of appeal:

1. *Appeal de novo.* This takes the form of a re-trial at which both sides are free to call new evidence and present new arguments. All previous rulings of law, fact, and discretion are ignored and the appellate court reaches a fresh decision on the merits of whatever is disputed.

2. *Appeal stricto sensu.* Here the appellate court examines the correctness of the trial court's rulings of law, fact, and discretion based on the evidence presented at the original trial. No new evidence may be adduced.

3. *Review.* The legality of the procedure by which a decision was reached or the court's jurisdiction to reach it is reviewed. Affidavit evidence of impropriety in the conduct of the trial may be given. The merits of the decision reached by the lower court are irrelevant.

4. *Rehearing.* This is something in between an appeal *de novo* and an appeal *stricto sensu*. It is not a re-trial but, if an error of fact or a procedural irregularity is alleged, the appellate court may receive additional evidence. Even without the benefit of fresh evidence, the court may draw fresh inferences from the transcript of the evidence presented at the original trial and on that basis reach a decision.

---

[1] [1995] QB 324.   [2] (1993) 98 Cr. App. R 361.

THE ENGLISH CRIMINAL APPEAL PROCESS:
A SUMMARY

INTRODUCTION

In England the criminal appeal process is largely a product of legislation. The key statutes are the Magistrates' Court Act 1980, the Criminal Appeal Act 1968, the Supreme Court Act 1981, and the Administration of Justice Act 1970. These determine rights of appeal and the consequences of an appeal. They are supported by extensive rules made under delegated law-making powers. Because the appeal process developed in a piecemeal fashion the criminal appeal regime is complex and riddled with anomalies. For example, the prosecution can appeal against acquittals for the least serious offences but not the most serious, and the accused has an automatic right of appeal against convictions for minor offences but not against convictions for really serious ones.

APPEAL TO THE CROWN COURT

95 per cent of criminal cases are disposed of by lay justices of the peace or stipendiary magistrates in the lowest criminal court, the magistrates' court. Provided that he pleaded 'not guilty', a defendant convicted by magistrates may appeal against a conviction to the Crown Court. Grounds of appeal need not be stated because the appeal is *de novo*, a re-trial of the original charges (Supreme Court Act 1981 section 79(3)). Evidence is presented afresh unless the defendant agrees to evidence from the first trial being read into the record. At the re-trial guilt or innocence is determined by a judge, usually sitting with two lay justices of the peace who have no previous connection with the case. The lay justices must accept the judge's decision on questions of law but can override his decision on the facts. By section 48(2) of the Supreme Court Act 1981 the Crown Court has power to quash, vary, or confirm any part of the decision reached in the magistrates' court and may exercise any power that the magistrates could exercise. A fresh sentence may be passed (Supreme Court Act 1981 section 48(4)). All defendants convicted in a magistrates' court can appeal against their sentence to the Crown Court. The issue for the Crown Court is not whether the original sentence is reasonable, but whether it is the one that the Crown Court would have passed. If it is not, the Crown Court will substitute what it deems to be the appropriate punishment.

APPEAL TO THE DIVISIONAL COURT OF THE QUEEN'S BENCH DIVISION OF THE HIGH COURT

Instead of appealing to the Crown Court a defendant convicted by magistrates may appeal to the Divisional Court of the Queen's Bench by what is known as 'case stated'. The prosecution may do the same after an acquittal. Appeal by case stated also lies at the instigation of either party from the determination of the Crown Court which has heard a defence appeal against conviction or sentence. By section 111 of the Magistrates' Court Act 1980 and section 28 of the Supreme Court Act 1981 an appeal by case stated is required to be on the ground that the determination is 'wrong in law or is in excess of jurisdiction'. This criterion rarely permits a complaint about a sentence. Appeal by case stated is, in effect, an appeal *stricto sensu* limited to issues of law. The stated case sets out the charge or charges being appealed against, the court's findings of fact, the submissions made to the court, the court's decisions on those submissions, and the question of law for the determination of the Divisional Court. There is no mention of evidence unless the error of law complained of is that there was no evidence to justify the decision reached, which is treated as if it were a matter of law. At the appeal hearing the case statement forms the focal point of argument and nothing new in the way of facts or evidence may be added. The Divisional Court may substitute an acquittal for a conviction or a conviction for an acquittal or return the case to the magistrates' court for a re-trial or with a direction to acquit or to convict.

A judicial review is another way that a case tried in a magistrates' court, or the Crown Court on appeal, can be challenged in the Divisional Court of the Court of Queen's Bench. Like appeal by case stated, judicial review is open to both sides but, unlike appeal by case stated, it is possible to seek a judicial review before there has been a final determination in the lower court. Judicial review, a procedure best known for keeping government bodies and officials in check, is the means by which an excess of jurisdiction,[3] unreasonableness, an 'error on the face of the record', or a breach of the rules of natural justice by an inferior court can be rectified. Judicial review is a two-stage procedure. First an application is made for permission to apply for judicial review. If permission is granted, there is an application for judicial review. Affidavit evidence may be presented, but only on the issues subject to review. No evidence on the merits of the defendant's conviction or acquittal is admissible. The available remedies are certiorari by which the decision of the lower court is quashed, prohibition, which is used to stop actions in excess of jurisdiction, and mandamus, by which the lower court is compelled to perform a duty. These orders may be given singly or in combination and are all discretionary. A decision at a judicial review hearing to quash a conviction voids the decision of the lower court. If the decision quashed is that of the Crown Court dismissing an appeal against conviction the original conviction of the magistrates will stand. The Divisional Court may not quash an acquittal in judicial review proceedings unless the original trial was a nullity and the defendant therefore never was in jeopardy of being convicted. Appeals both by case stated and judicial reviews are usually heard by two judges. There is a further appeal in both cases from the Divisional Court to the House of Lords, the highest court in the land.

---

[3] This includes all errors of law material to the decision: *R. v. Greater Manchester Coroner, ex parte Tal* [1984] 3 All ER 240.

APPEAL TO THE COURT OF APPEAL (CRIMINAL DIVISION)

The most serious criminal offences are tried on indictment in the Crown Court by a judge and, if the defendant pleads 'not guilty' to any count, a jury. An appeal by the defence against conviction, sentence, or both lies to the Court of Appeal (Criminal Division). An appeal against conviction is heard by a court of three (Supreme Court Act 1981 section 55), of whom at least one will be a regular judge of the Court of Appeal, a Lord Justice of Appeal. It is normal for at least one of the others to be a High Court judge (Supreme Court Act 1981 section 9) or a circuit judge (Criminal Justice and Public Order Act 1994 section 52) experienced in the conduct of criminal trials. The appeal judges arrive in court with a summary of the case prepared by the Registrar of Criminal Appeals, a skeleton argument submitted by the appellant's counsel, a transcript of the summing up, and, if appropriate and if it still exists, of the evidence. The appeal takes the form of a re-hearing though the court has a tendency to act more like a court of review. The legislation itself is clear enough. The court of Appeal is directed by section 2(1) of the Court of Appeal Act 1968 to allow an appeal against conviction and quash the conviction if '*they think* that the conviction is unsafe' (italics added). Otherwise the appeal must be dismissed. The court itself has confirmed that a conviction must be quashed if the appeal judges have a 'lurking doubt' about it.[4] When a conviction is quashed the court has a discretion to order a re-trial, order a *venire de novo* (possible only where the original conviction was a nullity) or substitute a conviction for an alternative offence. The court may, and often does, choose to make no order. A further appeal by either party lies to the House of Lords. An appeal against a sentence passed after trial on indictment where there is no appeal against conviction is heard by two judges, and the prosecution is not usually represented. If the appeal succeeds the court may quash the sentence and substitute another provided the overall sentence is not more severe than that imposed by the Crown Court.

The defence right to appeal a conviction, sentence, or both is not matched by an equivalent prosecution right to appeal against an acquittal or a sentence. Since 1972, however, the Attorney-General has been able to refer a point of law for the consideration of the Court of Appeal following an acquittal of a defendant tried on indictment in the Crown Court (Criminal Justice Act 1972 section 36). The actual acquittal is not affected whatever the Court of Appeal decides. Since 1988 the Attorney-General has also been able to refer to the Court of Appeal for rectification of an unduly lenient sentence passed on a defendant convicted in the Crown Court after a trial on indictment of certain serious offences (Criminal Justice Act 1988 sections 35, 36). A sentence is unduly lenient if it falls outside the range of sentences that a judge could reasonably consider appropriate.[5] Sentence references are relatively uncommon.

---

[4] *R. v. Cooper* (1968) 53 Cr. App. R 82, 86; *R. v. Sprange*, unreported, 1 July 1998.
[5] *Attorney-General's Reference (No. 4 of 1989)* (1990) 90 Cr. App. R 366, 371.

SOME ISSUES RAISED BY DEFENCE APPEALS AGAINST CONVICTION

THE VOLUME OF APPEALS

Criminal appeals generate a considerable workload for appellate courts at all levels, add to the bill for prosecuting offenders, and delay the closure of cases. The State and the judiciary have therefore seen fit to devise stratagems to stem the volume of appeals. At various times all of the following have been used.

THE LEAVE REQUIREMENT

Leave is not required to appeal against a summary conviction to the Crown Court or the High Court. This reflects the law's historic suspicion of trial by laymen. Appeals by the defence following trial on indictment, however, require leave unless the appeal is against conviction on a question of law alone. Leave may be obtained from the trial judge (which is rare), a single judge of the Court of Appeal, or, if this is refused, a full Court of Appeal. Appeal by the prosecution against an unduly lenient sentence also needs leave (Criminal Justice Act 1988 section 36(1)). The framers of the Criminal Appeal Act 1907 believed that the requirement of leave was necessary to prevent the disposal of genuine complaints being delayed by a large number of unfounded ones. In 1965 the Donovan Committee also recommended the retention of the filter process on this ground.[6] According to the *Judicial Statistics 1999*[7] in that year the leave process sifted out in excess of 5,500 applications out of a total of 8,274 appeals against conviction, sentence, or both. An explanatory memorandum to the Protocol states that a requirement of leave is not incompatible with the right of appeal guaranteed by Article 2 of Protocol 7 of the European Convention on Human Rights.

Criminal appeals to the House of Lords from both the Divisional Court and the Court of Appeal are subject to a very stringent leave requirement. The lower court must certify that the case raises a point of law of general public importance and leave to appeal must be given either by that court or by the Appeals Committee of the House of Lords (Administration of Justice Act 1960 section 1(2); Criminal Appeal Act 1968 section 33(2)).

RESTRICTING THE NUMBER OF APPEALS

Once leave to appeal is refused or the appeal is dismissed by the Court of Appeal the correctness of a conviction on indictment cannot be re-argued before the Court of Appeal[8] except on a reference by the Criminal Cases Review Commission. The 'one appeal' rule simultaneously achieves closure and keeps the workload of the Court of Appeal within bounds. A defendant convicted summarily by a magistrates' court can

---

[6] *Report of the Interdepartmental Committee on the Court of Criminal Appeal,* Cmnd 2755 (1965) para. 112.
[7] London: Lord Chancellor's Department, 2000.   [8] *R. v. Pinfold* (1988) 87 Cr. App. R 15.

appeal to the Crown Court, and then appeal again by case stated to the High Court. But the second appeal must be on a question of law or jurisdiction.

PENALIZING AN UNSUCCESSFUL APPEAL

To discourage frivolous appeals the Criminal Appeal Act 1907 specified that, if an application for leave to appeal failed, the entire period spent in custody while appealing was not to count toward the sentence unless the court directed otherwise (section 14(3)). In 1966 the statutory presumption was reversed so that it now requires a special direction for the time spent in prison to be discounted (Criminal Appeal Act 1968 section 29(1)). A 1980 Practice Direction[9] advises single judges not to make an order if counsel settled the grounds of appeal but allows the full court to do so. The thrust of the Practice Direction is to discourage the renewal of hopeless applications to the full court. The power to make a loss-of-time order is rarely used. It has always been controversial because its effect is to punish a convicted person for appealing. In 1986 Monnell and Morris, two appellants who were directed to lose time by a full court, unsuccessfully challenged this direction in the European Court of Human Rights.[10] The supranational court decided that the loss of time ordered by the full court was fair (as required by Article 6), was not discriminatory (as required by Article 14), and, because the loss of time was part of the overall sentencing procedure that followed their conviction, there was no infringement of Article 5 (which requires sufficient causal connection between conviction and deprivation of liberty). Defendants who appeal from the magistrates' court to the Crown Court cannot be penalized for appealing by a loss-of-time directive, but they do face the risk of an increase in sentence. On an appeal against sentence or conviction appeal, the Crown Court can pass any sentence it thinks appropriate, provided that the new sentence is within the sentencing limits of the magistrates' court (Supreme Court Act 1981 section 48(4)).

RESTRICTING THE GROUNDS OF APPEAL

A fourth means of shutting the flood-gates is to limit the grounds of appeal. The number of appeals from magistrates' courts that reach the High Court is controlled by the requirement that the appeal must involve a legal or jurisdictional point (which comes to much the same thing). The grounds upon which a convicted defendant may appeal to the Court of Appeal are not so limited, but the well-known reluctance of the Court of Appeal to substitute its own views of the evidence for that of the jury operates as a *de facto* barrier. Counsel simply will not sign grounds of appeal if the defendant's only complaint is that the jury reached the wrong verdict and there are not very good grounds for questioning the outcome.

DISMISSAL FOR HARMLESS ERROR

'Harmless error' is a term coined by the American courts to signify an error that does not affect the safety of the trial outcome. Until 1995 the Court of Appeal dealt with

---

[9] [1980] 1 All ER 555.   [10] (1998) 10 EHRR 205.

errors of this character by applying 'the proviso'. This provision allowed the appeal judges to dismiss an appeal 'notwithstanding that they are of opinion that the point raised in the appeal might be decided in favour of the appellant . . . if they consider that no miscarriage of justice has actually occurred'. The Court of Appeal generally applied the proviso when satisfied that a reasonable jury would inevitably have convicted had no error occurred.[11] But not always. In a study of 300 cases in 1990 for the Royal Commission on Criminal Justice,[12] Malleson could detect no reason why the proviso was considered (let alone applied) in some appeals and not in others. Since counsel had no idea whether the court would apply the proviso in any given case, the proviso probably had little or no deterrent effect on the numbers of convicted persons who appealed, as it might have done if applied in a consistent, predictable fashion.

APPEALS ALLEGING JURY ERROR

As the Royal Commission on Criminal Justice noted,[13] most appeals against conviction on indictment that allege only jury error do not prosper. There are several reasons for this. First, the jury gives no reasons. How is the court to know whether the jury made a mistake either in the assessment of the facts or in the application of the law to those facts? Judges sometimes ask juries about their reasons to assist them in sentencing the defendant, but the jury cannot be compelled to answer and the practice is frowned upon. If anyone else were to ask the jury about why it convicted, that person would fall foul of section 8 of the Contempt of Court Act 1981, which prohibits any inquiry which might lead to disclosure of matters discussed in the jury room and, in any case, the Court of Appeal will not admit evidence of jury-room discussions in case this puts pressure on the jurors and undermines their right to decide without giving reasons. The Court of Appeal also attaches great importance to the finality of jury verdicts. Initially, the Court of Appeal refused to interfere with a verdict for which there was a scintilla of evidence:

It must be understood that we are not here to re-try the case where there was evidence proper to be left to the jury upon which they could come to the conclusion at which they arrived . . . Here there was evidence on both sides, and it is impossible to say that the verdict is one which the jury could not properly have arrived at [*per* Lord Alverstone CJ].[14]

In response to legislative reform, the Court of Appeal has softened its approach. It nevertheless remains difficult to persuade the court that a conviction is unsafe if the defence is unable to come up with fresh evidence. A desire for closure is reinforced by a belief that the jury is in a better position than the appeal judges to assess the evidence because the jurors heard and saw the witnesses. Sir Frederick Lawton once said that 'reading a transcript of evidence is not conducive to raising a lurking doubt'.[15] The judges know from experience that miscarriages of justice are possible

[11] *DPP* v. *Stirland* [1944] 2 All ER 13, 14.
[12] *Review of the Appeal Process*, Research Study 17 (London: 1993).
[13] *Report*, Cm. 2263 (1993) paragraph 10.3. [14] *R.* v. *Williamson* (1908) 1 Cr. App. R3.
[15] 'Judging Without Prejudice', *The Times*, 23 Oct. 1990, 38.

wherever there are issues of evidence credibility, and that certain kinds of evidence, such as identification evidence, are suspect. However, by itself, this awareness is not a reason to doubt a jury's verdict if there is evidence upon which the jury could convict. Most of the appeal judges also believe that it is for the jury and not them to determine guilt. Lloyd LJ in *R. v. McIlkenny* put it thus:

Since justice is as much concerned with the conviction of the guilty as the acquittal of the innocent, and the task of convicting the guilty belongs constitutionally to the jury, not to us, the role of the Criminal Division of the Court of Appeal is necessarily limited. Hence it is true to say that whereas the Civil Division of the Court of Appeal has appellate jurisdiction in the full sense, the Criminal Division is perhaps more accurately described as a court of review.[16]

APPEALS ALLEGING LAWYER ERROR

When the Court of Criminal Appeal was set up the then Attorney-General, Sir John Walton, expected that the miscalculations and omissions of the defence lawyers would constitute a valid ground of appeal:

Supposing they had a case which was ill-conducted by the counsel for the prisoner, supposing he neglected to put questions which he ought to have put, supposing there was evidence which he might have called but had not called—all these were matters essential to enable a Court of review to deal with the case satisfactorily and to form a judgment as to whether a conviction ought or ought not to stand.[17]

The court itself consistently displayed, in the words of the counsel who advised on an appeal in *R. v. Ram*,[18] 'powerful psychological and legal reluctance . . . to allowing the re-opening of calculated decisions made by a defendant's legal representatives'. In 1989, in *R. v. Ensor*,[19] the court set as the standard for intervention 'flagrantly incompetent advocacy'. The court, perhaps in anticipation of critical comments by the Royal Commission on Criminal Justice, took a more flexible line in *R. v. Clinton*.[20] Instead of concentrating on the nature of counsel's error, the court said it would concentrate on its effect, but the court added that counsel's error would have to be 'in defiance of or without proper instructions' or against 'all the prompting of reason and good sense' to have an impact on the trial outcome. That this is not always so is demonstrated by *R. v. Boal*[21] where the conviction of a defendant who pleaded guilty because of a mistaken (but excusable) misunderstanding of the law on the part of his counsel was quashed. Nevertheless, the court likes to find 'flagrant incompetence',[22] or at least 'significant fault'[23] before it intervenes. An unwise tactical decision will not do. In *R. v. Ram* Beldham LJ remarked:

[16] (1992) 93 Cr. App. R 287, 311.   [17] HC Debs., 31 May 1907, vol. 175 col. 229.
[18] *The Times,* 7 Dec. 1995.   [19] [1989] 2 All ER 586.   [20] [1993] 2 All ER 998, 1004.
[21] [1992] 3 All ER 177, 183.   [22] *R. v. Donnelly* [1998] *Crim. LR* 131.
[23] *R. v. Ullah* [2000] *Crim. LR* 108.

There seems to be an increasing tendency to believe that it is only necessary to assert the fault of trial counsel to sustain an argument that the conviction is unsafe or unsatisfactory. Whether this is due to a mistaken interpretation of the observations on this subject by the Royal Commission on Criminal Justice we do not know; but we do see far reaching implications in the Commission's suggestion (ch. 9, para. 59) that even a reasonable decision of counsel could be the cause of a miscarriage of justice. Like the Commission, the court could not countenance a case in which the defendant is serving a prison sentence for no other reason than a mistake on counsel's part, but equally where counsel's judgement has been reasonable there is a strong public interest that the legal process should not be indefinitely prolonged on the ground, for example, that a defendant's case advanced within a different legal framework might have stood a greater chance of success. The advantages claimed for the adversarial system of justice of necessity depend greatly on the skill and judgement of trial counsel.

APPEALS FROM GUILTY PLEAS

The desire for closure is particularly strong where an appellant pleaded guilty. The circumstances in which a guilty-plea conviction can be upset on appeal were examined in *R. v. Chalkley*. Auld LJ said[24] that there were two:

(a) when the guilty plea was mistaken or without intention to admit the truth of the offence charge;

(b) 'where the effect of an incorrect ruling of law on admitted facts was to leave an accused with no legal escape from a verdict of guilty on those facts', an exceedingly rare occurrence.

An appeal would not be entertained where the guilty plea was entered because of an erroneous ruling by the trial judge that destroyed all hope of acquittal but did not make acquittal a *legal* impossibility. This is because, Auld LJ explained, a plea of guilty is an acknowledgment of the truth of the facts constituting the offence charged, the more so if counsel puts forward an explanation for the alleged conduct in mitigation of sentence.[25] In adopting this position the court ignored the possibility that the defendant might have intentionally pleaded guilty in the face of inevitable conviction in order to obtain a sentence discount or, if mentally feeble, for some misguided reason.[26] One wonders what the European Court of Human Rights would make of the Court of Appeal's position. Is a judicial process fair that leaves a defendant without remedy against an erroneous ruling by a judge that deprived him of a realistic chance of acquittal, and sometimes of certain acquittal,[27] because he thought he had no practical option but to plead 'guilty'? Even the factually guilty are entitled under Article 6 to a fair trial. In *R. v. Rajcoomar*[28]. Richards J, delivering the judgment of the Court of Appeal, asserted that, after an unequivocal plea of 'guilty', 'there can[not] be

---

[24] [1998] 2 All ER 155 to 169.   [25] *Ibid.* at 169, 171.

[26] *R. v. Lee* [1984] 1 All ER 1080, 182–3.   [27] *R. v. Hewitson* [1999] *Crim. LR* 307.

[28] [1990] *Crim. LR* 728.

any question of the conviction based on that admission of guilt being rendered unsafe by reference to an alleged abuse of process'. Surely, if a trial is 'an affront to the public conscience' (words used by Mustill LJ in *R. v. Mullen*[29] to describe an abuse of process), so too is the resulting conviction. As the law stands, if as a result of a mistaken ruling by the judge on, say, the admissibility of a damaging confession or damning scientific evidence, the defendant loses the chance of being acquitted, he must continue to contest his guilt in order to preserve the right of appeal. This cannot be in anyone's interests. The answer may be, as the Law Commission has recommended,[30] the introduction of a right of interlocutory appeal up to the close of the prosecution case. If the defendant both forgoes an appeal *and* pleads guilty there is no unfairness in denying him an appeal against conviction. It was tentatively suggested in *Chalkley* that the defendant might announce that he was pleading guilty to avoid an unnecessary trial, and that he reserved the right to appeal, but this would entail losing the opportunity to mitigate sentence and might not be effective. A judge might refuse to accept a conditional plea of guilty.

FRESH EVIDENCE

The public interest is best served by requiring the parties to present their case fully at trial. The Court of Appeal is therefore understandably cautious about allowing an appellant to tender fresh evidence on appeal, but, consistent with the fact that the appeal is a re-hearing, it does have a broad discretion to receive evidence. By section 23(2) of the Criminal Appeal Act 1968 in considering whether to exercise this discretion the court is bound to have regard to:

(a) whether there is a reasonable explanation for the failure to adduce the evidence at the trial, *and*

(b) whether the evidence (i) appears to be capable of belief; (ii) may afford any grounds for allowing the appeal; (iii) would have been admissible at the trial on an issue which is the subject of the appeal.

The court frequently hears witnesses give evidence *de bene esse* to help it decide (b)(i). Under the current version of section 23(2) none of the matters mentioned in (a) and (b) is a precondition: 'it is possible for [the] Court to receive evidence, when all four matters are not satisfied, provided the Court has regard to them'.[31] The ultimate touchstone for admitting evidence on appeal is whether this is 'necessary or expedient in the interests of justice' (section 23(1)). The court may thus receive evidence proffered by the Crown in refutation of fresh evidence offered by the defence[32] and in *R. v. Gilfoyle*[33] the court held that it could, on its own initiative, review a decision at the trial that evidence for the prosecution was inadmissible and, if it concluded that the

---

[29] [1999] 2 Cr. App. R 143.

[30] *Prosecution Appeals Against Judges' Rulings*, Law Com. CP No. 158 (London: HMSO, 2000).

[31] *Per* Rose LJ, *R. v. Sale*, The Times, 18 May 2000.   [32] *R. v. Lattimore* (1975) 62 Cr. App. R 53.

[33] (1996) 1 Cr. App. R 302.

evidence was relevant and admissible, receive that evidence. Since 1969 the court has accepted that it may also admit evidence of matters arising subsequent to the trial.[34]

Opinions have differed over the years on how the court should proceed once it has decided to admit fresh evidence. In the leading case, *Stafford* v. *DPP*,[35] Lord Cross said that fresh evidence appeals fall into three categories: those in which the fresh evidence convinces the appeal judges that a conviction is unsafe, those in which the appeal judges are convinced that the fresh evidence is of insufficient weight to make a difference, and those in between which are suitable for a new trial. In the years that followed the court treated most cases as falling into the two extremes. A research study for the Royal Commission on Criminal Justice by Malleson *Review of the Appeal Process* (above) found that a retrial was ordered in just two out of fourteen cases in which fresh evidence was admitted in the first six months of 1990. This was because it was the court's policy to assess for itself the strength of the evidence against the appellant, new and old. Perhaps the highpoint was the first Birmingham Six reference[36] where Lord Lane CJ said:

[T]he question which in the end we have to decide is whether in our judgment, in all the circumstances of the case, including both the verdict of the jury at trial upon the evidence they heard and the fresh evidence before this court that we have heard, the convictions were safe and satisfactory.

Lord Lane CJ certified as a point of law for an appeal to the House of Lords: 'whether on a proper construction of section 2(1) . . . in cases where fresh evidence has been admitted under section 23 . . . a conviction can be unsafe or unsatisfactory only if the Court of Appeal concludes that it has a reasonable doubt about guilt in the light of that evidence' but leave to appeal was refused by both Lord Lane and by the House of Lords. The Court of Appeal's approach was heavily criticized by Lord Devlin in his book *The Judge*,[37] as a usurpation of the role of the jury. His view was that when evidence that was relevant, capable of belief, and *capable* of making a difference was admitted the conviction was automatically unsafe. In these circumstances the court should quash the conviction and, in most cases, order a re-trial. There is much to be said for Lord Devlin's view where the new evidence is not conclusive of innocence and a re-trial is a practical possibility. The appeal judges, relying partly on a transcript of evidence given at the original trial and partly on the fresh evidence, are never as well placed to decide whether the prosecution has proved its case beyond a reasonable doubt as a jury who hear the whole of the relevant evidence. Since *Callaghan* the court has moved some way toward Lord Devlin's position. In 1992 in *R.* v. *Clemmett* the court said that it was 'not for this court to substitute itself for a jury and to assess the evidence, particularly as we have not heard the rest of the evidence at the trial. . . . [I]t is in the public interest that this matter should be cleared up, but it ought not to be done by this court'. In 1998 in *R.* v. *McNamee*[38] the court endorsed similar remarks made by Lord Carswell in *R.* v. *Clegg* a Northern Ireland case. Lord Carswell said, 'It is not for an appellate court to attempt to resolve conflicting issues of fact or opinion,

---

[34] *R.* v. *Ditch* (1969) 53 Cr. App. R 627.   [35] [1973] 3 All ER 762, 767–8.
[36] *R.* v. *Callaghan* (1989) 88 Cr. App. R 40, 47.
[37] P. Devlin, *The Judge*, Oxford: Oxford University Press, 1979, 157ff.   [38] Unreported 17 Dec. 1998.

which will remain the province of the criminal court of first instance' and that '[i]f it considers that a reasonable tribunal of fact might properly resolve the conflict in favour of the appellant, and so be left with a reasonable doubt about his guilt, the court should then allow the appeal and quash the conviction, giving consideration to the question whether to order a new trial'. A re-trial was ordered in *McNamee* notwithstanding that the Crown had made out a 'very strong case' that the appellant was indeed guilty and 'that, as a matter of probability, a jury would still have found him guilty if they had the material that we had' (*per* Swinton Thomas LJ). Under Lord Lane CJ, the appeal would, in all probability, have been dismissed.

FRESH LAW

In the forty-five years that elapsed between the conviction of Derek Bentley and the referral of his case back to the Court of Appeal[39] there were significant changes in the law. Giving judgment in that case, Lord Bingham said that the Court of Appeal (and by analogy any other appellate court) when hearing an appeal must apply: (1) the common law as understood at the time of the appeal, irrespective of whether the common law, at the time of appeal, has been supplanted by statute law; (2) the statute law in force at the time of the trial (as interpreted at the time of the appeal); (3) the standards of procedural fairness that apply at date of the appeal hearing; (4) the criteria for reviewing an appeal in force when the appeal is heard.

As Lord Bingham appreciated, these rules may result in the appeal judges applying 'legal rules and procedural criteria which were not and could not reasonably have been applied' during the trial. The *Bentley* rules can work against, as well as for, the defendant. Lord Bingham does not explain why reform to the common law effected by statute is to be ignored but not reform achieved through the judicial process. Did he have in mind the theory of the common law that says that the judges merely declare law that has always existed? Or, as is more likely, was it in recognition of the fact that the common law (unlike most statute law) operates retrospectively?

Defendants are allowed twenty-eight days within which to make an appeal to the Court of Appeal. May a defendant bring an appeal out of time to take advantage of a change in the law? Waiving the normal time limit is a matter for the discretion of the single judge and, if an extension is refused, on a renewed application, the full Court. In *R. v. Hawkins*[40] Lord Bingham advised judges to 'eshew undue technicality and ask whether any substantial injustice has been done'. Applications to extend the time to appeal because of a change in the law are not received with very much enthusiasm. If leave were too readily granted, the court would be inundated with appeals every time it, or the House of Lords, changed the common law, re-interpreted a statute, or imposed higher standards of procedural fairness. This would undermine finality in criminal litigation and would be grossly unfair to defendants who had exhausted their right of appeal before the law had changed. In *R v. Mitchell*[41]. Geoffrey Lane LJ stated:

[39] *R. v. Derek Bentley*, unreported, 30 July 1998.   [40] 1997) 1 Cr. App. R 234, 240.
[41] 1977) 65 Cr. App. R 185, 178.

It should be clearly understood . . . that the fact that there has been an apparent change in the law or, to put it more precisely, that previous misconceptions about the meaning of a statute have been put right, does not afford a proper ground for allowing an extension of time in which to appeal against conviction.

Unusually, in *Mitchell* leave to appeal against a conviction out of time was given because the effect of the intervening decision (one of statutory interpretation) was to establish that the defendant's conduct (to which he had pleaded guilty) was not criminal. There was also an outstanding appeal against sentence. To have refused to waive the normal time-limit for an appeal against conviction would have left the court 'to determine what the correct sentence was for an offence which had not been committed'.

THE APPEAL STANDARD: FAIR TRIAL OR SAFE CONVICTION?

In 1995 section 2(1) of the Criminal Appeal Act 1968 was amended, so that instead of the three grounds for allowing a defence appeal against conviction that had, with slight modifications, existed since 1907, namely a wrong decision of any question of law, a material irregularity in the course of the trial, or an unsafe or unsatisfactory conviction, there now exists but one ground that, in the opinion of the appeal judges 'the conviction is unsafe'. As a conviction cannot simultaneously be unsafe and inevitable, there was no need to retain the proviso to cater for harmless errors. Since then there has been controversy about what the court should do if the trial is unfair because of some flaw in the trial or a pre-trial irregularity but the evidence against the appellant is so overwhelming that no reasonable jury would have failed to convict the defendant had everything been done properly. In these circumstances the conviction may be 'unsatisfactory', but can it be said to be 'unsafe'? A study published by Knight of the application of the proviso during the first sixty years of the court's life shows that the court had occasionally refused to apply the proviso because of the gross nature of an error in the trial regardless of lack of prejudice to the defendant.[42] Under the revised wording of the legislation, could the Court of Appeal still do this? Should it even contemplate doing this? The answer to the second question has never really been in doubt. Article 6 gives a defendant a right to a fair trial. As far as the Strasbourg Court is concerned, a trial may be unfair even though the members of the Court of Appeal are *not* 'left in doubt that the appellant was rightly convicted'[43] and are satisfied that no reasonable jury would have failed to convict had the trial been properly conducted.[44] The Court emphasized the distinction between a conviction that was safe and a trial that was fair in *Condron* v. *UK*:[45] 'the question whether or not the

---

[42] (*Criminal Appeals: A Study of the Power of the Court of Appeal Criminal Division on Appeals Against Conviction* (London: HMSO, 1970) 10).

[43] *Per* Bingham LJ, *R.* v. *Graham* [1997] 1 Cr. App. R 302, 308.

[44] *R.* v. *Davis*, unreported, 17 July 2000.   [45] Application No. 35718/97, 2 May 2000, para. 65.

rights of the defence guaranteed to an accused under Article 6 . . . were secured in any given case cannot be assimilated to a finding that his conviction was safe in the absence of any inquiry into the issue of fairness'. Initially, at least, the Court of Appeal took a restrictive view of its powers. In *R. v. Chalkley*, Auld LJ said that '[t]he Court has no power under the substituted section 2(1) to allow an appeal if it does not think the conviction unsafe but is dissatisfied in some way with what went on at the trial'.[46] If this is right, then, contrary to Article 13 of the Convention, the defendant has no effective remedy in domestic law against a breach of Article 6 when the appellate judges are satisfied that the prosecution has proven the appellant's guilt, because quashing a conviction is often the only effective means available in English law to mark procedural unfairness. Subsequently, in a case in which abuse of process was alleged, the House of Lords was split on whether the *Chalkley* approach to section 2(1)[47] was correct (with a majority in favour of *Chalkley*) and Auld LJ himself seems to have had second thoughts, because in *R. v. McDonald*[48] he floated the idea that the court might have an inherent power to quash 'a conviction when it considers that the court below should have stayed the proceedings' as an abuse of process. These differences of opinion and the absurdity of the Divisional Court being able to rectify abuse of process in relation to a summary trial, but the Court of Appeal being impotent to do so for a trial on indictment, persuaded another Court of Appeal, in *R. v. Mullen*,[49] to look to *Hansard* to discover what Parliament had really intended by section 2(1). From *Hansard* it was discovered that the Home Secretary, the Minister of State, and the Under-Secretary of State (along with the senior judiciary) had all regarded section 2(1) as merely restating in compendious form the established practice of the Court of Appeal. *Mullen* settled that for a conviction to be safe it must be one that could lawfully take place. It could not settle whether the trial had to be in all other respects fair, though Rose LJ, who delivered the judgment of the court, expressed the opinion that ' "unsafe" bears a broad meaning'. This left the way open for the Court of Appeal to quash convictions resulting from any trial that has infringed Article 6. In *R. v. Smith*[50] in a reserved judgment Mantell LJ described the continuance of the trial after a submission of 'no case' to answer was mistakenly rejected as 'fundamentally unfair' and said that, even had there been evidence before the court of an admission of guilt by the defendant during cross-examination (which there was not), the court would have quashed the conviction.[51] When the opportunity presented itself in *R v. Davis*, which was a reference by the Criminal Cases Review Commission founded in part on the failure of the prosecution to disclose material information, Mantell LJ summed up the law in these terms:

The court is concerned with the safety of the conviction. A conviction can never be safe if there is doubt about guilt. However, the converse is not true. A conviction may be unsafe even where there is no doubt about guilt but the trial process has been 'vitiated by serious unfairness or significant misdirection'.

[46] [1998] 2 All ER 155, 172.   [47] *R. v. Martin* [1998] 1 Cr. App. R 347.   [48] [1998] *Crim. LR* 808.
[49] [1999] 2 Cr. App. R 143.   [50] [2000] 1 All ER 263.
[51] But see *R. v. Doldur, The Times,* Dec. 1999 in which Auld LJ indicated that *Chalkley* applied to any irregularity falling short of an abuse of process. He also disagreed that evidence by the defendant after a submission of 'no case' should be ignored if the judge's ruling of that point was appealed.

R. v. *Francom*,[52] a judgment of Lord Woolf, is to similar effect. The rejection of the *Chalkley* interpretation of section 2(1) signals rather more than a return to the pre-1995 practice. Then it was exceptional for the Court of Appeal to treat an error as 'proviso proof'. Now any error that renders the trial fundamentally unfair should result in the conviction being quashed. Still to be settled is whether a breach of Article 6 always constitutes fundamental unfairness. In *R. v. Davis* Mantell LJ thought not: 'we reject . . . [counsel's] contention that a finding of a breach of Article 6.1 by the ECHR leads inexorably to the quashing of the conviction. . . . The effect of any unfairness upon the safety of the conviction will vary according to its nature and degree' (*per* Mantell LJ).[53] Passages in *Francom* suggest that Lord Woolf thinks otherwise: 'we would expect this court to be approaching the issue of lack of safety in exactly the same way as the ECHR approaches lack of fairness'. Perhaps Mantell LJ had in mind cases in which trial or pre-trial unfairness was cured by the appeal itself, a possibility recognized by the European Court of Human Rights.[1] Be that as it may, a substantial proportion of breaches of Article 6 will require the conviction to be quashed as 'unsafe'. The consequence will not be a lot of palpably guilty defendants being set free. Where the unfairness occurred during the trial the Court of Appeal can often rectify the fault by directing a re-trial. This was an option that was not open to the Court of Appeal for most of the period studied by Knight, and probably explains why the court so rarely refused to apply the proviso when there was compelling evidence of guilt.

THE ISSUE OF PROSECUTION APPEALS

Many Continental countries allow the prosecution to appeal against an acquittal on grounds of law or fact, and the appellate court will reverse the acquittal if the appeal succeeds. In England acquittals by a jury are always final. Various reasons in support of the English rule have been offered. First, that if the prosecution appeal were to succeed, save in rare cases where the facts were not in dispute, the accused would have to undergo the trauma of submitting to judgment a second time either at the hands of the appeal judges or a fresh jury. Continental countries obviously do not regard this as an intolerable burden, neither does the Court of Appeal when it orders a re-trial following a successful defence appeal. Other objections include loss of public confidence in the criminal justice system if an acquittal is overturned and the possibility that juries may become less conscientious. These are not convincing reasons because these risks attach equally to the defence appeals that are, at the present time, permitted. The most compelling argument is that a prosecution right of appeal undermines the jury's ability to acquit an obviously guilty defendant whom the jury thinks should not have been prosecuted. Almost every year at least one such case is reported in

---

[52] Unreported, 31 July 2000.   [53] *R. v. Davis*, unreported, 17 July 2000.
[54] *R. v. Condron*, Application No. 35718/97, 2 May 2000, para. 65.

the press. The jury's *de facto* right to put conscience ahead of the law offers some protection against oppression through the application of unpopular laws. But it simultaneously prevents utterly perverse acquittals from being redressed. Which, on balance, is more important? The argument does not, in any event, apply when the acquittal is directed by the judge or is the result of a misdirection by the judge in the summing up. Throughout the common law world prosecution appeals against acquittal on the ground of error of fact are not permitted, but Canada and New Zealand permit a full appeal against acquittal on a ground that involves a question of law. This includes a directed acquittal. This corresponds to the position in England when a defendant is acquitted by magistrates where the prosecution is entitled to state a case for the High Court or to apply for a judicial review on a legal point.

CONCLUSION

Criminal appeals are integral to the legitimacy of the criminal justice system in England and Wales. While the purpose of the criminal appeal is to correct and deter error and unfairness and to promote consistency it also serves to validate the criminal justice system. The public has confidence in English criminal justice because it knows that if something goes wrong there is a way to put it right. This confidence will be maintained only so long as the appeal process works well. To be effective it must be flexible. One can detect in the judgments of the Court of Appeal throughout the twentieth century a tension between, on the one hand, the principle of trial by jury and finality and, on the other hand, fair treatment of all convicted defendants, including those who pleaded guilty and against whom there is much evidence. The court, particularly now that Article 6 of the European Convention is part of domestic law, must not, in the interests of finality and certainty, shackle itself with rules that make it overly difficult for defendants to complain of injustice. In the interpretation of 'unsafe' adopted in *R. v. Chalkley* the Court of Appeal was in danger of making this mistake, but its regressive response to the change in the wording of section 2(1) of the Criminal Appeal Act 1968 has lately been reversed. As on most other occasions when the tension has become obvious, due process has triumphed in appeal matters over crime control.

Further Reading

Recent Literature

This literature was published after completion of the chapter and is not referred to in it.

AULD, R. (2001) *A Review of the Criminal Courts of England and Wales,* chap. 12
www.criminal-courts-review.org.uk.

EDMOND, G., 'Constructing Miscarriages of Justice: Misunderstanding Scientific Evidence in High Profile Criminal Appeals' [2002] 22 *Oxford J. of Legal Studies* 53–89.

EMMERSON, B., and FRIEDMAN, D., 'Retrospectivity under the Human Rights Act', Matrix Public Law Seminar **www.matrixlaw.co.uk/seminars/documents/7Mar02/ RetrospectivitySEMINAR.pdf.**

MALLESON, K., and ROBERTS, S., 'Streamlining and Clarifying the Appellate Process' [2002] *Crim. LR* 272–282.

SAMUELS, A., 'Should There be a Right of Appeal as Opposed to the Right to Appeal for Leave to Appeal?' (2001) 165 *Justice of the Peace* 122–123.

TAGUE, P., 'Faulty Adversarial Performance by Criminal Defenders in the Crown Court' (2001) 12 *King's College Law Journal* 137–173.

For a detailed account of criminal appeals procedures consult *Taylor on Appeals* (Sweet & Maxwell, 2000) and *Blackstone's Criminal Practice 2001* (Blackstone Press, 2001).

Recent Cases

These cases were decided after completion of the chapter.

R. v. *Togher* [2001] 3 All ER 463, [2001] 1 Cr. App. R 33 (retrospectivity).

R. v. *Kansal (No. 2)* [2001] UKHL 62, [2001] 3 WLR 1562, [2002] 1 All ER 257 (retrospectivity).

R. v. *Jamil* [2001] EWCA Crim. 1687 (fresh evidence on appeal).

R. v. *Pendleton* [2001] UKHL 66, [2002] 1 WLR 72, [2002] 1 All ER 524 (fresh evidence on appeal).

R. v. *Hanratty*, *The Times*, 16 May 2002 (fresh evidence on appeal).

27

MISCARRIAGES OF JUSTICE AND THE CORRECTION OF ERROR

Clive Walker

INTRODUCTION

One expects in a fair and effective criminal justice system that evidence for guilt will be both overwhelming and clearly more convincing than the defendant's claim to innocence. But mistakes are inevitable. Memories are often fragile and may be masked by emotion, and strong inducements encourage both prosecution and defence to be selective in their versions of reality. How far should a criminal justice system be alive to these possibilities of error, and how should it respond?

The answer to the first question is that the values of liberty and justice demand that a very high priority be given to ensuring that state coercive powers are exercised only in justified circumstances. Ultimately, the imposition of official sanctions, such as imprisonment or the imposition of a fine, must be justifiable to the individual affected and must also be acceptable within the norms of society. The result is that a special premium is placed on the values of liberty and justice—more so than on the righting of a criminal wrong. 'It is better that ten guilty persons escape than that one innocent suffer'.[1]

The answer to the second question, how should a criminal justice system respond to the possibility of error, has in large part been examined in this book. Many of the safeguards must reside within the legal rules and the internal working cultures fostered by training and management within institutions such as the police, prosecution, forensic science, judiciary, and advocates. Of further relevance are the appeal courts which, as described in the previous chapter, provide an outlet for certain types of doubt and grievance to be addressed. Yet, no matter what care is expended at each stage of the criminal justice process, the possibility of error remains. So this chapter will consider the nature of what may be called 'residual error' within the criminal justice process in England and Wales, the mechanisms put in place to respond to such residual error, and their performance in recent times.

---

[1] Blackstone, *Commentaries on the Law of England* (1765–9) iv, 27.

RESIDUAL ERROR

A 'miscarriage' means literally a failure to reach an intended destination or goal. A miscarriage of justice is, therefore, *mutatis mutandis*, a failure to attain the desired end-result of 'justice'. Justice is about distributions, about according persons their fair shares, and treatment. As far as the impact of the criminal justice system is concerned, one could argue that fair treatment in the dispensation of criminal justice in a liberal, democratic society means that the State should treat individuals with equal respect for their rights and for the rights of others. It does not follow that individual rights must always be treated as absolute, for it is rationally coherent to accept limitations for the sake of preserving the rights of others or competing rights. The primacy of individual autonomy and rights is central to the well-known due-process model outlined by Packer,[2] which recognizes that the possibility of human fallibility and error can thereby yield grave injustice, as when the system convicts the innocent or even convicts without respecting procedural rights. The due-process model does not underpin much of the daily operation of the English criminal justice system, especially those parts of the system which involve routinized and unsupervised encounters between police and citizen. Yet, it should certainly be to the fore when those encounters become more formalized and more is affected by the operation of the criminal justice system, several are at risk, including humane treatment, liberty, privacy and family life, and even the very right to existence in those jurisdictions which operate capital punishment. The potential costs to the individual will be substantial if he or she becomes subject to the criminal justice system. Nevertheless, criminal and anti-social activities also have a real adverse effect on the enjoyment of rights by others. Hence it is justifiable and necessary for the criminal justice system to take steps against the rights of suspects and convicts, by way of loss of liberty, property, or other proportionate means, in order to protect the rights of others.

One possible definition of 'miscarriage' in the context of criminal justice will now be suggested, and it is one which reflects an individualistic rights-based approach to miscarriages of justice. A miscarriage occurs whenever suspects or defendants or convicts are treated by the State in breach of their rights, whether because of, first, deficient processes or, secondly, the laws which are applied to them or, thirdly, because there is no factual justification for the applied treatment or punishment, or, fourthly, whenever suspects or defendants or convicts are treated adversely by the State to a disproportionate extent in comparison with the need to protect the rights of others, or, fifthly, whenever the rights of others are not effectively or proportionately protected or vindicated by state action against wrongdoers or, sixthly, by state law itself. Each of these six categories will now be illustrated.

(1) The treatment of individuals in breach of their rights because of unfair processes will occur when individuals are subjected to arrest or detention without due cause or to unfair treatment to procure confessions. As well as

---

[2] H. L. Packer, *The Limits of the Criminal Sanction* (Stanford, Cal.: Stanford University Press, 1969) 153.

these breaches of rights perpetrated by the police, a breach may occur at the stage of a trial. Failures can arise through biased judges, perverse juries, and the suppression or mishandling of evidence. A defendant may also be failed by lawyers who fail through inadequate preparation or performance. Some observers attempt to distinguish between those who are really 'innocent' and the wrongfully convicted, and those who are acquitted 'on a technicality'. However, the emphasis here is on the breach of rights, and rights to due process have a central importance in assuring righteous treatment. Accordingly, even a person who has in fact and with intent committed a crime could be said to have suffered a miscarriage if convicted by processes which did not respect basic rights.

(2) Another conceivable category of persons suffering a miscarriage because of a denial of their rights concerns those who fall foul of laws which are inherently unjust rather than unjustly applied. In a responsive, liberal democracy, such failures of the system should be few and far between. However, claims along these lines have been made by persons convicted of failure to pay taxes to finance nuclear weapons or of homosexual activities by adults.

(3) The third category of miscarriage occurs where there is no factual justification for the treatment or punishment. A conviction, perhaps because of mistaken identity, of a person who is in fact innocent would obviously fall into this category of breach of rights (ultimately of humanity and liberty) and indeed might be defined as a core case. Persons enjoy a 'profound right not to be convicted of crimes of which they are innocent'.[3]

(4) Illustrations of miscarriages resulting from disproportionate treatment in terms of rights may include the granting of arrest or extensive search powers in respect of trivial anti-social conduct, or excessively harsh charges or sentences. Similarly, the imposition of conditions during punishment which serve little purpose other than degradation (as opposed to deterrence or the objectives of restorative justice), and therefore do not ultimately bolster respect for rights, should be treated as a miscarriage of justice.

(5) The fifth type of miscarriage, a failure to protect and vindicate the rights of potential or actual victims, can arise in various ways. For example, a lack of police officers to guard against violent attackers could be a breach of rights.[4] A refusal to prosecute particular types of suspects, whether through intimidation, bias, or political manipulation or corruption, may also be viewed as a miscarriage.[5] A failure to vindicate rights may equally occur when a jury perversely refuses to convict an individual, through intimidation or bias. As well as substantive outcomes, victims may also be treated unjustly by the process, a point which is often raised in relation to rape survivors, especially those who have to

---

[3] R. Dworkin, *A Matter of Principle* (Oxford: Clarendon Press, 1986) 72.

[4] See: *Osman v. UK.*, App. No. 23452/94, Reports 1998-VIII, *The Times*, 5 Nov. 1998.

[5] See *Report by the Police Complaints Authority on the Investigation of a Complaint against the Metropolitan Police Service by Mr N. and Mrs D. Lawrence*, Cm 3822 (1997).

face the cross-examination of their alleged assailants or are required to produce corroboration.[6]

(6) A sixth type of miscarriage is the existence and application of laws which are inherently unfair to victims. To continue the theme raised in the last category, the treatment of the sexual history of rape survivors has raised concerns, though the difficulty of balancing fairness to the accused is acute, and the rights of the accused have tended to be treated as more important. One may offer two reasons for this priority, that the loss of rights tends to be more acute in the case of the suspect/convict in the sense that, for example, liberty is immediately threatened, and, secondly, that the loss of rights is entirely a matter of state responsibility whereas the victim has suffered primarily through the actions of third parties.

These six categories may be termed direct miscarriages. In addition, it may be possible to derive from their infliction a seventh, indirect, miscarriage which affects the community as a whole. A conviction arising from deceit or illegality is corrosive of the State's claims to legitimacy on the basis of its criminal justice system's values, such as respect for individual rights. In this way, the 'moral integrity of the criminal process' suffers harm.[7] Moreover, there may be practical detriment in terms of diminished confidence in the forces of law and order, leading to fewer active citizens aiding the police and fewer jurors willing to convict even the blatantly 'guilty'. It is arguable that this indirect form of miscarriage can exist independently as well as contingently.

It is not intended in this commentary to give a full chronology of *causes célèbres* around which discussions about miscarriages of justice have taken place in England and Wales. However, a few examples from recent times will help to illustrate some of the categories listed above and also to explain why reforms have occurred.[8]

(1) The Guildford Four (Paul Hill, Carole Richardson, Gerard Conlon, and Patrick Armstrong) were convicted of pub bombings on behalf of the Irish Republican Army (IRA) in Guildford and Woolwich. An appeal against conviction failed in 1977 despite the fact that other IRA defendants awaiting trial had by then claimed responsibility. However, other new evidence was eventually amassed (including alibis and medical conditions) which persuaded the Home Secretary to order further investigations and to refer the case back to the Court of Appeal. Once it was discovered that detectives in the Surrey Police involved in the case had fabricated statements (especially of Armstrong) and suppressed possible exculpatory evidence, the Director of Public Prosecutions decided not to contest the convictions, which were quashed in 1989. This outcome immediately prompted reconsideration of the Maguire Seven case. Suspicion first fell on the Maguire household when Gerard Conlon (one of the Guildford

---

[6] A. McColgan, 'Common Law and the Relevance of Sexual History Evidence' (1996) 16 *Oxford J. of Legal Studies* 275.

[7] A. L.-T. Choo, *Abuse of Process and Judicial Stays of Criminal Proceedings* (Oxford: Clarendon Press, 1993) 10.

[8] For details of these cases see C. Walker and K. Starmer, *Miscarriages of Justice* (London: Blackstone Press, 1999) chap. 2.

Four) made statements to the police that his aunt, Anne Maguire, had taught him to manufacture bombs. The police raided her house and convictions were obtained mainly on the basis of forensic tests which were said to show traces of nitroglycerine. The Court of Appeal, on a reference back in 1990, grudgingly overturned the convictions because of the possibility that third parties had left the traces in the house and so caused innocent contamination (the non-disclosure of evidence was also a material irregularity in the case). However, the May Inquiry's *Interim* and *Second Reports*[9] on the Maguire case more realistically cast doubt on whether the tests used could in any event be taken to be conclusive proof of the knowing handling of explosives.

(2) The next blow to confidence in the criminal justice system was the Birming-ham Six case in 1991. The six (Patrick Hill, Gerry Hunter, Richard McIlkenny, Billy Power, Johnny Walker, and Hughie Callaghan) had been convicted along with three others of bombings in two Birmingham pubs in 1974. The attacks had caused the most deaths of any IRA incident in Britain and were the signal for the passage of the Prevention of Terrorism Acts. The prosecution evidence rested upon three legs: confessions, which the defendants claimed had been beaten out of them; forensic tests, which the defendants claimed were inher-ently unreliable and had been performed negligently by Dr Skuse (the forensic scientist employed by the police to examine the material); and highly circum-stantial evidence, such as links to known Republicans and the movements and demeanour of the defendants. After the defendants had been refused leave to appeal in 1976, there was a referral back to the Court of Appeal in 1988. The court was then not persuaded, but further revelations about the police fabrica-tion of statements (especially of McIlkenny) and new uncertainties about the quality of the forensic tests eventually secured their release in 1991. That outcome was swiftly followed by the establishment of the Runciman Commission[10] (described below).

(3) The next Irish-related case of relevance is that of Judith Ward, who was convicted in 1974 of delivering the bombs which resulted in twelve deaths on a British Army coach. The conviction was once again undermined by the unreliability of the forensic evidence (Skuse's name appears once more) and of the confessions she made (though this time more because of her mental instability than because of police mistreatment of her). In the background were allegations of non-disclosure of evidence by the prosecution to the defence. Ward's case was referred to the Court of Appeal unilaterally by the Home Office and she was released in 1992 after the prosecution declined to contest the matter. The court's judgment was particularly censorious of the non-disclosure of evidence by named forensic scientists and prosecution counsel.

(4) Another long-running case is that involving the murder of Carl Bridgewater, a newspaper delivery boy who was killed when he interrupted a burglary at Yew

---

[9] Sir John May, *Interim Report on the Maguire Case*, HC, Session 1989–90, 556 and *Second Report on the Maguire Case*, HC Session 1992–3, 296.

[10] (1992) 96 Cr. App. R 1.

Tree Farm, near Stourbridge. Michael Hickey, Vincent Hickey, James Robinson, and Patrick Molloy were imprisoned in 1979. The convictions rested largely on the confession of Molloy, who died in prison in 1981. Molloy, who was denied access to a solicitor, later retracted his confession and claimed he had been tricked by police who showed him a confession by Vincent Hickey, and his refutation was given credence by later electrostatic tests on the police papers, which revealed the imprint of a fake confession. The case was referred back to the Court of Appeal in 1996 (an appeal had been refused in 1989 following a referral back in 1987). The men were released in 1997.

(5) The Tottenham Three (Winston Silcott, Engin Raghip, and Mark Braithwaite) were convicted of the murder of PC Blakelock during the Broadwater Farm riot in 1985. On a referral back to the Court of Appeal in 1991, it was shown that in the case of Silcott notes of the interview were altered by the police, that Raghip's confession was unreliable because of his mental state; and that Braithwaite had been unfairly denied a lawyer.

(6) Release after an even longer period of imprisonment, thirteen years after his original appeal, was ordered in the case of Stefan Kiszko. His conviction for murder was accepted as unsustainable in the light of the medical evidence that he was unable to produce the sperm found on the murdered girl. The processing of this evidence by the prosecution counsel also gave rise to concern.

It will be evident that the largest catalogue of contemporary miscarriages has concerned Irish 'terrorist' cases. Amongst the reasons behind this tendency to lapse from acceptable standards are, first, that terrorist action creates, and is designed to create, extraordinary tension, fear, and panic. These reactions are intended to be induced in the forces of authority, such as the police, just as much as in sectors of the public. Secondly, official reaction to terrorism often involves a conscious departure from the normal due-process ideology of the criminal justice system and a tendency towards the holding of grand 'State trials'. Hence, Lord Denning's comment in response to the Guildford Four case was that even if the wrong people were convicted, 'the whole community would be satisfied'.[11] Nevertheless, there have also occurred various miscarriages which do not relate to Irish terrorism. Though less prominently discussed, this catalogue of cases may in a sense be even more significant, since they have occurred in more commonplace circumstances and under 'normal' policing regimes.

Aside from these notorious cases, some indication should be given of the number of possible miscarriages overall. The Home Office revealed that up to 1991 it received about 700–800 petitions per year.[12] This implies a strong duty on the part of the State to be vigilant about miscarriages and to be willing to rectify them, even if at some cost to aggregate (collective) welfare.

As for rights, evidence presented to the Runciman Commission from a survey of Crown Court cases found that 'problematic' convictions occurred at a rate of 2 per

---

[11] *The Times*, 17 Aug. 1990, 14.
[12] *Memoranda to Royal Commission on Criminal Justice* (London: Home Office, 1991) para. 4.47.

cent (250 cases *per annum*) in the view of judges and 17 per cent (about 2,000) in the view of defence lawyers.[13] Actual rates of application after 1997 to the Criminal Cases Review Commission are related below.

Miscarriages result from a multiplicity of causes, and individual prisoners have often been subjected to more than one form of abuse of authority. However, it is possible from this limited survey to form a picture of what are the recurrent forms of miscarriage in practice.[14]

(1) The most obvious danger is the falsification of evidence. For example, it has been recognized for some time that informers who are co-accused may well have self-serving reasons for exaggerating the role of the defendant. The police are also in a powerful position to manipulate evidence, for example by 'verballing' the accused—inventing damning statements or passages within them. The Birmingham Six and Tottenham Three cases involved such behaviour which is no more excusable because sometimes it is said to have been done in a noble cause.

(2) Both the police and lay witnesses may prove to be unreliable when attempting to identify an offender, especially if the sighting was momentary and in a situation of stress.

(3) The evidential value of expert testimony has also been overestimated in a number of instances only for it later to emerge that the tests being used were inherently unreliable, that the scientists conducting them were inefficient, or both. The Maguire Seven, Birmingham Six, *Ward*, and *Kiszko* cases all fit into this category.

(4) The next common factor concerns unreliable confessions as a result of police pressure, physiological or mental instability or a combination of all of these. Examples include the Guildford Four, Birmingham Six, *Ward*, and Tottenham Three cases.

(5) A further issue may be the non-disclosure of relevant evidence by the police or prosecution to the defence. The investigation of a case is by and large reliant on the police. They speak to all possible witnesses and arrange for all kinds of forensic testing. The defence has neither the financial resources to under-take such work nor the opportunities in terms of access. Yet, several cases, the Guildford Four, Maguire Seven, and *Ward*, demonstrate that the police, forensic scientists, and prosecution cannot be relied upon fairly to pass on evidence which might be helpful to the accused, despite there being no other agency which might uncover it in the interests of justice.

(6) The conduct of the trial may produce miscarriages. For example, judges are

---

[13] M. Zander and P. Henderson, *Crown Court Study*, Royal Commission on Criminal Justice Research Study No. 19 (London: HMSO, 1993) 171.

[14] The CCRC (*Third Annual Report* 1999–2000 (Birmingham: CCRC, 2000) 9) relates the following causes in the 80 cases referred to the Court of Appeal to date: police/prosecution failings = 27; scientific evidence = 26; non-disclosure = 23; new evidence = 23; defective summing up = 11; defective legal arguments = 10; false confessions = 6; defence lawyer failings = 6.

sometimes prone to favour the prosecution evidence rather than acting as impartial umpires, as is alleged in connection with the Birmingham Six. A failure to appreciate the defence's submissions either in law or fact can result in unfairness in their rulings or directions to the jury, as in the Maguire Seven case. Equally, defence lawyers are not always beyond reproach, and may not be as competent or assertive as they should be. Legal-aid funding takes a much smaller proportion of public funds than police and prosecution work.

(7) The next problem concerns the presentation of defendants in a prejudicial manner. An insidious way of achieving this effect is the perjorative labelling of them as 'terrorists'. Similarly, the obvious and heavy-handed security arrangements accompanying trips to court and the defendant's quarantined appearance in the dock inevitably convey an impression of guilt and menace. Prejudice can also arise through media commentaries.

(8) There are the problems associated with appeals and the procedures thereafter. Common difficulties include the lack of access to lawyers and limited legal aid funding, so there has to be reliance on extra-legal campaigns which may or may not be taken up by the media, depending upon factors which have little to do with the strength of the case. The Court of Appeal has made the task even more difficult because of its interpretations of the grounds for appeal. Once the courts are exhausted, complainants have, until recently, had to rely upon an amateurish and secretive review by Home Office officials rather than an independent inquiry.

THE MECHANISMS TO REDRESS RESIDUAL ERROR

The prime mechanism for a reconsideration of official policies on the redress of residual error has been the Royal Commission on Criminal Justice (the 'Runciman Commission'), which reported in 1993.[15] In keeping with many other facets of British public life, Royal Commissions tend to be exercises in bureaucracy and pragmatism rather than philosophy and principle. Accordingly, the Runciman Commission expended little effort on conceptualizing miscarriages of justice, but without much further ado simply emphasized the need for 'the effectiveness of the criminal justice system in England and Wales in securing the conviction of those guilty of criminal offences and the acquittal of those who are innocent', as well as 'the efficient use of resources'. The approach of the Commissioners was criticized sharply, as it encouraged lobbying by official interest groups on grounds unrelated to any analysis of past cases and allowed greater political freedom for the government of the day to interpret, meld, and select from the reform agenda.

For the purposes of the present chapter, attention will be confined to its proposals relating to post-appeal mechanisms to deal with residual errors. Prior to the

---

[15] *Runciman Report*, Cm. 2263, (1993). See chap. 1, paras. 5, 16.

Runciman Report, for an appellant who maintained he or she had been wrongfully convicted but whose appeal under section 1 of the Criminal Appeal Act 1968 had been unsuccessful, the only option available was to lodge a petition with the Home Office. Under section 17 of the Criminal Appeal Act 1968 the Home Secretary was empowered to refer a case back to the Court of Appeal where a person had been convicted on indictment, for a new determination on conviction or sentence or both, as 'he thought fit'. The fitful scrutiny by the Home Secretary's backroom staff and the politically charged reluctance to use the referral power under (the now abolished) section 17 of the Criminal Appeal Act 1968 contributed to an inadequate review system. A proposal for an independent tribunal eventually came to find official favour and was given personal support by the Home Secretary in reaction to the Second Report of the May Inquiry[16] into the Guildford and Maguire cases.[17] The *Runciman Report* acceded to these pressures and recommended a replacement of the reviews and referrals through the Home Office.[18] The idea has been implemented after 1 April 1997 in the shape of the Criminal Cases Review Commission (CCRC) by Part II of the Criminal Appeals Act 1995.

The role of the Criminal Cases Review Commission in respect of allegedly wrongful convictions is in many ways similar to that previously performed by the Home Office. It has no power to determine the outcome of cases for itself but, if certain criteria are established, can refer a case back to the Court of Appeal. However, there are some critical differences between the old and new procedures, and in all cases the new procedures are to be preferred.

PREPARATION OF THE APPLICATION

In the past, a convicted person had to persuade the Home Secretary to intervene by forwarding a petition to the Home Office. As the Home Office, acting through its C3 department, received around 700–800 such petitions every year, it was vital that an individual petition was clearly written and well drafted if it was to catch the eye of the relevant officials. In some circumstances a prisoner may have been able to persuade a legal advisor to work on their behalf for little or no remuneration, but such occasions were rare. The establishment of the CCRC is designed in part to remove some of these initial practical obstacles from the petitioner. Though in the vast majority of cases an applicant will still have to bring his or her case to the attention of the CCRC, much more has been done to make the application process user-friendly. The CCRC also encourages the use of legal advice, though the rules about public funding have not changed.

[16] N. 9 above.

[17] Sir John May, *Report of the Inquiry into the Circumstances Surrounding the Convictions Arising out of the Bomb Attacks in Guildford and Woolwich in 1974*, Second Report (1992–93 HC 296) paras. 10.6, 12.24.

[18] *Runciman Report*, n. 15 above, chap. 11. This was considered further in Home Office, *Criminal Appeals and the Establishment of a Criminal Cases Review Authority* (London: Home Office, 1994).

RESOURCES

The Commission is far better resourced than C3. In addition to the fourteen Commission members, it employs dozens of case-workers. Its annual budget of £4–£5 million also represents a substantial increase in resources when compared to the estimated £750,000 annual running cost of C3. However, whether even these enhanced resources are adequate can be determined only by experience, and in practice, as shall be described, the CCRC has faced an early financial crisis.

CONSIDERATION OF THE APPLICATION

A petition before the Home Office was evaluated by civil servants who, operating within strict self-imposed guidelines, would not consider referring cases to the Home Secretary without new evidence or other considerations of substance not available at the original trial. If the petition, however, appeared to provide *prima facie* grounds for re-examining the case, then further investigations could be carried out. With just twenty-one officers, C3 was under-staffed and under-resourced for the task it was expected to perform. If C3 was of the opinion that a miscarriage of justice might have occurred, the matter would then be passed on to the Home Secretary, who had the final decision in regard to a referral to the Court of Appeal. However, as far as the Home Secretary was concerned, the overriding principle governing the use of his discretionary power was the need to avoid the appearance of any executive interference with the role of the judiciary, and so he would normally refer a case only if there was 'new' evidence available.

This reluctance to refer could be overcome only by a body truly independent of the executive and therefore unfettered by the constitutional constraints experienced by successive Home Secretaries. The constitutional independence of the Commission is provided for in section 8(2) of the Criminal Appeal Act 1995, whereby it 'shall not be regarded as the servant or agent of the Crown or as enjoying any status, immunity or privilege of the Crown'. The Home Secretary is not involved with the selection procedure, does not decide the ways in which the Commission should do its work, and, crucially, is not involved in its decision-making role. At least one-third of the Commission's membership must be legally qualified, and under section 8(6) at least two-thirds 'shall be persons who appear to the Prime Minister to have knowledge or experience of any aspect of the criminal justice system'. As established in April 1997 the Commission has fourteen members, ten of whom are part-time. They will have fixed terms of five years renewable to a maximum of ten years. The apparent desire to appoint members with wide-ranging legal experience in addition to a discerning lay element must also be welcomed when compared to the cohort of civil servants responsible for evaluating petitions in C3 who lacked any formal legal training. However, there are criticisms that the current Commission membership derives too heavily from prosecution interests and that it also largely reflects the white, male, middle-class background that is so often a feature of judicial institutions in the United Kingdom.

As well as by Commissioners, much sifting work is undertaken by case-workers. For each application, a Case Review Manager, with a Commissioner acting as a mentor, starts to obtain the basic required documentation, arranges for directions to be issued and the preservation of papers by the relevant authorities, and considers the cases for any special priority. A preliminary assessment will also be made at this stage to establish eligibility on the grounds that appeal rights have been exhausted and that there are grounds on which an appeal would be likely to succeed, if the grounds for application were true (if not, the case goes forward as a 'short form of review'). If successful at this stage the case then undergoes a more intensive, Stage 2, review, when a Case Review Manager and a Commissioner are assigned to work on the case. The case-worker peruses the documentation, makes inquiries, and, in consultation with the assigned Commissioner, takes a preliminary view on referral. If the case-worker is not satisfied that there is a real possibility that the conviction would be reversed were the case referred back, the applicant is sent a 'short form' of reasons and is given twenty-eight days to make a response. Rejections are finally made by a single Commissioner, in consultation with the Case Review Manager. If, on the other hand, the Case Review Manager and Commissioner believe that there may be a possibility of reversal, then the case is presented to a quorum of three Commissioners who take the final decision whether to refer. Following a referral to the Court of Appeal, the CCRC's involvement ceases.

RE-INVESTIGATIONS

Most applicants will still be faced with the problem of trying to persuade the Commission to use its resources in carrying out further investigations. As the quality of re-investigations under the old reference procedure was heavily criticized, it is vital to the success of the Commission that it is seen to have thorough and, as far as is possible, transparent investigative processes. But the government stood fast against giving the Commission an ability to investigate cases with its own staff:[19]

The Government has no intention of funding a team in the Commission whose job would be to operate as a mini police force, duplicating work which could, and should, be done by the police. . . . We envisage its doing investigative work from time to time but, generally the right people to investigate will be the police.

Consequently, there are no CCRC in-house investigative staff. Instead, investigations are mainly carried out by the police under the supervision of the Commission. Under section 19 of the 1995 Act the Commission can require the appointment of an investigating officer to carry out inquiries, and can insist that the investigating officer be from a different police force from the one which carried out the original investigation. The Commission can also direct that a particular person shall not be appointed or, should it be dissatisfied with his or her performance, it can require under section 20 that the officer be removed. As Malet suggests, 'In short, the 1995 Act takes a trusting attitude to the police',[20] and this relationship represents a major concern for the future effectiveness of the CCRC.

[19] HC Debs, vol. 263, cols. 1371–72, 17 July 1995.
[20] D. Malet, 'The New Regime for the Correction of Miscarriages of Justice' (1995) 159 JP 716, at 765–6.

DISCLOSURE OF EVIDENCE

The Commission has a wide power to obtain documents from public bodies under section 17 of the 1995 Act 'where it is reasonable to do so'. The provisions of section 17 do not extend to any information in regard to a minister's previous consideration of the case, though this limit is of diminishing importance. As regards disclosure of information to the applicant, in *R. v. Secretary of State for the Home Department, ex parte Hickey (No. 2)*,[21] Simon Brown LJ ensured through his judgment that when the Home Secretary was minded to reject an applicant's petition on the basis of evidence gathered in any further inquiries, the applicant should be given an opportunity to make representations upon such material before a final decision is made. There is no general duty under the 1995 Act to disclose all the information gathered during any re-investigation, the government preferring to rely upon the flexible standard of fairness in *Ex parte Hickey*.

REFERRAL TO THE COURT OF APPEAL

In order to refer a case to the Court of Appeal, the CCRC under section 13(1) of the Criminal Appeal Act 1995, must 'consider that there is a real possibility that the conviction ... would not be upheld were a reference to be made ... '. This 'real possibility' can be realized through 'an argument, or evidence, not raised in the proceedings'. This is effectively wider than the Home Office review and may ensure the criteria for referrals are more easily satisfied. No longer will there be a need to provide 'new evidence' as interpreted by the Home Office. At the same time, the Act left much to be determined by the interpretations of the CCRC and also the receptivity of the Court of Appeal, which will have to be second-guessed by the CCRC. More radical solutions would have been to give the Commission the power to determine applications or at least to make recommendations to the Court of Appeal either to acquit or to order a retrial, placing the onus on the judges to find reasons to disagree. However, these ideas could be seen as interfering too much with judicial independence and the finality of verdicts.

In terms of design, the CCRC is an important and innovative reform which does recognize the possibility of residual error and places state facilities on call for their correction. However, there are at least two potential design problems. One concerns the level of resources, which is designed to render the CCRC reliant upon the police for investigation and also could leave it struggling to cope with its case-load. The second is that the CCRC's powers end with a referral, so that it is ultimately dependent on the receptivity and performance of the Court of Appeal, which has emerged relatively unscathed from the Runciman reforms.

---

[21] [1995] 1 All ER 490.

PERFORMANCE OF THE CCRC

The CCRC has been widely accepted, in theory and in practice, to be a great improvement on its predecessors, the C3 Department of the Home Office and an equivalent unit in the Northern Ireland Office. Not only is it an independent body, separate from both the executive and the judiciary, but it has enhanced resources, staffing, and even, arguably, expertise. Most importantly, its receptive approach and attitude is in complete contrast to the reluctance, endemic in the governmental departments, to reinvestigate cases with thoroughness.

The CCRC began work on 1 April 1997 with 270 cases transferred to it from the Home Office and twelve from the Northern Ireland Office. In its first three years of operation, 2,914 new applications have been received; perhaps in the light of this workload, the CCRC has not yet exercised its power under section 14 of the 1995 Act to review a suspected miscarriage in the absence of an application.

The CCRC has powers under section 19 to appoint an outside Investigating Officer. By the end of August 1999, Investigating Officers (invariably from the police) had been appointed in thirteen cases. In the three completed reviews all were appointed from forces different from those whose investigations had led to the original convictions. The modest use of section 19 reflects the possibility that more limited fact-finding can arise from the commissioning by the case worker (under section 21) of specific independent reports, such as by engineers, forensic scientists, and psychiatrists. In addition, the Commission itself has adopted the practice of carrying out for itself as much fieldwork as is practicable (including interviews with witnesses, lawyers, and the applicant). But it is a disappointing replication of Home Office practices that police officers have invariably been employed as investigators. It seems that the financial consideration that the police provide their services for free to the CCRC will prove weighty in both the short and long term.

By 31 March 2000, eighty cases had been referred to the Court of Appeal. Of these, just thirty-five had been determined (in twenty-seven of which convictions or sentences were quashed or reduced). The first case to be considered was that of *Mattan*.[22] It is an encouraging sign that Rose LJ expressly recognized that 'the Criminal Cases Review Commission is a necessary and welcome body, without whose work the injustice in this case might never have been identified'. Similarly, in *R. v. Criminal Cases Review Commission, ex parte Pearson*,[23] Lord Bingham asserted that 'it is essential to the health and proper functioning of a modern democracy that the citizen accused of crime should be fairly tried and adequately protected against the risk and consequences of wrongful conviction'. This approbation would have been of little comfort to Mahmood Mattan, who was hanged in 1952, but it provided great encouragement to others and gave the CCRC a good start in its relationship with the Court of Appeal.

Of the cases which have reached judgment to date, the case of Derek Bentley (who

---

[22] *R. v. Mattan, The Times*, 5 Mar. 1990.
[23] [2000] 1 Cr. App. R 141.

was hanged in 1952),[24] decided in July 1998, was perhaps the most remarkable, not only because of its history but also because it gave rise to the alarming implication that older convictions can become vulnerable simply by the application of current standards of due process. The Court of Appeal relied essentially upon the unfair conduct of the trial and directions to the jury by Lord Goddard CJ, an issue which had been raised without success in the appeal immediately following conviction in 1952. This prospect has become less likely since the decision in *Gerald* in November 1998.[25] Rose LJ expressed mild annoyance that the referral (concerning a conviction for grievous bodily harm in 1987) had been made at all: 'we venture to express a measure of surprise that, in this case, in which, as will emerge, there is no new evidence and the points which form the substance of the appeal were never canvassed in evidence or argument at trial, the Commission has thought it appropriate to [refer]'. A corresponding approach has been established in regard to sentencing referrals in the case of *R. v. Graham.*[26]

Since only a small number of cases have so far been dealt with by the Court of Appeal, it is premature to make a final appraisal of the success of the scheme under the 1995 Act. Nevertheless, the CCRC has on the whole been well received by the legal profession and other criminal justice agencies, as shown by the submissions to the House of Commons' Home Affairs Select Committee's survey, *The Work of the Criminal Cases Review Commission.*[27] The Select Committee considers that it has made a 'good start'.[28]

However, this positive picture must be balanced with some difficulties. One problem concerns the meaning of the statutory test for referral. The CCRC's decisions on referral are governed by section 13 of the 1995 Act. This provides that there must be a 'real possibility' that the original conviction, finding, or sentence[29] would not be upheld as 'safe' were the conviction to be referred back to the Court of Appeal. In the case of a conviction, the 'real possibility' must be as a result of an argument or evidence not raised in the original proceedings, or of 'exceptional circumstances' such as wholly inadequate defence representation. While 'real possibility' itself is not defined in the Act, early indications suggest that the test prescribed in section 13(1)(a), although imprecise, denotes a contingency which in the Commission's judgement is 'more than an outside chance or a bare possibility, but which may be less than a probability or a likelihood or a racing certainty'.[30] Whether this formula provides a sufficiently clear signal of society's determination to avoid miscarriages remains to be seen.

Next, the backlog of cases before the CCRC causes some anxiety. By the end of

---

[24] *The Times*, 31 July 1998.   [25] [1999] *Crim. LR* 315.

[26] LEXIS, 23 Feb. 1999 (CA).

[27] Home Affairs Select Committee, *The Work of the Criminal Cases Review Commission*, Cm 2263 (1999).

[28] *Ibid.*, para.19.

[29] An additional problem was encountered by Iain Hay Gordon in 1998 (see *Criminal Cases Review Commission's Reference under s 14(3) of the Criminal Appeal Act 1995* [1998] NI 275). A 'guilty but insane' verdict under the Trial of Lunatics Act 1883 did not amount to a conviction, finding, or sentence for the purposes of s. 10 of the 1995 Act until amended by the Criminal Cases Review (Insanity) Act 1999.

[30] *R. v. CCRC, ex parte Pearson* [2000] 1 Cr. App. R 141, *per* Bingham LCJ.

August 1999, a total of 2,763 submissions had been received by the CCRC. Of these, 1,194 awaited completion, with 445 actively being worked on. In total, 1,124 cases have been completed (including those deemed ineligible, fifty-four referrals, and 142 refusals to refer). The overall daily intake has been around four, while the disposal rate has been around two. Even before the CCRC started work in 1997, concern was voiced that it would be swamped with new applications, especially from applicants who had derived no satisfaction from C3. These fears soon materialized. By 31 March 1998, 1,096 new cases had been received, with an accumulation of 851 cases awaiting review; by 31 March 1999, there was an additional intake of 1,034 cases and combined queue of 1,105. Recognizing the implications of such a backlog, the CCRC made a bid for more money in January 1998 in order to increase the number of Case Review Managers from twenty-seven to sixty. This request was refused, but the Home Secretary awarded the CCRC a further £1.28 million in February 1999, enabling it to increase its work-space and to appoint twelve more Case Review Managers (plus four more administrative staff) for the financial year 1999–2000. Concern persisted that the work was still piling up as the CCRC moved into its third year, and that this would itself create injustice as well as damaging confidence and demoralizing staff. There was also the danger that some of these dissatisfied customers might begin legal action against the CCRC for the injustice of delay. Assuming its own complaints mechanism is exhausted without satisfactory redress, the possibilities include judicial review[31] and an action based on the Human Rights Act 1998.

Taking the case backlog and delay as the most pressing problems, the Select Committee advanced four possible strategies: that the CCRC should reassess its approach to referrals; that it should greatly increase its productivity; that its resources must be significantly increased; or some combination of the foregoing. The issue of increased resources has already been considered, and the Select Committee inquiry itself deserves credit for its part in the pressure which prompted the change of heart in the Home Office. The remainder of this commentary will therefore concentrate on the approach to referrals and productivity.

APPROACH TO REFERRALS

The Select Committee argued that the CCRC could take a changed approach to its investigation of cases in that it could 'prune the amount of detailed work done' with no loss of effectiveness, describing its investigative processes as 'highly technical and formulaic'.[32] This feature, it is contended, has contributed greatly to the large backlog of cases that has now built up. It could be contended that in looking for a 'real possibility' that a conviction would be reversed by the Court of Appeal, the CCRC should not be second-guessing the Court of Appeal and referring only those cases which are sure to be overturned. The high success rate in the Court of Appeal combined with the low number of cases referred seems to be indicative of this tendency. However, there are problems with a more cursory review. The risks arise that less

---

[31] For a successful application, see R. v. CCRC, ex parte Cleeland, 31 Mar. 2000 (DC).
[32] Select Committee, Report, n. 27 above, paras. 26, 44.

obvious grounds for referral will be overlooked, so that cases are not referred or are referred on weaker grounds than necessary, with no certainty that the necessary investigative work will be undertaken in time by defence lawyers, prosecutors, or appellate judges.[33] A major criticism levelled at the Home Office was its inability or reluctance to investigate thoroughly those cases which initially appeared to have little chance of success. If at this early stage in the life of the CCRC the quality of preliminary investigation is reduced, honed down to a mechanical filtration and rejection process with eligibility thresholds being effectively increased, the CCRC will quickly become as discredited as the previous system. There is also the danger of incurring the wrath of the Court of Appeal if a sizeable proportion of referrals fails.

PRODUCTIVITY

As regards improvements to the CCRC's working practices suggested by the Select Committee, the following are the more substantial or more controversial changes advocated.

First, the Select Committee suggested that the CCRC should publicize the availability of legal advice in order that a greater proportion of the applications received meet the eligibility criteria.[34] In this way private lawyers could act as gatekeepers for the CCRC, saving the time of the Case Review Manager who would otherwise have to check for eligibility (around 25 per cent of applications are ineligible, mainly because of the failure to exhaust appeals). To a certain extent this goal has been pursued through the production of the CCRC's video, 'Open to Question', which may have contributed to the increase from 10 to 30 per cent in applications prepared with legal assistance from 1997 to the end of March 2000. The utilization of private lawyers is not, of course, an overall saving to the public purse if their work is paid for from the Legal Aid Fund, but there may be savings in regard to the cost of unjust imprisonment.

The Select Committee also considered various permutations in priorities. In this regard, the CCRC has rightly given little prominence to summary cases (they amount to 7 per cent of the workload)[35] but instead has adopted a system of priority which largely favours those in custody in date order of receipt. But it also gives priority to two more dubious categories.[36] One is the cases falling under the short form of review procedure. In other words, weaker cases are accelerated, which must improve the statistical returns but hardly makes much sense in terms of justice. Secondly, there is priority for those cases transferred from the Home Office and Northern Ireland Office, yet one wonders whether so much effort should be expended on old cases which involve files of gargantuan proportions but no live defendants and arguably no live issues for the contemporary criminal justice process.

---

[33] The Court of Appeal can now direct the CCRC to carry out investigations but, up to 31 March 2000, just 3 matters had been referred under the Criminal Appeal Act 1995 s. 15.

[34] Select Committee, *Report*, n. 27 above, para. 47.

[35] Summary cases are altogether excluded from the Scottish CCRC scheme (see n. 37 below).

[36] Select Committee, *Report*, n. 27 above, paras. 38, 39.

Another area (not considered by the Select Committee) where savings could be made concerns the establishment on 1 April 1999 of a separate Scottish CCRC.[37] It is arguable that valuable resources and time are being dissipated through the process of institutional establishment and subsequent maintenance, whereas a unified United Kingdom Commission could have operated earlier and more efficiently and effectively through the dissemination of practices and experiences. Though Scotland has a distinct criminal process, its differences should not be reflected in expensive offices and equipment or the reinvention of working systems. So the separation is explained by the pandering to historical symbolism rather than a determination to combat miscarriages of justice.

Some of the recommendations of the Select Committee could result in a clearing of the backlog of cases awaiting consideration without being detrimental to those cases. However, the principal tone of its Report is one of bureaucratic efficiency involving a cut in standards. The appropriate responses should be a lobby for more resources or the reconsideration of priorities within existing resources. It is heartening that these have indeed been the responses of the CCRC, which agrees with the Select Committee's combination approach, but focuses on productivity and resources. Conversely, it rightly cautions against a more superficial approach to the examination of applications.[38] Fortunately, the crisis has now receded somewhat through a combination of factors. One is that extra resources have produced a greater capacity within the CCRC, and further subventions in 1999 have allowed for the number of Case Review Managers to rise to fifty. The second is that the flow of applications significantly diminished in 1999–2000 to just 774, taking the level back to the rates pertaining before the CCRC came into existence, and perhaps suggesting that the interest it generated amongst existing prisoners has now run its course. Accordingly, by 31 March 2000, the case accumulation had been reduced to 886 and was falling at a modest rate.

CONCLUSIONS

The CCRC has started well and has gained widespread support and confidence. There are signs that a combination of reforms in working practices plus further resources are overcoming its early difficulties. With more resources further work could be undertaken by the CCRC. It has been shown that legal advice is vital to the conduct of applications. In addition, an emergent agenda is the compensation of the wrongfully imprisoned and abused.[39] Wider meanings of reparation, such as rehabilitation,

---

[37] See Criminal Procedure (Scotland) Act 1995 s. 194A–L, as inserted by the Crime and Punishment (Scotland) Act 1997 s. 25. In its first year it received 127 applications (including 19 transferred from the Scottish Office) and reached 14 decisions (with 2 referrals): *First Annual Report 1999–2000* (Glasgow: 2000). It has 7 commissioners and 4 case-workers.

[38] *Second Annual Report 1998–99* (Birmingham: 1999) 7.

[39] See C. Walker and K. Starmer, *Miscarriages of Justice* (London: Blackstone Press, 1999) chap. 12.

restoration of dignity and reassurance of non-repetition, are also not presently considered by the CCRC.

Criminal justice systems should be judged, *inter alia*, by the number of injustices produced by them in the first place, and, secondly, by their willingness to recognize and correct those mistakes. The British system could improve on both counts. The institution of the CCRC is much to its credit, but the failure to reform the Court of Appeal may yet undermine its future.

Further Reading

BELLONI, F., and HODGSON, J., *Criminal Injustice* (London: Macmillan, 2000).

Committee on Criminal Appeals and Alleged Miscarriages of Justice, *Report*, Cm 3245 (1996).

Criminal Cases Review Commission web page, **www.ccrc.gov.uk/**.

FIELD, S., and THOMAS, P. A. (eds.), *Justice and Efficiency*, special volume of (1994) 21(1) *Journal of Law & Society* (special issue, Blackwell, London).

GREER, S., 'Miscarriages of Justice Reconsidered' (1994) 57 *MLR* 58.

HILL, P., and YOUNG, M., *Rough Justice* (London: BBC, 1983).

—— and —— *More Rough Justice* (London: Penguin, 1986).

Home Affairs Select Committee, *The Work of the Criminal Cases Review Commission* (1998–99 HC 106) and Government Reply (1998–99 HC 569).

Home Office, *Criminal Appeals and the Establishment of a Criminal Cases Review Authority: A Discussion Paper* (London: HMSO, 1994).

JAMES, A., TAYLOR, N., and WALKER, C., 'The Criminal Cases Review Commission: Economy, Effectiveness and Justice' [2000] *Crim. LR* 140.

JESSEL, D., *Trial and Error* (London: Headline, 1994).

JUSTICE, *Miscarriages of Justice* (London: JUSTICE, 1989).

Lord Chancellor's Department, Home Office and Law Officer's Department, *The Royal Commission on Criminal Justice: Final Government Response* (London: Home Office, 1996).

McCONVILLE, M., and BRIDGES, L. (eds.), *Criminal Justice in Crisis* (Aldershot: Edward Elgar, 1994).

MALLESON, K., 'A Broad Framework' (1997) 147 *JP* 1023.

MAY, SIR JOHN, *Report of the Inquiry into the Circumstances Surrounding the Convictions Arising out of the Bomb Attacks in Guildford and Woolwich in 1974, Interim Report* (1989–90 HC 556).

—— *Second Report* (1992–93 HC 296).

—— *Final Report* (1993–94 HC 449).

MULLIN, C., *Error of Judgment* (3rd edn., Dublin: Poolbeg, 1990).

NOBLES, R., and SCHIFF, D., *Understanding Miscarriages of Justice* (Oxford: Oxford University Press, 2000).

Northern Ireland Office, *Criminal Appeals and Arrangements for Dealing with Alleged Miscarriages of Justice in Northern Ireland* (Belfast: Northern Ireland Office, 1994).

PATTENDEN, R., *English Criminal Appeals 1844–1994* (Oxford: Clarendon Press, 1996).

Royal Commission on Criminal Justice, *Report*, Cm 2263 (1993).

ROZENBERG, J., *The Search for Justice* (London: Hodder & Stoughton, 1994).

Scottish Criminal Cases Review Commission web page, **www.sccrc.co.uk**.

SMITH, J.C., 'Appeals against Conviction' [1995] *Crim. LR* 920.

WALKER, C., and STARMER, K., *Justice in Error* (London: Blackstone Press, 1993).

——and—— *Miscarriages of Justice* (London: Blackstone Press, 1999).

WOFFINDEN, B., *Miscarriages of Justice* (2nd edn., Sevenoaks: Coronet, 1989).

28

RESTORATIVE JUSTICE
Assessing the prospects and pitfalls

Carolyn Hoyle and Richard Young

INTRODUCTION

The term 'restorative justice' as yet has no settled meaning. Indeed, and partly because of this lack of agreement, a recent United Nations document proposing 'basic principles' on the use of restorative justice deliberately avoided defining the term.[1] For the purposes of this chapter, we will take restorative justice to encompass a diverse and developing set of values, aims, and processes which have as their common factor attempts to repair the harm caused by criminal behaviour. It may address a wide range of such harms, including both material and psychological damage, as well as damage to relationships and the more general social order. It should be noted at the outset that restorative justice generally presupposes that the offender has acknowledged responsibility for an offence. In other words restorative justice is not concerned with fact-finding but with an appropriate response to an admitted offence. Its realm is that of sentencing, not that of the criminal trial.

The chapter begins with the rise of restorative justice and an examination of emergent definitions. Next there is a description of the recent statutory reforms that have introduced restorative-justice practices into the mainstream youth justice system of England and Wales, and a consideration of various potential uses for restorative justice and examines the debates concerning what is appropriate territory for restorative interventions. The chapter ends with a discussion of the problems and tensions within restorative justice, focusing especially on the arguments for keeping it away from state control.

---

[1] 'Basic principles on the use of restorative justice programmes in criminal matters', ECOSOC Resolution 2000/14, adopted 27 July 2000. Discussed in D. van Ness, 'Proposed United Nations Basic Principles on the Use of Restorative Justice: Recognizing the Aims and Limits of Restorative Justice' in A. von Hirsch, J. Roberts, A. Bottoms, K. Roach, and M. Schiff (eds.), *Restorative Justice and Criminal Justice: Competing or Reconcilable Paradigms?* (Oxford: Hart, forthcoming 2002).

THE RISE OF RESTORATIVE JUSTICE

The modern Anglo-American professional and bureaucratic criminal justice system, with decisions on whether to prosecute concentrated in the hands of the State, did not emerge until the latter part of the nineteenth century. While this system has swung at different times between rehabilitative/welfarist and retributive models of punishment, both have focused primarily on the offender. The unintended consequence has been the marginalizing of both victims and communities from the day-to-day workings of the criminal process. The feelings shared by many victims were summed up in an oft-cited article by Christie, which argued that the State had 'stolen the conflict'; and that in so doing had usurped the ability of victims to seek reparation and recompense for the harms they had suffered.[2]

Although mainstream policy remained concerned mainly with prosecution, the 1970s and 1980s saw the start of new initiatives that tried to embrace victims in what could be seen as proto-restorative ways. The first 'victim–offender reconciliation programme' was founded in Kitchener, Ontario, in 1974. Later, various American community programmes brought together victims and offenders, usually after a court had passed sentence. These mediation schemes aimed at providing individual reparation and reconciliation. By the mid-1990s, there were over 300 such programmes in North America,[3] as well as a number of similar schemes in England and Wales.[4]

The 1980s saw the first attempts to include 'the wider community', however defined, in such programmes. For example, indigenous Canadian peacemaking processes provided the inspiration for 'sentencing circles', group mediation involving offenders, victims, their families, and other community members—which focus on the harms done by offences and seek consensus on their resolution.[5] These mainly local models[6] began to catch the attention of criminal justice agents, academics, and policy-makers throughout the English-speaking world. Although they encompassed a broad range of aims and practices, most of them found themselves classified under a new umbrella label, 'restorative justice'. Claims were soon being made that this was a far better way of doing justice than the mainstream system could provide. In 1990 Howard Zehr inaugurated what has since become something of a restorative

---

[2] N. Christie, 'Conflicts as Property' (1977) 17 *British Journal of Criminology* 1.

[3] M. Umbreit, 'Restorative Justice through Juvenile Victim–Offender Mediation' in L. Walgrave and G. Bazemore (eds.), *Restoring Juvenile Justice* (Amsterdam: Kugler Publishers, 1998).

[4] See J. Dignan and P. Marsh, 'Restorative Justice and Family Group Conferences in England' in A. Morris and G. Maxwell (eds.), *Restorative Justice for Juveniles: Conferencing Mediation and Circles* (Oxford: Hart, 2001) for a description of 4 of the best-known family-group conferencing projects in England, and T. Marshall and S. Merry, *Crime and Accountability* (London: HMSO, 1990) for a discussion of victim offender mediation.

[5] See H. Lilles, 'Circle Sentencing: Part of the Restorative Justice Continuum' in Morris and Maxwell, n. 4 above; and B. Stuart, 'Circle Sentencing: Turning Swords into Ploughshares' in B. Galaway and J. Hudson (eds.), *Restorative Justice: International Perspectives* (Monsey, NY: Criminal Justice Press, 1996).

[6] See H. Blagg, 'Aboriginal Youth and Restorative Justice' in Morris and Maxwell, n. 4 above, for a critique of claims that restorative justice practices reflect indigenous patterns of community association.

justice fanfare by suggesting that it could become a fully-functioning alternative to established criminal justice, a new 'lens' through which to perceive crime.[7]

DEFINING RESTORATIVE JUSTICE

A review of the literature suggests that there are more definitions of restorative justice than there are programmes. Some emphasize core values and principles, some focus on outcomes and aims, whilst still others apply the term to specific processes or programmes. In considering the various definitions of restorative justice and the debates over what it does and should mean, it is important to note that for some the problem of defining the concept is rooted in the name itself. Hence alternatives, such as 'relational justice', 'positive justice', and 'reintegrative justice', are occasionally adopted. Others have tried to move away from the word 'justice', but have so far failed to come up with a credible alternative.

RESTORATIVE JUSTICE VALUES

Most restorative justice advocates agree that its core values include: mutual respect; the empowerment of all parties involved in the process (except the facilitator); neutrality of the facilitator; accountability; consensual, non-coercive participation and decision-making; and the inclusion of all the relevant parties in meaningful dialogue. In particular, the inclusion of victims is held by most to be an extremely important value, although there is disagreement over what it means to participate. Many consider that a victim's participation should be direct, through attending a meeting with 'their' offender and others affected by the offence. Others feel that participation can be indirect, through a mediator, for example, or through a representative at a meeting.

Not all restorative-justice advocates share these values. There is, for example, some disagreement over the notion of non-coercive participation and decision-making. In many cases offenders have little choice but to participate in a restorative meeting or accept a restorative sentence, since the alternative is usually a harsher process or sentence or is presented as such. Less obviously, many victims who participate in restorative encounters may do so out of a sense that it is their public duty to help the offender or the State. Where this sense of duty is fostered by those running restorative processes, the victim's participation, whilst not coerced, is arguably not fully voluntary. It can, therefore, be misleading to describe restorative processes as involving voluntary participation. Most people, however, agree that people should not be directly forced into participating in restorative processes. There is no agreement on whether coercion is appropriate to enforce restorative outcomes.[8]

---

[7] H. Zehr, *Changing Lenses: A New Focus for Criminal Justice* (Scottsdale, Penn.: Herald Press, 1990).

[8] J. Dignan, 'The Crime and Disorder Act and the Prospects for Restorative Justice' [1999] *Crim. LR* 48.

Whilst there is some divergence over specific restorative justice values, some, if adhered to, can be said to impose their own 'procedural safeguards'. They should avoid many of the potential pitfalls of restorative justice (discussed below). For example, they should reduce the risk of 'compulsory attitudinizing',[9] insincere apologies produced through the coercive effect of a process which aims to encourage offenders to express regret and to make good harms. Such a degree of coercion would be contrary to the value of mutual respect and would undermine the meaningful nature of the dialogue, since a coerced apology is unlikely to be regarded as sincere by other participants.

THE AIMS OF RESTORATIVE JUSTICE

Restorative justice embraces multiple aims. This allows restorative justice to appeal to a broad spectrum of interest groups and political positions. However, the difficult choices that must be made when the various aims come into conflict with one another have yet to be properly addressed. The sweeping nature of statements made about the aims of restorative justice are well illustrated by Marshall's argument that restorative justice should prevent re-offending, help victims more effectively, and recreate community.[10] Others focus more on the restorative process itself, arguing that this should seek to restore all three groups which are recognized as stakeholders in the offence, the offenders, the victims, and the wider community.[11] It should restore their material and emotional loss, safety, damaged relationships, dignity, and self-respect.

Another key aim for many adherents to restorative justice is to move the victim back into the system. The last decade in England and Wales has seen other attempts to achieve this within the mainstream criminal process. A series of 'Victims' Charters' has been at best a limited success. While they marked the system's recognition of victims' needs and vulnerabilities, they have done little to change the way it works in practice. Evaluation of a pilot scheme which introduced Victim Impact Statements into court cases found them counterproductive. They raised victims' expectations, but had no effect on outcomes, leaving many victims bewildered and dissatisfied.[12] One problem with such statements is that they are essentially static. They presuppose a lack of dialogue between offender and victim, and thus do not carry any potential for views to be reconsidered in the light of such a dynamic interaction.

By contrast many restorative-justice practitioners seek to trigger a *genuine* apology from the offender directly to the victim and to promote greater mutual understanding. In a restorative meeting an apology is unlikely to be perceived to be genuine or satisfactory unless it comes after the offender has heard how their actions have caused harm, to both the victim and others. To arrive at restoration and reconciliation

---

[9] A risk highlighted by A. von Hirsch in a seminar paper given at All Souls College, Oxford, 25 Apr. 2001.

[10] T. Marshall, 'Seeking the Whole Justice', ISTD Conference, *Repairing the Damage: Restorative Justice in Action*, 20 Mar. 1997, 10.

[11] J. Braithwaite, 'Restorative Justice: Assessing Optimistic and Pessimistic Accounts' in M. Tonry (ed.), *Crime and Justice: A Review of Research* (Chicago, Ill.: University of Chicago Press, 1999), xxv.

[12] C. Hoyle, E. Cape, R. Morgan, and A. Sanders, *Evaluation of the 'One Stop Shop' and Victim Statement Pilot Projects* (London: Home Office RDSD, 1998).

victims need to tell their 'stories', and, just as important, be listened to. Restorative justice also gives offenders a voice. It encourages them, indeed requires them, to talk about what they did and to explain how they think their actions may have affected others. In an effort to hold them accountable, they are denied the chance of allowing someone else to speak for them, as a lawyer would in court. Through dialogue it is hoped that victims' feelings of anger or fear towards 'their' offender, or crime more generally, will be alleviated and that offenders will experience genuine remorse and develop a greater sense of victim empathy.

Some advocates of restorative justice have made bold claims for its quantifiable outcomes, especially in relation to reducing re-offending. We would argue that delivering justice fairly is a more important aim for any criminal justice system. If restorative justice treats people fairly and with respect, and encourages them to treat others in this way, this would be an improvement on the established criminal justice process. In other words, restorative justice is best thought of as a more legitimate way of doing justice. Any reductions in offending behaviour that may be achieved through restorative justice should be regarded as a welcome bonus rather than as a necessary condition for success. Given the complex factors that generate and sustain offending behaviour, it is realistic to assume that restorative justice interventions will usually have little impact on re-offending, and still less on crime rates (see further below). Where restorative justice could have a real impact is on a community's sense that crime is responded to in a just way, i.e. by holding offenders accountable for their actions to those they have harmed.

RESTORATIVE JUSTICE PROCESSES AND PROGRAMMES

The term 'restorative justice' was used by Zehr to describe, and indeed promote, existing practices of victim–offender mediation in North America (see above). As part of this promotional strategy he contrasted these emerging restorative schemes with established 'retributive' criminal justice. Zehr summed up the retributive model's approach to crime as follows:

Crime is a violation of the state, defined by lawbreaking and guilt. Justice determines blame and administers pain in a contest between the offender and the state directed by systematic rules.

He described the restorative justice model as viewing crime in a fundamentally different way:

Crime is a violation of people and relationships. It creates obligations to make things right. Justice involves the victim, the offender and the community in a search for solutions which promote repair, reconciliation, and reassurance.[13]

Like other advocates, he argues for a shift towards restorative justice by describing the established criminal justice system in at times reductionist and misleading ways. His 'retributive justice' is an extremely negative model, while restorative justice has the

---

[13] Zehr, n. 7 above.

answer to all its evils. He gets close to arguing that the aim of retributive justice is to inflict pain (by which he means punishment), whereas restorative justice has more positive aims of restoring participants, reintegrating offenders, and repairing harms.

Other commentators have, by contrast, argued that the supposed conflict between restorative and retributive justice has been considerably overstated.[14] Marshall, for example, shows how restorative justice could blend with state justice, and how both have positive features to offer. He argues that restorative justice 'is complementary to criminal justice, not antithetical to it',[15] and that Zehr's crude dichotomy does an injustice to both. Marshall, in a much quoted definition, sees restorative justice as:

a process whereby all the parties with a stake in a particular offence come together to resolve collectively how to deal with the aftermath of the offence and its implications for the future.[16]

This definition emphasizes restorative justice as a process. It makes clear that victims and offenders must come together in a face-to-face meeting and that they themselves must determine the outcome of that meeting. Hence it is a definition that fits with 'conferencing', direct mediation (rather than 'shuttle' mediation), and 'circles'. It allows for restorative justice to work alongside the established criminal process rather than positing it as a wholly new alternative system. Notwithstanding this flexibility, Bazemore and Walgrave argue that Marshall's definition is too restrictive, and advocate the inclusion of judicially-imposed community service (as long as the intent is to bring 'healing' to victims and the offended 'community').[17] The importance of this is that it allows for a 'restorative response' even in cases where offenders and/or victims refuse to enter into dialogue with one another. Others disagree with this position, arguing that judicial sentences, even if they include a reparative component, cannot be said to be restorative, as they do not arise from a process which allows all of those harmed by an offence to come together to discuss and find ways of resolving the damage done. Even those, such as Bazemore and Walgrave, who diverge from this view, concede that the best outcomes are achieved when victims and offenders are brought together in a face-to-face meeting.

One way out of this definitional maze is to accept McCold's argument that there is a 'core' model of restorative justice in which offenders and victims enter into dialogue. The process involved in bringing the victim and offender together under this model has four steps: the acknowledgment of the wrong; the sharing and understanding of the harmful effects; agreement on terms of reparation; and the reaching of an understanding about future behaviour. He defines as 'pure models of restorative justice' all those meetings which seek to move the victim and offender through these steps,

---

[14] K. Daly and R. Immarigeon, 'The Past, Present and Future of Restorative Justice: Some Critical Reflections' (1998) 1 *Contemporary Justice Review* 21.

[15] Marshall, n. 10 above, at 9.

[16] T. Marshall, 'Criminal Mediation in Great Britain 1980–1996' (1996) 4 *European Journal on Criminal Policy and Research* 21 at 37.

[17] G. Bazemore and L. Walgrave, 'Restorative Juvenile Justice: In Search of Fundamentals and an Outline for Systemic Reform' in G. Bazemore and L. Walgrave (eds.), *Restorative Juvenile Justice: Repairing the Harm of Youth Crime* (Monsey, NY: Criminal Justice Press, 1999).

arguing that the various models (for example, mediation, community conferencing, sentencing circles, etc.) differ only in their details.[18]

It is not possible within the scope of this chapter to describe all the many existing models which come under the restorative-justice rubric. We will provide an outline of one influential model: restorative conferencing as used by the Thames Valley Police, England, and in Canberra, Australia. Both of these schemes derive from a scripted model of police-led conferencing in Wagga Wagga, Australia, in the early 1990s.[19] It, in turn, was inspired by the theory of 'reintegrative shaming' set out by John Braithwaite in his seminal work, *Crime, Shame and Reintegration*.[20] He argues that crime is best responded to by processes which shame criminal *behaviour*, whilst maintaining respect and concern for the *person* who committed the offence.

In Canberra, offenders who fully admit their crime can be diverted from court if they agree to attend a conference. The police facilitate a discussion about the offence, the harm caused, and how this might be repaired, with all of those who have been affected by the offence. An outcome agreement is reached which might involve only an apology to the victim(s) or might entail material reparation (a financial payment or an undertaking to carry out work for the victim or for the wider community).

The Thames Valley Police model, which covers the English counties of Berkshire, Buckinghamshire, and Oxfordshire, differs from the Canberra scheme in two main ways. First, in Canberra conferencing is offered to offenders and victims whose relatively serious cases would normally not be considered for diversion from court. In Thames Valley conferencing is used mainly for less serious cases which would be diverted in any event. Secondly, reparation agreements reached in Thames Valley Police conferences are not legally binding and the police can do little if promises are not kept. Conversely, in Canberra the police monitor the agreement and have the powers to reconvene the conference or, rarely, send the matter to court if the offender fails to 'pay up'.

The current Thames Valley Police script requires the facilitator to arrange for all those affected by an offence to attend a meeting in which the participants sit on chairs arranged in a circle. He or she will introduce everybody by indicating their relationship to the offence and their reasons for being there. After explaining that participants are free to leave at any time, the facilitator sets out the focus of the meeting, making clear that discussion should concentrate on the offender's *behaviour*, not the offender, thus promoting the notion that the criminal act is to be condemned rather than the

---

[18] P. McCold, *Restorative Justice Practice—The State of the Field 1999* (Real Justice website www.realjustice.org/Pages/vt99papers/vt_mccold.html.

[19] See R. Young and B. Goold, 'Restorative Police Cautioning in Aylesbury: From Degrading to Reintegrative Shaming Ceremonies?' [1999] *Crim. LR* 126 and R. Young, 'Just Cops doing "Shameful" Business? Police-led Restorative Justice and the Lessons of Research' in Morris and Maxwell, n. 4 above, for analysis of the Thames Valley model and D. Moore, L. Forsythe, and T. O'Connell, *A New Approach to Juvenile Justice: An Evaluation of Family Conferencing in Wagga Wagga* (Wagga Wagga: Charles Stuart University, 1995) for a description of the Canberra programme and its origins.

[20] J. Braithwaite, *Crime, Shame and Reintegration* (Cambridge: Cambridge University Press, 1989). The link between Braithwaite's theoretical book and the practice of conferencing is discussed in K. Daly, 'Conferencing in Australia and New Zealand: Variations, Research Findings, and Prospects' in Morris and Maxwell, n. 4 above.

actor as a person. The facilitator explains that everyone will be helped by specific scripted questions to tell their own story and that everyone will get a chance to respond to what other people have said. In this way the facilitator should be able to create a safe, empowering forum where everyone feels able to talk openly about the offence and to ask relevant questions of the others, regardless of age, social status, or relationship to the offence. Finally, the facilitator explains that the meeting will ultimately focus on how the harm caused by the offence might be repaired.

Following these introductory remarks the offender is asked about thoughts and feelings at the time of the offence, and subsequently, and to identify who has been harmed by the offence. Similar questions are then put to the victim, any victim supporters present, and finally to any supporters of the offender. This order of speakers is seen as important for two main reasons. First, it allows the victim to hear the offender taking responsibility for the offence right at the start of the process, thus alleviating any anger the victim may feel. Secondly, inviting the victim group to speak prior to the offenders' supporters is meant to reduce the risk that the latter will seek to downplay the seriousness of the matter, something that might aggravate the victim. Thus it can be seen that the scripted process does not simply aim to promote communication between the participants, but rather seeks to encourage *constructive dialogue*. Once this has been achieved, the prospects of the participants achieving restorative outcomes (whether this be an apology or something more) are much improved. In practice, victims, offenders, and their respective supporters can find that they have more in common than they imagined. Offenders' supporters (particularly parents) often experience feelings such as powerlessness, hurt, and anger in the aftermath of an offence, reactions normally associated with victims. Similarly it can be argued that offenders harm themselves when the crimes they commit result in damage to valued relationships and to their status within society.[21]

Once the multi-faceted nature of the harm that can be caused by a criminal offence is accepted it becomes clear that a genuinely restorative process must address a range of damaged relationships, not only between victims and offenders, but also between offenders and their communities and with society as a whole.[22] Offenders must also be encouraged to learn from the process, in order to address the factors which may have contributed to their offending in the first place. Where the offender needs help to overcome those factors, the State should provide it since this is consistent with its duty to promote social integration. From the victim's point of view, ' "restoration" is not simply about material reparation, but about seeking to restore the security, safety, self-respect, dignity and, most importantly, sense of control'.[23] The same should also hold

---

[21] See further R. Young, 'Integrating a Multi-victim Perspective into Criminal Justice through Restorative Justice Conferences' in A. Crawford and J. Goodey (eds.), *Integrating a Victim Perspective within Criminal Justice* (Aldershot: Ashgate, 2000).

[22] T. Marshall, 'Grassroots Initiatives Towards Restorative Justice: The New Paradigm?' in A. Duff, S. Marshall, R. E. Dobash, and R. P Dobash (eds.), *Penal Theory and Practice: Tradition and Innovation in Criminal Justice* (Manchester: Manchester University Press, 1994) 245.

[23] A. Morris and L. Gelsthorpe, 'Something Old, Something Borrowed, Something Blue, but Something New? A Comment on the Prospects for Restorative Justice under the Crime and Disorder Act 1998' [2000] *Crim. LR* 18 at 20.

true both for the offender and for the other parties harmed by the offence. Following these definitions, to what extent has the criminal justice system of England and Wales introduced measures which are truly restorative?

RESTORATIVE JUSTICE MOVES INTO MAINSTREAM CRIMINAL JUSTICE IN ENGLAND AND WALES

The British Labour government which came to power in 1997 was keen to shake off some of the more punitive aspects of criminal justice policy brought in by the previous administration and identify 'a third way' for its policies.[24] In its first year in office, the government published a White Paper, *No More Excuses*, presaging the introduction of restorative-justice principles and practices into the youth justice system.[25] Legislation to put this plan into effect quickly followed: the Crime and Disorder Act 1998 (CDA) and the Youth Justice and Criminal Evidence Act 1999 (YJCEA).[26]

The CDA replaced police cautions for young offenders with 'reprimands' and 'warnings'.[27] Reprimands are relatively informal measures aimed at first-time offenders who have committed minor offences. Warnings are intended for offenders whose offence is too serious for a reprimand or who have already been reprimanded on a previous occasion. Second warnings should be given only in exceptional circumstances.

Before a warning is carried out, the offender is referred to a new multi-agency Youth Offending Team (YOT). YOTs comprise a probation officer, a police officer, a social worker, a representative of the local health authority, and a person nominated by the chief education officer. They are responsible for co-ordinating the provision of youth justice in local areas, for assessing offenders' needs, and for delivering programmes aimed at promoting desistance. Their work is overseen by a national advisory body set up under the 1998 Act, the Youth Justice Board of England and Wales. When the government issued advice on how YOTs should function, it recommended restorative-justice initiatives such as that already being undertaken by Thames Valley Police (described in above).

The CDA also provides scope for restorative justice by the power given to the courts to impose Reparation Orders on young offenders. These orders require them to make some sort of reparation to the victim—although only with their consent—or to the

---

[24] For a detailed examination of the various Labour Party consultation papers spelling out the Party's aims for youth justice, and the Reports which influenced them, see J. Fionda, 'New Labour, Old Hat: Youth Justice and the Crime and Disorder Act 1998' [1999] *Crim. LR* 36.

[25] Home Office, *No More Excuses—A New Approach to Tackling Youth Crime in England and Wales*, Cm 3809 (1997).

[26] There were various attempts in the preceding decades to introduce restorative interventions into criminal and civil justice but these were, in the main, unsuccessful. See G. Davis, *Making Amends: Mediation and Reparation in Criminal Justice* (London: Routledge, 1992).

[27] This was in part an attempt to stop the practice of giving repeat cautions to young offenders, something which the government thought was bringing cautioning into disrepute and failing to tackle recidivism.

wider community. Reparation can be material (acts or work done by the offender) and/or symbolic (an apology). Action Plan Orders provide another possibility for restorative interventions. Drawn up by the YOT, these put young offenders under supervision for three months of intensive community intervention with the aim not only of punishment, but also of reparation and rehabilitation. Again, these orders create the potential for consultation with victims.

The YJCEA introduced a new mandatory sentence of referral to a Youth Offender Panel for most young offenders pleading guilty and appearing before a youth or magistrates' court for the first time.[28] YOTs are responsible for administering the order and setting up the panels. Any work a panel recommends should be informed by principles of restorative justice: making restoration to the victim, achieving reintegration into the law-abiding community, and taking responsibility for the consequences of offending behaviour. The panel has to set out a programme for the offender and then agree a 'contract' for its completion. Contracts are likely to include agreements to make reparation to victims, or to do unpaid work for the community, as well as requirements to attend mediation sessions with the victim. Offenders are also likely to find themselves required to participate in programmes aimed at reducing re-offending. These 'contracts' are coerced, rather than volunteered and approved by all of the affected parties.

Whilst there are clearly many restorative elements in the CDA and the YJCEA, the Acts send out contradictory messages. In policy circles and in government briefings to the media the reparation element of restorative justice is talked up at the expense of the reintegration of offenders. Moreover the emphasis is on practical outcomes rather than the quality of the process. This increases the danger that the courts, in issuing reparation orders, will push for material outcomes (the offender paying back in terms of money or tasks) rather than symbolic reparation (an apology).[29] Most advocates feel that the alleged transformatory potential of restorative justice cannot be realized by imposing a reparation order. Rather, a face-to-face meeting or at least some type of shuttle mediation is necessary if there is to be any hope of changing people's attitudes and behaviour.

The government's emphasis on reparation may partly be a response to critics of the victim–offender mediation schemes of the 1980s who pointed out that these schemes were focused on offender needs rather than victim needs.[30] It is also an attempt to feed the presumed appetite of the public for greater victim involvement in the criminal justice process. In the current political climate, however, where the two main British political parties are battling it out to see who is the toughest on crime, we should not underestimate the government's fear of being seen to be pushing a 'soft' option. Regrettably, the coercive nature of the various orders detracts from the 'balanced approach' of restorative justice which should pay equal heed to victims, offenders, and the wider community.

---

[28] It is not intended that any other sentence should be imposed with the referral order.

[29] Dignan, n. 8 above, at 57.

[30] J. Dignan 'Repairing the Damage: Can Reparation Work in the Service of Diversion?' (1992) 32 *British J. of Criminology* 453.

The transition from the punitive, exclusionary policies and rhetoric of the previous Conservative government to the supposedly inclusive, restorative measures of the post-1997 Labour government has been neither smooth nor complete.[31] There are many exclusive and punitive measures in the CDA (consider, for example, the anti-social behaviour orders, curfew orders, and the extension of imprisonment for persistent juvenile offenders) and the restorative elements do not go far enough along the road of restorative justice for some critics.[32] As Morris and Gelsthorpe have argued, 'restorative justice [is] just one theme in a broadly punitive and controlling piece of legislation'.[33] They conclude that under the current legislation in England and Wales restorative conferencing, or other forms of restorative justice, could not become an integral part of the youth justice system.

UNREALIZED POTENTIAL?

Two simple but seemingly controversial questions are: who, and what type of offences, is restorative justice for? Initially, especially in England and Wales, initiatives targeted on young offenders, first-time offenders, and minor offences. The Youth Justice Board funded the establishment and evaluation of some forty-six 'restorative justice programmes' across the country.[34] These programmes represent an eclectic mix of philosophies and practices, but they are all schemes dealing with relatively minor offences committed by young people. However, there are a number of different schemes in this and in other countries which use restorative interventions for adult offenders and for more serious crimes. The programmes in Thames Valley, England, and Canberra, Australia, referred to above, both deal with adult offenders as well as juveniles, and both can deal with moderately serious offences. More recently, the Home Office of England and Wales has set up experiments to evaluate the effectiveness of restorative justice for adults involved in fairly serious offences. Family-group conferences in New Zealand are used for all but the most serious offences, and in South Australia conferences are being held for relatively serious offences.[35]

Probably the most serious cases dealt with by way of restorative practices have occurred in North America, where Mark Umbreit has used victim–offender mediation and dialogue in cases of homicide and sexual assault.[36] Umbreit has also held a

---

[31] C. Hoyle and D. Rose, 'Labour, Law and Order' (2001) 72 *The Political Quarterly* 76.

[32] The mandatory nature of the YJCEA referral order can similarly be criticized for being confused and potentially non-restorative. See Fionda, n. 24 above; and C. Ball, 'The Youth Justice and Criminal Evidence Act 1999—Part I: A Significant Move Towards Restorative Justice, or a Recipe for Unintended Consequences?' [1999] *Crim. LR* 211 for critical reviews of these two Acts.

[33] Morris and Gelsthorpe, n. 23 above, at 18.

[34] The authors (with Aidan Wilcox) are national evaluators of these programmes. See R. Young and C. Hoyle, 'Examining the Guts of Restorative Justice' (2000) 40 *Criminal Justice Matters* 32 for a description of the programmes and the evaluation.

[35] Daly, n. 20 above.

[36] M. S. Umbreit, W. Bradshaw, and R. B. Coates, 'Victims of Severe Violence Meet the Offender: Restorative Justice Through Dialogue' (1999) 6 *International Review of Victimology* 321.

mediation session between the family of a murder victim and his killer, shortly before the murderer's execution. Although Umbreit has argued that this experience helped both parties to develop a sense of 'closure' and resolution,[37] it seems to us grotesque that any involvement with the State's taking of a further human life could be described as restorative. A reintegrative state execution is a contradiction in terms.

There are some interesting examples of restorative practices being employed for behaviours which, whilst not criminal, are harmful either to the offender or to others. For example, restorative techniques are used in some schools to deal with cases of bullying, truancy, minor offences committed in school, and with conflict between staff and pupils.[38] At the other end of the scale are the various possible applications for restorative justice within prisons, as a response to conflicts between inmates, and even between inmates and prison officers.[39] In Canada 'circles of support' are formed to help plan for and deal with the release of serious sexual offenders (often guilty of pædophilia) into the community at the end of their prison sentences. Circles agree on a programme to facilitate a reintegration plan to reduce the fears within the community, and to try to reduce the likelihood of re-offending, by holding the released prisoner accountable to the plan and by providing him with the necessary community resources.[40]

Other imaginative uses include: restorative justice in the workplace; with neighbours trapped in apparently irresolvable disputes; with residents and local authority bodies in conflict, and as alternative dispute resolution in civil cases. Thames Valley Police have recently started to use restorative conferencing techniques to deal with complaints made by members of the public against the police as well as internal police disciplinary matters. Fresno, California, has also used a form of dispute resolution to deal with allegations of police brutality.[41]

One example where such conferencing might prove beneficial is domestic violence cases where many victims are currently unwilling to co-operate with a criminal prosecution.[42] Morris and Gelsthorpe have argued that '[r]estorative justice processes increase women's choices, provide women not only with the support of family and friends, but also with a voice, and, through this, may increase women's safety'.[43] Braithwaite and Daly, a little more cautiously, have argued the legal system should adopt escalating responses to domestic violence which might begin with a restorative conference but might ultimately lead to prison.[44]

---

[37] M. Umbreit, Second International Conference on Restorative Justice, Fort Lauderdale, Florida, 7–9 Nov. 1998.

[38] Daly, n. 20 above.

[39] See C. Hoyle, 'Restorative Justice in the Thames Valley: Changes in the Complaints and Discipline Process' (2001) 133 *Prison Service Journal* 37 for a critical examination of restorative justice within the prison setting.

[40] D. van Ness, A. Morris, and G. Maxwell, 'Introducing Restorative Justice' in Morris and Maxwell, n. 4 above.

[41] Van Ness *et al.*, n. 40 above.

[42] C. Hoyle, *Negotiating Domestic Violence: Police, Criminal Justice and Victims* (Oxford: Clarendon, 1998).

[43] A. Morris and L. Gelsthorpe, 'Re-visioning Men's Violence Against Female Partners' (2000) 39 *Howard Journal* 422.

[44] J. Braithwaite and K. Daly, 'Masculinities, Violence and Communitarian Control' in T. Newburn and E. Stanko (eds.), *Just Boys Doing Business: Men, Masculinities and Crime* (London: Routledge, 1994).

Whilst some argue that this type of response is likely to come about in England and Wales,[45] it is highly controversial. Critics argue that restorative justice used for domestic violence brings with it dangers of intimidation and emotional pressures. Stubbs, for example, has argued that it is dangerous to assume that victims of domestic violence are able to assert their own needs and promote their own interests in the presence of the person who has perpetrated violence against them, and that requiring such victims to participate may be disempowering and punitive. However, many victims of domestic violence already feel completely disempowered by abusive relationships.[46] Restorative justice has the potential to give victims a voice, to feel more in control of their lives and to provide a supportive community, not to mention the potential to change the attitude and behaviour of the perpetrator. Such cases would need to be selected carefully and would also need a great deal of preparatory and follow-up work. Nevertheless, restorative justice could play a useful role in responding to disputes and offences which would otherwise receive no statutory attention.

Advocates of the use of restorative justice as a response to racial conflicts attract similar criticisms to those who argue in favour of restorative measures for dealing with domestic violence. However, Hudson believes that in relation to both racial and family violence, 'restorative justice . . . enables the parties to be equally represented; it enables other narratives to be heard; it empowers standpoints which are otherwise powerless and excluded, or at least circumscribed'.[47] Restorative principles helped to inform conflict resolution at the Truth and Reconciliation Commission established to tackle the historic human rights abuses in South Africa.[48] Indeed, Desmond Tutu explicitly sees the Truth and Reconciliation Commission as a restorative-justice process.[49]

Corporate and 'white-collar' crimes are rarely discussed in the restorative-justice literature and there are few restorative initiatives designed to tackle these offenders. The obvious exception to this rule is Braithwaite, who found through empirical study that the regulation of corporate crime in most countries was rather 'restorative'. He argued that instead of trying to make the response to corporate crime more like the state response to street crime, it might be preferable to make street-crime enforcement more like corporate-crime enforcement. He found that 'communitarian' regulation has had considerable success in securing a more responsible approach to compliance with the law by institutions as diverse as coal-mining firms, nuclear-power plants, and nursing homes.[50]

---

[45] K. Paradine and J. Wilkinson, 'Home Truths', *Police Review*, 25 Feb. 2000, 26.

[46] C. Hoyle and A. Sanders, 'Police Response to Domestic Violence: From Victim Choice to Victim Empowerment?' (2000) 40 *British Journal of Criminology* 14.

[47] B. Hudson, 'Restorative Justice: The Challenge of Sexual and Racial Violence' (1998) 25 *Journal of Law and Society* 249.

[48] See A. Skelton and C. Frank, 'Conferencing in South Africa: Returning to Our Future', in Morris and Maxwell, n. 4 above.

[49] See his foreword to J. C. Consedine, *Restorative Justice: Healing the Effects of Crime* (Christchurch: Ploughshares Publications, 1997).

[50] Braithwaite, n. 11 above.

adva

For most governments and policy advisors, as well as for many criminal justice practitioners, the most attractive feature of restorative justice is its possible capacity to reduce re-offending. Recent data from the United Kingdom, New Zealand, and Canberra suggest that these models of restorative justice may indeed have some such reductive effect, at least in some types of case. In the United Kingdom, Hoyle, Young, and Hill[51] found some reductions in offending patterns, but only in cases involving identifiable victims (whether present at the conference or not). Maxwell and Morris, dealing with New Zealand, found evidence consistent with a reduction in re-offending even when other important factors such as adverse early experiences and subsequent life events were taken into account:

> Critical factors for young people are having a conference that is memorable, not being made to feel a bad person, feeling involved in the conference decision-making, agreeing with the conference outcome, completing the tasks agreed to, feeling sorry for what they had done, meeting the victim and apologising to him or her, and feeling that they had repaired the damage.[52]

These are factors which reflect key restorative values, processes, and outcomes. Of course not all 'restorative' processes actually reflect restorative values, nor do they all achieve restorative outcomes. Sometimes practitioners fail to implement the restorative model successfully and sometimes the participants act in ways inconsistent with restorative values and outcomes. Where this is so the New Zealand evidence suggests that there will be no impact on recidivism. Furthermore, the methodology adopted in the New Zealand study does not allow us to be confident that the relationship between 'good' conferences and reductions in offending is a causal one. It could be that these conferences went well only because the offenders were predisposed to be co-operative and remorseful and that they would have reduced their offending even in the absence of a conference.

lisa d

One way of circumventing this problem is randomly to allocate offenders willing to meet their victims into either restorative or non-restorative processes and then see which group offends at the higher rate following the intervention. The Canberra evaluation (RISE)[53] adopted this method and found that, when compared to court appearances and based on a one-year follow up, the effect of diversionary conferences is to cause a big drop in offending rates by violent offenders, a small increase in offending by drink drivers, and no difference in repeat offending by juvenile property offenders or shoplifters.[54] In light of the fact that the great bulk of criminal offences are against property this is a somewhat discouraging result. On the other hand the public is generally (and rightly) more concerned about violent offences. If restorative

---

[51] C. Hoyle, R. Young, and R. Hill, in von Hirsch *et al.* (Oxford: Hart, 2000).

[52] G. Maxwell and A. Morris, 'Family Group Conferences and Reoffending' in Morris and Maxwell, n. 4 above 261.

[53] Strang, n. 4 above.

[54] L. Sherman, H. Strang, and D. Woods, *Recidivism Patterns in the Canberra Reintegrative Shaming Experiments (RISE)* (Canberra: Centre for Restorative Justice, Research School of Social Sciences, Australia National University, 2000).

justice can achieve reductions in re-offending by violent offenders that will be a major benefit to society even if overall rates of crime were little affected.

The fact that restorative justice in Canberra appears to have produced a slight increase in re-offending by drink drivers (compared with what would have happened if they had gone to court instead) highlights the point that attempts to reduce offending can have unintended consequences. As Maxwell and Morris[55] note, further research is needed in order to ascertain just what it is about the restorative process which appears to impact on re-offending. Whilst most people acknowledge that the data on re-offending are as yet equivocal, for many desistance remains the Holy Grail. James Dignan warns against this:

There is always a danger that any initiatives may come, fleetingly, to be seen as 'magic bullet solutions' to the problem of crime—perhaps based on over-optimistic assessments of their potential in order to secure funding and support—only to be discarded when their independently evaluated performance fails to match up to these over-inflated and often unrealistic claims.[56]

Further research may support the findings of Hoyle, Young, and Hill that restorative sessions can change some offenders' behaviour. However, they are unlikely to affect offending rates in societies generally, given that most offences remain undetected, most offenders give up offending by a certain age regardless of the criminal sanctions imposed, and those who give up offending, especially with regard to property and drug offences, are often replaced by new entrants to the criminal labour market.[57]

There are, of course, other ways of measuring success, and there should be as much interest in these as cuts in re-offending. Potential benefits of restorative justice include: victim satisfaction (the evaluation of the Canberra programme shows moderate improvements in the satisfaction of conference victims as compared to victims whose cases went to court, as does research carried out in Pennsylvania);[58] improvements in offenders' relationships with their families; reductions in truanting and exclusions from schools; and *reductions* in offending and/or *changes* in offending behaviour which, whilst not amounting to desistance, clearly indicate a move away from recidivism or towards the cessation of particularly unacceptable behaviour.

To realize its full potential it seems to us that restorative justice needs to transcend the focus on small crimes, juveniles, and first-time offenders.[59] As Lord Walgrave has argued:

To actualise its potential fully, a maximalist version of restorative justice must be developed, with the aim of providing restorative outcomes to a maximum number of crimes in a

---

[55] N. 4 above.   [56] Dignan, n. 8 above, at 57.

[57] F. Zimring and G. Hawkins, *Incapacitation: Penal Confinement and the Restraint of Crime* (Oxford: Oxford University Press, 1995).

[58] For Canberra see H. Strang, 'Justice for Victims of Young Offenders' in Morris and Maxwell, n. 4 above, and the RISE website for up-to-date results of the evaluation: **www.aic.gov.au\rjustice\rise**. For Pennsylvania see P. McCold and B. Watchel, *Restorative Policing Experiment: The Bethlehem Pennsylvania Police Family Group Conferencing Project* (Pipersville, Penn.: Community Service Foundation, 1998).

[59] Braithwaite, n. 11 above; Maxwell and Morris, n. 52 above.

maximum number of possible situations and contexts, including those where voluntary agreements are not possible and coercion is needed.[60]

It is crucial, if restorative justice is to realize its potential that its virtues are not exaggerated and that its pitfalls are not ignored. Restorative-justice advocates would be better placed spending less time celebrating its successes and more time critically evaluating, and guarding against, its intermittent failings.

UNRECOGNIZED PITFALLS?

Perhaps the greatest tension in restorative justice is to be found in the question whether it should be integrated into the mainstream state justice system and, if so, to what extent. Some argue that restorative-justice programmes should be kept independent of mainstream criminal justice because their aims and practices are so different.[61] Others say that restorative justice should be an integral part of criminal justice, and could even help to reform it.[62]

There are deep pitfalls in attempts to divorce restorative justice from the State. In particular, rejecting the due-process protections and other checks and balances which accompany state-administered justice entails grave risks. Both critics and advocates of restorative justice have expressed concerns about the limited scope for protecting defendants' rights in restorative-justice processes.[63] Even Braithwaite, a passionate restorative-justice advocate, has warned that '[r]estorative justice practices can trample rights because of impoverished articulation of procedural safeguards'.[64] Few argue that there is no legitimate role for the State in restorative justice. Disagreements typically arise around the question of the extent and nature of the State's role.

WHO SHOULD FACILITATE CONFERENCES?

There is concern about whether it is appropriate for conferences to be led by the police, with an understandable fear that police facilitation places too much power in their hands. The danger is that officers will investigate, arrest, judge, and punish someone without there being sufficient legal safeguards in place against the abuse of these considerable powers.[65] It has been argued that the police are exploiting the

---

[60] L. Walgrave, 'On Restoration and Punishment' in Morris and Maxwell, n. 4 above.

[61] T. Marshall, 'Results of Research from British Experiments in Restorative Justice' in B. Galaway and J. Hudson (eds.), *Criminal Justice, Restitution and Reconciliation* (Monsey, NY: Criminal Justice Press, 1990).

[62] L. Walgrave and I. Aertsen, 'Reintegrative Shaming and Restorative Justice: Interchangeable, Complementary or Different?' (1997) 4 *European Journal on Criminal Justice Policy and Research* 67.

[63] See, e.g., D. van Ness, 'Legal Principles and Process' in Walgrave and Bazemore, n. 3 above.

[64] Braithwaite, n. 11 above, at 101.

[65] See A. Ashworth, 'Is Restorative Justice the Way Forward for Criminal Justice?' (2001) 54 *Current Legal Problems* 347 and R. White, 'Shame and Reintegration Strategies: Individuals, State Power and Social Interests' in C. Alder and J. Wundersitz (eds.), *Family Conferencing and Juvenile Justice: The Way Forward or Misplaced Optimism?* (Canberra: Australian Institute of Criminology, 1994).

vogue for restorative justice to expand their punitive function, and, given half the chance, will abuse it.[66] Harry Blagg suggests the police-led Wagga Wagga model of restorative conferencing in Australia 'has led to the supplementation and extension of already significant police powers over young people'.[67] White notes that the police are generally called upon to play contradictory roles in their contact with young people (for example, law enforcement, welfare assistance, peacekeeping) and this creates conflict between the police and some young people, which means that they will not be considered by some to be neutral facilitators.[68]

For many restorative-justice advocates part of its appeal is in dealing fairly with indigenous populations who have felt themselves unfairly and systematically discriminated against by established criminal justice processes. Restorative justice is held up as the fairer, more accountable alternative, rooted in the local community and taking into account the context within which people experience crime and societal responses to it. It is argued that restorative justice has the potential to empower particular communities by taking seriously their distinctive cultural norms. As Weitekamp has argued:

This is even more important at times of massive migration and in countries where many cultures exist and where often different understandings of justice can lead to major problems and, eventually, to processes of marginalisation, segregation, and social exclusion.[69]

However, Cunneen has argued, in a powerful critique of police involvement in community conferencing in indigenous communities in Australia, that:

In most jurisdictions, community conferencing has reinforced the role of state police and done little to ensure greater control over police discretionary decision-making.[70]

In his view it is particularly problematic for a police service which is not seen by indigenous people as legitimate to try to bring about reintegrative shaming. He cites research evidence from Australia which found that the police presence increases the reluctance of Aboriginal people to attend meetings and contributes to a non-communicative atmosphere for those who do. He makes the point that in New Zealand there were significant reforms to policing practices at the same time as the introduction of family-group conferences. These included tighter controls on police powers in relation to young people, whereas '[t]he Australian variations have simply seen conferencing as expanding the options available to police'.[71]

In New Zealand, the role of facilitator is taken by a 'youth justice co-ordinator', normally a social worker. Police officers, while never running conferences, are legally obliged to attend as participants. As such, they have a right of veto on the process like

[66] D. Sandor, 'The Thickening Blue Wedge in Juvenile Justice' in *ibid.*

[67] H. Blagg, 'A Just Measure of Shame?: Aboriginal Youth and Conferencing in Australia' (1997) 37 *British Journal of Criminology* 481.

[68] White, n. 65 above.

[69] E. G. M. Weitekamp, 'Mediation in Europe: Paradoxes, Problems and Promises' in Morris and Maxwell, n. 4 above, at 155.

[70] C. Cunneen, 'Community Conferencing and the Fiction of Indigenous Control' (1997) 30 *Australian and New Zealand Journal of Criminology* 1.

[71] *Ibid.*, at 7.

anyone else, but, in theory, they do not hold more power than the others. However, the officers' professional experience means that they can, in principle, steer the conference away from suggestions of reparation that appear to be disproportionate. Some, thus, see them as representing the public interest. Moreover, social work-led conferencing is not without its problems. Maxwell and Morris have found, for example, that many families attending conferences have had negative experiences with social workers. They argue that social welfare and restorative justice values are not necessarily reconcilable, and that where conferences have met restorative objectives and reflected restorative values this has happened despite being placed in a social welfare setting rather than because of it.[72]

Restorative cautioning in the Thames Valley is police-led, although occasionally conferences are co-facilitated with representatives from other state agencies, often social workers, and sometimes from voluntary organizations. However, conferences are usually delivered as part of a caution (for adults) or a warning (for juveniles), and so a police officer has to be present at the meeting. However, police officers, or any other person for that matter, cannot choose to facilitate a conference in Thames Valley in whatever way they see fit. Thames Valley Police trains all facilitators to deliver conferences in a fair way and requires them to follow a script, which charts a path towards a genuinely restorative process and outcomes. Facilitators are told in their training that they should act as neutral facilitators, not as professionals with their own agendas. Restorative conferences are supposed to empower not police officers, but the other participants. The facilitator should enable all participants to reach a restorative resolution which meets *their* needs. In theory, at least, it should matter little who facilitates the process. However, our research has observed conferences where police facilitators did use their power in an unacceptable way.[73] This points to the importance of strategies for securing full implementation of restorative blueprints.

From this discussion it might seem that the ideal solution would be for the facilitator to be drawn from an entirely independent agency specializing in restorative justice. This, however, would have enormous cost implications, and it seems unlikely that the State would be willing to provide the necessary funds. Strategies must therefore be devised to guard against the risk of facilitators allowing the agendas of the agencies in which they are based to dominate the restorative process. Such strategies might include the monitoring by peers or supervisors of practice standards, occasional top-up training, and the encouragement of independent research into practice 'on the ground'. Another possibility is for legal advice and representation to be provided to the participants as a check on any potential unfairness or abuse of power. This suggestion is so controversial that it merits separate discussion.

SHOULD LEGAL ADVICE BE MADE AVAILABLE?

One obvious role of the State—in any functional system—is to provide due-process checks and balances on both the process and outcome of the administration of justice.

---

[72] Maxwell and Morris, n. 52 above, at 261.   [73] See Young, n. 19 above.

If restorative justice is not made subject to state scrutiny, it will remain effectively outside the rule of law. Most people who are concerned about police and prosecution powers are in favour of suspects' and defendants' rights. They approve of legal frameworks which provide 'equality of arms'. In other words, they welcome the role of legal advisors in the justice system. Some restorative-justice advocates, however, do not wish to see lawyers involved in the restorative-justice process, or at least wish to see that role greatly restricted.[74] Their fear is that lawyers will impede the taking of responsibility by the offender and that they will monopolize the process. Another concern is that professional advice is not always in the interests of the parties. As Crawford asserts, 'It is questionable whether it is wise to involve lawyers whose traditions and organizational culture are rooted in partisan advisory and representative roles. Rights-based forms of representation may run counter to the logics of broader interest-based negotiation.'[75]

One might argue that if restorative justice is being used in a diversion scheme, with no risk of re-entry into the criminal process, then legal representation is less crucial. However, if restorative schemes are being used effectively to sentence people, legal representation should be encouraged, if not mandated, as otherwise the guarantees against disproportionate outcomes are too weak. More broadly Shapland has argued that lawyers should be admitted into most restorative-justice processes because the key human rights elements of obtaining and clarifying information, advising, and, in rare instances, acting as advocates where defendants are unable to speak themselves, are as pertinent to restorative justice as to well-run criminal courts.[76] However, she concedes that they need to be trained to act in a different manner from that envisaged by adversarial ideology. In other words, rather than be combative, they need to act in a way which furthers restorative values.

At present, in England and Wales, there is no requirement for young people who are offered a reprimand or a warning to have access to legal advice. Similarly, offenders who are given referral orders by the courts will rarely be legally represented in their dealings with youth offender panels. The proposition that offenders *should* have legal representation during a conference or other restorative process has provoked hostility. Ball, in her critical review of the YJCEA, quotes Paul Boateng, formerly Minister of State and Deputy Home Secretary, articulating the government's determination to deny young offenders legal representation:

I can think of nothing more destructive to the objectives of the [Youth Justice and Criminal Evidence Bill] than involving lawyers in youth offender panels. . . . Lawyers see themselves as a shield, not as a means of encouraging or engineering the involvement of a young person in a process that requires them to confront their offending and address the means of preventing them offending in future. Therefore we see the removal of legal representation as a

---

[74] M. Wright, *Restoring Respect for Justice* (Winchester: Waterside Press, 1999).

[75] A. Crawford, 'The Prospects for Restorative Youth Justice in England and Wales: A Tale of Two Acts' in K. McEvoy and T. Newburn (eds.), *Criminology and Conflict Resolution* (London: Palgrave, 2002).

[76] J. Shapland, 'Restorative Justice and Criminal Justice: Just Responses to Crime?', draft paper for the Toronto Symposium on Restorative Justice, May 2001. See generally K. Warner, 'The Rights of the Offender in Family Conferences' in Alder and Wundersitz n. 65 above.

positive step. We do not believe that it will have a negative impact on the young person. There is nothing coercive about the process.[77]

This thinking produced the government's official *Guidance for Youth Offender Panels*, insisting that young people should not be legally represented at a youth offender panel meeting. But Article 6(3)(c) of the European Convention on Human Rights provides that a person who is the subject of criminal proceedings is entitled to employ a lawyer of his choice for each stage of the criminal process, with free legal assistance where justice so demands. As Ball points out, this aspect of the YJCEA does not comply with this. Such concerns have resulted in the government deciding that YOTs should, after all, have the power to allow legal representatives to attend youth offender panel meetings. However, there is at present no legal aid available for panel meetings so this change is likely to have little impact in practice.[78] It seems that the government is content on this issue to pay mere lip-service to the protection of human rights.

CONCERNS ABOUT PROPORTIONALITY

There is a danger that reparation arrangements, be they imposed or voluntary, will place a disproportionate burden on an offender. The present government of England and Wales is extremely risk-averse and, as is evidenced by many features of the CDA (such as local curfew orders and child safety orders), is keen to intervene in young people's lives in a rather intrusive way, even when they have as yet committed no offence. The language of 'nipping it in the bud' is used to justify more and more interventions and might conceivably be used to justify overly harsh reparation agreements.

Just-deserts theorists are particularly concerned that the influence of victims or the wider community could result in disproportionate reparation agreements.[79] Reparation orders under the CDA 1998, discussed above, should not, in theory, result in offenders paying back in a way that is disproportionate to the offence. This is because the Act states that reparation requirements shall be commensurate with the seriousness of the offence. But, as Wasik has argued, there is a poor fit between reparation and desert, and allowing victims to influence the form that reparation should take can lead to inconsistency and injustice.[80]

Fears over disproportionate reparation agreements might be ignored if restorative justice were being used only for diverting low-level cases from court. However, now that reparation is part of a referral order, one cannot escape the fact that it has become a form of sentencing in its own right. Arguments about proportionality and consistency in sentencing thus become harder to disregard. Cavadino and Dignan are essentially advocates of restorative justice, but they recognize the need for such public interest considerations to be taken into account in responding to the offence:

[77] Ball, n. 30 above, at 221.   [78] See Crawford, n. 75 above.

[79] A. Ashworth, 'Victims' Rights, Defendants' Rights and Criminal Procedure' in A. Crawford and J. Goodey (eds.), *Integrating a Victim Perspective within Criminal Justice* (Aldershot: Ashgate, 2000).

[80] M. Wasik, 'Reparation: Sentencing and the Victim' [1999] *Crim. LR* 478. See also L. Zedner, 'Reparation and Retribution: Are They Reconcilable?' (1994) 57 *Modern Law Review* 228.

The protection of the human rights of potential victims via crime reduction gives us the 'general justification' for having a system of punishment; while the desirability of conveying correct moral messages about the relative wrongfulness of different actions that affect human rights argues for a general principle of proportionality in the amount of punishment imposed on individual offenders.[81]

However, they argue that the principle of proportionality need not be strict, and can give way at times to other aims, such as the restoration of the victim. Their model allows for reparation agreements of both a material and symbolic nature, and for victims to play a role in making decisions about appropriate reparation. Their solution to this apparent conundrum is to set upper and lower limits on the amount of reparation to which an offender should be liable. Proportionality could also be a fallback for those cases where the various parties cannot agree on reparation. Within 'retributive limits', victims and offenders would be encouraged to agree on forms of reparation that they considered to be appropriate.

Others suggest that restorative justice and proportionality are incompatible concepts. Indeed, Braithwaite and Pettit have explicitly developed the theories of reintegrative shaming and restorative justice in critical opposition to a just-deserts model.[82] The limits upon restorative justice for critics such as Braithwaite are to be found in international human rights instruments rather than in any philosophical commitment to proportionality. Such critics might be wise to recall that the rehabilitation movement of the 1960s fell out of favour because of a perception of disproportionate sentences.

The fairness of restorative outcomes cannot be judged only by the standard of proportionality (whether that standard be broadly or narrowly defined) but must also reflect other core values of restorative justice, such as mutual respect and empowerment. Hence the *amount* of reparation should not be the only issue. Offenders should not be asked to perform degrading or stigmatizing tasks as part of a reparation agreement. The now notorious example from the Canberra restorative conferencing programme of participants in a conference agreeing that the young offender would wear a T-shirt stating 'I am a thief' contradicts the fundamental values of restorative justice.

THE INFLUENCE OF STATE AGENDAS ON RESTORATIVE JUSTICE

Arguments for a purely communitarian restorative approach to crime partly stem from a rejection of the criminal justice system and all its perceived ills. As Weitekamp has argued, 'The old systems of criminal justice do not seem to work properly anymore and people are looking for alternatives.'[83] Furthermore, incorporating restorative justice as part of mainstream criminal justice (as in the Thames Valley model) attracts concerns about state control and limited community involvement. On

---

[81] M. Cavadino and J. Dignan, 'Reparation, Retribution and Rights' in A. von Hirsch and A. Ashworth (eds.), *Principled Sentencing: Readings on Theory and Policy* (2nd edn., Oxford: Hart, 1998) 351.

[82] J. Braithwaite and P. Pettit, *Not Just Deserts* (Melbourne: Oxford University Press, 1990).

[83] Weitekamp, n. 69 above.

the other hand, any process which purports to change behaviour and to facilitate agreements between people who might ordinarily be assumed to be opposed to one another needs to be accountable. Local, individualized justice can be punitive (whether through 'negative shaming' or through particularly harsh reparation agreements) and tainted by prejudice. A safe and accountable process would look to protect the rights—and the safety—of all participants. This is properly the agenda of the State. It is thus our position that there is nothing necessarily wrong with the State seeking to shape the agenda of restorative justice.

An institutionalized response to criminal offences, in particular to the more serious offences, ultimately requires some input from one or other of the criminal justice agencies—even if only for societal recognition of the legitimacy of the process. Criminal justice cannot be a merely private affair but necessarily involves a public dimension. If offences are not seen to be dealt with effectively vigilantism becomes more likely and there is even a danger of undermining the general deterrent effect of the criminal law. Furthermore, courts are needed for those offenders who do not plead guilty or who do not wish to accept an outcome proposed by other participants during a restorative intervention. More pragmatically, purely community-based restorative-justice schemes with no statutory basis tend to receive only a small number of, usually non-serious, referrals.

There are, however, undeniably tensions created by attempts to graft restorative justice on to established systems of criminal justice. When restorative justice is fitted into the main criminal justice system, as is the case in England and Wales, it has to be delivered in line with the general goals of criminal justice at any one time. Currently in England and Wales the managerialist thinking behind Labour's law-and-order policies, which can be seen in the establishment of the Youth Justice Board and Youth Offending Teams (see above), have found expression in a determination to speed up the process of youth justice (and of course to measure the 'improvements'). To bring about the reduction of 'delays' in the system, the government has introduced 'fast tracking' and statutory time limits. Fast-tracking was purportedly introduced to reduce the risk of re-offending and to meet the needs of the victim but, as Dignan, who evaluated the Youth Justice Pilot projects, noted, it could have the opposite effect of 'diminish[ing] the prospects for victims to receive direct reparation or take part in mediation'.[84]

This must be of concern to those whose task it is to deliver restorative interventions. Most advocates of restorative justice recognize that any attempt to bring together all parties affected by an offence takes sensitive preparation. Sometimes victims, especially in more serious cases, may not be prepared to meet their offender until some months have elapsed following the offence. This may be possible for restorative meetings at the warning stage, but not for panel meetings as a result of a referral order (panel meetings are supposed to be held within fifteen working days of the first court appearance). There needs to be a balance between holding meetings soon enough so that people's memories of the experience (and their desire for a just

---

[84] J. Dignan, 'Victim Consultation and Reparation: Preliminary Lessons from Pilot Youth Offending Teams' (2000) 47 *Probation Journal* 134.

resolution through dialogue) have not faded, and delaying them long enough for the co-ordinator to be able adequately to prepare all participants and be sensitive to their wishes not to rush into things. If co-ordinators are under pressure to 'deliver justice' as quickly as possible this balance will be in jeopardy.

Such tensions are bound to occur in a system which expresses such a bewildering mix of aims as that established in England and Wales. We nonetheless adhere to the position that it is better for restorative-justice advocates to seek to engage with, and transform certain aspects of, established criminal justice (even in the knowledge that their efforts will, at least in the short term, result in partial failure and questionable compromises) than to insist on an independent and thus marginalized setting for restorative interventions.

CONCLUSION

Just a couple of decades ago there was little focus on the victim's role in dispute resolution and responding to criminal offences. Now it is taken for granted that victims should have a role to play, and the debates are centred on the type of role.[85] Should they, for example, have the right to meet 'their offender' and explain the harms they have suffered? Or should they be able to take a more active role in the court process, as a '*partie civile*', or an auxiliary prosecutor, for example? These are now considered to be legitimate questions. Similarly, two decades ago it would have been unheard of to ask offenders what, if anything, they felt that they should do to make amends to their victims. Today, in restorative conferencing, this is considered good practice.

Across the world restorative justice is evolving in different jurisdictions, in some cases quite rapidly, with different types of advocates driving its progress. It appears that it is here to stay, at least for the foreseeable future. What this will mean in practice, however, is still to be determined. It will almost certainly develop in diverse ways in a variety of settings, dependent on the perceived problems of each jurisdiction and the methods for dealing with those problems that statutory and voluntary bodies have traditionally used. The danger has to be that, in the rush to introduce restorative interventions into different systems, programmes will be developed which are poorly thought out and badly implemented. There will be a proliferation of schemes calling themselves restorative justice, many of which will be anything but restorative in their aims and practices.

To persuade different communities or sentencers to give restorative justice a chance necessitates promoting confidence in the product. In their quest for acceptance advocates may be relying too heavily on criticisms of the criminal justice system. Some seem to feel that in order to promote a new way of doing justice it is necessary to

---

[85] A. Sanders, 'Victim Participation in Criminal Justice and Social Exclusion' in C. Hoyle and R. Young (eds.), *New Visions of Crime Victims* (Oxford: Hart, forthcoming).

destroy the reputation of the old. Reports of the death of criminal justice are greatly exaggerated. The restorative-justice literature is replete with various unfair, sometimes meaningless, comparisons of the court with the conference. This may prove to be a risky strategy. Further analysis, which measures the work of the courts against their own objectives, might show that they are reasonably successful in achieving the aims of a fair criminal justice system. Moreover, it may be a mistake for restorative-justice advocates to suggest that there is a well-founded crisis of confidence in established criminal justice. Whilst public opinion surveys have shown that courts in England and Wales are strongly criticized for being too lenient, these same surveys have found that people's criticisms are based on mistaken assumptions about actual court practice.[86] In reality sentencing is broadly in line with public preferences even if the public has yet to realize this.[87] The established sentencing system may not deserve as much scorn as its detractors would have us believe. Restorative justice should be given the chance to be tried and tested on its own merits rather than being marketed as a complete alternative to established criminal justice.

Further Reading

Bazemore, G., and Walgrave, L. (eds.), *Restorative Juvenile Justice* (Monsey, NY: Criminal Justice Press, 1999).

Braithwaite, J., *Crime, Shame and Reintegration* (Cambridge: Cambridge University Press, 1989).

Crawford, A., and Goodey, J. (eds.), *Integrating a Victim Perspective within Criminal Justice* (esp. Part III) (Aldershot: Ashgate, 2000).

Galaway, B., and Hudson, J. (eds.), *Restorative Justice: International Perspectives* (Monsey, NY: Criminal Justice Press, 1996).

Marshall, T., *Restorative Justice: An Overview* (London: Home Office, 1999).

Morris, A., and Maxwell, G. (eds.), *Restorative Justice for Juveniles: Conferencing, Mediation and Circles* (Oxford: Hart, 2001).

Von Hirsch, A., Roberts, J., Bottoms, A., Roach, K., and Schiff, M. (eds.), *Restorative Justice and Criminal Justice: Competing or Reconcilable Paradigms?* (Oxford: Hart, forthcoming 2002).

[86] M. Hough and D. Moxon, 'Dealing with Offenders: Popular Opinion and the Views of Victims in England and Wales' in N. Walker and M. Hough (eds.), *Public Attitudes to Sentencing: Surveys from Five Countries* (Aldershot: Gower, 1987); M. Hough and J. Roberts, *Attitudes to Punishment: Findings from the British Crime Survey*, Home Office Research Study 179 (London: Home Office, 1998).

[87] N. Russell and R. Morgan, *Research report—1, Sentencing of Domestic Burglary* (London: Sentencing Advisory Panel, Mar. 2001); **www.sentencing-advisory-panel.gov.uk/saprr1.htm**.

29

MONITORING AND UNDERSTANDING CRIMINAL JUSTICE

Statistics, Research, and Evaluation

A. Keith Bottomley

It should already be clear to readers of this book that the processes of law enforcement and the administration of criminal justice in contemporary societies are subject to the influence of a wide range of political and cultural forces. As a result, criminal procedure and practices are not just shaped by the 'law in books' that can be properly understood only by qualified lawyers but are informed by and accountable to the interests of the wider community, comprising many different audiences. In order to understand the complexities of criminal justice it is essential to have a basic knowledge of the operation of the system in action, against which its objectives and aspirations may be measured.

The aims of this chapter are quite modest. First, the wider context of criminal justice will be considered and attention drawn to a useful conceptual framework suggested by James and Raine in their monograph, *The New Politics of Criminal Justice*.[1] This will be followed by a review of the primary sources of statistical information relating to the operation of the criminal justice system in England and Wales, focusing particularly on the annual official volume of *Criminal Statistics England and Wales*.

This information will then be subjected to critique and interpretation, in the light of the sort of questions that may be raised by members of the public, commentators, and politicians. There will then be a short discussion of some of the issues surrounding attempts to compare criminal justice systems across jurisdictions, before briefly reviewing the prospects for the development of more informed, reflective and self-critical criminal justice practice.

---

[1] A. James and J. Raine, *The New Politics of Criminal Justice* (London: Longman, 1998).

CRIMINAL JUSTICE IN CONTEXT

The law enforcement and criminal justice processes intervene and serve to mediate between public fears and experience of criminal victimization and the way society responds to suspected and/or convicted offenders. The reluctance or ambivalence in many quarters about referring to the totality of these processes as a 'system' reflects the divergent aims and objectives for criminal justice as a whole and the various underlying or manifest conflicts that are apparent at different stages in what, for those caught up in it, may seem very much like a 'production line', with little light at the end of the tunnel. Andrew Ashworth made the point well in the introduction to his evaluative study of the criminal process:

Although many who speak and write about criminal justice tend to refer to 'the criminal justice system', it is widely agreed that it is not a 'system' in the sense of a set of co-ordinated decision-makers. . . . None the less, the inappropriateness of the term 'system' should not be allowed to obscure the practical interdependence of the various agencies. Many depend on other agencies for their case-load or for their information, and decisions taken by one agency impinge on those taken by others.[2]

Ashworth was keen to stress from the outset the need to avoid the dominance of a 'rationalist' notion that decisions are taken by individuals independently and based on objective information.[3]

In their valuable critique of the 'new politics' of criminal justice, James and Raine portray criminal justice policy as being shaped by the interplay of four key dynamics: politicization, managerialism, administrative processing, and 'public voice'. They argue that 'each dynamic has contributed its own logic and rationale based on its own set of values, each has made its own distinctive mark on policy and practice, and each has its own legitimacy, though each is often at odds with the others'.[4]

The significance of the James and Raine model for any attempt to monitor and evaluate criminal justice is that it provides a lens through which existing statistics and monitoring data can be viewed. In particular it must be recognized that most existing data are the products of administrative processing of the activities and decisions of the police, lawyers, sentencers, and penal practitioners that provide records of those activities without always a clear sense or appreciation of how this information may subsequently be used by other interested parties. In fact this information has increasingly been used by managers to monitor performance and account for increasing levels of expenditure, and this has encouraged the manipulation of statistics (especially the 'key performance indicators') to maximize the apparent achievement of the internal objectives of the workforce and/or its managers.

These often rather cynical developments have served seriously to undermine the

---

[2] A. Ashworth, *The Criminal Process: An Evaluative Study* (2nd edn., Oxford: Oxford University Press, 1998) 22–3.

[3] *Ibid.*, at 9.

[4] James and Raine, n. 1 above, at 4.

more idealistic objectives for official statistics set out more than a generation ago by the government-appointed Departmental Committee on Criminal Statistics (Perks Committee, 1963–7), which stated:

We should like to emphasise that in our view criminal statistics should serve not only to inform Parliament and the public; they should be capable of use as a basis for decisions by the authorities responsible for legislation, law enforcement and the treatment of offenders, and for research.[5]

The increasing managerialism of criminal justice towards the end of the twentieth century required all agencies to become more efficient and cost-effective, at a time of increasing politicization of 'law and order'. Thus routine statistical information took on a new significance and a whole set of new meanings for professional and political accountability.

The counter-argument and dimension that James and Raine were keen to emphasize was the need for increased *public voice and participation*:

The argument is that some of the main problems for criminal justice policy and practice during the period under review reflected the fact that public opinion was not always suf-ficiently understood or taken into account by the politicians and policy-makers and, con-versely, that the public were generally not well informed either about the circumstances surrounding the problem of crime or about the criminal justice agencies and their responses.[6]

This is the context within which the review of statistical information about the criminal justice process that follows should be viewed.

OFFICIAL STATISTICS ON THE OPERATION OF THE CRIMINAL JUSTICE SYSTEM

The most obvious starting point for those wishing to discover reliable information about crime and the criminal justice processes in England and Wales is the annual volume of *Criminal Statistics England and Wales* that have been published in some form or another for almost 150 years. The scope and depth of the information con-tained in this volume (and its accompanying four volumes of Supplementary Tables) have increased significantly during the last thirty years, so that arguably they provide the most comprehensive data set to be found anywhere in the world.

Although we shall not dwell too much for present purposes upon the base-line data provided in *Criminal Statistics* relating to 'notifiable offences recorded by the police', these constitute a crucially important statistic from which Parliament and the public derive their knowledge of crime trends and the backcloth against which they interpret their personal and collective experience of crime and the fear of crime. Furthermore,

---

[5] W. Perks, *Report of the Departmental Committee on Criminal Statistics*, Cmnd 3448 (1967) para. 29.

[6] James and Raine, n. 1 above, at 65.

the police role in discovering crime and responding to reports of crime from victims and other members of the public highlights the importance of these primary 'gate-keepers' of criminal justice, whose decisions directly impact upon the subsequent stages of the process by the way they influence the nature and extent of the offences and suspected offenders dealt with by the courts and penal agencies.

DETECTION OF OFFENDERS: POLICE 'CLEAR-UP' RATES

Official information about crime and criminal justice can be divided fairly crudely into that which relates to the nature and extent of offences that may have been committed and that which relates to offenders, or those persons who are suspected and (some) eventually convicted of specific offences. Just as there is a huge gap in our knowledge of the true extent of crimes that are committed in the community (although these are now increasingly being filled by the findings of successive nation-wide British Crime Surveys of victimization) so also are there very large gaps in our knowledge of the offenders who are responsible both for reported/recorded offences and even more for those offences that escape the official notice of the authorities. A good illustration of the fundamental limitation on our knowledge of offenders, and the somewhat spurious reassurance that official statistical discourse may appear to provide, is shown by considering the statistic of the police 'clear-up' rates.

Each year *Criminal Statistics* provides details of the number of recorded indictable offences that have been 'cleared up' by the police in each offence group. In 1999–2000, following changes in the rules according to which the police were permitted to count crimes as 'cleared up', the overall clear-up rate for police forces in England and Wales dropped to just 25 per cent—compared to 29 per cent in the previous year, when different counting rules were used. However, throughout most of the 1990s (as in previous decades), there were large and consistent differences in the clear-up rates for different offence groups, ranging from three-quarters of offences of violence against the person and sexual offences to less than one-fifth of criminal damage and 20–25 per cent of offences of burglary. This wide gap between the clear-up rate of personal and property offences is largely due to the fact that there are very few clues as to the identity of most property criminals, whereas a large proportion of violent and sexual offenders are either known to or can be more readily identified by the victim. Fur-thermore, there are some offences that become known or reported to the police only when there is a suspected offender, for example possession of illegal drugs or shoplifting.

When interpreting the police clear-up rate, it is also important to be aware of the various ways in which an offence may be regarded for official purposes as 'cleared up'. Although a majority of offences are recorded as cleared up when the police charge, summons, or caution the suspected offender, significant numbers of offences are cleared up by being 'taken into consideration' by the court when the offender has been convicted of one or more primary offences and admits to other offences of a similar kind. Until the change of rules in 1999, the police were also permitted to count as cleared-up crimes those to which convicted prisoners admitted during prison interviews with the police. These so-called 'prison write-offs' accounted for an average of over 200,000 offences a year between 1988 and 1998 or about one in six of the total cleared-up crimes.

Information is also provided in *Criminal Statistics* about the clear-up rates of the different police forces in England and Wales. Thus, in 1999, the clear-up rates of police forces in England ranged from 14 per cent in the London Metropolitan Police to 35 per cent in Cumbria, and in Wales from 26 per cent in South Wales to 60 per cent in Dyfed-Powys. Some of the variation is due to the different 'offence-mix' of recorded crimes in police force areas, and some is due to different police force practices and priorities in the way that they clear up crime in their area, which the changes of 1999 were intended to address and reduce.

ARREST, BAIL, AND REMAND DECISIONS

If we shift our focus of attention from the recording and detection/clearing up of crime to the initial action taken against those suspected of having committed crimes, then in the final short chapter of *Criminal Statistics* we find information about the proportion of suspects arrested and charged by the police to appear at magistrates' courts (46 per cent in 1999) compared to the proportion summonsed[7] to appear in the same year (54 per cent). Less than ten years previously the proportion arrested and charged was only 35 per cent (1991), with 65 per cent summonsed. However, the percentage of those arrested and charged who were held in custody by the police until their first court appearance remained relatively stable throughout the 1990s, at 15 per cent or less.

Just over two million people a year are proceeded against in magistrates' courts in England and Wales, of whom approximately seven out of ten are dealt with at their first appearance. In 1999, 98,000 people were remanded in custody by magistrates, representing just 15 per cent of all those remanded. The rest were granted bail, with or without conditions (see Chapter 15, in this volume).

An increasing percentage of those committed for trial at the Crown Court are being committed in custody, rising from 18 per cent in 1990 to 28 per cent in 1999. There continues to be a high correlation between being remanded in custody and subsequently being given a custodial sentence, with 79 per cent of those pleading guilty after being committed for trial in custody being sentenced to immediate imprisonment in 1999, compared to 41 per cent of those committed on bail. Almost a quarter (23 per cent) of all those remanded in custody at magistrates' courts and the Crown Court were acquitted or not proceeded with, as were 30 per cent of those remanded on bail.

45,200 people were proceeded against for failing to surrender to bail in 1999, a fall of 1,300 compared to the previous year, reversing the rising trend over recent years. For the second year in a row, 12 per cent of all those bailed failed to appear at court to answer the charges against them.

---

[7] Such individuals will be given a formal notice to appear at court without having been arrested by the police.

CAUTIONING OF OFFENDERS

One of the most significant trends in the criminal process in the second half of the twentieth century was the steady and eventually quite dramatic increase in the proportion of known offenders who were cautioned by the police and thereby diverted from prosecution and spared a formal court appearance and trial/sentence. In the 1960s this trend was particularly noticeable with regard to juvenile offenders, but by the 1990s significant proportions of all age groups and both sexes were being cautioned by the police instead of being recommended to the Crown Prosecution Service for prosecution. It was only in the final years of the century that the cautioning rate started to decline slightly, following a change in government policy towards the alleged over-use of this practice in a climate of 'tougher justice'.

The cautioning rate for indictable offences across all age groups reached a peak of over 40 per cent in the mid-1990s (1992–5), when the cautioning rate for summary offences was also at an all-time high of 18 per cent. By 1999, the former rate had dropped to 34 per cent, whilst the cautioning rate for summary offences remained at 18 per cent. The drop in the cautioning rate occurred for both males and females in all age groups, but it was still the case that in 1999 almost seven out of ten males aged 12–14 were cautioned for indictable offences, as were almost nine out of ten girls of the same age. Furthermore, over one fifth of adult males aged 21 and over were cautioned in that year, as were over one third of adult women.

Criminal Statistics provides further interesting information on the variation between police forces in the extent to which cautioning was used in 1999, ranging from 22 per cent of persons in all age groups in Durham to 51 per cent in Surrey. The reader's attention is also drawn to the findings of a Home Office research study that reported significant differences between police forces in England and Wales in their cautioning of 14–17-year-old males during the 1990s, having discovered more than a 35 percentage point difference between the highest and lowest forces.

Reference is also made in the same section to the findings of research into the effectiveness of cautioning in reducing subsequent reconvictions or, at least, into the success of the police in identifying those offenders who are least likely to reoffend however they are dealt with. This measure of the effectiveness of cautioning appears to show that it declines after the first caution, with just 11 per cent of those cautioned with no previous criminal history being reconvicted within two years compared to 42 per cent reconvicted of those with two or more previous cautions.

COURT PROCEEDINGS AND SENTENCING

Traditionally, the major focus of the annual volume of official *Criminal Statistics* had been on court proceedings and the sentencing of offenders. Although the expanded coverage of other sorts of crime data in the main volume means that this is no longer quite so true, the additional volumes of Supplementary Tables provide a wealth of detail about proceedings in magistrates' courts (Volume 1), proceedings in the Crown Court (Volume 2), recorded offences, and court proceedings by police force areas (Volume 3) and sentencing data for individual Petty Sessional Divisions in which magistrates' courts are grouped (Volume 4). For present purposes the basic information about sentencing in England and Wales will be examined, to illustrate the kind of data routinely available relating to this central function of the criminal justice process. However, before examining sentencing, it is necessary to summarize the information that is recorded about court proceedings, including venue, plea, and convictions.

Throughout the 1990s an average of approximately 1.9 million defendants were proceeded against each year in magistrates' courts, of whom half a million were facing charges for indictable offences, and of whom 800–900,000 were charged with summary motoring offences. Of all the cases that were completed by the Crown Prosecution Service in magistrates' courts each year 12 per cent were discontinued or the charges were withdrawn, with a further 6–10 per cent written off, because the defendant could not be traced and/or the case was adjourned *sine die.*

Over 80 per cent of all cases finally dealt with in magistrates' courts in 1994–9 resulted in a guilty plea conviction, with a further 5–8 per cent resulting in a conviction after trial. However, almost three-quarters of those who pleaded not guilty at magistrates' courts each year were convicted.

Following a change in procedure in October 1997, with the introduction of plea before venue, there was an increase in the number committed by magistrates' courts for sentence at the Crown Court, but a fall in the number committed for trial. Thus, in 1999 20,400 persons were committed for sentence and 72,300 committed for trial at the Crown Court. Over two-thirds of the triable-either-way offences committed for trial at the Crown Court in 1999 were because magistrates had declined jurisdiction, rather than because the defendant had elected to be tried at the Crown Court.

Approximately 90 per cent of all cases which proceeded to a hearing in the Crown Court during the 1990s resulted in a conviction (with a 1–2 percentage drop in 1998–9). 60 per cent of those tried for indictable offences in the Crown Court in 1999 pleaded guilty (ranging from 34 per cent of those charged with sexual offences to 76 per cent of those charged with burglary). 35 per cent of all those pleading not guilty in the Crown Court were convicted, ranging from 80 per cent of those facing summary motoring offences to 21 per cent of those charged with criminal damage. However, on average, one third of those acquitted following a not guilty plea in the Crown Court were discharged by the judge, e.g. because witnesses refused to testify or evidence was deemed insufficient.

Moving on to information about sentencing, *Criminal Statistics England and Wales* provides detailed information about sentencing trends, although from a criminological perspective the data are somewhat limited. They include sentencing in magistrates' courts and the Crown Court, by age, sex, offence, and type of sentence imposed, enabling a number of key trends to be identified over significant periods of time. However, it is important to stress that information about offenders sentenced for particular types of crime should not be interpreted as providing information about the characteristics of all offenders, as a long process of selection and attrition occurs between committing a crime and being detected, convicted, and sentenced for it. Nevertheless, important trends do emerge from the analysis of sentencing statistics, which are of relevance to court administrators, practitioners, and policy-makers.

The total number of offenders sentenced in England and Wales during the past five or six years has remained fairly stable at around 1.4 million per year, of whom just under a quarter are sentenced for indictable offences. The number sentenced in magistrates' courts has risen from 245,000 (1994) to 268,000 (1999). Similarly, the number sentenced in the Crown Court has risen from 68,500 (1994) to 74,000 (1999).

Sentencing trends in recent years have witnessed a steady decline in the use of fines, so that by the end of the 1990s only 27 per cent of those sentenced for indictable offences in all courts were fined. In contrast, there has continued to be a steady increase in the use of community measures, so that now almost three out of every ten convicted indictable offenders receive some form of community sentence.

The trend in the use of custodial sentences has been somewhat more uneven, but there has been quite a significant overall increase since the early 1990s. Immediate custodial sentences in magistrates' courts have increased from 7 per cent of indictable offenders in 1994 to 12 per cent in 1999; whereas, in the Crown Court, the increase has been from 52 per cent (1994) to 63 per cent (1999). By the end of the decade, therefore, 23 per cent of all indictable offenders were being sentenced to immediate custody.

When examining information about the sentencing of young offenders in England and Wales, it has to be remembered that a majority of such offenders are in fact cautioned, rather than prosecuted and found guilty in the Youth Courts (see above). Thus, the increase in the number of young offenders sentenced by the courts during the last few years has been largely due to the reduction in the number of those cautioned rather than to an overall increase in the number of young offenders proceeded against. Similarly, the impact of gender is such that in every age group a higher proportion of females than males are cautioned, with comparably fewer prosecuted and sentenced.

Very few children aged 10–11 years are now prosecuted for indictable offences, although increases were recorded in 1999, when 555 boys of that age were sentenced, compared to forty-seven girls. The majority received absolute or conditional discharges, with approximately one third receiving community sentences.

The number of males and females aged 12–14 sentenced for indictable offences increased steadily during the last decade, from fewer than 5,000 males in 1991 to 8,300 in 1999; and from 600 females (1991) to 1,400 (1999). Moreover, this trend was accompanied by a decrease in the proportion receiving court discharges. Almost half the males in this age group (48 per cent) now receive community sentences, as do 38 per cent of the females.

The number of sentenced males aged 15–17 years increased to 35,000 in 1998–99, after a low of 26,200 in 1993. Similarly, the number of females sentenced in 1999 was 5,200 compared to 3,100 in 1993. As with all young offenders, the proportions discharged and fined by the courts have steadily declined in the last few years, with comparable increases in the proportions receiving community sentences, which now comprise 40 per cent or more of this age group. There have been significant increases in the numbers and proportions of sentenced indictable offenders in this age group who have been given immediate custodial sentences. 16 per cent of males were sentenced to immediate custody in 1999, compared to 10 per cent in 1990, as were 6 per cent of females in 1999, compared to 2 per cent in 1990.

Gender differences in the use of custodial sentences are confirmed by the statistics of adults sentenced for indictable offences. Approximately one quarter of all male indictable offenders aged 18–20 were sentenced to custody in the late 1990s, compared to 11 per cent of females, but the proportion of the latter had increased more rapidly from just 3 per cent in 1990 (compared to 15 per cent of males sentenced to immediate custody). However, there has been relatively little fluctuation in the proportion of males and females aged 18–20 who have been given community sentences during the past decade, with 30 per cent of males and 36 per cent of females receiving such sentences in 1999.

The number of persons aged 21 and over sentenced for indictable offences increased between 1993 and 1999, from 183,100 males and 27,600 females in 1993 to 195,100 males and 34,800 females in 1999. Significant decreases in the proportions fined during this period were mirrored by increases in the proportions sentenced to immediate custody. Thus, 28,000 males were given immediate custodial sentences in 1999 (compared to 18,000 in 1993), and 16,000 females were sentenced to immediate custody in 1999, compared to 7,000 in 1993.

In order to begin to make much sense of these gender comparisons and interpret their significance in terms of possible discrimination on the part of sentencers, it is necessary to probe beneath the surface of simple statistics of this sort, but as we shall see (below) even sophisticated research studies are unable to provide all the answers.

OTHER SOURCES OF STATISTICAL DATA

There are several other annual series of official statistics relating to the criminal justice system in England and Wales, from which additional information may be gleaned. These include *Judicial Statistics*, with additional information about court proceedings, pleas, verdicts, etc. *Probation Statistics*, which give full details of the varied work carried out by the Probation Service, including pre-sentence reports, the supervision of offenders in the community and on licence after release from prison; and *Prison Statistics*, with comprehensive data on all categories of prisoners held in custody before trial/sentence and after conviction/sentence and also reconviction statistics of persons released from prison (discussed below).

To supplement these major annual publications, the Home Office publishes Statistical Bulletins which give advance summaries of statistical data to be published in more detail subsequently, as well as data that are not published elsewhere. This latter group of Statistical Bulletins that are published annually include: *Operation of Certain Police Powers under PACE* (e.g. stops and searches, detention in police custody); *Police Complaints and Discipline, Deaths in Police Custody; Statistics of Drug Seizures and Offenders Dealt With;* and *Statistics of Mentally Disordered Offenders.*

In addition, each year other important data and/or research findings are published by the Home Office in its *Statistical Bulletins* series. Recently these have included the main and supplementary findings from the British Crime Survey, analyses of reconviction data of offenders sentenced to community penalties and also those released from prison, and the criminal careers of people born between 1953 and 1973.

Finally, perhaps, to be mentioned in this section are the important Home Office publications under section 95 of the Criminal Justice Act 1991, especially *Statistics on Race and the Criminal Justice System* and *Statistics on Women and the Criminal Justice System*, which are published quite frequently at irregular intervals, which provide a starting point for the sort of more detailed critique that we must now consider.

INTERPRETATION AND EVALUATION

Regularly published statistical information about activities and decision-making within the criminal justice system of the kind reviewed in the previous section provides a necessary starting point for monitoring some of the complexities of criminal justice but are not sufficient on their own to promote a fuller understanding of the competing aims, objectives, and values inherent in any such system. In this section we shall raise some of the questions that need to be answered if official information is to meet the needs of the audiences identified by the Perks Committee, as long ago as 1967, and the contemporary stakeholders identified by James and Raine (see above). There is space here simply to raise some of the salient questions and point the reader in the general direction of where answers or partial answers may be found. The discussion that follows will focus upon: (i) police effectiveness, (ii) sentencing, and (iii) reoffending rates.

Police effectiveness

This is not the place to enter into the minefield debate of the extent to which police activities *per se* may directly influence the crime rate. Rather we shall take up the story at the point when decisions have been taken by the police to record certain incidents and reported events as *prima facie* 'crimes'. The traditional role of the police from hereon is to make further inquiries and carry out investigations with a view to proceeding against the suspected offender(s) who may then eventually be cautioned or prosecuted and convicted for the offence(s) in question.

In the context of the above scenario, as far as the police are concerned, one of their primary tasks is to 'clear up' as many recorded crimes as possible, within the due-process constraints of fair investigation and detection of likely suspects. Unfortunately, the statistic that tends to be used as a measure or 'key performance indicator' (KPI) of police success in this respect shows a 'clear-up' rate of 25–30 per cent, which by most standards appears to be low. Moreover, when it is recognized that this statistic has often in the past been inflated by some arguably rather dubious (albeit officially sanctioned) clear-up methods, then this apparently low level of performance leaves the police even more vulnerable and exposed to criticism for 'not doing their job' well enough.

In the present managerialist climate, combined as it is with increasingly frequent outbursts of moral panic and 'populist punitiveness' on the part of the news media, public opinion, and politicians alike, the calming message from research that the police will always face inherent difficulties in 'solving' the majority of property crimes falls largely upon deaf ears. In fact the nature of crime and the characteristics of offenders are such that the police will never on their own be able to improve their success rate without a dramatic transformation of victim awareness and community involvement in crime detection.

Similar problems of interpretation surround the statistics on the exercise of police stop and search powers under PACE (Police and Criminal Evidence Act 1984), which are published each year in the Home Office *Statistical Bulletin* series. Recorded stops and searches of persons and vehicles by the police increased from just under 110,000 in 1986 to over 1 million by 1997–98. However, in 1999–2000 there was an unprecedented drop of 21 per cent in the total number of stops and searches under PACE—almost certainly due to the aftermath of the Stephen Lawrence Inquiry Report, which recommended a more targeted, intelligence-led use of stops and searches, focused on more serious crime and more persistent offenders.[8]

But what should be read into statistics of this sort? At one level, certain doubts must be raised by the considerable variation between police forces in the use of these powers, just over a fifth of which in 1999/2000 took place in the London Metropolitan Police area. The rate of stops and searches for England and Wales as a whole in that year was 1,630 per 100,000 general population, but wide variations existed, ranging from 336 per 100,000 in Nottinghamshire to 7,300 in Cleveland. Some of these differences may be attributable to the patterns of crime in the different areas, but these seem unlikely to explain such large variations in practice.

An obvious measure of effectiveness appears to be the number of such stops/searches that result in an arrest. In fact, this measure of 'success' declined from 17 per cent of stops and searches leading to arrest in 1986 to 10 per cent in 1996–98, but it increased in 1999/2000 to 13 per cent—the highest rate since 1993, apparently confirming the greater targeting of stops and searches following the Lawrence Inquiry.

The single most important cause for concern surrounding police stops and searches (since the original PACE legislation) has always been that of the racial/ethnic dimension. The Home Office publication (under section 95 of the Criminal Justice Act 1991), *Statistics on Race and the Criminal Justice System* now provides regular monitoring of this aspect of stops and searches. In 1999/2000, 8 per cent of stops and searches were of black people and 4 per cent Asian, whereas those ethnic groups comprised less than 2 per cent and 3 per cent, respectively, of the general population (aged 10 and over) of England and Wales.[9]

However, to complicate matters further, recent research for the Home Office by Miller, Quinton, and Bland (2000) revealed that resident population figures provide a poor indication of the population actually 'available' to be stopped and searched in those public places where stops and searches take place. Their overall conclusion was:

while comparisons between the number of recorded stops and searches and the numbers in the resident population remain important in describing the different experiences of stop and search for different ethnic communities, they provide a poor indication of overall police bias in the use of stops and searches.[10]

---

[8] *Operation of Certain Police Powers under the Police and Criminal Evidence Act 1984*, Home Office Statistical Bulletin 3/01 (London: Home Office, 2001).

[9] Home Office, *Statistics on Race and the Criminal Justice System 2000* (London: Home Office, 2000).

[10] *Ibid.*, at 1.

The proportion of stops and searches that resulted in an arrest was generally higher for Blacks and Asians than for Whites, suggesting perhaps that the higher level of stops and searches of certain ethnic groups was to some extent justified by the outcomes.

It is nevertheless very salutary to examine the statistical evidence for possible racial bias at other stages of law enforcement and the administration of criminal justice that is set out in *Statistics on Race and the Criminal Justice System 2000*. These show, for example, that the number of black people arrested for notifiable offences relative to the population was on average four times higher than the proportion of white people arrested, but on the other hand in nearly all police forces there was a lower use of cautioning for suspected black offenders than for both white and Asian offenders.[11]

Sentencing

Sentencing and its consequences are at the very heart of the criminal justice process. As has already been illustrated, *Criminal Statistics* provides basic monitoring data for sentencing trends, according to age, sex, and offence type, with additional detailed information by level of court, Petty Sessional Divisions, and Police Force Areas contained in the volumes of Supplementary Tables. But in order to understand and interpret sentencing practice at a more meaningful level, it is necessary to consult the findings of the extensive body of criminological research literature dating back almost half a century (or longer in the USA).

The best of this research (such as the classic studies by Roger Hood)[12] adopts a rigorous methodology that enables conclusions to be reached about the factors that appear to influence sentencing by magistrates and judges and go some way towards explaining the widespread disparities that exist in most jurisdictions. At the heart of sentencing disparities in magistrates' courts in England and Wales are differences in community attitudes towards and experiences of crime in their locality, plus also the maintenance of court traditions and practices as mediated by key personnel.[13] It is unfortunate that independent academic research into judicial sentencing practices in the Crown Court has received much less support from the authorities and thus lags behind the strong tradition of research into sentencing by lay magistrates.[14]

However, in keeping with contemporary concern, information is now regularly made available and published by the Home Office on the impact of race and gender on sentencing, following the requirements of section 95 of the Criminal Justice Act

---

[11] *Statistics on Race and the Criminal Justice System 2000*, at 19–20.

[12] R. G. Hood, *Sentencing in Magistrates' Courts* (London: Stevens, 1962); R. G. Hood, *Sentencing the Motoring Offender* (London: Heinemann, 1972); R. G. Hood, *Race and Sentencing: A Study in the Crown Court* (Oxford: Clarendon Press, 1992).

[13] See e.g. R. Tarling, *Sentencing Practice in Magistrates' Courts*, Home Office Research Study 58 (London: HMSO, 1979); H. Parker, M. Sumner, and G. Jarvis, *Unmasking the Magistrates: The 'Custody or Not' Decision in Sentencing Young Offenders* (Milton Keynes: Open University Press, 1989).

[14] See A. Ashworth *et al.*, *Sentencing in the Crown Court: Report of an Exploratory Study* (Oxford: Centre for Criminological Research, University of Oxford, 1984); D. Moxon, *Sentencing Practice in the Crown Court*, Home Office Research Study 103 (London: HMSO, 1988); C. Flood-Page and A. Mackie, *Sentencing Practice: An Examination of Decisions in Magistrates' Courts and the Crown Court in the Mid-1990s*, Home Office Research Study 180 (London: Home Office, 1998).

1991. In addition to sentencing data, *Statistics on Women and the Criminal Justice System 2000* presents detailed statistics covering patterns of female offending, arrest and police disposals of women, remand and mode of trial, community penalties, women in custody (the longest chapter), reconvictions, victims of crime, and female practitioners in the criminal justice system.

Although this publication makes frequent references to relevant research findings, as well as collating published official statistics on women in the criminal justice system, the information by and large is presented in a descriptive rather than analytical or critical fashion. Thus the short chapter on sentencing brings together the basic data published in *Criminal Statistics*, confirming that for indictable offences as a whole, women are more likely than men to be discharged or given a community sentence and are less likely to be fined or sentenced to custody. When sentenced to custody, women receive shorter sentences on average than men, which partly reflects the different types of offences committed by women. In 1999, 7,500 females were sentenced to custody for all offences, of which by the far the most common was shoplifting (for which 2,100 women were sentenced to custody), followed a long way behind by fraud (470), wounding (440), and drug possession/supply (360). Only 340 women were sentenced to custody in 1999 for any kind of burglary.[15]

Reference is made to the findings of the Home Office Research Study (HORS) 170, *Understanding the Sentencing of Women*, edited by Hedderman and Gelsthorpe.[16] This studied the sentencing of 13,000 men and women aged 21 and over for offences of shoplifting, violence, and drugs, taking into account the comparative criminal histories of the male and female offenders. Female shoplifters were less likely than comparable males to receive a prison sentence, but more likely to be sentenced to a community penalty or discharged by the court, rather than fined. Men and women were equally likely to receive a custodial sentence for a first violent offence, although among repeat offenders women were less likely than men to receive a custodial sentence.[17]

No reference was made, however, to the second research project reported in HORS 170, based on a series of interviews with 189 lay and eight stipendiary magistrates, investigating their attitudes towards women offenders and the reasoning behind their sentencing decisions:

From these discussions it emerged that magistrates saw offenders broadly in terms of whether they were primarily 'troubled' or 'troublesome'; and the group a [male or female] offender fell into was determined by factors such as motive for the offence, degree of provocation, relationship to the victim, abuse of drugs or alcohol, and mental state. It was also affected by the way an offender behaved in court, by the way magistrates perceived other courtroom 'players' and the information they provided, and by magistrates' awareness of how their decisions might be seen by others. Together these factors shaped magistrates' views of an appropriate sentence.[18]

---

[15] Home Office, *Statistics on Women in the Criminal Justice System 2000* (London: Home Office, 2000) 21.

[16] C. Hedderman and L. Gelsthorpe (eds.), *Understanding the Sentencing of Women*, Home Office Research Study 170 (London: Home Office, 1997).

[17] *Ibid.*, at vii.   [18] *Ibid.*, at 25.

The juxtaposition of fairly dry statistical data, on the one hand, and interpretive research interviews and analysis on the other serves to highlight the limitations of statistics *per se* and the need for further interpretation and evaluation, wherever possible.

If the reader turns to *Statistics on Race and the Criminal Justice System 2000* in the hope of finding comparable information on sentencing patterns by ethnic background, they will be disappointed by what they find there. At the outset it is admitted that 'a major gap in the current information available on the way that ethnic minorities are dealt with by the criminal justice system is the lack of data concerning the prosecution and sentencing process'.[19] Accordingly, a very short chapter describes some analysis of a study of CPS decisions on ethnic minorities under the age of 22[20] and reports some preliminary findings from a pilot study of the introduction of ethnic monitoring in magistrates' courts in five police force areas. The level of analysis was limited due to the small number of ethnic minority cases in many areas, so that neither age, offence type, nor previous convictions could be taken into account—all of which are known to be related to sentencing patterns of different ethnic groups. In view of the serious limitations of the methodology, and despite variations being apparent in the sentencing of the courts in the five areas, relatively few differences were found in the sentencing of the various ethnic groups:

the use of custody was similar for white offenders (12 per cent) to that of black offenders (11 per cent) and Asian offenders (10 per cent). In general, black offenders were slightly more likely to be sentenced to community sentences than white offenders and Asian offenders, and less likely to be given a discharge.[21]

Reference was also made to research by Roger Hood on a sample of persons sentenced in Crown Court in the West Midlands, which indicated that there were sentencing differences between ethnic groups even when such relevant factors were taken into account.[22]

Reoffending rates

Perhaps, for many people, the primary indicator for judging the effectiveness of the sentencing of offenders should be the rate of reoffending following different sentences. This is another good example of where basic statistical data are of limited use on their own for assessing the relative success of different sentences in reducing reoffending.

The most comprehensive reconviction statistics are to be found in the annual *Prison Statistics England and Wales*. The latest volume, for 1999, provides a detailed analysis of the reconvictions of prisoners within two years of their discharge from prison in 1996. 57 per cent of all prisoners were reconvicted of a standard-list offence within two years, comprising 47 per cent of all females, 52 per cent of adult males, and 76 per cent of male young offenders. Reconviction rates varied according to the type

---

[19] Home Office, *Statistics on Race and the Criminal Justice System 2000* (London: Home Office, 2000) 37.

[20] B. M. Mhlanga, *Race and Crown Prosecution Decisions* (London: TSO, 1999).

[21] See Home Office, n. 18 above, at 38.

[22] R. G. Hood, *Race and Sentencing: A Study in the Crown Court*, n. 12 above.

of original offence, so that 76 per cent of those serving sentences for burglary were reconvicted within two years of their discharge, as were 70 per cent of those sentenced for theft and handling but only 19 per cent of those serving sentences for sexual offences were reconvicted within two years.[23]

It was emphasized that an offender's propensity to reoffend is affected by many other factors than the experience of custody and that care should be taken when interpreting the basic reconviction rates as 'they only give a limited picture of the pattern of convictions', with no indication, for example, of the seriousness of the offences concerned and, obviously, no information about reoffending that is undetected![24]

The chapter ends with a comparison of the reconviction rates after custody and community penalties. The reconviction rates for those commencing probation, community service, or combination orders in the first quarter of 1996 were 60, 50, and 59 per cent, respectively—with an overall rate for community penalties of 56 per cent. The comparable reconviction rate for those discharged from prison in 1996 was 57 per cent. It was pointed out that, in making comparisons of this sort, it is also necessary to take account of differences in the characteristics of the two groups of offenders (e.g. age, sex, and number of previous convictions). After making the necessary adjustments very little difference indeed was found between the reconviction rates after custody and all community penalties.[25]

These conclusions are very much in line with the findings reported in a series of Home Office *Statistical Bulletins*, published in the 1990s, comparing the reconviction rates of those discharged from prison with those sentenced to community penalties. Together they confirm that in respect of the sentencing aim of reducing offending there is currently very little to choose between the effectiveness of different sentences.

As a tantalizing gender postscript to this discussion it is instructive to consider the reconviction rates for males and females, as summarized in *Statistics of Women in the Criminal Justice System 2000*. The reconviction rates for prisoners discharged in 1996, according to age and gender, were 52 per cent for adult men, 45 per cent for adult women, 76 per cent for young men, 57 per cent for young women.

Similarly, the reconviction rates for those commencing community penalties in 1996 were 57 per cent for all men, 46 per cent for all women.

However, when account is taken of the number of previous convictions of male and female offenders, much of the differential disappears, or is reversed. For example, the reconviction rate for women prisoners with three to six, seven to ten, and eleven or more previous convictions is actually higher than that of comparable male prisoners. It is only women prisoners with none or 1–2 previous convictions whose reconviction rates are lower than males.[26]

A similar, but slightly less marked, effect is found when comparisons are made between men and women sentenced to community penalties. Overall, 57 per cent of all males given community penalties are reconvicted, compared to 46 per cent of all

[23] Home Office, *Prison Statistics England and Wales 1999*, Cm 4805 (2000) 150.
[24] *Ibid.*, at 151.   [25] *Ibid.*, at 157.
[26] See Home Office, n. 14 above, at 35–6.

females. However, when account is taken of the number of previous convictions, the reconviction rate of females with one to two, three to six, and seven to ten previous convictions is only 2–3 per cent lower than comparable males sentenced to community penalties, whereas, for women with either none or eleven or more previous convictions the rate is 7–8 per cent lower than comparable males.[27]

COMPARING CRIMINAL JUSTICE SYSTEMS

Having drawn attention to some of the many problems and pitfalls in interpreting statistical information about the criminal justice system in a single jurisdiction, it stands to reason that attempts to draw comparisons between the operation and effectiveness of criminal justice systems of different countries is fraught with even greater problems. The inherent difficulty of this task was recognized at the beginning of one of the most painstaking and comprehensive attempts of this sort, to draw together the criminal justice statistics of the major European countries:

the issue of whether or not it is feasible to use official criminal justice statistics for decision-making in crime policy or for conducting scientific studies is one of the classic debates of criminology. The problems involved are even more serious when it comes to international comparisons, because nations differ widely in the way they organise their police and court systems, the way they define their legal concepts, and the way they collect and present their statistics. In fact, the lack of uniform definitions of offences, of common measuring instruments and of common methodology makes comparisons between countries extremely hazardous.[28]

We shall use the example of the *European Sourcebook of Crime and Criminal Justice Statistics* to illustrate the possibilities and limitations of exercises of this kind, concentrating for present purposes on comparisons between European criminal justice statistics rather than comparisons of crime rates which have now been transformed by data from the International Crime Victimization Surveys.[29] The *European Sourcebook* is divided into four main sections: (1) Police statistics (2) Prosecution statistics (3) Conviction statistics (4) Correctional statistics. It includes data from up to thirty-six separate European jurisdictions, for the period 1990–6, although as some data are incomplete not all countries are included in every part of the analysis.

The section on *police statistics* mainly covers recorded crime statistics and so need not detain us long, apart from noting that the Sourcebook recognizes that police statistics are not a good measure of crime, as victims often do not report crimes and,

---

[27] N. 14 above, at 36.

[28] European Committee on Crime Problems, *European Sourcebook of Crime and Criminal Justice Statistics* (Strasbourg: Council of Europe, 1999).

[29] See J. J. M. van Dijk, P. Mayhew, and M. Killias, *Experiences of Crime Across the World: Key Findings of the 1989 International Crime Survey* (2nd edn., Deventer: Kluwer, 1991); P. Mayhew and J. J. M. van Dijk, *Criminal Victimisation in Eleven Industrialised Countries: Key Findings from the 1996 International Crime Victims Survey* (The Hague: Wetenschappelijk Onderzoek en Documentatiecentrum, 1997).

when reported to the police, not all such incidents are recorded as crime for official statistical and investigative purposes. Furthermore, the role of the police as 'gatekeepers' of the criminal justice process varies across jurisdictions, as in some countries the prosecuting authorities may initiate criminal proceedings without having received a police report. It is also noted:

The position of the police in the criminal justice system is not only relevant to the extent to which crime recorded at police level may be seen as a measure of the input into the criminal justice system. It may also directly influence the number of offences recorded and their classification. Firstly, in some countries the police may be quite independent in its activities, while in others they work under the close supervision of the prosecutor or the court. Secondly, the police may have the power to 'label' the incidents they investigate as specific offences, or they may have to leave this task to the prosecutor.[30]

The section on *prosecution statistics* presents data for thirty-two jurisdictions. The nature and role of the prosecuting authorities vary widely between the countries surveyed and so it is unwise to attach too much weight to the differences in outcome that the statistics reveal. In most European countries prosecutions are dealt with by a special authority, either a public prosecutor or an investigating judge, with power to prosecute or not prosecute those arrested or proceeded against by the police. The proportion of those initially investigated and proceeded against who were eventually brought to court varied from 12–13 per cent in France and Germany to three-quarters or more in England and Wales, the Former Yugoslavian Republic of Macedonia (FYRO), Hungary, and Finland, with an overall mean of 49 per cent.[31]

The title of chapter 3, *Conviction Statistics*, is somewhat misleading, in that it does not provide data on pleas and acquittals to compare with convictions, but simply lists the number of persons convicted for each major offence, per 100,000 population in each country. It then gives data on the sentencing patterns for a selection of offences, including homicide, rape, robbery, theft, theft of motor vehicle, burglary, and drug offences. More detailed analysis is provided on those offences where the data are more complete and where the legal/operational definitions are more comparable across jurisdictions. This confirms the variation in sentencing found in England and Wales.

For example, 30 per cent of those sentenced for *rape* in nine countries were given suspended sentences. On the other hand, 90 per cent or more convicted rapists were sentenced to imprisonment in Scotland, Romania, France, and Sweden. Where custodial sentences were imposed, the average length was five years, but in some countries (e.g. England and Wales) life sentences could be and were imposed for this offence. Average sentences of just three years were found in Norway and Sweden.[32]

There was considerable variation in the definition of drug offences in the European countries surveyed, with similar wide variations in the sentences imposed, from 96 per cent given prison sentences in FYOR Macedonia to 5 per cent in Poland.[33]

Further details about the use of imprisonment and community penalties were presented in a chapter on *correctional statistics*. The rate of community supervision

---

[30] See European Committee on Crime Problems, n. 28 above, at 30.
[31] *Ibid.*, at 97. [32] *Ibid.*, at 114. [33] *Ibid.*, at 115.

measures varied from over 300 per 100,000 population in Northern Ireland, Lithuania and Moldova, to eight (in Cyprus), ten (Albania), and thirteen (Portugal). In comparison, the custodial detention rates (1990–7) varied from 415 per 100,000 population in Ukraine to thirty-nine in Slovenia and forty in Cyprus.[34] More detailed information about the use of imprisonment across Europe (including pre-trial and sentenced prisoners) can be found in the Council of Europe's *Penological Information Bulletin*. Details are provided about the age and offences of prisoners, their average sentence lengths and time served, and also various forms of community 'probation'.[35]

Finally, it is worth noting that the *European Sourcebook* project intended to collect and analyse comparative reconviction rates following different sentences. However this plan had to be abandoned, due to the many technical and methodological problems involved, with little standardization between countries either in the type of information or the way in which it was collected:

Indeed, choosing different offender characteristics, follow-up periods and recidivism criteria, it is possible to synthetically increase or decrease recidivism rates. Therefore, care should be taken in interpreting reconviction rates, even within one country, and special care should be taken when comparing rates across countries. Neither should it be forgotten that reconviction rates are in fact 'rates of recapture' whilst recidivism rates may vary with the efficiency of the different criminal justice systems.[36]

This is perhaps an appropriately cautious note on which to end this discussion of the problems of comparing criminal justice systems.

FUTURE PROSPECTS

What conclusions and lessons for the future emerge from this review of statistics and information about criminal justice in the UK and other countries?

The operation and evaluation of the criminal justice system are too important to be simply left in the hands of the agencies and practitioners themselves. Comprehensive data collection and reliable information systems are essential prerequisites for developing the necessary self-awareness and understanding of criminal justice procedures and outcomes. Despite the complex legal frameworks within which criminal justice systems operate and to which they are accountable, wide discretion is permitted to the key decision-makers, whether they be police officers responding to a reported crime incident, lawyers advising on pleas and mode of trial, or sentencers choosing appropriate penalties.

Merely to record and tabulate the decisions and outcomes does not constitute satisfactory monitoring of their actions or enable proper evaluation to be made of

---

[34] European Committee on Crime Problems, n. 28 above, at 181, 187.

[35] See, e.g., Council of Europe, *Penological Information Bulletin* No. 22 (Council of Europe: Strasbourg, 2000).

[36] See European Committee on Crime Problems, n. 28 above, at 180.

their work. Furthermore, in an increasingly managerialist environment, there is a real risk that statistics and agency records become liable to manipulation to create the best possible impression of efficiency and effectiveness. Examples of statistics and practices that are particularly vulnerable to this sort of 'massaging' include the number of recorded crimes, the police 'clear-up' rate, stops and searches, pleas, and reconviction rates. Criminal justice managers owe it both to their staff and to the wider audiences and 'stake-holders' to ensure that the pervasive pressures towards improved performance do not lead to serious distortions of the messages communicated by official statistics and 'Key Performance Indicators' (KPIs).

Similarly, although it may be a somewhat naïve and idealistic aspiration, politicans of all parties should avoid (ab)using statistics to curry favour with their public constituencies. The late twentieth century saw a disconcerting rise in 'populist punitiveness', not only in the UK but also in many other European countries and across the USA. [37]

Getting 'back to basics' in the understanding of criminal justice means endorsing the objectives of the Perks Committee (see above) to produce statistics that serve to inform Parliament and the public in an honest and responsible way and at the same time to provide the basis for what we now call 'evidence-based' practice for legislators, law enforcement agents, sentencers, and the penal services. Arguably, the 'public voice' should be heard more loudly in Parliament and the corridors of Whitehall, but only if this voice is fully informed and educated about the reality of the crime problem and the criminal justice response.

We need to be able to dig beneath the surface of official statistics and interpret the true significance (or otherwise) of managerially driven KPIs. There must be a greater commitment in all quarters to the production of meaningful information that renders criminal justice more directly accountable to the community it is intended to serve. Only in this way will increased public participation be a force working constructively towards social progress and the enhancement of the quality of life and rights of all citizens.

Further Reading

In addition to the official publications of criminal justice statistics in England and Wales, to which references have been made throughout this chapter, a useful summary is to be found in G. C. Barclay and C. Tavares (eds.), *Digest 4: Information on the Criminal Justice System in England and Wales* (London: Home Office, 1999). A comprehensive academic guide to the interpretation of crime statistics is M. A. Walker (ed.), *Interpreting Crime Statistics* (Oxford: Clarendon Press, Oxford, 1995). For an earlier analysis see A. K. Bottomley and K. Pease, *Crime and Punishment: Interpreting the Data* (Milton Keynes: Open University Press, 1986).

The best general review of the criminal justice process, from a legal evaluative perspective, is by A. Ashworth, *The Criminal Process: An Evaluative Study* (2nd edn., Oxford: Oxford University Press, 1998). Useful chapters on different stages are to be found in M. Maguire,

---

[37] For the rise of 'tough justice' in England and Wales see I. Dunbar and A. Langdon, *Tough Justice: Sentencing and Penal Policies in the 1990s* (London: Blackstone Press, 1998).

R. Morgan, and R. Reiner (eds.), *The Oxford Handbook of Criminology* (2nd edn., Oxford: Clarendon Press, 1997).

Information from the most recent crime victimization survey in England and Wales is to be found in C. Kershaw *et al.*, *The 2000 British Crime Survey, England and Wales*, Home Office Statistical Bulletin 18/00 (London: Home Office, 2000).

Finally, an excellent critique of the legal, cultural, and sociological issues surrounding the comparative study of criminal justice is D. Nelken (ed), *Contrasting Criminal Justice: Getting from Here to There* (Aldershot: Ashgate/Dartmouth, 2000).

INDEX